ADVANCES IN

EXPERIMENTAL
SOCIAL PSYCHOLOGY

VOLUME 17

Theorizing in Social Psychology:
Special Topics

CONTRIBUTORS TO VOLUME 17

Nancy Cantor

Shelly Chaiken

Joel Cooper

John F. Dovidio

Alice H. Eagly

Russell H. Fazio

Kenneth J. Gergen

Linda J. Keil

John F. Kihlstrom

Roderick M. Kramer

Howard Leventhal

Charles G. McClintock

ADVANCES IN

Experimental

Social Psychology

EDITED BY

Leonard Berkowitz

DEPARTMENT OF PSYCHOLOGY
UNIVERSITY OF WISCONSIN—MADISON
MADISON, WISCONSIN

VOLUME 17

Theorizing in Social Psychology:
Special Topics

 1984

ACADEMIC PRESS, INC.
(Harcourt Brace Jovanovich, Publishers)
Orlando San Diego New York London
Toronto Montreal Sydney Tokyo

ACADEMIC PRESS, INC.
Orlando, Florida 32887

United Kingdom Edition published by
ACADEMIC PRESS, INC. (LONDON) LTD.
24/28 Oval Road, London NW1 7DX

LIBRARY OF CONGRESS CATALOG CARD NUMBER: 64-23452

ISBN 0-12-015217-7

PRINTED IN THE UNITED STATES OF AMERICA

84 85 86 87   9 8 7 6 5 4 3 2 1

CONTENTS

Equity and Social Change in Human Relationships

Charles G. McClintock, Roderick M. Kramer, and Linda J. Keil

A New Look at Dissonance Theory

Joel Cooper and Russell H. Fazio

Cognitive Theories of Persuasion

Alice H. Eagly and Shelly Chaiken

Helping Behavior and Altruism: An Empirical and Conceptual Overview

John F. Dovidio

CONTRIBUTORS

Numbers in parentheses indicate the pages on which the authors' contributions begin.

Nancy Cantor (1), *Department of Psychology, University of Michigan, Ann Arbor, Michigan 48106*

Shelly Chaiken (267), *Department of Psychology, Vanderbilt University, Nashville, Tennessee 37240*

Joel Cooper (229), *Department of Psychology, Princeton University, Princeton, New Jersey 08540*

John F. Dovidio (361), *Department of Psychology, Colgate University, Hamilton, New York 13346*

Alice H. Eagly (267), *Department of Psychological Sciences, Purdue University, West Lafayette, Indiana 47907*

Russell H. Fazio (229), *Department of Psychology, Indiana University, Bloomington, Indiana 47405*

Kenneth J. Gergen (49), *Department of Psychology, Swarthmore College, Swarthmore, Pennsylvania 19081*

Linda J. Keil (183), *Department of Psychology, University of North Carolina, Chapel Hill, North Carolina 27514*

John F. Kihlstrom (1), *Department of Psychology, University of Wisconsin, Madison, Wisconsin 53706*

Roderick M. Kramer (183), *Department of Psychology, University of California, Los Angeles, California 90024*

Howard Leventhal (117), *Department of Psychology, University of Wisconsin, Madison, Wisconsin 53706*

Charles G. McClintock (183), *Department of Psychology, University of California, Santa Barbara, California 93106*

ix

PREFACE

This is the second of our two special volumes dealing with theorizing in contemporary social psychology. The first book, Volume 16, offers an overview of the perspectives guiding theory development throughout the entire field. This volume singles out several research areas within social psychology for particular attention and looks at the theoretical conceptions now emerging in these more specialized areas.

The topics covered in this book also vary in breadth. The first two chapters are devoted to the study of the self, a subject that is now of concern to almost every part of social psychology. It is difficult to think of any research area that would not benefit from a fuller analysis of the nature and operation of the self. Because of these widespread implications, and the great interest in the self throughout the behavioral sciences, research and theorizing have inevitably followed different approaches, and the first two chapters reflect these differences. Kihlstrom and Cantor have adopted the relatively new information-processing perspective and show how the concepts and methods employed in the study of memory and information processing generally can contribute in important ways to our understanding of the self-concept. Gergen, on the other hand, follows a much older tradition, phenomenology, one not especially familiar to American psychologically oriented social psychologists but better known to sociologists and philosophers, especially in Europe. Whatever their preference, advocates of each side would do well to consider the other perspective's arguments and observations.

The third chapter, dealing with equity and social exchange, is also far-ranging in scope. A number of theorists have attempted to apply equity and social exchange conceptions to a wide variety of areas—including social interactions, close relationships, helpfulness, and work and pay in economic settings—maintaining that humans frequently consider fairness in their calculation of costs and benefits in their encounters with others. Human behavior, these theorists contend, reflects a moral order, and we cannot have a truly adequate social psychology unless we know what rules govern judgments of fairness and how these judgments affect social conduct. In this chapter, McClintock, Kramer, and Keil examine the current status of the theorizing in this area and point the way to future developments.

The latest conventional wisdom in social psychology holds that the field is now overly dominated by ''cold'' cognitive formulations and should pay greater attention to emotion and affect. Such an admonition does not mean, of course, that cognitions have only a minor role in emotions, and in his chapter (Chapter 4), Leventhal offers an information-processing analysis of emotions that incorporates recent developments in the study of cognitive processes. This formulation is essentially a network analysis, similar in important respects to the conceptions offered by other investigators such as Gordon Bower and Peter Lang, and represents an impressive challenge to the Schachter–Singer theory of emotions that is now so popular in social psychology.

If there is a growing interest today in the study of emotions, there has also been a decline in the number of publications concerned with the theory of cognitive dissonance since the heyday of this theory. Nonetheless, if social psychology is ever to be a cumulative discipline in which future research builds systematically on what has been discovered in the past, it should not forget its earlier concerns as it pursues its current interests. Every once in a while we must have a summary statement of what has been learned so far in a particular research area so that this accumulated knowledge can serve as a foundation for later investigations. Cooper and Fazio (Chapter 5) provide such a summary in their integrative review of dissonance research. In one sense, this survey narrows the scope of the theory since it identifies the limited conditions under which dissonance effects are most likely to arise; cognitive dissonance is not the product of opposing cognitions, as Festinger had originally held, but comes about only under more limited circumstances. But, on the other hand, dissonance theory concepts are still applied to a broad range of phenomena so that the formulation remains exceedingly important.

The final two chapters deal with the end-products of social psychological processes rather than with the processes or mechanisms that affect behavior. In Chapter 6, Eagly and Chaiken review research on a topic having a fairly extensive history in social psychology—persuasion. This subject has long been the ground, and even battleground, on which widely different theoretical perspectives have contested for disciplinary popularity. Testifying to the present dominance of cognitive analyses, the authors concentrate on cognitive theories of persuasion and demonstrate the fruitfulness of these formulations. The final chapter, by Dovidio, covers one of the newest research topics in social psychology—helpfulness. Because of its youthfulness as well as its complexity, this research area still lacks overarching theoretical analyses, but Dovidio shows how particular concepts can help us understand bystander reactions to emergency situations. As a scholarly review, this essay is also an answer to those critics who maintain that social psychology has not accomplished much. Social psychologists first began to investigate helpfulness in the late 1950s but the research in this area did not really take off until the 1960s. Much has been learned in this relatively brief period of time, as Dovidio shows.

Indeed, all the chapters testify to our field's accomplishments. Having been in social psychology for about 30 years now, I have no doubt that we have come far in the past several decades, and the chapters in this volume represent a considerable advance over what was known in their respective areas at the time I was a graduate student. But we obviously still have a long, long way to go. These essays can help spur the future development in our discipline.

MENTAL REPRESENTATIONS
OF THE SELF*

John F. Kihlstrom

DEPARTMENT OF PSYCHOLOGY
UNIVERSITY OF WISCONSIN
MADISON, WISCONSIN

Nancy Cantor

DEPARTMENT OF PSYCHOLOGY
UNIVERSITY OF MICHIGAN
ANN ARBOR, MICHIGAN

This puzzling problem arises when we ask, "Who is the I who knows the bodily me, who has an image of myself and sense of identity over time, who knows that I have propriate strivings?" I know all these things and, what is more, I know that I know them. But who is it who has this perspectival grasp? . . . It is much easier to *feel* the self than to *define* the self (Allport, 1961, p. 128).

*Preparation of this paper was supported in part by Grant #MH-35856 from the National Institute of Mental Health, United States Public Health Service, and in part by Grant #BNS-8022253 from the National Science Foundation.

ADVANCES IN EXPERIMENTAL
SOCIAL PSYCHOLOGY, VOL. 17

The self, like consciousness and intelligence, is a problematic topic within personality and social psychology. We all share the intuition that each of us has a self and that each of us is conscious or intelligent; but it has not been easy to articulate just what the self (or consciousness or intelligence) is or what it does. In this essay we seek to sketch out a preliminary theory of the self viewed from the perspective of cognitive social psychology. We begin with Allport's assertion (1961, p. 137) that "the human mind is able to regard itself as an object in much the same way that it regards objects in the outer world." Accordingly, we define the self as one's mental representation of oneself, no different in principle from mental representations that a person has concerning other ideas, objects, and events and their attributes and implications. In other words, the self is a concept, not unlike other concepts, that is stored in memory as a knowledge structure, not unlike other knowledge structures. This idea is not so new: Others also have had the same intuition (Bower, 1981; Greenwald, 1981; Keenan & Baillet, 1980; Kuiper & Derry, 1981; Mancuso & Ceely, 1980; Markus & Sentis, 1982; Markus & Smith, 1981). However, we attempt to go further than prior investigators in integrating the literature on the self-concept with research on memory and categorization, as represented by Anderson's (1976) ACT model of memory and Smith and Medin's (1981) view of concepts as prototypes or examplars. In this way we are able to paint a picture of what the self looks like and examine the ramifications of a particular set of theoretical commitments. Our coverage is highly selective: To perform our task adequately would require the space of a monograph—and, we suspect, about a decade's worth of research. For overviews of other topics, as well as different perspectives on material covered here, we refer the reader to other volumes (Buss, 1980; Gergen, 1971; Lynch, Norem-Hebeisen, & Gergen, 1981; Suls, 1982; Wegner & Vallacher, 1980).

I.   Cognitive and Social Processes in Personality

The framework for this discussion is provided by an emerging theory of personality (Cantor & Kihlstrom, 1982; Kihlstrom & Cantor, 1983) that has its roots in the work of Lewin (1935), Kelly (1955), Mischel (1968, 1973), and Bandura (1977). In this approach, the psychology of personality is conceived as a general psychology, in which our knowledge of biological, cognitive, social, and developmental processes is synthesized into a comprehensive view of the way that people attempt to understand, respond to, and change the physical and social world in which they live. Like all theories of personality, it begins with the everyday observation of wide individual differences in behavior and experience, thought and action. Unlike many established theories, however, it also takes account of the apparent fact that human thought and action is quite flexible and responsive to change in both the intrapsychic and interpersonal context in which it takes place. Rather than offering a taxonomy of people in terms of some set of stable categories or dimensions, or for that matter a taxonomy of situations, the theory places primary emphasis on the general processes out of which human individuality is constructed. These general processes are both cognitive and social in nature.

The fundamental fact of human existence is human intelligence: our enormous capacity to understand ourselves and the world around us, and our ability to communicate that understanding to others through language. Our responses to events are largely determined by the meanings that we give to them, to the options we perceive to be available, and to the anticipated outcomes of both events and actions. We are also social animals: All of our thought and action takes place in the context, explicit or implicit, of other people. Therefore it follows that the most important mental processes implicated in personality are those involved in social cognition: mental representations of the self, other people, and the situations in which interpersonal interactions take place; the procedures by which we construct and reconstruct our impressions and experiences and make evaluations, attributions, and other judgments of people and events in the social world; and the effects of social cognition on social behavior.

This is not to deny a role for biological processes in personality. After all, human intelligence is a product of our phylogenetic heritage—though it should be said, contrary to the suggestion of the sociobiologists, that our biological capacity to generate new knowledge and transmit it to the next generation has enabled cultural evolution to outstrip biological evolution (e.g., Gould, 1981). Some individual differences in temperament—activity level and response intensity, for example—are observable immediately after birth and may reflect the individual's genetic and biochemical endowment. However, it is important to remember that genotypes represent only potential, and that the phenotype is shaped by environmental factors: immediately after birth the program for shaping personality passes from the genes and hormones to the environment (e.g., Money & Ehrhardt, 1972).

Although this cognitive–social approach to personality acknowledges the effects of the social context on human thought and action, it is not a form of disguised situationism. People are in part creatures of their social environment, to be sure, but they are equally creators of that environment. Although situational demands shape and constrain cognition, emotion, and action in various ways, people are capable of acting behaviorally and cognitively to transform the situations impinging on them. This fact is of utmost importance because, after all, people respond not to situations but to *mental representations* of situations. Their responses cannot be understood without reference to the way they construct perceptions, reconstruct memories, arrive at judgments, make predictions, and choose among available options. The interaction between a person and the situation is cognitively mediated and is best characterized as reciprocal determinism. Although this implies mutual influence and a powerful role for the environment, in the final analysis, the balance of power favors cognitive control over environmental control. The social centext can coerce behavior, but it has less impact when it comes to the way people think. As long as people have access to information they are free.

II.   The Self-Concept in a System of Social Concepts

The self is a concept about oneself, and as such, it is part of the individual's organized system of concepts concerning his or her social and physical world. Again, this conceptual system is the foundation of cognition. As Bruner has noted, every act of perception is an act of categorization. Some categories can be defined by enumeration—that is, by preparing an exhaustive list of all the instances of a category (e.g., the letters of the alphabet) or by finding a rule that generates all the instances (e.g., the integers in the mathematical system). More commonly, however, categories are defined by attributes—the perceptual, functional, and relational features shared by members of the category (e.g., animal species, tools, and kinship). A great deal of attention has been devoted to the question of just how clusters of attributes combine to define a category (see reviews by Rosch & Lloyd, 1978; Smith & Medin, 1981). According to the *classical view* attributed to Aristotle and employed in much early research on concept formation (e.g., Bruner, Goodnow, & Austin, 1956; Hull, 1920), a concept is a summary description of an entire class of objects or events. Its attributes are singly necessary (i.e., every instance possesses every defining feature) and jointly sufficient (i.e., every object or event that possesses all the defining features is an instance of the concept) to define the category; and it is located in a hierarchical system characterized by perfect nesting (i.e., within any particular branch of the hierarchy, all the defining features of superordinate categories are also defining features of subordinate categories). This all-or-none arrangement of features means that category members are quite homogeneous and that there are sharp boundaries between the various categories.

Although such a definition may be satisfactory when it comes to defining proper sets and certain artificial categories, a number of problems arise when it is employed with respect to natural categories (Wittgenstein, 1953). Smith and Medin (1981) summarize a variety of conceptual and empirical objections, not one of which is sufficient alone to destroy the classical view, but when taken together make for quite a devastating package. For example, it is often unclear how to categorize some objects, and it has proved quite difficult to specify the necessary and sufficient features that ostensibly define many natural categories.

Moreover, people find some instances to be better representatives of a concept than others. These variations in perceived typicality are related to the distribution, across category members, of *nondefining* features. Finally, there is good evidence that people base their category judgments on these nondefining features, rather than on attributes that are necessary and sufficient to define a category. These findings seem to lead to the conclusion that *natural* categories at least are organized along lines that are different from the classical view of concept structure.

A more recent development is the *prototype view* (Rosch, 1975), which in its early forms argued that the features of the summary descriptions are only probabilistically associated with category membership. Accordingly, no feature is singly necessary and no set of features jointly sufficient to define a concept. Also, the hierarchical system is characterized by imperfect nesting: Within any particular branch the subsets do not possess all the features of supersets. With correlated rather than defining attributes, category members can be quite heterogeneous, and there are no sharp boundaries between contrasting categories. Perhaps the most important implication of the prototype view is that instances can vary in typicality, meaning that some are better representatives of the category than others. Such categories are represented by a prototype instance, concrete or abstract, that contains many features that are correlated with category membership and few features that are correlated with membership in contrasting categories. In determining feature overlap, particular attention is paid to central features, which show high correlations, rather than to peripheral ones, whose correlations are low.

Smith and Medin (1981) have proposed a third formulation, the *exemplar view,* which holds that categories are represented by several typical examples rather than by a single abstract summary. Thus, categorization involves matching a test item to each of many focal instances, rather than to any single best example; if there is a good match between the item and any of these focal instances, the item is labeled as a member of the category. In actual practice, an exemplar can be either a specific instance or a subordinate category. The point is merely that there may be no single summary representation of a category at any level. Perhaps the best evidence favoring this view is that people often do seem to make use of multiple exemplars when they assign objects to categories. This viewpoint, however, is relatively new and has not yet been systematically explored. (For yet a fourth alternative, see Keil, 1979.)

Although the exemplar approach has not yet been applied to the problem of social categorization, the prototype approach has. In a series of studies, Cantor (Cantor, 1980; Cantor & Mischel, 1979; Cantor, Mischel, & Schwartz, 1982; Cantor, Smith, French, & Mezzich, 1980) has shown that both intuitive and professional psychologists follow the prototype view of social categorization, recognizing (for example) that there are no sharp boundaries between extraverts and introverts and that some individuals are more typical extraverts than others. Perhaps the most telling documentation of this point involves the categories of psychopathology (Cantor *et al.*, 1980). In the past, the diagnostic rules appeared to assume that the various mental illnesses were proper sets defined by necessary and sufficient features (certainly many criticisms of these rules assumed that this was so), but data collected by Cantor *et al.* indicate that psychiatrists actually construe these categories as fuzzy sets represented by prototypes and actually perform a feature-matching process when assigning real cases to categories. These findings strongly support the proposition that other person categories are also represented by prototypes and that category judgments operate along probabilistic, feature-matching lines.

Oneself is a person in the individual's social world, and so it seems natural to conclude that the self-concept is embedded in his or her overall hierarchical organization of person concepts. Just where in such a hierarchy the self-concept lies, however, is a difficult question. From one point of view, oneself is a highly specific instance and so would seem to belong at the most subordinate level of a categorical system, along with other specific individuals of the person's acquaintance. Imagine, if you will, a hierarchical structure, such as that depicted in Fig. 1, containing such superordinate concepts and contrasts as person–nonperson and good–bad person (Rosenberg, 1976) at the very top, various broad categories of good and bad people (Norman, 1963) and subtypes of these (Cantor & Mischel, 1979) arrayed in the middle, and oneself and others arranged along the bottom as specific instances of these. From another point of view, the self-concept is located at an extremely superordinate level. Among the earliest distinctions acquired by the developing infant is that of self–not self (Flavell, 1977); and we sort other people into social categories more readily than we classify ourselves (Nisbett, Caputo, Legant, & Maracek, 1973). These considerations suggest that the self-concept might stand alone in the hierarchical system, with all the usual social categories branching out under the superordinate concept "other", as in Fig. 2.

In any event, the self-concept, as a concept, is represented by a prototype consisting of some set of central and peripheral features. The question is, prototype *of what?* Prototypes, whether represented as feature sets (Rosch, 1975) or as points in multidimensional space (Krumhansl, 1978; Posner & Keele, 1968; Reed, 1972), are summaries of a multitude of specific instances; whereas there are lots of extraverted people in the world, there is only *one* of each of *us*. If there is a self-prototype, then it must be abstracted from observations of ourselves in specific situational contexts. This suggests that there might be a whole hierarchy of *selves* (rather than a single, unitary self), gathered together at various levels of abstraction: for example, the self alone versus with people: with acquaintances versus strangers; with family versus friends versus coworkers; with mother versus father versus spouse; and so on, yielding a structure along the lines of Fig. 3.

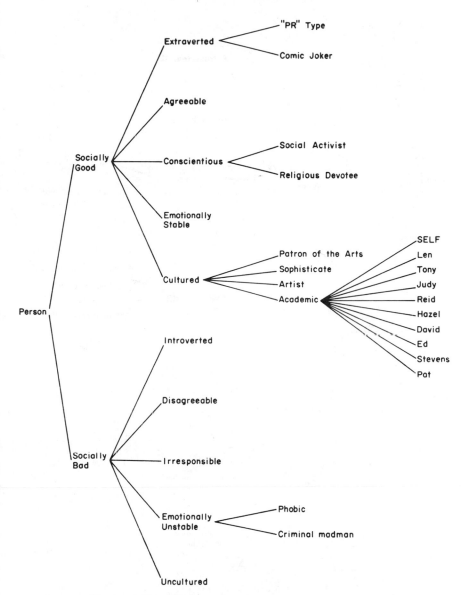

Fig. 1. A hierarchical structure of context-specific self-concepts.

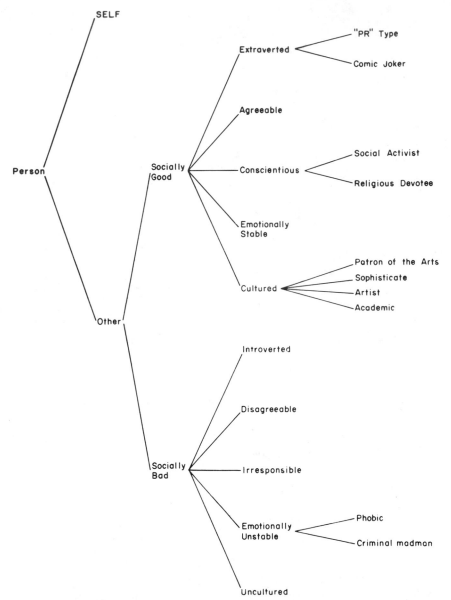

Fig. 2.   The self as a unitary concept on a separate branch within a hierarchical structure of persons.

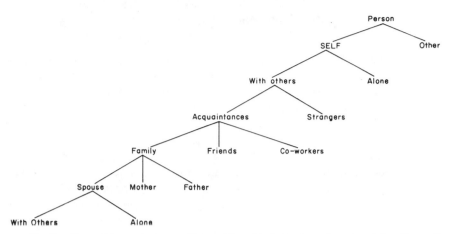

Fig. 3. The self as an instance within a hierarchical structure of persons (after Cantor & Mischel, 1979).

Each of these selves would be represented by a prototypical self-in-context, abstracted from multiple observations within similar situations. Given the exemplar view, of course, there may be no single, unitary, superordinate, summary self-concept at all—only a set of coequal typical selves.

If there is a conceptual hierarchy of selves, analogous to the conceptual hierarchies found in mental representations of other people (Cantor & Mischel, 1979), is there some level within the system that is preferred for self-definition and self-description? Within the domain of natural objects, for example, Rosch and her colleagues (Rosch, Mervis, Gray, Johnson, & Boyes-Brehm, 1976) found that stimuli were categorized most readily at some intermediate level (e.g., chair) compared to the very abstract superordinate (e.g., furniture) or very concrete subordinate (e.g., kitchen chair) levels. When consensual prototypes at each level were constructed, Rosch et al. found that the prototypes at these levels differed in terms of both richness (the number of features associated with category membership) and differentiation (the number of features shared with alternative categories within the same branch of the hierarchy). This intermediate level, which Rosch et al. called *basic*, appears to optimize both richness and differentiation. Interestingly, children learn the names of basic levels first during the course of vocabulary acquisition, and these names are preferred when people are asked to name category instances. Cantor (e.g., Cantor & Mischel, 1979; Cantor et al., 1982) has provided evidence for a basic level of social categorization that, like natural-object categorization (Murphy, 1982; Murphy & Smith, 1982), maximizes distinctiveness. It remains to be seen whether such a basic level can be found in a hierarchy of selves.

III. How Many Selves Have We?

The view of the self-concept as a concept may help resolve a long-standing dispute among personality psychologists, as to whether the self is to be construed as unitary or fragmentary (Epstein, 1973). Many theorists have conceived of the self as a unitary structure representing the core of personality. James (1890) was an early proponent of this view. He distinguished between the *self as knower,* closely identified with the self-referential nature of consciousness, and the *self as object of what is known.* Whereas James distinguished among three aspects of the self-as-object—the *material self,* consisting of the individual's body, family relationships, and possessions; the *social self,* representing the individual as she or he is viewed by others; and the *spiritual self,* comprising his or her emotions and drives—these were not so much different selves as they were aspects of a single conception of oneself, forming a coherent unity. A similar unitary concept is apparent in the work of Snygg and Combs (1949), who considered the self to consist of those characteristics of a person that were stable rather than changeable, and Rogers (1951), who included in the self those characteristics of a person over which she or he is aware and has control. Perhaps the most thorough description of the unitary self comes from Allport (1955), who defined the *proprium* (an alternative name for the self-concept) as those aspects of personality that the person him- or herself regards as central to his or her own personality. For Allport, all of these facets are woven into a single, unified sense of oneself—a sense that transcends particular contexts and is good for all places and all times.

Other psychologists, working within a more sociological tradition, have argued that we seem to have many selves rather than a single, unitary, monolithic self-concept. James (1890) himself, of course, argued for a multiplicity of social selves. An early example of this point of view is Cooley (1902), who initially defined the self as consisting of whatever attributes were associated with first-person pronouns. Cooley held that the individual perceives him- or herself largely the way others do—the "looking-glass self." From this point of view, each person possesses as many selves as there are significant others in his or her social environment. A similar notion was suggested by Mead (1934), who argued that a person has as many selves as there are social roles for him or her to play. Of course, Mead understood that some social roles are not central to the person; these selves are, correspondingly, not so important. Perhaps the most thorough analysis of the self-concept from the fragmentary point of view has been provided by Sarbin (1952). Anticipating later developments in cognitive social psychology, he argued that social behavior was organized around various cognitive structures, including the self-structure. The self-structure consists of two substructures, somatic and social. For Sarbin, each of us possesses a number of "empirical selves" corresponding to the different social roles that we are called on to play. Sarbin goes on to connect this fragmentary view of the self with the unitary view by postulating "pure ego" as a cross section of these different empirical selves. Gergen (1971) drew upon these notions in his argument that we possess multiple selves corresponding to our multiple social identifications.

Greenwald (1982) has argued for a division of personality into four systems: body, verbal, self, and social. These systems do not necessarily form a coherent unit: For example, they may have different sources of knowledge available to them, or they may serve quite different adaptive functions. Accordingly, they may on occasion appear to conflict, resulting in a discrepancy between verbal and nonverbal communication, attitudes and behavior, cognition and emotion, and so forth. Whereas Greenwald raises the possibility of the nonunity of the *person,* however, it is not clear whether he is willing to entertain the possibility of the nonunity within the self or any other subsystem.

This issue is of more than academic interest because a number of syndromes of psychopathology appear to involve the fragmentation of the self into coexisting, but not consistent, selves. Consider, for example, Bleuler's (1911/1950) classic description of schizophrenia as entailing a split between cognition, conation, and emotion. Bleuler observed that despite superficial differences in symptomatology, all schizophrenics seemed to share a lack of internal consistency between thoughts, motives, and affects. A patient might giggle when told of the death of his mother or describe a severe pain in an objective, detached manner. More to the point, perhaps, it is a fascinating set of disorders of memory that are labeled functional because they do not seem to be associated with any pathological change in the functioning of the central nervous system: fugue and multiple personality (for reviews see Kihlstrom, 1984; Nemiah, 1979, 1984).

The Case of Ansel Bourne

As reported by James (1890), Ansel Bourne began life as a devout Baptist, but later in life became an atheist. In middle age he was suddenly struck deaf, mute, and blind—apparently a religious conversion experience, because he became an itinerant preacher soon after he recovered. Eventually he settled down and became a carpenter. Shortly after opening his business, he withdrew money from his bank account to pay some bills and promptly disappeared from Greene, Rhode Island. He awoke one morning 2 months later in Norristown, Pennsylvania, to find that he had been living there for the previous 6 weeks as a storekeeper. He had no memory for the events of the past 2 months, however; nor had he spoken of his previous life while in Norristown. Under hypnosis, Bourne was able to recount the events of the 2 lost months with considerable accuracy; however, none of this material was accessible to him in the normal waking state.

A number of similar cases have been described by many authors (for a review see Kihlstrom, 1984). The characteristic features of *fugue* are an amnesia that covers the victim's entire personal history, resulting in a loss of identity and of access to relevant clues by which the individual could retrieve or reconstruct his or her identity, and relocation or wandering, which gives the syndrome its name. Nevertheless, the person's general fund of information and repertoire of cognitive and behavioral skills is not affected. The victim suddenly awakens to his or her original identity or to an awareness that she or he does not know who she or he is. The fugue, which essentially consists of an amnesia for all that went before the episode, ends with an amnesia for the events of the fugue.

The Misses Beauchamp

As described by Prince (1906), Miss Beauchamp (pronounced Beecham) was a conscientious, hard-working, and proud college student from a good family (B-I). She presented herself for treatment of neurasthenia, and Prince, as was his usual practice, attempted a cure by means of hypnosis. In the course of treatment, he discovered that when hypnotized, Miss Beauchamp became a more intense version of her normal waking self (B-II). However, at one point during the treatment she manifested a dramatic change in personality: She became very childlike and fun-loving, with no sense of adult responsibility; and she expressed a passionate dislike for her usual intellectual and religious activities (B-III). Later on in treatment, yet another aspect of Miss Beauchamp appeared: In addition to disliking cultural, intellectual, and religious affairs, she now manifested a quick temper and irritability (B-IV). Investigations showed that these different patterns of personality were manifested outside of the clinical context as well. Ordinarily this state of affairs would not be particularly remarkable, except that these patterns of personality were separated by an amnesic barrier. The Miss Beauchamp who presented herself for treatment appeared to know nothing about her activities when she was in her childlike or irritable state. B-III, when interviewed, appeared to have no memory for the activities of B-I or B-IV; and B-IV had no acquaintance with B-I or B-III. B-II had access to the memories of B-I, but B-I showed a complete amnesia for the events and experiences that transpired during hypnosis. The asymmetrical pattern of amnesia produced complex patterns of control over action in which, for example, the childlike Miss Beauchamp would play pranks on the other two. On vacations, Prince corresponded with each of the three major personalities on virtually a daily basis.

Many other cases of multiple personality have been reported in the literature (for a review see Kihlstrom, 1984). Taylor and Martin (1944) have described a number of features that may serve to distinguish the alternate personalities, including: general quality, propriety of behavior, gender identity or sexual orientation, age, local anesthesias or paralyses, and language or quality of speech.

Interestingly, they found no clear pattern of "normality" or "pathology" in the personalities—often the less frequently appearing personalities, for example, were better adjusted than the more frequently appearing ones. By far the most cases in the literature involve only two or three personalities, separated by a pattern of symmetrical or asymmetrical amnesia and marked by alterations in control over behavior.

These cases have clear implications for theories concerned with conscious, subconscious, and unconscious thought and action (Hilgard, 1977; Kihlstrom, 1984; Nemiah, 1979). In the present context, however, they are interesting chiefly because they seem to represent extreme cases of the fragmentation of selfhood. Probably most of us present different sides of ourselves in different contexts, depending on the demands of the situation, our personal goals and intentions, and so forth. For the present it remains to be seen whether various configurations of personality characteristics are sufficiently different from each other to constitute different selves in any meaningful sense. If they do, this will not mean that there is no stable core to personality. From the prototype view, the separate contextual selves are subordinate categories or instances, united by a superordinate prototype. Even if the prototype view should prove to be wrong, it would not follow that these selves represent unrelated exemplars. For most of us, our contextual selves are united by a continuously running autobiographical record: Just as we awaken in the morning knowing that we are the same person who went to sleep the night before, we are aware of the activities of our different selves. When our spouse self is activated, we can still remember what we did in our college-professor self or our jogger self and—equally important—we are aware of having shifted from one to the other and of why. In the final analysis, our personal histories provide for the continuity that is the essence of selfhood (Hilgard, 1949; James, 1890).

IV. The Self-Concept in a System of Social Memory

The self-concept is a mental representation of a particular person—oneself—and as such is part of the individual's wider knowledge concerning objects and events in his or her social world. This social knowledge, in turn, constitutes a portion of the individual's entire memory system. This system stores structured and organized representations of knowledge and forms the cognitive basis of perception, memory, thought, and action. In order to understand the structure of the self-concept and its influence on cognition and action, it is necessary to understand how conceptual information is represented within the memory system.

Hastie and Carlston (1980) have offered an important overview of the system for social memory within the framework of a generic multistore model of the mind (e.g., Bower, 1975). Following their arguments, we find it useful to maintain two somewhat independent distinctions within the memory system: between declarative and procedural knowledge (Winograd, 1975) and between episodic and semantic memory (Tulving, 1972). *Declarative knowledge* is factual knowledge concerning the nature of the physical and social world: what words, numbers, and other symbols mean, what attributes objects possess, where and when certain events happened, and the like. *Procedural knowledge* is knowledge of how to manipulate and transform declarative knowledge: mathematical operations; rules of syntax, inference, and judgment; and strategies for acquiring, storing, and retrieving memories, motor skills, and the like. *Episodic memory* is memory for personal experiences: Such memories include features describing the spatial and temporal context in which events occurred and are embedded in one's personal autobiographical record. *Semantic memory,* by contrast, may be thought of as the person's mental lexicon, consisting of categorical information stored without reference to the context in which it has been acquired and used. Semantic memory contains world knowledge in addition to lexical knowledge, which is why some theorists (e.g., Hastie & Carlston, 1980) prefer the term *generic memory*. Hermann (1982) has provided a concise historical summary of the development of the episodic–semantic distinction in memory that argues for a third form of long-term memory—*skill memory*—that is roughly analogous to procedural knowledge. This taxonomic structure is complicated somewhat by the additional concept of metamemory (Flavell & Wellman, 1976) or knowledge about memory: one's awareness of what facts are available in storage (even if they are not immediately accessible) and what procedures are available for encoding new facts, retrieving old ones, and performing other cognitive tasks.

From a cognitive point of view, the structural features of personality may be identified with that subset of the individual's declarative knowledge that is relevant to social interaction; it includes both semantic and episodic memory. The semantic aspect includes the individual's implicit theories of personality, categorical knowledge concerning generalized types of people and social situations, descriptions of historical events, and detailed representations of both the self and particular other persons. Episodic memory includes the individual's record of personal experiences, embedded in a context of personal space and time; it also includes the individual's memory for the actions and experiences of other people, insofar as they involve the person him- or herself. In other words, the structure of personality is tantamount to the individual's store of knowledge concerning the individual's understanding of him- or herself, significant other people, and the world in which they live. This is the knowledge by which individuals understand what transpires in their social world and plan their responses accordingly. Assuming that people are presented with a standard stimulus situation, individual differences in social behavior are caused by individual differences in declarative social knowledge.

Theoretically, a declarative memory may be characterized as a bundle of features describing an object or event and the context in which it was perceived (Tulving & Watkins, 1975); precisely which features are encoded depends on a number of factors, including the amount of attention devoted to each aspect of the stimulus, what unseen aspects are inferred on the basis of prior knowledge, the way in which each feature is recoded during perceptual and postperceptual processing, and the like (Bower, 1967, 1972). Such a memory is commonly represented graphically as a set of nodes representing concepts that are interconnected by directed pathways that represent predicate relationships between them,

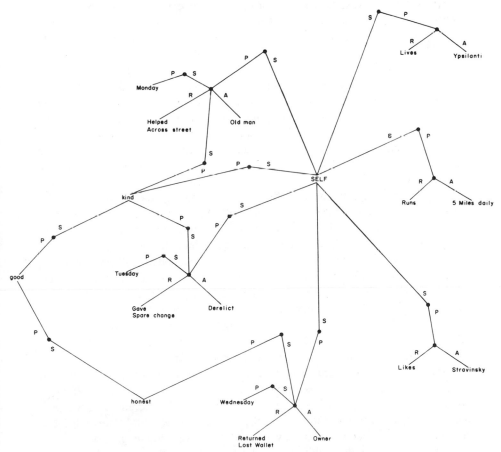

Fig. 4.   A portion of the self as a node in a simplified network of declarative memories (after Bower & Gilligan, 1979). S=Subject; P=Predicate; R=Relation; A=Argument.

as in the ACT system of Anderson (Anderson, 1976, 1981a, 1981b; Anderson & Bower, 1973). Both episodic and semantic memories can be represented in this format.

Figure 4, which has been adapted from Bower and Gilligan (1979), shows a small portion of a (fictional) subject's mental representation of her own personality. In this propositional network, she describes herself as living in Ypsilanti, as a runner, as liking Stravinsky, and as a kind person (semantic memories). She also is recorded as having helped an old man across the street on Monday, having given a derelict some spare change on Tuesday, and having returned a lost wallet to its owner on Wednesday (episodic memories). Helping old men and derelicts are acts described as kind, and returning a wallet is honest. Note that there is a direct link between the self and the adjective *kind,* but not between self and *honest.* In other words, *kind* is part of the self-concept because the person can readily access that information about herself; but *honest* is a descriptor that can only be generated by inference, after retrieving information about specific life episodes. Further distinctions among directly linked attributes may be represented by the strength of the associative pathway. The more central the feature is to the self-concept, the stronger will be the link between self and attribute. Both *kind* and *honest* are socially desirable adjectives, and so—if asked—this subject would be able to describe herself as *good*; but this is apparently not the way she usually thinks about herself. Other people, and the individual's relationships with them, may also be directly associated with the self-concept. Given this analysis, it seems likely that the self-concept has more propositional information associated with it, episodic and semantic, than any other concept in memory.

In the same way, the dynamic features of personality may be identified with the subset of the individual's procedural knowledge that guides the organization and transformation of social information and the transformation of social cognition into interpersonal behavior. These procedures include the interactional skills that the individual employs in the course of social exchange, self-presentational strategies, scripts for social interaction, preferred strategies of focusing on different sources of social information, the rules (algorithms and heuristics) by which people form impressions of themselves and others and make other social judgments, and the processes involved in encoding and retrieving social and personal information. In other words, this procedural knowledge represents the rules by which the individual makes inferences about missing information, formulates predictions about the future, and generates and tests plans for responding to current and anticipated events. Again, given a standard stimulus, individual differences in response will be a product of individual differences in the procedural knowledge brought to bear on the situation. Procedural knowledge can be represented in much the same way as declarative knowledge—as a set of nodes representing goals, conditions, and actions that can be taken to achieve the goals if the conditions have been met. The nodes are interconnected by directed pathways to form a *production system* (Anderson, 1976).

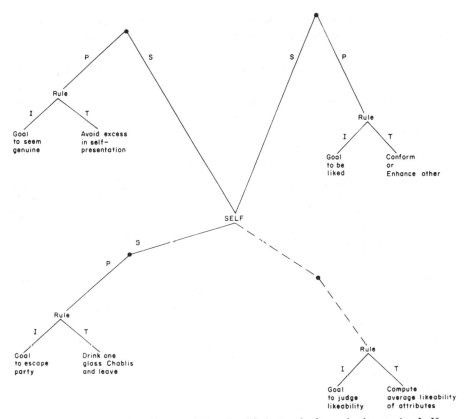

Fig. 5.   A portion of the self as a node in a simplified network of procedural memories. I=If; T=Then. Solid lines indicate direct introspective access to the production system (metaknowledge); broken lines indicate no such access.

Figure 5 shows a small portion of our fictional subject's procedural knowledge. One propositional network indicates that her evaluation of another person's likability is given by the weighted average of his or her desirable and undesirable characteristics; another indicates that when the individual finds herself at a party, she should stay just as long as it takes to consume one glass of Chablis and then go home; a third indicates that in order to get another person to like her, she should conform to his or her expectations. Note that the party and likability production systems are directly linked with her self-concept node, whereas the weighted-averaging rule is not (it is, of course, linked indirectly, but we do not have room to show these connections). This demonstrates one way to think about metacognition: Our subject is quite aware of how she behaves at parties and has encoded this feature as part of her self-concept; she is not aware that she uses a weighted-averaging rule to form global impressions of other people. She might be able to figure this out and incorporate this new knowledge (about her knowledge) into her self-concept. Nisbett and Wilson (1977) have argued that much of the individual's procedural social knowledge is of this nonconscious type, which is outside of reportable awareness.

A good example of consciously accessible procedural knowledge may be found in the self-presentation strategies discussed by Goffman (1959) and Jones (Jones 1964; Jones & Pittman, 1982). Strategic self-presentation, or impression management, involves deliberately attempting to shape another person's view of us. The purpose may be to gain power over that person in some specific social interaction or simply to inculcate an impression that is congruent with the actor's own self-concept. Jones and Pittman have discussed a number of such strategies, including ingratiation, intimidation, self-promotion, exemplification, and supplication. For example, people seem to know intuitively that they can create an image of likeability through conformity, other-enhancement, favor doing, and even self-enhancement (Jones & Wortman, 1973). They also seem to know intuitively that one can be too good to be true and that the strategy will be most successful if it is employed subtly and without excess. Jones and Pittmann note a number of factors that will determine whether the individual will engage in such strategic behavior and if so, precisely which form the impression management will take. Among these are opportunities, resources, incentives, the subjective probability of success, and the appropriateness of the behavior within a particular interaction setting. In the present context, perhaps the most interesting of these constraints is legitimacy: whether the particular impression being constructed is consistent with the actor's self-concept. When there is congruence, they suggest that the performance will be more convincing. Thus, declarative knowledge (one's impression of oneself) seems to have an impact on the use of procedural knowledge (impression-management strategies) to create an impression of oneself in others. When these impressions are consistent with the actor's own self-concept, we may speak of *authentic* self-presentation. On other occasions, we may deliberately attempt to shape another's impressions of us in ways that are quite divergent from the way we view ourselves, in order to gain the advantage in some specific social interaction: In this case, *strategic* self-presentation would seem to be a more appropriate label. Jones and Pittman (1982) have described some of the factors that determine whether self-presentation will be strategic or authentic. For example, under conditions of high task-involvement or emotionality, people may be more likely to reveal their "true selves"—to behave in accordance with their self-concept.

Even when self-presentation is initially incongruent with the self-concept, the possibility remains that people may actually come to see themselves in terms of the impressions that they are trying to create. Despite the actor–observer difference in causal attributions (Jones & Nisbett, 1971), the fundamental attribution error (Jones & Davis, 1965; Ross, 1977) appears to affect self-perception as well as the perception of other people (Jones, 1979; Watson, 1982). Thus, through dissonance reduction (Festinger, 1957) or self-perception (Bem, 1967, 1972), people may come to infer an attribute of themselves that was not present before. In this case, what started out as strategic self-presentation may turn into authentic self-presentation. Darley and Fazio (1980) have reviewed evidence for a similar change in self-description, if not self-concept, arising as part of the sequence of the self-fulfilling prophecy (Rosenthal & Rubin, 1978; Snyder, 1981). The conditions under which these transformations occur, if indeed they do, and those under which the changes are maintained are unknown at present. Perhaps its deliberate, intentional quality fades into the background as strategic behavior becomes routinized, so that the behavior comes to be seen as natural. If a behavior is accompanied by awareness of strategic goals, or of situational constraints, it may be discounted and declared irrelevant to the self-concept. If these goals or constraints can be internalized, however, the new attribute may very well become part of the self-concept and be consistently displayed. Finally, Bowers (1973, 1975) has shown that when people are unaware of the situational control of their behavior, as when it takes the form of a posthypnotic suggestion covered by amnesia (Kihlstrom, 1984; Kihlstrom & Evans, 1979), the behavior may persist even after the contingencies have been removed.

Although the feature-list discussions of concept structure are useful in showing what kinds of information are stored in memory as part of the self-concept, models such as ACT are useful in showing how this information is retrieved from memory when it is required. Basically, ACT holds that each feature of a memory probe, when perceived, activates its corresponding concept node in memory. Activation then spreads out from each of these nodes along associative pathways. When a number of activated pathways intersect, the corresponding proposition (or portion thereof) is compared with the specifications of the query, and if there is a good match, the item corresponding to the proposition is retrieved. The spread of activation is determined by two principal factors: the strength of the associative link between concepts and the number of propositional links emanating from a particular concept node. If the associative link is strong, activation spreads more rapidly. If there are many associative links leading from a concept, activation will spread more slowly because it has to be distributed among many pathways. The interference among such associative links is the theoretical explanation for the fan effect, in which it takes longer to recognize sentences as having been studied when a particular concept implicated in this sentence has been associated with many different propositions. This interference effect has been documented a number of times (Anderson, 1981; Smith, 1981) and is a primary reason for taking propositional network theories such as ACT seriously as models of memory.

Whereas a number of investigators have conceptualized the self as a node in a propositional network (e.g., Bower & Gilligan, 1979; Markus & Sentis, 1982), Rogers (1981) has entered an objection. He points to the common finding that decisions concerning the self—such as whether an adjective like *honest* is self-descriptive—are made more rapidly than corresponding decisions regarding other people. If, as seems likely to be the case, more information is associated with the self-concept than with any other node in the system of social memory, the fan effect would seem to predict precisely the opposite—decisions about the self should take longer than decisions about other people, about whom much less is likely to be known. Smith and his colleagues (Smith, Adams, & Schorr, 1978; see also Reder & Anderson, 1980) have pointed to a similar paradox within the domain of recognition memory, and their resolution may be applicable to Rogers' objection as well. For Smith *et al.*, the notion that more we learn about a concept, the more interference we suffer seems to contradict our intuitions that we are better able to answer questions about topics of which we are more knowledgeable. Smith (1981) has described a number of ways that this knowledge can be organized in order to reduce the number of propositional links emanating from a given concept. For example, the information can be divided into various superordinate categories; they can be integrated by some common theme; or propositions that are perfectly correlated can be represented together. In any event, the net effect is to reduce the number of propositional links fanning off any given conceptual node—reducing associative interference and speeding the spread of activation throughout the network. Smith (1981) has shown that a hierarchically organized propositional network with five levels and five nodes per level could hold 3225 different propositions while having a minimal negative effect on the speed with which activation spreads throughout the network. If the self-concept is the richest node in the memory network, it is also likely to be the best organized one. Thus the absence of a fan effect does not appear to be critical for the idea that the self is a memory structure organized along the lines described in the ACT model.

V.   Assessment of the Self-Concept

The self-concept, as a concept, may be construed as a set of features that are characteristic of the person and also distinguish him or herself from other individuals. What sort of features are represented in the self-concept? Ifthe research reviewed by Wylie (1974, 1979) is taken as representative, most investigators appear to think that the self-concept has mostly to do with self-esteem—with the person's global assessment of him- or herself as good or bad, happy or sad, competent or inadequate, liked or unliked, and so forth. However, the analysis of the self-concept as a node in social memory indicates that it may be linked with a wide variety of other nodes and propositions representing narrower features of personality, specific events, social skills and strategies, and even other people. This has certainly proved to be the case for concepts concerning other people.

For example, Cantor and Mischel (1979) found that the features associated with concepts concerning representative broad classes of people included information concerning physical appearance, material possessions, socioeconomic status, and specific behaviors, as well as dispositions of various levels of generality. Thus, it seems appropriate to cast a broader net in assessing the self-concept in order to produce a more complete listing of its contents (Kihlstrom & Nasby, 1980).

Unfortunately, most techniques that have been developed to assess the self-concept are reactive in that they ask the individual to rate him- or herself on a set of dimensions chosen by the investigator. For example, Carl Rogers (1951) employed a Q-sort technique in which the subject sorted 100 broad self-referent statements into categories representing different levels of self-descriptiveness. Typically, these distributions were forced to conform to a normal distribution. T. B. Rogers (1977) employed a similar technique in which subjects rated a set of adjectives on a 1–9 scale of self-descriptiveness, although these self-ratings did not need to conform to any particular distribution set a priori. Although such techniques are convenient, it is unclear whether such ratings capture all that is important in the self-concept—if the term is to refer to the way the individual construes him- or herself. There is sometimes a tremendous difference between an individual's willingness to describe him- or herself in a particular way and an individual's actual thinking of him- or herself in that way. The propositional theory of memory (Anderson, 1980) indicates why this is so. The self-concept node is connected directly to a number of other nodes, but indirectly—through still other nodes—to every other node in the memory system. For this reason, an individual is able to retrieve a great deal of information about him- or herself—indeed, everything that is accessible in memory; but to consider all of a person's knowledge to be part of his- or her self-concept surely distorts the meaning of the construct beyond all recognition. It might be better to restrict the features of the self-concept to those nodes that are more or less directly linked to the node that represents the self. But how to find them?

Markus (1977) recognized this problem. Like Rogers (1977), she employed self-ratings on a set of experimenter-determined dimensions to assess the self-concept; but she also required that the subjects rate each term both for its *self-descriptiveness* and for its *importance* to his or her own self-concept. Markus defined people as *schematic* in a particular domain if they considered an attribute to be extremely self-descriptive (or extremely nondescriptive) and if they considered the attribute to be extremely important to their self-concept. In the same way, individuals were defined as *aschematic* in a domain if the attribute was rated as only moderately descriptive and *unimportant* to their self-concept. The use of the importance rating is an important advance because it gets us closer to people's actual self-concepts. In the final analysis, it may be useful to disentangle *descriptiveness* from *importance*; since some moderately descriptive attributes may, none the less, be quite important in specifying the self-concept. Markus's (1977) instrument can be easily modified to provide independent assessments of descriptiveness and importance.

Even so, the technique still asks the subject to use the experimenter's categories to describe him- or herself. This will not be a problem if the dimensions employed in the assessment can be defined with a high degree of consensus between investigator and subject, as is the case with Markus's (1977) work. However, this problem may also be solved by employing free-response approaches to the assessment of the self-concept, in which individuals describe themselves in their own words. For example, Jones (Jones, Sensenig, & Haley, 1974) gave subjects 20 minutes to list self-descriptive words and phrases, which were then coded into 97 categories and submitted to multidimensional scaling. This scaling solution yielded four broad dimensions, which were held to be the central features of the self-concept: evaluation; impulsiveness–inhibition; stereotyped masculinity–femininity; and communality with others. Although this approach allowed individuals to speak for themselves in their own words, it is still limited by its ultimate reliance on investigator-defined coding categories. The effect of these, of course, is to translate the subject's self-definition into the investigator's constructs—again introducing the possibility that the individual's self-concept will be distorted. Thus the principal advantage of the free-response technique—that it represents the person's own view of him- or herself—has been sacrificed to the convenience of aggregated data analysis. If any aspect of personality deserves idiographic assessment, however, it is the self-concept. Accordingly, some method of assessment is needed that will preserve individuals' characterizations of themselves, while at the same time permitting investigators to derive general principles concerning the structure and function of the self-concept.

In an extensive line of research, McGuire and his colleagues (e.g., McGuire & McGuire, 1981, 1982) have taken just such an approach to the analysis of free-response self-descriptions. They have employed two free-response tests to assess both the general self concept (i.e., "Tell me about yourself") and physical (i.e., "Describe what you look like") aspects of the self-concept. In their first study, these tests were administered to a group fo 252 sixth-graders, and the responses were subjected to a content analysis. This content analysis is less a translation than it is a categorization of responses, thus staying fairly close to the subjects' own words. The following distribution of categories was obtained: habitual activities (hobbies, sports, skills), 24%; significant others, 20%; attitudes, interests, hopes, and preferences, 17%; school status, 15%; demographic information, 12%; self-evaluation, 7%; physical characteristics, 5%; and miscellaneous, 1%. By this evidence, the self-concept contains much more than self-esteem information. Indeed, it is extremely rich and varied, consisting of behaviors as well as traits and representing the individual's relationships with other people.

McGuire's approach asks subjects to describe themselves in the abstract, without any reference to the context in which they observe themselves. However, consideration of the structure of natural categories has led us to propose that most individuals have several self-concepts associated with different social contexts and organized either as subordinate categories under a superordinate prototype or as exemplars. One approach to the assessment of these contextual selves would be to ask subjects to indicate how they perceive themselves in various social situations. The danger with this approach is that the situations selected by the investigator may not be particularly relevant to the individual subject, again introducing the possibility that the subject's self-concept will be distorted by the assessment process. What is needed is an idiographic approach that will allow the subject to select *both* the situations *and* the attributes for self-description.

An important step towards such an approach has been taken by Pervin (1976), who has adapted Rosenberg's (1976) technique for assessing the personal constructs employed by individuals in impression formation. Rosenberg asked his subjects to list all the different people whom they encounter in their lives, and then elicited free descriptions of each. Pervin (1976) asked his subjects to list all the different situations that they encounter, defining a situation in terms of a specific location, time, activities, and interaction partners. Then they were asked to describe each situation, as well as their own feelings and behaviors in each. These responses were then collated by computer, and the subjects made a final rating of the applicability of each descriptor to each situation. This resulted in a Situation × Descriptor matrix for each individual subject that then can be subjected to various multidimentional analyses to reveal factors or clusters of situations.

Pervin (1976) originally offered his procedure as a technique for the assessment of person-by-situation interactions. In research in progress, Kihlstrom has adapted the procedure for the assessment of context-specific self-concepts. Briefly, subjects list all the situations that they encounter in the ordinary course of everyday living and then freely describe themselves in each of these situations. These responses are then collated, and a computer presents every combination of situation and self-description to the subject for a final rating. These ratings are then used to generate a similarity matrix for the situations, and cluster analysis is employed to reveal a hierarchy of context-specific selves.

Anderson's (1976) ACT model of memory suggests other ways in which the assessment of the self-concept may be improved. Recall that in the ACT system (or any other network model of memory, for example) the network is entered by activating one or more nodes related to information supplied by some query. Activation then spreads to other nodes, with the latency of activation inversely proportional to the number of propositional links that must be traversed. The responses of subjects to free-description procedures of the sort employed by

McGuire (McGuire & McGuire, 1982) and Pervin (1976) may be construed as the products of just such a process. Obviously, given enough time a subject could list the entire contents of accessible memory in response to the simple query, "Describe yourself"; but few of these responses would be appropriately considered to be features of his or her self-concept. Even with time constraints more closely conforming to the conditions of the typical experiment, however, subjects may list attributes that are not closely related to their self-concepts simply because they have the opportunity to do so. This situation may be easily corrected by placing very severe time constraints on subjects, as McGuire does. Alternatively, the investigator may allow subjects to generate items freely, but to take spew order into consideration. Presumably, those items appearing earliest in the subject's list of self-descriptions are more closely linked to the self-concept than those appearing later.

In a similar manner, reaction time may offer a way to improve the validity of reactive measures of the self-concept. The problem with reactive measures is that subjects may affirm characteristics contained in standard personality questionnaires or adjective checklists, even though these attributes do not represent the way in which the subject thinks about him- or herself. However, reaction-time measures may help distinguish between those attributes that are central to the self-concept and those that are not. Consider a typical reactive self-assessment in which the subject must rate him- or herself on a dimension such as "cultured". ACT suggests that such a self-appraisal would begin by activating two nodes in the memory system—one for "self" and one for "cultured". Alternatively, the person must activate nodes representing prototypically cultured acts and episodes from his or her own autobiographical memory. In either case, activation would spread out from both nodes; and if the two pathways intersected, the subject would give an affirmative response. Obviously, features that are more closely associated with the self-concept will yeild faster response latencies.

Some data already exists on this point. For example, a number of investigators have found an inverted U relating self-descriptiveness to reaction time for both personality adjectives (Kuiper & Derry, 1981; Rogers, 1981) and attitudinal statements (Judd & Kulik, 1980). The usefulness of reaction time in assessing the self-concept is most clearly demonstrated in some experiments by Markus and her colleagues. For example, Markus (1977) classified subjects as self-schematic or aschematic for the attribute of independence (or dependence), yielding three groups: self-schematic for independence, self-schematic for dependence, and aschematic for this dimension. Later, these same subjects rated a larger set of adjectives, including a number of items conceptually related to independence and dependence, on a dichotomous scale of self-descriptiveness. Not surprisingly, subjects who were self-schematic for independence rated more independent adjectives as self-descriptive; and those who were self-schematic for dependence rated more dependent adjectives in this way. However, independent adjectives were also endorsed at substantial rates by subjects previously classified as self-schematic for dependence, and many subjects classified as self-schematic for independence endorsed dependent items as self-descriptive. The response latency data was more revealing. Self-schematics for independence showed shorter latencies when rating themselves on independent rather than dependent adjectives; similarly, self-schematics for dependence showed shorter latencies when rating themselves on dependent rather than independent adjectives. Subjects who were aschematic for this dimension showed no difference in response latencies for independent and dependent items. Similar findings have been obtained in the domain of gender-role orientation (Markus, Crane, Bernstein, & Siladi, 1982). Subjects may say many things about themselves for a variety of reasons. Shorter response latencies seem to indicate that the subject needs less time to find a reason—perhaps because that particular feature is already closely associated with the self-concept.

VI. Acquisition of the Self-Concept

From a cognitive point of view, the declarative and procedural knowledge involved in social cognition develops in the same manner as the other declarative and procedural aspects of the cognitive system: In other words, they are largely learned. To be sure, work in perceptual and linguistic development indicates that certain rudimentary knowledge structures are innate; and some research with infants suggests that certain social–cognitive processes, such as those involved in face perception and recognition, are included in this category. Moreover, the clear developmental trends that have been found on such social–cognitive tasks as impression formation and causal attribution may reflect the general course of cognitive development, as children acquire both a larger data base and the cognitive capacity to integrate large amounts of information (for reviews see Ruble & Rholes, 1981; Surber, 1984, in press). However, just as children employ innate linguistic structures to acquire whatever language they are immersed in, so too the vast bulk of the child's specific declarative and procedural social knowledge must be acquired through social learning that takes place within a particular familial and sociocultural framework.

Flavell (1977) has summarized a number of aspects of the development of the self-concept. He notes that one of the earliest tasks of psychological development is for the child to distinguish him- or herself from others—a goal that is probably not accomplished until early childhood. During infancy, however, children do seem to develop an awareness of their bodies, as indicated by recognition of their own mirror images (Amsterdam, 1972; see also Gallup,

1977). Among the first signs of conservation is the child's sense that he or she remains the same person despite the physical changes associated with growth and maturation. Just as others (e.g., Kuiper & Derry, 1981; Markus & Smith, 1981) have noted an association between self-perception and the perception of other people, so Flavell (1977) notes an association between the development of self- and other-perception. For example, descriptions of both self and others show age-related increases in richness, differentiation, and the use of trait terms. McGuire and McGuire (1982) have traced the development of the "social" (as opposed to the "physical") self in a study involving children in grades 1, 3, 7, and 11. The subjects each described themselves orally for 5 minutes, and the resulting tape recordings were transcribed and coded. They found that as a child matures, other people occupy a diminishing proportion of the features given in a self-description and that references to specific other people are replaced by references to general categories of people. Moreover, an increasing proportion of significant others come from outside the family: for example, teachers rather than parents, friends and schoolmates rather than siblings. These age trends, in turn, are theoretically related to the child's developing autonomy, so that his or her self-concept is less and less tied to his or her relationships with other people.

How are features encoded as part of the self-concept? McGuire and his colleagues (e.g., McGuire & McGuire, 1981) have strongly argued that one tends to encode those features of oneself (and others, for that matter) that are unusual in some way. Although this *distinctiveness postulate* was derived principally from perceptual theory (McGuire et al., 1979), it is consistent with the literature on categorization and memory processing. For example, Cantor (Cantor, 1980; Cantor & Mischel, 1979), following Rosch (1978), has argued that person concepts are represented in a hierarchy of prototypes. Each of the prototypes consists of a number of features correlated with category membership, but not correlated with membership in contrasting or alternative categories. In other words, the features possessed by the category prototype have cue validity because they serve both to identify instances of the category and keep the category relatively distinct from other categories. As another example, Hastie (1981) has shown that memory encoding processes selectively favor those aspects of a stimulus that are surprising or otherwise inconsistent with one's general impression. If we can extend this schematic principle to the problem of perception and memory of the self, then it follows that individuals will tend to encode those attributes of themselves that make them stand out in their social contexts.

Evidence from studies of the spontaneous self-concept appears to favor McGuire's (McGuire & McGuire, 1982) distinctiveness postulate. In a series of studies, attributes spontaneously generated by subjects (usually children) have been compared to the distribution of these same attributes within the individual's reference group. The general finding is that attributes are more likely to appear in the self-concept when the individual occupies minority status with respect to them. For example, schoolchildren are more likely to mention their age if they are atypically young or old compared to their classmates; to mention their birthplace if they are not native to the city or country in which they are currently residing; to mention hair and eye color, weight, and height if they are statistically abnormal in these respects (McGuire & Padawer-Singer, 1976); and to include gender as part of the self-concept if the respondent's sex is the minority in his or her classroom (McGuire & Padawer-Singer, 1976) or in his or her household (McGuire, McGuire & Winton, 1979). Sinistrals are more likely to mention handedness than dextrals (McGuire & McGuire, 1980); and individuals who wear eyeglasses are more likely to mention this fact if very few (as opposed to relatively many) of their classmates also have corrected vision (McGuire & McGuire, 1981). Black and Hispanic children are more likely to mention their ethnic identification than white children, and such descriptions are more likely when the child's ethnic group is a weak (as opposed to strong) minority in his or her classroom and when the school is ethnically heterogeneous (McGuire, McGuire, Child & Fujioka, 1978). Not all of these effects have been consistently obtained—compare McGuire and Padawer-Singer (1976) and McGuire and McGuire (1981) on age and height, for example—but overall the hypothesis has fared rather well, sustaining some subtle predictions (McGuire et al., 1978).

Again, the results are in line with what we would expect, given the structure of the self as a concept and as a node in a memory system. The self does not contain an unorganized, exhaustive list of features and attributes. Rather, it is selective, emphasizing features that are characteristic of the self but not of other people. This line of research needs to be investigated with respect to mental as well as demographic and physical attributes. It follows from the distinctiveness hypothesis that those attitudes, traits, behaviors, and significant others that are encoded as part of the self-concept will also be relatively distinctive. Testing this aspect of the hypothesis, however, one immediately encounters some problems. First, McGuire (McGuire & McGuire, 1982) was able to employ objective measures of such attributes as birthplace, age, gender, and race. But how are honesty, profeminism, acting in a shy manner at parties, and being friendly with Joe to be measured objectively? Perhaps, for these types of tests, the distinctiveness hypothesis has to be stated in terms of *perceived* distinctiveness, rather than *actual* distinctiveness. Of course, in the final analysis it is perceived distinctiveness that matters, even in the case of attributes that are easy to measure objectively.

This proposed extension of the distinctiveness hypothesis raises the whole question of the relationship between self-perception and the perception of other people. In fact, the self-concept appears to affect the perception of others in a variety of ways (for reviews see Kuiper & Derry, 1981; Markus & Smith, 1981). For example, Shrauger and Patterson (1974) found that those categories that featured prominently in their subjects' descriptions of other people were also rated as highly self-descriptive. Similarly, Ross (Ross, 1977; Ross, Green, & House, 1977) has observed a "false consensus" effect, whereby individuals appear to believe that other people share their attitudes and experiences. These findings are reminiscent of the psychoanalytic concept of projection, except that projective attribution is not restricted to undesirable qualities. Moreover, as Holmes (1968, 1978) has pointed out, the projective attribution of undesirable qualities is as commonly directed to desirable as well as to undesirable targets and does not lead to more favorable evaluation of these qualities or any other kind of stress reduction. Such findings, however, appear to conflict with McGuire's research that indicates that the self-concept favors attributes that *distinguish* self from others. By this reasoning, individuals should perceive other people as different from themselves. In fact, there is some evidence that favors this point of view as well (e.g., Nisbett, Borgida, Crandall, & Reed, 1976). Given this state of the evidence, Markus and Smith (1981) were only able to conclude that "overall, the person–perception research has unambiguously demonstrated only that self-relevant qualities . . . can figure in the description of others. It has not succeeded in specifying the nature, the direction, or the outcome of the influence of the self-structure on perceiving others" (p. 237).

A distinction between self-concept and self-description may help to resolve this ambiguity. Perhaps, we perceive ourselves as different from others with respect to those attributes that form our self-concept; when it comes to attributes that are merely self-descriptive, however, we may perceive ourselves as similar to other people. This hypothesis bears some similarity to the assimilation–contrast model of social judgment proposed by Sherif and Hovland (1961) and to the notion that one's self-appraisal provides a benchmark for the perception of others in domains that are highly self-relevant (Berkowitz, 1960). Along these lines, Markus and her colleagues have collected evidence that subjects with self-schemata in domans such as independence and masculinity are more sensitive to these characteristics when displayed by other people, compared to those who are aschematic in these domains (for a review see Markus & Smith, 1981). Similarly, Kuiper and his colleagues (e.g., Kuiper & Derry, 1981) have suggested that subjects make faster judgments of others with respect to attributes that form part of their self-concept, as compared to irrelevant attributes. Most recently, Fong and Markus (1982) have found that individuals with self-schemata for extraversion or introversion seek more self-relevant information (i.e., about a target's own extraversion or introversion) than aschematics and are more confident in rating the target on extraversion–introversion than on other dimensions.

According to the cognitive view of personality (Cantor & Kihlstrom, 1982), personality change occurs whenever the individual acquires new declarative and procedural social knowledge or begins to make different choices among options that are already available. Whereas our emphasis on the potential for cognitive and behavioral change opens us up to the charge that we think that people are infinitely malleable, we ourselves prefer to be thought of as meliorists. Again, except in totalitarian environments, the possibility of coercive change is limited by the availability of a wide range of alternatives from which the individual can freely choose. More to the point, perhaps, is the possibility that all this emphasis on flexibility and change has left the individual without any stable core of personality—in other words, without a self. This is not the case. Instead, the individual's self-concept provides for continuity amidst change, through the record of autobiographical memory; and change may be limited to those directions that are congruent with the individual's overall self-concept.

VII. Is the Self Unique?

So far we have discussed the self as a concept and as a knowledge structure, as if oneself were just another person represented in social memory. The question naturally arises as to whether the mental representations of oneself differ in some way from one's representations of other people. From a structural point of view, we think the answer is clearly no: The self-concept is organized along the same lines as concepts representing others. From a functional point of view, however, the answer is not so clear. A number of special properties have been attributed to the self, with respect to the way in which it is involved in social information processing.

In a review of the literature on the role of the self in memory, Greenwald (1981, pp. 223–224) found evidence for three related effects:

1. Material that is actively generated by the learner is more easily recalled than material passively received (the *self-generation effect*).
2. Material that is encoded with reference to the self is more easily recalled than is material otherwise encoded (the *self-reference effect*).
3. Material associated with a persisting task is more easily recalled than is material associated with a completed task (the *ego-involvement effect*).

Of these, the self-reference (or *egocentric perspective*) effect has been the object of considerable study (for reviews see Keenan & Baillet, 1980; Kuiper & Derry, 1981; Rogers, 1981). The earliest experiments in this series involved conventional procedures employed in the study of verbal learning, except for the stimulus materials. For example, Rogers (1977, Experiment 3) presented subjects with 60 personality questionnaire items written either in the first or third person. Half the subjects in each group were simply asked to study the items; the remaining subjects were asked to decide if the item was self-descriptive. On a subsequent recognition test consisting of the 60 targets and 60 lures, memory was better for the items written in the first person (i.e., fewer misses and fewer false alarms); this was especially the case for subjects who had made a self-referent decision at the time of encoding. A subsequent study of incidental memory presented trait adjectives under various orienting conditions, following the "depth of processing" paradigm; items for which self-referent decisions were made were better recognized than items associated with orthographic, phonemic, or semantic decisions (Rogers, Kuiper, & Kirker, 1977). An experiment by Klein and Kihlstrom (1984) coupled the depth-of-processing procedure with the hypermnesia procedure of Erdelyi (e.g., Erdelyi & Becker, 1974; Erdelyi & Kleinbard, 1978). Their subjects studied a list of 64 trait adjectives (half socially desirable and half undesirable) under orthographic, phonemic, semantic, and self-referent orienting conditions, and then they were surprised with a test of free recall. Initial recall was highest for items studied under the self-referent condition. Then the subjects were given two further recall trials, separated by 7-minute "think" intervals with no further opportunity to study the items. Recall improved significantly over the trials, but only for items studied in the self-referent condition. A subsequent replication by Mross and Kihlstrom (1984) has confirmed these findings.

The effect of self-reference on memory can also be seen in another type of experiment that employs idiographically constructed sets of stimulus materials. For example, Perry (Perry, 1979; cited in Rogers, 1981) gathered self-ratings on a large set of adjectives and then constructed for each subject an individualized wordlist consisting of adjectives varying in degree of self-descriptiveness. Following a study trial under conditions of intentional learning, free recall was found to be best for those items that were judged to be highly self-descriptive. A similar experiment by Rogers, Rogers, and Kuiper (1979) explored recognition memory. The subjects rated themselves on a set of 84 adjectives and later studied half of these (drawn from all levels of self-descriptiveness). Memory testing showed no effect of self-descriptiveness on correct recognition; however, there was significantly more false recognition of unstudied items judged earlier to be highly self-descriptive, compared to false recognition of nondescriptive terms. Bower and Gilligan (1979) found a equivalent self-reference effect, whether or not the item was judged in an episodic memory task (in which the subject was asked to recall a specific personal experience in which she or he manifested the characteristic) or in a semantic memory task (the subject had to determine whether the item was self-descriptive).

However, it is not at all clear that this effect is unique to the self. For example, memory is also enhanced if the orienting task involves deciding whether the trait adjective is descriptive of some other person who is familiar to the subject. For example, Bower and Gilligan (1979) found that memory for trait adjectives was also enhanced if they were judged with respect to the subject's mother, but not if they were judged with respect to Walter Cronkite. Similarly, Kuiper and Rogers (1979) found that self-referent adjectives were better recalled than adjectives rated early in the term with respect to a course instructor, who was then an unknown quantity (Experiment 1), but not later in the term when the subjects were presumably better acquainted with their target. Keenan and Baillet (1980) compared the effects of rating adjectives with respect to seven different targets (i.e., Jimmy Carter, a teacher or a boss, a favorite fiction character, a friend, a parent, a best friend, and the self) and found that the memorability of an item was a direct function of the familiarity of the target. However, Keenan and Baillet (1980) found the familiarity effect only for judgments of personality attributes, but not for judgments of physical attributes. Thus, effects similar to those produced by referring stimulus information to the self-schema are also produced by referring it to schemata representing familiar others. It seems likely, as others have suggested (Bower & Gilligan, 1979; Keenan & Baillet, 1980), that both effects can be explained in terms of the degree of cognitive elaboration received by stimulus items at the time of encoding (Anderson & Reder, 1979; Jacoby & Craik, 1979). Assuming that the self is a very rich structure with many links to other nodes in the memory system, such items are associated with more (and more effective) potential retrieval cues as compared to items that have been encoded with respect to more impoverished memory structures. But there is nothing unique about self-reference in this respect.

Although these sorts of principles can be used to explain self-related increases in *accurate* memory, it is not clear that they can account for the biases that occur in perception and memory concerning oneself. Greenwald (1980), beginning with the metaphor of the self as a personal historian that preserves a record of autobiographical memory, has outlined three such cognitive biases; some of these are at least partially related to the effects of self-reference on memory.

1. Memory is best for information that is highly relevant to the self, and people overestimate their own importance as an influence or target of social interactions *(egocentricity)*.
2. People readily perceive themselves as responsible for positive outcomes and tend to deny responsibility for negative outcomes *(beneffectance)*.
3. People tend to seek information that confirms their theories about themselves and to revise their autobiographical memory so that it accords with their current self-concept *(cognitive conservativism)*.

Of these effects, egocentricity and beneffectance appear to be the best documented (Greenwald, 1980; Ross, 1981; Snyder, Stephan, & Rosenfeld, 1976). Interestingly, they seem to interact with each other. For example, self-relevant information appears to dominate perception and memory, and self-generated material is easier to remember than corresponding material produced by others; but under a threat to self-esteem, the "reverse Zeigarnik effect" (Kihlstrom, 1981) favors the recall of successes as opposed to failures. Even when outcomes are determined entirely by chance or experimental manipulations, there is a tendency for people to assert that they had control over them; but while one's success is typically ascribed to one's own ability or efforts, blame for one's failures is typically assigned to task difficulty or the poor performance of partners. It remains to be seen, however, whether a similar sort of bias intrudes on attributions concerning other people—especially people who are positively regarded or who are perceived as similar to oneself. Intuition suggests that we do not readily countenance blame assigned to our friends and that we are more likely to share responsibility for good outcomes with friends than with enemies or strangers.

The conservation of the self-concept was demonstrated clearly in a study by Markus (1977). Her subjects were classified as self-schematic for independence (Independents), for dependence (Dependents), or as aschematic on this dimension (Aschematics), and then they engaged in a variety of tasks. In one case, they were presented with a number of adjectives related to independence–dependence and asked to recall instances in which they had behaved in the manner described by the word. Dependents supplied more behavioral evidence for dependent than for independent adjectives, whereas Independents showed the opposite trend; the Aschematics gave equal amounts of evidence for both dependent and independent characteristics. In addition, the subjects' self-ratings on these dimensions were compared during the initial self-schema assessment. Independents and Dependents showed considerable test–retest reliability in these self-ratings, whereas Aschematics did not. Finally, when asked to predict their future behavior, Independents and Dependents were more confident in their prediction of future schema-congruent and schema-incongruent behavior, as compared to Aschematics. Thus, both memory of the past and predictions of the future are in line with the self-concept.

In a second study, Markus (1977) studied the responses of these subjects to information that was incongruent with their self-concepts. After participating in an ostensible test of suggestibility, Independents were informed that they were highly suggestible and Dependents were informed that they were highly resistant to suggestion; half the Aschematics were given each type of bogus feedback. When asked to evaluate the test, the Independents and Dependents were quite critical, rating it as considerably less valid than Aschematics. In addition, self-ratings of suggestibility were more influenced by the feedback in the Aschematics than in the Independents or Dependents. Finally, when asked to rate themselves again on the adjectives that contributed to the initial self-schema assessment, the Independents and Dependents showed longer response latencies as compared to their initial ratings; however, the response latencies of Aschematics did not change. Nevertheless, the self-ratings themselves were more reliable for the Independents and Dependents than they were for the Aschematics. Apparently, subjects who were self-schematic for independence or dependence were more likely to consider, but ultimately reject, information that is incongruent with their self-concepts. Aschematics, by contrast, readily incorporated this new information into their self-descriptions.

Of course, this conservation of the self-concept may simply be a special case of the well-known proclivity of the intuitive scientist generally toward theory-conservation (Nisbett & Ross, 1980; Snyder, 1980; Wason & Johnson-Laird, 1972). When testing hypotheses about other people, for example, people selectively appear to seek out or retrieve theory-consistent data as opposed to information that might potentially disconfirm the theory (Snyder & Cantor, 1979; Snyder & Swann, 1978). These tendencies can be seen even when the individual is directly confronted with information that is incongruent with his or her hypothesis. For example, Hastie (1980, 1981) found that people are more likely to attempt to explain behavior that is incongruent with an initial impression—presumably in a manner that preserves that impression. Experimentally induced impressions of other people, and even oneself, have also been shown to persist even when the basis for the original impression is completely discredited by later information (Ross, Lepper, & Hubbard, 1975; Ross, Lepper, Strach, & Steinmetz, 1977). Perhaps the self-concept is most resistant to change of all the representations of people stored in social memory; but this probably reflects a quantitative, rather than a qualitative, difference between self and other.

Perhaps the most radical argument for the similarity of concepts of self and others is implicit in Bem's self-perception theory (Bem, 1967, 1972; see also Locksley & Lenauer, 1981). Self-perception theory argues against the notion of direct, introspective self-knowledge and asserts instead that we typically make judgments about our own traits, states, attitudes, and other personality characteristics in the same way that we make them about other people—that is, by inferring them from observations of behavior and the social context in which it occurs. However, there is at least one important way in which self-perception is different from the perception of other people. Although people show a marked tendency to attribute the behavior of other persons to their internal dispositions (Heider, 1958; Jones & Davis, 1965)—the "fundamental attribution error" described by Ross (Ross, 1977; Nisbett & Ross, 1980)—people tend to make situational attributions concerning themselves (Jones & Nisbett, 1971). For example, Nisbett et al. (1973) asked subjects to complete an adjective checklist describing either themselves or some familiar acquaintance. In addition to the usual continuous scale, the subjects were also given the option of responding "it depends on the situation". Although descriptions of other persons tended to be polarized, with the attributes described as highly characteristic or not at all characteristic of the person, the descriptions of the subjects themselves were strongly biased toward situational specificity. In a recent review of self–other differences in causal attibution, Watson (1982) found that the evidence, though complicated, strongly supported the Jones–Nisbett hypothesis.

A number of explanations have been offered for this actor–observer difference in attribution. One possibility lies in the differences in the attentional focus of actors and observers. Heider (1958) suggested that the observer's attention was focused on the actor and that his or her "behavior engulfs the field," leading to a dispositional attribution. However, the gaze of the actors themselves is quite literally directed outward on the field. Another reason may be the wealth of knowledge concerning our own behavior that we possess by virtue of our record of autobiographical memories. This may provide extra information concerning the consistency and distinctiveness of our own behavior that, if available to observers, would also lead them to make situational attributions. Watson (1982), in his review, concluded that there was no evidence that differences in information level, as such, produced the actor–observer difference. Nevertheless, the question underscores an important difference between mental representations of self and others: the wealth of autobiographical information that we possess about ourselves. Therefore, an important topic of research on the self-concept concerns the manner in which autobiographical memories are represented in the cognitive system and the manner in which they are retrieved.

Recently, a number of investigators have reopened the study of autobiogaphical memory, including intensive studies of individual memories (e.g., Linton, 1975, 1978) and early recollections (e.g., Kihlstrom & Harackiewicz, 1982; White & Pillemer, 1979). One promising method of inquiry has employed a cued-recall procedure originally devised by Galton and reintroduced by Crovitz (Crovitz & Quina-Holland, 1976; Crovitz & Schiffman, 1974), Robinson (1976), and Chew (1979). Such studies are beginning to address both the declarative and procedural features of autobiographical memory: how the individual episodes are related to each other in an organized scheme and the way in which these experiences are retrieved and reconstructed. For example, Chew (1979), in a study of high-school seniors, found that response latencies in a cued-recall task were longer for remote memories (i.e., from ages 3–7) than for recent ones (ages 13–17), suggesting a serial activation process that works backward from the present. However, the temporal distributions of memories within remote and recent epochs were quite different, and the latency differences were substantially reduced when high-imagery nouns were used as cues. Although temporal organization is an important factor in retrieval (Kihlstrom & Evans, 1979), other factors complicate the picture.

Although the matter of autobiographical memory is most sensibly raised in the context of the self, it is obvious that social memory may contain rather detailed histories of other individuals as well. Thus, despite the obvious importance of the autobiographical record to the self-concept, the availability of autobiographical memory represents only a quantitative difference between self and others. Of course, our knowledge of other people, especially our intimate acquaintances, is closely related to our knowledge of ourselves. As McGuire

(McGuire & McGuire, 1982) has shown, we define ourselves at least partly in terms of others who are significant for us. We know the attributes of other people because we have observed their behavior, compared it to our own, and encoded it in terms of our personal construct systems; we know their histories to the extent that we personally shared their experiences. Perhaps self-reference and familiar-other-reference have similar effects on memory because we cannot think of one without thinking of both.

A quantitative difference that borders on the qualitative, perhaps, is the extent to which the self-schema is chronically activated in memory. Consider, for example, a recent experiment by Bargh (1982), employing procedures popularized by Schneider and Shiffrin (Schneider & Shiffrin, 1977; Shiffrin & Schneider, 1977). Subjects were classified as self-schematic for independence, self-schematic for dependence, or aschematic for these attributes, following the procedure developed by Markus (1977). They then performed a dichotic listening task in which they were required to shadow a list of words presented to one ear while ignoring those presented to the other. In one condition the subjects were asked to attend to a channel over which a series of adjectives was presented and to ignore a channel over which a series of nouns was presented; in the other, they were instructed to attend to the nouns and ignore the adjectives. The adjective list was constructed so that the middle third contained items related to independence, but the first and last thirds did not. Allocation of attentional capacity to each channel was measured by latency of response to probe stimuli presented twice while independent adjectives were being read and twice while unrelated adjectives were being read. When subjects attended to the adjectives, their processing capacity was increased during the time that independent adjectives were being read. Thus, even in the absence of any explicit self-reference instructions, the self-schema appears to facilitate the processing of self-relevant information. When subjects attended to the nouns, their processing capacity was decreased during this time. Apparently, self-relevant information coming over the unattended channel was picked up without conscious intent and outside of conscious awareness (subjects showed poor memory for the items, nouns or adjectives, presented over this channel), consuming some attentional resources. The effect is not unlike that observed in an airport waiting room or some similar situation in which individuals are responsive to their names read over the public-address system, though they remain oblivious to other messages that are not self-relevant. This automaticity suggest that the central feature of the self-concept, in contrast to other nodes in the memory system, may be chronically activated.

Are there any truly qualitative differences between self-perception and the perception of other people, differences that would render the self-concept unique? Probably not—not, that is, unless one is willing to grant that individuals have some degree of direct introspective access to their own mental states: what they are perceiving, remembering, thinking, and feeling while they are behaving. These ideas and experiences are by their very nature denied to outside observers except through verbal reports. Therefore, they can never form part of our knowledge of other people. This is not to say that our introspections are always accurate. Nisbett and Wilson (1977) suggest that under some circumstances we can be entirely wrong about the reasons for what we think and do. Subjects can be shown to be responsive to experimental contingencies manipulated by experimenters, even though they do not manifest any awareness of these contingencies in the accounts that they give of themselves (see also Bargh, 1982; Dixon, 1971; Eriksen, 1962). Experimenters are not always in a position to contradict, on the basis of behavioral evidence, the subjective reports given by subjects (e.g., Malcolm, 1959). Nor can it be denied that subjective states themselves are often the product of inference and other constructive activity, based on what individuals observe themselves doing. But self-observations of behavior and the context in which it occurs cannot be the sole, or even the major, data base employed in self-perception. Otherwise we would find ourselves constantly in the predicament of the poor creature in Margaret Haskins Durber's (1980) "A Book Report on Minnesota Birds":

> We say, "To err is human." Perhaps to err is also avian.
>
> When a bird is lost, however, we don't call
>   the National Guard or the Navy in,
> We just look up and say, "Good heavens, what is that
>   black-throated gray warbler doing here
>   where all this snow and ice is?
> Maybe the bird looks down and sees it's Minnesota
>   and has an identity crisis
> He says, "If I'm here in the winter, maybe I'm *not*
>   a black-throated gray warbler,"
> And broods and broods about it and feels harbler and harbler,
> Until he's too depressed to warble a single note,
> For how can he know for sure he's a black-throated gray warbler
>   if he can't see this throat?

In work in progress, Kihlstrom and his colleagues have begun to explore the process of self-perception within the domain of hypnosis. Upon termination of hypnosis it is common for subjects to make some general comment concerning what their experience of hypnosis was like. These comments typically range from reports that "nothing happened" or of being "wide awake" to reports of having been "moderately" or "deeply" hypnotized and can be quantified by simple scaling procedures (see the review by Tart, 1979). Other investigators have focused their efforts on exploring the ways in which these depth reports are affected by contextual factors, such as the definition of the situation as hypnosis and the wording of the scale (Radtke & Spanos, 1981). This approach, in contrast has focused on the behavioral and subjective information employed by subjects in making their judgments and the mannner in which this information is integrated in making a global retrospective judgment of their experience. In the experiments, the subjects receive an administration of a standardized procedure consisting of an induction of hypnosis accompanied by 12 representative hypnotic suggestions. After termination of hypnosis, the subjects provide dichotomous ratings of each suggestion according to both their subjective impressions of its success and a behavioral criterion set by the investigator. In some studies the subjects also report on subjective experiences, such as loss of awareness or feelings of automaticity or compulsion; this information is collected either in the form of questionnaire responses or free descriptions. Finally, the subjects provide an overall retrospective judgment of the depth of hypnosis achieved during the session on a 1–10 scale. Our studies consistently show that the subjective experience ratings of either the success of individual suggestions or of overall alterations in consciousness are more important determinants of the subjects' global depth ratings than the publicly observable behavioral responses. It remains to be seen whether the hypnosis results can be generalized to other self-appraisals—though an abundance of data on emotional states indicates that they can (e.g., Leventhal, 1980, 1983). If so, it would seem necessary to revise self-perception theory to allow the process to take account of strictly private, subjective experiences as well as publicly observable aspects of behavior and its social context. The availability of experiential as well as behavioral and contextual information may be the only qualitative difference between concepts of self and of others.

VIII.   What is Missing?

In this chapter, we attempt to adopt two complementary theoretical perspectives in cognitive psychology and pursue their implications for research and for theory on the structure and function of the self-concept. It should be clear that these implications should be construed as hypotheses rather than conclusions. We do not yet know, for example, whether self-concepts are better thought of as summary prototypes or as multiple exemplars—or, frankly, whether the distinction makes a difference. We do not know whether there are multiple self-concepts and, if so, whether these are represented as self-in-context, self-as-different-type-of-person, both, or something else entirely. We do not know how the various types of self-knowledge—declarative and procedural, episodic and semantic—influence each other within an organized memory system. We do not know much about the relative importance of distinctiveness and consensus in determining the features of the self-concept. We do not know to what extent the self-concept has unique properties and to what extent we are simply the people we know best. But we believe that these questions might not have arisen from a pretheoretical framework. That is the virtue of having theories, taking them seriously, and pushing them as far as they will go. The work on concepts and categories and on memory networks has contributed a great deal to our thinking about the self. Now, in conclusion, it is time to consider some of the things that have been left out.

In focusing on the attributes of the self-concept, for example, we have intentionally given short shrift to self-esteem. In part, this grievance is redressed by the huge volume of research and theory on this topic that has been produced elsewhere. But the fact remains that we have not paid too much attention to the emotional and motivational aspects of selfhood. Certainly the self is tied to a great deal of affect: Most of us are more emotionally involved with ourselves than with others. Some of these issues may be discussed in the context of such biases in self-perception as egocentricity and beneffectance. But it is not yet clear whether these biases represent the intrinsic liabilities of the human cognitive system, or alternatively whether the cognitive effects revealed on are products of noncognitive emotional and motivational processes. At the same time, in our defense, this chapter is concerned with cognitive aspects of the self. Even within this domain, however, there are problems that must be confronted.

So far, we have discussed self-assessment as if it were adequately represented by a process involving direct look up of features associated with the self-concept. According to ACT, activation spreads out from the self-node until it arrives at other nodes, which are then reported to be part of the self-concept; or, in response to a query as to whether a particular feature is in one's self concept, activation spreads out from both nodes, one representing the self and one representing the feature, and the attribute is affirmed if their pathways intersect within some critical period. According to the probabilistic view of categorization, a category is accessed and its attributes are looked up directly in a feature list. However, there are reasons for thinking that such processes do not necessarily, or even usually, describe the process of self-appraisal. Subjects are asked to say an almost infinite number of things about themselves on reactive self-assessment procedures: Consider the 17,953 traits listed by Allport and Odbert (1936) and the mass of self-statements generated since Woodworth's research (1919) by those in the business of constructing personality questionnaires; consider as well the fact that subjects are capable of making fairly differentiated judgments about themselves on Likert-type scales, as well as more global ones on dichotomous scales. We simply doubt that there are that many different meters in the head. If not, then most instances of self-assessment must represent the product of judgment and inference.

How then do we come to form impressions of ourselves as intelligent or extraverted, profeminist or antinuclear, tired or forgetful, or anxious or depressed? We want to argue that such self-appraisals represent the product of a prototype-matching process similar to that employed in forming impressions of other people (e.g., Cantor & Mischel, 1979). When asked to decide whether someone else is an extravert, subjects appear to match the attributes of the target person with those of a prototypical representative of that category, paying particular attention to central rather than peripheral features, the presence of attributes central to contrasting or alternative categories, and the situations in which category-consistent attributes are displayed. If there is a close match, then the target is assigned to the category. If oneself is a person, just like anyone else, then self-perception should be based on the same principles as those that guide the perception of other people. Perhaps when asked whether we are friendly or conscientious, we compare the features of our self-concept with those of the relevant category prototype and say yes if we find substantial overlap. Although this proposal may seem similar to self-perception theory in many respects, it differs in arguing that people take into account private, subjective experience as well as publicly observable behavior and environmental context in making inferences about themselves. Although agreeing that the process of self-perception is similar to that of other-perception (even if self-perception takes account of additional information that is not directly available when forming impressions of other people), it goes beyond self-perception by linking social cognition with our knowledge of perception and categorization in other domains.

From the prototype or exemplar view of categorization, the features of the self-concept are lists of words denoting its attributes; from the point of view of ACT, the self is a set of interconnecting nodes forming a propositional network. The question immediately arises as to whether there are nonlinguistic, nonpropositional representations of the self. Is there literally a self-image? The fact that nonhuman primates and preverbal human infants recognize themselves in mirrors suggests that there is; so does the fact that certain thin people of our acquaintance picture themselves as fat or potentially so. Similarly, our emotional and motivational states—what it is like when we are happy or sad, what turns us on and off—may be difficult or impossible to articulate. Arguably, these internal states can be represented as the production systems that construct them; but it is not clear that this solves the problem. In much the same way, it is possible that some aspects of our personality are nonrepresentational. For example, some of our distinctive characteristics may reflect the operation of conditioned habits rather than cognitive processes. In the ACT model, stimulus-response (S-R) associations of this type are represented as production systems in procedural knowledge, but this gambit may imply to some critics that the model, by making all behavior cognitive by definition, is unconstitutionally vague and broad. Alternatively, some of our characteristics may be mediated by dissociated or repressed mental structures and processes that are not normally accessible to phenomenal awareness (Kihlstrom, 1984). This is a complicated issue. Certainly, habits and subconscious mental contents and processes are potentially important parts of personality, but are they parts of the self? Intuitively, it would seem that an attribute should not be considered as part of the self unless it figures in the individual's self-awareness.

This brings us back to the problem articulated by Allport (1937, 1961), as typified by the epigram to this chapter. We have treated the self as an object of knowledge—as a mental representation of a thing that exists in the physical and social world and in some kind of relation to other such things. This is the phenomenal self, with the person him- or herself as the object of regard. We have had nothing to say abut the self as knower, except, obviously, to identify it with the cognitive system that encodes, retrieves, and transforms information. But the matter of the self-as-knower is not simply a matter of information processing. Rather, it is a matter of the executive, the portion of the cognitive system that monitors and controls the rest and forms the basis for the experiences of phenomenal awareness and intentionality. We identify our ideas, our percepts, our memories, and our actions as ours. This problem of consciousness and metacognition remains the great mystery.

REFERENCES

Allport, G. W. *Personality: A psychological interpretation.* NY: Holt, 1937.
Allport, G. W. *Becoming.* New Haven: Yale University Press, 1955.
Allport, G. W. *Pattern and growth in personality.* NY: Holt, Rinehart, & Winston, 1961.
Allport, G. W., & Odbert, H. S. Trait-names, a psycho-lexical study. *Psychological Monographs,* 1936, *47*(Whole No. 211).
Amsterdam, B. Mirror self-image reactions before age two. *Developmental Psychology,* 1972, *5,* 297–305.
Anderson, J. R. *Language, memory, and thought.* Hillsdale, NJ: Erlbaum, 1976.
Anderson, J. R. *Cognitive psychology and its implications.* San Francisco: Freeman, 1981. (a)
Anderson, J. R. Concepts, propositions, and schemata: What are the cognitive units? In H. E. Howe & J. H. Flowers (Eds.), *Nebraska Symposium on motivation, 1980* (Vol. 28): *Cognitive processes.* Lincoln, NE: University of Nebraska Press, 1981.(b)
Anderson, J. R., & Bower, G. H. *Human associative memory.* Washington, DC: Winston, 1973.
Anderson, J. R., & Reder, L. M. An elaborative processing explanation of depth of processing. In L. S. Cermak & F. I. M. Craik (Eds.), *Levels of processing in human memory.* Hillsdale, NJ: Erlbaum, 1979.
Bandura, A. *Social learning theory.* Englewood Cliffs, NJ: Prentice-Hall, 1977.
Bargh, J. A. Attention and automaticity in the processing of self-relevant information. *Journal of Personality and Social Psychology,* 1982, *43,* 425–436.
Bem, D. J. Self-perception: An alternative interpretation of cognitive dissonance phenomena. *Psychological Review,* 1967, *74,* 183–200.
Bem, D. J. Self-perception theory. In L. Berkowitz (Ed.), *Advances in experimental social psychology* (Vol. 6). NY: Academic Press, 1972.

Berkowitz, L. The judgmental process in personality functioning. *Psychological Review*, 1960, *67*, 150–162.

Bleuler, E. *Dementia praecox, or the group of schizophrenias*. NY: International Universities Press, 1950. (Original work published 1911)

Bower, G. H. A multicomponent theory of the memory trace. In K. W. Spence & J. T. Spence (Eds.), *The psychology of learning and motivation* (Vol. 1). NY: Academic Press, 1967.

Bower, G. H. Stimulus-sampling theory of encoding variability. In A. W. Melton & E. Martin (Eds.), *Coding processes in human memory*. Washington, DC: Winston, 1972.

Bower, G. H. Cognitive psychology: An introduction. In W. K. Estes (Ed.), *Handbook of learning and cognitive processes* (Vol. X). Hillsdale, NJ: 1975.

Bower, G. H. Mood and memory. *American Psychologist*, 1981, *36*, 129–148.

Bower, G. H., & Gilligan, S. G. Remembering information related to one's self. *Journal of Research in Personality*, 1979, *13*, 420–432.

Bowers, K. S. Hypnosis, attribution, and demand characteristics. *International Journal of Clinical and Experimental Hypnosis*, 1973, *21*, 226–238.

Bowers, K. S. The psychology of subtle control: An attributional analysis of behavioral persistence. *Canadian Journal of Behavioral Sciences*, 1975, *7*, 78–95.

Bruner, J. S., Goodnow, J. J., & Austin, G. A. *A study of thinking*. NY: Wiley, 1956.

Buss, A. H. *Self-consciousness and social anxiety*. San Francisco: Freeman, 1980.

Cantor, N. Perceptions of situations: Situation prototypes and person-situation prototypes. In D. Magnusson (Ed.), *The situation: An interactional perspective*. Hillsdale, NJ: Erlbaum, 1980.

Cantor, N., & Kihlstrom, J. F. Cognitive and social processes in personality. In G. T. Wilson & C. M. Franks (Eds.), *Contemporary behavior therapy: Conceptual and empirical foundations*. NY: Guilford, 1982.

Cantor, N., & Mischel, W. Prototypes in person perception. In L. Berkowitz (Ed.), *Advances in experimental social psychology* (Vol. 12). NY: Academic Press, 1979.

Cantor, N., Mischel, W., & Schwartz, J. A prototype analysis of psychological situations. *Cognitive Psychology*, 1982, *14*, 45–77.

Cantor, N., Smith, E. E., French, R. DeS., & Mezzich, J. Psychiatric diagnosis as prototype categorization. *Journal of Abnormal Psychology*, 1980, *89*, 181–193.

Chew, B. R. *Probing for remote and recent autobiographical memories*. Paper presented at the 87th Annual Meeting of the American Psychological Association, New York, September 1979.

Cooley, C. H. *Human nature and the social order*. NY: Scribner, 1902.

Crovitz, H. F., & Quina-Holland, K. Proportion of episodic memories from early childhood by years of age. *Bulletin of the Psychonomic Society*, 1976, *7*, 61–62.

Crovitz, H. F., & Schiffman, H. Frequency of episodic memories as a function of their age. *Bulletin of the Psychonomic Society*, 1974, *4*, 517–518.

Darley, J. M., & Fazio, R. H. Expectancy confirmation processes arising in the social interaction sequence. *American Psychologist*, 1980, *35*, 867–881.

Dixon, N. F. *Subliminal perception: The nature of a controversy*. NY: McGraw-Hill, 1971.

Durber, M. H. A book report on Minnesota birds. Poem read on *A prairie home companion*, November 15, 1980.

Epstein, S. The self-concept revisited, or a theory of a theory. *American Psychologist*, 1973, *28*, 404–416.

Erdelyi, M. H., & Becker, J. Hypermnesia for pictures: Incremental memory for pictures but not words in multiple recall trials. *Cognitive Psychology*, 1974, *6*, 159–171.

Erdelyi, M. H., & Kleinbard, J. Has Ebbinghaus decayed with time? The growth of recall (hypermnesia) over days. *Journal of Experimental Psychology: General*, 1978, *4*, 275–289.

Eriksen, C. W. (Ed.) *Behavior and awareness*. Durham, NC: Duke University Press, 1962.

Festinger, L. *A theory of cognitive dissonance*. Evanston, IL: Row, Peterson, 1957.

Flavell, J. H. *Cognitive development*. Englewood Cliffs, NJ: Prentice-Hall, 1977.

Flavell, J. H., & Wellman, H. M. Metamemory. In R. V. Kail & J. W. Hagen (Eds.), *Memory in cognitive development*. Hillsdale, NJ: Erlbaum, 1976.

Fong, G., & Markus, H. Self-schemas and judgments about others. *Social Cognition*, 1982, *1*, 191–204.

Gallup, G. G. Self-recognition in primates: A comparative approach to the bidirectional properties of consciousness. *American Psychologist*, 1977, *32*, 329–338.

Gergen, K. J. *The concept of self*. NY: Holt, Rinehart, & Winston, 1971.

Goffman, E. *The presentation of self in everyday life*. Garden City, NY: Doubleday, 1959.

Gould, S. J. *The mismeasure of man*. NY: Norton, 1981.

Greenwald, A. G. The totalitarian ego: Fabrication and revision of personal history. *American Psychologist*, 1980, *35*, 603–618.

Greenwald, A. G. Self and memory. In G. H. Bower (Ed.), *The psychology of learning and motivation* (Vol. 15). NY: Academic Press, 1981.

Greenwald, A. G. Social psychology from the perspective of the self. In J. Suls (Ed.), *Psychological perspectives on the self*. Hillsdale, NJ: Erlbaum, 1982.

Hastie, R. Memory for behavioral information that confirms or contradicts a personality impression. In R. Hastie, T. F. Ostrom, E. Ebbesen, R. Wyer, D. L. Hamilton, & D. Carlston (Eds.), *Person memory: The cognitive basis of social perception*. Hillsdale, NJ: Erlbaum, 1980.

Hastie, R. Schematic principles in human memory. In E. T. Higgins, P. Herman, & M. P. Zanna (Eds.), *Social cognition: The Ontario symposium*. Hillsdale, NJ: Erlbaum, 1981.

Hastie, R., & Carlston, D. Theoretical issues in person memory. In R. Hastie, T. F. Ostrom, E. Ebbesen, R. Wyer, D. L. Hamilton, & D. Carlston (Eds.), *Person memory: The cognitive basis of social perception*. Hillsdale, NJ: Erlbaum, 1980.

Heider, F. *The psychology of interpersonal relations*. NY: Wiley, 1958.

Hermann, D. J. The semantic-episodic distinction and the history of long-term memory typologies. *Bulletin of the Psychonomic Society*, 1982, *20*, 207–210.

Hilgard, E. R. Human motives and the concept of the self. *American Psychologist*, 1949, *4*, 374–382.

Hilgard, E. R. *Divided consciousness: Multiple controls in human thought and action*. NY: Wiley (Interscience), 1977.

Holmes, D. S. Dimensions of projection. *Psychological Bulletin*, 1968, *69*, 248–268.

Holmes, D. S. Projection as a defense mechanism. *Psychological Bulletin*, 1978, *85*, 677–698.

Hull, C. L. Quantitative aspects of the evolution of concepts. *Psychological Monographs*, 1920, (Whole No. 23).

Jacoby, L. L., & Craik, F. I. M. Effects of elaboration of processing at encoding and retrieval: Trace distinctiveness and recovery of initial context. In L. S. Cermak & F. I. M. Craik (Eds.), *Levels of processing and human memory*. Hillsdale, NJ: Erlbaum, 1979.

James, W. *Principles of psychology*. NY: Holt, 1890.

Jones, E. E. *Ingratiation: A social-psychological analysis*. NY: Appleton-Century-Crofts, 1964.

Jones, E. E. The rocky road from acts to dispositions. *American Psychologist*, 1979, *34*, 107–117.

Jones, E. E., & Davis, K. E. From acts to dispositions: The attribution process in person perception. In L. Berkowitz (Ed.), *Advances in experimental social psychology* (Vol. 2). NY: Academic Press, 1965.

Jones, E. E., & Nisbett, R. E. The actor and the observer: Divergent perceptions of the causes of behavior. In E. E. Jones, D. E. Kanouse, H. H. Kelley, R. E. Nisbett, S. Valins, & B. Weiner (Eds.), *Attribution: Perceiving the causes of behavior*. Morristown, NJ: General Learning Press, 1971.

Jones, E. E., & Pittman, T. S. Toward a general theory of strategic self presentation. In J. Suls (Ed.), *Psychological perspectives on the self*. Hillsdale, NJ: Erlbaum, 1982.

Jones, E. E., & Wortman, C. *Ingratiation: An attributional approach*. Morristown, NJ: General Learning Press, 1973.

Jones, R. A., Sensenig, J., & Haley, J. V. Self-descriptions: Configurations of content and order effects. *Journal of Personality and Social Psychology*, 1974, *30*, 36–45.

Judd, C. M. & Kulik, J. A. Schematic effects of social attitudes on information processing and recall. *Journal of Personality and Social Psychology*, 1980, *38*, 569–578.

Keenan, J. M., & Baillet, S. D. Memory for personally and socially significant events. In R. S. Nickerson (Ed.), *Attention and performance VIII*. Hillsdale, NJ: Erlbaum, 1980.

Keil, F. L. *Semantic and conceptual development*. Cambridge, MA: Harvard University Press, 1979.

Kelly, G. A. *The psychology of personal constructs*. NY: Norton, 1955.

Kihlstrom, J. F. On personality and memory. In N. Cantor & J. F. Kihlstrom (Eds.), *Personality, cognition, and social interaction*. Hillsdale, NJ: Erlbaum, 1981.

Kihlstrom, J. F. Conscious, subconscious, unconscious. In K. S. Bowers & D. Meichenbaum (Eds.), The unconscious reconsidered. NY: Wiley, 1984.

Kihlstrom, J. F., & Cantor, N. *Modern personology: Cognitive and social processes in personality*. Book in preparation, 1984.

Kihlstrom, J. F., & Evans, F. J. Memory retrieval processes in posthypnotic amnesia. In J. F. Kihlstrom & F. J. Evans (Eds.), *Functional disorders of memory*. Hillsdale, NJ: Erlbaum, 1979.

Kihlstrom, J. F., & Harackiewicz, J. M. The earliest recollection: A new survey. *Journal of Personality*, 1982, *50*, 134–148.

Kihlstrom, J. F., & Nasby, W. Cognitive tasks in clinical assessment: An exercise in applied psychology. In P. C. Kendall & S. I. Hollon (Eds.), *Cognitive-behavioral interventions: Assessment methods*. NY: Academic Press, 1980.

Klein, S., & Kihlstrom, J. F. *Self-reference, incidental recall, and hypermnesia*, Manuscript in preparation, 1984.

Krumhansl, C. L. Concerning the applicability of geometric models to similarity data: The interrelationship between similarity and spatial density. *Psychological review*, 1978, *85*, 445–463.

Kuiper, N. A., & Derry, P. A. The self as a cognitive prototype: An application to person perception and depression. In N. Cantor & J. F. Kihlstrom (Eds.), *Personality, cognition, and social interaction*. Hillsdale, NJ: Erlbaum, 1981.

Kuiper, N. A., & Rogers, T. B. Encoding of personal information: Self-other differences. *Journal of Personality and Social Psychology*, 1979, *37*, 499–514.

Leventhal, H. Toward a comprehensive theory of emotion. In L. Berkowitz (Ed.), *Advances in experimental social psychology* (Vol. 13). NY: Academic Press, 1980.

Leventhal, H. A perceptual-motor theory of emotion. In L. Berkowitz (Ed.), *Advances in experimental social psychology* (Vol. 15). NY: Academic Press, 1983.

Lewin, K. *A dynamic theory of personality*. NY: McGraw-Hill, 1935.

Linton, M. Memory for real-world events. In D. A. Norman, D. E. Rummelhart, & the LNR Research Group (Eds.), *Explorations in cognition*. San Francisco: Freeman, 1975.

Linton, M. Real world memory after six years: An *in vivo* study of very long term memory. In M. M. Gruenberg, P. E. Morris, & R. N. Sykes (Eds.), *Practical aspects of memory*. NY: Academic Press, 1978.

Locksley, A., & Lenauer, M. Considerations for a theory of self-inference processes. In N. Cantor & J. F. Kihlstrom (Eds.), *Personality, cognition, and social interaction*. Hillsdale, NJ: Erlbaum, 1981.

Lynch, M. D., Norem-Hebeisen, A. A., & Gergen, K. (Eds.), *Self-concept: Advances in theory and research*. NY: Ballinger, 1981.

McGuire, W. J., & McGuire, C. V. Salience of handedness in the spontaneous self-concept. *Perceptual and Motor Skills*, 1980, *50*, 3–7.

McGuire, W. J., & McGuire, C. V. The spontaneous self-concept as affected by personal distinctiveness. In M. D. Lynch, A. A. Norem-Hebeisen, & K. Gergen (Eds.), *Self-concept: Advances in theory and research.* NY: Ballinger, 1981.

McGuire, W. J., & McGuire, C. V. Significant others in self-space: Sex differences and developmental trends in the social self. In J. Suls (Ed.), *Psychological perspectives on the self.* Hillsdale, NJ: Erlbaum, 1982.

McGuire, W. J., McGuire, C. V., Child, P., & Fujioka, T. A. Salience of ethnicity in the spontaneous self-concept as a function of one's ethnic distinctiveness in the social environment. *Journal of Personality and Social Psychology,* 1978, *36,* 511–520.

McGuire, W. J., McGuire, C. V., & Winton, W. Effects of household sex composition on the salience of one's gender in the spontaneous self-concept. *Journal of Experimental Social Psychology,* 1979. *15,* 77–90.

McGuire, W. J., & Padawer-Singer, A. Trait salience in the spontaneous self-concept. *Journal of Personality and Social Psychology,* 1976, *33,* 743–754.

Malcolm, N. *Dreaming.* London: Routledge & Keegan Paul, 1959.

Mancuso, J. C., & Ceely, S. G. The self as memory processing. *Cognitive Therapy and Research,* 1980, *4,* 1–25.

Markus, H. Self-schemata and processing information about the self. *Journal of Personality and Social Psychology,* 1977, *35,* 63–78.

Markus, H., Crane, M., Bernstein, S., & Siladi, M. Self-schemas and gender. *Journal of Personality and Social Psychology,* 1982, *42,* 38–50.

Markus, H., & Sentis, K. The self in social information processing. In J. Suls (Ed.), *Psychological perspectives on the self.* Hillsdale, NJ: Erlbaum, 1982.

Markus, H., & Smith, J. The influence of self-schemas on the perception of others. In N. Cantor & J. F. Kihlstrom (Eds.), *Personality, cognition, and social interaction.* Hillsdale, NJ: Erlbaum, 1981.

Mead, G. H. *Mind, self, and society.* Chicago: University of Chicago Press, 1934.

Mischel, W. *Personality and assessment.* NY: Academic Press, 1968.

Mischel, W. Toward a cognitive-social learning reconceptualization of personality. *Psychological Review,* 1973, *80,* 252–283.

Money, J., & Ehrhardt, A. A. *Man and woman, boy and girl: Differentiation and dimorphism of gender identity from conception to maturity.* Baltimore, Johns Hopkins University Press, 1972.

Mross, E. F., & Kihlstrom, J. F. *Encoding processes and the recovery of inaccessible memory.* Manuscript in preparation, 1984.

Murphy, G. L. Cue validity and levels of categorization. *Psychological Bulletin,* 1982. *91,* 174–177.

Murphy, G. L., & Smith, E. E. Basic-level superiority in picture categorization. *Journal of Verbal Learning and Verbal Behavior,* 1982, *21,* 1–20.

Nemiah, J. C. Dissociative amnesia: A clinical and theoretical reconsideration. In J. F. Kihlstrom & F. J. Evans (Eds.), *Functional disorders of memory.* Hillsdale, NJ: Erlbaum, 1979.

Nemiah, J. C. The unconscious and psychopathology. In K. S. Bowers & D. Meichenbaum (Eds.), *The unconscious reconsidered.* NY: Wiley, 1984.

Nisbett, R. E., Borgida, E., Crandall, R., & Reed, H. Popular induction: Information is not always informative. In J. S. Carroll & J. W. Payne (Eds.), *Cognition and social behavior.* Hillsdale, NJ: Erlbaum, 1976.

Nisbett, R. E., Caputo, C., Legant, P., & Maracek, J. Behavior as seen by the actor and as seen by the observer. *Journal of Personality and Social Psychology,* 1973, *27,* 154–164.

Nisbett, R., & Ross, L. *Human inference: Strategies and shortcomings of social judgment.* Englewood Cliffs, NJ: Prentice-Hall, 1980.

Nisbett, R. E., & Wilson, T. D. Telling more than we can know: Verbal reports on mental processes. *Psychological Review,* 1977, *84,* 231–259.

Norman, W. T. Toward an adequate taxonomy of personal attributes: Replicated factor structures in peer nomination personality ratings. *Journal of Abnormal and Social Psychology*, 1963, *66*, 574–583.

Osherson, D. N., & Smith, E. E. On the adequacy of prototype theory as a theory of concepts. *Cognition*, 1981, *9*, 35–58.

Perry, D. *Self-reference as an aspect of memory for connected discourse. Unpublished master's thesis, University of Calgary, 1979.*

Pervin, L. A. A free-response description approach to the analysis of person-situation interaction. *Journal of Personality and Social Psychology*, 1976, *34*, 465–474.

Posner, M. I., & Keele, S. W. On the genesis of abstract ideas. *Journal of Experimental Psychology*, 1968, *77*, 353–363.

Prince, M. *The dissociation of a personality: A biographical study in abnormal psychology.* NY: Longmans, 1906.

Radtke, H. L., & Spanos, N. P. Was I hypnotized? A social-psychological analysis of hypnotic depth reports. *Psychiatry*, 1981, *44*, 359–376.

Reder, L. M., & Anderson, J. R. A partial resolution of the paradox of interference: The role of integrating knowledge. *Cognitive Psychology*, 1980, *12*, 447–472.

Reed, S. K. Pattern recognition and categorization. *Cognitive Psychology*, 1972, *3*, 382–407.

Robinson, J. A. Sampling autobiographical memory. *Cognitive Psychology*, 1976, *8*, 578–595.

Rogers, C. R. *Client-centered therapy.* NY: Houghton-Mifflin, 1951.

Rogers, C. R., & Dymond, R. F. (Eds.). *Psychotherapy and personality change: Co-ordinated studies in the client-centered approach.*

Rogers, T. B. Self-reference in memory: Recognition of personality items. *Journal of Research in Personality*, 1977, *11*, 295–305.

Rogers, T. B. A model of the self as an aspect of the human information-processing system. In N. Cantor & J. F. Kihlstrom (Eds.), *Personality, cognition, and social interaction.* Hillsdale, NJ: Erlbaum, 1981.

Rogers, T. B., Kuiper, N. A., & Kirker, W. S. Self-reference and the encoding of personal information. *Journal of Personality and Social Psychology*, 1977, *35*, 677–688.

Rogers, T. B., Rogers, P. J., & Kuiper, N. A. Evidence for the self as a cognitive prototype: The "false alarms" effect. *Personality and Social Psychology Bulletin*, 1979, *5*, 53–56.

Rosch, E. Cognitive representations of semantic categories. *Journal of Experimental Psychology: General*, 1975, *104*, 192–223.

Rosch, E. Principles of categorization. In E. Rosch & B. B. Lloyd (Eds.), *Cognition and categorization.* Hillsdale, NY: Erlbaum, 1978.

Rosch, E., & Lloyd E. B. (Eds.). *Cognition and categorization.* Hillsdale, NJ: Erlbaum, 1978.

Rosch, E., Mervis, C. B., Gray, W., Johnson, D., & Boyes-Brehm, P. Basic objects in natural categories. *Cognitive Psychology*, 1976, *8*, 382–439.

Rosenberg, S. New approaches to the analysis of personal constructs in person perception. In A. W. Landfield (Ed.), *Nebraska Symposium on Motivation.* Lincoln, NE: University of Nebraska Press, 1976.

Rosenthal, R., & Rubin, D. B. Interpersonal expectancy effects: The first 345 studies. *Behavioral and Brain Sciences*, 1978, *3*, 377–415.

Ross, L. The intuitive psychologist and his shortcomings. In L. Berkowitz (Ed.), *Advances in experimental social psychology* (Vol. 10). NY: Academic Press, 1977.

Ross, L., Green, D., & House, P. The false consensus phenomenon: An attributional bias in self-perception and social perception processes. *Journal of Personality and Social Psychology*, 1977, *13*, 279–301.

Ross, L., Lepper, M. R., & Hubbard, M. Perseverance in self perception and social perception: Biased attributional processes in the debriefing paradigm. *Journal of Personality and Social Psychology*, 1975, *32*, 880–892.

Ross, L., Lepper, M. R., Strach, F., & Steinmetz, J. L. Social explanation and social expectation: The effects of real and hypothetical explanations upon subjective likelihood. *Journal of Personality and Social Psychology,* 1977, *35,* 817–829.

Ross, M. Self-centered biases in attributions of responsibility: Antecedents and consequences. In E. T. Higgins, P. Herman, & M. P. Zanna (Eds.), *Social cognition: The Ontario Symposium.* Hillsdale, NJ: Erlbaum, 1981.

Rotter, J. B. *Social learning and clinical psychology.* Englewood Cliffs, NJ: Prentice-Hall, 1954.

Ruble, D.N., & Rholes, W. S. The development of children's perceptions and attributions about their social world. In J. H. Harvey, W. Ickes, & R. F. Kidd (Eds.), *New directions in attribution research* (Vol. 3). Hillsdale, NJ: Erlbaum, 1981.

Sarbin, T. R. A preface to a psychological analysis of the self. *Psychological Review,* 1952, *59,* 11–22.

Schneider, W., & Shiffrin, R. M. Controlled and automatic human information processing (Vol. I): Detection, search, and attention. *Psychological Review,* 1977, *84,* 1–66.

Sherif, M., & Hovland, C. I. *Social judgment.* New Haven: Yale University Press, 1961.

Shiffrin, W., & Schneider, R. M. Controlled and automatic human information processing (Vol. II): Perceptual learning, automatic attending, and a general theory. *Psychological Review,* 1977, *84,* 127–190.

Shrauger, J. S., & Patterson, M. B. Self-evaluation and the selection of dimensions for evaluating others. *Journal of Personality,* 1974, *42,* 569–585.

Smith, E. E. Organization of factual knowledge. In H. E. Howe & J. H. Flowers (Eds.), *Nebraska Symposium on motivation, 1980* (Vol. 28): *Cogntive processes.* Lincoln, NE: University of Nebraska Press, 1981.

Smith, E. E., & Medin, D. L. *Categories and concepts.* Cambridge, MA: Harvard University Press, 1981.

Snyder, M. Seek, and ye shall find: Testing hypotheses about other people, In E. T. Higgins, C. P. Herman, & M. P. Zanna (Eds.), *Social cognition: The Ontario Symposium.* Hillsdale, NJ: Erlbaum, 1980.

Snyder, M. On the self-perpetuating nature of social stereotypes. In D. L. Hamilton (Ed.), *Cognitive processes in stereotyping and intergroup behavior.* Hillsdale, NJ: Erlbaum, 1981.

Snyder, M., & Cantor, N. Testing hypotheses about other people: The use of historical knowledge. *Journal of Experimental Social Psychology,* 1979, *15,* 330–342.

Snyder, M., Stephan, W. G., & Rosenfeld, D. Egotism and attributions. *Journal of Personality and Social Psychology,* 1976, *33,* 435–441.

Snyder, M., & Swann, W. B. Hypothesis-testing in social interaction. *Journal of Personality and Social Psychology,* 1978, *36,* 1202–1212.

Snygg, D., & Combs, A. W. *Individual behavior.* NY: Harper & Row, 1949.

Suls, J. (Ed.) *Psychological perspectives on the self* (Vol. 1). Hillsdale, NJ: Erlbaum, 1982.

Surber, C. F. The development of achievement-related judgment processes. In J. Nicholls (Ed.), *The development of achievement motivation.* Greenwich, CT: JAI Press, 1984.

Surber, C. F. Developmental changes in inverse compensation in social and nonsocial attributions. In S. Yussen (Ed.), *The development of reflection.* NY: Academic Press, in press.

Tart, C. T. Measuring the depth of an altered state of consciousness, with particular reference to self-report scales of hypnotic depth. In E. Fromm & R. E. Shor (Eds.), *Hypnosis: Developments in research and new perspectives.* NY: Aldine, 1979.

Taylor, W. S., & Martin, M. F. Multiple personality. *Journal of Abnormal and Social Psychology,* 1944, *39,* 281–300.

Tulving, E. Episodic and semantic memory. In E. Tulving & W. Donaldson (Eds.), *Organization of memory.* NY: Academic Press, 1972.

Tulving, E., & Watkins, M. J. Structure of memory traces. *Psychological Review,* 1975, *82,* 261–275.

Wegner, D. M., & Vallacher, R. R. *The self in social psychology*. NY: Oxford University Press, 1980.

Wason, P. C., & Johnson-Laird, P. N. *Psychology of reasoning: Structure and content*. Cambridge: Harvard University Press, 1972.

Watson, D. The actor and the observer: How are their perceptions of causality different? *Psychological Bulletin*, 1982, *92*, 682–700.

White, S. H., & Pillemer, D. P. Childhood amnesia and the development of a socially accessible memory system. In J. F. Kihlstrom & F. J. Evans (Eds.), *Functional disorders of memory*. Hillsdale, NJ: Erlbaum, 1979.

Winograd, T. Computer memories: A metaphor for memory organization. In C. N. Cofer (Ed.), *The structure of human memory*. San Francisco: Freeman, 1975.

Wittgenstein, L. *Philosophical investigations*. NY: Macmillan, 1953.

Woodworth, R. S. *Personal data sheet*. Chicago: Stoelting, 1919.

Wylie, R. C. *The self-concept* (Vol. 1). Lincoln, NE: University of Nebraska Press, 1974.

Wylie, R. C. *The self-concept* (Vol. 2). Lincoln, NE: University of Nebraska Press, 1979.

ACKNOWLEDGMENTS

We thank our colleagues Anthony G. Greenwald, Judith M. Harackiewicz, Reid Hastie, Hazel Markus, David M. Neves, Edward E. Smith, Stevens S. Smith, and Patricia A. Register for their comments during the preparation of this paper.

THEORY OF THE SELF: IMPASSE AND EVOLUTION*

Kenneth J. Gergen

DEPARTMENT OF PSYCHOLOGY
SWARTHMORE COLLEGE
SWARTHMORE, PENNSYLVANIA

I. Introduction

The origins of human concern with the self are no less ancient than the process of historical accounting itself. Already within the Homeric world there

*Preparation of this chapter was facilitated by a grant from the National Science Foundation (NBS 78-09393). Appreciation is also expressed to Marianthi Georgoudi, Mary Gergen, Deborah Kemler, Mansur Lalljee, Morris Rosenberg, Barry Schwartz, and Wolfgang Stroebe for their critical reading of the manuscript in earlier draft.

ADVANCES IN EXPERIMENTAL
SOCIAL PSYCHOLOGY, VOL. 17

was broad concern with the extent to which states of consciousness were subject to demonic intervention. Aristotle's inquiry into the character of the soul may be considered a direct predecessor to contemporary self-research. Such questions as how it is possible to know oneself, what is the character of the true self, what are the origins and implications of self-love, how does self-alienation develop, how is self-definition linked to the social order, what value is to be placed on the state of selflessness, and whether selves should be considered origins of action have continued over the centuries to command attention. Such thinkers as Pascal, Spinoza, Locke, Descartes, Berkeley, and Hume may all be credited with significant contributions to this legacy. Such work also formed the grounding context for the development of self-inquiry within early psychology. By the late 1800s there was already available to thinkers in the Western tradition a history of pertinent questions and a rich vocabulary of understanding (see Robinson, 1982; Verhave & van Hoorn, 1984). Many of the central features of today's psychology of the self may be importantly linked to these estimable traditions.

Contemporary inquiry into the self also owes a more immediate debt to twentieth century developments. Three major pillars of contemporary work may be identified. First, James's (1890) seminal work on the senses of identity and the configuration of self-esteem legitimated research on the self within what became the domain of *experimental psychology*. Although such work was muted with the hegemony of the behaviorist movement and its penchant for observables, the work of such notables as Koffka (1935), Hilgard (1949), and Woodworth (1958) insured safe passage of self-concerns within the experimental tradition. The second pillar of contemporary study is lodged within *psychoanalytic theory*. The impact of Freud's (1933) early writings on the ego cannot be overestimated in this respect. His concerns became extended, modified, and popularized through Horney's (1950) later writings on self-love, Adler's (1927) inquiries into the sense of inferiority, Sullivan's (1953) treatment of the "self dynamism," Jung's (1939) elaboration of the individuation process, and Erikson's (1950) explorations of identity development. The third formative influence of significance was furnished by the *symbolic interactionist* writings, particularly those of Mead (1934) and Cooley (1902). Much of the continuing dialogue between social psychologists and sociologists can be traced to the common theoretical discourse emerging within this domain (cf. Kaplan, 1975; McCall & Simmons, 1966).

Between 1940–1960 most psychological research on the self could trace its theoretical roots to one of these three seminal sources. However, because the dominant orientation within psychology was (and continues to be) neo-behaviorist stimulus-organism-response (S–O–R) and the major method of research was (and continues to be) experimentation, theoretical conceptions particular to these disparate contexts tended to become integrated and homogenized. Differing theoretical perspectives often lost their unique configurations as various facets of each theory could readily be translated into the relatively atheoretical

S–O–R format. Thus, for example, perceptual and learning processes, central within the experimental domain, might be related (either as determinants or products) to level of self-esteem, a variable drawn from the clinical sphere. Or one's success in the eyes of others, critical to the interests of the symbolic interactionist, might serve as the independent variable in a study of learning; and various ego defense mechanisms might serve the same role in studies of perception of others' regard. Many of the seminal contributions within this early period have been collected in volumes edited by Gordon and Gergen (1968), Hamachek (1965), and Stoodley (1962). Results of the many lines of related research are carefully reviewed by Wylie (1961, 1968).

Although these various traditions of inquiry were firmly entrenched within psychology, more generally it would be unfair to say that they gained a focal position within social psychology. Researchers in the areas of social influence and race prejudice often employed self-constructs (particularly self-esteem) in their research (cf. Clark & Clark, 1947; Hovland & Janis, 1959). Goffman's (1955, 1959) writings had begun to stimulate interest in self-presentational strategies; and dissonance researchers had become increasingly concerned with the relationship between self-conception and dissonance arousal (Aronson, 1968). However, the renaissance of the self in social psychology may properly be traced to the "cognitive revolution" within psychology. As concept formation and related processes commanded increasing attention within the field at large, it became increasingly apparent to social psychologists that the self-concept might play a critical role in guiding human conduct. The growth of attribution theory in social psychology added further vitality to such concerns. Research into people's perceptions of themselves and others as causal sources of their actions (Jones & Nisbett, 1971; Seligman, 1975) and into the social origin of emotional attribution (Nisbett & Schachter, 1966; Schachter, 1964; Valins, 1966) spoke directly to questions of long-standing importance to self-theory. These developments, combined with Bem's (1972) captivating reinterpretation of dissonance findings in terms of self-perception, the rekindling of philosophic interest in the self (Mac-Murray, 1978; Mischel, 1977), the revitalization of self-concerns in the developmental sphere (Lewis & Brooks-Gunn, 1979), and the lively and continuing input from both the sociological (Rosenberg, 1979) and psychoanalytic spheres (Kohut, 1971) have now earned self-study a central place within the social psychological literature. Many basic texts now devote an entire chapter to the self, thus placing such concerns on a par with the traditional areas of attitude change, social influence, group psychology, and the like. Other volumes have been exclusively built around issues of self-perception (Gergen, 1971, Hewit, 1976, Kleinke, 1978). These volumes, combined with a plethora of edited integrations (Fillipp, 1979; Giovannini, 1979; Lynch, 1981; Rosenberg & Kaplan, 1982; Suls, 1982; Suls and Greenwald, 1983; Wegner and Vallacher, 1980) suggest that the hegemony of self-inquiry is currently at hand.

A review of the full panoply of inquiry into the self is well beyond the scope of the present chapter. Such a review would require a volume in itself. However, the present context does furnish a needed opportunity to move beyond the infinity of detail and to take a more general account of the progress and problems within the field. How have the major conceptions been altered; what critical problems have been discovered; and what can be anticipated from a continuation of present investments? These and similar questions are the central concern in the present treatment. The chapter is divided into three sections. At the outset it is essential to deal with the place of empirical data in evaluating the progress of inquiry. Although the traditional crucible for assessing inquiry into self has been considered empirical, an assaying of developments in adjoining domains suggests that this criterion has been overemphasized. Invited is greater theoretical boldness and attention to alternative criteria for evaluation. This discussion will set the stage for tracing major evolutions in understanding within the present renaissance of self-inquiry. Particular attention will be given to (1) the concept of self-knowledge, (2) the concern with the self as agency, and (3) the shift from structural to process orientations. As will be shown, alterations in these domains together suggest a major evolution in the dominant image of human functioning in social psychology. Finally, discussion will center on the limitations of "the concept" as a theoretical implement and consider means of moving beyond existing barriers in future undertakings.

II. The Place of Observation in Self-Research

As we have seen, much early inquiry into self originated either within the psychoanalytic or symbolic interactionist domain. By virtue of training, interest, and ideology investigators within these domains did not typically attempt to ground their ideas in systematic empirical research. However, with the emergence of what Koch (1959) and others have seen as the development of a self-conscious scientism in American psychology, concern with the empirical basis of psychological knowledge became paramount. Such concern has been no less evident in research on the self; well over 90% of contemporary contributions to this literature reflect the outcomes of empirical research. In effect, contemporary inquiry into the self has become virtually synonymous with systematic empirical research. Further, as evidenced in most primary reviews of the past several decades (Bem, 1972; McGuire, 1968; Wylie, 1961, 1968), critical discussion centers on the empirical validity of relevant propositions. Although the process of empirical research has played a substantial role in establishing the identity of psychology as a science and has allayed suspicions that self-investigation is personal bias masquerading in scientific terminology, it is a propitious point at which to reassess the traditional posture of the field. A variety of significant changes have occurred in the intellectual context in which self-research has been carried out. Such changes suggest that empirical work does not play the pivotal role traditionally assumed in the advancement of knowledge. As the empirical crucible for theoretical evaluation recedes in importance, new considerations emerge. The theorist is invited to speculate more boldly and to broaden substantially the range of criteria for theoretical evaluation. Four such concerns are particularly germane.

A. THE EMPIRICAL UNDERDETERMINATION OF THEORY

Logical empiricist philosophy of the kind that has dominated traditional thinking about psychological research placed a strong emphasis on the relationship between theoretical statements and observation. As often stated, theoretical statements not subject to correction through observation are candidates for mysticism; theoretical terms that cannot be linked to sense data through operational definition are open to suspicion. Yet, much has changed within the philosophy of science since this period, and during the present "post-empiricist" era (Thomas, 1979), the demands for strict linkages between theoretical language and observation are seldom voiced. As Quine (1960) has compellingly demonstrated, there is never more than a loose fit between theoretical terms and observation. The spatio–temporal coordinates for even the simplist term (e.g., rabbit) are never precise and often shift as the context is altered. In a related line of argument, Quine (1953) has shown how empirical tests of a theory seldom yield unequivocal results; most theories typically contain a host of auxiliary and unarticulated assumptions. Any empirical findings that appear to disconfirm one's theory can typically be explained in terms of one or more of these auxiliary assumptions. The major premises of a theory may thus remain relatively inviolate whereas minor assumptions are altered. It is on such grounds as these that philosophers such as Lakatos (1970) argue for the empirical assessment, not of particular theoretical propositions, but of the outcomes of long-term research programs. Others, such as Laudan (1977) are willing to abandon the attempt at approximating truth through empirical work and to settle for "problem solving" as the criterion for evaluating scientific progress.

In addition to these various revisions in the traditional view, Hanson (1958) has made a strong case to the effect that what is taken to be empirical data is determined by preliminary theoretical suppositions. Thus, argues Hanson, one cannot set out to study the world of given facts; one must already possess some form of theoretical template to determine what is to be counted as a fact. Theoretical distinctions are not thus inductively generated through the careful assaying of real world differences; rather, one's theoretical distinctions largely determine what counts as similar or different within the stimulus world. When extended, Hanson's argument suggests that theories should primarily be viewed as lenses for perceiving the world; once a given lens is employed, the theory cannot be falsified through observation. Observations essentially become defined in terms of the theory.

Although critiques have been launched against each of these various lines of argument, it is generally agreed among philosophers of science that, at a minimum, even the most compelling of natural science theories are empirically underdetermined. To illustrate in the case of self-research, we may consider the extended line of research on self-awareness (cf. Carver & Scheier, 1978; Duval & Wicklund, 1972; Wicklund, 1975, 1982). As generally argued in this domain, when one's attention is focussed on oneself, evaluative criteria become salient. With the enhanced saliency of such criteria, one becomes increasingly concerned with one's actions and the extent to which they are consistent with the criteria. Thus, both children and college students are shown to cheat less when self-aware (Diener & Wallborn, 1976). People may also be induced to work harder (Wicklund & Duval, 1971), to perform less adequately (Brockner, 1979), to be more helpful (Wegner & Schaefer, 1978), to display more social sensitivity (Feingstein, 1979), to reciprocate disclosure (Shaffer, Smith, & Tomarelli, 1982), and to bring their behavior into line with their standards (Pryor, Gibbons, Wicklund, Faslor, & Hood, 1977) under similar conditions. Yet, the status of self-awareness as an explanatory instrument is to be considered an emergent rather than a given. That is, its meaning and implications are continuously undergoing alteration. The dependency of self-awareness processes on past learning, anticipation of the future, various drive states, gender differences, age variations, attitudes toward self or the environment, specific values, state of generalized arousal, and so on, are all left unspecified. Each of these concepts may figure in the development of auxiliary propositions that may be employed in sustaining the theory across a vast range of conflicting empirical findings.

As further seen, from the present perspective the theory could not have been derived from observation itself. One could not deduce a proposition such as "self focused attention enhances the salience of evaluative criteria," by merely observing the movement (or sounds) of the human body through time and space. Rather, given the proposition, one comes to understand human activity in its terms. The mere existence of a mirror in front of a person is hardly worthy of note in daily life. Yet in the hands of the self-awareness researcher, it becomes a "stimulus for self-focused attention"—with its attendant consequences of making salient standards of evaluation. The theory has thus transformed the observation world, sensitizing one to certain features while obscuring others.

B.   VALUATIONAL IMPLICATIONS OF SCIENTIFIC THEORY

Coupled with the receding importance attached to the factual grounding of theory has been an enhanced concern with the moral, ethical, and ideological prescriptions embedded within sociobehavioral theory. Such concerns are hardly novel to the sciences. Weber's (1949) analysis of the value-impregnated character of theoretical distinctions, Mannheim's (1952) elucidation of the ideological basis of social theory, and Marx's (1954) critique of the self-serving character of capitalist economic theory are all classic in this regard. Although such concerns were largely obscured during psychology's age of self-conscious scientism, they have now returned to demand lively attention. Thus, for example, social psychological theories have been criticized for their implicit commitment to an ideology of self-contained individualism along with their concomitant denigration of interdependent or communal forms of social organization (cf. Hogan & Emler, 1978; Sampson, 1977, 1978, 1981). Similarly, traditional conflict theory has been derogated for its rendering the have-nots in society invisible (Apfelbaum & Lubek, 1976), Kohlberg's theory of moral development for its bias toward masculine values (Gilligan, 1982), cognitive theory for its abrogation of concern with "real world" problems (Sampson, 1981), and traditional gender distinctions within the sciences for their sustaining a rigid dichotomy in social patterning (Kessler & McKenna, 1978). As it is argued, such biases filter outward into the society and serve to shape common conceptions and values. Thus, social theory contributes to the configuration of society (Gergen, 1982b).

To illustrate, the compelling work of Synder and his colleagues (Snyder, 1974, 1979; Snyder & Campbell, 1982; Snyder & Monson, 1975) on self-monitoring introduces a 25-item measure designed to sort people with respect to their conceptions of self as either pragmatic or principled in their relationships with others. Much of the research in this domain thus attempts to demonstrate that persons who fall toward one end of this dimension, as opposed to the other, differ in the ways they characteristically process information and carry out social relationships (cf. Dabbs, Evans, Hopper, & Puruis, 1980; Elliott, 1979; Snyder & Cantor, 1980; Snyder & Gangestad, 1982). Yet, regardless of the robustness of the empirical findings, it is clear that this particular conceptualization carries with it a variety of valuational implications. It facilitates the tendency to divide the world into types and to see people as falling into separate social categories. It may be argued that such a tendency fosters a sense of social devisiveness, engenders feelings of us versus them, or feeds people's feelings of alienation at not belonging. Also one discovers in the work the implicit critique of the pragmatic person for being unprincipled and of the principled person for being socially insensitive. It could be otherwise; pragmatism could be elevated in status to a form of moral principle, and a principled orientation could be viewed as the most efficacious in contributing to the broad social good. Again, this is not to question the findings or the significance of the research. It is rather to raise concerns over the ethical and ideological implications of selecting one interpretive or theoretical schema over another. Given the decreasing emphasis placed on empirical outcomes in evaluating theory, such concerns gain in relevance. To the extent that self-theory is underdetermined with respect to data, inquiry is invited into its broad prescriptive implications within the society.

C. THE EFFECTS OF METHOD ON THEORY

A third concern with the role of observation centers on methodology. To the extent that the major crucible for judging theories of the self is the product of empirical method, then theoretical developments become dependent on methodology. Theoretical structure cannot easily be elaborated beyond the limits of available methods. The investigator is simultaneously invited to cast theoretical structures in forms favored by the logic of existing methods. For example, as Thorngate (1976) has argued, the systematic use of analysis of variance designs has discouraged the development of highly complex, multivariate theories. Similarly, McGuire (1973) has demonstrated how the exclusive use of experimentation has impeded the development of theories employing concepts of bidirectional effects and feedback loops. Pepitone (1981) has demonstrated how the demand for experimental research has militated against the growth of small group theory. As the present author (Gergen, 1982b) has argued, a commitment to the experimental method hinders the development of diachronic, contextualist, and rule–role theories of human interaction. In this light we find that the exclusive use of empirical evidence as the benchmark for assessing theoretical accomplishments has the implicit effect of limiting the domain of theoretical possibilities.

It is largely for these reasons that McGuire and his colleagues (McGuire & McGuire, 1982; McGuire, McGuire, & Winton, 1979; McGuire & Padawer-Singer, 1976) have turned to nonexperimental methods in the study of the self-concept. As McGuire (1981) has argued, research should primarily be concerned with generating hypotheses rather than testing them. Given an hypothesis, McGuire proposes it is usually possible to develop an experimental demonstration. However, a premium is to be placed on research that is more open-ended with respect to outcome. Thus, following the early symbolic interactionist method of asking people to describe themselves (cf. Bugental, 1964; Gordon, 1968; Kuhn & McPartland, 1954), the McGuires simply ask respondents "tell us about yourself." Using this method it is found, for example, that people tend to describe themselves in ways that are distinctive or set them apart from their usual social background and that females are more likely than males to define themselves in relation to others.

D. THE INTERPRETIVE BASIS
   OF OBSERVATION STATEMENTS

A final line of argument suggests that in the case of self-inquiry the empirical baseline is particularly problematic. The self-theorist confronts a cluster of enigmas that may well occlude the passage to empirical substantiation. First it is to be noted that the domain of fundamental interest in most self-inquiry is hypothetical. Theorists attempt to explore, for example, the contours of self-conception, to discover the effects of self-awareness, to determine the causes and effects of self-esteem level, or to trace the operation of self-schemata within the larger context of information processing. The knowledge that is sought, then, is knowledge about psychological mechanisms and/or processes along with their origins and behavioral implications.

Of course, such concerns are hardly unique to self-theorists, and psychologists of many stripes have long confronted the problem of how to ground theory of the opaque in the concrete and observable. The most widely accepted answer to this challenge since the publication of MacCorquodale and Meehl's (1948) famous paper on hypothetical constructs lies in the realm of inference. As it is argued, one is permitted to infer the state of various hypothetical entities or processes on the basis of systematic observation of the individual's behavior. Thus, for example, it is generally held that agreement with a statement on Rosenberg's (1979) test of self-esteem, such as, ''On the whole, I am satisfied with myself,'' would permit the investigator to infer a state of enhanced self-esteem. Similarly, McGuire and McGuire (1982) might use a child's statement ''I am Polish'' (in response to the interviewer's request, ''Tell us about yourself'') as a means of inferring ''salience of ethnicity'' to the child's self-concept. In Wicklund's (1982) study of self-awareness, subjects' affective ratings are used to infer phenomenological states of discomfort.

This means of constructing an objective grounds for knowledge of psychological states has remained relatively secure until the resurgence of concern with the processes of interpretation (hermeneutics) in the behavioral sciences (cf. Bauman, 1978; Gauld & Shotter, 1977; Geertz, 1973; Giddens, 1976; Rabinow & Sullivan, 1979; Taylor, 1971). As argued in this domain, people do not generally respond to others' overt actions, but to the meaning of these actions. The primary task of the actor, and indeed the scientist, is thus to determine the intentions underlying various actions. In an extension of this view, Gergen (1982b) has argued that most terms for behavioral description do not thus refer to the observable activities of individuals; they refer to the underlying disposition, motive, or intention. Such terms as aggression, altruism, friendliness, competitiveness, and so on do not then refer to specific movements of the body through space and time. Rather, such terms refer to what the individual is attempting to accomplish through such actions. Thus, if one depresses the trigger of a pistol and the result is the death of a neighbor, one is not permitted to call the act a murder until one has penetrated the state of mind of the actor. Did he intend or mean to kill? The spatio–temporal event is itself uninformative on this score; triggers may be pressed in precisely the same manner whether they are pointed in the direction of targets, persons, or the air. Even when the result of this movement is another's death, the actions themselves do not count as murder. The essential question is whether the individual was motivated to kill, which is a matter of psychological disposition.

From this perspective the traditional attempt to anchor psychological variables in observables is rendered problematic. This is so because each of the putative behaviors that serves as the empirical anchor for inferring psychological states is found, upon closer inspection to depend on an inference in its own right. That is, the terms describing the actions used as the basis of inference do not themselves refer to the actions per se but to underlying dispositions, motives, or intentions—all psychological states. To illustrate, in determining level of self-esteem, the movement of the respondent's arm and fingers in checking "strongly agree" in response to the statement "On the whole, I am satisfied with myself" is inconsequential. From the researcher's perspective, the writing implement could be controlled by the respondent's toes or carried in his teeth. It is not the observable activity that is in question, but what the individual *means* by it. Similarly, the child's verbal utterance "I am Polish" is not of fundamental concern in determining the underlying salience of ethnicity to the self-concept. If the child were trained from birth to utter these and only these particular words, the investigator would be little inclined to accept them as an indicator of the underlying concept. It is what the child means by the utterances that is fundamentally in question. And, the precise phonemes used by an individual in reporting on his or her internal states are of no interest to the self-awareness investigator. Of critical concern is what the individual is *trying* to say.

As this line of argument suggests, what have been traditionally accepted as behavioral anchors for hypothetical constructs are essentially cues to further inference. The language of behavioral operations is not, in fact, tied to observables but is itself a language of hypothetical constructs. One thus attempts to determine a hypothetical state of self-esteem by assaying yet another hypothetical state of intention, meaning, or motive. One essentially employs one language of hypotheticals to verify or instantiate another.

One might attempt to reduce the domain of possible interpretations by employing the traditional means of establishing discriminant validity (cf. Jackson, 1981; Marsh & Smith, 1982; Shoemaker, 1980). However one need only extrapolate from the previous line of reasoning to realize the inadequacies of such a solution. Each of the multimeasures employed for purposes of triangulation is itself in need of interpretation. Thus, one is furnished not with multiple data points but with multiple sources of inference. The constraints upon such inferences are not furnished by the data but by the investigator's theoretical skills. To illustrate, consider the means by which one would determine whether a given measure was a valid indicator of self-esteem. The following items are from two separate self-esteem tests and a measure of self-monitoring.

"On the whole, I am satisfied with myself." (Rosenberg, 1979)
"I can usually take care of myself." (Coopersmith, 1967)
"I can look anyone in the eye and tell a lie for a right end." (Snyder, 1979)

In establishing discriminate validity for the initial measure, the investigator might hope that responses on the first and second would be positively correlated but unrelated to responses on the third. Yet, such an outcome might result if the respondent was *trying* (intending or motivated) through agreement with the first two items to express his or her desire for others' approval, generalized satisfaction with the quality of life, hopes for the future, or fear that the opposite of the statements were true. None of these intentions might be at work in responding to the third item. Or, to set the case more squarely, the individual who has high self-esteem might employ the last of the items to inform the investigator of his or her outstanding capacities, whereas responding to the first two items for one or more of the mentioned reasons. In this case the attempt at discriminate validity would yield perfect results but be perfectly in error. And, by the same token, all or none of the items might be used as a vehicle for the individual to express his or her state of self-esteem. Again, agreement to the words does not furnish an objective anchoring for one's inferences about the hypothesized intentions of the respondent.

It is important that this line of argument not be confused with radical behaviorist attacks on "psychologizing." Although often obscured, the behaviorist's attempt to describe ongoing activity is subject to the same process of implicit inference as that of the self-investigator. When an operant trainer describes the actions of an animal as "pressing a bar," he or she is referring not to the actual movements of the animal itself but to its intentions or motives. If the animal pressed the bar inadvertently or accidentally, the investigator would be loath to count the action as a proper bar press. If the animal's paws were pressed to the bar by another experimenter or the animal were shot through a cannon and on its way through the apparatus triggered the bar pressing apparatus, one would be disinclined to say that the animal pressed the bar. In none of these cases did the animal intend to press the bar. By the same token, self-investigators who would hope to avoid the perils of psychological inference by confining their analysis to the overt self-presentational activities of the individual do not escape the interpretive problem. For example, Goffman's (1959) seminal volume *The Presentation of Self in Everyday Life* generally confines itself to the description of ongoing activity, while avoiding the complexities of the psychological underpinnings. More recent investigations of self-presentation (cf. Arkin, 1980; Jones and Pittman, 1982; Reis, 1981; Richardson and Cialdini, 1981; Schlenker, 1980; Schneider, 1981), although retaining a concern with psychological resources, are in a position to follow Goffman in this respect. However, again we find that descriptions of self-presentation do not generally refer to the objective actions of the person. No matter what the attire in which others may dress it or in what position the limbs may be placed, a corpse cannot present itself. This is primarily because the dead, by contemporary convention, possess no intentions or motives. Self-presentation does not depend, after all, on a bodily configuration but on a state of mind.

To conclude, there is ample reason to believe that the traditional demand for observational support for theories of the self has been greatly overextended. Given more general philosophic views on the underdetermination of theory, assessments of the prescriptive implications of social theory, and the constraints placed upon theory by traditional commitments to empirical testing, one may view existing demands for verification as overly constraining. Moreover, as we examine more closely the traditional process for rendering accounts of psychological phenomena objective, we find it open to serious difficulty. Essentially, theories of the self rely for their major support on other more informal and often unarticulated theories of psychological process. The self-theorist appears largely to anchor his or her interpretations of psychological structure and mechanisms in other interpretations about people's internal status. The claim to objective validity for such accounts is, as yet, without substantial warrant.

Two significant lessons may be drawn from this analysis. First, future theorists should be encouraged to expand manyfold the breadth and depth of their theoretical speculations. Theories of the past several decades have seldom been constituted by more than a handful of often self-evident propositions. This unduly simplistic and unimaginative form of theorizing is virtually demanded by the presumption that theories should not precede their evidential grounds except by a small margin. From the present perspective, the bridle of empirical justification should be considerably slackened and theorists invited to think boldly and provocatively. It is just such theoretical speculation that can challenge intellectual inquiry more generally and enhance broad public consciousness. Also the richness of future empirical work will be concomitantly enhanced.

In addition, however, the present analysis suggests that the range of criteria for evaluating theories of the self should be broadly enriched. Whether such theories are grounded at every point in a base of systematic observation is not the only, and perhaps far from the most important, question to ask of a theory. Attention may appropriately be directed to such matters as the general value of the theory within the history of thought, the extent to which the theory renders a solution to problems of broad scope within the culture, and its moral and ideological influence on the culture. Such matters are amplified in the following discussion.

III.   Evolution in the Concept of the Self

In his challenging work, *Divided Existence and Complex Society,* Van den Berg argues that the emergence of the concept of "plural selves" can be traced to the onset of the Industrial Revolution (c. 1760). With the revolution came a splitting and pluralizing of the social structure. The result on the level of intellectual analysis was a fundamental shift in the concept of the human mind. Thus, in the 1600s Pascal spoke of the "single soul" of man, and in the early 1700s

Berkeley discoursed on the single center of the individual which could be called "soul" or "self." However, with the Industrial Revolution one finds in Adam Smith's writing the sense of self buffeted by the changing character of the surrounding culture. Such pluralization of culture has been particularly endemic to North America. Thus, James's (1890) argument that the individual has "as many social selves as there are individuals who recognize him" (p.178) along with Mead's (1934) later view that multiple personalities are a normal consequence of life in a complex social world appear to reflect the character of the contemporary culture. From this perspective we find that the intellectual accounts of the self may be used as signal indicators of the times. Embedded in such writings are significant clues for understanding oneself and one's relationship to the cultural surroundings. Self-conceptions are embedded in and reflect upon the cultural system (Gadlin, 1978; Harré, 1984; Smith, 1981). Through theoretical conceptions of the self, one acquires, although through a glass darkly, an image of one's own historical condition.

Yet, in addition to furnishing insights into the culture and one's activities within it, theories of the self serve in their own right as inputs into the social process. Such theories inform the society as to what the individual can or cannot do, to what limits may be placed over human functioning, and to what hopes may be nurtured for future change. Further, they inform society as to rights and wrongs, designate those activities to be viewed with suspicion or approbation, and indicate who or what is to be held responsible for our present condition. In this light it is imperative that periodic attention be given to the central forms of conceptualization within the field: What major shifts have occurred in the dominant views of human functioning? In what important ways, if any, do they deviate from traditional forms of understanding? What do such conceptualizations appear to be saying about the general character of human activity? And what are the implications for such changes within the intellectual and social sphere more generally? Again, full treatment of such issues would carry us well beyond the constraints of the present medium. However, in the service of enhancing theoretical self-consciousness, opening debate on a variety of important issues, and placing contemporary theory within the broader intellectual context exploration will be opened on three related fronts. Analysis will center on the concept of self-knowledge, the self as origin, and the shift from structure to process in self-theory. As it is argued, when considered in tandem, present theoretical trends possess broad and significant implications both for science and the culture more generally.

A. FROM SELF-KNOWLEDGE TO COMMUNAL CONSTRUCTION

The Delphic inscription "Know thyself" has served as an intellectual emblem in Western culture for over 2000 years, and the underlying rationale for this injunction is readily appreciated. As often reasoned, the inner world of motives, thoughts, and feelings is an ambiguous one, and the correct identification can often be critical to the individual's well-being. If such psychological wellsprings are disregarded or mistakes are made in their identification, then one's behavior may often militate against one's true interests. For example, one might make major life decisions violating his or her fundamental values, ideology, or emotional commitments, with much resultant suffering. Moral opprobrium is also attached to those who are insensitive to their internal states. One may fail to realize that what he or she sees as acts of good will are actually a means of demonstrating prowess over others. The individual's self-deception may be justifiably vilified. It is not only to internal states that one must attend in the quest for self-knowledge. It is also essential that one be able to identify properly one's overt behavior—to see it for what it is. If people fail to realize that their actions are callous and cruel, for example, they will be debilitated in their interaction with others. It is important that one not be deluded about the true character of one's activities.

In earlier years broad support for such beliefs could be found in the psychological literature, and much empirical work was employed in the service of furthering the traditional outlook. The classic works of Freud (1933) and Jung (1939) stressed the opacity of psychological events, explained why the process of recognition was impeded, and furnished a variety of means for the individual (typically guided by an analyst) to tap the basic repositories of the mind. Neoanalytic theorists such as Horney and Sullivan were far more sanguine regarding the possibility for self-knowledge. In their eyes the defenses erected against accurate recognition were far less potent than suggested by Freud. Similar optimism regarding the possibility for self-knowledge was later reflected in Rogers's (1959) work. For Rogers, repressive or obfuscating processes are set in motion when the individual internalizes others' conditions of acceptance. In one's natural state, argues Rogers, psychological wellsprings are essentially transparent. It is primarily when one incorporates others' views about the relative merits of various impulses, feelings, values, desires, and the like that one begins to distort or inaccurately perceive.

Within clinically oriented circles such themes have changed little over the past 50 years. Kohut's (1971, 1979) imaginative theorizing has done much to thrust concern with the self to the center of modern psychoanalytic thought. However, Kohut's work retains a deep respect for the unconscious and the individuals' potential for distorting psychological contents. Within the social psychological literature the same theme recurs sporadically. For example, drawing from thinking in personality (Mischel, 1974), cognitive psychology (Wason & Johnson-Laird, 1972), and phenomenology (Fingarette, 1969), theorists Gur and Sackheim (1979) argue for self-deception as a state in which an individual holds two contradictory beliefs, but due to motivational dynamics, is unaware of one of the beliefs.

Optimism regarding the possibility of self-knowledge has been wedded to the companionate assumption of *natural kinds*. This view, amply illustrated in early scientific work, holds that the world is made up of classes of particulars, such as various species of animal, chemical elements, and racial groupings. Knowledge commences when one begins to isolate and develop a taxonomy for the various kinds. Within most philosophical circles the doctrine of natural kinds has been widely discredited, and most contemporary philosophy of science has moved strongly (though not exclusively) in an instrumentalist direction. From the instrumentalist perspective, theoretical languages constitute devices for organizing one's experiences. Thus, there may be a wide variety of competing theoretical orientations, each of which may have instrumental value relevant to particular ends. Such shifts in perspective at the philosophic level have been accompanied by a movement within social psychology constituting little short of a major disjunction in the Western tradition. In effect, discourse on the self within modern social psychology not only poses a major challenge to the preceding centuries, but opens a variety of rich intellectual vistas. This view requires elaboration.

1. The Social Construction of Psychological Events

To appreciate fully the character of the contemporary revolution in orientation, it is necessary to distinguish between knowledge of psychological events and knowledge of overt conduct. With respect to the identification of events in the "internal world," the breakthrough of singular significance was embodied in Schachter's (Schachter, 1964; Schachter & Singer, 1962) two-factor theory of emotion. From an historical perspective, this theory accomplished two important ends. First, it proposed a fundamental alteration in the character of the things to be known. Reinforced by a belief in natural kinds, it was traditionally believed that emotional terms stand in rough correspondence to an array of independent physiological states. The major problem was to determine how many states exist and to develop an appropriate set of labels for them. Schachter's work threw this line of thinking into sharp question. To what entities or physiological states did the widely variegated vocabulary of emotions refer? With no convincing answer available to this question, the conclusion seemed inescapable that the linguistic variations were not mirrors of physiological states but were products of social convention. Over time the emotional language had become reified. In place of these reifications Schachter proposed that there was only a single entity, a generalized and amorphous state of arousal. Suddenly the hoary problem of emotional identification was dissolved; there was no set of entities to be identified.

Schachter's (1964) second accomplishment was that of lodging the process of psychological knowledge within the social sphere. Traditionally it was believed that the individual alone had access to his or her private states, and as a result, it was the individual who was left with the problem of accurate identification. From Schachter's perspective the individual-centered tradition is found wanting. It is no longer the individual who is at the center of knowledge production but the social group. The individual's act of labeling is but a by-product of social interchange. It is the social group that furnishes the vocabulary with which emotional identification is to proceed, along with the rules for proper vocabulary use.

It is in this context that one can readily appreciate why the many attempts (cf. Marshall & Zimbardo, 1979; Maslach, 1979; Plutchik & Ax, 1967) to discredit Schachter's research have done little to dislodge it. The theory is both innovative and compelling in its coherence. Attempts to discredit the theory through argument and evidence may create doubts about the theory's validity, but just as in the case of psychoanalytic theory, they do not detract from the catalytic power of the perspective. Further, they do not furnish an alternative scaffolding of similar consequence. Schachter's work has succeeded in stimulating research over a vast area. A substantial number of research studies have attempted to demonstrate the way in which people can be aroused in one context and then influenced through subsequent information to label this arousal in ways not suggested by the initial context (cf. Rule & Nesdale, 1976; Zillmann, 1978). One obtains what Zillmann (1978) and his colleagues term an "excitation transfer" effect. For Zillmann such a process plays a critical role in understanding aggression. Berscheid and Walster (1974) employ much the same logic to explain what people feel to be romantic love. Other studies have employed false physiological feedback as a means of influencing attributions of emotions (Berkowitz & Turner, 1972; Valins, 1966; Valins & Ray, 1967). Perhaps the most active line of research to be stimulated by Schachter's work has been concerned with clinical application. As investigators have attempted to demonstrate, by altering information inputs systematic changes may be produced in various behavioral indicators of pain (Davison & Valins, 1969; Nisbett & Schachter, 1966), fear (Ross, Rodin, & Zimbardo, 1969), and insomnia (Lowery, Denney, & Storms, 1979; Storms & Nisbett, 1970).

These various lines of work have served to obscure various details of Schachter's early theory. Most important among these subtle alterations has been a steadily diminishing importance placed on "generalized arousal," either as the amorphous object of one's internal perception or as the prod to the outward search for proper label. Rather, as both the work on false physiological feedback and reattribution suggest, generalized arousal may play no necessary role in the attribution of emotional states. Both environmental and false physiological cues may be sufficient to alter one's conclusions about his or her emotions. As Leventhal (1980) concludes from his review, arousal appears unnecessary as an input to emotional experience. Leventhal himself has furnished an extensive elaboration of the "cognition–arousal" orientation and added the important concept of "expressive motor processing" to the vocabulary of understanding.

However, the latter concept has the function of replacing emotional entities of the traditional variety with generic, expressive motor mechanisms. In effect, this extension retains a strong biological base. The culmination of the view of emotion as social construction is found in Averill's (1980, 1983) constructivist view of emotion. For Averill, emotion *is* a form of social role, a syndrome of behaviors guided by the culture's rules of appropriate conduct. Thus, the same emotional role (e.g., romantic, hopeful, or sad) might be related to varying physiological states, and any given physiological state might be associated with a wide number of emotional roles. This full severing of the link between social construction and physiology is of particular significance inasmuch as it (1) renders the theory invulnerable to attacks on the initial and most tenuous assumption of generalized and undifferentiated arousal (cf. Pribram, 1980; Stein, 1978), and (2) removes the possibility for reducing social psychological analysis to physiology. In effect, it is a fully social view of emotion.

The undermining of the traditional belief in emotional knowledge and the relocation of such knowledge in the social rules of understanding has not been complete. Theorists have yet to confront critically, for example, the various arguments for the evolution of emotions in animals (cf. Plutchik, 1980; Scott, 1980; Weinrich, 1980) and for the universality of emotional expression (Eibl-Eibesfelt, 1980; Ekman, Friesen, & Ellsworth, 1972; Izard & Buechler, 1980). Such explorations continue to sustain the traditional belief in emotional knowledge, and it is incumbent on the social constructionists to reconcile their position with such explanations.

Concomitant with the erosion of belief in emotional knowledge has been a progressive socialization in what is assumed to be knowledge of cognitive process. Of particular importance, Schachter's student Nisbett has essentially recapitulated the major lines of his mentor's thesis in challenging the belief that people can identify their mental processes (Nisbett & Bellows, 1977; Nisbett & Wilson, 1977). With strong support garnered from the domain of cognitive study, it is argued that people are aware of the products of their mental processes but generally have little if any access to the processes giving rise to these products. Interestingly, most of Nisbett's experimental work on the issue has dealt not with people's ability to recognize mental states, but with their capacity to identify the environmental conditions preceding various actions. Subjects are asked to identify aspects of the environment that may have influenced their actions, and either because no cues or very subtle cues are supplied, subjects typically cannot locate the environmental source. However, if the identification of external contingencies were acceptable as an indication of one's awareness of mental states, a moot assumption at best, then any instance in which subjects could identify an environmental event preceding their action (e.g., "I ran from the room because a fire broke out") would stand as evidence for the assumption that people could correctly identify the cognitive processes responsible for their actions. In effect, empirical work of the sort used to demonstrate lack of awareness of mental conditions could easily be used to show an acute awareness of such states. Further criticisms of the Nisbett work have been mounted by Shotter (1981), White (1980), Smith and Miller (1978), and Sabini and Silver (1981). However, although such criticisms do weaken certain aspects of the initial argument, they do not succeed in rendering support for the traditional view that persons can be accurate in identifying the cognitive processes underlying their actions. This latter conclusion finds further strength in the work of Zajonc (1980) and Wilson (1979), who employ their data to argue that people are unable to identify the processes (in particular, enhanced sense of familiarity) responsible for their affective preferences.

In the long run it will prove difficult to sustain the case for the social construction of psychological knowledge on the basis of empirical findings. The preceding discussion of the interpretive character of evidence in this domain demonstrates why this is likely to be so. Thus, as an alternative to the empirical orientation, the attempt has been made (Gergen, 1982b) to secure the case through conceptual analysis. That is, a critical examination of the assumptions entailed by a belief in self-knowledge is undertaken, with the aim of assaying their coherence and plausibility. This form of analysis raises questions of fundamental difficulty for the traditional view. Four problems are of particular note:

a. *Process in Search of Itself*   To say that one can identify one's own psychological states places an arduous burden on theoretical speculation. Such a conclusion would entail a concept of mind in which psycbological process could essentially ascertain its own states. Rather than a single stream of consciousness, one would be forced into a mental dualism in which one level of process acted as a sensing and recording device and a second process furnished the stuff to be sensed and recorded. Such a dualism is sufficiently awkward that one is led to conclude that the assumption of internal perception is a reconstructed form of the subject–object dichotomy represented in the traditional metaphor of external perception. In this case the object is displaced inward, and one is left with the image of an inward eye in the process of perceiving itself.

b. *Internal Perception as Self-Biased*   If one can perform the theoretical circumlocution necessary to justify this kind of internal dualism, one faces a second problem of no less magnitude. Specifically, if both the sensing process (subject) and the sensed data (object) are constituents of the same psychological structure, what safeguards (if any) could be placed over misperception? Could the processes one hoped to identify not hinder or distort the very task of identification itself? For example, self theorists such as Fromm (1939), Hilgard (1949), and Pepitone (1968) posit just the kind of psychological processes that would obscure the very entities (states, drives, and intentions) one hoped to identify. All that is taken to be true of psychological states could be but the substitution in consciousness for the opposite of what is true. On what grounds could one argue that internal processes do not operate in this way?

c. The Ambiguous Properties of Psychological States   A third difficulty emerges when one inquires into the properties of mental states that would enable them to be identifed. What is the size, shape, color, sound, or smell, for example, of an intention, a thought, a motive, a desire, a need, or a hope? Even the questions seem ill-conceived. If one closes one's eyes, sits in silence, and turns one's attentions inward, what entities or states does one encounter? One seems to confront a murky, and unarticulated opacity.

d. The Infinite Regress of Recognition Rules   Finally, one is at a loss to understand how it would be possible, if one did sense a psychological state, to identify a second instance of it. Typically it is said that recognition of this sort depends on the application of recognition rules. The rules essentially specify what properties must be present for one to conclude that a given state is being experienced. Thus, it might be said, if one experiences simultaneously the properties of "warmth," "pain," and a "pounding sensation," one may conclude that an alpha state has been experienced. Yet, it may be asked, on what grounds is one to decide he or she has experienced the constituent properties of warmth, pain, and so on? One is thrown back once again on the logic of recognition rules. One knows one feels warmth when the following properties are present: (1)_____, (2)_____, (3)_____ (one is at a loss to specify the particular characteristic of warmth, in this case, lending further support to the preceding arguments for ambiguity). Yet, should these qualities or properties be supplied, the question again emerges as to the process of recognition, and one is forced into an elaboration of third-order recognition rules. As evident, one has entered into an infinite regress.

2. Social Subjectivity in Judgments of Self-Behavior

The attempt to relocate psychological knowledge in the social sphere has played a robust and catalytic role in the self-theory of the recent decades. A similar shift may be discerned in the case of knowledge of one's behavior. That is, inquiry has begun to raise increasing question with the assumption of natural kinds of behavior and the concomitant belief that a person can be accurate or inaccurate, biased, or self-deceived when reporting on his or her activities. However, developments in this realm have proceeded at a slower pace than in the preceding case, possibly because a successful relocation of behavioral knowledge within the social sphere would pose a lethal threat to the traditional view of behavioral science as "truth teller."

The seeds for a social constructionist view of behavioral knowledge have long been latent within the symbolic interactionist theory. As argued by both Mead (1934) and Cooley (1902), one's understanding of his or her actions is principally dependent on the opinions communicated to the individual by significant others. This view leaves the individual's knowledge of the self fully dependent on the social surroundings. Yet when this view is extended to its logical outcome, one is led to the conclusion that there is no behavioral knowledge outside of social opinion. That is, if each individual is dependent on others to decide when an action is aggressive, intelligent, cautious, and the like, then what is the source of truth in such matters? On what grounds could any individual be singled out as furnishing an accurate portrayal rather than a reflection of social opinion? Symbolic interactionist accounts have generally remained silent on this question.

A similar message lies implicit in the continuing line of research on social comparison. As Festinger (1954) initially proposed, people frequently lack objective information with which to evaluate their various capacities and attributes. As a result, they often compare themselves with others to reach an adequate self-definition. However, when the theory is pressed we find that adequacy in this case is more appropriately viewed as a normative concept rather than a surrogate for objectivity. That is, one draws conclusions that are acceptable within the immediate social milieu. However, such conclusions are not thus rendered the more accurate. The subjectivity of social comparison is clarified by two lines of argument. First, there is nothing in the process of scanning comparison information that insures an objective outcome. As researchers have been abundantly aware (cf. Gruder, 1977; Mettee & Smith, 1977), people have an immense latitude of choice in which others they attend to, and this choice of comparison targets can largely determine what conclusions one draws from comparison. Depending on which targets are chosen for comparison, which reference group is employed for which performance, and within which temporal period, different conclusions may be reached (Albert, 1977; Israel, 1956; Suls & Mullen, 1982). It is this fact that has enabled investigators to argue that people can use social comparison to increase their self-estimates (Singer, 1966; Thornton & Arrowood, 1966), defend against threats to self-esteem (Hakmiller, 1966; Pepitone, 1964; Samuel, 1973), determine the relative desirability of an action (Mettee & Smith, 1977), identify existing norms (Ruble, in press), and maintain self-definition (Tesser & Campbell, 1980). It is the choice of search strategies that also determine whether one perceives the self as consistent (Aboud, 1982). In effect, all conclusions are possible, depending on one's choice of targets.

The second problem with social comparison as a source of objective judgments stems from the fact that the basis for such comparisons is not frequently observable, but is the result of inference. For example, as demonstrated by Suls and others (Sanders, Gastorf, & Mullen, 1979; Gastorf & Suls, 1978; Suls, Gaes, & Gastorf, 1979), if one is trying to assess another's ability (in order to judge his or her own ability), one is faced with an attributional problem. Ability is an inferred construct and the process of deciding whether another's performances reflect ability (as opposed to, for example, motivation, mood, physical stamina, quality of the competition, etc.) does not proceed unproblematically to an inexorable conclusion. Goethals and Darley (1977) once argued that accuracy may best be approximated when one selects for comparison someone who is similar to self on all the attributes (other than ability) that might lead one to mistake the other's performance as ability (e.g., motivation or physical stamina). However, this argument does not easily salvage the case because most related attributes also are based on inference rather than observation. As Darley and Goethals (1980) conclude in their recent work, "It is very difficult to conceive of a performance . . . that conclusively disconfirms an already arrived at inference about the performer's underlying dispositions" (p. 16). One must infer motives, moods, stamina, and so on. Inference thus rests upon inference. In effect, although not directly assaulting the problem of objectivity through social comparison, such a challenge lies implicit in much of the research in this domain.

A more direct confrontation with the problem of objectivity in self-knowledge has been furnished by research on processes of personal inference. In part such work is a reflection of the more general shift from behaviorist to cognition accounts of human activity. More immediately, however, contemporary work owes a debt to the groundbreaking work of Jones and Nisbett (1971) on the one hand, and Kahneman and Tversky (1973) on the other. In both cases the investigators argue that information-processing sets (focus of attention, cognitive heuristics, etc.) lead people to draw mistaken or erroneous conclusions about the world. Such cognitive sets lead either to a "fundamental attribution error" in the former case or to a blindness to base rate probabilities in the latter.

Wide-ranging research programs have since emerged, most of which is consistent with the traditional belief that certain cognitive sets yield erroneous conclusions whereas others enhance accuracy (cf. Miller & Ross, 1975; Nisbett & Ross, 1980). However, within much of the inquiry on the self, a significant deviation from this tradition may be discerned, one that strongly echoes the constructionist elements identified earlier in this section. At the outset, a number of investigators set out to demonstrate that actors do not, as Jones and Nisbett (1971) suggested, necessarily furnish more correct views of the cause of their actions. Demonstrations have been arranged to show that both actors and observers might direct their attention in many different ways (internally, situationally, historically, etc.). Thus the conclusions reached about the causal source of one's actions are largely a function of which scanning strategy is employed (cf. Duncan & Laird, 1980; Ellis & Holmes, 1982; Miller & Norman, 1975; Taylor & Fiske, 1978; Wong & Weiner, 1981). Similarly, as a given action slips into the historical past, one may come to see the action increasingly as a result of the situation. When the implications of this work are extended, the assumption of accuracy in attribution is placed in jeopardy.

This latter view becomes more fully articulated among investigators sensitive to the social function of self-attribution. In this domain, attribution is often viewed as a form of social accounting, and thus, not a report of a mental event or a "reading of the world" so much as an attempt to gain social ends. For example, Pettit (1981) speaks of the uses of such accounts in "silencing questions" of various kinds. Lalljee (1981) points to aspects of the relationship between the account giver and the listener along with the social consequences of various accounts as important determinants of explanation. Harré (1981) has outlined the expressive aspects of the self-accounting (or attributional) process. Tedeschi and Riess (1981) have described the process of account giving as a problem in impression management. In this same vein Gergen and Gergen (1982) have attempted to demonstrate the nonempirical character of casual attributions. As it is shown, "the facts" themselves cannot in principle dictate or determine the locus of causality; thus the same array of facts permit one to make wide-ranging accounts of causality with equal empirical validity.

The concern with the effects of cognitive sets on the conclusions reached through observational scanning is scarcely limited to the domain of causal attribution. On the basis of their review of research on detection of covariation, Jennings, Amabile, and Ross (1982) venture that organisms, human and otherwise, are likely to see those covariations and only those that their own history, and indeed the history of the species, disposes them to see. By this argument, even the scientist's specification of the "true" covariation among events would be moot. Snyder and Swann (1978) have attempted to demonstrate how people review information in such a way as to confirm existing hypotheses. Swann and Read (1981) have extended the implications of this work to argue that people use their social interactions as opportunities to verify or confirm their self-conceptions. Thus, they seek social feedback that they believe will confirm their self-conceptions, elicit desired reactions from others, and later will preferentially recall feedback that confirms self-conception. With respect to the individual's future predictions about the self, Sherman (1980) has shown how people will erase errors in such predictions by changing their behavior so as to produce confirmation. On a more general theoretical level, Greenwald (1980) has likened the self to a totalitarian political organization. This organization is essentially intent on sustaining itself and thus marshalls information from the environment and from memory in its service. This proposal is itself sustained in Greenwald's (1981) review of the literature on the self and memory. In a similar vein, Wicklund and Gollwitzer (1982; Gollwitzer, Wicklund, & Hilton, 1982) have proposed a theory of "symbolic self-completion" in which it is ventured that people actively strive for a standard of excellence in defining themselves. When faced with shortcomings, they engage in symbolic activity designed to cover up or reduce the magnitude of the shortcomings.

Most investigators in the domain have been reluctant to extend the implications of their work so as to challenge the traditional belief in the objective grounding of behavioral knowledge. Yet, to the extent that personal perspective and data scanning techniques determine what is true of the self, then the foundation for objectivity in such matters stands in jeopardy. Such a possibility has been explored by the present author (Gergen, 1982b) on grounds developed in the preceding analysis of the place of empirical research in the evaluation of theory. As ventured in this case, the prevailing vocabulary for describing human actions does not, in fact, refer to the overt actions but to the individual's underlying dispositions, motives, or intentions. To identify an action as aggressive, dominating, altruistic, cooperative, and so on would ultimately require an assessment of the individual's intentions in such cases. Yet, as we have also seen, such assessments primarily furnish additional material that requires motivational interpretation in order to be rendered intelligible. From this analysis, one is led to conclude that the language of "person description" is akin to mathematical formulation. That is, person descriptors operate as symbols within abstract systems, and the employment of such symbols depends on the rules governing such systems. In the case of mathematics, one can point to any ongoing event and say, "Let's call that X." Similarly, in the case of human activity, one may meaningfully define virtually any act as aggression, altruism, dominance, submissiveness, and so on. Any observable motion of the body may thus serve as a potential candidate for any descriptor. This free-floating character of the language of person description is demanded, so the analysis proceeds, because the multiplex and everchanging character of ongoing activity prohibits ostensive definition of behavioral terms. From this standpoint, self-knowledge becomes a form of communal artifact. Because the rules of self-description are engendered through a process of social negotiation, then what may be said (known) about the self is dependent on existing agreements within the culture (or subculture) as to what is sensible.

To summarize, inquiry into both the perception of internal states and overt activities has increasingly challenged traditional beliefs in objectively grounded knowledge of the self. In the former case the view has become increasingly prevalent that what passes as knowledge of the self is a product of social interchange. Self-understanding is thus a product, not of accurate observation, but of employing conventional rules of understanding. Although the social constructionist view has not generally been applied to the case of behavioral knowledge, recent investigation has succeeded in laying the groundwork for such a move. If knowledge of one's behavior is not built up through induction, as the tradition suggests, but is a product of one's cognitive set, then one is prompted to inquire into the origins of such sets. At least one compelling answer to this question is that such cognitive search strategies are acquired through social interchange. As Vygotsky (1978) has reasoned, cognitive processing is largely a reflection of social process. If this argument can be elaborated and sustained, social psychologists will have succeeded in executing a major revolution in perspective. Knowledge will essentially be viewed as an artifact of social process.

B. FROM MECHANISM TO AGENCY

Evolution in the conception of self-knowledge has hardly taken place in an intellectual vacuum. A full account of this shift should be sensitive to the intellectual, ideological, and political ethos of the discipline's development. Although such an account cannot be rendered in the present context, it is appropriate and useful to view this shift toward a social-centered epistemology as it is related to other alterations in self-theory. In particular, a significant link may be discerned between this shift and the emergence of concern with the self as an active agent. The behaviorist orientation, long adopted by psychologists, more generally, strongly militates against the view of the self as the origin of action. With its programmatic aim of developing laws or principles relating environmental antecedents to behavioral consequences, the behaviorist orientation twice impugns the concept of human agency. It does so, first, in its location of the causal force for human activity: From the behaviorist perspective the cause of behavior is removed from the person and placed within the environment. Stimulus configurations and/or reinforcement contingencies are viewed as the source of human patterning. The general deployment of hypothetical, psychological constructs has not generally helped reinstate intentional processes. As typically argued, such constructs or variables are to be anchored in or tied operationally to both antecedent conditions and consequent behaviors. Thus, most psychological constructs come to function as mere integers in a three-step (S-O-R) process in which the stimulus retains its function as "first case." The behaviorist orientation also threatens the concept of agency in its committed search for laws and principles, a search suggesting that human actions are, like the movement of the planets or the tides, subject to inexorable determination. To the extent that the research focus is on the lawful relationship among observables, the concept of intention is obscured.

Self-psychologists with clinical and/or symbolic interactionist leanings have been reticent to adopt a strongly articulated form of behaviorist (or neo-behaviorist) theory. However, methodological neo-behaviorism came to have such a strong, general grip over the discipline of psychology that self-formulations were inevitably to give way. Thus from roughly 1940–1960 most psychological research on the self was committed to an S-O-R formulation, with stimulus preceding and determining the character of internal mechanisms and the latter determining the character of behavioral responses. The chief theoretical entity to emerge from this tradition was the mechanism of the *self-concept*. Although wide variations exist in the usage of the term, and other terms such as *percept, image, definition, schema* and *prototype* are sometimes used synonymously, the self-concept is most frequently viewed as a relatively enduring organization of self-referring categories (see Giovannini *et al.,* 1974; Gordon, 1968; Tomé, 1979, for extended accounts of structural properties). The self-concept is further believed to act as a guide or standard against which one's conduct can be compared. Typically, this representation is said to possess a strong evaluative component, thus favoring a conflation of self-concept and self-esteem. The mechanistic character of the self-concept is revealed in its passive character; it is generally viewed as the product of environmental influence. Without environmental inputs it is generally believed to remain inert or stabilized. This mechanistic orientation to the self has been embodied in hundreds of research studies since the 1950s (e.g., Wylie, 1974, 1979).

Research in the neo-behaviorist model has been of two major varieties. First, there has been a general attempt to trace variations in the self-concept to various social conditions or inputs. Thus, for example, researchers have concentrated on self-esteem as affected by child-rearing patterns (see Coopersmith, 1967), consensus in others' appraisals (Backman, Secord, & Pierce, 1982), membership in various socioeconomic structures (cf. Davidson & Lang, 1960; Trowbridge, 1972), age (cf. Back & Gergen, 1968; Rosenberg, 1965; Rosenberg & Simmons, 1971), gender (cf. Becker & Dileo, 1967; McCarthy & Rafferty, 1971; Schroeder, 1973), and racial groups (cf. Clark & Clark, 1947; Gregor & McPherson, 1966; Simon, 1974). Other representative research has examined the impact of social approval under varying conditions on one's level of self-acceptance (cf. Deutsch & Solomon, 1959; Gergen, 1965; Jones, Hester, Farina, & Davis, 1959; Shrauger & Schoeneman, 1979). The second major line of research in the neo-behaviorist mold has attempted to trace the effects of possessing a certain configuration of self-conception on resulting behavior. In this vein, investigators have been concerned with the influence of self-esteem on variations in academic and task performance (Baliff, 1981; Coopersmith & Gilberts, 1981; Trope, 1983), attraction toward others (cf. Kiesler & Baral, 1970; Walster, 1965), influencibility (cf. Hovland & Janis, 1959; Silverman, 1964), and various forms of deviance, criminality, drug addiction, and aggression (see Kaplan, 1975, for review).

Yet the concept of a stable structure of conceptions that simply reflects environmental inputs and gives direction to behavior has never proven fully satisfying for most self-psychologists. Concepts of the self as agent were deeply woven into early theories of the self. Adler viewed the self as the "mover of mental life;" for Hilgard (1949) the self played an integrating and organizing function; for Allport (1943) the self was equated with the *proprium* or center of thought, and given a regnant function in guiding human action. It is the present contention that such concepts, although not in name, are returning full force to the theoretical scene. In large measure, the way for this return has been presaged by the generalized deterioration of the romance with the neo-behaviorist paradigm in psychology (cf. Argyris, 1980; Chein, 1972; Gergen, 1982b; Koch, 1971; Sarason, 1981). This deterioration has raised widespread questions regarding the intellectual, empirical, ethical and ideological outcomes of research in the

S-O-R paradigm. In part the return to agency has also resulted from the cognitive revolution and the gradual replacement of mechanistic theory with organismic theories (Reese & Overton, 1970) of cognitive processing. This shift toward the internal has essentially given a rebirth to the possibility of self-as opposed to environmentally- originated action. However, in social psychology the preceding discussion of the social basis of knowledge would also appear significant. If knowledge is not data driven as the behaviorist tradition suggests, but is constructed by interacting individuals as the accumulating literature on the self suggests, then one is inclined to grant to the individual a certain power of agency. The individual is liberated within this perspective from mechanistic dependency on environmental inputs, as he or she masters and contributes to the rules of understanding within the social sphere.

It is against this backdrop that one may appreciate the subtle insinuation of agency into otherwise traditional research frameworks. Two major forms of agency smuggling can be discerned. On the one hand, forms of agency are frequently inserted *between the incoming stimulus and the conception of self*. For example, Markus and Sentis (1982) speak of self-schemas in the mechanistic tradition and argue for their importance in the process of coding and memory. However, as they go on to argue, ''An important aspect of schemata is their dual nature: A schema is at once a *structure* and a *process*'' (P. 44). Upon closer inspection it is found that the concept of process involves the importation of a voluntarist agent. As they describe, ''A strong hypothesis or model (a schema) exists for the incoming stimuli, and the processing system uses the model to operate on the input data'' (p 44). In effect, the theory proposes a structural schema *and* a processing system, the latter granted the powers of employing the schema as it seems fit in sorting incoming stimuli. Much the same importation of agency is found in the steadily accumulating research on self-serving bias in causal attribution (cf. Arkin, Appelman, & Burger, 1980; Bradley, 1978). As investigators frequently argue in this case, the individual engages in an autonomous search for information that will serve or be consistent with a positive self-conception. A particular configuration of self-conception is thus created by the decision-making agent. The second form of agency restoration results from insinuating additional processes *between the structure of self-conception and the subsequent behavior*. In this case, the self-conception does not dictate behavior in a mechanical fashion but serves as a repository of information that may be consulted by the agent for purposes of making decisions about behavior. Thus, for example, in research on self-esteem maintenance (cf. Swann & Read, 1981; Tesser, 1983), the individual's level of self-esteem does not directly determine his or her actions. Rather, one autonomously carries out actions that he or she expects to sustain or contribute to a high level of self-esteem.

One of the most concerted attempts to reconcile the concept of mechanistic structure with that of active agency has been made by Bandura (Bandura, 1977,

1982). It is a particularly interesting attempt, inasmuch as it is far more forthright in its concern with agency than any of the aforementioned cases and yet, does not ultimately succeed in making the transition. As Bandura argues, much traditional behaviorist theory has been at fault in its "one-sided determinism," that is, in its viewing persons mainly as respondents to environmental stimuli. As he further maintains, most interactionist solutions, which hold that behavior is a function of the environment and the person, are also at fault because they view both the environment and person variables to be functioning independently. Bandura terms his own solution "reciprocal interactionism" in that it assumes that the environment and the person (along with behavior) are all continuously in the process of influencing each other. From this perspective, Bandura (1982) then goes on to describe various "mechanisms of agency." These include the individual's observations of the self, the creation of one's own incentives, the valuation of activities, the attribution of cause, comparing the self with others, and the creation of one's own incentives.

Although this is a significant step in the direction of a theory of agency, in the final analysis the neo-behaviorist orientation prevails. In accounting for the origin of these various "self-regulative mechanisms," as they are termed, Bandura looks to the process of learning. The self-sustaining mechanisms are essentially products of environmental determination. In effect, self-control is reduced to a composite of learned (environmentally induced) dispositions. In asking why people engage in self-regulation, Bandura again looks toward the environment. As he says, "A variety of external factors serve as reciprocal supports for the exercise of self-influence" (1982, p. 15). And, "Self-influences do not operate unless activated, and there are many factors that exercise selective control over their activation" (1982, p. 19). Again, agency becomes ultimately a pawn to environmental contingency and thus loses its essential function as origin.

Other theorists are similar in their attempts to account for agency within a neo-behaviorist framework. For example, in Mischel and Mischel's (1977) analysis of self-control, the individual is granted power to control his or her actions. However, as the theorists also maintain, this control depends in turn on (1) learned dispositions and (2) situationally induced motivation. "Self-control" thus appears in the theory as the internal or psychological surrogate for external control. The shift toward agency remains incomplete. Similarly, theorists such as Duval and Wicklund (1972), Wicklund (1975, 1979), and Carver and Scheier (1981) have carried out wide-ranging research on self-awareness and self-regulation. Yet in both cases, self-focused attention is viewed as a determined product of environmental influences, and its specific mode of operation thereafter follows mechanical principles. For Duval and Wicklund (1972), human activity is the automatic result of demands for aversive drive reduction; for Carver and Scheier (1981) it is the result of an inexorable tendency to reduce the discrepancy between one's activity and an internal standard (the latter, a product of learning).

These theories may be usefully compared with competing models of self-consciousness. In Buss's (1980) work on self-consciousness and anxiety, mechanistic underpinnings are implicit but unelaborated. In Hull and Levy's (1979) model of self-awareness, the self is finally granted autonomous organizing capacities.

This struggle toward the concept of an autonomous self-agency is also evident in Greenwald's (1980, 1982) challenging analysis of ego or self-functioning. As Greenwald proposes, the self organizes memory, manages knowledge, and maintains itself in the midst of diverse and everchanging circumstances (see also Muller, in press). However, again the shift to voluntarism is a conservative one. For as Greenwald maintains, the ego's operation is constrained by a range of biases, including that of fabricating its history in relationship to itself, of its self-serving attribution, and of its resistance to change. Greenwald does not, like many theorists, go on to attribute these biases to environmental influences. In this way he joins with organismically oriented cognitive theorists. However, on Greenwald's account, the ego is not furnished with the capacity to choose against such biases. It is determined by its own formal properties.

Outspoken voluntarist positions have begun to emerge. Among the most visible are those of Rychlak (1977, 1981), Harré (Harré, 1979; Harré & Secord, 1972), Smith (1978, 1980), and Deci (Deci, 1980; Deci & Ryan, 1980). Rychlak proposes a *telic* or final cause model of human functioning to replace traditional explanation, which employs sufficient cause as an explanatory base. The individual is not *responding* to conditions, argues Rychlak, but acting out purposes for self-determined ends. Similarly, full powers of agency are granted to the individual within Harré and Secord's (1972) ethogenic formulation. As Harré (1977) proclaims, "An actor is an agent . . . he is involved in the genesis of his actions. . . . He generates his actions in accordance with a preformed plan, scenario, script, rule or habit . . . which he may himself have constructed" (p. 320). Thus Harré grants the individual the power of mental rehearsal, self-intervention (the voluntary termination of a line of activity), and reflexive consideration of ongoing actions. Smith (1978, 1980) proposes that by reinstigating a voluntary process, psychology may succeed in becoming a truly humanistic discipline. Deci (1980) goes on to argue that people not only possess powers of self-determination but an intrinsic need to be self-determining.

Voluntarist commitments are also found among modern adherents to Kelly's (1955) personal construct theory. As investigators such as Mancuso (1977), Landfield (1977), and Bannister and Agnew (1976) maintain, the individual possesses choice in his or her construction of the self and through powers of self-reflexiveness may autonomously review and reinterpret. This view is further sustained by important philosophic accounts of person description. As philosophers such as Peters (1958), Taylor (1964), Abelson (1977), and others have demonstrated, it proves virtually impossible to describe or understand human action without the concept of agency. To describe in full detail a person's precise physical movements through space and time (a behavioral account) gives us little useful information; to say that the person is "intending to rob a bank" is almost fully informative. Further, to say that the individual is robbing presumes some form of intentionality. By definition, one could not be engaging in a robbery if he or she had no intention to do so, regardless of how others defined the action. Further, those who have replaced the language of cognitive mechanisms with that of heuristics (cf. Wong & Weiner, 1981) take an important step toward voluntarism. According to common convention, one cannot excercise control over an automatic mechanism; however, one is free to select from available heuristic devices. In the same way those who speak of "coping strategies" to be used against problematic self-evaluations (Bowerman, 1975) reinstigate the concept of agency; by common understanding one is free to select a coping strategy or not.

How is one to evaluate the general shift from mechanistic to agential explanations in the history of self-inquiry? Surely from the broad cultural standpoint there is much to be applauded. Many would argue that the concepts of duty, right, obligation, morality, choice, freedom, and responsibility have played an enormously important role in the emergence of civilized culture. All are obviated if the concept of agency is lost from the vocabulary of understanding persons (Shotter, 1975). And as frequently argued, to conceive of the human as a robot or an automaton, conceptions invited by the imagery of environmentally driven mechanisms, is to open the door to various forms of human debasement (cf. Argyris, 1980; Hampden-Turner, 1970).

Although debate on such matters should not be foreclosed, more immediate concern within psychology may be directed to the implications of agency (voluntarism) for the science itself. For decades the concept was assiduously avoided within psychology because of its threat to the prevalent view of science. If persons could act as the spontaneous originators of their actions, then the causal chain among contingencies was broken. One could not set out to examine the laws governing the relationship between antecedents and consequences as certain events (vis., intentions) possess no antecedents. As Skinner (1971) and others argued, such a view would discourage any assessment of the environmental conditions under which behaviors occur. On this account, the concept of agency promotes systematic ignorance. Added to these arguments has also been the problematic character of intention as a hypothetical construct. As indicated earlier, the traditional logic of such constructs demands that they be anchored operationally to both antecedent conditions and subsequent responses. Yet, if the individual can initiate his or her own actions, a link between environmental conditions and psychological construct cannot be established. The traditional logic must give way, and a threat is thus posed to the assumption of fundamental principles of human behavior.

However, with the benefit of hindsight and the generalized erosion of scientism, it has become apparent that such misgivings have been overly drawn. Although some would disagree (cf. DeCharms & Shea, 1976; McClure, 1980), there are strong grounds for arguing that the concept of intention is not subject to empirical evaluation. All actions that may be explained mechanistically can be explained with equal facility in a voluntarist language (Gergen & Gergen, 1982). Intentions are intelligible constructs for explaining human action. As such, they compete with other explanations such as cognitive structure, association, motive, attitude, dissonance reduction, and so on. Yet, the selection of explanatory form does not alter the pattern of observables nor must it constrain the search for reliable relationships among events. For example, that people often respond to attack with aggression may be an interesting fact. However, the pattern remains regardless of whether it is explained in terms of volition, learned associations, conceptual structure, or genetic proclivity. Nor are any of these deterministic explanations superior to the voluntarist form in specifying what other conditions might be taken into account as exceptions to or deviations from this pattern.

It further seems clear that the traditional logic of hypothetical constructs should not impede the development of voluntarist accounts. As we have already seen, there are formidable difficulties in anchoring psychological constructs to observations. Upon closer inspection it was found that the results of such attempts are primarily an elaboration of understandings about the relationship among hypothetical constructs. The difficulties in making an empirically based case for intention or volition as the source of an activity are no greater than arguing that motives, concepts, plans, heuristics, or associations are the generic sources. If the rules of science qua science do not then require abandoning the concept of the self as agency, there would seem ample reason on the cultural level for nurturing the recent theoretical developments.

C. FROM STRUCTURE TO PROCESS

The concept of knowledge in its traditional sense is intimately connected with the concept of static structure. To know that "X is the case" fundamentally requires that there be an object of knowledge, X. The term "object" is to be carefully regarded in this case, as it implies some form of spatio–temporal endurance. That is, for there to be knowledge there must be a structured datum that permits sensory interrogation. Thus one can scarcely speak of knowledge in the case of a unique and fleeting instant of sensation. In this same sense, the concept of self-knowledge carries with it the associated implication of a structured set of characteristics, features, dispositions, or the like that endure across time and that permit interrogation, a fresh look, a deeper probing, or consensual validation to be reached. Psychologists have fallen heir to this assumption, and indeed, the structural–mechanistic language of the neo-behaviorists plays a congenial counterpoint to the assumption that one can acquire knowledge of psychological structures. However, we have also seen the gradual erosion in social psychology of the concept of self-knowledge. As this edifice begins to crumble, the way is opened for reconsideration of enduring mental structures. If there is no "thing" to be known, as theorists suggest with increasing frequency, then such concepts as construct system, schema, prototypes, enduring dispositions, esteem level, scripts and so on become less compelling. Without generating mischief, one can scarcely argue for the social construction of mental entities on the one hand, while employing just such psychological constructs to explain the process of social construction on the other. Moreover, as the concept of agency gains ascendance, concern with perduring entities is discouraged. One's focus shifts from the internal repository of past experience, as embodied in psychological structure, to the agency of action. In effect, the above conceptual alterations in the field have, in combination with other factors to be described, lent themselves to a reconsideration of the enduring character of self-conception.

Perhaps the clearest instantiation of the shift from structure to process is represented in the decline of trait research in self-psychology. Essentially, the self-concept (and its by-product, self-esteem) form the mainstay of the structural orientation. The concept of the self constitutes the enduring essential that typically furnishes the basis for continuity and/or repetition in behavior over time. As we have also seen earlier, research in the neo-behaviorist format has generally been concerned with tracing the formation of the self-concept (through environmental inputs) and its subsequent effects on behavior. Yet this S-O-R orientation and its accompanying assumption of enduring, trait-like entities has been the focus of a variety of assaults, and little but its vestiges remain. One of the earlier attacks on the assumption of enduring conceptual structures was made by the present author. Research was carried out to sustain the view that level of self-esteem does not endure in the traditional sense, but is constantly changing as one is exposed to ongoing feedback from others (Gergen, 1965), as one presents various social "faces" or personas to others (Gergen, 1965), as one compares oneself with others (Morse & Gergen, 1970), and as one scans one's memory in various ways (Gergen & Taylor, 1966). From this standpoint (see Gergen, 1977 for a full review), the concept of a steady, structured state seems misleading. Rather, the individual's level of self-esteem is viewed as "in-motion"—not an enduring characteristic but a continuously re-created by-product of ongoing relationships. This view is elaborated and extended in Zurcher's (1977) treatise on the mutable self and Martindale's (1980) treatment of subselves.

This line of argument has also been congenial to the growing concern in personality research with temporary states of readiness. In an attempt to validate various trait measures, investigators frequently employed experimental techniques to manipulate individuals into either high or low states of the dimensions of interest (e.g., self-esteem, achievement needs, and power needs). If the manipulated groups subsequently differed significantly and in the appropriate direction on the relevant measure, confidence in the validity of the measure was thereby increased. However, this same practice carried with it a hidden threat to the very orientation it was designed to sustain. If individuals were vulnerable to such situational influence during the testing procedure, were they not equally mobile without? If all trait-like activity were situationally induced, then the concept of the trait as a stable entity would indeed be obliterated.

This logical extension was never fully articulated within the trait domain, however, as the discipline found a convenient means of conceptual foreclosure: the trait versus state distinction. As frequently argued, persons possess enduring traits together with wavering states. (See also Turner's 1968 distinction between "self-concept" as an enduring structure and "self-image" as a situationally vacillating view of the self.) Yet, as is also clear, this dualism is both awkward and unwieldy. Are traits and states to be viewed as differing mental conditions governed by differing processes and having different ranges of effects? How is one to differentiate the effects of social feedback, or any other situational input, on the state as opposed to the trait? Do states and traits tend toward harmony; how are conflicts between them to be resolved? Such questions border on the nonsensical. One is invited, rather, to think in terms of traits as a set of recurring states of similar variety or a multiplicity of traits that are potentially inconsistent. It would appear that the trait–state distinction furnishes only a temporary and ill-gotten tranquility.

A further blow to the concept of enduring structures was struck by Mischel's (1968, 1969) analysis of the predictive capacity of trait measures in psychology. As this analysis indicated, trait measures could seldom account for more than 10% of the variance in various behaviors of interest and were thus of questionable consequence to the discipline. Such an analysis lent strong support to various situationist arguments (Bowers, 1973), which are more favored in the experimental wing of the discipline. In the hands of critics such as Jones and Nisbett (1971), self-esteem as a personality variable appeared to be merely the fictional result of misattribution. People used "traits" to explain behavior when they failed to see that behavior was actually under situational control.

Such attacks on the concept of trait have understandably stimulated a broad attempt at retrenchment. The major form of rebuttal has been empirical in character. Through the inventive research of Epstein (1977), Bem and Allen (1974), Block (1977), McCrae (1982), Lord (1982), and others, a strong attempt was made to furnish more exacting and more powerful empirical demonstrations of the endurance of basic personality dispositions. Even Mischel (1973) took much of the sting out of his early criticism by arguing that although traits had questionable cross-situational endurance, "cognitive styles" did demonstrate consistency. Both trait and style are, however, members of the same family of constructs, designating as they do enduring structures or dispositions. To admit one is to render the other more acceptable.

In the final analysis it would appear that the question of the relative potency of traits versus situations will not be answered via empirical research. The major problem is that there is no clear means of separating analytically the effects of traits versus situations. All effects traditionally attributed to situations may with equal validity be explained as personality effects; all so called "personality effects" may with equal force be viewed as situational effects in disguise (Gergen & Gergen, 1984). To illustrate the former case, subjects who capitulate to an experimenter's demands for obedience do not, as is typically concluded, unequivocally demonstrate the power of situational pressure. It may be ventured equally that such effects are dependent on the particular personalities of the obedient subjects. If the majority of the subjects were more "morally principled," for example, there might be no situational effects. From this perspective Milgram's (1974) classic research tells us nothing about the power of situations; rather it furnishes insight into the modal personality characteristics in the samples under study. To turn the question about, when individual difference measures successfully predict behavior, we are not necessarily informed about the power of the personality as opposed to situations. Rather, it may be argued, personality indicators are merely measures of the accumulated effects of past situations. They are shorthand indexes of one's exposure to previous situations. From this perspective, the concept of personality trait is expendable. All human action may be understood as a function of situational inputs.

The prevailing resolution to the trait versus situation clash has been that of interactionism. As widely maintained, to understand human behavior requires that both the situation and the personality be taken into account (cf. Bowers, 1973; Magnusson & Endler, 1977). Yet, the concept of interactionism bears careful scrutiny at this juncture. Several meanings have been attached to the term, some trivial, others of profound implication for the future study of the self. Interactionism, as a term in an analysis of variance research design, in which personality and situational variables are both employed, is of little conceptual significance and may be disregarded. The interaction term must be interpreted, and it is the interpretation, not the amount of variance accounted for, that is of theoretical significance. As we have just seen, for example, experimental effects purported to be situational may be interpreted as the products of personality, and vice versa. Further, interpretations of interactionism as the summation of unidirectional effects of personality and situational variables (Olweus, 1977) pose no particular problems for the structural or static view of self. For example, within this framework one might argue that under certain conditions, self-esteem has strong effects on behavior, whereas under other conditions the effects are minimal. Such a formulation enables the concept of self-structure to be retained intact. However, it is a third view of interactionism that is of chief interest in this case, the view of interactism as a reciprocal influence (cf. Bandura, 1982; Bowers, 1973; Endler and Magnusson, 1976; Mischel, 1973; Overton & Reese, 1973). In this bidirectional view, the person both influences and is influenced by the situation. Thus, for example, one's high self-esteem might lead one to boast, which would in turn cause others to react with criticism, which in turn could lower one's self-esteem. The lowered self-esteem might lead one to doubt oneself publicly, which might elicit others' praise, thus increasing once again one's self-esteem.

The perspective of reciprocal interactionism carries with it three consequences of substantial significance to the character of self-study. First, when reciprocal interactionism is embraced, the concept of enduring psychological structure is rendered obsolete. It is replaced by a view of the self that is in a state of continuous movement as it interacts with a continuously changing environment. In effect, as reciprocal interactionism gains in credibility, self-structure is replaced by self-process as the appropriate image of psychological functioning. Second, and of equally broad implication from the perspective of reciprocal interactionism, traditional methodological tools cease to be functional. Most available methods and associated statistics are designed to accommodate some form of stimulus–response model. That is, they confine themselves to the immediate outcomes of a given stimulus on behavior. Such techniques are ill-suited to a conception of individuals in continuous, interactive interchange with the environment. They enable one to appreciate only a minute segment in a broad sequence of interdependent events. In this sense, experimental data yield snapshots when the demand of the reciprocal interactionist is for moving pictures. Necessitated then are diachronic methodologies, techniques sensitive to cross-time change among interacting entities. Inroads have been made in the development of such methods (cf. Gottman, 1981; Hibbs, 1974; Kenny & Campbell, 1984; Simonton, 1984; Warner, Kenny, & Stoto, 1979), but the territory remains largely uncharted.

Finally, reciprocal interactionism poses problems for the traditional segmentation of the environment and the person. Once it is agreed that the two are in a state of continuous, ongoing interchange, then the theorist is discouraged from considering either abstracted from the other. To attempt the latter would be tantamount to developing theories dealing with the independent movements of each component of a machine without considering the principles by which the totality operates. Thus, when reciprocal interactionism is taken seriously, the theorist is encouraged to consider larger systems of interdependent events. The unit of analysis shifts from the individual person to the system of interacting persons. Rather than thinking of the relationship between the self and other, the theorist is challenged to think in terms of joint action (Shotter, 1980), mutually created sequences (Pearce & Cronen, 1980), or collusive patterning. Rather than thinking in terms of one person, *A's,* altruistic actions, and *B's* response, for example, the level of analysis might shift to the creation and maintenance of donor–recipient interaction patterns. It is the form of the relationship rather than the isolated actions of separated individuals that would be described and explained by theory. Again, overtures have been made to the development of such theories. Social ecologists and dialectic theorists have been particularly concerned with such possibilities. However, the latitude for creative theoretical work in this domain is both immense and little explored.

Poised for entry into the interactionist arena is a final domain of self-inquiry in which the process orientation has figured prominently, the domain of self-presentation. Goffman's (1959, 1963) groundbreaking work has been prophetic in a certain respect, as it has been vitally committed to a voluntarist base, has generally eschewed the concepts of mental mechanisms, has been periodically concerned with interdependent units (e.g., teams, the concept of *with*, and collective rituals), and has placed a strong emphasis on temporally unfolding processes. This concern with the individual as molding his or her career is further amplified and extended in Tomkins's (Tomkins, 1979; Carlson, 1981) script theory of personality in which the individual is viewed as a playwright who constructs his or her drama from the earliest weeks of life. Certain of these elements, namely the concern with self-agency and process, have also been integral to the experimental work of E. E. Jones and his colleagues (Baumeister & Jones, 1978; Jones, 1964; Jones & Pittman, 1982). This work has been concerned, for example, with the ways in which people alter their self-presentation for purposes of ingratiation (Jones, 1964; Jones & Wortman, 1973), handicap themselves in order to defend against the implications of failure (Jones & Berglas, 1978), and undergo changes in their views of the self as they interact with others (Jones, Gergen, & Davis, 1962; Jones, Rhodewalt, Berglas, & Skelton, 1981). Of interest in light of the present arguments is that this research initially made considerable use of the mechanistic implement of the self-concept. However, as the work has progressed, this language of the enduring structure has been replaced by one emphasizing temporally contingent change. The *phenomenal self* (akin to the self-image) has replaced the self-concept. As Jones and Pittman (1982) point out in their most recent review, "the phenomenal self; (1) shifts from moment to moment as a function of motivational and situational cues and (2) is constantly evolving and changing in ways that incorporate or come to terms with one's actions or outcomes" (p. 233).

A similar emphasis on both voluntarism and process may be located in much additional inquiry into self-presentation. As argued by Schneider (1981) and by Jellison (1981), people are faced with the task of making themselves *appear* to have an enduring character or a "true self." They strategically manage their public presentations in order to bring off this impression. In effect, the theorists thus view people as agents in process, whereas the "enduring structure" is removed from inside the head and placed within the social arena. Other theorists have taken much the same view toward self-esteem. That is, it is not a private conception of the self as "good" toward which the person aspires, but a publicly acceptable image. Thus, people may manage situations so that they may "bask in reflected glory" (Richardson & Cialdini, 1981), avoid seeming at fault for errors (Tedeschi & Riess, 1981), or make modest public claims about themselves (Arkin, 1980) in order to ensure that the public image is in good order. As investigators in this area have shown, it is also possible to employ this process-oriented view of human functioning to account for a broad number of activities traditionally viewed within the mechanistic framework. It is possible to view as voluntarily managed people's behavior in psychological experiments (Alexander & Rudd, 1981; Page, 1981), their change in attitudes (Haas, 1981; Jellison, 1981), aggression (Athens, 1980; Felson, 1981), and prosocial action (Tedeschi & Riordan, 1981). Most of this work continues to use the individual as the unit of explanation. However, in certain cases, such as Athen's (1980) and Luckenbill's (1977) portrayal of violent crime as a social achievement, investigators have succeeded in shifting focus from the individual to the level of interaction.

Closely allied with inquiry into impression management have been developments in understanding self-disclosure. Much early research in this domain was strongly mechanistic in character. One viewed disclosure as a learned pattern or personality trait (see Cozby's 1973 review). However, with the seminal writing of Jourard (1964) and Altman and Taylor (1973), attention shifted importantly to patterns of disclosure produced jointly by participants during the development of a relationship. Thus participants may voluntarily increase or decrease disclosure as matters of attraction, reciprocity, and relevant rules shift in a relationship over time (Archer & Berg, 1978; Davis, 1977; Lynn, 1978). Theoretical interest thus shifts to the self-disclosing process within groups (typically dyads) of interdependent persons.

D.   THE EMERGING IMAGE OF HUMAN ACTION

In the mid-1950s, inquiry into the self was largely a derivative of the neo-behaviorist paradigm that prevailed more generally throughout the psychological sciences. Theory and research were critically concerned with the internal structures or mechanisms of the individual, and the laws governing the ways in which these internal entities were (1) engendered or altered by environmental influences and (2) figured in the subsequent determination of behavior. Knowledge about these psychological entities was viewed as both obtainable and subject to verification. Both the individual and the scientist could thus be right or wrong regarding matters psychological. In effect, the guiding metaphor of the discipline was the human-as-machine. As machine the individual was essentially a passive device, subject to understanding through systematic exposure to various stimuli.

Social life was essentially a secondary byproduct of the particular configuration and juxtaposition of individual machine-units. Knowledge of social interaction was thus, in principle, a derivative of the laws governing the psychological functioning of individuals.

As the present review has attempted to demonstrate, with steadily increasing force social psychological research on the self has come to pose a major challenge to this entire colligation of interdependent assumptions. Research on self-attribution established perhaps the first significant beachhead. As this work has made increasingly clear, there is good reason to view the world of psychological entities not as a world of natural kinds, but as a world of socially generated constructions. Such constructions do not appear subject to correction through observation (or inference), but are generated, sustained, and altered through social interchange. This view is now in the process of being extended from the psychological to the behavioral realm.

Closely allied with this alteration in understanding has been a liberation in self-inquiry of the concept of human agency. With increasing boldness social psychologists have come to rely on an explanatory language granting the individual autonomous powers of self-direction. The stimulus world thus loses its powers of inexorable determination, and the individual becomes a creature of reasons as opposed to causes. As has also become increasingly clear, this explanatory language can neither be dislodged empirically nor does it obviate the search for order in contemporary behavior patterns. If psychological mechanisms may be considered social constructions and the social process is carried out by self-directing agents, then the concept of internal machinery ceases to be compelling. Rather, one's attention shifts to social processes unfolding over time. Social life is no longer a juxtaposition of disconnected S–O–R sequences, but a phenomenon in continuous and coherent emergence. The metaphor of the *machine* is replaced by the metaphor of the *the dialogue, the dance, the drama* or *religious ritual,* as it is the latter in which voluntary agents are united in an ongoing, interdependent process.

At the beginning of this chapter it was pointed out that social psychological research on the self posed a dramatic challenge to the 2000 year old beliefs in self-knowledge. However as is also apparent, if the current trends in self-inquiry are extended and proliferated, the discipline of psychology more generally may undergo a substantial evolution. For, as the present work suggests, that which is taken to be psychological knowledge is more properly to be viewed as a product of social interchange. From this perspective an understanding of social life is not to be derived from knowledge of psychological principles. Rather, what are taken to be psychological principles are derivative from the ongoing process of negotiation and conflict among persons. Thus understanding community is prior to and establishes the grounds for psychological knowledge. The mechanistically oriented, individual-centered, law-producing investments of the discipline thus give over to a communitarian perspective. Forms of social process and their potentials and failings become focal concerns of the discipline. The outcomes of research would not be laws for putative purposes of prediction and control, but rendered understandings that can stimulate the social process that is science and more generally challenge the common conventions of the society.

To what degree can one anticipate such an evolution? This is indeed a difficult and many-faceted question, depending as it does not only on intellectual developments but on political, pragmatic, and ideological matters. With respect to the growth of ideas alone, we find that we are now only at the horizon of a new understanding. Conceptual developments are frequently piecemeal. For example, the "script" (Abelson, 1981; Schank & Abelson, 1977; Wilson & Capitman, 1982) as a theoretical implement represents an important contribution to the shift from the static structure of the self-concept to a process orientation. Yet, the script ultimately stands as well as a static device, the execution of which would lead to automaton-like behavior. Ziller (1973) proposes a shift from the concept of self, to "self–other" concepts, and in so doing takes an important step toward reciprocal interactionism. Yet, these self–other units are finally consigned to the cognitive structure of the individual. In much contemporary self-inquiry, remnants of the earlier S–O–R paradigm peacefully coexist with concepts central to the newly evolving image. Evolution will depend, in part, on whether such inconsistencies are challenged. Further, much contemporary work on the self is sustained by the creative efforts of artificial intelligence investigators. The prevailing machine metaphor is now the computer, and it seems clear that time will be required for the full intellectual unpacking of its implications. And too, the difficult task lies ahead of creating new conceptions. Social psychologists are only beginning to develop concepts of cross-time process and to shift the focus of understanding from the level of the individual to that of interdependence. Innovative work is much needed in these domains.

Some inspiration for these latter endeavors may be furnished by investigators who have turned their attention to developmental changes in social activity. Previously cited was the work of Lewis and Brooks-Gunn (1979) who have charted the course of the child's capacity for self-recognition and self-knowledge. Others have also enhanced sensitivity to the alterations in self conception in the early and middle years (cf. Fincham & Jaspers, 1979; Hormuth, 1982; Loevinger, 1976; Lynch, 1981; Norem-Hebeisen, 1981; O'Malley & Backman, 1979; Phillips & Zigler, 1980). Investigators have also expanded tbe concern with developmental process to the life span. Thus, both Ruble (in press) and Suls and Mullen (1982) have begun to explore the age-related changes in self-evaluation through social comparison. A variety of investigations have begun on the way in which biographic (Bertaux, 1981) life accounts (Gagnon, 1981) or self-narratives (Gergen & Gergen, 1982) develop through the social process over time. And investigators such as Blank (1982), Ryff (1982), and L'Ecuyer (1979) have carried out extensive work on changing patterns of self-attribution over the life span. Blank's (1982) volume is of special interest to the present discussion inasmuch as it represents a full-scale exhortation to social psychologists to adopt a developmental orientation to social pattern. Such work may play a vital role in the shift toward process theories of self.

Perhaps the most imposing obstruction to the present reconstitution of understanding remains "the concept." Deeply engrained within the Western tradition is the belief that people possess ideas, that ideas are basic constituents of thought processes, and that thought processes are essential to the survival of the species. The favored instantiation of "the idea" in contemporary psychology is the concept. As it is argued, concepts are essential in enabling the person to organize or sort incoming stimuli, to store and retrieve information, to weight values and probabilities, and to direct action. Such assumptions are realized in self-inquiry in the traditional importance attached to the "self-concept." It is thus to the theoretical status of the concept in general and the self concept in particular that our critical focus must finally be turned. After examining a number of fundamental problems inherent in the assumption of the concept, we can consider an alternative orientation to self-study that will vivify more fully a form of inquiry favored by the newly emerging views of human functioning.

IV.   The Limitations of "the Concept" in Psychological Theory

As we have seen, the vast share of traditional research on the self has relied on some form of mental mechanism and most typically "the concept," as the central explanatory locus for understanding human behavior. Further, with the general cognitive revolution in psychological theorizing, strong encouragement has been furnished to those employing the language of conceptualization. The self-schema, the cognitive prototype, and the script may all be considered by-products of the cognitive turn, each embodying the structural features of the concept but embedding them in differing linguistic contexts. Yet, as the previous analysis suggests, the status of the concept as the cornerstone of self-theory deserves closest scrutiny. First, in our discussion of the place of empirical research in self-inquiry, we encountered major difficulties with the process of assessing or inferring mental structures, As it was found, with each inference to the psychological level, the researcher commits him- or herself to yet other inferential assumptions. Thus, there appears to be little intelligible means of fully anchoring knowledge about self-concepts to empirical observables. Further difficulties with the concept may be derived from the above review of developments in the theory of self-knowledge. As we saw, there is emerging agreement that knowledge of mental states is problematic. Differentiation among states is difficult, access to cognitive process seems denied, and there are conceptual impediments to understanding how one could identify a mental state. The implication of these arguments for the concept is transparent: There would appear to be no fully satisfactory way in which the individual him- or herself could report with fidelity on the character of his or her concepts, schemata, prototypes, and the like.

The reemergence of *agency* in theories of the self does not raise problems of such fundamental significance for the assumption of the concept. As we saw, both agency and structure can legitimately figure in the same theoretical account (e.g., one may voluntarily *select* from one's repertoire of *concepts*). However, to the extent that explanatory stress is placed on agential functions, conceptual structures tend to recede in theoretical significance. Further problems for the concept emerged in the final treatment of process theory. As indicated, conceptual structures become increasingly less serviceable to theoreticians as they turn their attention to the reciprocal relationship across time between the person and the environment. As process-oriented theories gain increasing credence, the concept is shorn of explanatory significance.

However, these particular discussions do not penetrate with sufficient depth the problematic character of the concept. Required at this juncture is a sharper focus on the construct. This assessment can be limited to two fundamental problems, both of which have proved perdurably recalcitrant to solution. Such solution would seem essential if the concept is to be justifiably sustained in psychological theory.

A. THE IMPASSE OF ORIGIN

Any theory of mental structure or process may appropriately be asked to furnish an account of origin. If concepts are the chief vehicle through which the world is understood or comprehended and the chief basis for action in the world, one may well ask for reasons of both intellectual curiosity and pragmatic concern, how these conceptual structures are developed. Further, one major constraint that might justifiably be placed over the positing of psychological entities is that of intelligible origin. Otherwise there are few safeguards against a theorist arguing that human conduct is guided by impulses sent from extraterrestial beings, by powers of black magic, by cosmic reverberations, or by memories of one's prehistoric being. To be sure, a variety of accounts have been offered for the genesis of conceptual structure. However, an appreciation of the inherent problems in the prevailing explanations can proceed more effectively after establishing the broader context of concern.

At the outset, it has long been recognized within the philosophy of science that observation cannot properly serve as the principle impetus to conceptual construction. One can neither derive concepts from sense data nor derive higher-order abstractions from primitive concepts (Fodor, 1981). For example, in scanning the horizon, one's visual experience would permit one to distinguish simply between "figure" and "ground," or conversely, to make as many conceptual distinctions as there are possible sensory discriminations (along with distinctions representing all possible combinations and permutations of such discriminations). Nature would not appear to dictate one's choice in such matters. One is not required by the nature of the stimulus world to form any particular conception of it. The most compelling argument of this variety within recent philosophy is that of Norwood Hanson (1958). As he argues, what counts as a fact in the stimulus world depends on one's conceptual standpoint. On this account, one brings to experience certain forms of understanding that operate much like lenses; they determine, for example, whether the sky is viewed as an overall Gestalt, whether we distinguish among nimbus, cumulus, and cirrus clouds, or whether the clouds simply become a peripheral background for one's focal observation of a flight of geese. In effect, what are taken to be facts are thus products of conceptual perspectives. Yet, however, compelling Hanson's account, one is left with the problem of explaining the initial genesis of such perspectives.

It is at this juncture that many thinkers, from Kant to the present, have turned to nativist accounts of concept origin. Thus, it is proposed, humans must be genetically equipped to make certain basic distinctions. For Kant, human nature enables the individual to comprehend space, time, causality, and other elementary aspects of the world. In contemporary psychology there are few adherents to a Kantian perspective. Perhaps the most significant neo-Kantian proposal has been put forward by Chomsky (1968). As he argues, the individual must possess an innate knowledge of language, the positing of which is essential to account for the rapid language development of the child. The possibility of an innate knowledge of language continues to provoke debate (cf. Cooper, 1978; Fodor, 1975, 1981).

Yet, substantial problems also inhere in the nativist orientation to concept origin. One first confronts the problem of how the fundamental set of concepts was acquired. How did the basic repertoire of rudimentary concepts come to be part of human nature? One might wish to fall back on the process of natural selection at this point, but such reliance does not fully solve the problem. The existence of the concept would still have to precede selection. One must first possess a concept in order for it to be favored by selection. It might be argued that the basic repertoire represented a genetic mutation common to an entire species. However this proposal stretches the borders of credulity. It might also be argued that the initial concepts resulted from common experience within the culture. However this proposal would commit one to some form of

Lamarkianism. For most contemporary scientists, the view that acquired concepts are genetically transmitted would be most unwelcome.

Further, should a means be found for rendering plausible the nativist argument for a rudimentary conceptual repertoire, one is puzzled to understand how the individual would ever acquire additional concepts. If the stimulus world were segmented into things that move versus stable entities, for example, on what basis would one develop a concept of *phasic sequences* of stability and change? As the latter concept would not, on this account, be a product of genetic makeup, how are we to understand its origins? The most obvious route to solution is to consider environmental demands. For example, one might wish to argue that the more differentiated concept of phases meets certain functional requirements; it enables the individual to solve certain problems threatening its well-being. Yet, as we see, the recognition of a functional requirement or a problem to be solved itself would require a preliminary conceptualization or framework of understanding. Problems do not inhere in environments; they would appear to be derived from conceptual perspectives. In effect, one may effectively posit a fundamental set of genetically preferred concepts, but the problem of further elaboration and proliferation of the basic set thrusts the theorist back into the clutches of the initial dilemma. Few nativist theorists have wished to offer more than a handful of genetic preferences. To do otherwise would be to enter a fool's paradise in which all concepts, from the Beatles to black holes, would be said to inhere in the genetic code.

As is apparent, both the environmental (empiricist) and the nativist (rationalist) orientation to concept origin confront a range of seemingly implacable problems. Against this background we may profitably consider the major accounts within psychology of concept development in general and of self-concept in particular. As can readily be appreciated, there are no existing nativist explanations for the full and differentiated structure of the conceptual domain. Although nativist and environmentalist accounts share certain characteristics (Fodor, 1981), to this reviewer's knowledge virtually all present accounts in psychology are fundamentally environmentalist in orientation. These may conveniently be divided into three basic types: reinforcement, communication and mapping theories. We may consider each in turn.

Reinforcement accounts of concept development have been popular within general psychology since the publication of Hull's (1920) classic work on concept attainment. Such theories typically though not exclusively cast the concept-learning process into the metaphor of the hypothesis test. Thus, for example, Restle (1962) describes a variety of hypothesis testing strategies of concept attainment, each based on the assumption that concepts are learned through environmental provisions of success and failure. Similarly, Bower and Trobasso (1964) view concepts as depending, at least in part, on error signals from the environment. In Levine's (1966) work, correct responses are emphasized as opposed to errors. In a model placing greater emphasis on cognitive mediation, Simon and Kotovsky (1963) propose that people form a hypotheses about the sequential pattern to which they are exposed and then test the adequacy of the hypothesis against subsequent exposures. For self-theorists, reinforcement assumptions have long occupied an important position. Thus, for James (1980), the development of self-esteem was said to be dependent upon exposure to success and/or failure. In Diggory's (1966) research on self-esteem, task success plays the same function. In Coopersmith's (1967) analysis of self-esteem development in children, parentally enforced limits on the child's activities play a pivotal role. Epstein (1980) has proposed that the self-concept is developed in much the same manner as scientific theory: It thus comes to reflect the results of hypothesis testing and is corrected through falsification (the latter a conceptual surrogate for punishment in reinforcement theory).

Yet, informed by the earlier analysis, we see that reinforcement theories are fundamentally inadequate to the challenge of origin. In particular, it is apparent that in order for reinforcement (correct outcomes, errors, or other forms of environmental feedback) to correct or modify one's self-concept, the individual must already possess a conceptual repertoire. Two conceptual forms are required, one specific and the other more general. On the specific level, the individual must possess an hypothesis or a critical concept for which reinforcement would be relevant. One must presumably possess an hypothesis or criterion such as "Am I a good or bad X" in order for environmental feedback to function as a corrective or verifying device. On a more general level, the reinforcement model requires that the individual possess a prior concept of reinforcement. If one cannot conceptualize an event as a success or an error, then he or she simply remains uninformed. If children cannot distinguish between a parental admonishment and the remainder of the "booming, buzzing confusion," if they cannot place into their meaning system the words *good* versus *bad*, then environmental feedback fails to influence or extend their conceptual repertoire. Yet, it is precisely the origins of such distinctions that theories of reinforcement (and their derivatives) are designed to explain. In effect, reinforcement accounts do not offer a satisfactory explanation of conceptual development because reinforcement cannot function without a conceptual structure already intact.

Reinforcement accounts may be contrasted with a second family of explanations, those that trace concept development to some form of social communication. Direct reward and punishment are unnecessary for learning to occur on this account; rather the individual develops a concept of the self through participation in the communication process. It was this view that Sullivan (1947) advanced in his concern with the way "reflected appraisal" shapes the self-dynamism. Similarly, for Veblen (1889/1934) one's self-esteem is the product of others' communicated regard. Both Cooley (1902) and Mead (1934) adopted a similar but more complex orientation. For Cooley, it was not the direct fact of others' communication that shaped one's self-conception but the imagined view of others that was significant. In contrast, Mead proposed that one's self-concept is the result of one's projecting oneself into the others' role or standpoint toward oneself. This general concern with the communication process in the shaping of self-conception continues to be represented in much contemporary theory and research (cf. Jones, 1973; McCall, 1977; Rosenberg, 1979; Shrauger, 1975). Although not explicitly a communications theory, Bandura's (1976) account of the emergence of self-reinforcement bears close resemblance to the communication paradigm. As it is said, the child observes the behavior of models toward both themselves and toward itself. As a result of such observations the child adopts the patterns of such models in carrying out self-rewarding (or punishing) actions. Similarly, the work of Bandura and others (Bandura & Schunk, 1981; Ryckman, Robbins, Thornton, & Cantrell, 1982) on perceived self-efficacy assumes that people derive their perceptions from observations of their own mastery.

Yet, as should be apparent, *communication* in the present explanatory framework stands in the same problematic position as reinforcement did in the preceding account. That is, it is difficult to discern how another's communication (or action) could be intelligible without already granting a conceptual repertoire to the individual. Thus, for the symbolic interactionist, recognition and understanding of others' communications about oneself would presumably depend on one's possessing a conceptual structure that would render such communications meaningful. Similarly, in the case of social learning theory, for the child to emulate an adult model would require a preliminary conceptualization of meaningful actions. The child would have to understand that the model had rewarded him or herself and that there were similar circumstances in which it would be legitimate to reward oneself as well. In effect, analyses centering on the communication process are subject to the same critical defect as other environmentalist theories. They do not appear adequate to the problem of developing mental structure.

The third process for explaining concept origin may be termed *mapping*. This approach generally assumes that through various mental and physiological mechanisms (typically left unspecified), concepts come to resemble the range of real-world entities or events. In the case of Posner and Keele (1968), it is proposed that people abstract essential features from a range of stimuli. This approach is recently exemplified in Rosch's widely cited (1978) theory of "natural categories." As she argues, through observation of objects in the real world, people become acquainted with the structure of real-world attributes. They observe that such attributes are not randomly distributed, but appear in recurring, structural combinations. Thus, for example, certain creatures have wings, beaks, feathers, and claws. Continued exposure to such a confluence of features lends itself to the formation of the natural category *bird*. Although more equivocal regarding the extent to which such categories operate as maps of real-world events (as opposed to socially derived distinctions), various accounts of self-prototypes (cf. Cantor & Mischel, 1979; Kuiper, 1981) draw sustenance from the Rosch (1978) account. Ziller's (1973) analysis of self–other schemata also posits a mapping device. While otherwise distinct from this line of inquiry, Bem's (1972) investigation of self-observation also presumes some form of mapping process. From Bem's standpoint knowledge of the self appears to be built inductively from observations of one's own behavior. Thus, behavioral constructs should presumably operate as maps of actual occurrences.

The precise details by which mapping occurs have not been elaborated in any of the just mentioned analyses. The process by which the individual searches the environment, registers certain configurations, disregards others, creates hypotheses about co-occurrences, moves logically from discriminate sensations to general abstractions, and so on—all critical to the intelligibility of a mapping theory—are left opaque. As the preceding analysis further indicates, any such account would encounter rather formidable problems. In particular, the theorist confronts the problem of understanding how the individual would come to recognize the features, objects, or properties of the world at the outset. How would it be possible to recognize the features of a configuration without a preliminary concept of those features? In the Rosch formulation (1978), for example, how does one come to recognize the constituent features of feathers, beak, wings, etc, which enter into the generation of the natural category bird? Must one not already possess a category system in which such features are rendered sensible and discriminant in order for recognition to occur?

As the present analysis has demonstrated, in spite of the immense importance of understanding the origins of self-conception (along with other structural mechanisms serving similar theoretical functions), theorists have yet to render a satisfactory account. Not only does the process of concept development thus remain obscure, but neither nativist nor empiricist formulations appear to offer convenient avenues of solution. One might speculate on the possibility of some form of compromise among existing solutions. Although neither the empiricist nor the nativist position alone is satisfactory, one might hope that a combination of the two would suffice. One might look forward to an interactionist solution of some variety. Do not the inherent processes of the organism along with stimulus properties of the real world interact with each other to engender conceptual structure? One does not wish to foreclose on such a possibility prematurely. However, if processes of neither variety are capable of rendering a logically coherent account, the resort to interactionism would seem more attractive in the contemplation than the realization. Such a theory would presumably require that one make intelligible the means by which an unarticulated concept interacts with an unrecognized event in order to give form to the first and substance to the latter. The empiricist cannot account for the origin of concepts without resorting to internal generation, and the nativist cannot account for internal generation without recourse to events in the external world. One is ill-disposed to see how a confluence of conundrums will readily yield to a satisfying solution. In effect, the hoary problem of the origin of ideas remains to haunt self-inquiry, and no convenient solution is in sight.

B. THE IMPASSE OF EFFECT

Our concern with the viability of the concept in psychological theory must now be extended in yet a second direction. In particular, we must consider the relationship between concept and action. What explanation may be rendered for the putative effects of cognitive structure on behavior? Such an account might generally be demanded of psychological terms on both theoretical and practical grounds. In the former case, the demand places reasonable constraints over the range of psychological vocabulary. It would seem suspicious to populate the psychological realm with constructs devoid of behavioral implications. On the practical level, if theoretical constructs do not possess behavioral implication, such constructs may be impugned for their lack of practical or real-world applicability. As is widely agreed, linking psychological mechanisms and/or processes to observable behavior is a crucial task for the theorist.

The importance of this challenge is equaled by its complexity. In the case of structural terms such as the concept (and its near relatives), the problems are particularly obdurate. Not only is the self-theorist confronted by the array of difficulties encountered by psychological theories in general, but there are more specialized problems indigenous to the particular domain. Given space limitations, we shall limit our concern to two problems that self-inquiry shares in common with most other psychological domains and then two enigmas of special pertinence to the domain of self-theory.

On the more general level, the self-theorist shares with most other psychologists the Cartesian conundrum of accounting for causal linkages between differing ontological realms. If one posits a dualism constituted by psychological mechanisms and/or processes on the one hand, and corporal movements on the other, how is one to understand how event of the first kind can influence events of the second? As in the present case, how does a conception of self exert a force over the movements of the body? Because of the complexity of this problem, many investigators have simply suspended judgment and plunged into research exploring the relationship between measures of "psychological states" and "behavioral events" (cf. Kaplan, 1975; Shavelson & Stuart, 1981; Snyder and Campbell, 1982). As it is hoped, systematic relationships between such measures can later be cashed out in terms of causal linkages, even if the particular character of these linkages is presently clouded. Others accede to the early behaviorist view that hypothetical constructs such as self-concept are paralleled by particular physiological states. On this account we may ultimately anticipate the physiological reduction of psychological constructs. Still others have resisted this view in its implication that psychology is merely a temporary holding operation to be dissolved by advances in physiology. Psychological theory, as it is advanced, is an independent realm of discourse and not reducible to the discourse of physiology. Again, a full elucidation of the dimensions of this problem cannot be undertaken at this juncture. The major point is that the mind–body problem has not yielded to any broadly compelling solution in psychology. Until a solution is reached, the self-theorist continues under threat of embarassment.

A second pervasive and perplexing problem was elucidated by Ryle (1949) in his classic work, *The Concept of Mind*. As Ryle argued, it is both imparsimonious and obfuscating to posit psychological processes lying behind and responsible for human actions. If one observes an overt action called "intelligent," it is unnecessary and misleading to posit an internal process (e.g., "thought") responsible for this action. Whatever is attributed to the internal domain is merely another way of talking about one's observations of the external. No additional information is given. In addition to the unnecessary duplication of terminology, positing an internal process responsible for an external action leads to an infinite regress of explanation. How, asks Ryle, does one account for the operation of the internal process? This account must presuppose the existence of yet another psychological process, the operation of which itself requires explanation, and so on. For example, many investigators attempt to explain "sorting behavior" in terms of "conceptual operations." But what triggers these particular conceptual operations, one might ask. One is not required by the nature of the stimulus world to use any particular concepts for the task of sorting. Thus, a second-order prompting process might be invoked to explain why certain concepts were employed and not others. Yet, this prompting process is also in need of explanation. Why does it prompt (or make salient) certain concepts and not others? A prompting primer might be envisioned, leading once again to the question of its origins, and so on. The problems raised by Ryle remain unanswered and largely unheeded by the contemporary research community.

The third enigma for present consideration is particularly germane to theories employing concept-like entities. Concepts are traditionally viewed as abstractions from reality. They are not thus eidetic images of the world, but categories into which events are placed according to restricted criteria. Yet, if knowledge of the self is stored in this abstracted form, one rapidly confronts the question of how such knowledge may be applied in particular instances. How is one to employ a system of abstractions for generating concrete, particularized actions? For example, if one conceptualized oneself as a friendly person and wished to act consistently with this conception, how would one determine what constituted a friendly action in a given situation? The concept itself is essentially indeterminant in this respect. The abstraction friendly does not in itself recommend or favor any particular set of bodily movements. Virtually any movement of the body may be viewed as friendly or unfriendly depending on the confluence of circumstances. This problem appears to yield to solution if one resorts to a second-order construct or rule, namely one that prescribes the precise character of friendly actions in a given circumstance. This second-order construct (possibly viewed as a hierarchial substructure of the more general class, friendly) might inform the individual, ''On occasions of meeting a friend, a smile and a greeting are normal.'' Yet, as we see, this application rule is also in the abstract form and leaves important questions unanswered. In particular it does not inform one about the particulars of what it is to meet a friend, to smile, or to greet. What is now required is a subapplication rule, that informs one, for example, that a friend is one who has given you support and that smiling is a form of turning the corners of the mouth in the upward direction. Yet, how is the individual to determine when support has been given and what constitutes turning the corners of the mouth upward? These are, after all, abstractions without specified particulars.

As rapidly discerned, the problem of applying conceptual knowledge to concrete circumstance casts one back upon subsidiary conceptualizations (specification rule), which must be defined in terms of still other conceptualizations (rules), and so on in an infinite regress. In effect there appears to be nothing within the process of abstract or conceptual thought that enables one to make exit to the realm of concrete action. One is essentially left to rove the dictionary of the mind, as it were, continuously defining concepts in terms of other concepts.

One might resist the implications of this argument by attaching some form of eidetic imagery to the conceptual structure. Particularly lower level concepts, it might be ventured, have various images associated with them, and it is these images and not the conceptual criterion that furnish the paradigm for action. However, it should also be realized that to the extent the concept becomes eidetically saturated, the traditional value assigned to the conceptual apparatus is weakened. One of the major attractions of the concept as a theoretical device is that it allows one to understand how the individual can transcend or avoid absorption by the buzzing confusion of particulars. With the tools of abstract thought, it is said, the individual can develop adaptive strategies that generalize across ranges of diverse particulars. Yet, to the extent that abstract categories are suffused with images of particulars, they lose this adaptive capacity. As storage and processing in the eidetic form is enhanced, the power of abstraction as a generalizing device deteriorates.

The final enigma of particular concern to self-theorists is the problem of linking the static with the vital, that is, furnishing an intelligible explanation for how an immobile structure, such as the self-concept or schema, can form the basis of mobile action. A concept of self as pragmatic, for example, does not itself motivate pragmatic action. Self theorists have long been aware of this issue and have tried through a variety of means to furnish answers. However, the existing forms of solution prove, on closer inspection, to offer little redress. One form of solution, for example, is to argue that the self-concept has motivational properties (Combs & Snygg, 1949). However, to grant such vitality to a structure places an excessive strain on the metaphor of psychological mechanism. By far the most popular mode of solution is to posit one or more motivational sources. These sources move the individual to action, whereas the self-concept furnishes either a direction or criterion for action. In Rosenberg's (1979) synthesis, for example, the individual is said to be motivated by a desire for enhanced self-esteem and self-consistency (including the attempt both to act in accord with self-conception and to maintain one's self-concept intact). The specification of these motives enables Rosenberg to incorporate wide-ranging inquiry in sociology (cf. Kaplan, 1975; Stryker, 1982), social psychology (cf. Jones, 1973; Wortmann, Costanzo & Witt, 1973), and clinical psychology (cf. Murphy, 1947; Rogers, 1959).

Yet, one is forced at this juncture to inquire more directly into the motivational process and particularly into the relationship between motives and concepts. At the outset one confronts the problem of information transmission between the two domains. If motivation is to succeed in maintaining a given self-concept, the motivational source would appear to require some means of (1) identifying the character of the self-concept that it is attempting to maintain and (2) holding it in place for a sufficient duration that it could direct action across time. In effect, the theorist would be required to supply motives with devices for concept recognition and retention. The motive then becomes an automation or a form of homonculus that possesses all the features of the concept—thereby rendering the latter redundant. There is, further, the problem of accounting for both the origin and effects of motives. If motives are learned and have effects according to the character of situations, some apparatus is required to account for the recognition of differeing situations. Yet, such a proposal leads us again into familiar and forbidding territory. How is one to account for the origin of this recognition system? Is it innate, and if not, how could learning occur without a recognition system already intact? Further, how can this system, as a static structure, mobilize action? What motivates the motive, and how does it translate its conceptual imperatives to movements in space and time? For example, how does the concept of self as "needing self-esteem" in itself move one to do anything in particular? In effect, at the present juncture the discipline is without a satisfactory view of how the concept instigates action.

V.   From Self-Concept to the Ethnopsychology of Self

As the preceding discussion demonstrates, theoretical reliance on the concept and its various relatives (prototypes, schemas, scripts) places one in a tenuous form of equilibration. The theorist confronts a precipitous plunge into incoherence in the attempt to relate the conceptual world either to inputs from the empirical world, on the one side, or to subsequent action on the other. This is not to say that such theoretical problems are principally insoluble. However, they have remained steadfastly recalcitrant to solution, in spite of the fact that in several cases they have occupied some of the finest minds of the Western culture over many centuries. Even today's romance with cognitive mechanisms appears to be reaching an impasse (cf. Allport, 1975; Cohen, 1977; Newell, 1973). In effect, we find ourselves at the present historical juncture with a disembodied system of hypotheticals, one that cannot easily be tied to any form of observable input or behavioral outcome. Rather than an indefinite and potentially unproductive continuation of the traditional perspective, it would seem an auspicious juncture to consider alternative theoretical orientations toward the self. One such alternative seems particularly advantageous as it avoids most of the pitfalls outlined previously whereas simultaneously aligning itself with the evolution in self-inquiry. The intellectual roots of this orientation may be traced to Wittgenstern's (1963) inquiries into the function of psychological terminology within various linguistic practices. His concerns were later extended within what came to be known as analytic or ordinary language philosophy. Treatments of such terms as intention (Anscombe, 1957), motivation (Peters, 1958), sense data (Austin, 1962), emotion (Kenny, 1963), and mind (Ryle, 1949) are all useful precursors of the present proposal. The proposal itself may be termed ethnopsychological and can be briefly outlined as follows.

At the outset the vast study of the self furnishes a rich sample of the *language forms* employed by people in describing and explaining themselves. Research in which persons evaluate or rate themselves, explain their motives, describe their emotions, reveal their memories, indicate their plans, evaluate their actions, and so on all contribute to this repository of language samples. By and large, such materials have been used to infer the state of psychological structure. That is, they are viewed as bases for inferring the individual's conceptual repertoire, level of self-esteem, attributional rule system, and so on. Yet, as we saw in our initial discussion, it is the assumption of inference that creates many of the problems just elaborated. As we found, for example, there is no apparent means of validating such inferences empirically; each inference depends on yet another inference for its sustenance. Further, the theorist is typically led to positing conceptual structures for which the origins and effects remain shrouded in mystery. Yet, one is not required by virtue of the samples to assume that they reflect upon or reveal the structural features of the mind. Rather, one may focus on self-description as language.

From this perspective we may view samples of self-talk (self-evaluation or self-description) as contributions to an ethnography of the culture. The scientist discovers, in this case, the conventions and limitations of what participants in contemporary culture may intelligibly say about themselves. For example, present research does demonstrate the facility with which people can talk about various cognitive, emotional, and behavioral aspects of the self. In the cognitive realm they talk about their abilities to reason, remember, plan, intend, and the like. In the emotional realm there appears to be a broad spectrum of terms (viz., fearful, happy, depressed, anxious, etc.) that are used to describe one's states. In effect, existing samples of self-description may contribute to an ethnography of the means by which people depict their psychologcal processes, traits, dispositions, and activities. In this sense they form the beginning of an ethnopsychology, that is, an exploration of the common linguistic practices of accounting for one's internal states or conditions.

Yet, it must be emphasized, extant materials form only a beginning. A host of significant questions remain as yet unaddressed. Two classes of question would seem of particular moment. First, more fully elaborated accounts are needed of the rules governing the language of self-description. There are clearly a wide number of rule-governed limits placed upon what people can say at present about their thoughts, emotions, and so on. For example, one is permitted to say that their reasoning faculties have deteriorated, but not that they are resuscitating themselves. One can describe one's emotions as weak or powerful but not as submissive or authoritarian. And one can say of one's aggression that it is triggered by frustration but not so convincingly by affection. Further, there would appear to be widespread rules governing the relationship between one's self-description and the accompanying description of the environment. Given a particular description of the environmental context, certain accounts of the self become more or less appropriate; as self-description is elaborated, restrictions may be placed over what may be said about the environmental context. Thus, to say that one has been insulted (description of an environmental event) increases the likelihood that one will describe his or her emotional reaction as hostility rather than passion. Or, to say that an individual experiences passion virtually requires that the target be described in desirable as opposed to derogatory terms.

Certain inroads into these domains have begun to emerge. For example, both Smedslund (1980) and Ossario (1978) bave outlined what they believe to be basic components of person description. Sabini and Silver (1981) have furnished insights into the way various moral terms (viz., envy, greed, anger, etc.) function within social relationships. Mummendey, Bornewasser, Loschper, and Linneweber, (1984) have begun to assess the social processes underlying the use of the concept "aggression"; Gergen and Gergen (1983) have outlined linguistic procedures essential for employing the term "altruism"; and Averill (1980) has furnished the groundwork for viewing emotion terms as social conventions. Yet, these are only bare beginnings for what could be a vast and immensely absorbing enterprise.

The exploration of contemporary rules, their rigidity, and their distribution within the culture furnishes but one important focal point for future exploration. A second form of inquiry would attempt to throw the contemporary conventions of self-talk into relief through comparative analysis. Much needed are studies of contrasting cultures and/or historical periods. The discovery of broad similarities in constructs (e.g., the concept of intentions) might suggest the possibility of fundamental components of person-talk more generally. The elucidation of cross-cultural and transhistorical variations would enhance contemporary sensitivity to the arbitrary and potentially delimiting character of contemporary convention. For example, do other cultures possess the kind of gender-related requirements for emotional self-description that pervade contemporary Western culture? Or, are there viable alternatives for the kind of emotional self-description used in our culture during the mourning period? In effect, the documentation of contrasts may play an emancipatory role in the society more generally. Again, important beginnings have been made in this domain (cf. Heelas & Lock, 1981; Needham, 1972; Shweder & Bourne, 1982); however, future exploration seems immensely promising.

As can be seen, an ethnopsychological approach to self-inquiry not only enables the investigator to extricate him- or herself from the conundrum of the concept, but also extends the historical tendencies described earlier. First, such an orientation is fundamentally concerned with the process of social construction. Language is essentially the medium of construction; in selecting words one makes ontological commitments. The emphasis on self-talk is also harmonious with assumptions of self-agency. To the extent that self-talk is governed by rules or convention, the individual retains the power of choice. One is not required by dint of genes or conditioning to obey a rule or to follow a convention; one is granted the power to abstain. To the extent that one views language in diachronic perspective, an ethnopsychology is also process oriented. It assumes the possibility for cross-time evolution in prevailing rules. This orientation toward process also enables one to shift the focus of concern from the self-contained individual to the system of relationship. Utterances do not become a language until there is social assent. The construction of the self is not thus carried out by individuals in isolation, but requires complicity, negotiation, and collusion— terms that all refer to relationships and not to single individuals. This latter point underscores the view to be taken of the scientist in this domain. Although traditional canons of objectivity may be maintained in reporting on language use in itself, such reports themselves are not the ultimate end of the research process. Rather, it is the rendering of a more general process of social construction that is at stake, and this rendering must be viewed as underdetermined by the data at hand. The theorist, then, is engaged in an interpretive enterprise. Interpretations may be justified or rendered meaningful and compelling by the use of linguistic exemplars. However such exemplars cannot ultimately invalidate an interpretive form.

In this light we finally see that the ethnopsychological investigator confronts the opportunity for significant creative work. Social psychologists themselves represent a subculture with their own evolving rules for describing psychological processes and mechanisms. As we have seen, this language has undergone substantial alteration over the years, alteration with significant implications for the surrounding culture. Further, the patterns of the culture can be much affected by the language of the guild, as frequently evidenced by the broadscale entry of disciplinary language into the common vocabulary of the educated culture (see Moscovici, 1961). However, as purveyors of languages, the discipline may also engage in the tactical expansion of available linguistic practices. They may invent languages to help sustain or alter the present configuration of the culture. For example, on the level of personal enhancement, psychologists might develop languages enabling people to account for their social actions as aesthetic expressions, as forms of moral exploration, or as means of linking themselves with the past—to name but a few possibilities. In each case, forms of theoretical articulation could contribute substantially to people's sense of personal fulfillment. On the more collective level, we have already touched on the need for a fully intelligible account of the self as a public entity. Other accounts might be useful in enhancing social solidarity, building community, or fostering a sense of interdependency among nations. In effect, the theoretical psychologist may act as an innovative agent of social change. The fruits of the discipline in this case are new forms of linguistic practice, practices that may furnish meaningful and useful alternatives to those that now restrict or cripple the human capacities.

REFERENCES

Abelson, R. *Persons, A study in philosophical psychology.* NY: St. Martin's Press, 1977.
Abelson, R. P. Psychological status of the script concept. *American Psychologist,* 1981, *36,* 715–729.
Aboud, F. *Cognitive bases of perceived self-integration.* Unpublished manuscript, McGill University, Canada, 1982.
Adler, A. *Practice and theory of individual psychology.* NY: Harcourt, 1927.
Albert, S. Temporal comparison theory. *Psychological Review,* 1977, *84,* 585–603.
Alexander, C. N., Jr., & Rudd, J. Situated identities and response variables. In J. T. Tedeschi (Ed.), *Impression management theory and social psychological research.* NY: Academic Press, 1981.
Allport, D. A. The state of cognitive psychology. *Quarterly Journal of Experimental Psychology,* 1975, *27,* 141–152.
Allport, G. W. The ego in contemporary psychology. *Psychological Review,* 1943, *50,* 451–478.
Altman, I., & Taylor, D. A. *Social penetration: The development of interpersonal relationships.* NY: Holt, Rinehart & Winston, 1973.
Anscombe, G. E. M. *Intention.* Oxford: Blackwell, 1957. Reprinted 1976.
Apfelbaum, E., & Lubek, I. Resolution *vs.* revolution? The theory of conflicts in question. In L. Strickland, F. Aboud, & K. J. Gergen (Eds.), *Social psychology in transition.* NY: Plenum, 1976.

Archer, R. L., & Berg, J. H. Disclosure reciprocity and its limits: A reactance analysis. *Journal of Experimental Social Psychology,* 1978, *14,* 527–540.

Argyris, C. *Inner contradictions of rigorous research.* NY: Academic Press, 1980.

Arkin, R. M. Self-presentation. In D. M. Wegner & R. R. Vallacher (Eds.), *The self in social psychology.* NY: Oxford University Press, 1980.

Arkin, R. M., Appelman, A. J., & Burger, J. M. Social anxiety, self-presentation and the self-serving bias in causal attribution. *Journal of Personality and Social Psychology,* 1980, *38,* 23–35.

Aronson, E. Dissonance theory: Progress and problems. In R. Abelson, E. Aronson, W. McGuire, T. Newcomb, M. Rosenberg, & P. Tannenbaum (Eds.), *Theories of cognitive consistancy: A source book.* Chicago: McNally, 1968.

Athens, L. H. *Violent criminal acts and actors: A symbolic interactionist study.* Boston: Routledge & Kegan Paul, 1980.

Austin, J. L. *Sense and sensibilia.* New York: Oxford University Press, 1962.

Averill, J. R. A constructivist view of emotion. In R. Plutchik & H. Kellerman (Eds.), *Emotion: Theory, research, and experience.* NY: Academic Press, 1980.

Averill, J. R. *Anger & aggression.* NY: Springer Verlag, 1983.

Averill, J. R., & Boothroyd, R. On falling in love in conformance with the romantic ideal. *Motivation and Emotion,* 1977, *1,* 235–247.

Back, K. W., & Gergen, K. J. The self through the latter span of life. In C. Gordon & K. J. Gergen (Eds.) *The self in social interaction* (Vol. 1) *Classic and contemporary perspectives.* NY: Wiley, 1968.

Backman, C., Secord, P., & Pierce, J. Resistance to change in the self-concept as a function of consensus among significant others. In M. Rosenberg and H. Kaplan (Eds.), *Social psychology of the self-concept.* Arlington Heights, IL: Davidson, 1982.

Baliff, B. The significance of the self-concept in the knowledge society. In M. Lynch, A. Norem-Hebeisen, & K. Gergen (Eds.), *Self-concept: Advances in theory and research.* MA: Ballinger, 1981.

Bandura, A. Self-reinforcement. Theoretical and methodological considerations. *Behaviorism,* 1976, *4,* 135–155.

Bandura, A. Self-efficacy: Toward a unifying theory of behavior change. *Psychological Review,* 1977, *84,* 191–215.

Bandura, A. The self and mechanisms of agency. In J. Suls (Ed.), *Psychological perspectives on the self.* Hillsdale, NJ: Erlbaum, 1982.

Bandura, A., & Schunk, D. H. Cultivating competence, self-efficacy, and intrinsic interest through proximal self-motivation. *Journal of Personality and Social Psychology,* 1981, *41,* 586–598.

Bannister, D., & Agnew, J. The child's construing of self. In J. K. Cole (Ed.), *Nebraska Symposium on Motivation,* 1975 (Vol. 24). Lincoln, NE: University of Nebraska Press, 1976.

Bauman, Z. *Hermeneutics and social science.* NY: Columbia University Press, 1978.

Baumeister, R. F., & Jones, E. E. When self-presentation is constrained by the target's knowledge: Consistency and compensation. *Journal of Personality and Social Psychology,* 1978, *36,* 608–618.

Becker, G., & Dileo, D. T. Scores on Rokeach's Dogmatism Scale and the response set to present a positive social and personal image. *Journal of Social Psychology,* 1967, *71,* 287–293.

Bem, D. Self-perception theory. In L. Berkowitz (Ed.), *Advances in experimental social psychology* (Vol, VI), NY: Academic Press, 1972.

Bem, D. J., & Allen A. On predicting some of the people some of the time: The search for cross-situational consistancies in behavior. *Psychological Review,* 1974, *81,* 506–520.

Berkowitz, L., & Turner, C. Perceived anger level, instigating agent, and aggression. In H. London & R. E. Nisbett (Eds.), *Cognitive alteration of feeling states.* Chicago: Aldine, 1972.

Berscheid, E., & Walster, E. A little bit about love. In T. Huston (Ed.), *Foundations of interpersonal attraction.* NY: Academic Press, 1974.

Bertaux, D. *Biography and society.* Beverly Hills, CA: Sage, 1981.

Blank, T. O. *A social psychology of developing adults.* NY: Wiley, 1982.

Block, J. Advancing the psychology of personality: Paradigmatic shift or improving the quality of research. In D. Magnusson & N. S. Endler (Eds.), *Personality at the crossroads: Current issues in interactional psychology.* Hillsdale, NJ: Erlbaum, 1977.

Bowerman, W. R. Causal cognitions and self-evaluations: Implications for stress and stress management. In T. G. Sarason, C. D. Spielberger, & P. B. Defares (Eds.), *Stress and anxiety* (Vol. II). New York: Halstead, 1975.

Bowers, G. Concept identification. In R. C. Atkinson (Ed.), *Studies in mathematical psychology.* Stanford: Stanford University Press, 1984.

Bowers, K. Situationism in psychology: An analysis and critique. *Psychological Review,* 1973, *80,* 307–336.

Bradley, G. W. Self-serving biases in the attribution process: A re-examination of the fact or fiction question. *Journal of Personality and Social Psychology,* 1978, *36,* 56–71.

Brockner, J. Self-esteem, self-consciousness and task performance. Replications, extensions and possible explanations. *Journal of Personality and Social Psychology,* 1979, *37,* 447–461.

Bugental, J. F. T. Investigations into the self-concept (Vol. III): Instructions for the W-A-Y method. *Psychological Reports,* 1964, *15,* 643–650.

Buss, A. H. *Self-consciousness and social anxiety.* San Francisco: Freeman, 1980.

Cantor, N., & Mischel, W. Prototypes in person perception. In L. Berkowitz (Ed.), *Advances in experimental social psychology* (Vol. 12). NY: Academic Press, 1979.

Carlson, R. Studies in script theory (Vol 1): Adult analogs of a childhood nuclear scene. *Journal of Personality and Social Psychology,* 1981, *40,* 501–510.

Carver, C. S., & Scheier, M. F. Self-focusing effects of dispositional self-consciousness, mirror presence, and audience presence. *Journal of Personality and Social Psychology,* 1978, *36,* 324–332.

Carver, C. S., & Scheier, M. F. *Attention and self-regulation: A control-theory approach of human behavior.* NY: Springer-Verlag, 1981.

Chein, I. *The science of behavior and the image of man.* NY: Basic Books, 1972.

Chomsky, N. *Language and mind.* NY: Harcourt, Brace, & World, 1968.

Clark, K. B., & Clark, M. P. Racial identification and preference in Negro children. In T. M. Newcomb & E. L. Hartley (Eds.), *Readings in social psychology.* NY: Holt, Rinehart, & Winston, 1947.

Cohen, G. The state of cognitive psychology: Problems and panaceas. In J. Kroll (Ed.), *The psychology of cognition.* NY: Academic Press, 1977.

Combs, A., & Snygg, D. *Individual behavior: A new frame of reference for psychology.* NY: Harper, 1949.

Cooley, C. H. *Human nature and the social order.* NY: Scribner, 1902.

Cooper, D. E. *Knowledge of language.* NY: Humanities Press, 1978.

Coopersmith, S. *The antecedents of self-esteem.* San Francisco: Freeman, 1967.

Coopersmith, S., & Gilbert, R. Behavioral academic self-esteem. In M. D. Lynch, A. A. Norem-Hebeisen, & K. J. Gergen (Eds.) *Self-concept: Advances in theory and research.* Cambridge, MA: Ballinger, 1981.

Cozby, P. Self-disclosure: A literature review. *Psychological Bulletin,* 1973, *2,* 73–91.

Dabbs, J. M., Evans, M. S., Hopper, C. H., & Purvis, J. A. Self-monitors in conversation: What do they monitor? *Journal of Personality and Social Psychology,* 1980, *39,* 278–284.

Darley, J. M., & Goethals, G. R. People's analysis of the causes of ability-linked performances. In

L. Berkowitz (Ed.), *Advances in experimental social psychology* (Vol. 13). NY: Academic Press, 1980.

Davidson, H. H., & Lang, G. Children's perceptions of their teachers' feelings toward them related to self-perception, school achievement and behavior. *Journal of Experimental Education*, 1960, *29*, 107–118.

David, J. D. Effects of communication about interpersonal process on the evolution of self disclosure in dyads. *Journal of Personality and Social Psychology*, 1977, *35*, 31–37.

Davis, J. D. When boy meets girl: Sex roles and the negotiation of intimacy in an acquaintance exercise. *Journal of Personality and Social Psychology*, 1978, *36*, 684–692.

Davison, G., & Valins, S. Maintainance of self-attributed and drug attributed behavior change. *Journal of Personality and Social Psychology*, 1969, *11*, 25–33.

DeCharms, R., & Shea, D. Beyond attribution theory: The human conception of motivation and causality. In L. Strickland, F. Aboud, & K. Gergen (Eds.), *Social psychology in transition*. NY: Plenum, 1976.

Deci, E. L. *The psychology of self-determination*. Lexington, MA: Lexington, 1980.

Deci, E. L., & Ryan, R. M. The empirical exploration of intrinsic motivational processes. In L. Berkowitz (Ed.), *Advances in experimental social psychology*. NY: Academic Press, 1980.

Deutsch, M., & Solomon, L. Reactions to evaluations by others as influenced by self evaluation. *Sociometry*, 1959, *22*, 93–112.

Diener, E., & Wallborn, M. Effects of self-awareness on antinormative behavior. *Journal of Research in Personality*, 1976, *10*, 107–111.

Diggory, J. C. *Self-evaluation concepts and studies*. NY: Wiley, 1966.

Duncan, J. W., & Laird, J. D. Positive and reverse placebo effects as a function of differences in cues used in self-perception. *Journal of Personality and Social Psychology*, 1980, *39*, 1024–1036.

Duval, S., & Wicklund, R. A. *A theory of objective self-awareness*. NY: Academic Press, 1972.

Eibl-Eibesfelt, I. Strategies of social interaction. In R. Plutchik & H. Kellerman (Eds.), *Emotion, theory, research and experience* (Vol I). NY: Academic Press, 1980.

Ekman, P., Friesen, W. V., & Ellsworth, P. *Emotion in the human face*. NY: Pergamon, 1972.

Elliott, G. C. Some effects of deception and level of self-monitoring on planning and reacting to a self-presentation. *Journal of Personality and Social Psychology*, 1979, *37*, 1282–1292.

Ellis, R. J., & Holmes, J. G. Focus of attention and self-evaluation in social interaction. *Journal of Personality and Social Psychology*, 1982, *43*, 67–77.

Endler, N. S. & Magnusson, D. (Eds.) *Interactional psychology and personality*. Washington, DC: Hemisphere, 1976.

Epstein, S. Traits are alive and well. In D. Magnusson & N. S. Endler (Eds.), *Personality at the crossroads*. NY: Halsted, 1977.

Epstein, S. The self-concept, a review and the proposal of an integrated theory of personality. In E. Staub (Ed.), *Personality: Basic issues and current research*. Englewood Cliffs, NJ: Prentice-Hall, 1980.

Erikson, E. H. *Childhood and society*. NY: Norton, 1950.

Feingstein, A. Self-consciousness, self-attention and social interaction. *Journal of Personality and Social Psychology*, 1979, *37*, 75–86.

Felson, R. B. An interactionist approach to aggression. In J. T. Tedeschi (Ed.), *Impression management theory and social psychological research*. NY: Academic Press, 1981.

Festinger, L. A theory of social comparison processes. *Human Relations*, 1954, *7*, 117–140.

Filipp, U. S. H. *Selbstkonzept-Forschung: Probleme, Befunde, Perspektiven*. Stuttgart: Klett-Cotta, 1979.

Fincham, F., & Jaspars, J. Attribution of responsibility to the self and others in children and adults. *Journal of Personality and Social Psychology*, 1979, *37*, 1589–1602.

Fingarette, H. *Self-deception*. London: Routledge & Kegan Paul, 1969.

Fodor, J. A. *The language of thought*. NY: Corwell, 1975.

Fodor, J. A. *Representations*. Cambridge, MA: MIT Press, 1981.

Freud, S. *A new series of introductory lectures on psychoanalysis*. (W. J. H. Sprott, trans.). NY: Norton, 1933.

Fromm, E. Selfishness and self love. *Psychiatry*, 1939, *2*, 507–523.

Gadlin, H. Child discipline and the pursuit of self: An historical interpretation. In *Advances in child development and behavior*. NY: Academic Press, 1978.

Gagnon, N. On the analysis of life accounts. In D. Bertaux (Ed.), *Biography and society*. Beverly Hills, CA: Sage, 1981.

Gastorf, J., & Suls, J. Performance evaluation via social comparison: Performance similarity versus related attribute similarity. *Social Psychology*, 1978, *41*, 297–305.

Gauld, A., & Shotter, J. *Human action and its psychological investigation*. London: Routledge & Kegan Paul, 1977.

Geertz, C. *Interpretation of cultures*. NY: Basic Books, 1973.

Gergen, K. J. The effects of interaction goals and personalistic feedback on presentation of self. *Journal of Personality and Social Psychology*, 1965, *1*, 413–425.

Gergen, K. J. *The concept of self*. NY: Holt, Rinehart, & Winston, 1971.

Gergen, K. J. The social construction of self-knowledge. In T. Mischel (Ed.), *The self, psychological and philosophical issues*. Oxford, England: Blackwell, 1977.

Gergen, K. J. From self to science: What is there to know? In J. Suls (Ed.), *Psycholgical perspectives on the self* (Vol. 1). Hillsdale, NJ: Erlbaum, 1982.

Gergen, K. J. *Toward transformation in social knowledge*. NY: Springer, 1982. (b)

Gergen, K. J., & Gergen, M. Explaining human conduct: Form and function. In P. Secord (Ed.), *Conceptual issues in the human sciences*. Beverly Hills, CA: Sage, 1982.

Gergen, K. J. & Gergen, M. M. The social construction of helping relationships. In J. D. Fisher, A. Nadler & B. DePaulo (Eds.), *New directions in helpings* (Vol. 1). New York: Academic Press, 1983.

Gergen, K. J., & Taylor, M. G. *Role playing and modifying the self-concept*. Paper presented at the meetings of the Eastern Psychological Association, March 1966, New York.

Giddens, A. *New rules of sociological method*. NY: Basic Books, 1976.

Gilligan, C. *In a different voice*. Cambridge, MA: Harvard University Press, 1982.

Giovannini, D. (Ed.). *Identita personale: Teoria e ricerca*. Bologna: Zanichelli, 1979.

Giovannini, D., Palmonari, G., Speltini, G., Bariand, F., & Tomé, H. Rodriguez. Aspetti comparativi dello studio della struttura dellii-identità in adolescenti. In D. Giovannini (Ed.), *Identità personale: teoria e ricerca*. Bologna: Zanichelli, 1979.

Goethals, G. R., & Darley, J. M. Social comparison theory: An attributional approach. In J. Suls & R. Miller (Eds.), *Social comparison processes: Theoretical and empirical perspectives*. Washington, DC: Hemisphere/Halsted, 1977.

Goffman, E. On face-work: An analysis of ritual elements in social interaction. *Psychiatry*, 1955, *18*, 213–231.

Goffman, E. *The presentation of self in everyday life*. NY: Doubleday, 1959.

Goffman, E. *Stigma: Notes on the management of spoiled identify*. Englewood Cliffs, NJ: Prentice-Hall, 1963.

Gollwitzer, P. M., Wicklund, R. A., & Hilton, J. L. Admission of failure and symbolic self-completion. *Journal of Personality and Social Psychology*, 1982, *43*, 358–371.

Gordon, C. Self-conceptions: Configurations of content. In C. Gordon & K. J. Gergen (Eds.), *The self in social interaction* (Vol. 1) *Classic and contemporary problems*. NY: Wiley, 1968.

Gordon, C., & Gergen, K. J. (Eds.), *The self in social interaction* (Vol 1): *Classic and contemporary problems*. NY: Wiley, 1968.

Gottman, J. *Time-series analysis: A comprehensive introduction for social scientists.* MA: Cambridge University Press, 1981.

Greenwald, A. G. The totalitarian ego. Fabrication and revision of personal history. *American Psychologist,* 1980, *35,* 603–618.

Greenwald, A. G. Self and memory. In G. H. Bower (Ed.), *Psychology of learning and motivation* (Vol. 15). NY: Academic Press, 1981.

Greenwald, A. G. Is any*one* in charge? Personalysis versus the principle of personal unity. In J. Suls (Ed.), *Psychological perspectives on the self.* Hillsdale, NJ: Erlbaum, 1982.

Gregor, A. J., & McPherson, D. A. Racial attitudes among white and negro children in a deep-South standard metropolitan area. *Journal of Social Psychology,* 1966, *68,* 95–106.

Gruder, C. L. Choice of comparison persons in evaluating oneself. In J. M. Suls & R. L. Miller (Eds.), *Social comparison processes.* NY: Hemisphere, 1977.

Gur, R. C., & Sackheim, H. A. Self deception: A concept in search of a phenomenon. *Journal of Personality and Social Psychology,* 1979, *37,* 147–169.

Hakmiller, K. Threat as a determinant of downward comparison. *Journal of Experimental Social Psychology,* 1966 (Suppl. *1*), 32–39.

Hamachek, D. E. (Ed.). *The self in growth, teaching, and learning.* Englewood Cliffs, NJ: Prentice-Hall, 1965.

Hampden-Turner, C. *Radical Man: The process of psychosocial development.* Cambridge, Schenkman, 1970.

Hanson, N. R. *Patterns of discovery.* London: Cambridge University Press, 1958.

Harré, R. Expressive aspects of descriptions of others. In C. Antaki (Ed.), *The psychology of ordinary explanations of social behavior.* NY: Academic Press, 1981.

Harré, R. *Personal being.* Oxford: Blackwell, 1984.

Harré, R., & Secord, P. F. *The explanation of social behavior.* Oxford: Basil, Blackwell, & Mott, 1972.

Hass, R. G. Presentational strategies and the social expression of attitudes: Impression management within limits. In J. T. Tedeschi (Ed.), *Impression management theory and social psychological research.* NY: Academic Press, 1981.

Heelas, P. & Locke, A. *Indigenous psychologies.* London: Academic Press, 1981.

Hewitt, J. *Self and society: A symbolic interactionist social psychology.* Boston: Allyn & Bacon, 1976.

Hibbs, D. Problems of statistical estimation and causal inference in time-series regression models. In H. L. Costner (Ed.), *Sociological methodology.* San Francisco: Jossey-Bass, 1974.

Hilgard, E. R. Human motives and the concept of the self. *American Psychologist,* 1949, *4,* 374–382.

Hogan, R. T., & Emler, N. P. The biases in contemporary social psychology. *Social Research,* 1978, *45,* 478–534.

Hormuth, S. E. *Commitment, role transitions and self-concept change: Relocation as a paradigm.* NATO-Symposium on Role Transitions, Madison, WS, 1982.

Horney, K. *Neurosis and human growth.* NY: Norton, 1950.

Hovland, C. I., & Janis, I. L. (Eds.). *Personality and persuasibility.* New Haven, CT: Yale University Press, 1959.

Hull, C. L. Quantitative aspects of the evolution of concepts: An experimental study. *Psychological Monographs,* 1920, *28,* 123–125.

Hull, J. G., & Levy, A. S. The organizational functions of the self: An alternative to the Duval and Wicklund model of self-awareness. *Journal of Personality and Social Psychology,* 1979, *37,* 756–768.

Israel, J. *Self-evaluation and rejection in groups. Three experiments and a conceptual outline.* Uppsala, Sweden: Almqnist & Wiksells, 1956.

Izard, C., & Buechler, S. Aspects of consciousness and personality in terms of differential emotions theory. In R. Plutchik & H. Kellerman (Eds.), *Emotion, theory, research and experience*. NY: Academic Press, 1980.

Jackson, S. E. Measurement of commitment to role identities. *Journal of Personality and Social Psychology*, 1981, *40*, 138–146.

James, W. *The principles of psychology* (Vol. 2). NY: Holt, 1890.

Jellison, J. M. Reconsidering the attitude concept: A behavioristic self-presentation formulation. In J. T. Tedeschi (Ed.), *Impression management theory and social psychological research*. NY: Academic Press, 1981.

Jennings, D. L., Amabile, T., & Ross, L. Informal covariation assessment: Data-based *vs.* theory-based judgements. In A. Tversky, D. Kahneman, & P. Slovic (Eds.), *Judgement under uncertainty: Heuristics and biases*. NY: Cambridge University Press, 1982.

Jones, E. E. *Ingratiation*. NY: Appleton-Century-Crofts, 1964.

Jones, E. E., & Berglas, S. Control of attributions about the self through self-handicapping strategies: The appeal of alcohol and the role of under-achievement. *Personality and Social Psychology Bulletin*. 1978, *4*, 200–206.

Jones, E. E., Gergen, K. J., & Davis, K. E. Some determinants of reactions to being approved or disapproved as a person. *Psychological Monographs*, 1962, *76*, (2, Whole No. 521).

Jones, E. E., Hester, S. L., Farina, A., & Davis, K. E. Reactions to unfavorable personal evaluations as a function of the evaluator's perceived adjustment. *Journal of Abnormal and Social Psychology*, 1959, *59*, 363–370.

Jones, E. E., & Nisbett, R. *The actor and the observer: Divergent perceptions of the causes of behavior*. Morristown, NJ: General Learning Press, 1971.

Jones, E. E., & Pittman, T. S. Toward a general theory of strategic self-presentation. In J. Suls (Ed.), *Psychological perspectives on the self*. Hillsdale, NJ: Erlbaum, 1982.

Jones, E. E., Rhodewalt, F., Berglas, S., & Skelton, J. A. Effects of strategic self-presentation on subsequent self esteem. *Journal of Personality and Social Psychology*, 1981, *41*, 407–421.

Jones, E. E., & Wortman, C. *Ingratiation: An attributional approach*. Morristown, NJ: General Learning Press, 1973.

Jones, S. C. Self and interpersonal evaluations: Esteem theories versus consistency theories. *Psychological Bulletin*, 1973, *79*, 185–199.

Jourard, S. *The transparent self*. Princeton, NJ: Van Nostrand Insight, 1964.

Jung, C. G. *The integration of the personality*. NY: Farrar & Rinehart, 1939.

Kahneman, D., & Tversky, A. On the psychology of prediction. *Psychological Review*, 1973, *80*, 237–251.

Kaplan, H. B. *Self attitudes and deviant behavior*. Pacific Palisades, CA: Goodyear, 1975.

Kelly, G. *The psychology of personal constructs*. NY: Norton, 1955.

Kenny, A. *Action, emotion and will*. London: Routledge & Kegan Paul, 1963.

Kenny, D. A., & Campbell, D. T. Methodological considerations in the analysis of temporal data. In K. Gergen & M. Gergen (Eds.), *Historical social psychology*. Hillsdale, NJ: Erlbaum, 1984.

Kessler, S. J., & McKenna, W. *Gender: An ethnomethodological approach*. NY: Wiley, 1978.

Kiesler, S., & Baral, R. The search for a romantic partner: The effects of self-esteem and physical attractiveness on romanitc behavior. In K. Gergen & D. Marlowe (Eds.), *Personality and social behavior*. MA: Addison-Wesley, 1970.

Kleinke, C. *Self-perception: The psychology of personal awareness*. San Francisco: Freeman, 1978.

Koch, S. (Ed.). *Psychology: A study of a science* (Vol. III). NY: McGraw Hill, 1959.

Koch, S. Reflections on the state of psychology. *Social Research*, 1971, *38*, 669–709.

Koffka, K. *Principles of gestalt psychology*. NY: Harcourt, Brace, & World, 1935.

Kohut, H. *The analysis of the self*. NY: International University Press, 1971.

Kohut, H. The two analyses of Mr. Z. *The International Journal of Psychoanalysis*, 1979, *60*, 1–27.

Kuhn, M. H., & McPartland, T. S. An empirical investigation of self attitudes. *American Sociological Review*, 1954, *19*, 68–76.

Kuiper, N. A. Convergent evidence for the self as a prototype: The "inverted URT Effect" for self and other judgments. *Personality and Social Psychology Bulletin*, 1981, *7*, 438–443.

Lakatos, I. Falsification and the methodology of scientific research. In I. Lakatos & A. Musgrave, (Eds.), *Criticism and the growth of knowledge*. Cambridge: Cambridge University Press, 1970.

Lalljee, M. Attribution theory and the analysis of explanations. In C. Antaki (Ed.), *The psychology of ordinary explanations of social behavior*. NY: Academic Press, 1981.

Landfield, A. W. Interpretive man: The enlarged self-image. In J. V. Cole (Ed.), *Nebraska Symposium on Motivation, 1976*. Lincoln, NE: University of Nebraska Press, 1977.

Laudan, L. *Progress and its problems*. Berkeley: University of California Press, 1977.

L'Ecuyer, R. Le development du concept du soi chez les personnes agees de 60 a 100 ans. In D. Giovannini (Ed.), *Identita personale: Teroia e ricerca*. Bologna: Zanichelli, 1979.

Leventhal, H. Toward a comprehensive theory of emotion. In L. Berkowitz (Ed.), *Advances in experimental social psychology*. NY: Academic Press, 1980.

Levine, M. Hypothesis behavior by humans during discrimination learning. *Journal of Experimental Psychology*, 1966, *71*, 331–336.

Lewis, M., & Brooks-Gunn, J. *Social cognition and the acquisition of self*. NY: Plenum, 1979.

Loevinger, J. *Ego Development*. San Francisco: Jossey-Bass, 1976.

Lord, C. G. Predicting behavioral consistency from an individual's perception of situational similarities. *Journal of Personality and Social Psychology*, 1982, *42*, 1076–1088.

Lowery, G. R., Denney, D. R., & Storms, M. D. The treatment of insomnia: Pill attributions and nonpejorative self-attributions. *Cognitive Therapy and Research*. 1979, *3*, 161–164.

Luckenbill, D. F. Criminal homicide as a situated transaction. *Social Problems*, 1977, *25*, 176–186.

Lynch, M. D. Self-concept development in childhood. In M. D. Lynch, A. A. Norem-Hebeisen, & K. J. Gergen (Eds.), *Self-concept: Advances in theory and research*. Cambridge, MA: Ballinger, 1981.

Lynn, S. J. Three theories of self-disclosure exchange. *Journal of Experimental Social Psychology*, 1978, *14*, 466–479.

MacCorquodale, K., & Meehl, P. E. On a distinction between hypothetical constructs and intervening variables. *Psychological Review*, 1948, *55*, 95–107.

McCall, G. J. The social looking-glass: A sociological perspective. In T. Mischel (Ed.), *The self, psychological and philosophical issues*. Oxford: Blackwell, 1977.

McCall, C. J., & Simmons, J. L. *Identities and interactions*. NY: The Free Press, 1966.

McCarthy, B., & Rafferty, J. E. Effects of social desirability and self concept scores on the measurement of adjustment. *Journal of Personality Assessment*, 1971, *35*, 576–583.

McClure, J. *Paradigms of attribution and illusion: A critical analysis*. Unpublished master's thesis, University of Aukland, 1980.

McCrae, R. R. Consensual validation of personality traits. *Journal of Personality and Social Psychology*, 1982, *43*, 293–303.

McGuire, W. J. The nature of attitudes and attitude change. In G. Lindzey & E. Aronson (Eds.), *The handbook of social psychology* (Vol. 3). Addison-Wesley: Reading, MA: 1968.

McGuire, W. J. The yin and yang of progress in social psychology: Seven Koans. *Journal of Personality and Social Psychology*, 1973, *26*, 446–456.

McGuire, W. J. The development of theory in social psychology. In R. Gilmour & S. Duck, (Eds.), *The development of social psychology*. London, Academic Press, 1980.

McGuire, W. J., & McGuire, C. V. The spontaneous self-concept as affected by personal distinctiveness. In M. D. Lynch, A. A. Norem-Hebeisen, & K. G. Gergen (Eds.), *Self concept: Advances in theory and research*. Cambridge, MA: Ballinger, 1981.

McGuire, W. J., & McGuire, C. V. Significant others in self space: Sex differences and developmental trends in the social self. In J. Suls (Ed.), *Psychological perspectives on the self.* Hillsdale, NJ: Erlbaum, 1982.

McGuire, W. J., McGuire, C. V., & Winton, W. Effects of household sex composition on the salience of one's gender in the spontaneous self-concept. *Journal of Experimental Social Psychology,* 1979, *15*, 77–90.

McGuire, W. J., & Padawer-Singer, A. Trait salience in the spontaneous self-concept. *Journal of Personality and Social Psychology,* 1976, *33*, 743–754.

Macmurray, J. *The self as agent.* Atlantic Highlands, NJ: Humanities Press, 1978.

Magnusson, D., & Endler, N. S. (Eds.). *Personality at the crossroads: Current issues in interactional psychology.* Hillsdale, NJ: Erlbaum, 1977.

Mancuso, J. C. Current motivational models in the elaboration of personal construct theory. In J. K. Cole (Ed.), *Nebraska symposium on motivation,* 1976 (Vol. 24). Lincoln, NE: University of Nebraska Press, 1977.

Mannheim, K. *Essays on the sociology of knowledge.* London: Routledge & Kegan Paul, 1952.

Markus, H., & Sentis, K. The self in social information processing. In J. Suls (Ed.), *Psychological perspectives on the self.* Hillsdale, NJ: Erlbaum, 1982.

Marsh, H. W., & Smith, I. D. Multitrait-multimethod analyses of two self-concept instruments. *Journal of Educational Psychology,* 1982, *74*, 430–440.

Marshall, G. D., & Zimbardo, P. G. Affective consequences of inadequately explained physiological arousal. *Journal of Personality and Social Psychology,* 1979, *37*, 970–985.

Martindale, C. Subselves. In L. Wheeler (Ed.), *Review of personality and social psychology* (Vol. I). Beverly Hills, CA: Sage, 1980.

Marx, K. *Capital: A critical analysis of capitalistic production.* Moscow: Foreign Languages, 1954.

Maslach, C. Negative emotional biasing of unexplained arousal. *Journal of Personality and Social Psychology,* 1979, *37*, 953–969.

Mead, G. H. *Mind, self and society.* Chicago: University of Chicago Press, 1934.

Mettee, D. R., & Smith, G. Social comparison and interpersonal attraction: The case for dissimilarity. In J. M. Suls & R. L. Miller (Eds.), *Social comparison processes: Theoretical and empirical perspectives.* Washington, DC: Hemisphere, 1977.

Milgram, S. *Obedience to authority.* NY: Harper & Row, 1974.

Miller, D. T., & Norman, S. Actor-observer differences in perceptions of effective control. *Journal of Personality and Social Psychology,* 1975, *31*, 503–515.

Miller, D. T., & Ross, M. Self-serving biases in the attribution of causality: Fact or fiction? *Psychological Bulletin,* 1975, *82*, 213–225.

Mischel, T. Understanding neurotic behavior: From "mechanism" to "intentionality." In T. Mischel (Ed.), *Understanding other persons.* Totowa, NJ: Rowman & Littlefield, 1974.

Mischel, T. *The self, psychological and philosophical issues.* Oxford: Blackwell, 1977.

Mischel, W. *Personality and assessment.* NY: Wiley, 1968.

Mischel, W. Continuity and change in personality. *American Psychologist,* 1969, *24*, 1012–1018.

Mischel, W. Toward a cognitive social learning reconceptualization of personality. *Psychological Review,* 1973, *80*, 252–283.

Mischel, W., & Mischel, H. N. Self-control and the self. In T. Mischel (Ed.), *The self: Psychological and philosophical issues.* Oxford: Basil Blackwell, 1977.

Morse, S. J., & Gergen, K. J. Social comparison, self-consistency and the presentation of self. *Journal of Personality and Social Psychology,* 1970, *16*, 148–159.

Moscovici, S. *La psychoanalyse, son image et son public.* Paris: P. V. F., 1961.

Muller, J. P. Cognitive psychology and the ego: Empirical support for Lacan. *Psychoanalysis and contemporary thought* (Vol. 5). In press.

Mummendey, A., Bornewasser, M., Löschper, G., & Linneweber, V. It is always somebody else who is aggressive. *Zeitschrift für Sozialpsychologie,* 1982, *13.* 1984.

Needham, R. *Belief, language and experience.* Chicago: University of Chicago Press, 1972.

Newell, A. You can't play twenty questions with nature and win. In W. G. Chase (Ed.), *Visual information processing.* NY: Academic Press, 1973.

Nisbett, R. E., & Bellows, N. Verbal reports about causal influences as social judgments: Private access versus public theories. *Journal of Personality and Social Psychology,* 1977, *35,* 613–624.

Nisbett, R. E. & Ross, L. *Human inference: strategies and shortcomings of social judgment.* Englewood Cliffs, NJ: Prentice-Hall, 1980.

Nisbett, R. E., & Schachter, S. Cognitive manipulation of pain. *Journal of Experimental Social Psychology,* 1966, *2,* 227–236.

Nisbett, R. E., & Wilson, T. D. Telling more than we can know: Verbal reports on mental processes. *Psychological Review,* 1977, *84,* 231–259.

Norem-Hebeisen, A. A. A maximization model of self-concept. In M. D. Lynch, A. A. Norem-Hebeisen, & K. J. Gergen (Eds.), *Self-concept: Advances in theory and research.* Cambridge, MA: Ballinger, 1981.

Olweus, D. A critical analysis of the "modern" interactionist position. In D. Magnusson & N. Endler (Eds.), *Personality at the crossroads: Current issues in interactional psychology.* NY: Halsted, 1977.

O'Malley, P. M., & Backman, J. G. Self-esteem and education: Sex and cohort comparisons among high school seniors. *Journal of Personality and Social Psychology,* 1979, *37,* 1153–1159.

Ossorio, P. G. *What actually happens.* Columbia: University of South Carolina Press, 1978.

Overton, W. F., & Reese, H. W. Models of development: Methodological implications. In J. R. Nesselroade & H. W. Reese (Eds.), *Life-span developmental psychology: Methodological issues.* NY: Academic Press, 1973.

Page, M. M. Demand compliance in laboratory experiments. In J. T. Tedeschi (Ed.), *Impression management theory and social psychological research.* NY: Academic Press, 1981.

Pearce, W. B., & Cronen, V. E. *Communication, action and meaning.* NY: Praeger, 1980.

Pepitone, A. *Attraction and hostility.* NY: Atherton, 1964.

Pepitone, A. An experimental analysis of self-dynamics. In C. Gordon & K. Gergen (Eds.), *The self in social interaction* (Vol. 1). NY: Wiley, 1968.

Pepitone, A. Lessons from the history of social psychology. *American Psychologist,* 1981, *36,* 972–985.

Peters, R. S. *The concept of motivation.* London: Routledge & Kegan Paul, 1958.

Pettit, P. On actions and explanations. In C. Antaki (Ed.), *The psychology of ordinary explanations of social behavior.* NY: Academic Press, 1981.

Phillips, D. A., & Zigler, E. Children's self-image disparity: Effects of age, socioeconomic status, ethnicity and gender. *Journal of Personality and Social Psychology,* 1980, *39,* 689–700.

Plutchik, R. *Emotion: A psychoevolutionary synthesis.* NY: Harper & Row, 1980.

Plutchik, R., & Ax, A. F. A critique of determinants of emotional state by Schachter and Singer. *Psychophysiology,* 1967, *4,* 79–82.

Posner, M. I., & Keele, S. W. On the genesis of abstract ideas. *Journal of Experimental Psychology,* 1968, *77,* 353–363.

Pribram, K. The biology of emotion and other feelings. In R. Plutchik & H. Kellerman (Eds.), *Emotion, theory, research and experience* (Vol. 1). NY: Academic Press, 1980.

Pryor, J. B., Gibbons, F. X., Wicklund, R. A., Fazio, R. H., & Hood, R. Self-focused attention and self-report validity. *Journal of Personality,* 1977, *45,* 513–527.

Quine, W. V. O. *From a logical point of view.* Cambridge, MA: Harvard University Press, 1953.

Quine, W. V. O. *Word and object.* Cambridge, MA: Technology Press of M.I.T., 1960.

Rabinow, P., & Sullivan, W. (Eds.). *Interpretive social science: A reader.* Berkeley: University of California Press, 1979.

Reese, H. W., & Overton, W. F. Models of development and theories of development. In L. R. Goulet & P. B. Baltes (Eds.), *Life-span developmental psychology: Research and theory.* NY: Academic Press, 1970.

Reis, H. T. Self-presentation and distributive justive. In J. T. Tedeschi (Ed.), *Impression management theory and social psychological research.* NY: Academic Press, 1981.

Restle, F. A. The selection of strategies in cue learning. *Psychological Review,* 1962, *69,* 320–343.

Richardson, K. D., & Cialdini, R. B. Basking and blasting: Tactics of indirect self-presentation. In J. T. Tedeschi (Ed.), *Impression management theory and social psychological research.* NY: Academic Press, 1981.

Robinson, D. N. Cerebral plurality and the unity of self. *American Psychologist,* 1982, *37,* 904–910.

Rogers, C. Therapy, personality and interpersonal relationships. In S. Koch (Ed.), *Psychology: A study of a science* (Vol. III). NY: McGraw-Hill, 1959.

Rosch, E. Principles of categorization. In E. Rosch & B. B. Lloyds (Eds.), *Cognition and categorization.* Hillsdale, NJ: Erlbaum, 1978.

Rosenberg, M. *Society and the adolescent self-image.* Princeton, NJ: Princeton University Press, 1965.

Rosenberg, M. *Conceiving the self.* NY: Basic Books, 1979.

Rosenberg, M., & Kaplan, H. *Social psychology of the self-concept.* Arlington Heights, IL: Davidson, 1982.

Rosenberg, M., & Simmons, R. G. *Black and white self-esteem: The urban school child.* Washington, DC: American Sociological Association, 1971.

Ross, L., Rodin, J., & Zimbardo, P. G. Toward an attribution therapy: The reduction of fear through induced cognitive-emotional misattribution. *Journal of Personality and Social Psychology,* 1969, *12,* 279–288.

Ruble, D. H. The development of social comparison processes and their role in achievement-related self-socialization. In E. T. Higgins, D. H. Ruble, & W. W. Hartup (Eds.), *Developmental social cognition: A socio-cultural perspective.* In press.

Rule, B. G., & Nesdale, A. R. Moral judgment of aggressive behavior. In R. G. Geen & F. C. O'Neal (Eds.), *Perspective on aggression.* NY: Academic Press, 1976.

Runyon, W. M. *Life histories and psychobiography: Exploration in theory and method.* NY: Oxford University Press, 1982.

Rychlak, J. F. The case of a modest revolution in modern psychological science. In R. A. Kasschau & C. N. Cofer (Eds.), *Psychology's second century.* NY: Praeger, 1981.

Rychlak, J. F. *The psychology of rigorous humanism.* NY: Wiley, 1977.

Ryckman, R. M., Robbins, M. A., Thornton, B., & Cantrell, P. Development and validation of a physical self-efficacy scale. *Journal of Personality and Social Psychology,* 1982, *42,* 891–900.

Ryff, C. D. Self-perceived personality change in adulthood and aging. *Journal of Personality and Social Psychology,* 1982, *42,* 108–115.

Ryle, G. *The concept of mind.* NY: Barnes & Noble, 1949.

Sabini, J., & Silver, M. *The moralities of everyday life.* Oxford: Oxford University Press, 1981.

Sampson, E. E. Psychology and the American ideal. *Journal of Personality and Social Psychology,* 1977, *35,* 767–782.

Sampson, E. E. Scientific paradigms and social values: Wanted—a scientific revolution. *Journal of Personality and Social Psychology,* 1978, *36,* 1332–1343.

Sampson, E. E. Cognitive psychology as ideology. *American Psychologist,* 1981, *36,* 730–743.

Samuel, W. On clarifying some interpretations of social comparison theory. *Journal of Experimental Social Psychology,* 1973, *9,* 450–465.

Sanders, G., Gastorf, J., & Mullen, B. Selectivity in the use of social comparison information. *Personality and Social Psychology Bulletin,* 1979, *5,* 377–380.

Sarason, S. *Psychology misdirected.* NY: Free Press, 1981.

Schachter, S. The interaction of cognitive and physiological determinants of emotional state. In L. Berkowitz (Ed.), *Advances in experimental social psychology* (Vol. 1). NY: Academic Press, 1964.

Schachter, S., & Singer, J. L. Cognitive, social and physiological determinants of emotional state *Psychological Review,* 1962, *65,* 121–128.

Schank, R. C., & Abelson, R. P. *Scripts, plans, goals and understanding.* NY: Wiley, 1977.

Schlenker, B. R. *Impression management: The self concept, social identify, and interpersonal relations.* Monterey, CA, Brooks-Cole, 1980.

Schneider, D. J. Tactical self-presentations: Toward a broader conception. In J. T. Tedeschi (Ed.), *Impression management theory and social psychological research.* NY: Academic Press, 1981.

Schroeder, C. C. Sex differences and growth toward self-actualization during the freshman year. *Psychological Reports,* 1973, *32,* 416–418.

Scott, J. P. The function of emotions in behavioral systems: A systems theory analysis. In R. Plutchik & H. Kellerman (Eds.), *Emotion, theory, research and experience.* NY: Academic Press, 1980.

Seligman, M. E. P. *Helplessness.* San Francisco: Freeman, 1975.

Shaffer, D. R., Smith, J. E., & Tomarelli, M. Self-monitoring as a determinant of self-disclosure reciprocity during the acquaintance process. *Journal of Personality and Social Psychology,* 1982, *43,* 163–175.

Shavelson, R. J., & Stuart, K. R. Application of causal modeling methods to the validation of self-concept interpretations of test scores. In M. D. Lynch, A. A. Noren-Hebeisen, & K. J. Gergen (Eds.), *Self-concept, advances in theory and research.* Cambridge, MA: Ballinger, 1981.

Sherman, J. On the self-erasing nature of errors of prediction. *Journal of Personality and Social Psychology,* 1980, *39,* 211–221.

Shoemaker, A. I. Construct validity of area specific self-esteem scale. *Educational and Psychological Measurement,* 1980, *40,* 495–501.

Shotter, J. *Images of man in psychological research.* London: Methuen, 1975.

Shotter, J. Action, joint action and intentionality. In M. Brenner (Ed.), *The structure of action.* Oxford: Blackwell, 1980.

Shotter, J. Telling and reporting: Prospective and retrospective uses of self-ascriptions. In C. Antaki (Ed.), *The psychology of ordinary explanations of social behavior.* NY: Academic Press, 1981.

Shrauger, J. S. Responses to evaluation as a function of initial self-perceptions. *Psychological Bulletin,* 1975, *82,* 581–596.

Shrauger, J. S., & Schoeneman, T. J. Symbolic interactionist view of self-concept: Through the looking glass darkly. *Psychological Bulletin,* 1979, *86,* 549–573.

Shweder, R. A., & Bourne, E. J. Does the concept of the person vary cross-culturally? In H. A. Marsala & G. M. White (Eds.), *Cultural analysis of mental health and therapy.* Dordrecht, Holland: Resdell, 1982.

Silverman, I. Self-esteem and differential responsiveness to success and failure. *Journal of Abnormal and Social Psychology,* 1964, *69,* 115–119.

Simon, H. A., & Kotovsky, K. Human acquisition of concepts for sequential patterns *Psychological Review,* 1963, *70,* 534–546.

Simon, R. J. An assessment of racial awareness, preference, and self identity among white and adopted non-white children. *Social Problems,* 1974, *22,* 43–57.

Simonton, D. K. Generatioal time-series analysis: A paradigm for studying socio-cultural influences. In K. Gergen & M. Gergen (Eds.), *Historical social psychology.* Hillsdale, NJ: Erlbaum, 1984.

Singer, J. E. Social comparison-progress and issues. *Journal of Experimental Social Psychology,* 1966, (Suppl. 1) 108–110.

Skinner, B. F. *Beyond freedom and dignity.* NY: Random House, 1971.

Smedslund, J. Analyzing the primary code. In D. Olson (Ed.), *The social foundations of language: Essays in honour of J. S. Bruner.* NY: Norton, 1980.

Smith, E. R., & Miller, F. D. Limits on perception of cognitive processes: A reply to Nisbett and Wilson. *Psychological Review*, 1978, *85*, 355–362.

Smith, M. B. Perspectives on selfhood. *American Psychologist*, 1978, *33*, 1053–1063.

Smith, M. B. Attitudes, values and selfhood. In H. E. Howe & M. M. Page (Eds.), *Nebraska Symposium on Motivation, 1979.* Lincoln, NE: University of Nebraska Press, 1980.

Snyder, M. The self-monitoring of expressive behavior. *Journal of Personality and Social Psychology*, 1974, *30*, 526–537.

Snyder, M. Self-monitoring process. In L. Berkowitz (Ed.), *Advances in experimental social psychology* (Vol. 12). NY: Academic Press, 1979.

Snyder, M., & Campbell, B. H. Self-monitoring: The self in action. In J. Suls (Ed.), *Psychological perspectives on the self.* Hillsdale, NJ: Erlbaum, 1982.

Snyder, M., & Cantor, N. Thinking about ourselves and others: Self-monitoring and social knowledge. *Journal of Personality and Social Psychology*, 1980, *39*, 222–234.

Snyder, M., & Gangestad, S. Choosing social situations: Two investigations of self-monitoring processes. *Journal of Personality and Social Psychology*, 1982, *43*, 123–135.

Snyder, M. L., & Monson, T. C. Persons, situations, and control of social behavior. *Journal of Personality and Social Psychology*, 1975, *32*, 637–644.

Snyder, M., & Swann, W. B., Jr. Behavioral confirmation in social interaction: From social perception to social reality. *Journal of Experimental Social Psychology*, 1978, *14*, 148–162.

Stein, L. Reward transmitters, catecholamines and opioid peptides. In M. A. Lipton, A. DiMascio, & K. R. Killam (Eds.), *Psychopharmacology: A generation of progress.* NY: Raven, 1978.

Stoodley, B. H. *Society and self.* Glencoe, IL: Free Press, 1962.

Storms, M., & Nisbett, R. Insomnia and the attribution process. *Journal of Personality and Social Psychology*, 1970, *2*, 319–328.

Stryker, S. Identity salience and role performance: The relevance of symbolic interaction theory for family research. In M. Rosenberg & H. B. Kaplan (Eds.), *Social psychology of the self-concept.* Arlington Heights, IL: Davidson, 1982.

Sullivan, H. S. *Conceptions of modern psychiatry: The first William Alanson White Memorial Lectures.* Washington, DC: The William Alanson White Psychiatry Foundation, 1947.

Sullivan, H. S. *The interpersonal theory of psychiatry.* NY: Norton, 1953.

Suls, J. (Ed.). *Psychological perspectives on the self* (Vol. 1). Hillsdale, NJ: Erlbaum, 1982.

Suls, J., Gaes, G., & Gastorf, J. Evaluating a sex-related ability: Comparison with same-, opposite-, and combined-sex norms. *Journal of Research in Personality*, 1979, *13*, 294–304.

Suls, J. & Greenwald, A. G. *Psychological perspectives on the self* (Vol. 2). Hillsdale, NJ: Erlbaum, 1983.

Suls, J., & Mullen. B. From the cradle to the grave: Comparison and self-evaluation across the life-span. In J. Suls (Ed.), *Psychological perspectives on the self.* Hillsdale, NJ: Erlbaum, 1982.

Swann, W. B. Jr., & Read, S. S. Self-verification processes: How we sustain our self conceptions. *Journal of Experimental Social Psychology*, 1981, *17*, 351–372.

Taylor, C. *The explanation of behavior.* London: Routledge & Kegan Paul, 1964.

Taylor, C. Interpretation and the sciences of man. *The Review of Metaphysics*, 1971, *25*, No. 1.

Taylor, S. F., & Fiske, S. T. Salience, attention and attribution: Top of the head phenomena. In L. Berkowitz (Ed.), *Advances in experimental social psychology* (Vol. 10). NY: Academic Press, 1978.

Tedeschi, J. T., & Riess, M. Identities, the phenomenal self, and laboratory research. In J. T. Tedeschi (Ed.), *Impression management theory and social psychological research.* NY: Academic Press, 1981.

Tedeschi, J. T., & Riordan, C. A. Impression management and prosocial behavior following transgression. In J. T. Tedeschi (Ed.), *Impression management theory and social psychological research*. NY: Academic Press, 1981.

Tesser, A., & Campbell, J. Self-definition: The impact of the relative performance and similarity of others. *Social Psychology Quarterly*, 1980, *43*, 341–347.

Tesser, A. & Campbell, J. Self-definition and self-evaluation maintenance. In J. Suls & A. G. Greenwald (Eds.), *Psychological perspectives on the self*. (Vol. 2). Hillsdale, NJ: Earlbaum, 1983. __

Thomas, D. *Naturalism and social science*. Cambridge: Cambridge University Press, 1979.

Thorngate, W. Possible limits on a science of social behaviour. In L. A. Strickland, F. E. Aboud, & K. J. Gergen (Eds.), *Social psychology in transition*. NY: Plenum, 1976.

Thornton, D., & Arrowood, A. Self-evaluation, self-enhancement, and the locus of social comparison. *Journal of Experimental Social Psychology*, 1966 (Suppl. 1), 40–48.

Tomé, H., Rodriguez, H., & Bariaud, F. La struttura dell identità: Ricerca su popolazioni di adolescenti Francesi. In D. Giovannini (Ed.), *Identità personale: teoria e ricerca*. Bologna: Zanichelli, 1979.

Tomkins, S. S. Script theory: Differential magnification of affects. In H. E. Howe, Jr., & R. A. Dienstbier (Eds.), *Nebraska Symposium on Motivation* (Vol. 26). Lincoln: University of Nebraska Press, 1979.

Trope, Y. Self-assessment in achievement behavior. In J. Suls & A. Greenwald (Eds.), *Psychological perspectives on the self* (Vol. 2). Hillsdale, NJ: Erlbaum, 1983.

Trowbridge, N. T. Self-concept and socio-economic status in elementary school children. *American Educational Research Journal*, 1972, *9*, 525–527.

Turner, R. The self-conception in social interaction. In C. Gordon & K. Gergen (Eds.), *The self in social interaction* (Vol. 1). NY: Wiley, 1968.

Valins, S. Cognitive effects of false heart-rate feedback. *Journal of Personality and Social Psychology*, 1966, *4*, 400–408.

Valins, S., & Ray, A. Effects of cognitive desensitization on avoidance behavior. *Journal of Personality and Social Psychology*, 1967, *7*, 345–350.

Van den Berg, J. H. *Divided existence and complex society*. Pittsburgh: Duquesne University Press, 1974.

Veblen, T. *The theory of the leisure class*. NY: Modern Library, 1934. (Original work published 1899).

Verhave, T. & Van Hoorn, W. (1984) The temporalization of the self. In K. J. Gergen and M. M. Gergen (Eds.), *Historical social psychology*. Hillsdale, NJ: Erlbaum.

Vygotsky, L. S. In M. Cole, V. John-Steiner, S. Scribner, & E. Souberman (Eds.), *Mind in society*. Cambridge, MA: Harvard University Press, 1978.

Walster, E. The effect of self-esteem on romantic liking. *Journal of Experimental Social Psychology*, 1965, *1*, 184–197.

Warner, R., Kenny, D., & Stoto, M. A new round robin analysis of variance for social interaction data. *Journal of Personality and Social Psychology*, 1979, *37*, 1742–1757.

Wason, P. C., & Johnson-Laird, P. N. *Psychology of reasoning: Structure and content*. London: Batsford, 1972.

Weber, M. *The methodology of the social sciences* (E. A. Shils & H. A. Finch, trans). Glencoe, IL: Free Press, 1949.

Wegner, D. M., & Schaefer, D. The concentration of responsibility: An objective self-awareness analysis of group size effects in helping situations. *Journal of Personality and Social Psychology*, 1978, *36*, 147–155.

Wegner, D., & Vallacher, R. *The self in social psychology*. NY: Oxford University, 1980.

Weinrich, D. Toward a sociobiological theory of the emotions. In R. Plutchik & H. Kellerman (Eds.), *Emotion, theory, research and experience* (Vol. 1). NY: Academic Press, 1980.

White, P. Limitations on verbal reports of internal events: A refutation of Nisbett and Wilson and of Bem. *Psychological Review,* 1980, *87,* 105–112.

Wicklund, R. A. Objective self-awareness. In L. Berkowitz (Ed.), *Advances in experimental social psychology* (Vol. 9). NY: Academic Press, 1975.

Wicklund, R. A. The influence of self on human behavior. *American Scientist,* 1979, *67,* 187–193.

Wicklund, R. A. How society uses self-awareness. In J. Suls (Ed.), *Psychological perspectives on the self.* Hillsdale, NJ: Erlbaum, 1982.

Wicklund, R. A., & Duval, S. Opinion, change and performance facilitation as a result of objective self awareness. *Journal of Experimental Social Psychology,* 1971, *7,* 319–342.

Wicklund, R. A. & Gollwitzer, P. M. *Symbolic self-completion.* In J. Suls & A. G. Greenwald (Eds.), *Psychological perspectives on the self* (Vol. 2). Hillsdale, NJ: Erlbaum, 1982.

Wilson, T. D., & Capitman, J. A. Effects of script availability on social behavior. *Personality and Social Psychology Bulletin,* 1982, *8,* 11–19.

Wilson, W. R. Feeling more than we can know: Exposure effects without learning. *Journal of Personality and Social Psychology,* 1979, *37,* 811–821.

Wittgenstein, L. *Philosophical investigations* (G. Anscombe, trans.).NY: Macmillan, 1963.

Wittgenstein, L. In G. H. von Wright & H. Nyman (Eds.), *Remarks on the philosophy of psychology* (Vols. I & II). Oxford: Blackwell, 1980.

Wong, P. T. P., & Weiner, B. When people ask "why" questions, and the heuristics of attributional search. *Journal of Personality and Social Psychology,* 1981, *40,* 650–663.

Woodworth, R. S. *Dynamics of behavior.* NY: Holt, 1958.

Wortman, C., Costanza, P., & Witt, J. Effect of anticipated performance on the attributions of causality to self and others. *Journal of Personality and Social Psychology,* 1973, *27,* 372–381.

Wylie, R. C. *The self-concept* (Vol. 1). Lincoln: University of Nebraska Press, 1974.

Wylie, R. C. *The self-concept* (Vol. 2). Lincoln: University of Nebraska Press, 1979.

Zajonc, R. Feeling and thinking: Preferences need no inferences. *American Psychologist,* 1980, *35,* 151–175.

Zanna, M. P., Goethals, G., & Hill, J. F. Evaluating a sex-related ability: Social comparison with similar others and standard setters. *Journal of Experimental Social Psychology,* 1975, *11,* 86–93.

Ziller, R. C. *The social self.* NY: Pergamon, 1973.

Zillmann, D. *Hostility and aggression.* Hillsdale, NJ: Erlbaum, 1978.

Zurcher, L. *The mutable self: A self concept for social change.* Beverly Hills, CA: Sage, 1977.

A PERCEPTUAL–MOTOR THEORY OF EMOTION

Howard Leventhal

DEPARTMENT OF PSYCHOLOGY
UNIVERSITY OF WISCONSIN—MADISON
MADISON, WISCONSIN

ADVANCES IN EXPERIMENTAL
SOCIAL PSYCHOLOGY, VOL. 17

I. Goals for an Emotion Model

I begin by enumerating the desirable features that an adequate theory of emotion should possess and then employ this list in examining the pertinent research. Although this may seem to reverse the appropriate order for scientific discourse, it will, I believe, force a focus on the key issues in evaluating the theory to be presented.

1. A theory of emotion must describe a mechanism that constructs subjective, emotional experience. With this requirement, I am following the lay person in assigning significance to subjective experience as the phenomenon under study. In my view, subjective experience is worthy of explanation in its own right, independent of any role that emotional experience might have in controlling behavior.

If emotion is a perceptual experience, like the experience of distance or of objects, it is clear that it is private and accessible to study only through the use of indicators such as verbal reports, expressive and instrumental responses, and physiological reactions. All of these indicators are responsive to a wide range of environmental and organismic conditions, including many that are "nonemotional." Hence, each indicator is subject to considerable distortion. As a consequence, in order to understand the operation of the mechanism that constructs emotion, an investigator must search for patterns in these indicators under selected environmental conditions.

The great potential for error might lead to despair unless we recognize that the study of perception has advanced despite its similar reliance on indicators and on the lack of direct access to the mechanisms controlling the phenomena of interest. It is my judgment that verbal reports and their related response methods (rating scales, checklists, etc.) are the best available indicators for the study of emotion in adult subjects and that we must rely upon them to interpret the meaning of other indicators such as autonomic response. Such a procedure is particularly appropriate in the early stage of research when verbal reports can be used to assess the many facets of perceptual–emotional experience.

2. A model for the construction of emotional experience must be sufficiently complex to account for clearly noticeable attributes of that experience. These attributes include the following:

a. *Emotional experiences are often fragile;* they appear and disappear with great rapidity.
b. In contrast to the typically rapid fluctuation of acute emotional episodes, *some aspects of emotion are also relatively stable.* For example, moods may be sustained for long periods of time, and feelings toward specific,

highly significant objects, while at times contradictory, may remain positive (or negative) for very long periods of time.

   c. *Emotional experience is felt as internal to the experiencing individual,* that is, as within the self.
   d. *Emotional experience varies in intensity, some emotions being strong, others weak.*
   e. *Emotional experience varies in quality or color.* Some emotions are negative, others positive, and they vary in quality within these broad categories. Negative feelings include anger, disgust, and fear; and positive feelings include joy, sexual excitement, interest, and self-satisfaction.
   f. *Emotions are usually experienced as involuntary reactions.* Because emotions are typically experienced as involuntary, people conclude that emotionally motivated behavior is also involuntary and not subject to the same evaluative norms as rational or volitional behavior. The involuntary nature of emotional experience also causes the psychological self to appear detached from the physical self and its actions, the helpless observer of an impassioned body that is difficult, if not impossible, to control.

   3. *The model should account for the universality of emotional experience and the emotional behavior accompanying the experience.* There are two aspects of this universality:

   a. *Emotional experience and its accompanying expressive behavior appear over the individual lifespan.* Emotions occur early in development, far earlier than the development of language and the occurrence of efforts to inculcate emotions into the infant's repertoire of responses. Emotions appear to serve a communicative function from birth until death.
   b. *Emotional experience and reactions appear to be experienced, understood, and similarly evoked across widely differing cultures.*

   4. *A theory of emotion should account for the intertwining of emotional reactions and cognition.* Many, if not most, acute emotional reactions are related to the perception of specific external stimuli events or to internal imagery and conceptual elaboration of external events (e.g., Lazarus, 1980; Plutchik, 1980). It is clear that several different types of cognition are involved in emotion:

   a. *Simple perceptual cues* (e.g., loud noises or rapidly approaching objects) appear innately connected to emotional reponses.
   b. *Complex perceptions of meaningful objects* (e.g., guns [Berkowitz & Geen, 1967]) *and imagery* generated while awake (Grossberg & Wilson,

1968) or asleep (Dement, 1972; Witkin & Lewis, 1967, pp. 148–201) are able to evoke strong emotional reactions.

c. *Abstract ideas* presented verbally or thought of spontaneously *also generate emotional reactions,* although thoughts seem less able to do this than perceptions or images.

A model of emotion must take into account, therefore, the varieties of cognitive processes linked to emotion.

5. *The model must account for the complexity of the elicitation of emotion.* As described in number 4, emotion can be elicited by a variety of cognitive processes, including the perception of external stimuli, the interpretations imposed on these stimuli, and the internally generated imagery and thought. Emotion can also be elicited, however, by such responses as physiological changes (e.g., shaking, sweating, or changes in the heartbeat), which may or may not be perceived, and instrumental reactions or their consequences (e.g., fatigue generated by depression).

a. *Emotions can be elicited by illness* in at least two ways: through the perception or meaning assigned to illness symptoms and by the direct influence of illness on the physiological substrate (autonomic and central nervous system) that contributes to mood and emotion.

b. *Emotion has a complex relationship to voluntary instrumental action.* There appear to be at least two distinct aspects to the relationship of emotion to other volitional actions:

(1) *Emotions frequently arise during gaps, breakdowns* (Dewey, 1894, 1895), *or interruptions* (Mandler, 1962, 1975) *of ongoing instrumental behavior.*

(2) *Emotions can be experienced and integrated with ongoing motivated behavior.* Examples include the positive effect experienced as one gradually inserts the pieces in a puzzle or the anger that is part of an aggressive move to the basket against an opponent in basketball.

II. Past Theories

Three types of theory have occupied center stage in psychological discussions of emotion: body arousal, central neural, and cognition arousal. I believe that none of the three addresses all or even most of the previously mentioned issues. What is more serious, however, is that the concepts and/or the logical structure of current formulations may actually deny the existence of at least one of the commonly observed phenomena of emotional experience and behavior.

Formulations that deny observation have intrinsic shortcomings for the understanding of emotion. I briefly review these positions and then present an updated version of my own perceptual–motor model.

A. BODY REACTION THEORY

James was but one (although the best remembered) of a line of psychologists and philosophers who rejected the commonsense thesis that the perception of an emotion-provoking object leads first to emotional feelings and then to expressive, autonomic, and overt instrumental action. He argued instead "that the bodily changes followed directly the perception of the exciting fact, and that our feelings of the same changes as they occur is the emotion" (James, 1890/1950, p. 449). James adopted a simple psychophysical parallelism: For every subjective emotional experience there must be a correlated bodily reaction pattern, just as for every visual or auditory sensory experience there must be correlated activity in the nervous system at a particular locus or at a particular rate.

There are two major reasons why James (1890/1950) adopted the notion that emotional experience is produced by behavior: (1) Neurophysiological studies had identified only sensory, associative, and motor areas in the brain—there was no neural "center" for emotion—and (2) the hypothesis was obviously consistent with his own introspective observation. Indeed, bodily reactions, particularly those that are felt but not directly visible, have a compelling quality that can stimulate lengthy psychological, philosophical, medical, and commonsense speculation regarding their origins and meaning (Leventhal, Meyer, & Nerenz, 1980). James's hypothesis had two other virtues as well. It made sense of the everyday observation that emotions are experienced within the perceiver and not as events in the environment, and it provided a clue to the mechanisms responsible for the differentiation of emotional states.

There are at least five points on which James' hypothesis is unclear:

1. James was quite ambiguous about the responses that created subjective feelings. His more dramatic statements implied that overt instrumental reactions as well as covert internal ones produced subjective feelings.
2. Although he was not consistent on the point, he also seemed to believe that nonvoluntary visceral rather than voluntary expressive responses provided the most important feedback for emotion.
3. James was unclear in specifying whether or not people were directly aware of bodily reactions when experiencing an emotion.
4. James did not give an adequate account of how a particular object (e.g., a bear, baby, cartoon, or dead body) comes to elicit a particular set of reactions.

5. James actually presented two theories of emotion, one for turbulent emotion involving bodily feedback and another for the subtler aesthetic emotions or "genuinely cerebral forms of pleasure and displeasure" that involved "an absolutely sensational experience, an optical or auricular feeling that is primary, and not due to the repercussion backwards of other sensations elsewhere consecutively aroused" (James, 1890/1950, p. 468). It is of course desirable to integrate both types of experience within a common framework.

B. CENTRAL NEURAL THEORY

Cannon (1927) presented a well-known five-point critique of James's (1890/1950) hypothesis that subjective feelings are based on feedback from visceral reactions. Three of the five points are applicable to subjective feelings in a natural setting. They are:

1. The viscera are relatively insensitive and insufficiently supplied with receptors to provide sufficient sensory feedback.

2. The same viseral responses occur for different feeling states, making impossible a functional dependence of subjective feeling quality upon visceral reaction.

3. The latency of many visceral responses greatly exceeds that of the subjective emotional reactions they are supposed to cause (Grossman, 1967, pp. 498–563; Lehmann, 1914; Nakashima, 1909).

The two remaining points pertain to results of experimental studies.

4. The artificial induction of visceral change, through injection of such pharmacological agents as epinephrine, induces the autonomic and visceral reactions observed during naturally elicited emotion but do not give rise to subjective feeling states (Cantril & Hunt, 1932; Landis & Hunt, 1932; Maranon, 1924).

5. The surgical separation of the viscera from the central nervous system, also occasionally achieved by accident, does not eliminate emotional behavior.

Cannon (1927) recognized that his criticisms of James (1890–1950) were unlikely to deal a fatal blow to a "famous doctrine . . . so strongly fortified by proof and so repeatedly confirmed by experience" (Perry, 1926, quoted in Cannon, 1927, p. 106) unless he provided a clear theoretical alternative. The alternative hypothesis was that feeling states depended upon central neural activity: "The peculiar quality of the emotion is added to simple sensation when the thalamic processes are aroused" (p. 120). In short, "thalamic processes are a source of affective experience . . . and the feeling tone of a sensation is the product of thalamic activity" (p. 118). Muscular feedback did not elicit affect, although Cannon argued it might help sustain it.

Cannon's argument was closely related to his neurological studies of the role of hypothalamic and thalamic centers in emotional expression. He saw a close relationship between expressions and feelings but did not regard the relationship as causal. The signals emanating from the thalamic centers caused both the expressive response and when they arrived at the cortex, the subjective feeling of emotion. Therefore, Cannon concluded, the thalamus is not the place in which subjective emotional experience happens (see Cannon, 1931; Newman, Perkins, & Wheeler, 1930). Cannon also took careful note of the fact that not all stimuli are capable of activating the emotion centers of the thalamus and suggested that eliciting stimuli may come from both external and internal sources.

Cannon made two additional important points. First, he believed that the feeling and expressive systems were partially independent of one another because the expressive and cortical areas receiving thalamic impulses were influenced by other parts of the brain. Second, Cannon (1929) believed visceral activity was irrelevant for emotional experience. "The processes going on in the thoracic and abdominal organs in consequence of sympathetic activity are truly remarkable and various; their value to the organism, however, is not to add richness and flavor to experience, but rather to adapt the internal economy so that it spite of shifts of outer circumstance the evenness of the inner life will not be profoundly disturbed'' (p. 358). Emotions that require exertion, such as fear and anger, have common adrenergic effects that are useful in maintaining internal stability.

The central neural theory pointed to ways of constructing more complex models of the relationship between expression and feeling and the neurological pathways and neurochemical changes underlying moods and subjective feeling states. The main contribution of the model to psychological theory was the proposition that subjective feelings are generated by special centers in the central nervous system and need not be compounded or created by nonemotional processes. The theory had little effect on psychological research, however, because it was phrased in physiological rather than psychological language. Because Cannon (1927, 1931) failed to specify the mental structures involved in the elicitation and processing of emotion, he provided no guidance for the subsequent study of environmental events that create feeling, thought, and expressive and instrumental action. Cannon (1927) came very close to specifying such a model, but the main impact of his writing for psychological theories of emotion was its negative, anti-Jamesian influence.

C. COGNITION–AROUSAL THEORY

Three factors seem to be particularly important for the development of cognition-arousal theory. The first is the failure of the central neural analysis to develop a convincing case for the existence of emotion centers capable of ac-

counting for the diversity of human feeling. The second is the failure of past
theories, both body feedback and central neural, to deal with the elicitation of
emotion, that is, the problem of stimulus decoding and response selection (Angier, 1927; Gardiner, 1894). The last reason is the conviction (unshaken by
Cannon's 1931 critique) that autonomic activation is necessary, if insufficient, to
create feeling states (Maranon, 1924; Ruckmick, 1936; Russell, 1927/1960;
Schachter, 1964; Schachter & Singer, 1962). As a consequence, numerous authors suggested that subjective emotions were products of bodily arousal combined with the cognition of emotion-eliciting events (e.g., Russell, 1927/1960;
Sully, 1902). Schachter (1964) restated this formulation in the three following
propositions:

> 1. Given a state of physiological arousal for which an individual has no immediate explana-
> tion, he will "label" this state and describe his feelings in terms of the cognitions available
> to him . . . precisely the same state of physiological arousal could be labeled "joy" or
> "fury" or any of a great diversity of emotional labels, depending on the cognitive aspects
> of the situation.
> 2. If the individual has a completely appropriate explanation . . . for his arousal . . . no
> evaluative needs will arise, and the individual is unlikely to label his feelings in terms of the
> alternative cognitions available.
> 3. Given the same cognitive circumstances the individual will react emotionally or describe
> his feelings as emotions only to the extent that he experiences a state of physiological
> arousal. (p. 53)

The propositions made clear that although both arousal and cognition are
necessary for emotion, neither is sufficient. The arousal component defines an
experience as emotional and locates it in the self. Arousal, however, is neutral
and undifferentiated; it varies in intensity, not in quality, and provides a charge
or a drive (Hull, 1930, 1932, 1943; Spence, 1958) but does not direct behavior
(Zillmann, 1978, pp. 335–368). For Schachter, however, arousal is also a conscious psychological event that stimulates a need to know that leads the individual to look outward for the cause of his arousal. The search generates the
cognitive component that specifies the quality (anger, fear, joy, etc.) of the
feeling state; that is, "cognition arising from the immediate situation as interpreted by past experience provides the framework within which one under-
stands and labels his feeling" (Schachter, 1964, pp. 50–51). Thus, by starting
from the bottom up (arousal through search to cognition) instead of from the top
down (perception to emotion), Schachter introduces symmetry and goes beyond
James (1890/1950) by spelling out specific processes (e.g., awareness and labeling of arousal) in the construction of emotion. Although Schachter agrees with
James that autonomic reactions are necessary for feeling and suggests that the
autonomic component of the feeling matrix is involuntary, occurring either spontaneously or by chemical elicitation, he also believes that the emotion's cognitive
component is obviously more subject to volitional control. The formulation also

makes clear that environmental perception and interpretation are necessary for emotion and suggests that the clearer the environment, the clearer the individual's feelings. The model falls back on common sense, however, in responding to the impact set of issues regarding why different stimuli arouse different emotions. Finally, the model suggests that the integration of arousal and cognition is postattentive (occurring after awareness) and multiplicative. If one is completely unaroused or if one confronts a completely benign environment, there can be no emotional experience.

III. The Perceptual–Motor Model

A. OVERVIEW

The key issue separating the prior analyses is whether or not emotion has a separate existence. Central neutral theory votes *yes;* emotion is supposedly a product of specific affective processes in the brain. By contrast, both arousal and cognition-arousal theory vote *no;* for them; emotion is either feedback from bodily reactions or the amalgamation of feedback from bodily reactions with cognition. The *no* votes have had the edge in directing research because they point to more readily manipulated and measured factors for the study of emotion. The central neural position appears to expose emotion only to neurophysiological investigation. However, the availability of measures is no assurance of their relationship to emotional processes. Cognition–arousal theory, for example, may deal with social influence processes instead of the mechanisms underlying emotion.

As Cannon (1931) noted, it seems difficult if not impossible to eradicate the notion of arousal feedback, for it fits our intuitive experience of emotion too well. It is also clear that arousal and cognitive processes are indeed involved with emotion, as they are with all behavior. The issue, however, is whether these processes are the necessary and sufficient mechanisms for defining emotional experience or whether some other mechanism defines emotional experience, and arousal and cognition participate with it in the organism's total response to emotion-provoking situations.

I think it impossible to construct an adequate theory of emotion with no other concepts than arousal and cognition. Emotion must be *added* as a unit— indeed, as a complex system—into the cognition-arousal framework. The emotion mechanism I have proposed (Leventhal, 1974b, 1979, 1980; Leventhal & Mosbach, 1983) uses a more general systems approach to describe the mechanisms that control behavior (see Carver & Scheier, 1981, 1982; Leventhal, 1970; Leventhal & Nerenz, 1983). The general model postulates that behavior is constructed and controlled by *parallel* systems that are arranged in *stages*. One of these systems controls *objective* or problem-oriented behavior. The other controls *emotional* or affect-oriented behavior. Both systems are conceptualized as a sequence of stages for representing the environment, responding to it, and testing response outcomes. The first stage in each of the parallel systems involves processing information to create either a representation of the problem space in the problem-oriented system or a representation of an emotion in the affect-generating system. The second stage is the selection of a coping response to reach the goals defined by the representation. The third stage is the appraisal or testing of the degree to which the response has reduced or expanded the gap between the goal and the individual's current state (see Carver, 1979; Lazarus, 1966; Miller, Galanter, & Pribram, 1960; Powers, 1973).

The postulate of parallel processes (Fig. 1) was initially proposed to deal with the observed independence of emotional and problem-oriented responses to health threats (Leventhal, 1970). The two systems are seen as independent but in constant interaction at all three stages of processing. The parallel hypothesis has also played an important role in conceptualizing the mechanisms within each step or stage of the control system. For example, the representation of pain in response to a noxious stimulus is the experience of an emotion combined with the perceptual attributes of the noxious stimulus. The experience does not usually separate the emotion from the stimulus attributes. For example, pain combines distress and anxiety with the burning heat or the pricking coldness of the stim-

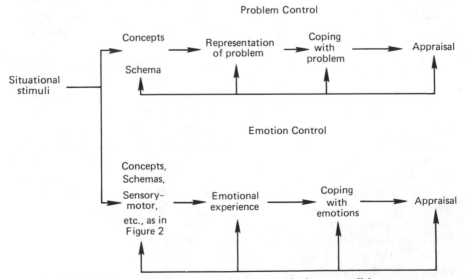

Fig. 1.   The parallel-processing model: the stages in the two parallel systems.

ulus. The mechanism underlying the construction of this perceptual representation appears to involve the action of both sensory–perceptual and emotional-processing systems from the very point of contact with the noxious stimulus (Casey, 1973; Leventhal & Everhart, 1979; Melzack, 1973; Melzack & Wall, 1965).

The primary focus of the perceptual–motor theory of emotion has been the elaboration of the mechanism presumed to underly the generation of the emotional experience in the first or representation stage of stimulus processing. This mechanism decodes or interprets stimulus information to generate an emotional response. A series of postulates or assumptions about the interpretive mechanism is at the core of the model. The three most important of these are:

1. There is a basic set of stimulus-senstive expressive-motor templates, each of which generates a different emotional experience and expressive-motor reaction. These experiences and motor reactions are relatively primitive or unenriched in the newborn, but do not long remain that way.
2. There are at least two different types of cognitive memory systems that store information about the environmental conditions evoking the just described expressive-motor reactions: (a) One makes an analog record of the eliciting conditions, the expressive-motor and autonomic response accompanying them, and the subjective emotion itself. (b) Another makes an abstract, self-reflective record of the situation and one's response to it. Thus, the innate expressive-motor reaction is recoded in memory in at least two new or different forms.
3. These systems are simultaneously active and interactive in the generation of emotional behavior.

B. FUNDAMENTAL ASSUMPTIONS ABOUT THE NATURE OF THE SYSTEM

Elsewhere, we have proposed four fundamental features of this emotion-generating system. They are as follows:

1. Hierarchical Processing

The concept of hierarchical processing is basic to our model. Every emotion is composed of components and operations at several levels. These components vary from emotion to emotion and may also vary from moment to moment for the same emotion. The hierarchical nature of the system also ties emotion to several types of cognition, including sensations, perceptions, images, and ideas.

There are two hierarchies involved in emotional processing. First, the central nervous system forms a hierarchy with the peripheral machinery of the body, using information from the body and the body's motor mechanisms for constructing emotional reactions. Second, within the central nervous system we postulate a hierarchical processing system consisting of at least three levels (see Fig. 2):

   a. Expressive-Motor Level. The expressive-motor mechanism is the basic processor of emotional behavior and experience. It includes an innate set of central neuromotor programs for generating a distinctive set of expressive reactions and feelings in response to specific releasing stimuli in the newborn and the developing child (Izard, 1971).

   b. Schematic Level. The schematic mechanism is an automatic processing system that involves the coding of emotional experience in memory. It is not a memory about emotional reactions; it is an analog record of the reactions. The schematic system combines the subjective feelings and expressive-motor reactions with stimulus inputs and other motor reactions, particularly autonomic responses. Instrumental reactions are less tightly linked to schemata than autonomic or expressive-motor responses. This system can be conceptualized as a record of conditioned emotional reactions.

   c. Conceptual Level. The conceptual system includes a set of abstract propositions or rules about emotional episodes and a set of rules for voluntary response to emotional situations and to emotions themselves. The rules or propositions that made up this system emerge from self-observation and from variations in voluntary efforts to cope with emotion-provoking situations and subjec-

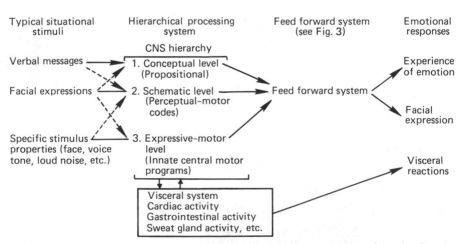

Fig. 2.   Model of the hierarchical processing system for the construction of emotional reactions: (1) the three levels of Central Neural Processing (CNS) and (2) the relation of CNS to the visceral system.

tive feelings. Rules or propositions for creating emotion are easy to verbalize. For example, we can observe and comment on our emotional reactions by making statements such as "The near-miss with that car really upset me" or "I seem to feel butterflies in my stomach and shaky all over whenever I have a close call."

The voluntary motor component of the conceptual system is separate from the motor system that is linked to automatic or schematic processing (Geschwind, 1975). It provides the individual with the capacity to perform specific expressive and instrumental "feeling" responses voluntarily. This system is crucial for developing voluntary control over emotional experience and behavior. The comparison between voluntary (intended) and automatic (unintended) expressive-motor impulses is important for subjective feeling.

I want to make clear at the outset that the model does not require feedback from peripheral or motor (autonomic or facial-motor) activity for emotional experience. This is clearly true for emotional experience in adults and is also likely in neonates. However, even though we claim that peripheral motor activity is not necessary for emotional experience and behavior, we are not suggesting that it is irrelevant to them. Autonomic facial-expressive and postural-peripheral motor activity feeds back into and is integrated with central emotional processing, but none of these feedback loops is believed to be *necessary* for the experience of an emotion. These subtleties may seem academic, but they are critical in differentiating the perceptual-motor model from other theories. For example, the cognition-arousal model proposed by Schachter and Singer (1962) argues that autonomic activity is necessary for emotion and that cognition without autonomic activity is cold or emotionlike but not emotional. Similarly, the revised Darwinian perspective of Tomkins (1962, 1980) suggests that some type of differentiated facial feedback is necessary to feel different types of emotion. The perceptual–motor position argues that genuine emotion can be experienced solely on the basis of central motor activity (though this may be a rare case) and that autonomic activity is not necessary for emotion. It also argues that emotion can be independent of what we commonly call cognition or reason (if only expressive-motor activity is present) and that emotion can be associated with several types of cognition (perceptual, schematic, and conceptual). The perceptual–motor model also suggests that the activation of autonomic and other types of motor activity can arouse emotion if it has been associated with central-neutral emotion processes in the past (Grossman, 1967 pp. 498–563; Izard, 1971; Leventhal, 1974b, 1979, 1980; Tomkins, 1962).

2. Simultaneous Action

All three processing mechanisms in the central-neural hierarchy and the accompanying bodily machinery are active in emotion-provoking situations.

Thus, one cannot separately observe conceptual, schematic, or expressive-motor action. It is only possible to observe the product of their interaction. There are two ways to study the contribution of a particular component to the total system: We may vary a factor that primarily affects activity on one of the three levels, or we may develop an analytic model that links specific independent variables to responses (verbal expression, facial activity, etc.) presumed to reflect activity in a particular mechanism.

Although each of the levels is involved in every emotional response, the degree and the nature of their involvement may vary from occasion to occasion. They will also vary at different times in the life cycle because the degree and type of cognitive involvement changes with development (Piaget, 1968). On the other hand, I hypothesize that the expressive-motor system changes very little over much of the life span.

3. Meaning Domains

Emotions are processed in meaning domains. With experience, an individual develops an increasingly rich and differentiated store of knowledge that is linked to a wide variety of emotional memories and emotional experiences (Paddeley, 1982; Bower & Cohen, 1982; Mandler, 1962). The phrase "meaning domain" refers to specific content areas that include the self-identity and its component roles (e.g., the self as child, student, or father) as well as content areas such as illness, work, and sports. Each domain contains a history of emotional experiences such as joy, interest, pain, and anxiety. The activation of a meaning domain or its components will activate the emotions integrated with it. For example, we can expect different emotional reactions from a woman hospitalized with uterine cancer and a woman in childbirth, even though each may experience the same sensations during a medical examination. The cancer patient may perceive the pain as confirming her terminal illness and become severely frightened and anxious. The pregnant woman, in contrast, may feel happy and exhilarated as the same sensations remind her of the impending birth.

Each meaning system or domain changes in structure and complexity with development and with increased experience in that content area. The construction of emotion by expressive-motor response to a sensory cue is how the neonate gives sensory–motor meaning to that external reality. In the infant, undifferentiated wholes (e.g., the human face) or specific components (e.g., high-pitched tones of voice) may stimulate these expressive reactions and subjective feelings. In turn, these reactions may be conditioned to perceptual memories and linked to autonomic reactions. Long exposures to such combinations, either over repeated occasions or from a single long-lasting occasion, can lead to well-structured schemata that form the core of an interpersonal meaning domain (e.g., an attachment) for mediating emotional behavior. As systems of this type become well-structured and join feelings, expressions, and autonomic responses to perceptual memories, they will form what Piaget called concrete operational systems (Piaget & Inhelder, 1971). As an area of the affective system grows to include conceptual and volitional rules, it takes on the characteristics of a formal operational system. Because meaning domains are organized by specific contents or by specific emotions, they tend to be segregated. For example, an individual may be differentially mature in some domains but not in others and may be able to exert volitional control over anger and fear but not over joy and love.

4. Multiple Routes of Activation

The entire emotional system, including overt emotional reactions and subjective feelings, can be stimulated to activity by processing at any level of the system. The speed and clarity with which emotion will be experienced and the cognitive content accompanying emotional arousal will vary according to which levels of the system are active. For example, if an emotional sequence is initiated by activity at the visceral or autonomic level (from the bottom up in Fig. 2), emotional behavior and experience may be relatively ambiguous because autonomic activity accompanies many types of intense activity. The feeling state would become more distinct and be experienced as fear, anger, joy, and so forth when a central expressive-motor program is activated by either external stimulation (e.g., seeing or imitating the behavior of a stooge [Schachter & Singer, 1962; Walters & Parke, 1964]) or through cognitive activity that stimulates central expressive-motor activity. At some point, all levels of processing will be active, and expressive-motor processing will nearly always play a central role in the active generation of feelings.

IV. Elaboration of the Model

I have provided an overview of my assumptions regarding the fundamental structure and function of the emotional processing system. The definition of terms and the description of the processes are presented briefly and without supportive evidence. The goal of the present section is to define further and spell out the functions of each system and to tie them to observations. In this section I focus on data relevant to the expressive-motor, schematic, and conceptual levels of neural processing.

A. EXPRESSIVE-MOTOR PROCESSING

I have suggested that a central, emotional sensory–motor program generates both expressive action and feeling and that this system is operative at birth.

Although we have no way of testing whether the system generates emotional feelings in the newborn, I believe this is a plausible assumption given that many central states (imagery, dreams, thought during anticipation of exposure to counter-attitudinal arguments, etc.) are accompanied by motor responses in adults (Cacioppo & Petty, 1981) and that there is continuity of emotional behavior from childhood to adulthood. Hence, I argue that expressive-motor processing provides the earliest emotional "meaning" for situational experiences. It is an innate meaning system that defines events with a "feeling" quality. The presumed link between the feeling and motor response is the reason for labeling the system an expressive-motor system.

Much data support the hypothesis of a central motor mechanism that generates both innate expressive-motor reactions and subjective emotional experiences. First, there are data describing the structure and function of the facial muscles. This musculature is highly differentiated (Ekman, Friesen, & Ellsworth, 1972; Izard, 1971, 1977; Tomkins, 1962) and therefore able to express a full range of differentiated feelings (Leventhal, 1979, 1980). The face also has extensive connections to central neural areas implicated in emotional response (Gellhorn, 1964). Second, there is considerable evidence showing that facial expressions of emotion are recognized with high accuracy both within and across cultures (Ekman & Friesen, 1971; Izard, 1971; Tomkins & McCarter, 1964). Third, there are data showing that expressive behavior develops in the blind as well as in the normally sighted child (Eibl-Eibesfeldt, 1980). This demonstrates that expressive-motor behaviors are not learned. Fourth, emotional states seem to be sufficiently tied to expressive behavior to allow for predictions of subjective feelings from recordings of facial muscle activity invisible to the unaided observer (Schwartz, Fair, Mandel, Salt, & Klerman, 1976). Facial muscle activity can also predict an observer's judgment of emotion (Ekman & Friesen, 1975), and in some circumstances, the emotional experience of the person observed (Leventhal & Sharp, 1965). Finally, there is abundant evidence to support the hypothesis that specific emotional states are keyed to particular eliciting cues. For example, nausea–disgust is related to taste and upset of the gastro–intestinal tract (Garcia, 1981); pain–distress is related to noxious stimulation rather than threat; and fear is stimulated by specific visual and auditory cues, such as a rapidly approaching shadow or an abrupt, loud sound.

The most astonishing evidence for the linking of expressive patterns to specific outer cues has been reported by Field, Woodson, Greenberg, and Cohen (1982). These investigators studied a group of 74 babies with a mean age of 36 hours. An adult held each baby upright, sustained its alertness by performing two knee bends and making two clicking sounds with his or her tongue, and then fixed a happy, sad, or surprised expression on his or her face. The baby and the model were videotaped using a split-screen setup, and a rater (who could not see the model) scored the baby's affective expression. There were two important findings. First, the babies' expressions actually matched the model's at greater than chance levels (surprise was matched 76% of the time; happiness and sadness on 58% and 59% of their respective trials). Second, the babies showed clear signs of learning; when exposed repeatedly to the same expression, the infants fixated it less (habituated), whereas their fixations increased markedly when the model changed expressions. The evidence for learning is of most relevance to our discussion of schematic emotion. The evidence exhibited by the babies' matching the model's expression is relevant to our expressive-motor hypothesis. These data, however, can be interpreted in several ways. First, one could argue that the infant was simply copying the model's facial expression. Intentional behavior of this complexity, however, is difficult to attribute to the newborn. Second, the response could also be a simple reflex—the equivalent of a knee jerk. Such a minimalist interpretation ignores the entire body of data on expressive behavior and subjective feelings. A third, and perhaps more plausible, interpretation is that the model's expressions stimulated the babies' emotional responses and their consequent expressive behaviors. Thus, a subjective state accompanied or preceded the motor display.

The previously mentioned list of findings provides evidence for the existence of an innate expressive-motor system. It is important to note, however, that the data provide no direct evidence of relationships between expressive reactions and subjective feeling states. Second, it is important to realize that neither the cognitive content nor the subjective experience that accompanies an expression in the newborn will match the cognitive content or subjective experience accompanying a similar expression in an individual with an emotional history. Simple expressive-motor reactions and their accompanying subjective states are "minimal" emotions. They are unlikely to be experienced as related to specific outer events and response consequences because environmental probabilities and the assessment of coping strategies are dependent upon experience.

These data, particularly those on infants, suggest a variety of hypotheses about the functions and operations of the expressive-motor system. For example, the cries of distress and the vigorous face, head, and arm movements that the infant generates in response to the placement of a cloth over his or her face serve both to dislodge the obstruction and to signal a caregiver who can remove the threat. In this example, emotion has communicative and survival functions. Another important function of expressive responses is to establish and sustain the interaction between the caregiver and the infant by allowing both parties to develop social-emotional schemata (perceptual memories joined to affect). These schemata are the base for the further development of mutual affective stimulation and attachment, and more complex forms of mutual modeling behaviors (Prazelton, Koslowski, & Main, 1974).

The stimulus specificity of different expressive-motor affective states is an extremely important aspect of emotional communication. Although the identification of the cues relevant to different affects is largely an empirical issue, many of these stimulus–response specificities can be anticipated. Garcia (1981) suggests that the favored relationship of taste cues to the conditioning of nausea–disgust is predictable because the sensory organs involved, the mouth and tongue, are part of the biological system that forms the body component of that emotional-motor complex. Similarly, distress, a response to noxious stimuli applied to the body (Mandler & Kessen, 1979), serves to inhibit responses that may cause further damage to injured parts of the body. It is more difficult to detect the stimuli specific to emotions that are responsive to specific external events, but there has been some progress in this area and more will follow (see review in Leventhal, 1980).

Finally, to repeat a prior comment, most theorists who recognize the importance of facial motor reactions in emotion have hypothesized that sensory feedback from the facial muscles creates subjective feelings (Izard, 1971; Tomkins, 1962). I do not. I suggest that a motor mechanism located in the central nervous system can create feelings in the absence of peripheral feedback (Leventhal, 1980; Leventhal & Mosbach, 1983). I discuss this mechanism in a later section.

B. SCHEMATIC PROCESSING

It is hypothesized that emotional schemata are integrations of separate perceptual codes of the visual, auditory, somesthetic, expressive, and autonomic reactions that are reliably associated with emotional experiences; they are an analog memory of the emotional experience itself (see Hurvich, 1969, p. 503). Schematic memories represent a recoding of expressive-motor reactions in combination with perceptual memories and memories of motor events (autonomic and instrumental). Thus, I do not conceive of schemata as associations of perceptual (situation) memories with the original expressive-motor codes; I believe the motor acts (expressive, autonomic) to be recoded in a common locus with the perceptual memories in schema formation. Schematic processing refers to the combination or coding of new situational inputs with these memories. These emotional memories play a critical role in the creation of ongoing emotional experience.

The cognitive component of emotional schemata in neonates is likely to include little more than sensory features (e.g., tastes for nausea-disgust or shadows or approaching images for fear) or generalized patterns, such as a smile, that are not specific to an object or person. Initially, it may require prolonged and intense attention to stimuli to elicit the infant's expressive-motor reactions. However, once the key features of the stimulus are coded and joined with feeling and motor components, processing becomes rapid and automatic. Attention is then required only to bring the stimulus into the receptor field in order to activate the schematic unit. Repeated activation, particularly under novel conditions, will add to and enrich the schema. Thus, what initially was a simple expressive-motor emotional reaction is linked to a schema of increasingly complex content and structure, and different stimulus inputs may be needed to elicit the same type of emotion at different ages (Campos, Emde, & Caplovitz, 1983).

The Field, *et al.* (1982) study mentioned in the prior section can serve as a starting point for describing the formation of social-emotional schemata. Picking up, smiling at, and cooing at an alert infant generate an audio–visual perceptual pattern likely to stimulate a return smile. The parental smile and vocalization will be stored in the infant's perceptual memory, along with memory traces of the infant's subjective emotional experience and expressive-motor behavior. Traces of autonomic reactions will also be included. The strength of the motor traces will depend to a great extent on the way the parent interacts with the infant. If the parent is vigorous and intensifies the infant's expressive display and autonomic arousal, the baby's memory structure will incorporate high levels of feeling and autonomic display. In the natural environment, these interchanges are likely to take place more often when acting to satisfy the infant's needs: during feeding, diaper changing, and so forth. Needs are a trigger to interaction (Sullivan, 1953), but the emotional reponse appears to integrate the interpersonal exchange and to structure the memory.

1. Functions of Schematic Processing

I will list and briefly discuss seven functions of schematic processing.

1. Automatic Processing. The main function of schematic emotional memory, in my judgment, is to provide a rapid (i.e., automatic) perceptual–emotional appraisal of current situations parallel to volitional cognitive activity. Thus, these schemata shape our subjective experience of objects and events without effort and without awareness of their activity (Panagis & Leventhal, 1973; Safer, 1978; Zajonc, 1980). just as perceptual memory schemata shape the organization of objects in our perceptual field (Allport & Pettigrew, 1957; Broadbent, 1977). Indeed, there is evidence to suggest that the emotional schemata for objects and situations need not overlap with the nonemotional perceptual schemata for these settings (see Ericksen, 1958, pp. 169–227; Wilson, 1979; Zajonc, 1979).

2. Creating Expectations. Like other schemata or categories (Broadbent, 1977), emotional schemata act as filters to focus attention on particular stimulus features and to generate anticipation about later experiences. Thus, schemata expand emotional experience and behavior by adding environmental and response expectations to expressive-motor events. The significance of this addition can be seen in animals raised without exposure to noxious stimulation. When exposed to shocks or burns, they show sensory–motor arousal (i.e., they express distress), but they fail to anticipate or avoid injury. They are not able to learn that outer events cause harm or that their own behavior can be followed by avoidance of that harm (Melzack & Scott, 1957). Similar evidence has been found for animals raised without early experience of food deprivation on their first exposure to deficits: They do not respond with organized affect (Hebb, 1966).

   3. Solidifying Episodic Memories. Emotional schemata also play a critical role in the development of memory systems or knowledge domains; emotionally directed attention appears to be longer lasting than attention directed by novelty because expressive and autonomic components of emotion are less easily habituated. Emotions play a major role in stimulating rehearsal of perceptual features and responses to objects (e.g., a lover's face) and situations (Isen, Shalker, Clark & Karp, 1978). By directing attention and rehearsal in this way, schematic processing is central to the formation of specific episodic memories. As a consequence, much of emotional memory appears to join feelings and expressive, autonomic, and instrumental responses to situationally specific stimuli and images. For example, being insulted or snubbed can arouse a strong feeling of anger toward a person, and the review of this event can elaborate a highly specific memory of a situation of feelings of hurt and anger.

   4. Prototype Formation and Generalization. Schemata also participate in the generalization of emotional experiences as perceptual memories become general or prototypic (Posner, 1973). These generalizations take place along features or dimensions that are particularly salient (or modal) characteristics of the set of concrete episodes that originally evoked that particular class of emotion. Thus, anger and fear may generalize to concrete features of power and status such as physical size and dress, whereas depression generalizes to situations of punishment for failure following effort (Abramson, Seligman, & Teasdale, 1978). These affectively based attributions are automatic and "unreasoned."

   5. Creating New Emotion Blends. Emotional schemata are critical to the development of new emotions. Situations may evoke combinations of basic expressive-motor reactions (e.g., emotions of fear, joy, anger, or sadness), and these combinations will be recorded in perceptual schematic memory. Blends of this sort can generate new feelings states (Ekman *et al.,* 1972). It is therefore possible to talk of automatically elicited emotions such as intimacy, pride, and empathic distress.

   6. Organizing and Accumulating Emotional Experience. Emotional schemata serve to organize experience. Two aspects of their organizing properties can be distinguished. The first is the linking of feeling to objects: Schemata focus the individual on the object of affective desire or aversion and bathe the perception of the object in a specific emotional feeling. The expressive and autonomic behaviors that are included in the feeling are relatively nonsalient because the integration of the outer stimulus with the subjective emotion dominates the field of consciousness (Krueger, 1928/1968; Mathews, 1971; Peters, 1970, pp. 187–203). In this respect emotional experience is a form of tacit knowledge, which is compared to the perception of depth in stereoscopic viewing (Polanyi, 1968). The viewer uses two monocular views, the particulars, to build a unified experience of a scene in depth. The particulars are necessary for the unified view, but the unified view goes beyond them. Indeed, the construction of the unified view is accomplished by a processing mechanism separate from that used to construct the perception of the separate monocular images (Wolfe, 1983). We believe that schemata serve a similar role in integrating particulars (expression, situational perceptions, etc.) to create a unified emotional experience. And the tightness or degree of integration of the schemata may depend upon a specific processing mechanism that is affected by factors such as attentional set (Isen & Means, 1983), sex differences, individual differences, and so forth.

The second organizing aspect of schematic processing is seen in the collative or cumulative nature of emotion. The components of emotion appear to combine in an additive or even multiplicative fashion; they do not seem to average (Anderson, 1965; 1971). This collative property is inherent in the very concept of emotional schemata. Seemingly unrelated events (e.g., object perception and expressive behavior) are combined to form a feeling about something. Strengthening any one of these elements (e.g., by increasing the intensity of spontaneous expression or heightening autonomic activity) will increase the intensity of the emotional experience.

The fine studies of the generalization of arousal conducted by Zillmann and his associates (Zillmann, 1978, pp. 335–368) illustrate this collative function. In these studies, Zillmann found that the intensity of arousal from a prior task, such as pedaling an exercise bicycle, added to and strengthened a subsequent but unrelated emotional experience, such as sexual arousal. It is important to note that this cross-situational or cross-emotional addition occurred for active emotions (e.g., generalization occurred from vigorous exercise to anger-motivated attacks). Such generalizations appear to occur as long as (1) both emotions typically involve extensive autonomic activity and (2) there is a situational cue to action for the second emotional state (Zillmann, Katcher, & Milavsky, 1972). Zillmann also pointed out that generalization of autonomic arousal from a prior to a later situation does not occur when the arousal is so intense that it is clearly perceived as belonging to the prior situation. The subject then knows he or she is shaking and breathing hard from the earlier exercise and not from the later anger. As arousal declines to less noticeable levels, it readily adds into the subsequent expression of anger.

The collative process requires, however, that the arousal remain a background factor and not be salient in perception (Cupchik & Leventhal, 1974,

Reisenzein & Gattinger, 1962). In summary, the studies illustrate that the components of emotions collate automatically unless checked by alternative organizations of the perceptual field (e.g., arousal as part of earlier exercise).

7. *Stabilizing Object Relationships.*   Finally, emotional memory has the additional function of establishing stable object relationships; that is, positive and negative attitudes, as well as attachments and aversions. Stable object relationships are critical for maintaining a secure social support network and maintaining positive and avoiding negative experiences with specific objects and events. The basic core of the problem of attitude change that has occupied so much of the energy of social psychologists (McGuire, 1968, pp. 1130–1188) is very likely a problem of changing schematic emotional memory. More dramatic examples of emotionally based attitudes are seen in behavior therapy studies of such phenomena as snake phobias (e.g., Lang, 1979). One important aspect of the attitude problem is developing techniques for distinguishing attitude domains in which there is close involvement with emotional memory from those in which there is little. Beliefs or opinions with little emotional involvement are likely to be easy to change and may often be based on inferences from one's own behavior (Bem, 1972; Leventhal, 1974b pp. 52–126). The durability of schematic emotional memory is seen in attribution studies in which reattribution alters overt behavior but fails to reduce subjective emotional reports (Calvert-Boyanowsky & Leventhal, 1975). Resistance to therapeutic action is also visible in cases of phantom pain, a problem that is discussed in detail in the following section.

2. *Behavioral Evidence for Schematic Processing*

Evidence for schematic emotional processing varies from the anecdotal to the experimental. The anecdotal examples are perhaps more persuasive because of their extraordinary quality. For example, Janis (1958) reports fascinating instances of the arousal of early imagelike memories during the psychoanalytic therapy of a 39-year-old woman who elected minor surgery to remove varicose veins in her legs. The fear associated with the impending surgery led to vivid, dreamlike recall of childhood experiences, such as seeing a crippled boy while looking out a train window and seeing an amputee move himself about on a small wheeled platform. The memory images were linked to the present by the fear and threat of injury to the legs.

Other examples of such emotional memory range from mild experiences of déjà vu to the vivid, uncontrollable, and unwanted intrusion into REM sleep (Witkin & Lewis, 1967, pp. 148–201) and waking life of scenes from previous viewings of upsetting and gory films (Horowitz, 1970). Recent studies have shown that mood induction (e.g., by listening to sad or happy music) reduces subjects' ability to put mood-relevant, intrusive thoughts out of mind (Sutherland, Newman, & Rachman, 1982) and to influence the accessibility of such imagery and thought (Teasdale & Fogarty, 1979; Teasdale, Taylor, & Fogarty, 1980).

The behavioral significance of emotional imagery is nicely illustrated in an experimental study by Turner and Layton (1976). Turner and Layton constructed four lists of paired associates, two of neutral words (one high and one low in imagery value) and two of aggressive words (one high and one low in imagery value). Their subjects learned one of these lists before performing a second task—administering shocks (as "teachers") whenever a confederate made errors in a learning task. Those subjects who learned the words high in aggressive imagery administered the strongest shocks to the confederate. Subjects who learned words high in agressive meaning but low in imagery delivered shocks of the same intensity and duration as subjects learning neutral words. The imagery value of the words was critical in activating overt agressive action to situational cues.

Perhaps the most vivid example of the concreteness and specificity of schematic emotional memory is the phenomenon of phantom pain (Melzack, 1971, 1973; Morgenstern, 1970, pp. 225–245; Simmel, 1962). Following the amputation of a body part (either by surgery or by accident), an individual may come to experience a phantom limb replete with the sensations and pain that were present prior to the loss. The imagery can be exceptionally vivid and the pain intense. It can be accompanied by subjective distress and anxiety, high levels of autonomic arousal (sweating and heart racing), and complete facial motor displays.

It is necessary to postulate a central memory structure to account for phantom (and other) pain experiences (Engel, 1959; Nathan, 1962) because efforts to explain these experiences on the basis of more peripheral events have been uniformly unsuccessful (e.g., Morgenstern, 1970, pp. 225–245). The importance of central memory processes is forcefully emphasized in cases in which a painful phantom is experienced postsurgically even though surgery occurred several weeks after spinal cord injuries had destroyed all communication between central and peripheral sensory–motor machinery (Cook & Druckmiller, 1952; Li & Elvidge, 1951).

Phantom pain has other properties consistent with the hypothesis of emotional schematic memory. For example, it is far more likely to occur when pain has existed in the body part prior to amputation, and the sensory properties of the pain following loss are usually similar if not identical to those experienced beforehand (Melzack, 1973; Morgenstern, 1970, pp. 225–245; Simmel, 1962). In some cases the pain memory is clearly selected on the basis of its emotional significance. Henderson and Smyth (1948) report such a case. An amputee had sprained an ankle in combat and was then hit by shrapnel in the sprained leg. This latter injury produced severe pain and eventually led to the amputation. However, the soldier attributed his misfortune to the sprain, which had hampered his movement and was responsible for his wound; and it was the painful sensations of the sprain that appeared in the phantom.

The emotional quality of the phantom pain memory is also illustrated by cases in which a phantom that has been dormant for months or years is re-aroused by emotionally distressing life experiences (Melzack, 1973). Phantoms and phantom pain are also dependent upon a reasonably mature memory system; they do not appear in children under 4–6 years of age (Simmel, 1962). It could be that the cognitive imagery system must reach a minimal level of development before a person can establish relatively firm, affectively laden pictorial or concrete memories of amputated body parts. Recent data suggest that self-descriptions of 3- to 5-year-olds are less oriented to body image than was previously suspected (Keller, Ford, & Meachem, 1978). In summary, because the reported observations all point to the existence of a concrete memory system linking body image with pain experience, they provide good support for the hypothesis of an emotional memory.

3. Neuropsychological Evidence for Schematic Processing

Although we do not have a precise notion of the nature of the schematic memory structure, I do not believe it can be represented as a set of nodes in an associative network. The analogic properties of schemata, (i.e., the ease of access to them by stimulus shapes that mimic the shape of the response) and the tightness of the linkages between their elements suggest that spatial or pattern factors play an important role in the formation of these memory structures. One was of thinking of them is as a set of components that fall in a common cortical field or column. A column is a vertical section through the layers of the cortex that allows for a combination of sensory and motor events to be represented in each layer. These events are closely linked to one another because of their spatial proximity and because excitation appears to flow downward in the column (from the topmost sensory layer) and to be restricted to the column by lateral inhibition. These columns can be conceptualized as discrete, automatically activated units that arouse a pattern of behavioral responses comprising each of the components of emotion (expressive, autonomic, etc.).

The previous speculation converges with accumulating evidence about the difference in function, structural organization, and biochemical basis of the different cerebral hemispheres (Carmon & Nachson, 1973; Harnad & Doty, 1977; Safer & Leventhal, 1977; Tucker, 1981). The sum of the evidence suggests the occurrence of extensive right hemispheric activity involving concrete perceptual imagery in association with emotional states (Cohen, Rosen & Goldstein, 1976; Davidson, Schwartz, Pugash, & Bromfield, 1976). One could argue that emotional schemata are one form of code used in right hemispheric processing of stimuli. The right hemisphere is especially suited for the formation of emotional schemata because it appears to be well designed to integrate information across modalities; it can integrate perceptual, expressive-motor, and autonomic information (Semmes, 1968; Tucker and Williamson, 1984). Although the final word is yet to be written on the meaning of hemispheric differences (e.g., Kinsbourne, 1974), the evidence is consistent with the existence of the type of memory integrations underlying emotional schemata.

C. CONCEPTUAL PROCESSING

Conceptual processing deals with two aspects of emotion. First, it is important for the conclusions that we draw about our feelings—our guesses as to what internal events and actions make up emotion, as well as the causes and consequences of emotion. Although these beliefs are based on information gleaned from sensory–motor and schematic processing, there is no reason to assume that they accurately reflect these processes (see Mandler, 1975; Nisbett & Wilson, 1977). However, the incomplete and inaccurate aspects of conceptualizations of emotion are not the important issues. The key issues are to be found in attempting to answer the questions of how people formulate their conceptions, what information they use to do so, and what rules they adopt in making generalizations.

Second, it is hypothesized that conceptual processes are closely related to deliberately controlled, skilled motor performance and to propositional thinking. Conceptual processes can regulate and control expressive-motor and schematic processing by controlling attention and voluntary action. The development of conceptual structures that can match schematic and expressive-motor mechanisms may be crucial for the integration and control of emotional experience (see Lang, 1979, for a related perspective).

The conceptual system contains a verbal component used for recording and interpreting information about emotional experiences and a performance component underlying the volitional production and control of emotional reactions. Both conceptual codes are generated by abstracting information from specific emotional episodes; both are more flexible than the concrete perceptual memories comprising schematic processing; and both retain information in a sequential format that is useful for the regulation of temporal action sequences. They are therefore useful for reasoning, regulating ongoing sequences of behavior, directing attention to particular events, and generating specific responses to deal with these events.

1. The Verbal Conceptual Component

The verbal conceptual system is a way of representing and communicating about feelings, but it is not a representation of the feelings themselves. We recall that we felt a particular way following a specific incident, that we acted on the feeling, that the acts had specific consequences, and that we can talk about how we felt. Communication about feelings seems relatively simple and direct for most lay persons, if not for most psychologists (Davitz, 1970), but the verbal conceptual system often seems removed from and unable to control emotional processes. A key reason for this is that verbal conceptualizations abstract a limited portion of the features of any emotional episode, and the features on which the abstractions are based are those most salient to attention at the time that the abstraction is formed (often after the episode). Concrete circumscribed objects and unexpected or particularly vivid features of stimulation are attended to more intently than familiar events and contextual factors, so that the former are more likely to be selected out and perceived as causes of emotion (Bowlby, 1973). For example, one might be startled and frightened by an unexpected sound in a darkened house and attribute one's fear to the sound, failing to recognize that the darkness played an equal role in stimulating the fear reaction. Similarly, being alone may be a critical contextual factor for the arousal of fear and the formation of phobias to a wide variety of stimuli (Bowlby, 1973; Bronson, 1968). The well-documented fear of strangers also reflects a partial error in causal explanation. Sroufe and Waters (1976) concluded that fear of strangers is readily elicited in 9-month-old infants under laboratory conditions but is seldom seen in the home when the mother is present. In a safe familiar context, strangers provoke positive affective reactions because the figure of the stranger is more salient than the context for the investigator as well as for the child, and investigators were slow to recognize the importance of the latter in stimulating fear reactions. The schematic and expressive-motor systems respond strongly to contextual cues, leading to an inconsistency between them and the actor's post hoc conceptual representation of the process. The sense that emotion is provoked from outside and is not under voluntary control is another consequence of post hoc attention to the figure and of failure to recognize the contribution of context as a stimulus to the automatic memory system that generates emotion.

2. Performance Conceptualizations

Earlier presentations (Leventhal, 1974; 1979; Leventhal & Everhart, 1979) of the perceptual–motor model of emotion discussed evidence for performance conceptualizations but did not differentiate them sharply from verbal–conceptual processing. Performance conceptualizations are abstract, sequential representations of the perceptual and motor responses that are organized in analogic, spatial, or holistic form in emotional schemata. Performance codes must abstract cues and responses from critical junctures or starting points in the motor portion of automatic schemata (see Carver & Scheier, 1981, 1982; Powers, 1973, for a description of hierarchical control processes) in order to exert partial control over schematic and expressive-motor processing systems. Individuals develop performance codes by active participation; they thrust themselves into emotional situations, deliberately enact grief, anger, joy, and fear, and practice expressing and generating feeling.

Performance codes play a critical part in emotional life. When they are present, the volitional system can swiftly generate a sequence of voluntary responses to match spontaneous expressive outputs from the schematic system (see Fig. 1). This volitional performance system can anticipate emotional behaviors through self-instruction. The schematic code, in contrast, is more similar to a conditioned response and is situationally governed. The performance system can greatly reduce the impact of emotionally provocative situations by anticipating the automatic processing systems.

Studies on the lateralization of cerebral functioning provide some data to support the separation of conceptual from schematic processing and to suggest that performance plays an important role in generating conceptual emotional codes. Earlier in the section on neuropsychological evidence for schematic processing, I cited data that suggested that the right hemisphere of the brain plays a major role in the automatic processing of emotional schemata. There is reason to suspect, however, that highly skilled individuals can perform emotional tasks (e.g., recognition of emotional expressions) as well with the left hemisphere as they can with the right. Trained musicians, for example, are equally proficient in melody recognition (a task with emotional properties) with either the left or right hemisphere, and their left hemisphere skills greatly exceed those of nonmusicians (Bever & Chiarello, 1974; Davidson & Schwartz, 1977). Skill also appears to have important consequences for musical performance. For example, skilled performers and novices display sharply different reactions to making an error in a run of notes. The novice returns to the start of the run to repeat the sequence, whereas the skilled musician appears to anticipate the error and continues virtually uninterrupted. Practice at painstakingly slow rates as well as at normal tempos appears to be the skilled musician's method of constructing both a voluntary sequential code and an automatic schema of the passage. The voluntary code seems to run ahead of the automatic output and generate the appropriate next response when an error is detected in the automatic output. There is sometimes, however, a momentary decline in the tonal expressiveness of the performance.

Practice and skill in generating voluntary emotional reactions should have similar effects for emotional judgments. Safer (1981) tested this hypothesis in a series of studies in which subjects were shown a pair of faces in sequence; the first face was exposed for 8 seconds at the center of the visual field and the second was briefly flashed (50 milliseconds) to one or the other side of the central point of fixation after the central face was removed. The second flash was received by only one side of the brain. Two experiments were run. In one, subjects were asked to judge whether the two pictures were the same or different.

This was a pattern-judgment task. In the other experiment, subjects were asked whether the emotional expressions had been the same or different. This was an emotion-judgment task. Safer reasoned that female subjects would be more likely to develop volitional emotion codes because the female role encourages the open expression, performance, and practice of complex emotional reactions (Hoffman, 1977). He expected, therefore, that females would show greater accuracy than males with left hemisphere judgments. Safer found that female subjects were equally accurate in judging emotional expressions in the left and right hemispheres, and their left hemisphere performance greatly exceeded that of male subjects. Accuracy in judging emotional expressions in the right hemisphere was equal for both female and male subjects. In the pattern judgment experiment, both female and male subjects showed substantially better performance with the right hemisphere.

Although Safer's (1981) data describe only the recognition of emotional expressions, other data suggest that sex differences exist for generating expressions. Noller (1980) found that the ability to express emotional tone was substantially lower for members of poorly adjusted marriages than for members of well-adjusted marriages, and the emotional expressions generated by females were given higher clarity ratings and more accurately judged than were the expressions generated by males. Similarly, Lang and his associates (Lang, 1979; Lang, Kozak, Miller, Levin, & McLean, 1980) reported that females are better than males at generating complete (subjective, expressive, and autonomic) emotional reactions when instructed to do so. This deficit in voluntary emotional performance can be overcome with practice.

The separation of performance and verbal conceptual codes from automatic, emotional schemata receives further support from studies of the behavioral control of emotion. For example, both modeling and desensitization procedures are effective in reducing snake phobias, but modeling is even more effective in reducing reported fear and phobic behavior when the observer is encouraged to engage actively in behaviors of looking at, approaching, and touching snakes. Modeling with active participation also appears to produce a longer lasting therapeutic effect, suggesting that active participation helps to develop control of stimulus-elicited emotion or automatically processed emotion (Pandura, Blanchard, & Ritter, 1969). Lang (1979) has contrasted passive and active imagery in desensitization and found more complete reduction of phobias when the imagery included the participant's actively engaging in behavior involving snakes. McKechnie (1975) reports having successfully treated a case of phantom pain by using a desensitization procedure in which the patient imagined himself actively relaxing and using the painful phantom. These findings and others similar to them (see Zillmann, 1978) suggest the value of distinguishing between emotional schematic codes, which automatically connect with perceptual inputs, and conceptual performance codes, which can connect perception with a volitional self-representation that permits control over otherwise automatic affective behavior.

V. Relationships between the Processing Systems

Postulating a hierarchy of mechanisms for processing emotion raises a variety of interesting questions about their interactions. These questions focus on such issues as the antecedent of emotional reactions, the conditions giving rise to emotional behavior with or without emotional experience, and the change in emotional experience and behavior accompanying personality development.

A. THE ANTECEDENTS OF EMOTIONAL PROCESSING

Each of the systems generating emotional behavior and experience is sensitive to somewhat different cues. At the earliest moments in life, emotional behavior appears to be generated by an innate system whose function does not depend on past learning. Processing in this system is initiated by specific, yet generic, stimulus attributes (e.g., eyes or pitch of voice) rather than by stimulus identity (e.g., Mom's voice) or meaning (Hebb, 1949). We should be able to represent the stimulus gradients that initiate expressive-motor processing in ways similar to the representations of the stimulus gradients (texture, disparity, movement, etc.) involved in the generation of spatial perception cues (E. J. Gibson, 1970; J. Gibson, 1950).

The literature on emotional response in infants supports the hypothesis that dimensional or gradient cues are important for early expressive behavior. Such stimuli as an object's rate of approach ("looming") and lightness or darkness (Bowlby, 1973) are important for provoking startle and withdrawal responses (the beginnings of fear affect) and smiling reactions (Sroufe & Waters, 1976). Features of the expressive responses emitted by adults provide a source of stimulation that is able to capture the infant's attention and elicit an expressive response. Brazelton et al. (1974) observed head turning and visual search in the neonate in response to high-pitched vocalizations by an adult. They also found distinctively different motor reactions, such as smooth cycling of arms and legs, when the infant was fixating an adult face as compared to fixating a physical object (see also Condon & Sander, 1974). These stimuli are dimensional; any adult (parent, friend, or stranger) can stimulate the expressive reactions in the infant if his or her speech lies within the range of critical values for the features of pitch and rate. By contrast, particular faces and voices whose identification requires a categorical process only become important with development (Kagan, 1970).

Although the newborn's expressions can be externally controlled, Emde (1979) has suggested that there is a great deal of spontaneous expressive-motor activity in newborns that is generated largely by internal (noncognitive) factors that gradually come under the control of increasingly specific external stimuli. For example, the mildly hungry infant makes a variety of expressive cues to stimulate expression and feeling in the adult caregiver. The expressive behavior in the caregiver can then evoke expressiveness in the infant. Once it is brought under external control, expression becomes an interactional trait (Emde, 1979). Developmental changes of this sort are obviously of critical importance for the emergence of emotional schemata. However, the concept of schemata may be too limited to deal with the emergence of emotional interaction traits. Interaction traits seem to refer to regularities over time that are more aptly described by such concepts as emotional scripts (Abelson, 1976; Leventhal & Everhart, 1979) rather than emotional schemata. The term schemata seems best to describe less temporally expanded emotional events.

It is clear that emotional schemata are likely to be activated by many of the same stimuli that activate expressive-motor processing. With repeated exposure to specific emotion-eliciting events, emotional schemata become increasingly complex, and a situation must match its schemata more precisely to stimulate an emotional reaction. For example, as infants first learn to distinguish faces, they smile at strangers and at frightening masks as well as at their mothers (Spitz & Wolf, 1946). With development they become more discriminating and smile at familiar faces but show fear of strangers when in strange or "unsafe" environments (Schaffer & Emerson, 1964), whereas they might smile at both types of faces in familiar and "safe" environments (Sroufe & Waters, 1976). With further growth, yet new stimuli control fear. At kindergarten age, fears are elicited by vague, fantasylike events, whereas later still (e.g., in sixth grade) they become more realistic and focused on bodily injury and physical danger (Bauer, 1976). Because the stimuli that activate emotional reactions change with age—that is, with cognitive growth (Campos *et al.,* 1983)—investigators who focus upon a specific age or situation have been led to erroneous conclusions about the age at which that emotion first appears. For example, the ready elicitation of fear responses to strangers at 9 months of age was easily observed in the laboratory, and investigators concluded that fear reactions were first manifest at that time. They failed to notice either the earlier or later conditions for fear because they were focused upon a particular eliciting stimulus.

The continuity between expressive-motor and schematic processing is strongly suggested by the Ohman and Dimberg (1978) study, in which adults' skin conductance responses were conditioned to facial expressions. In this experiment, uncomfortable electric shocks served as the unconditioned stimulus for the skin conductance response, while happy, angry, or neutral faces were used as the conditioned stimuli. Although skin conductance was conditioned to all three conditioned stimuli with equal facility, extinction was extremely slow to the stimulus of the angry face. The features of angry caregivers probably have elicited fear reactions in all of us during childhood so that angry faces form a central part of our emotional fear schemata. These schemata and their autonomic and expressive components can be readily activated in later life. As Ohman and Dimberg (1978) suggest, therefore, the organism is prepared to acquire and retain particular emotionally based stimulus–response relationships (Seligman, 1970).

It is also clear that contextual cues contribute greatly to schematic emotion by affecting the relative strength or availability of selected schemata. For example, fear schemata are more available than joy schemata in unfamiliar and possibly unsafe environments. Moreover, although adults appear to give less emphasis to contextual cues in reporting on the source of their emotional disturbances, the cues still retain their potency as elicitors of emotional processing (Hebb, 1955).

The development of emotional schemata add at least two other types of antecedents to emotional reactions. First, man and other primates clearly respond emotionally to the disconfirmation of schema-based expectations. Hebb (1946) suggested that the violation of schemata is a critical source of affective experiences and reactions for all individuals and all species of primate. For example, many primates form a perceptual schema of the typical configuration of a member of their species. When this is violated by exposure to the torso, head, or the anesthetized body of a conspecific, the animal may respond with intense fear. This fear depends on the violation of the expected appearance of a normal animal and does not depend on prior negative experiences with severed heads or anesthetized animals.

The development of schemata both narrows and broadens the range of stimuli capable of evoking prolonged and intense emotional reactions. These reactions appear to be based both on the specific meaning of the stimulus and on deviations from expectations. The current situation is constantly compared with schemata-based expectations, and familiar and novel stimuli are highly likely to elicit emotion.

Finally, conceptual processes, both verbal and performance, are elicited by a variety of situational and social cues and can tune or increase the salience of specific sets of schemata. The gracious hostess verbalizes and performs expressions of delight to even the least desirable guest. The competitive "Type A" executive conceptualizes future situations as a threat to the self and to his or her perceptual schemata, and his coping resources are ready to see and to cope with threat well before it can materialize; hence, he speaks rapidly, with emphasis, and answers questions before the questioner completes them (Scherwitz, Berton, & Leventhal, 1977, 1978). Long-term interests, plans, and self-concerns direct affective responding and coping by bringing individuals into contact with affect-eliciting situations, by making emotion schemata salient, and by generating anticipatory emotional reactions to deal with them. The key to conceptual processing is the system's responsiveness to the symbolic stimuli of verbal information from oneself and others. It can therefore function as an anticipatory device for emotional control.

B. THE INTERACTION OF AUTOMATIC
    AND VOLITIONAL PROCESSING

1. The Feedback Hypothesis

Earlier in the section "Expressive Motor Processing," we reviewed a great deal of evidence implicating facial-motor activity in emotion when defining the substance and function of the expressive-motor system. Although this system is clearly involved in the expression of emotion, it is less clear how it is involved in the generation of subjective emotional experiences. One important hypothesis has been that of facial feedback; that is, that feedback from facial-motor activity is felt as emotional experience (Izard, 1971; Laird, 1974; Leventhal and Sharp, 1965; Tomkins, 1962), an hypothesis that is clearly one of James's (1890/1950) legacies.

James (1890/1950), however, emphasized patterned visceral activity rather than patterned facial expression. He rejected facial expressions because actors reported generating clear, intense expressions of emotion during performances without feeling the expressed affect. And most, if not all, of us can also recall at least one occasion on which we have smiled, frowned, or looked guilty in order to fit the demands of social conventions, without feeling the expressed emotion. James (1884) thought that this eliminated the face as the source of emotion, but he also made the following contradictory suggestion: "If we wish to conquer undesirable emotional tendencies in ourselves, we must assiduously, and in the first instance, cold-bloodedly go through the outward movements of those contrary dispositions which we prefer to cultivate" (p. 198). James appears to have believed that generating an opposing expression swiftly eliminates an unwanted emotion, but that the replacement of the unwanted emotion with the one we wish to cultivate is gradual. For him, therefore, facial expressions can more easily block than create feelings.

Although it is difficult to reject the facial feedback hypothesis, it is more difficult to reconcile it with these contradictory examples so as to make it acceptable. The facial-motor system is clearly adequately differentiated; there are 15 symmetrical muscle pairs plus the orbicular muscle (Izard, 1971, pp. 238, 239). It is constructed so as to facilitate patterned feedback (the muscle groups are unsheathed and can contract partially, can send afferent messages to the hypothalamus, and can show little afferent adaptation) and is highly responsive to stimulation (e.g., the newborn is more reactive when stimulated on the face and head than on other parts of the body). But none of this evidence, nor any of that already reviewed on judgment of expressions, the appearance of expressions in the neonate, and the orderly maturation of expression in blind children directly supports the feedback hypothesis. It is one thing to muster evidence to support the plausibility of the hypothesis that facial-motor activity is important for emotion; it is quite another to support the more specific hypothesis that patterned facial activity creates specific, subjective emotions through sensory feedback.

Two procedures have been used to attempt direct tests of the feedback hypothesis. In some studies, the facial expressions of subjects have been directly manipulated; in others, subjects have been instructed to exaggerate or minimize expressive reactions. Both kinds of investigation assume that expressive changes cause (or mediate) subjective feeling.

An early study by Pasquarelli and Bull (1951) supported James's (1890/1950) suggestion that expressions could block emotions but did not show that expressions could create feelings. While in a hypnotic trance, a subject was instructed to contract specific facial muscles as the experimenter touched them with a pointer. Once the expression was established, the subject was told not to move. He was then instructed to feel an emotion (but not to make an expression) that required an expressive-motor pattern either opposite or similar to that in which he had been locked. None of the subjects felt the suggested emotion when its facial pattern was opposite to the pattern molded under hypnosis. Thus, the earlier facial pattern blocked the emergence of the newer feeling.

Laird (1974) and Izard, Kidd, and Kotsch (undated) have attempted to create feelings in subjects by touching specific muscles on their faces and instructing the subjects to contract them. Like Pasquarelli and Bull (1951), these investigators avoided the use of words such as *smile* or *frown* to minimize the experimenter's demands to report specific emotions. The manipulation of the facial pose was crossed with a second variable, exposure to pictures whose contents should stimulate an emotion that might or might not be related to the pose. After the subject was set in a pose and exposed to a picture, he or she completed a mood-adjective checklist. These investigators found an association between expression and mood; specifically, negative and aggressive moods elicited by a picture were slightly to moderately enhanced by manipulated frowns, and elated moods were accentuated, although to a smaller degree, by experimentally established smiles.

The second set of experiments attempted to test the same hypothesis by using instructions to achieve expressive change. For example, Leventhal and Mace (1970) produced very large differences in positive expression among grade-school children shown a slapstick movie. They told some groups to feel free to laugh during the movie so that the experimenters could obtain a good recording of children's laughter and told other groups not to laugh so that they could obtain a good recording of the film sound-track. Lanzetta and Kleck and their associates (Lanzetta, Cartwright-Smith, & Kleck, 1976) used a negative stimulus (a series of electric shocks of varying intensity) to conduct similar studies. They told their subjects either to express or to hide their feelings so that an observer would (or would not) be able to judge the strength of the shock from their expressions. The data from these studies are not consistent with a simple feedback hypothesis. Leventhal and Mace (1970) found substantial sex differences. Female subjects gave more favorable subjective ratings to funny films when their expressive behavior was exaggerated by instructions, whereas the opposite occurred with men. The same results were obtained by several other investigators (Cupchik & Leventhal, 1974; Young & Frye, 1966). The Lanzetta and Kleck studies (Lanzetta et al., 1976), in contrast, are fairly consistent in showing direct associations between expressiveness and electrodermal measures of "emotionality" (or arousal). For example, both expressions and electrodermal activity are generally lower in the hidden-expression conditions and higher in the shown-expression conditions. Ratings of shock intensity do not consistently vary in association with the manipulations of expression.

What do these two sets of studies tell us about expressive behavior and subjective feeling? The first and most substantial finding is that investigators were far better able to alter subjects' expressive behavior than to modify their reports of subjective feeling. Changes in mood (e.g., Izard et al., undated; Laird, 1974), in ratings of films and cartoons (Cupchik & Leventhal, 1974; Leventhal & Cupchik, 1975; Leventhal & Mace, 1970), and in ratings of shocks (Kleck, Vaughan, Cartwright-Smith, Vaughan, Colby & Lanzetta, 1976; Lanzetta et al., 1976) were relatively small despite very large changes in expression. Feelings and judgments seem to be strongly tied to the stimulus—the shock level, the film, or the picture (see also Schachter & Wheeler, 1962). Second, it is clear that expressiveness is not always positively associated with subjective feeling. This is seen in the studies of humor conducted by me and my students (Cupchik & Leventhal, 1974; Leventhal & Cupchik, 1975, 1976; Leventhal & Mace, 1970) and in several of the conditions of the Lanzetta et al. studies (1976), for example, when subjects were practicing hiding or expressing emotion before being televised.

There are at least four arguments that could be made from these findings: (1) One might say that the studies failed to test the hypothesis that facial feedback is necessary for subjective feeling. This argument has been advanced by Hagar and Ekman (1981). (2) One might alter the hypothesis and suggest that the feedback is from some place other than the facial muscles (Tomkins, 1980). (3) One could conclude that the hypothesis is incorrect and that facial feedback and the facial motor system have little or nothing to do with subjective emotion. (4) One might suggest that while the facial-motor system is important for creating feelings, its operation is more complex than a simple feedback model would have us believe.

To appraise the feedback hypothesis adequately, we should carefully examine the logic of these studies. We can then turn to an alternative, feed-forward hypothesis.

2. Appraising the Feedback Hypothesis

We do not have to adopt absurdly rigid standards to maintain that the studies just reviewed generally fail to test the feedback hypothesis. In nearly all instances, the findings are correlational, and we cannot tell whether facial expression, feeling, or a third variable is responsible for the observed changes (Buck, 1980). Correlation is not causation. This is true whether the correlation is between the means of a set of dependent measures across experimental conditions or between scores across subjects within a condition. The studies by Lanzetta and his associates (1976) show a positive association between expression and autonomic indicators across treatments, but they do not show or even test the hypothesis that changes in expression cause changes in subjective feeling. This conclusion is no more reasonable than the conclusion that negative correlations of expression and autonomic response in studies of individual differences reflect some type of causal hydrodynamic process (Jones, 1950; Lanzetta & Kleck, 1970; Notarius & Levenson, 1979). Although their hypothesis may be right, their experiments do not test this hypothesis.

The experiments directly manipulating facial muscle response fare no better in testing the feedback hypothesis because they fail to rule out alternative ways in which expressive change may produce change in mood reports (see Buck, 1980). The procedure (manipulating single muscles and not asking for smiles and frowns) may avoid suggesting or demanding emotional reports, and the use of control subjects who heard the instructions may rule out a direct path from instructions to moods. This control, however, does not rule out somewhat less plausible though possible alternatives, such as subjects reporting mood change in response to the effortfulness of facial muscle change and not to its pattern or subjects recognizing the patterns that automatically stimulate a memory schema that creates the emotion.

Given the equivocal data and the difficulty of establishing adequate tests, we might expect investigators to conclude that the feedback hypothesis is incorrect (e.g., Buck, 1980; McCaul, Holmes, & Solomon, 1982; Tourangeau & Ellsworth, 1979). However, advocates of a hypothesis do not readily accept its demise (Kuhn, 1962). Tomkins (1980) has suggested that feedback is from the vasculature in the skin of the face and not from muscle action. Another defense has been that feedback is produced by invisible, micromomentary, expressive reactions whose minute changes generate subjective feeling states (e.g., Haggard & Isaacs, 1966). Schwartz and his associates recorded electromyogram (EMG) activity at specific muscle sites (corrugator, frontalis, masseter, and depressor) and have identified muscle patterns that distinguish between moods of sadness, anger, happiness, and a typical day's feelings, though no visible expressive changes were associated with the EMG results (Schwartz *et al.*, 1976). They also found that the happy pattern was attenuated in depressed individuals; when the subject's depression improved, the happy pattern became clearer (Schwartz, Fair, Mandel, Salt, Mieske, & Klerman, 1978).

However, this line of defense cannot protect the feedback hypothesis against four key problems: (1) The new evidence for the hypothesis is still correlational, and some other factors may mediate the reported associations (as yet there is no evidence for the vasculature hypothesis suggested by Tomkins (1980); (2) substantial changes in expression often fail to relate to substantial change in subjective feelings; (3) the changes observed in microexpressiveness precede changes in subjective reports by days or weeks (Schwartz *et al.*, 1978); and (4) the hypothesis is not consistent with clinical neurological data.

The failure to square with clinical neurological data is a serious blow to the feedback hypothesis. Investigators have typically used clinical reports to examine the relationship between patterned expressive behavior and subjective emotional states (e.g., James, 1890/1950, p. 445). Although the concerns of the practitioner may lead to sketchy and sometimes ambiguous reports, data obtained by clinical neurologists with a clear grasp of the contrasting implications of the Darwinian (1872/1904) and Jamesian (1890/1950) theses indicate that: (1) subjective emotions are present in patients lacking spontaneous facial expression; and (2) subjective emotions are absent in individuals showing extraordinarily intense expressive reactions. The first conclusion is based on data showing that patients completely lacking facial expression can still have a rich subjective life, as in the case of the patient with facial diplegia (absence of expressive-motor movement) who comments, "his greatest misfortune [that he was] forced to be joyful or sad without making any demonstration of his feelings to his fellow creatures" (Romberg, 1853, cited in S. A. K. Wilson, 1924, p. 315).

Data for the second statement come from the large number of patients who spontaneously and "at the slightest provocation" burst into intense laughter or crying without an appropriate accompanying subjective affect. This is seen in cases of double hemiplegia, pseudobulbar paralysis, and multiple sclerosis (S. A. K. Wilson, 1924, p. 300). More recent reviews by Ironside (1956) and Brown (1967) reinforce Wilson's observation. It now seems abundantly clear that subjective feelings arise in the absence of overt expressive behavior and fail to arise in its presence.

Given the clinical observations, it seems that there is no alternative but to reject a simple feedback hypothesis. Rejecting the feedback hypothesis, however, is not equivalent to denying involvement of expressive-motor mechanisms in the generation of subjective feelings. There are occasions when laughter "makes" us happy and tears make us sad, just as there are occasions when they do the opposite (Laird, in press). Abandoning this latter hypothesis would again separate the study of expression and emotional communication from that of subjective feelings. I believe that some kind of motor mechanism is involved in generating emotional experience. I will try to provide an initial guess as to its structure.

3. The Feed-Forward Hypothesis

It is important to remember that the feedback hypothesis was intended primarily to account for the rapid appearance and disappearance of specific subjective feelings and not for the production of longer lasting emotions and mood states. My analysis attempts to account for the same phenomena but avoids the pitfalls of assuming that feelings are a direct product of feedback from expression.

The mechanism was first suggested by the findings of our studies in which subjects rated the funniness of cartoons that were viewed and judged either in the presence or in the absence of audience laughter (Cupchik & Leventhal, 1974). Some subjects were asked to monitor their expressive behavior; they then rated these reactions before judging the cartoons. For female subjects, it was predicted and found that the observation and rating of one's own expressive behavior diminished the positive effects of audience laughter on the cartoon ratings. A similar finding has been reported showing that self-observation (by mirrors) can inhibit the inducement of emotion by suggestion (Scheier, Carver, & Gibbons, 1979).

This prediction regarding the effect of self-monitoring was based on the following assumptions: (1) Subjects' expressive behaviors can contribute to their feelings. (2) Expressive reactions create feelings only when they are spontaneous or involuntary (Leventhal, 1974a). (3) Hearing audience laughter intensifies spontaneous laughter. (4) The stimulus (the cartoon) combines with the feedback from the exaggerated laughter to create an emotion only when the combination occurs preattentively. (5) Increased expressiveness adds to the rating of the cartoons only when conditions 2, 3, and 4 are met (i.e., when laughter has been intensified, spontaneous, and combined preattentively with the cartoon). (6) Self-monitoring of expression disrupts these conditions by making the laughter voluntary and conscious.

It is, of course, impossible for a single experiment to verify so long a list of assumptions. The results, however, were consistent with them. Female subjects who monitored their own expressions gradually lost sight of differences in stimulus quality, suggesting that monitoring self-expressiveness disrupted both the automatic (nonvoluntary) preattentive integration of the feedback with the stimulus and the feelings and made the rating task confusing. Responses to the postexperimental questionnaire supported this interpretation. Because self-monitoring also increased expressiveness, it was clear that the reduced ratings of funniness did not occur because self-monitoring inhibited the expression of motor reactions and feelings, as was hypothesized in the Lanzetta *et al.* (1976) studies.

In a report published in *Nature*, Weiskrantz, Elliott, and Darlington (1971) confirm the hypothesis that feedback from peripheral stimulation has quite different effects on feeling, depending on whether it is generated by voluntary or by involuntary behavior. They exposed subjects to three tickling conditions: one where the bottom of the subject's foot was tickled by a stick moved by the experimenter, another where the stick was moved by the subject, and a third where the subject's hand rested on the experimenter's hand as the latter moved the stick. Reports of ticklishness were highest when the experimenter moved the stick.

Another type of data that suggested the feed-forward model of emotion came from studies of the effects of eye movements on visual perception. Eye movements generate movement of the retinal image, and movement of the retinal image can be seen as a movement in the outer world. In most instances, however, the outer world remains stable despite movement of the image. The stability is due to an interaction between a motor response set and the visual pattern (Gyr, 1972; Von Holst, 1954). When a person intends to move his or her eyes and then does so, the intentional set generates both an eye movement and a feed-forward motor signal that anticipates the new retinal location of the environmental projection and cancels out the perception of environmental movement. In contrast, externally generated pushes on the eyeball produce movement of the retinal image, which is seen as movement in the outer world (Von Holst, 1954).

All three types of data reviewed above—for humor, tickling, and eye movements—suggest that intentional movement creates feed-forward motor signals that anticipate feedback generated by changes in outer stimuli; that is, audible canned laughter, tactile stimulation, or retinal image movement. If the outer stimulation is unanticipated, it evokes a spontaneous motion—laughter, ticklishness, or visual movement. The three together suggest the following model for expressive behavior and emotion. The model is shown in Fig. 3. It was constructed to reflect the following assumptions:

1. There are separate volitional and spontaneous controls in the expressive-motor system. Subjective experience confirms this division of motor activity into spontaneous and volitional acts, and it is the spontaneous, expressive-motor process that generates the impulse to feel an emotion. Indeed, the term emotion is often used to mean external stimulus control in contrast to internal volitional control (Peters, 1970, pp. 187–203). The neurological literature previously cited (Brown, 1967; Geschwind, 1975; Ironside, 1956) also confirms the distinction.

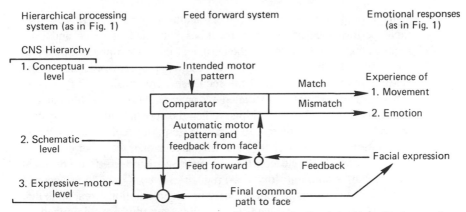

Fig. 3.   The feed-forward system. Each of the three levels of the hierarchical processing system (See Fig. 2) generate a motor pattern: the conceptual, an intentional-motor pattern; the schematic; and expressive-motor, an automatic-motor pattern. The two types of pattern enter a comparator. If they match, the experience is of an intended movement. If they mismatch, the experience is of a spontaneous emotion. (The type of emotion depends on the motor pattern.) The intended and automatic pattern compete for control of overt expression via the final common path to the face. Facial feedback enters the feed-forward loop where it can initiate as well as intensify (its usual effect) emotional experience.

2. The central nervous system contains all of the basic mechanisms neces-sary for emotional experience. By moving emotion into the central ner-vous system, where Cannon (1927) placed it, we need no longer puzzle over inconsistencies between outer expression and inner feeling. This does not deny the access of peripheral feedback to the central mecha-nism; it merely asserts that the necessary machinery for emotional expe-rience is centrally located. More specifically, the model postulates that the spatial and temporal patterning of emotional expression is centrally programmed and that separate programs exist for both spontaneous and volitional reactions (Geschwind, 1975).

Psychologists have historically given excessive weight to peripheral cuing hypotheses, perhaps because introspection confirms the signifi-cance of body cues (e.g., the bodily upset that follows emotional epi-sodes) for behavior. It is no surprise that an introspectively oriented psychologist such as James (1884) placed so much emphasis on pe-ripheral feedback for emotion. The same emphasis is seen in such behav-ioral concepts as response chaining (Hull, 1943) and response-produced cues (Dollard & Miller, 1950). These concepts exist in part because the fear of mentalistic concepts drove the behaviorists to the periphery. However, Lashley (1951) pointed out long ago that complex serial per-formances could not be carried out by a regulatory mechanism relying on signals going from center to periphery and back again at every step. The rapid performance of complex reactions patterned in space and time requires that signals be sent to the periphery in an appropriate spatial and temporal order by a central program. These programs encompass the starting and the end points of the sequence (Greenwald, 1970).

3. Emotional experience is mediated by an interaction of volitional and spontaneous central motor scripts. When the spontaneous motor system overrides the control of the voluntary system, we feel emotion. When the volitional system overrides the spontaneous one, we experience controlled action. It should come as no surprise, therefore, that volitional actions can be emotion- (distress-) reducing, even if they do not control outer stimulus events. Spontaneously provided emotional reactions that intensify the distress induced by a noxious stimulus are minimized by volitional performance (Geer, Davidson, & Gatchel, 1970; Weiss, 1970).

4. The interaction between the systems may involve a feed-forward mechanism. The basic assumption here is that external (or internal) stimuli provoke expressive-motor or schematic processing and that this processing generates an automatic motor response template that sends a pattern of motor signals (laughter, tears, frowning, etc.) in two different directions: (a) to the motor controls for the periphery (e.g., the face, where emotion can be displayed) and (b) to a comparator in the volitional motor system—a feed-forward path. The signals sent to the comparator over this feed-forward route are matched to a motor template generated in the voluntary system. If the spatial and temporal features of the two motor systems agree, the comparison will be experienced as a voluntary movement; that is, the information coming from the comparator cannot be distinguished from the completion of the instructions for an intended movement, and it is felt as such.

5. The feed-forward comparison process is automatic and preattentive. This point emphasizes that people are unaware of the steps in information processing that lead to the generation of expressive-reaction patterns and the comparison of the feed-forward signal with the volitional representation (Mandler, 1975; Nisbett & Wilson, 1977). Usually only the output of the comparison (i.e., emotion or willed movement) is conscious. Efforts to control emotion tend to be directed toward blocking out the stimulus that provokes automatic processing or inhibiting the expressive reactions that result from it. Neither alternative directly influences stimulus coding on the comparison of the two motor templates. Damage to the volitional system can lead to expressive display without emotion (as seen in clinical literature) because either the comparison process can no longer take place or its results are no longer accessible to awareness (Brown, 1967).

6. Facial feedback can intensify and sustain emotional experience when it arrives at the comparison point. Therefore, feedback can serve the same functions as the feed-forward signal from the automatic processing system, but it is not necessary for emotional experience.

The model (Fig. 1) has several advantages in addition to the obvious one of freeing subjective feeling states from direct ties to peripheral expressive-motor activity. One of the most important is the suggestion that volitional performance of automatic expressive actions can, as Cannon (1927) suggested, bring action under volitional control and eliminate emotion. This is critical in accounting for the humor data generated by Cupchik and Leventhal (1974) and Leventhal and Mace (1970), the tickling data of Weiskrantz *et al.* (1971), and a variety of clinical data suggesting that voluntary performance of emotionally motivated behaviors can remove these acts from emotional control. For example, deliberate stuttering has been recommended as a procedure for controlling stuttering caused by emotional anxiety (Dunlap, 1933). Fear reduction through desensitization (Lang & Lazovik, 1963) and guided participation (Bandura, Blanchard, & Ritter, 1969) also can be interpreted within this framework because both involve voluntary production of behaviors (images, approaching snakes, etc.) that are typically controlled by automatic emotional reactions.

The feed-forward hypothesis provides a central mechanism by which motor system interactions mediate felt and expressed emotion. We must not forget, however, that this mechanism operates within a larger system. Feedback can contribute to and help activate this system. Moreover, we should not assume that one cannot feel emotion in the absence of a feed-forward motor discharge. Although feed-forward signals may frequently accompany emotional experience and may be sufficient to create emotion, they may not be necessary to produce emotion in the adult organism. The latter, weak hypothesis would hold that feeling could be directly experienced from the elicitation of schematic emotional memory, as in phantom pain. There is no need to choose between the strong and the weak hypotheses at this time, although the weaker version of the hypothesis appears more likely. Izard's (1979) concept of reafference is consistent with this weaker hypothesis.

C. VERBAL INFLUENCE ON SCHEMATIC AND EXPRESSIVE REACTION

Another critical system interaction is the effects of verbal symbols on the availability of emotional schemata. Although we have argued that schemata are analog structures and not associative networks, the links between conceptual memory and schemata may be best described in associative terms, and variables suggested by associative theory may affect these links. For example, the repetition of sentences that are affectively positive or negative may intensify schematic imagery and generate affective experience (Parke, Ewall, & Slaby, 1972). Once the conceptual (symbolic) system cues schematic and expressive-motor processes, the schematic system will automatically recruit affect-relevant imagery and stimulate still more affective responding. (See Leventhal & Nerenz, 1983, for a model describing such activity in the interpretation of body symptoms on illness.)

Because verbal responses cannot directly control emotional reactions, the most likely ways to achieve emotional control by self-instructions are to block out emotion-provoking stimuli in order to generate imagery opposite to the affect or to suppress unwanted expressive reactions and to replace them with contrary ones. Self-instructions to suppress expression may actually increase the discrepancy between volitional and feed-forward motor signals, resulting in the so-called laughter-in-church phenomenon, in which the suppression of expressive reactions intensifies subjective feelings. Suppression of emotion by blocking stimulation through denial, dissociation, or thinking positive thoughts can remove unwanted material from conscious awareness by increasing the salience of schemata opposite in emotional sign. An example is the reduction of pain and distress through the generation of positive affective imagery (Barber & Hahn, 1962). Research indicates, however, that the pain and distress return at original levels once a blocking strategy stops (see Ahles, Blanchard, & Leventhal, 1983; Shacham, 1979).

Emotional control can also be achieved by the alternative strategies of instructing oneself to monitor stimulus features in order to generate an objective or nonemotional schema or to change the interpretation of the stimulus (Leventhal, Brown, Shacham, & Engquist, 1979; Leventhal & Johnson, 1983; Leyens, Cisneros, & Hossay, 1976). In this case, volitional or conceptually controlled monitoring affect emotion by altering schematic memory structures. The strategy appears to work best when attention to noxious body sensations begins at low levels of stimulation, when there is a plausible nonthreatening interpretation of the sensory experience, and when attention drifts elsewhere subsequent to adaptation. If automatic schematic processing is altered, the changes produced by monitoring will last even when monitoring stops.

The choice of control procedure appears to be determined by conceptual rules (i.e., ideas about what will work). Unfortunately, these rules may not accurately reflect either the nature of the environment or the nature of emotional processing mechanisms at lower levels of the hierarchy. Thus, individuals may prefer emotion control strategies that are inadequate. We will see examples of this in the following section.

1. The Schematization Hypothesis

During the past 15 years, two sets of studies of pain reaction have appeared in the psychological literature that provide ample illustration of how blocking and assimilation of information can alter emotional distress. Effects produced by both approaches can be conceptualized within the present framework. Pain cannot be understood or treated if it is conceptualized as a purely sensory system (Beecher, 1959; Melzack & Wall, 1970). Both neurological and behavioral data suggest that the emotional component of pain is generated parallel to the informational signals from the noxious stimulus and that both types of signal are integrated in emotional schemata or perceptual memories prior to experience (Leventhal & Everhart, 1979).

Nathan (1962) reports an ingenious demonstration by Hutchins and Reynolds consistent with this schematization hypothesis. They applied a nonpainful electrical stimulus to the trigeminal nerve of patients who had dental work weeks earlier under either nitrous oxide or injections of novocaine. For the patients who had received nitrous oxide, the electrical stimulus to the nerve re-created the pain of having one's teeth drilled because nitrous oxide works by reducing emotional distress without affecting the sensory signals sent to the brain. The electrical stimulus did *not* re-create the pain of drilling for patients who had received novocaine because novocaine blocks the transmission of impulses from the site of drilling to the central nervous system and prevents the formation of a pain schemata.

Using an analysis similar to that just presented, Johnson (1973) reasoned that a noxious stimulus could be experienced as either highly painful or mildly painful, depending on whether it was integrated with a schema of pain and distress or integrated in a nonthreatening schema of the sensory features of a stimulus. To encourage an objective sensory schematization, Johnson gave subjects in one of her experimental conditions detailed information about the sensory features of the stimulus by describing the numbness, aching, pins and needles, and discoloration of the fingers that would be caused by ischemia induced by a blood pressure cuff. Subjects given the sensory information reported significantly less distress during ischemic stimulation than did control subjects given a description of the experimental procedure. Two additional experiments showed that the difference could not be accounted for by differences in expectations of harm, preexposure fear level, or efforts to distract or turn away from the noxious stimulus. It was concluded that sensory information instructed subjects to monitor and detect the features of the stimulus in order to generate an objective schema of the noxious experience. This schema then captured subsequent inputs and prevented their coding into pain–distress schemata.

An alternative interpretation of the Johnson (1973) study is that subjects did not become startled or aroused when the stimulus finally impinged on them because they had accurate expectations about how it would feel. Epstein (1973) has suggested that accuracy of expectations alone does not protect a person against distress and disturbance during stimulus impact, although it may aid in coping with the stimulus situation afterward. The first of three studies by Leventhal *et al.* (1979) supported the first part of Epstein's suggestion. It compared distress reports during exposure to cold pressor stimulation for four groups of subjects. Subjects were given either sensory information about the cold pressor experience or procedural information about the cold pressor task, and then half of each group received a pain warning. The accuracy hypothesis predicted the lowest levels of distress for subjects given both sensory information and the pain warning because these subjects had the most accurate information. The schematization hypothesis, in contrast, predicted that a pain warning would facilitate the coding of the noxious input in terms of an emotional pain–distress schema. According to this position, reduction of distress should only occur when sensory information is given without a pain warning so that subjects form a schema of the stimulus features that does not incorporate pain and emotional distress. The results showed distress reduction only in groups given sensory information without a pain warning, and all other groups were virtually identical. Thus, the schematization hypothesis was supported (see also Hall & Stride, 1954; Staub & Kellett, 1972).

Another feature of the data that strengthens this interpretation is that the distress ratings initially climbed to approximately equally high levels in all of the groups before group differences appeared. Thus, the lower distress levels for the sensory-informed groups occurred because of the very much lower distress ratings in the last half of the cold pressor period. It takes time to form a new schema of the noxious stimulus, so the reduction of distress does not occur right away. Experiments 2 and 3, conducted by Shacham (Leventhal *et al.*, 1979), further corroborated the schematization hypothesis by showing that attending to the sensations during the first half of the immersion was as effective as attending throughout, whereas attending during the second half, after distress was activated, was of no value. Reduction of the emotional response was dependent on early attention to the physical sensations (see also Epstein, Rosenthal, & Szpiler, 1978).

2. Schematization versus Dissociative Strategies

Several new studies suggest clear differences between cognitive strategies, which take in stimulation and construct new schemata, and dissociative strategies, which block stimulus information and do not alter schemata. Shacham (1979) found that forming a clear image of the hand while it was immersed in cold water led, in time, to significant reductions in reported pain in comparison to a control condition. Her results were strong, however, only for subjects who scored high on tests of vividness of visual imagery. Again, the pain reduction effects were substantial on the second of a pair of cold pressor trials, even though the subjects generated hand imagery only on the first trial. By contrast, another group of subjects, who were told to think of the ice water as pleasant during the first trial but to do nothing during the second, showed pain only when they actively tried to block out the distressful stimulus. During the second trial, this group showed the same level of distress as did control subjects and more distress than did imagery subjects. The blocking (dissociative) strategy does not produce lasting pain–distress reduction. Studies of hypnotic analgesia highlight this contrast; hypnotic analgesia produces immediate pain–distress reductions of great magnitude, but these reductions vanish when the analgesia is removed (Hilgard, 1969; Knox, Morgan, & Hilgard, 1974; Lenox, 1970).

Recent research (Ahles *et al.*, 1983; McCaul & Haugtvedt, 1982; Reinhardt, 1979) demonstrates the need for a substantially long exposure in order to achieve distress reduction by sensation monitoring and shows sensation monitoring to be superior to blocking, with the passage of time. Ahles *et al.* (1983) also show that sensation-monitoring effects are durable even when subjects are no longer following monitoring instructions. Thus, automatic or preattentive schematic processing (a "lower" level of processing) has been altered by conceptual (voluntarily controlled) sensation monitoring. Interestingly, both McCaul and Haugtvedt (1982) and Ahles *et al.* (1983) show that subjects will prefer to distract rather than to monitor sensations when given the choice. What we have come to prefer may not correspond to what is actually best.

In summary, there is ample evidence that preparing people for a noxious stimulus by giving them sensory information and asking them to monitor their sensations can lead to marked drops in reported distress when these instructions are combined with a benign or neutral stimulus interpretation. Distress is reduced when sensation monitoring begins at low levels of stimulation, but the decrease in felt distress only appears in the latter half of the cold pressor trial or in a second trial after a period during which schema formation is presumed to occur. These outcomes seem quite different from those obtained with cognitive strategies, which call for dissociative blocking or reversal of thoughts, such as ignoring the stimulus, hypnotic analgesia, or thinking of it in a positive and pleasant way. The results are also more complex than what would be expected if distress reduction were simply a process of labeling autonomic or sensory information; both labeling and hypnosis should lead to immediate rather than delayed effects, and neither should reduce distress on subsequent exposures if removed. The effectiveness of monitoring sensations with benign expectations is undoubtedly dependent on the experience of the stimulus confirming the objective schema. The sensations produced by cold pressor do reach a peak and then diminish because of sensory adaptation. The adaptation checks against the neutral schema and further strengthens this objective schematization because the coded stimulus recruits less emotional response and lowers distress.

There is evidence suggesting that focusing on or analyzing the perceptual features of stimuli is an effective way of controlling emotional states other than pain. For example, Leyens *et al.* (1976) found significantly less aggression (in the form of delivering electric shocks) toward an insulting partner from subjects who had analyzed the aesthetic properties of slides designed to stimulate aggression than from subjects exposed to these same slides without an analytic de-centering set. Lazarus and associates found similar reductions in emotional response for subjects instructed to adopt an analytic or intellectualizing set to a stressful movie of a subincision rite by viewing it as though they were anthropologists (Speisman, Lazarus, Mordkoff, & Davison, 1964). These sets closely resemble those generated by sensory information and attention instructions and contrast with sets aimed at inducing denial, blocking, or avoidance of stimulation (e.g., see Lazarus & Alfert, 1964).

D. INTEGRATION OF THE PROCESSING SYSTEM

I have reviewed a number of interactions between the various components of the emotion-processing system. The feed-forward mechanism was formulated to deal with interactions between automatic and volitional motor mechanisms. To generate emotional states, both the automatic feed-forward motor reactions and the peripheral sensory feedback from expressive responses in the facial-motor system are compared to central voluntary motor templates. These effects are largely "bottom-up" phenomena, although the interaction can also proceed in a to-down manner; that is, the individual can ready an anticipatory volitional motor response and cancel the emotional property of either the feed-forward or feedback signal.

The focusing of attention to sensory features of noxious stimulation, on the other hand, is clearly a top-down phenomenon. Here it is the conceptual system that processes instructions and that then focuses attention in order to facilitate construction of a nonemotional schema. The volitional attentional act involves both peripheral motor and mental adjustments, or the directing and concentrating of attention on specific stimulus properties. Blocking strategies represent an alternative top-down approach to sensory input, and their effect is quite different from that seen with the attention to sensory features. Top-down strategies may alter emotional processing in other ways. The most obvious is problem solving, in which the conceptual or volitional direction of attention and of action removes the stimulus that provokes affect. Problem solving may be precluded, however, in environments in which the individual can exert relatively little control. One example is the work setting (Pearlin & Schooler, 1978). I focused on the two prior types of interaction rather than on problem solving because coping strategies such as sensation monitoring and blocking illustrate the difference between conscious or controlled processing and automatic or uncontrolled processing. They also show how controlled processing may produce effects at the automatic level that are inconsistent with consciously held expectations.

My discussion of the three levels of perceptual–motor processing also suggested that the emotion system is asymmetrical and that bottom-up effects cannot always be reversed by top-down processes (and, perhaps, vice versa). Indeed, in most instances automatic processes appear to be dominant in the generation of emotion. Achieving voluntary control seems to require special decisions (e.g., decisions to monitor specific sensations or to be ready to express a feeling before it is provoked by an external source) to counter the organizational thrust inherent in automatic processing. The asymmetry suggests that a complex nonassociative mechanism may be at work in the integration of processing across sensory–motor, schematic, and conceptual levels.

1. Moods (Neurochemical Events) and the Integration of Emotion

There are a number of findings that point to the presence of a mechanism for binding perceptions to emotional motor reactions in the creation of affective schemata and for integrating perception, expressive reactions, and affective schemata in the construction of temporary emotional states. First, active attentional effort is necessary to counter the integration mechanism so as to separate emotion from perception and to form new objective schemata (e.g., the pain studies on schematization of noxious stimuli). Second, substantial individual differences exist in the degree to which emotions are attached to situations or to one's own actions (Hare, 1970). Third, the segregation of memories by affective state appears to be similar to state-dependent memory, suggesting that integration occurs within a specific affective domain (see Paddeley, 1982; Bower, 1981; Bower & Cohen, 1982). Fourth, the suggestion of asymmetry among the processing levels (i.e., the swift upward impact of expressive-motor and schematic processing relative to the more complex downward action of conceptual to schematic and to expressive-motor action) suggests the existence of some type of complex integrative mechanism. And finally, separate integrative systems have been found in other perceptual systems; for example, the mechanism for binocular fusion is distinct from that for monocular perception (Wolfe, 1983).

I would guess that the integrative mechanism and that the process of integration are both attentional and neurochemical. Attentional processes play a critical role in bringing specific pieces of information to awareness at a common point in time and space. This is a key step for integration. Neurochemical processes, on the other hand, appear to be the base or envelope for integrating the components. Thus, specific neurotransmitter systems—for example, specific monoamines (serotonin, noradrenaline) or neuropeptides (dynorphin, leu-enkephalin, etc.)—integrate the units that generate specific moods, for example, euphoria, depression, and anxiety (Iversen, 1982; Maclean & Reichlin, 1981; vanPraag, 1982). Variation of the tonic levels in these systems, caused by alterations in production, uptake, or destruction of these neurotransmitters, appears to cause changes in mood. Differential activity in a neurotransmitter system not only alters specific moods; it tunes or sensitizes the schematic or the perceptual and motor traces related to that mood. Thus, although moods can be elicited by specific environmental events, their maintenance may depend upon the durability of changes in the balance of neurotransmitters that help sustain the mood. Emotions are quantitatively more intense than moods and based on activity in common neurochemical systems; but emotions also may be qualitatively different because they involve clear phasic discharges of automatic expressive-motor activity. Whether the motor reaction induces a subjective emotion beyond the neurochemically induced mood change will depend on the interaction of automatic and volitional processes as outlined in the feed-forward mechanism.

The speed and the duration of response of these neurochemical systems is sufficient to integrate the expressive reaction and its feed-forward process with perceptual impressions so as to build and sustain affective states and to generate emotional memory schemata from these episodes. Once schemata are formed, they function as perceptual memories of feelings and become part of feedback loops in settings in which mood sensitizes the schemata and the schemata and the expressive-motor sets help sustain mood (Beck, 1976). The distribution of these neurochemical substances throughout the body (e.g., the heart and gut) allows the peripheral machinery to interact with central nervous system processes to sustain and to amplify mood and to facilitate phasic emotional reactions.

2.   Culture and Language

Culture and language play a crucial role in the development of emotion (see Levy, in press), a role that is more clearly defined in the perceptual–motor model than in other emotion theories. Cognition-arousal models such as Schachter's (Schachter & Singer, 1962) gave culture and language the overwhelmingly key role in fixing the quality of emotion. The perceptual–motor model postulates that primary feelings are innate. But the model makes clear that culture and language play extremely important roles as determinants of attention and of the development of both affective schemata and propositional knowledge about affective experience and behavior. The existence of prewired or sensory–motor feelings and the concrete nature of emotion schemata generate special problems for culture. First, cultural and linguistic notions must match or fit preexisting structures, both to grab hold of and to shape these structures and to be accepted as plausible by the individual. Second, the multilevel nature of the processing system poses the opportunity for inconsistency in the way culture affects the individual because one processing level may match cultural definitions of feelings and their cause and another may not. The issues in this area are so numerous and so important that they deserve separate treatment. Hence, little more will be said about them in this chapter except for a few suggestions that I will make when discussing directions for future research.

VI.   New Directions in Emotion Theory

The perceptual–motor model incorporates many features of earlier theories such as those advanced by James (1884) and Schachter (1964) and provides a broad framework for the study of emotion. For example, James's (1884) hypothesis that autonomic arousal generates emotion is an example of bottom-up effects in which diffuse visceral activity serves as an automatic cue to emotion schemata whose history links them to autonomic activity. If, for example, socialization has discouraged overt behavioral responses to anger but has encouraged them to fear, autonomic arousal would be linked to fear and the individual would tend to experience fear when arousal is induced by ephinephrine or hypnotic suggestion (Marshall & Zimbardo, 1979; Maslach, 1979). Precisely which emotions or sets of emotions will be activated by autonomic arousal is an empirical and theoretical issue requiring study of socialization practices and the development of models that both identify the features of autonomic response that evoke emotion schemata and describe the similarity between the features of the schemata for different emotions.

The model also incorporates many aspects of Schachter's (Schachter & Singer, 1962) cognition-arousal theory, although it differs with it in important respects. The first and most important of the similarities is the postulate of an intimate connection between affective and cognitive processes. The most important of the differences is the perceptual–motor postulate that sensory–motor emotions are the basic entities integrated with cognition; emotion is not a product of the integration of an autonomic event with a cold cognition. Second, the perceptual–motor model differentiates between various types of cognitive processes and suggests different types of linkage between these cognitive processes and emotion. Defining the types of stimuli and cognitive decoders for different levels of emotion processing and describing how different types of cognition regulate or influence one another are major jobs for emotion theory.

A.   THE SEPARATION AND INTEGRATION
     OF COGNITION AND EMOTION

Zajonc (1980; Zajonc, Pietromonaco, & Bargh, 1982) has made the separation or integration of cognition and emotion a major issue for many emotion theorists. Zajonc appears to argue that emotional processes can be independent of and precede cognitive processing. His position has stimulated clinical psychologists to refocus interest on emotion (Rachman, 1980) and to rush to the defense of the cognitive affective link (Greenberg & Safran, in press; Lazarus, 1982).

It is difficult to see precisely what Zajonc (1980) has in mind when he proclaims the independence of emotion and cognition. He does not mean that emotion and cognition (i.e., perceptual responses to objective reality) are processed in parallel because he apparently rejects any similarity between his position and parallel models such as the one I presented in my summary in 1970 of the fear communication literature. His rejection may reflect the judgment that a parallel model assumes that the construction of objective and emotional reactions involves overlapping mechanisms (Leventhal, 1974b, 1979, 1980). Zajonc (1980) excludes such overlap by defining cognitive processes as conscious deliberate reasoning in contrast to emotional responding, which is defined as a separate form of automatic nonconscious processing. He supports this separation of affective and cognitive processing on the basis of a series of studies showing that frequent exposure to a stimulus will lead to higher ratings of it on a liking scale even though the subjects do not recognize the stimulus. It is difficult, of course, to understand how one can have an affective response to a stimulus without some type of recognitory reaction: Stimuli must be differentiated from one another if one of them is to elicit an emotional response and the others not. If this is the case, Zajonc's theory hinges on his particular way of labeling affective differentiations; he has decided they are noncognitive. There is, of course, nothing new about the finding that a stimulus may evoke independent (uncorrelated) verbal and autonomic reactions, though I know of no theorist who argues that this separation suggests that a cognitive process is not involved in both discriminations. The key issue is to better characterize the way in which the discrimination takes place and to see if the mechanisms involved in emotional discriminations are different from those involved in nonemotional discriminations of which the subject is also unaware. I would guess that the latter type of discriminative response is basic to the former.

Zajonc's (Zajonc, Pietromonaco, & Bargh, 1982) solution to this discrimination problem is the suggestion that affective discrimination involves a form of motor discrimination or motor memory. I have no difficulty with the idea that the liking reaction involves a motor reaction, but I cannot see how the motor reaction can be stimulus specific without some type of antecedent stimulus discrimination. In addition, Zajonc's formulation does not provide any insight into the nature of the motor process or suggest why it should be totally independent of motor and recognition processes involved in nonaffective perception, that is, why it is not cognitive. In summary, Zajonc's position exists as a distinctive statement on emotion only insofar as we accept his restricted definition of cognition, and his model contributes little to emotion theory. I do believe, however, that the experimental paradigm (repetition leading to liking) from which his theory emerged may help us to understand the nature of the automatic cognitive processes that generate liking reactions.

B. EMOTIONS AS NODES IN ASSOCIATIVE SPACE

One of the major challenges to emotion theory is how to represent emotion in memory. I have suggested that we must use at least three levels of representation: sensory–motor (innate level), schematic (perceptual memory of prior affective episodes), and conceptual (a propositional memory of ideas extracted from reflecting on emotion episodes). Bower and Cohen (1982) have suggested a similar division in which emotions and names or labels for emotion can be represented as separate nodes in an associative memory space. The distinction allows their computer model to generate emotion in response to stimulation and to talk about emotion with or without its activiation.

Bower and Cohen's (1982) model is significant for its richness of detail. Like the perceptual–motor model elaborated in the present chapter, it suggests a wide range of questions and specific hypotheses for experimental testing. There are a number of areas in which comparison between the two may prove to be of special interest and stimulate significant research. First, both models assume that emotions are recorded in memory; that is, they postulate that we store and retrieve the experience of an affect. Is this a reasonable assumption? If it is, how should we represent the emotional memory: as a node that is associatively linked to expressive, autonomic, and verbal nodes, as Bower and Cohen would suggest (1982, p. 298), or as a unified schema whose components are stored in a common physical location (Leventhal, 1979, 1980)? I do not believe that the memory of an emotion (e.g., of the subjective experience) is tied to its autonomic and expressive components with the same type of link that ties it to its verbal label. If the links were identical in nature and merely unequal in strength, I would expect greater symmetry of control between verbal and nonverbal aspects of emotional reactions. Whereas verbal controls can be strengthened with practice and verbal labels undoubtedly play a critical role in the articulation of the subtle emotions found in mature adults, it would be worthwhile to explore the difference between these types of connections and their implications for the socialization and control of emotions. I also think we could learn much by investigating the effects of verbal labeling on the differentiation of affective experience and facial expression.

A second pair of contrasting hypotheses emerges respecting the nature of state-dependent memory. Bower and Cohen's (1982) model suggests that the enhanced recall of events by emotion manipulations (i.e., the improved recall of material learned in a specific mood when recall is conducted in that same mood) is due to the associative linkage between the learned verbal materials with an emotion node. The perceptual–motor model, on the other hand, suggests that the enhanced recall also may be due to the activation or modulation of neural sectors by mood-specific neurotransmitter systems. If the first of these hypotheses is true, mood enhancements or mood decrements in recall would be proportional to variables that affect associative strength, for example, frequency of association, similarity of content, and so forth. If the second hypothesis is correct, emotional effects on memory should be relatively indiscriminate, with the arousal of a specific mood or emotion leading to the retrieval of a wide range of images and ideas that are mood congruent but otherwise unrelated. A clear test of these hypotheses may prove difficult because mood-assisted recall in most everyday situations will reflect some combination of associative and modulating effects (e.g., see Janis's description of the effects of threat on memory for remote events, 1958).

C. ELICITATION OF EMOTION

With but a few exceptions (e.g., Tomkins, 1962), emotion theories have had relatively little to say about the elicitation of emotion. What is particularly lacking is a theoretically organized description of the stimulus attributes that evoke specific emotions; that is, what attributes are key for the evocation of different emotion states. Many efforts in this area are so abstract that they are of little help in generating specific operations, though they may point toward sets of variables potentially related to the onset of specific emotions. For example, Plutchik (1980), from a "psychoevolutionary" point of view, and Kemper (1978), from a social structural point of view, focus on variables such as group membership and hierarchy or status as causes of pairs of emotions, such as approach and avoidance or anger and fear. Other theorists discuss equally abstract, though more process-oriented variables, such as interruption as causes of emotion (e.g., Mandler & Watson, 1966). The greatest degree of operational specificity exists in studies of specific emotions such as anger (Berkowitz, 1983) and depression (Beck, 1976; Brown & Harris, 1978; Depue, 1979).

It is clear that substantial theoretical and empirical effort is needed to go beyond our current commonsense approaches to the creation of emotional states. At least two quite different types of development seem possible. First, we can generate better organized descriptions relating specific emotions to specific meanings. I am using the term meaning in its broadest possible sense, that is, ranging from automatically perceived meaning to more conscious and deliberately generated meaning. Such studies would improve our understanding of the perception and interpretation of situations involved in affects such as depression and anger and generate theoretical and empirical analyses of the developmental histories of the prototypical experiences that elicit these emotions, for example, as in the study of attachment and loss attempted by Brown and Harris (1978) or Solomon (1974). What I am suggesting, therefore, is an effort to identify the stimuli that are critical for the earliest elicitation of specific emotions. This would require identifying the features of the stimuli that are coded in schematic memory and activated in new experiences of the emotion and then identifying the features that the individual conceptualizes as the sources of his fear, anger, joy or depression. I do not believe that the successive recodings of sensory–motor processes in the schematic record and of both in the conceptual record is a random process. Subsequent elicitation of an affect and its recoding is dependent upon prior codings. One important task is to describe this development. The job will not be easy because many if not most of the stimuli involved in early affect codes are expressive and visual rather than verbal.

Cognitive theorists would define the above task as describing the knowledge base that is interwoven with specific emotions. This definition of the problem points to at least one difference between the perceptual–motor model and the computer model advanced by Bower and Cohen (1982). Both models suggest that cognition elicits emotion and that emotion can alter cognition. Bower and Cohen (1982) claim, however, that the effects of emotion on cognition appear largely in recall and not recognition tasks because adaptive demands require that the sensory–perceptual system provide a relatively accurate picture of external reality uninfluenced by our affective states. Although I do not take issue with this bias, the model I have proposed suggests that acquired knowledge is represented in at least two ways: as schemata and as conceptual propositions. Hence, I can see no reason why emotion should not influence recognition tasks if the stimuli are heavily weighted with cues relevant to emotion schemata (e.g., pictures of faces or verbal utterances *rich in affective expression*). Bower (1981) rules out mood effects on recognition memory on the basis of a study that failed to find mood enhancement effects on the recognition of photographs of faces (initially viewed under specific mood states) taken from a high school yearbook. Because yearbook pictures tend to be rather nonexpressive, the finding is not surprising. Safer and Gage (Gage, 1983) are finding mood effects on recognition when the facial stimuli are rich in emotional expression. (See also the interesting study by Orr & Lanzetta, 1980.) In summary, it is clear that much systematic work remains to be done on the elicitation of emotion. This will require models that deal with how knowledge is represented and organized in the system and how emotion is integrated with it.

Chemical interventions, including diet, represent a second major way of influencing emotion. One unfortunate legacy of the Jamesian (1890/1950) and Schachterian (Schachter & Singer, 1962) views of emotion has been the focus on autonomic system activity as the physiological core of emotion and the belief that the physical system is relatively nondifferentiated and unable to support and define different affective states. From the perspective of the perceptual–motor model and from what is known of endocrine function, there is little reason to expect a peripheral injection of adrenaline to stimulate a central neural emotion process. Although the injection may speed heart rate and create emotionlike activity in various organs, it would not be at all surprising if exogenously induced adrenalin actually reduced the production of pituitary and hypothalamic releasing substances related to emotional arousal because most systemic changes in the levels of autonomic and endocrine substances generate feedback to curtail central neural production of the substances. If this were the case, the central neural changes would reduce the likelihood of evoking affective schemata and the individual would indeed be puzzled by the experience of active peripheral machinery without accompanying subjective affect or relevant cognitions.

The hypothalamic pituitary axis is extremely complex, including multiple endocrines and many peptides which have been implicated in emotion and mood change, and there is a growing body of data suggesting that endocrines and peptides have powerful affects on moods and emotion. For example, data from our laboratory are showing very clear relationships between steroid injections and the production of fairly intense states of euphoria and the suppression of aversive affective states such as nausea–disgust. Direct stimulation of emotion through such routes should provide further insight into the nature of affective processes and the impact of emotion on the organization of knowledge systems.

D. EMOTION AND INTERACTION

Most psychological treatments of emotion focus on the individual's experience or expression of emotion and its consequences for his or her later behavior. Emotion is conceptualized as a respondent, an automatically elicited event whose underpinnings lie in individual cognition and individual psychophysiology. Social psychological studies from this frame of reference focus on the way individuals cope with emotion (e.g., Folkman & Lazarus, 1980; Leventhal, 1970; Pearlin & Schooler, 1978) and the way emotion is perceived or read by observers (e.g., Ekman & Friesen, 1982; Hagar & Ekman, 1981). Emotions, however, are *operants* as well as respondents. They are affected by their consequences, and they are coping reactions in addition to being reactions to be coped with. Smiles elicit smiles, and this consequence feeds back to the initial smiler generating yet other expressive displays. And each of these expressive acts has its associated expectation (often implicit) that influences the decoding of expressive replies and determines the initial smiler's reaction to replies. Developmental psychologists claim that emotional responses have this interactive expectational character very early in life. If such patterns can be detected and described, we should be able to trace their development and operation in later interactive episodes. In my judgment, this area of research will make the most important contributions to furthering our understanding of the nature and function of emotion.

One might ask whether models of the system that mediates emotion, of which the perceptual–motor model is one type, will influence studies of interactive processes. I can see several possible ways in which this influence will occur. First, the differentiation of perceptual and conceptual processing from the postulate that each might have different rules for appraising stimuli and turning on emotion is important for the analysis of emotional communication that uses both expressive and verbal channels. Second, the postulate of sensory–motor processes provides a firm base for affective communication because it establishes a common language in subjective feeling and overt expression. Third, the model may help in the exploration of phenomena such as transference in which emotional schemata acquired early in life influence later interactions, oftentimes in inappropriate ways. Isen and her associates (Isen, Means, Patrick, & Nowicki, 1982) were not only among the first to explore the effects of emotion on social behavior, but have been in the forefront in exploring the way in which emotional states affect memory processes that then impact on social behaviors. Berkowitz has also addressed issues respecting the mediation of anger over the past 10 to 15 years (Berkowitz, 1974; 1982).

Finally, models of the system presumed to mediate emotional behavior may help us to understand how social factors shape the way individuals feel, express, and conceptualize their affects. Culture, through its institutions, definitions of roles, and invention of language to increase the specificity and durability of both institutions and roles establishes a formidable set of environmental factors for shaping our emotional lives (Levy, in press). Formidable though it may be, there are limits to the power of cultural factors. Models of the mediating system help define these limits. More important, however, these models may help us to articulate the processes involved in the interaction of biological (affective, cognitive, and motor) givens with culture. For example, roles and language may play a critical role in directing attention to environmental and internal events which will then shape emotional schemata or join specific subjective feelings to particular classes of object perceptions. Our research on the ways in which people both seek and make use of external information with respect to seeking help for and identifying illness threats (e.g., Leventhal, Nerenz & Steele, in press; Safer, Tharps, Jackson & Leventhal, 1979) suggests there is continual cross-checking between externally provided information and internal experience. For example, when people are told they have high blood pressure, they are likely to find symptoms to match their diagnosis (Leventhal, Meyer, & Nerenz, 1980); and when specific symptoms for this disorder are inadvertently suggested by their practitioners, they appear to check these out against their subjective experience (Leventhal, Nerenz, & Steele, in press). The process of learning about and acquiring new emotions is likely to show similar characteristics with individuals finding or inventing bodily sensations and causes for suggested affects, and rejecting or accepting suggestions as to how they (do or should) feel by comparing internal states to external suggestions. Levy's (in press) analysis of this problem provides an interesting set of suggestions for empirical research, as does Peters's (1970) suggestions on the education of emotion. Very little is known, however, about this important area.

VII. Conclusion

This chapter focuses on the requirements for a theory of the mechanisms that mediate the construction of emotional experience and expression, suggests that prior theories have failed to meet these requirements, and offers a model that might better meet investigators' needs. The model diverges from recent social psychological theorizing in arguing for the reality of emotional experience; that is, the qualities of emotion or primary emotional meaning are given by an innate sensory–motor structure and not derived from social influence. Further, it suggests at least two different ways in which emotional experiences are stored: schematic or perceptual memories and conceptual or reflective "verbal" memories. The modes of storage effect the organization of emotional processing and generate a series of problems for the elicitation and control of emotion.

I also make a number of specific suggestions about the operation of the expressive-motor component of the system (the feed-forward motor model) and offer an hypothesis about the structure of schemata (as spatial integrations in columns or tightly knit nodes rather than associative structures) in contrast to the structure of conceptual affective processes (as propositionally organized scripts). I then speculate about the integration of the system and the role of neurotransmitters, attentional processes, and culture for the integration of emotion schemata and for the organization of emotional states. Interactions among the components, such as bottom-up and top-down influences, are discussed within this framework. Finally, I suggest some areas of future study (e.g., the emotion–cognition interaction and the nature of emotion memory) and suggest that the study of emotional interactions holds the key to future advances in this area.

The model I've suggested is complex! It has multiple components capable of multiple types of interaction, some symmetrical, some not. It would be in error to have it otherwise, and it is a misperception of the role of theory to argue that complexity is a barrier to research. Sensible use of a model requires multiple approaches, and there is no reason why investigators should not pay careful attention to various aspects of emotional processes while holding others constant. Studies of the motor system make sense as do studies of memory. One need not study the entire system to add to our understanding of emotion. But studies of components can become meaningless if we lose sight of the whole, that is, when a single hypothesis, be it facial feedback, cognition time arousal, domains of meaning as determinants of cognition, and so forth, becomes *the* model and the complete phenomenon of emotion. Our goals should be to study the parts while keeping sight of the whole so that we are truly holding other factors constant and not denying or ignoring their existence. When we ignore major aspects of our emotion model and lose sight of emotion, we can be trapped by our own methods. When that happens, we will produce data specific to a set of operations and unrelated to the phenomenon under study.

REFERENCES

Abelson, R. P. Script processing in attitude formation and decision-making. In U. S. Carroll & J. W. Payne (Eds.), *Cognitive and social behavior*. Hillsdale, NJ: Erlbaum, 1976.

Abramson, L. Y., Seligman, M. E. P., & Teasdale, J. D. Learned helplessness in humans: Critique and reformulation. *Journal of Abnormal Psychology*, 1978, *87*, 49–74.

Ahles, T., Blanchard, E., & Leventhal, H. Cognitive control of pain: Attention to the sensory aspects of the cold pressor stimulus. *Cognitive Therapy and Research*, 1983, *7*, 159–177.

Allport, G., & Pettigrew, T. F. Cultural influence on the perception of movement: The trapezoidal illusion among Zulus. *Journal of Abnormal and Social Psychology*, 1957, *55*, 104–113.

Anderson, N. H. Averaging versus adding as a stimulus combination rule in impression formation. *Journal of Experimental Psychology*, 1965, *70*, 394–400.

Anderson, N. H. Integration theory and attitude change. *Psychological Review*, 1971, *78*, 171–206.

Angier, R. P. The conflict theory of emotion. *American Journal of Psychiatry*, 1927, *34*, 390–401.

Baddeley, A. D. Domains of recollection. *Psychological Review*, 1982, *89*, 708–729.

Bandura, A., Blanchard, E. B., & Ritter, B. Relative efficacy of desensitization and modeling approaches for inducing behavioral, affective and attitudinal changes. *Journal of Personality and Social Psychology*, 1969, *13*, 173–199.

Barber, T. X., & Hahn, K. W. Physiological and subjective responses to pain producing stimulation under hypnotically-suggested and wake imagined "analgesia." *Journal of Abnormal and Social Psychology*, 1962, *65*, 411–418.

Bauer, D. H. An exploratory study of developmental changes in children's fears. *Journal of Child Psychology and Psychiatry*, 1976, *17*, 69–74.

Beck, A. T. *Cognitive therapy and the emotional disorders*. NY: International Universities Press, 1976.

Beecher, H. K. *Measurement of subjective Responses*. London: Oxford University Press, 1959.

Bem, D. J. Self-perception theory. In L. Berkowitz (Ed.), *Advances in experimental social psychology* (Vol. 6). NY: Academic Press, 1972.

Berkowitz, L. Some determinants of impulsive aggression: Role of mediated associations with reinforcements for aggression. *Psychological Review*, 1974, *81*, 165–176.

Berkowitz, L. The experience of anger as a parallel process in the display of impulsive "angry" aggression. In R. G. Geen & E. Donnerstein (Eds.), *Aggression: Theoretical and empirical reviews*. NY: Academic Press, 1982.

Berkowitz, L., and Geen, R. G. Stimulus qualities of the target of agression: A further study. *Journal of Personality and Social Psychology*, 1967, *5*, 364–368.

Bever, T. G., & Chiarello, R. J. Cerebral dominance in musicians and nonmusicians. *Science*, 1974, *185*, 537–539.

Bower, G. H. Mood and memory. *American Psychologist*, 1981, *31*, 129–148.

Bower, G. H., & Cohen, P. R. Emotional influences on learning and cognition. In M. S. Clarke & S.

T. Fiske (Eds.), *Affect and cognition: The 17th Annual Carnegie Symposium on Cognition.* Hillsdale, NJ: Erlbaum, 1982.

Bowlby, J. *Separation: Anxiety and anger.* NY: Basic Books, 1973.

Brazelton, T. B., Koslowski, B., & Main, M. The origins of reciprocity: The early mother-infant interaction. In M. Lewis & L. A. Rosenblum (Eds.), *The effect of the infant on its caregiver.* NY: Wiley, 1974.

Broadbent, D. E. The hidden preattentive processes. *American Psychologist,* 1977, *32,* 109–118.

Bronson, G. W. The development of fear in man and other animals. *Child Development,* 1968, *39,* 409–431.

Brown, G. W. & Harris, T. *Social origins of depression: A study of psychiatric disorder in women.* London: Tavistock, 1978.

Brown, J. W. Physiology and phylogenesis of emotional expression. *Brain Research,* 1967, *5,* 1–14.

Buck, R. Nonverbal behavior and the theory of emotion: The facial feedback hypothesis. *Journal of Personality and Social Psychology,* 1980, *38,* 811–824.

Cacioppo, J. T., & Petty, R. E. Social psychological procedures for cognitive response assessment: The thought-listing technique. In T. Merluzzi, C. Glass, & M. Genest (Eds.), *Cognitive assessment.* NY: The Guilford Press, 1981.

Calvert-Boyanowsky, J., & Leventhal, H. The role of information in attenuating behavioral responses to stress: A reinterpretation of the misattribution phenomennon. *Journal of Personality and Social Psychology,* 1975, *32,* 214–221.

Campos, J. J., Emde, R. N., & Caplovitz, K. Emotional development. In R. Harre (Ed.), *The Blackwell encyclopedia dictionary of psychology.* Oxford: Basil Blackwell, 1983.

Cannon, W. B. The James–Lange theory of emotions: A critical examination and an alternative theory. *American Journal of Psychology,* 1927, *34,* 106–124.

Cannon, W. B. *Bodily changes in pain, hunger, fear and rage.* NY: Appleton, 1929.

Cannon, W. B. Again the James–Lange and the thalamic theories of emotion. *Psychological Review,* 1931, *38,* 281–295.

Cantril, H., & Hunt, W. A. Emotional effects produced by the injection of adrenalin. *American Journal of Psychology,* 1932, *44,* 300–307.

Carmon, A., & Nachson, I. Ear asymmetry in perception of emotional nonverbal stimuli. *Acta Psychologica,* 1973, *37,* 351–357.

Carver, C. S. A cybernetic model of self-attention processes. *Journal of Personality and Social Psychology,* 1979, *37,* 1251–1281.

Carver, C. S., & Scheier, M. F. *Attention and self-regulation: A control-theory approach to human behavior.* NY: Springer-Verlag, 1981.

Carver, C. S., & Scheier, M. F. Control theory: A useful conceptual framework for personality-social, clinical, and health psychology. *Psychological Bulletin,* 1982, *92,* 111–135.

Casey, K. L. Pain: A current view of neural mechanisms. *American Scientist,* 1973, *61,* 194–200.

Cohen, H. D., Rosen, R. C., & Goldstein, L. Electroencephalographic laterality changes during human sexual orgasm. *Archives of Sexual Behavior,* 1976, *5,* 189–199.

Condon, W. S., & Sander, L. W. Neonate movement is synchronized with adult speech: Interactional participation and language acquisition. *Science,* 1974, *183,* 99–101.

Cook, A. W., & Druckemiller, W. H. Phantom limb pain in paraplegic patients. *International Journal of Neurosurgery,* 1952, *9,* 508–516.

Cupchik, G. C., & Leventhal, H. Consistency between expressive behavior and the evaluation of humorous stimuli: The role of sex and self observation. *Journal of Personality and Social Psychology,* 1974, *30,* 429–442.

Darwin, C. *The expression of the emotions in man and animals.* London: Murray, 1904. (Original work published 1872).

Davidson, R. J., & Schwartz, G. E. The influence of musical training on patterns of EEG asymmetry during musical and non-musical self-generation tasks. *Psychophysiology,* 1977, *14,* 58–63.

Davidson, R. J., Schwartz, G. E., Pugash, E., & Bromfield, E. Sex differences in patterns of EEG asymmetry. *Biological Psychology*, 1976, *4*, 119–138.

Davitz, J. R. A dictionary and grammar of emotion. In M. B. Arnold (Ed.), *Feelings and emotion.* NY: Academic Press, 1970.

Dement, W. C. *Some must watch while some must sleep.* Stanford, CA: Stanford Alumni Association, 1972.

Depue, R. A. *The psychobiology of the depressive disorders: Implications for the effects of stress.* NY: Academic Press, 1979.

Dewey, J. The theory of emotion (Vol. I): Emotional attitudes. *Psychological Review*, 1894, *1*, 553–569.

Dewey, J. The theory of emotion (Vol. II): The significance of emotions. *Psychological Review*, 1895, *2*, 13–32.

Dollard, J., & Miller, N. E. *Personality and psychotherapy.* NY: McGraw-Hill, 1950.

Dunlap, K. *Habits, their making and unmaking.* NY: Liveright, 1933.

Eibl-Eibesfeldt, I. Strategies of social interaction. In R. Plutchik & H. Kellerman (Eds.), *Emotion: Theory, research, and experience.* NY: Academic Press, 1980.

Ekman, P., & Friesen, W. V. Constants across culture in the face and emotion. *Journal of Personality and Social Psychology*, 1971, *17*, 124–129.

Ekman, P., & Friesen, W. V. *Unmasking the face.* Englewood Cliffs, NJ: Prentice-Hall, 1975.

Ekman, P. & Friesen, W. V. Felt, false, and miserable smiles. *Journal of Nonverbal Behavior*, 1982, *6*, 238–252.

Ekman, P., Friesen, W. V., & Ellsworth, P. *Emotion in the human face.* NY: Pergamon, 1972.

Emde, R. N. *Levels of meaning for infant emotion: A biosocial view.* Paper presented at a seminar on emotion and cognition, Social Science Research Council, San Francisco, CA November 1979.

Engel, G. L. ''Psychogenic'' pain and the pain-prone patient. *American Journal of Medicine*, 1959, *26*, 899–918.

Epstein, S. Expectancy and magnitude of reaction to a noxious UCs. *Psychophysiology*, 1973, *10*, 100–107.

Epstein, S., Rosenthal, S., & Szpiler, J. The influence of attention upon anticipatory arousal, habituation, and reactivity to a noxious stimulus. *Journal of Research in Personality*, 1978, *12*, 30–40.

Eriksen, C. W. Unconscious processes. In M. R. Jones (Ed.), *Nebraska Symposium on Motivation* (Vol. 8). Lincoln, NE: University of Nebraska Press, 1958.

Field, T. M., Woodson, R., Greenberg, R., & Cohen, D. Discrimination and imitation of facial expression by neonates. *Science*, 1982, *218*, 179–181.

Folkman, S., & Lazarus, R. An analysis of coping in a middle-aged community sample. *Journal of Health and Social Behavior*, 1980, *21*, 219–239.

Gage, D. *Mood state-dependent memory and brain laterality.* Unpublished doctoral thesis, University of America, Washington, D.C., 1983.

Garcia, J. Tilting at the paper mills of academe. *American Psychologist*, 1981, *36*, 149–158.

Gardiner, H. N. Review of Professor James' theory of emotion by D. Irons. *Psychological Review*, 1894, *63*, 544–549.

Geer, J. H., Davidson, G. E., & Gatchel, R. I. Reduction of stress in humans through non-veridical perceived control. *Journal of Personality and Social Psychology*, 1970, *16*, 731–738.

Gellhorn, E. Motion and emotion: The role of proprioception in the physiology and pathology of the emotions. *Psychological Review*, 1964, *71*, 457–472.

Geschwind, N. The apraxias: Neural mechanisms of disorders of learned movement. *American Scientist*, 1975, *63*, 188–195.

Gibson, E. J. The development of perception as an adaptive process. *American Scientist*, 1970, *58*, 98–107.

Gibson, J. *The perception of the visual world.* Boston: Houghton, 1950.

Goldstein, L., Stolzfus, N. W., & Gardocki, J. F. Changes in interhemispheric amplitude relationships in the EEG during sleep. *Physiology and Behavior*, 1972, *8*, 811–815.

Greenberg, L. S. & Safran, J. D. Integrating affect and cognition: A perspective on the process of therapeutic change. *Cognitive Therapy and Research*, in press.

Greenwald, A. G. Sensory feedback mechanisms in performance control: With special reference to the ideo-motor mechanism. *Psychological Review*, 1970, *77*, 73–99.

Grossberg, J. M., & Wilson, H. K. Physiological changes accompanying the visualization of fearful and neutral situations. *Journal of Personality and Social Psychology*, 1968, *10*, 124–133.

Grossman, S. P. *Physiological psychology*. NY: Wiley, 1967.

Gyr, J. W. Is a theory of direct visual perception adequate? *Psychological Bulletin*, 1972, *77*, 246–261.

Hagar, J. C., & Ekman, P. Methodological problems in Tourangeau and Ellsworth's study of facial expressions and experience of emotion. *Journal of Personality and Social Psychology*, 1981, *40*, 358–362.

Haggard, E. A., & Isaacs, F. S. Micromomentary facial expressions as indicators of ego mechanisms in psychotherapy. In L. A. Gotschalk & A. A. Auerback (Eds.), *Methods of research in psychotherapy*. NY: Appleton, 1966.

Hall, K. R. L., & Stride, E. The varying response to pain in psychiatric disorders: A study in abnormal psychology. *British Journal of Medical Psychology*, 1954, *27*, 48–60.

Hare, R. D. *Psychopathy: Theory and Research*. NY: Wiley, 1970.

Harnad, S., & Doty, R. W. Introductory overview. In S. Harnad, R. W. Doty, L. Goldstein, J. Jaynes, & G. Krauthamer (Eds.), *Lateralization in the nervous system*. NY: Academic Press, 1977.

Hebb, D. D. On the nature of fear. *Psychological Review*, 1946, *53*, 259–276.

Hebb, D. O. *The organization of behavior*. NY: Wiley, 1949.

Hebb, D. O. The mammal and his environment. *American Journal of Psychiatry*, 1955, *111*, 826–831.

Hebb, D. O. *A textbook of psychology*. Philadelphia: Saunders, 1966.

Henderson, W. R., & Smyth, G. E. Phantom limbs. *Journal of Neurology, Neurosurgery and Psychiatry*, 1948, *11*, 88–112.

Hilgard, E. R. Pain as a puzzle for psychology and physiology. *American Psychologist*, 1969, *24*, 103–113.

Hoffman, M. L. Sex differences in empathy and related behaviors. *Psychological Bulletin*, 1977, *84*, 712–722.

Horowitz, M. J. *Image formation and cognition*. NY: Appleton, 1970.

Hull, C. L. Knowledge and purpose as habit mechanisms. *Psychological Review*, 1930, *37*, 511–525.

Hull, C. L. The goal gradient hypothesis and maze learning. *Psychological Review*, 1932, *39*, 25–43.

Hull, C. L. *Principles of behavior*. NY: Appleton, 1943.

Hurvich, L. M. Hering and the scientific establishment. *American Psychologist*, 1969, *24*, 497–514.

Ironside, R. Disorders of laughter due to brain lesions. *Brain*, 1956, *79*, 589–609.

Isen, A. M., & Means, B. The influence of positive affect on decision-making strategy. *Social Cognition*, 1983, *2*, 18–31.

Isen, A. M., Means, B., Patrick, R., & Nowicki, G. Some factors influencing decision-making strategy and risk taking. In M. S. Clarke & S. T. Fiske (Eds.), *Affect and Cognition*. Hillsdale, NJ: Erlbaum, 1982.

Isen, A. M., Shalker, T., Clark, M., & Karp, L. Affect, accessibility of material in memory and behavior. *Journal of Personality and Social Psychology*, 1978, *36*, 1–12.

Iversen, L. L. Neurotransmitters and CNS disease: Introduction *Lancet*, 1982, *2*, 914–918.

Izard, C. E. *The face of emotion.* NY: Appleton, 1971.

Izard, C. E. *Human emotions.* NY: Plenum, 1977.

Izard, C. E. Emotions as motivations: An evolutionary-developmental prospective. In R. Dienstbier (Ed.), *Nebraska Symposium on Motivation* (Vol. 27). Lincoln, NE: University of Nebraska, 1979.

Izard, C. E., Kidd, R. F., & Kotsch, W. E. *Facial expression as an activator of the subjective experience of emotion.* Mimeo, Vanderbilt University (undated).

James W. What is an emotion? *Mind,* 1884, *9,* 188–205.

James, W. *The principles of psychology* (Vol. 2). NY: Dover, 1950, (Original work published 1890.)

Janis, I. L. *Psychological stress.* NY: Wiley, 1958.

Johnson, J. E. The effects of accurate expectations about sensations on the sensory and distress components of pain. *Journal of Personality and Social Psychology,* 1973, *27,* 261–275.

Jones, H. E. The study of patterns of emotional expression. In M. L. Reymert (Ed.), *Feelings and emotions.* NY: McGraw-Hill, 1950.

Kagan, J. Attention and psychological change in the young child. *Science,* 1970, *170,* 826–832.

Keller, A., Ford, L. H., Jr., & Meachem, J. A. Dimensions of self-concept in preschool children. *Developmental Psychology,* 1978, *14,* 483–489.

Kemper, T. D. *A social interaction theory of emotions.* NY: Wiley, 1978.

Kinsbourne, M. Mechanisms of hemispheric interaction in man. In M. Kinsbourne & W. L. Smith (Eds.), *Hemispheric disconnection and cerebral function.* Springfield, IL: Thomas, 1974.

Kleck, R. E., Vaughan, R. C., Cartwright-Smith, J., Vaughan, K., Colby, C. Z., & Lanzetta, J. T. Effects of being observed on expressive, subjective and physiological responses to painful stimuli. *Journal of Personality and Social Psychology,* 1976, *34,* 1211–1218.

Knox, V. J., Morgan, A. H., & Hilgard, E. R. Pain and suffering in ischemia: The paradox of hypnotically suggested anesthesia as contradicted by response from the "hidden observer." *Archives of General Psychiatry,* 1974, *30,* 840–847.

Krueger, F. E. The essence of feeling. In M. Arnold (Ed.), *The Nature of Emotion: Selected readings.* Baltimore: Penguin Books, 1968. (Original work published 1928.)

Kuhn, T. *The structure of scientific revolutions.* Chicago: University of Chicago Press, 1962.

Laird, J. D. Self-attribution of emotion: The effects of expressive behavior on the quality of emotional experience. *Journal of Personality and Social Psychology,* 1974, *29,* 475–486.

Laird, J. D. The real role of facial response in the experience of emotion: A reply to Tourangeau & Ellsworth and others. *Journal of Personality and Social Psychology,* in press.

Landis, C., & Hunt, W. A. Adrenalin and emotion. *Psychological Review,* 1932, *39,* 467–485.

Lang, P. J. Language, image and emotion. In P. Pliner, K. R. Plankstein, & J. M. Spigel (Eds.), *Perception of emotion in self and others* (Vol. 5). NY: Plenum, 1979.

Lang, P. J., Kozak, M. J., Miller, G. A., Levin, D. N., & McLean, A. Emotional imagery: Conceptual structure and pattern of somato-visceral response. *Psychophysiology.* 1980, *17,* 179–192.

Lang, P. J., & Lazovik, A. D. Experimental desensitization of a phobia. *Journal of Abnormal and Social Psychology,* 1963, *66,* 519–525.

Lanzetta, J. T., Cartwright-Smith, J., & Kleck, R. E. Effects of nonverbal dissimulation on emotional experience and autonomic arousal. *Journal of Personality and Social Psychology,* 1976, *33,* 354–370.

Lanzetta, J. T., & Kleck, R. E. Encoding and decoding of nonverbal affect in humans. *Journal of Personality and Social Psychology,* 1970, *16,* 12–19.

Lashley, K. S. *The problem of serial order in behavior.* NY: Wiley, 1951.

Lazarus, R. S. *Psychological stress and the coping process.* NY: McGraw-Hill, 1966.

Lazarus, R. S. The stress and coping paradigm. In C. Eisdorfer, D. Cohen, A. Klienman, & P. Maxim (Eds.), *Theoretical bases for psychopathology.* NY: Spectrum, 1980.

Lazarus, R. S. Thoughts on the relations between emotion and cognition. *American Psychologist*, 1982, *37*, 1019–1010.

Lazarus, R. S., & Alfert, E. Short circuiting of threat by experimentally altering cognitive appraisal. *Journal of Abnormal and Social Psychology*. 1964, *69*, 195–205.

Lehmann, A. *Hauptgesetze des menschlichen gefuehlsebens*. Leipzig: Reisland, 1914.

Lenox, J. R. Effect of hypnotic analgesia on verbal report and cardiovascular responses to ischemic pain. *Journal of Abnormal Psychology*, 1970, *75*, 199–206.

Leventhal, H. Findings and theory in the study of fear communication. In L. Berkowitz (Ed.), *Advances in experimental social psychology* (Vol. 5). NY: Academic Press, 1970.

Leventhal, H. Attitudes: Their nature, growth and change. In C. Nemeth (Ed.), *Social Psychology*. Chicago: McNally, 1974. (a)

Leventhal, H. Emotions: A basic problem for social psychology. In C. Nemeth (Ed.), *Social psychology: Classic and contemporary integrations*. Chicago: McNally, 1974. (b)

Leventhal, H. A perceptual-motor processing model of emotion. In P. Pliner, K. Blankenstein, & I. M. Spigel (Eds.), *Perception of emotion in self and others* (Vol. 5). NY: Plenum, 1979.

Leventhal, H. Toward a comprehensive theory of emotion. In L. Berkowitz (Ed.), *Advances in experimental social psychology* (Vol. 13). NY: Academic Press, 1980.

Leventhal, H., Brown, D., Shacham, S., & Engquist, G. Effect of preparatory information about sensations, threat of pain and attention on cold pressor distress. *Journal of Personality and Social Psychology*, 1979, *37*, 688–714.

Leventhal, H., & Cupchik, G. The informational and facilitative affects of an audience upon expression and the evaluation of humorous stimuli. *Journal of Experimental Social Psychology*, 1975, *11*, 363–380.

Leventhal, H., & Cupchik, G. A process model of humor judgment. *Journal of Communication*, 1976, *26*, 190–204.

Leventhal, H., & Everhart, D. Emotion, pain and physical illness. In C. Izard (Ed.), *Emotions and psychopathology*. NY: Plenum, 1979.

Leventhal, H., & Johnson, J. E. Laboratory and field experimentation: Development of a theory of self-regulation. In R. Leonard & P. Wooldridge (Eds.), *Behavioral science and nursing theory*. St. Louis: Mosby, 1983.

Leventhal, H., & Mace, W. The effect of laughter on evaluation of a slapstick movie. *Journal of Personality*, 1970, *38*, 16–30.

Leventhal, H., Meyer, D., & Nerenz, D. The common sense representation of illness danger. In S. Rachman (Ed.), *Contributions to medical psychology* (Vol. 2). Oxford: Pergamon, 1980.

Leventhal, H., & Mosbach, P. Perceptual-motor theory. In J. T. Cacioppo & R. E. Petty (Eds.), *Social psychophysiology*. NY: Guilford, 1983.

Leventhal, H. & Nerenz, D. A model for stress research and some implications for the control of stress disorders. In D. Meichenbaum & M. Jaremko (Eds.), *Stress prevention and management: A cognitive behavioral approach*. NY: Plenum, 1983.

Leventhal, H., Nerenz, D. R., & Steele, D. Disease representations and coping with health threats. In A. Baum & J. Singer (Eds.), *Handbook of psychology and health*, vol. 4. Hillsdale, NJ: Erlbaum, in press.

Leventhal, H., & Sharp, E. Facial expressions as indicators of distress. In S. S. Tomkins & C. E. Izard (Eds.), *Affect, cognition and personality*. NY: Springer, 1965.

Levy, R. I. Emotion, knowing, and culture. In R. Shweder & R. LeVine (Eds.), *Culture theory*. New York: Cambridge University Press, in press.

Leyens, J., Cisneros, T., & Hossay, J. Decentration as a means for reducing aggression after exposure to violent stimuli. *European Journal of Social Psychology*, 1976, *6*, 459–473.

Li, C. L., & Elvidge, A. R. Observation on phantom limb in a paraplegic patient. *Journal of Neurosurgery*, 1951, *8*, 524–526.

Maclean, D., & Reichlin, S. Neuroendocrinology and the immune process. In R. Ader (Ed.), *Psychoneuroimmunology*. NY: Academic Press, 1981.

Mandler, G. Emotion. In R. Brown, E. Galanter, E. H. Hess, & G. Mandler (Eds.), *New directions in psychology* (Vol. 1). NY: Holt, 1962.

Mandler, G. *Mind and emotion*. NY: Wiley, 1975.

Mandler, G., & Kessen, W. *The language of psychology*. NY: Wiley, 1959.

Mandler, G., & Watson, D. L. Anxiety and the interruption of behavior. In C. D. Spielberger (Ed.), *Anxiety and behavior*. NY: Academic Press, 1966.

Maranon, G. Contribution a l'etude de l'action emotive de l'adrenaline. *Revue Francaise d'Endocrinologie*, 1924, *2*, 301–325.

Marshall, G. D., & Zimbardo, P. G. Affective consequences of inadequately explained physiological arousal. *Journal of Personality and Social Psychology*, 1979, *37*, 970–985.

Maslach, C. Negative emotional biasing of unexplained arousal. *Journal of Personality and Social Psychology*, 1979, *37*, 953–969.

Mathews, A. M. Psychophysiological approaches to the investigation of emotion and related procedures. *Psychological Bulletin*, 1971, *76*, 73–91.

McCaul, K. D., & Haugtvedt, C. Attention, distraction, and cold-pressor pain. *Journal of Personality and Social Psychology*, 1982, *1*, 154–162.

McCaul, K. D., Holmes, D. S., & Solomon, S. Voluntary expressive changes and emotion. *Journal of Personality and Social Psychology*, 1982, *42*, 145–152.

McGuire, W. J. Personality and susceptibility to social influence. In E. Borgatta & W. Lambert (Eds.), *Handbook of personality theory and research*. Chicago: McNally, 1968.

McKechnie, R. J. Relief from phantom limb pain by relaxation exercises. *Journal of Behavior Therapy and Experimental Psychiatry*, 1975, *6*, 262–263.

Melzack, R. Phantom limb pain. *Anesthesiology*, 1971, *35*, 409–419.

Melzack, R. *The puzzle of pain*. NY: Basic Books, 1973.

Melzack, R., & Scott, T. H. The effects of early experience on the response to pain. *Journal of Comparative and Physiological Psychology*, 1957, *50*, 155–161.

Melzack, R., & Wall, Patrick D. Pain mechanisms: A new theory. *Science*, 1965, *150*, 971–980.

Melzack, R., & Wall, P. D. Psychophysiology of pain. *International Anesthesia Clinics*, 1970, *3*, 3–34.

Miller, G. A. Galanter, E., & Pribram, K. H. *Plans and the structure of behavior*. NY: Holt, 1960.

Morgenstern, F. S. Chronic pain. In O. U. Hill (Ed.), *Modern trends in psychosomatic medicine*. NY: Appleton, 1970.

Nakashima, T. Contributions to the study of the affective processes. *American Journal of Psychology*, 1909, *20*, 157–193.

Nathan, P. W. Pain traces left in central nervous system. In C. A. Keele, R. Smith (Eds.), *The assessment of pain in man and animals*. Edinburgh: Livingston, 1962.

Newman, E. B., Perkins, E. T., & Wheeler, R. H. Cannon's theory of emotion: A critique. *Psychological Review*, 1930, *37*, 305–326.

Nisbett, R. E., & Wilson, T. DeC. Telling more than we can know: Verbal report on mental processes. *Psychological Review*, 1977, *84*, 231–259.

Noller, P. Misunderstandings in marital communication: A study of couples' nonverbal comunication. *Journal of Personality and Social Psychology*, 1980, *39*, 1135–1148.

Notarius, C. I., & Levenson, R. W. Expressive tendencies and physiological response to stress. *Journal of Personality and Social Psychology*, 1979, *39*, 1135–1148.

Notarius, C. I., & Levenson, R. W. Expressive tendencies and physiological response to stress. *Journal of Personality and Social Psychology*, 1979, *37*, 1204–1210.

Ohman, A., & Dimberg, V. Facial expressions as conditioned stimuli for electrodermal responses: A case for preparedness? *Journal of Personality and Social Psychology*, 1978, *36*, 1251–1258.

Orr, S. P., & Lanzetta, J. T. Facial expressions of emotion as conditioned stimuli for human autonomic responses. *Journal of Personality and Social Psychology,* 1980, *38,* 278–282.

Panagis, D., & Leventhal, H. *Effects of expressive feedback upon judgments of cartoon quality: An investigation of sex differences in the latencies of expressive and cognitive reactions.* Mimeo, University of Wisconsin, Madison, 1973.

Parke, R. D., Ewall, W., & Slaby, R. G. Hostile and helpful verbalizations as regulators of nonverbal aggression. *Journal of Personality and Social Psychology,* 1972, *23,* 243–248.

Pasquarelli, B., & Bull, N. Experimental investigations of the body-mind continuum in affective states. *Journal of Nervous and Mental Disease,* 1951, *113,* 512–521.

Pearlin, L. I., & Schooler, C. The structure of coping. *Journal of Health and Social Behavior,* 1978, *19,* 2–21.

Peters, R. S. The education of the emotions. In M. B. Arnold (Ed.), *Feelings and emotion: The Loyola Symposium.* NY: Academic Press, 1970.

Piaget, J. *Six psychological studies.* NY: Random House, 1968.

Piaget, J., & Inhelder, B. *Mental imagery in the child: A study of the development of imaginal representation.* London: Routledge & Kegan Paul, 1971.

Plutchik, R. *Emotion: A psychoevolutionary synthesis.* NY: Harper & Row, 1980.

Polanyi, M. Logic and psychology. *American Psychologists,* 1968, *23,* 27–43.

Posner, M. I. *Cognition: An introduction.* Glenview, IL: Free Press 1973.

Powers, W. T. Feedback: Beyond behaviorism. *Science,* 1973, *179,* 351–356.

Rachman, S. (Ed.), *Contributions to medical psychology* (Vol. 2). NY: Pergamon, 1980.

Reinhardt, L. C. *Attention and interpretation in control of cold pressor pain distress.* Unpublished doctoral dissertation, University of Wisconsin, Madison, 1979.

Reisenzein, R., & Gattinger, E. Salience of arousal as a mediator of misattribution of transferred excitation. *Motivation and Emotion,* 1962, *6,* 315–328.

Ruckmick, C. A. *The psychology of feeling and emotion.* NY: McGraw-Hill, 1936.

Russell, B. *An outline of philosophy* NY: Meridian Books, 1960 (Original work published 1927)

Safer, M. A. *Sex differences in hemisphere specialization for recognizing facial expressions of emotion.* Unpublished doctoral dissertation, University of Wisconsin, Madison, 1978.

Safer, M. A. Sex and hemisphere differences in access to codes for processing emotional expressions and faces. *Journal of Experimental Psychology: General,* 1981, *110,* 86–100.

Safer, M. A., & Leventhal, H. Ear differences in evaluating emotional tones of voice and verbal content. *Journal of Experimental Psychology: Human Perception and Performance,* 1977, *3,* 75–82.

Safer, M., Tharps, Q., Jackson T., & Leventhal, H. Determinants of three stages of delay in seeking care at a medical clinic. *Medical Care,* 1979, *17,* 11–29.

Schachter, S. The interaction of cognitive and physiological determinants of emotional state. In L. Berkowitz (Ed.), *Advances in experimental social psychology* (Vol. 1). NY: Academic Press, 1964.

Schachter, S., & Singer, J. E. Cognitive, social, and physiological determinants of emotional state. *Psychological Review,* 1962, *69,* 379–399.

Schachter, S., & Wheeler, L. Epinephrine, chlorpromazine, and amusement. *Journal of Abnormal Social Psychology,* 1962, *65,* 121–128.

Schaffer, H. R., & Emerson, P. E. The development of social attachments in infancy. *Monographs of the Society for Research in Child Development,* 1964, *29*(3, Whole No. 94).

Scheier, M. F., Carver, C. S., & Gibbons, F. X. Self-directed attention, awareness of bodily states and suggestibility. *Journal of Personality and Social Psychology,* 1979, *37,* 1576–1588.

Scherwitz, L., Berton, K., & Leventhal, H. Type A assessment and interaction in the behavior pattern interview. *Psychosomatic Medicine,* 1977, *39,* 229–240.

Scherwitz, L., Berton, K., & Leventhal, H. Type A behavior, self-involvement, and cardiovascular response. *Psychosomatic Medicine,* 1978, *40,* 593–609.

Schwartz, G. E., Fair, P. L., Mandel, M. R., Salt, P., & Klerman, G. L. Facial expressions and imagery in depression: An electromyographic study. *Psychosomatic Medicine,* 1976, *38,* 337–347.

Schwartz, G. E., Fair, P. L., Mandel, M. R., Salt, P., Mieski, M., & Klerman, G. L. Facial electromyography in the assessment of improvement in depression. *Psychosomatic Medicine,* 1978, *40,* 355–360.

Seligman, M. E. P. On the generality of the laws of learning. *Psychological Review,* 1970, *77,* 406–418.

Semmes, J. Hemispheric specialization: A possible clue to mechanism. *Neuropsychologia,* 1968, *6,* 11–27.

Shacham, S. *The effects of imagery monitoring, sensation monitoring and positive suggestion on pain and distress.* Unpublished doctoral dissertation, University of Wisconsin, Madison, 1979.

Simmel, M. L. The reality of phantom sensations. *Social Research,* 1962, *29,* 337–356.

Solomon, R. L., & Corbit, J. D. An opponent-process theory of motivation (Vol. I). Temporal dynamics of affect. *Psychological Review,* 1974, *81,* 119–145.

Speisman, J. C., Lazarus, R. S., Mordkoff, A., & Davison, L. Experimental reduction of stress based on ego-defense theory. *Journal of Abnormal and Social Psychology,* 1964, *68,* 367–380.

Spence, K. A theory of emotionally based drive (D) and its relation to performance in simple learning situation. *American Psychologist,* 1958, *13,* 131–141.

Spitz, R. A., & Wolf, K. M. The smiling response: A contribution to the ontogenesis of social relations. *Genetic Psychology Monographs,* 1946, *34,* 57–125.

Sroufe, L. A., & Waters, E. The ontogenesis of smiling and laughter: A perspective on the organization of a development in infancy. *Psychological Review,* 1976, *83,* 173–189.

Staub, E., & Kellett, D. S. Increasing pain tolerance by information about aversive stimuli. *Journal of Personality and Social Psychology,* 1972, *21,* 198–203.

Sullivan, H. S. *The interpersonal theory of psychiatry.* NY: Norton, 1953.

Sully, J. *An essay on laughter.* London: Longmans, Green, 1902.

Sutherland, G., Newman, B., & Rachman, S. Experimental investigations of the relations between mood and intrusive unwanted cognitions. *British Journal of Medical Psychology,* 1982, *55,* 127–138.

Teasdale, J., & Fogarty, S. Differential effects of induced mood on retrieval of pleasant and unpleasant events from episodic memory. *Journal of Abnormal Psychology,* 1979, *88,* 248–257.

Teasdale, J. D., Taylor, R., & Fogarty, S. T. Effects of induced elation-depression on the accessibility of memories of happy and unhappy experiences. *Behavioral Research and Therapy,* 1980, *18,* 339–346.

Tomkins, S. S. *Affect, imagery, consciousness* (Vol. 1). *The positive affects.* NY: Springer, 1962.

Tomkins, S. S. Affect as amplification: Some modifications in theory. In R. Plutchik & H. Kellerman (Eds.), *Emotion: Theory, research, and experience* (Vol. 1). NY: Academic Press, 1980.

Tomkins, S. S., & McCarter, R. What and where are the primary affects? Some evidence for a theory. *Perceptual and Motor Skills,* 1964, *18,* 119–158.

Tourangeau, R., & Ellsworth, P. C. The role of facial response in the experience of emotion. *Journal of personality and Social Psychology,* 1979, *37,* 1519–1531.

Tucker, D. M., Lateral Drain function, emotion, and conceptualization. *Psychological Bulletin,* 1981, *89,* 19–46.

Tucker, D. M., & Williamson, P. A. Asymmetric neural control systems in human self-regulation. *Psychological Review,* 1984, *91,* 185–215.

Turner, C. W., & Layton, J. F. Verbal imagery and connotation as memory-induced mediators of aggressive behavior. *Journal of Personality and Social Psychology,* 1976, *33,* 755–763.

van Praag, H. M. Neurotransmitters and CNS disease: Depression. *The Lancet,* 2 (No. 8310), 1982, pp. 1259–1264.

Von Holst, E. Relations between the central nervous system and the peripheral organs. *British Journal of Animal Behavior*, 1954, *2*, 89–94.

Walters, R. H., & Parke, R. D. Social motivation, dependency, and susceptability to social influence. In L. Berkowitz (Ed.), *Advances in experimental social psychology* (Vol. 1). NY: Academic Press, 1964.

Weiskrantz, L., Elliott, J., & Darlington, C. Preliminary observations on tickling oneself. *Nature: London*, 1971, *230*, 598–599.

Weiss, J. M. Somatic effects of predictable and unpredictable shock. *Psychosomatic Medicine*, 1970, *22*, 397–408.

Wilson, S. A. K. Some problems in neurology (Vol. II). Pathological laughing and crying. *Journal of Neurology and Psychopathology*, 1924, *4*, 299–333.

Wilson, W. R. Feeling more than we can know: Exposure effects without learning. *Journal of Personality and Social Psychology*, 1979, *37*, 811–821.

Witkin, H. A., & Lewis, H. B. Presleep experiences and dreams. In H. A. Witkin & H. B. Lewis (Eds.), *Experimental studies of dreaming*. NY: Random House, 1967.

Wolfe, J. M. Hidden visual processes. *Scientific American*, 1983, *248*, 94–103.

Young, R. O., & Frye, M. Some are laughing; some are not—why? *Psychological Reports*, 1966, *18*, 747–754.

Zajonc, R. B. Feeling and thinking: Preferences need no inferences. *American Psychologist*, 1980, *35*, 151–175.

Zajonc, R. B., Pietromonaco, P., & Bargh, J. Independence and interaction of affect and cognition. In M. S. Clark & S. T. Fiske (Eds.), *Affect and cognition*. Hillsdale, NJ: Erlbaum, 1982.

Zillmann, D. Attribution and misattribution of excitatory reactions. In J. H. Harvey, W.Ickes & R. F. Kidd (Eds.), *New directions in attribution research* (Vol. 2). Hillsdale, NJ: Erlbaum, 1978.

Zillmann, D., Katcher, A. H., & Milavsky, B. Excitation transfer from physical exercise to subsequent aggressive behavior. *Journal of Experimental Social Psychology*, 1972, *8*, 247–259.

EQUITY AND SOCIAL EXCHANGE IN HUMAN RELATIONSHIPS*

Charles G. McClintock

DEPARTMENT OF PSYCHOLOGY
UNIVERSITY OF CALIFORNIA
SANTA BARBARA, CALIFORNIA

Roderick M. Kramer

DEPARTMENT OF PSYCHOLOGY
UNIVERSITY OF CALIFORNIA
LOS ANGELES, CALIFORNIA

Linda J. Keil

DEPARTMENT OF PSYCHOLOGY
UNIVERSITY OF NORTH CAROLINA
CHAPEL HILL, NORTH CAROLINA

*The preparation of this chapter was supported by NSF Grant, BNS 80-16214.
The present chapter represents a revision and extension of an earlier chapter by C. McClintock and L. Keil entitled "Equity and Social Exchange" which appeared in J. Greenberg and R. Cohen (Eds.) *Equity and Social Justice,* NY: Academic Press, 1982.

ADVANCES IN EXPERIMENTAL
SOCIAL PSYCHOLOGY, VOL. 17

> All women have their value, men as well
> fetch market prices when they want to sell.
> If a woman wants to boast she's made a kill
> And bagged my heart. Alright! She'll foot the bill.
> One has to strike a bargain, and to make
> the scale weigh even, give and *take*.
>
> Acate in Moliere's *The Misanthrope*

If a social psychologist were to speculate about what characteristics are common to the behavior of children on a playground, traders in the stock market, knights on a medieval field of battle, contestants on a TV game show, or adversaries in a divorce proceeding, two would readily suggest themselves. First, in each there are multiple actors or groups of actors who interact with one another in order to exchange a variety of more or less valued physical or social resources, whether these be marbles, coupons, arrows, prizes or animosities. And second, in each setting there exist more or less elaborate codes of behavior defining fair or equitable procedures for carrying out the exchange, as well as rules specifying equitable or just ways to allocate resources following a given set of outcomes.

I. Equity

There are a large number of terms in English that have been employed to describe equity in human relationships: just, rightful, fair, impartial, equal, lawful, legitimate, dispassionate, appropriate, considered, and so forth. Some of these terms apply primarily to the outcomes of human transactions; others, principally to the procedures employed to achieve such outcomes. In addition to its many specific meanings, equity has been conceptualized in more abstract and functional terms by sociologists, anthropologists, and political scientists.

In sociology, for example, equity often is used to define a set of organizational rules and procedures by which authority is legitimatized in bureaucracies. Beginning with Weber (1947), various organizational theorists including Simon (1957) and Presthus (1960) have viewed the norm of equity as providing the moral rationale for the premise that those in authority have the *right* to demand obedience; those subject to authority, the *obligation* to obey. These and other organizational theorists have attempted to describe the various criteria that societies employ to legitimize distributions of authority and how these various distributions influence the functioning of organizations. Similar assumptions about equity are made by political theorists concerned with the relationship between social contracts and the doctrine of political obligation. Although legitimization, as Katz and Kahn (1978) observe, has not been used frequently as an explanatory construct in social psychology, Milgram's (1974) findings on subject's blind obedience to authorities are certainly consistent with Weber's theoretical assumptions concerning fairness towards others and the rights delegated to legitimate authority figures.

In social psychology a somewhat different and more specific definition of equity dominates most contemporary research and theory. Beginning with Homans's notion of distributive justice (1961), and following its subsequent formalization by Adams (1965, pp. 267–299), *equity* has been defined as a single rule that may be employed to determine what is a fair distribution of outcomes between interdependent actors. Namely, the rule of equity is assumed to assert that the distribution of outcome or gain should be proportional to one's own and other's relative inputs or contributions. This definition might be thought to set rather strict boundaries on what outcome distributions are equitable. However, by broadly defining what are relevant inputs, the concept of equity can include a diverse set of distributional criteria (Deutsch, 1975) including those of strict proportionality, equality, need and even divine right.

A. EQUITY IN RECIPROCATION OR IN ALLOCATION

Eckhoff (1974) in his brilliant treatise on justice notes that problems of justice or equity occur in situations in which there is *transfer* of resources, namely, when one party takes some action in relation to another party to which the latter attaches positive or negative value. Parties can be individuals, groups, or societies. Eckhoff distinguishes two major classes of transfer, namely those of reciprocation and of allocation. *Reciprocation* exists where there is give and take between two parties, and where one transfer is conditioned by another. This may occur when there is an exhange of positive resources, such as parents trading kisses with their children at bedtime, or the reciprocation may involve parties inflicting negative outcomes upon each other, as in warfare or marital conflicts.

The second major class of transfers Eckhoff defines as *allocations* of resources. Such allocations involve the division of one set of objects by an allocator between two or more recipients. In terms of fairness, one can talk about whether parents have fairly allocated presents to their children at Christmas time or whether the criminal justice system has allocated fair punishments to two offenders, one of whose crimes is considered more serious than the other's.

A somewhat similar distinction has been made by Gulliver (1969, pp. 24–68), who examined the ways conflicts of interest are settled in differing cultures.

After reviewing a number of societies of differing complexity, he concludes that whereas all of them possess negotiation procedures for the reciprocal transfer of resources between parties, only some have methods for arbitration. Arbitration in this instance implies that some individual or group external to the conflict of interest acts as an arbitrator, or in Eckhoff's terms, as an allocator of resources. Hence, negotiations represent universal first party reciprocated procedures for conflict resolution in which compulsion is exercised by the opposing party and not by an overriding external authority. Arbitration, on the other hand, implies resource allocation decisions being made by a third party, such as might be obtained in a binding labor arbitration. We return to this distinction later.

B. EQUITY AS A PROCEDURE OR AS AN OUTCOME

In the present chapter we are concerned principally with equity as a form of *outcome fairness*. There are, or course, a whole range of fairness phenomena that relate to the issue of the means or procedures of justice rather than to its outcomes. Although the distinction between fairness of procedure and the justice of outcomes has received considerable philosophical attention (e.g., Kames, 1760; Rawls, 1972; Rescher, 1966), relatively little attention has been given to issues of procedural fairness by social psychologists (Reis, 1984). Exceptions to this involve some emerging work on the relationship between justice procedures, outcomes, satisfaction, and perceived fairness (Brickman & Bryan, 1976; Folger, 1977; Folger, Rosenfield, Grove & Cockran, 1979; Thibaut & Walker, 1975).

C. EQUITY AND THE THEORY OF SOCIAL VALUE

One fundamental characteristic of actors who are in a relationship of reciprocation is that they are interdependent in terms of achieving outcomes. That is, the behavior pursued by one actor often affects both the actor's and the other's outcome. The obverse is true as well—others' behaviors affect both their own and the actor's outcomes. This relationship of interdependence has profound implications for the formation and expression of *human values*. It implies that as a social agent developing criteria for action, an individual must often consider the implications that his or her choices have for both his or her own and others' outcomes. Such a consideration is requisite to the extent that humans have been evolutionarily programmed and/or socialized to place value on others' outcomes. The functional necessity for considering others' outcomes is obvious: Given the necessity for reciprocation of resources, an actor's rewards and punishments and, in fact, survival are determined by others' behavior as well as his or her own and vice versa.

McClintock (1972, 1977) has, with the help of a number of colleagues and students, attempted to develop a general conceptual paradigm that enables one to define an actor's preference for certain outcomes for the self and others, in settings of outcome interdependence. Such preferences are presumed to reflect the actor's *social values* or orientation towards others. The paradigm first assumes that in situations of social interdependence, actors' access to outcomes they value is dependent to a large extent upon each other's preferences. This reciprocal dependence is a condition central to the theory of games (see Luce & Raiffa, 1957), as well as to many other statements concerning human relationship. Further, in an assumption that takes one beyond conventional game theory, the value paradigm assumes that "the attractiveness of a particular alternative for one actor may be influenced not only by the outcomes she (or he) receives but also by the outcomes she (or he) judges the other will receive" (McClintock, 1977, p. 54.). Thus, the paradigm admits the possibility that coactors are not necessarily, or only, self-interested beings indifferent to the fate of others.

These two assumptions combine to describe a social being who is interdependent with others as regards obtaining valued outcomes and who may prefer to distribute physical, psychological, and social resources between the self and others in a variety of ways. Hence, the structure of the interdependence as well as the specific self- or other-outcome preferences of participating actors are viewed as playing a major part in determining the functional character of exchange relationships (see Wyer, 1969, 1971).

The paradigm goes on to assume that there often exist consistent preferences for particular distributions of outcomes for the self and others by an actor that reflect relatively stable and internalized social values. One way to represent such preferences is as vectors in a two-dimensional space, in which the magnitude or quality of an actor's outcomes is defined on one axis and those of a coactor on the other (Griesinger & Livingston, 1973). Fig. 1 illustrates those linear vectors that define a subset of social values that are more or less frequently expressed in settings in which there are two or more interdependent actors. Included are preferences that maximize others' outcomes, joint outcomes, one's own outcomes, and the relative advantage of one's own over others' outcomes, and one that minimizes others' outcomes. Although there are an infinite number of possible outcome preference rules, those social values common both to naive as well as to scientific descriptions of human social behavior clearly seem to fall on those vectors that correspond to the principal own- and other-outcome axes, or with vectors 45° removed from these.

D. THE SOCIAL VALUES OF FAIRNESS

In a recent article, Van Avermaet, McClintock, and Moskowitz (1978) demonstrate that rules or preferences for equitable outcomes can also be charac-

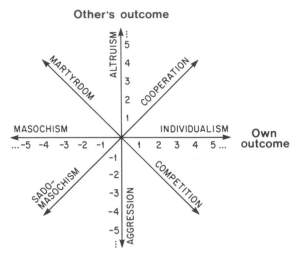

Fig. 1.   Vectors that define a subset of social values. (Given a particular value orientation, an actor should select that combination of available own and other's outcomes that has the greatest projection on the corresponding vector.)

terized as social values. For example, the two most frequently cited rules of fairness—proportional equity and equality—can be represented in a two-dimensional own- or other-outcome space. Given its proportional representation, however, equity does not take a linear form. Rather, as depicted in the example in Fig. 2, an individual intent upon maximizing the equity of his own and other's outcomes would follow a decision rule in which the ratio of the self to the other's outcomes would be proportional to the ratio of their respective inputs. Given that the other made twice the inputs as oneself, for example, an actor would prefer choices on a line with a slope value of 2 and would prefer those points in the outcome space for which the ratio between one's own and other's outcomes most closely approximates 2.

The dashed lines in Fig. 2 deserve brief comment. They represent indifference lines or curves, a concept developed by decision theorists to describe various combinations of two commodities between which a buyer has no preference. As depicted in Fig. 2, actors choosing equitably would prefer the combination of one's own and other's outcome points falling on the indifference line closest to the slope 2 line. However, they would be indifferent between the points defining a given indifference line because the ratio of one's own and other's outcomes to inputs falling on this line are proportionally equal. Indifference proves to be a very useful assumption in defining, prescribing, and measuring an actor's decision rules.

Whereas Fig. 2 depicts an instance of equity given 2 : 1 inputs, Fig. 3 illustrates an equality preference structure independent of inputs. The indifference curves in this instance run parallel to an equality ridge with a slope of

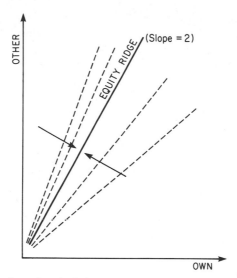

Fig. 2.   Equity, given the other's inputs are twice one's own inputs. (The most equitable distribution of one's own and other's outcomes would fall on the equity ridge. Dashed lines represent indifference curves defined by their proximity to the ridge and where the ratio of the self to the other's outcomes are proportional to the ratio of their respective inputs.)

one. Actors are again assumed to prefer their own and other's outcome combinations on those indifference curves most proximal to the ridge. Thus, both equality and equity as defined by any given own- or other-input ratio can be mapped onto the two-dimensional payoff space described in Fig. 1. The advantage of

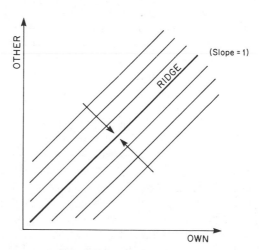

Fig. 3.   Equality given equal inputs by the self and the other. (Note indifference curves as defined in Fig. 2 are parallel to the equality ridge line.)

such a formal representation of social values is not merely that it graphically depicts possible preferences between various self- or other-outcomes. More importantly, it suggests ways to empirically test assertions about the relative dominance of various social goals and strategies.

It should be strongly emphasized that proportional equity and equality are only two of a number of patterns of outcomes between the actor and others that may be labelled as fair or just. A variety of systematic preference structures can be and have been defined as equitable: for example, winner-take-all, every man for himself, Pareto-optimality, the distribution of outcomes by need, and noblesse oblige.

E. ATTRIBUTIONS AND MISATTRIBUTIONS OF SOCIAL VALUES

One of the principal activities that actors who are in relationships of reciprocity pursue is the exchange between one another of various types of services, resources, and affect. Theories that describe these exchange processes are reviewed in the next section. Here, we want to point out why it is difficult at times for both a naive actor or observer, as well as a more sophisticated social scientist, to decode accurately the social values expressed by an actor within an interdependent relationship. The resulting inaccuracies in decoding pose a significant problem to both the actor and the other because they can raise the costs of maintaining the relationship and thereby jeopardize its viability. For the social scientist the misunderstanding of intentions behind acts may also reduce the validity and reliability of descriptions, explanations, and subsequent predictions of the choice behavior of actors in settings of reciprocity.

When an actor selects one of several ways to distribute outcomes between the self and the other, the behavior is subject to a variety of interpretations. One possible source of attributional confusion may occur when an act is interpreted as a goal rather than a. strategy. Mary's attributing John's act of giving her something as being an instance of ingratiation can markedly influence not only her view of him, but also what kinds of outcomes she will mediate for him in the future. Even if attributions are restricted to goal-oriented behaviors, there is still room for major errors. For example, suppose John had the opportunity to afford Mary $500 and himself $500, or to afford Mary $300 and himself $600, and he chose the second alternative. Mary could reasonably make the attribution that John was *not* behaving in a prosocial manner towards her. He did not choose to maximize either her outcome or their joint outcomes. Furthermore, he rejected the fairness norm of equality. However, Mary still does not have sufficient information to judge how antisocial John's behavior was intended to be. For his choice maximized his own outcome, his competitive advantage over her, and minimized Mary's outcome. Obviously, she does not have the information on the basis of John's choice to decide whether he was individualistic, competitive, or aggressive in motivation. Of course, which of these three orientations Mary chooses to attribute to John may affect her future behavior towards him, including the types of outcomes she would mediate for him. This, in turn, will influence John's subsequent behavior towards Mary, and so on.

II. Social Exchange Theories

In his ambitious analysis of social and economic behaviors, Engels (1880/1959) at one point argued, "Next to production, the exchange of things produced is the basis of all social structure. The final causes of all social changes . . . are to be sought not in men's brains, nor in man's better insight into eternal truth and justice, but in changes in the modes of production or exchange" (p. 90). Whereas equity theories focus specifically upon the fair or just distribution of resources, *social exchange theories* are concerned more broadly with the general processes and principles that govern the provision, trade, or transfer of more or less valued psychological, social, and material commodities or resources. Thus, equity may be viewed as one subset of these exchange processes; in one sense, a subset of regulative or procedural rules.

We should note from the outset that in ordinary usage *exchange* connotes any action or process whereby individuals donate, trade, barter, coerce, beg, or even steal in order to obtain valued objects or resources. As Blau (1964) has observed, "Neighbors exchange favors; children, toys; colleagues, assistance; acquaintances, courtesies; politicians, concessions; discussants, ideas; housewives, recipes. The pervasiveness of social exchange makes it tempting to consider all social conduct in terms of exchange, but this would deprive the concept of its distinctive meaning" (pp. 88–89). Consequently, social exchange theorists have generally adopted a more narrow and circumscribed conception of what constitutes exchange relations. There is general consensus among such theorists that social exchange entails the voluntary and intentional trade, transfer, or distribution of resources among actors; that the values or subjective utilities of these resources vary with the rewards and costs each individual associates with their acquisition, relinquishment, or possession; and that in exchange relations some kind of interdependence of outcomes exists between the actors. Excluded from most conceptions of social exchange is activity which is involuntary, relationships that are coercive, and situations in which compliance is dictated purely by conformity pressures. Thus, social exchange relationships are usually limited to those cases in which individuals can, to some degree at least, act in accord with their desires, preferences, and motivations.

However, it is *not* necessary to assume that individuals are entirely conscious of the utilities they attach to objects or outcomes they exchange, or even that an exchange has taken place. In some cases, individuals may be unaware that their relationship is based upon exchange. The physically unattractive man who exchanges his wealth and social power for his wife's elegance and uncommon beauty may never realize that there is a tacit ongoing exchange of their resources. If his wealth and power should diminish or her beauty fade, the stability of their relationship may be affected, necessitating a subtle renegotiation or reevaluation of its terms (e.g., the exchange of the loyalty they have developed for each other) or even its termination. Thus, it is not essential that exchange theories have "psychological reality" if they are otherwise useful predictive and explanatory systems.

Not surprisingly, anthropologists, sociologists, economists, and social psychologists have all at one time or another attempted to specify in their own terms, the processes and principles underlying the exchange of resources. In doing so, sociologists have been more inclined, for example, to think in terms of social groups and norms; anthropologists, in terms of institutional structures and cultural traditions; economists have preferred thinking in terms of material commodities and an interpersonal marketplace; whereas social psychologists are more comfortable with cognitive, motivational, and decisional processes occurring within the individual. Despite these differences, however, there has been considerable conceptual overlap, with cross-fertilization evident between the major exchange theories of each discipline. Emerson (1981), in an effort to define the common interdisciplinary ground of exchange theories, has noted that "the central concept in exchange theory carries a different name in the various disciplines the theory springs from: *reinforcement* in psychology; *value* in sociology; *utility* in economics and decision theory; *reward outcome* or *payoff* in social psychology" (p. 31–32). To a large extent, therefore, the kind of exchange theory one ends up with is determined by the kind of explanatory constructs posited and the primary unit of analysis preferred. In the remainder of this section, we briefly examine some of the more influential social exchange theories from anthropology, sociology, and economics. We are concerned primarily with their contributions to the development of a social psychological theory of exchange (See Emerson, 1976, 1981; McClintock & Keil, 1982; Roloff, 1981, for more detailed and complete reviews.

A.   THE ANTHROPOLOGICAL APPROACH TO EXCHANGE

One of the first social scientists to investigate the social nature of the exchange of resources was the anthropologist Mauss (1925/1954). Mauss examined the significance of the exchange of gifts in a number of simple societies. He observed that though gifts appeared to be offered in a voluntary manner within and between various societies, they were in fact given and repaid under obligation. He further noted that with regard to the nature of exchange, the process was strongly social in nature: "What they exchange is not exclusively goods and wealth, real and personal property, and things of economic value. They exchange rather courtesies, entertainments, rituals, military assistance, women, children, dances, feast, and fairs in which the market is but one part of a wide enduring contact" (p. 3).

Lévi–Strauss (1969), like Mauss, also examined the interparty exchange of goods within a variety of societies. He concluded that the exchange of goods is not only pervasive but has meaning far beyond the realization of simple economic values by permitting a participant "to gain security and fortify oneself against risks incurred through alliances and rivalry." (p. 76). He strongly argued against deductive forms of theorizing in which social exchange laws are deduced from economic principles that in turn are viewed to derive from more inclusive natural laws. In fact, he saw no need to distinguish economic laws from social laws of exchange. He proceeds to argue that the nature of the goods exchanged is actually irrelevant to understanding the process of exchange: "The exchange relationship comes before the things exchanged, and is independent of them. If the goods considered in isolation are identical, they cease to be so when assigned their proper place in the structure of reciprocity" (1969, p. 139).

The models of exchange proposed by Mauss, Lé-Strauss, and other anthropologists by and large fall within an emergent collectivist tradition that generally eschews as principles for explaining social behavior both the rational decision-making assumptions of economics and the individualistic reward and cost formulations of behavioral psychology. Whereas most social psychological theories of exchange ask how indiviudal actors behave and interact given the constraints of norms, roles, and other institutional arrangements, the more collectivist theories are concerned with understanding the origins and functioning of these institutional variables themselves. And whereas the former see individual self-interest, needs, and social values as the motivating forces propelling human action and interaction, the collectivist tradition postulates that understanding social phenomena, including the behavior of individuals, is dependent upon identifying and assessing those social processes that contribute more or less to the successful functioning of societies and subgroups within them. Consistent with this point of view, collectivists assume that the laws that govern such societal processes are emergent and hence irreducible to the level of the individual.

One of the more important insights that anthropologists have contributed to the social psychology of social exchange is their observation that there exist many extraindividualistic factors, for example, institutions, norms, and collective pressures, that influence exchange at the interpersonal level. Thus, any analysis that focuses only on interpersonal behaviors, as if the dyad were a complete or closed system in and of itself, may yield an oversimplified and inaccurate view of the determinants of exchange. These extraindividualistic factors may provide a stable context or environment within which individuals may negotiate exchange with relatively low risk and uncertainty. Thus, social psychological theories of exchange, an account of which is provided shortly, should always be viewed as *conditional* theories of individual behavior given the existence of a particular social and cultural context.

B.   ON DEFINING WHAT IS EXCHANGED

Although Mauss (1925/1954) was the first to attempt to classify the commodities typically exchanged in human social relationships, more recently Foa and Foa (1980) have continued this effort. They postulate the existence of six classes of exchangeable resources: status, love, services, information, material goods, and money. These they order along two dimensions, *particularism* and *concreteness*. Particularism is a dimension that defines the degree to which the specific individual with wbom the resource is to be exchanged constitutes a condition for the exchange to occur. Hence, one might expect that love would be the most particularistic resource and money, the least. The second dimension is one of symbolism, with status and information falling on the more symbolic end of the continuum and services and goods on the more concrete end. Foa and Foa use this classification scheme to help define similarity between resources, to predict which classes of resources are likely to be exchanged for one another, and to define the meanings imputed to such exchanges. For example, the meaning of exchanging love for money is quite different from that of exchanging love for status or for love.

Recently, McClintock (1982) has suggested that affect may serve not only as a by-product of the interpersonal exchange of resources, but it may function as a commodity for exchange in its own right. Affect is generally indicative of states of satisfaction and dissatisfaction. These, in turn, serve two functions in exchange relationships. First, the degree of satisfaction experienced can motivate participants either to continue or to terminate an exchange relationship. Second, the emotional cues associated with satisfaction or with dissatisfaction when directed towards or perceived by another can have utility for the other and can serve to encourage, persuade, or discourage the other to modify his or her behavior so as to produce more rewarding outcomes for oneself. In effect, the affect serves as a commodity that is exchanged for some valued future outcome. As Emerson (1981) has noted, "Beneficial events of all kinds whether they involve money, goods, smiles, or simply 'social attention,' are valuable in exactly the same general sense: people for whom they are beneficial act in a way that tends to produce them" (p. 31).

C. THE ECONOMIC MODEL OF EXCHANGE

Robbins (1932, p. 15) in an oft-quoted definition asserts that economics is "a science which studies human behavior as a relationship between ends and scarce means with alternative uses." In effect, Robbins argues that economics is concerned with how humans should and do make decisions or choices regarding the employment of scarce resources in the pursuit of preferred outcomes. Exchange processes become important because many economic decisions involve two or more interdependent actors. In the process of developing an economic exchange model, a general paradigm of human decision making has emerged that is applicable to human behavior in noneconomic as well as economic contexts. This decision making paradigm of rational choice, in fact, parallels that which provides the conceptual basis for the theory of social values described earlier in the section "Equity and the Theory of Social Values."

The theory of rational choice asserts that an individual actor should and often does make choices in a purposive manner so as to obtain preferred outcomes in an effective way, that is, so as to maximize the value of his or her outcomes. If an actor has complete control over achieving the outcomes available, he or she merely makes that choice that will access the most preferred goal. If, as is often the case, the likelihood that a particular outcome can be obtained is not certain, the actor is compelled to take into consideration both the probability of obtaining the outcome as well as its utility, thus, maximizing the expected value of his or her outcomes. In economics, the dominant value that is assumed to dictate human economic behavior is the maximization of one's *own* economic utilities or outcomes.

Given a theory of rational choice for maximizing the expected value of outcomes, economists next ask the question of whether one can define a preference space that would describe an actor's attempts to maximize outcomes in regard to preferred combinations of two or more commodities. To do so, they define indifference curves, namely, curves that can be mapped onto a two-dimensional geometrical outcome space. An indifference curve, as defined earlier in the section "The Social Values of Fairness", is given by a series of points; every point represents a particular combination of two or more commodities between which an actor is indifferent.

Generally, economists (see, MacCrimmon & Toda, 1969) assume in drawing sets of indifference curves that a consumer would prefer to have more of both commodities than less and that the consumer's choices are transitive; that is, the consumer has consistent preferences, and hence, indifference curves will not intersect. Finally, they assume that some notion of diminishing marginal utility applies, namely, the more a consumer has of a particular commodity, the less valuable will be the next additional unit of that commodity. In the theory of social values the two commodities that are used to map indifference curves are one's own and the other's resource outcomes. These commodities can be defined economically, but they can also be defined by outcomes that fall into Foa and Foa's (1980) other resource classes.

The most interesting part of economic theory as it relates to exchange theory concerns instances in which one has two buyers and/or sellers who each want something that the other has. In effect, much of economic theory and all of exchange theory is concerned with understanding the dynamics of actors' behaviors in settings in which the outcomes can be improved more within a relationship than outside of it. In some instances, to maintain acceptable levels of reinforcement, actors directly mediate rewards and/or costs for one another. In other instances, external constraints may make the rewards exchanged within a relationship, no matter how low, higher than the costs of leaving the relationship. The latter defines what is sometimes called an involuntary relationship.

Most major theories of economic exchange consider the case of bilateral monopoly in which two actors have something to trade or exchange and in which each attempts to maximize own profits. The economists again use the notion of indifference curves to represent this instance, but this time they map two or more actors' preference structures for the distribution of the two commodities to be traded in a geometric space, using what is in economics termed an *Edgeworth Box*. Blau (1964a), for example, uses such a box diagram to extend economic theory to an analysis of an exchange between two actors who possess two social rather than economic commodities, one being expert "problem-solving ability" and the other "resources of willing compliance", that is, the ability by deference to confer status or esteem upon others.

A simple depiction of Blau's (1964a) use of an economic model is given in the box diagram in Fig. 4. In effect, the box illustrates the bilateral relationship between Person A and Person B, who can trade the two social commodities in varying amounts. If one assumes that each person has some amount of each commodity prior to an exchange, then one can represent their initial position in the box, say at point X in Fig. 4. Also represented in the box are two indifference curves, one for Person A: $a_1 a_3$ and one for Person B: $b_1 b_3$. These two curves intersect and define the sets of outcomes between which both are indifferent. The space within the two sets of indifference curves defines a region *both* actors would simultaneously prefer in terms of the relative distribution of Blau's two commodities, problem-solving ability and willing compliance.

Once we have identified such a region, the next question becomes what actual trades should or will be made? Consider the point Y in the space. Both persons are better off here than at their present location X. However, note that there remain numerous points at which both would be even better off in terms of their preference structure. It can be seen, for example, that the optimal point for Person A is at a_2 and for Person B at b_2. In fact, a line connecting the two points defines the parties' maximum joint benefit. Economic theory argues that ex-

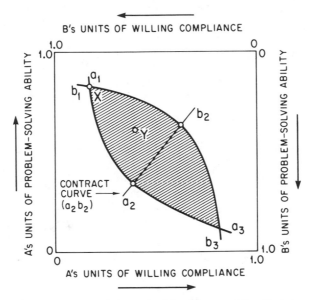

B's UNITS OF WILLING COMPLIANCE

A's UNITS OF WILLING COMPLIANCE

Fig. 4.   An Edgeworth box depicting a possible exchange relationship between Actor A and Actor B for the commodities of problem-solving ability and units of willing compliance. (Note that a_1, a_3 is an indifference curve for Actor A; b_1, b_3 for Actor B. Together they define a common region [shaded] of jointly preferred outcomes. Y represents an outcome preferred by A and B to X. Outcome a_2 is A's most preferred outcome; b_2 is B's. The line a_2, b_2 defines a contract curve, that is, the region of maximum joint benefit.)

changes will tend to occur along this a_2b_2 line, called the contract line, but that the particular point on the line is indeterminant a priori. In effect, this line represents a region in which bargaining is required because movement along either indifference curve away from the contract line will worsen one person's position at no added advantage to the other.

This bilateral monopoly model, as Cook and Emerson (1978) note, leaves the *specific* outcome of two-person exchange indeterminate along the contract line. Because economic theory is based upon a model of individual decision making in an asocial market in which actors, though more or less interdependent, tend to be numerous and strangers, there are no normative allocation rules once a contract line is reached. Social theories of exchange, on the other hand, address this indeterminancy. Namely, they are concerned with how concepts such as social value, equity, power, social comparison, distributive justice, profit, and so forth help to define the processes that influence the formation and maintenance of relations, as well as help to predict the specific outcomes that actors will obtain in exchange relationships.

Finally, one additional aspect of economic theory that has been important in the development of social exchange models is the theory of price. Both Blau (1964) and Homans (1974) in their theories of social exchange use the economic assumption that the actual or equilibrium price of a commodity is given by the intersection of demand and supply curves. For this to be obtained in economics, a number of assumptions must be made: such as, that the commodities are homogeneous; that there are large numbers of buyers and sellers; and that buyers and sellers have knowledge of the prices at which others are willing to buy and sell. Both Blau and Homans relax these assumptions. Blau (1964), for instance, utilizes the concept of price to help define the relative stability of relationships formed for the exchange of two resources, problem-solving ability and willing compliance (conformity). Homans (1974), in his social exchange theory, uses the theory of price in yet another way, namely to help explain why some members of a group are afforded more status than others. He argues, for example, that expert advice is characteristically in scarcer supply than conformity and hence engenders greater approval and status from the group. Again the pricing of advice or conformity may not be strictly determinant, and the setting of prices for these social commodities is subject to negotiation and the operation of various social decision rules. These two theories then, bilateral monopoly and price, are central in both theories of economic and of social psychological exchange.

D.   SOCIAL PSYCHOLOGICAL CONCEPTIONS OF EXCHANGE

Social psychological models of exchange, in contrast to anthropological and economic ones, have focused principally upon the exchange of resources between smaller numbers of actors (e.g., small closed groups). In fact, much of the research focuses on exchange between the two members of a single dyad. Further, although admitting the need for considering normative and institutional factors as well as decisions motivated by economic considerations, social psychologists place greater emphasis upon the structure of dyadic interdependence and interaction rather than institutional control and upon the centrality of social values in contrast to exclusively economic ones. As regards the latter, Olson (1965) has noted, "Economic incentives are not the only incentives . . . People are also motivated sometimes by the desire to win prestige, respect, friendship, and other social and psychological objectives" (p. 60).

There are three major social psychological theories of exchange. These differ primarily in terms of the kind of explanatory constructs employed: (1) Homans' theory, put forth in his *Social Behavior: Its Elementary Forms* (1961, 1974), uses principles derived from operant conditioning and behavioristic learning theories; (2) Blau's theory, presented in *Exchange and Power in Social Life* (1964a), extends Homan's theory considerably by introducing cognitive processes such as goals and purposes, as well as emphasizing the institutional bases of exchange; and (3) Thibaut and Kelley's theory sets forth a sophisticated analysis of the structure of interdependence underlying social coordination and exchange presented initially in *The Social Psychology of Groups* (1959), extended in Kelley and Thibaut's *Interpersonal Relations: A Theory of Interdependence* (1978), and more recently described in Kelley's *Personal Relationships* (1979).

Prior to a brief description of some of the more important assumptions in each of these three major social psychological models of exchange, we note some of the basic assumptions they share:

1. Human actors are outcome interdependent insofar as they mediate rewards and punishments for others who in turn mediate rewards and punishments for them.
2. Human beings tend to form and continue those relationships that are profitable in the sense that the rewards obtained outweigh the costs of maintaining the relationship. Continuance is based upon both parties finding the relationship mutually profitable.
3. Actors within a relationship are compelled to reciprocate rewards in order to assure ongoing exchange and stability. In effect, each must take into consideration the welfare of the other to assure his or her own welfare.
4. Exchange is not restricted to economic acitvities. Social exchange as Blau (1964a) has observed, is ubiquitous, and almost any resources that actors value may be exchanged, including material, social, and psychological ones.
5. The distribution of valued resources that actors possess prior to an exchange may or may not be symmetrical. Generally, an actor who has more of a valued resource or resources is assumed to have the capability to exercise commensurately more but not necessarily complete influence or power within the relationship.
6. Finally, although social psychological models differ in the degree to which they emphasize the centrality of various economic and psychological principles, they universally assume that the understanding of cultural or institutional arrangements is not sufficient for understanding the processes of social exchange. Rather, they see institutional factors as setting limits within which a variety of patterns of human interaction and exchange can occur.

1. Homan's Exchange Theory

Homans (1961, 1974) bases his theory of social exchange upon assumptions taken from Skinner's theory of operant conditioning (1973). He argues that even apparently complex social interactions are governed by, and hence can be analyzed in terms of, the same operant learning principles used to explain animal behavior. From this perspective, it is the reinforcements or consequences that follow emitted responses that determine the reward value of a behavior. These principles are presumed to provide entirely sufficient accounts of social exchange. "No new propositions [are needed] to describe and explain the social. With social behavior nothing unique emerges to be analyzed only in its own terms" (Homans, 1961, p. 30). This theoretical position contrasts, therefore, with the nonreductionism implicit in the anthropologist's consideration of the role of institutions, the sociologist's reliance on "emergent properties" in exchange relations, as well as the cognitive and decision theoretical assumptions concerning the future-oriented purposive nature of social action suggested by game theorists.

Homans defines the process of social exchange as consisting of the activities or behaviors of two persons who alternatively reinforce the activities of each other and thus influence the probability of future exchanges (1961, p. 30). Thus, for Homans, there is a behavioral interdependence whereby each actor's behaviors have reinforcing consequences that in turn shape the other's subsequent behaviors. A scientific analysis of their exchange behavior requires, therefore, a consideration of their unique reinforcement histories and differential responses to various reinforcers.

This model parsimoniously explains both prevalent and infrequent variations in social behavior. For example, the frequently observed commonalities in outcome distributions, for example, equality distributions, can be viewed as a resultant of similar and widespread patterns of prior reinforcement in a given society. Idiosyncratic or highly individualistic exchange behaviors, on the other hand, can be attributed to rarer or aberrant patterns of reinforcement. Homans' (1961) model of exchange helps illustrate how the contingencies of prior reinforcement present in various environmental settings help determine subsequent patterns of exchange. His analysis implies that as observers of current exchanges, we often mistakenly attribute causation to contemporaneous or future factors because the appropriate reinforcement history is not available or salient to us.

The concept of *value* in Homans' (1961) scheme is expressed in terms of the measure or magnitude of positive and negative reinforcement associated with the behaviors or resources exchanged. Homans argues that the behavioristic definition of the construct value is comparable to the economists' conception of utility, but avoids the necessity of assuming any cognitively mediated evaluative or rational decision processes. He notes further that there are two components of a value: first, that the resource, object, or behavior is in general reinforcing, and second, that the organism does not have sufficient quantity of that object, resource, or behavior. That is, there is a scarcity that increases the reward value of a resource or behavior. Thus, the value of a resource is dependent upon both its presence or availability in the environment and the receptivity of the organism towards it.

Because most social exchanges involve some expenditure of energy or investment of resources, the *costs* of the interaction also play a role in the exchange process. According to Homans, the "cost" of an exchange is the "value forgone" (1961, p. 58) implied by withdrawal or loss of a positive reinforcer. Taken together, the value and cost of the exchange are incorporated in its "psychic profit" which Homans defines simply as reward less costs. "No exchange continues," he argues, "unless both parties are making a profit" (1961, p. 61).

The major principles that Homans asserts govern the social exchange process are these (1961, 1976):

1. *Success Proposition.* The more often a given act is rewarded, the more likely an actor is to perform it (subject to the constraints stated in the deprivation–satiation proposition).
2. *Stimulus Proposition:* If in the past a particular event has resulted in an actor's behavior being rewarded, then the more similar the present event is to the past one, the more likely it is that the actor will again perform the same or a similar act.
3. *Value Proposition:* The more valuable the result of a person's action is to a person, the more likely he or she is to perform the action. Positive values imply both rewards and the avoidance or escape from punishment; negative values imply punishment, withholding rewards, or rewards forgone as a result of a given choice.
4. *Deprivation–Satiation Proposition:* The more recently a reward has been received, the less valuable any further unit of the reward.
5. *Aggression–Approval Proposition:* If a person does not receive an expected reward or receives less than expected, he or she will become angry or aroused and will be more likely to act aggressively as the results of such behavior become more valuable. Conversely, if a person receives an expected reward, and especially if more than expected is received, the person will be more likely to perform value-approving behavior.
6. *Rationality Proposition:* In choosing between alternative actions, a person will choose that one for which, as perceived at the time, the value of the results, multiplied by the probability of getting the results, is greatest. Homans does not mean here that we should view humans as calculators or rational decision-makers. On the contrary, he claims, "Although calculation for the long run plays its part in human affairs, we

make no allowance for it in our propositions. . . . The theory of games is good advice for human behavior but a poor description of it'' (1961, p. 81).

The final proposition, 6., summarizes Homans's (1961) first three propositions and is a restatement of the expected-value hypothesis that underlies most economic and social value models of human decision making. Homans believes that this proposition provides a link between his behavioral propositions and an economic model of human action and exchange without requiring the acceptance of their assumptions.

Although not stated in formal theoretical terms, Homans (1961) makes a number of assertions concerning the nature of social exchange that can be treated as derivatives of his fundamental psychological propositions. For example, he observes that exchange occurs when the action of one individual rewards another and vice versa and that an actor will approach that other person who is likely to offer the highest rewards in relationship to the costs of approach. He notes further that an *impersonal* relation exists when an actor enters into a single exchange with another for a single reward that is readily available elsewhere because it is the nature of the reward and not the identity of the particular person that is important. The relationship is a *personal* one when actors enter into multiple exchanges of reward that are specific to the particular actors involved.

The outcome of their interaction may be satisfactory or unsatisfactory to the parties involved. Conflict and anger may result if one actor perceives that another has achieved an unfair advantage. This leads to Homans's (1961) fourth well-known principle of distributive justice: An actor in an exchange relationship with another will expect the rewards of each to be proportional to the costs and the net rewards or profits of each person to be proportional to his or her investment, such that the greater the investment, the greater the profit.

Although there have been a number of insightful analyses and critiques of Homans's (1961) theory, we will limit our attention here to consideration of only one of the more central and frequently raised objections, a criticism that we believe to be in error. It has been claimed that Homans's analysis of social exchange is tautological, or circular. It seems as if he is saying that what is valuable are reinforcers, and yet the only way to tell if they are reinforcers is to see if the organism values them (i.e., expends effort and tolerates costs to obtain them). This criticism reveals two general misconceptions of his model. First, although psychologists typically analyze behavior in terms of antecedent and immediate processes, as Skinner (1973) has pointed out, there has been little systematic appreciation in most psychological theories of the fact that it is the consequences of behaviors that shape and maintain them. Second, as Emerson has noted (1981), the apparent circularity in Homans's analysis is not so much a theoretical flaw as it is a recognition of the fact that human behavior, like the behavior of most complex natural systems, is cybernetically regulated. Thus, though specific antecedent conditions may influence the range of behaviors emitted in a given context, it is the consequences of emitted behavior that affect the probability of future emission of that behavior.

2. Blau's Exchange Theory

In contrast to Homans' theory, Blau (1964a) argues that social exchange cannot be explained entirely in terms of the rewarding and punishing consequences of emitted behavior. "To be sure, each individual's behavior is reinforced by the rewards it brings, but the psychological process of reinforcement does not suffice to explain the exchange relation that develops. This social relation is the *joint product of the actions of both individuals,* with the actions of each being dependent on those of the other" (p. 4, italics ours). Central to Blau's conception of the exchange relationship is the assumption that the actor's behavior is directed towards goals that can only be attained by social means and that, consequently, exchange behaviors often represent strategic accommodations to others in order to achieve those goals. Thus, in contrast to Homans's (1961) depreciation of the role of decision making in exchange relations, Blau draws attention to the primacy of more purposive and rational processes underlying social exchange.

He also stresses the role of emergent properties in social relations. Although the immediate reciprocation of rewards may, for example, be important in the early stages of a relationship, later emergent qualities such as trust and commitment may lead to provision of rewards or benefits without expectation of short-term return or immediate compensation. These emergent properties add stability and adaptive flexibility to the relationship. "The limitation of psychological reductionism is that it tends to ignore these emergent characteristics of social life and explains it exclusively in terms of the motives that govern individual behavior" (Blau, 1964, p. 3).

By stressing the *mutual* dependence of outcomes, Blau (1964a) also identifies a number of basic social processes that underlie the associative tendencies of individuals. First, association with others may be facilitated by *intrinsic* attractions. For example, one individual may find it pleasurable or rewarding to be with an attractive, witty other, or with a similar other. More typical, however, are associations based upon *extrinsic* attractions. In these instances, one or more of the individuals in a relationship want something the others have. Social power, Blau claims, originates in these desired properties or assets. One of the obvious goals of an exchange relationship is the redistribution of resources so that each party obtains preferred outcomes. The kinds of rewards that are exchanged are not simply physically pleasurable but may take highly symbolic forms (e.g., self-esteem or status). Thus, relatively intangible and tacit rewards may be highly valued, despite the absence of obvious immediate positive reinforcement.

Blau's (1964a) conception of rewards is decidedly more cognitive than Homans's (1961). In characterizing social exchange processes, Blau assumes that rewards may be *spontaneous* (ends in themselves) or *calculated* (means to other ends). He distinguishes three types of costs that may affect the value of rewards: *investment costs* such as those associated with the acquisition of skills, *direct costs* such as occur when an actor complies to the other's demands in an exchange setting, and *opportunity costs* that include the alternative between pursuing and forgoing a given outcome. An actor is assumed to choose between alternative potential relationships or courses of action by first evaluating both prior and expected rewards and costs associated with each, and then selecting the one that maximizes net gains to the self.

Blau (1964a) further postulates that a fundamental characteristic of social exchange is that an actor who supplies a rewarding service to another obligates the other to furnish a benefit in return. In other words, exchanges create expectations regarding reciprocity (cf. Gouldner, 1960). Social exchange also differs from economic transactions insofar as the nature of the required return benefit is often diffuse, unstructured with regard to time, and dependent upon the perceived trustworthiness of the coactor.

Social exchange processes are also assumed to give rise to a differentiation in social power. An actor who services others' needs and who is independent of any services at the others' command attains power over others by making the satisfaction of others' needs contingent on their compliance or submission. Finally, Blau (1964a) describes dialectic processes that regulate the exchange process. Actors are motivated to maintain a balance between inputs and outputs and to stay out of debt in social transactions; which produces the strain towards reciprocity mentioned earlier. Simultaneously, actors aspire to achieve an exchange balance in their own favor by which they accumulate credit providing them status superior to that of others; hence, a strain towards imbalance is also evident in exchange relationships.

Blau (1964a) does not explicitly present a description of the needs and values of individual actors. Rather, he assumes them as given and goes on to define and evaluate the specific dyadic and group processes that guide the exchange of resources. In doing so, he examines such phenomena as impression formation and maintenance, the formation of groups, the differentiation of power and status, the emergence and functioning of group norms, the development of interpersonal trust, as well as a number of higher level collective processes.

It might seem at this point as if Blau's (1964a) conception of social exchange relationships is consistent with economic and "rational man" models, insofar as the individual is portrayed as systematically evaluating alternative outcomes and selecting that one which is best (i.e., maximizes his or her own gain or rewards). He is quick to point out, however, fundamental differences between social and economic exchanges. "In contrast to economic transactions, in which an explicit or implicit formal contract stimulates in advance the precise obligations incurred by both parties, social exchange entails unspecified obligations" (Blau, 1964a, p. 315). Because of these unspecified obligations, social exchange entails reliance upon emergent properties, such as mutual trust whereby one may make substantial investments with faith in long-term returns of a different sort. The coactors' commitment to these tacit rules and norms allows them to interact effectively with minimal negotiation of terms and perceived risk.

3. Thibaut and Kelley's Theory of Social Interdependence

Consistent with both Homans (1961) and Blau (1964a) Thibaut and Kelley (1959) assume that in order to be repeated social behavior must be reinforced or rewarded. More than other theorists, however, they have attempted to develop a comprehensive theory of social exchange and interaction by analyzing the structural features of social interdependence.

Thibaut and Kelley (1959) argue that the interaction between one actor and another can be depicted using a simple matrix in which rows represent one actor's behavioral choices; and columns, those choices available to the other. Entered in each cell of the matrix are outcomes that represent a composite of the rewards and costs experienced by the actor and by the other for a particular combination of their behaviors. The specific value of each outcome is a function of variables *exogenous* to the relationship, such as the needs of the actor and the resources of other, and *endogenous* variables, such as the prior history of dyadic interaction or existing incompatibilities between the actor's various response alternatives.

Kelley and Thibaut (1978) assume that individuals are highly selective in their interactions, seeking out those that are most likely to produce satisfaction. They further assume that an interaction between an actor and another will be initiated or will continue based upon the value of the outcomes experienced by both parties relative to two general criteria: (1) *Comparison level (CL)*, the standard one that is used to evaluate the attractiveness of a relationship in terms of beliefs about whether one deserves the outcome provided. If the outcomes fall above the comparison level, then the relationship is relatively satisfying; if they fall below, it is unsatisfying. The level is determined by one's prior history, real or symbolic, of outcomes experienced, and (2) the *Comparison level for alternatives (CL_{alt})*, the lowest level of outcomes that one will accept in a relationship, given available alternative relationships. When outcomes fall below the comparison level for alternatives, an actor may leave the relationship. The more above the CL_{alt} that one's outcomes are in a given relationship, the more one is likely to remain in that relationship. For example, an actor may remain in an intrinsically unsatisfying relationship (i.e., one in which the level of rewards are below the actor's CL) because these outcomes are still above the actor's CL_{alt}.

An actor is assumed to have power over another to the extent that variations in his or her behavior can affect the quality of the other's outcome. Two basic kinds of power are defined. Actors have *fate control* if they can affect another's outcome regardless of what the other does. Actors are said to have *behavior control* over another if they have available to them rewards and punishments that can be used to encourage the other to behave in one way rather than another.

Kelley and Thibaut's (1978) more recent theoretical work extends their prior structural analyses of game matrices as a way to depict formally the nature and levels of social interdependence. Game matrices were initially defined and formally explored by mathematicians and economists as a method for developing prescriptive models of rational choice, given varying structures of outcome interdependence and exchange. Subsequently, these matrix games have been used both theoretically and methodologically by social psychologists to explore empirically patterns of cooperation, competition, and bargaining in relationships in which two or more actors are outcome interdependent and in which the behaviors of each mediate rewards and punishments for themselves and others.

Kelley and Thibaut (1978), in particular, consider how the social values of individual actors and the objective nature of the interdependence structure between them interact to determine the "*total set* of outcome matrices—those correctly and those incorrectly understood—[that] account for all social behaviors" (p. 4–5). More specifically, Kelley and Thibaut (1978) and Kelley (1979) examine three factors or components of a given matrix that can help to account for the variance of self–other outcomes within it. The first factor they define as *reflexive control,* namely, the implications of the effects one's behavior has for one's own outcomes, independent of its effect upon another's outcome. The second, as described earlier, is fate control, or the degree to which one can unilaterally affect another's outcomes. The third, *behavior control,* reflects the degree to which combinations of one's own and other's actions can simultaneously influence each person's outcomes.

In summary, Thibaut and Kelley's (1959) conception of the exchange process focuses upon outcome interdependence. Individual rewards and costs, two major forms of evaluation of outcomes, and the capability to exercise control over one's own and another's outcomes and behaviors are initially defined at an individualistic level, albeit at the level of a very social individual who maximizes socially defined outcomes, such as status and prestige, and who values both his or her own outcomes with other's outcomes. For Thibaut and Kelley, the more fundamental understanding of social exchange and interdependence necessarily occurs at the level of an interacting dyad or group.

III. Equity and Social Exchange

The primary purpose of the present chapter is *not* to provide a comprehensive analysis either of equity or of social exchange theories. Rather we examine what has been set forth theoretically about the role equity plays within relationships of reciprocity or exchange. To do this, we believe it useful to characterize the current status of theories of fairness and exchange. In considering the relationship between equity and exchange one can assume that *equitable exchanges* may be characterized as that subset of all possible exchanges that are deemed fair, just, reasonable, or appropriate according to some criteria or standard. Understanding how these more or less formalized standards or rules influence reciprocal preferences or choice behaviors is requisite to explaining how considerations of fairness influence human interaction and exchange.

A. THE RELATIONSHIP BETWEEN EQUITY AND RECIPROCITY

There have been a number of ways in which fairness and justice have been defined and described in terms of their relationship to the processes of reciprocity and social exchange. Such definitions, as in decision theoretical models of human behavior, have been made both prescriptively and descriptively. An example of a prescriptive definition of equity is provided by Mauss (1925–1954, p. 69) in his study of the reciprocation of gift giving: "A wise precept has run right through human evolution, and we would be wise to adopt it as a principle of action. We should come out of ourselves and regard the duty of giving as a liberty, for in it there lies no risk. A fine Maori proberb runs: . . . 'Give as much as you receive and all is for the best.' "

Eckhoff (1974) also defines a prescriptive set of principles of justice common to a number of situations of reciprocity or exchange and illustrated by the following directives: "(1) good shall be repaid by good; (2) hurt can be repaid by hurt; (3) a wrong shall be righted; and (4) after receiving an advantage one may expect a disadvantage" (p. 30). Eckhoff defines the preceding principles as instances of *retributive justice* in exchange settings, differentiating them from the principle of justice that is central to allocation settings, namely, the familiar notion of *distributive justice*.

Malinowski (1922, p. 39) provides a more functional description of the relationship between fairness and social exchange. A fair relationship is characterized as "occurring within a standing partnership, or associated with definite social ties or coupled with mutuality in noneconomic matters" and as entailing "mutual dependence . . . being realized in the equivalent arrangement of reciprocal services" (p. 55). And it is the "equivalent arrangement of reciprocal services'' that defines for Malinowski how fair outcomes are achieved given various divisions of labor between interdependent actors.

Gouldner (1960, p. 88) takes a somewhat similar stance to that of Malinowski, assuming the existance of a universal norm of reciprocity that in effect defines the following requirements for fairness in human action: ''(1) People should help those who have helped them and (2) people should not injure those who have helped them.'' Gouldner then describes four conditions or standards that help to define the imputed value of the resource the potential reciprocator has received from a donor: (1) the intensity of the recipient's need, (2) the resources available to the donor, (3) the motives imputed to the donor, and (4) the nature of the constraints existing when the resource was donated. Given Gouldner's model, the utility of the resource initially transferred would be perceived to be greater if the recipient were in strong need, if the donor had little in the way of that resource to give (but gave), and if the donor gave without external pressures being applied and without thought of his or her own gain. In terms of social value theory, each of these conditions adds weight to the perception that the actor giving resources was concerned with increasing or maximizing another's outcomes as an end in itself. The norm of reciprocity then sets an expectation for some form of repayment as a requirement for fair exchange.

Homans (1961, 1974) defines fairness in exchange relationships in terms of the previously cited principle of distributive justice. In applying the principle of distributive justice descriptively, he uses both situations of reciprocity and of allocation. For example, Homans employs the principle of reciprocity to describe justice in the Norton Street Gang, originally described in Whyte's *Street Corner Society* (1943): ''The value of what a member receives by way of a reward from the members of the group in one field of activity should be proportional to the value to them of the activities he contributes to another field'' (p. 234). However, most of Homans's analysis of justice is based on descriptions of fairness in the Western Electric Company (Roethlisberger & Dickson, 1939) and in the Eastern Utilities Company (Homans, 1954). Justice in these industrial contexts is generally framed in terms of relationships of allocation or of complementarity (Gouldner, 1960) rather than of exchange and reciprocity. That is, Homans is not principally concerned in his analysis of fairness with the exchange of resources between the worker and management per se. Rather, he examines how given workers or a group of similar workers define and evaluate the fairness of the outcomes they are allocated by a corporation for their work investment relative to the outcomes others receive for their investment.

Thus, Homans assumes that equity is based upon a learned expectancy that outcomes to the self and others will conform to the rule of distributive justice. Violations of this distributive principle give rise to perceptions of unfairness, and to possible anger and guilt. It is a short conceptual step from Homans's assumption concerning expectancy violation, particularly as set forth in his 1974 book, to Festinger's (1957) assumptions regarding dissonance and dissonance reduction. Furthermore, it is the marriage of distributive justice and dissonance that has produced the dominant contemporary allocative theories of fairness in social psychology, namely, those advanced by Adams (1965) and by Walster, Berscheid, and Walster (1973).

Blau, in his 1964 book, accepts Homans's definition of distributive justice but also asserts that, rather than being derivable from the principles of operant conditioning, justice in exchange relationships is normatively given. He argues that equity represents "a social norm that prescribes just treatment and a moral principle" (p. 243), a norm that is reinforced initially by socializing third parties and that may be subsequently internalized by an actor, thereby producing feelings of guilt if violated. In effect, Blau argues that equity is initially a social fact that may become an individual social value.

In another paper Blau (1964b) criticizes Homans for deliberately limiting his evaluation of equity to the exchange of rewards and punishments between two persons and for not considering the more important normative aspects of justice. He is correct in asserting that Homans does not perform a normative analysis of equity, though Homans does use the construct of norms in other contexts. Blau then extends Homans's notion of distributive justice by examining how value becomes assigned to its principal components: the returns received for services and the investment costs incurred for providing them. He argues, using principles derived from the economic laws of supply and demand, that it is society that assigns values to the rewards and costs experienced and hence that defines the values attached to fairness in a relationship of direct exchange. And then, in characteristic fashion, Blau argues that an understanding of these more elementary processes can be used to help define more complex and higher level processes such as those that affect allocation decisions made by groups in settings of indirect exchange. In effect, Blau uses evidence gained from examining the processes of direct exchange between two actors as a beginning point from which to develop more complex theories of indirect exchange such as those, for example, that would help define social welfare.

Thibaut and Kelley (1959), in their initial statement on social interdependence, do not include fairness of equity in their analysis of the processes or rules that help to define the nature of interdependence relationships. They do note, however, in this initial statement that an individual's comparison level (CL) for outcomes provides a standard that may be used to evaluate both the goodness and the fairness of outcomes obtained within a relationship.

In their more recent theoretical statement, Kelley and Thibaut (1978) do relate two of the major constructs of fairness, equity and equality, to the interpersonal processes of negotiation and exchange. In their analysis of the structural properties of social interdependence, they set forth a two-stage decision process. They argue that an actor first uses a transformational calculus to translate objective own–other outcome matrices into effective or operational matrices. The calculus they suggest an actor employs is quite similar to that which was elaborated in our earlier discussion of social values in the section "Equity and the theory of social values," except that equity and equality as values are subject to bilateral negotiation and introduced as possible outcome rules during the second rather than the first stage.

Kelley and Thibaut (1978) argue that if, after the transformation process, actors' preferences are not perfectly correspondent, a second decision stage is entered during which actors may pursue individually or collectively three alternative courses of action: (1) They can act on their own in order to obtain the best available outcome for themselves, perhaps taking into account the other's likely behaviors; (2) They can behave in an agreed-upon coordinated way in the interest of providing both with better outcomes through time, given their respective effective matrices, than they could obtain by behaving independently; (3) They may behave in a coordinated way under the coercion produced when one or both actors threaten to lower the other's outcomes below what could be obtained through coordination.

Equity and equality become possible decision rules to be invoked by actors to define outcome distributions acceptable to both parties during this second stage. In discussing how equity and equality may be used in negotiation, Kelley and Thibaut (1978) claim that the actor and the other probably use both the value of the outcomes they could likely obtain by taking independent action, as well as the strength of the strategic threats they can employ, to influence the other as criteria for evaluating the goodness of various possible distributions of outcomes between the self and the other. The range of own- and other-outcome combinations that become negotiable are those that are bilaterally acceptable, given the two preceding criteria. In terms of the theory of bargaining or negotiation, these combinations define the *frontier* of a plot of all pairs of possible negotiated outcomes. This frontier is analogous to the contract curve depicted earlier in Fig. 4.

In situations in which actors have made differential inputs, Kelley and Thibaut (1978) argue that one would expect an advantaged actor to seek the equitable frontier point, whereas the nonadvantaged actor would maintain that the equal outcome frontier point would indeed represent a fairer distribution of resources. In regard to the resulting impasse, the same that Cook and Emerson (1978) address in their analysis of the indeterminacy of bilateral monopoly models of economic exchange, Kelley and Thibaut observe, "At this point our model has made its predictions about the progress of negotiation, and must leave some uncertainty about the outcome. In general, we might expect the final agreement to be some compromise between those indicated by the two arguments" (p. 293).

Kelley and Thibaut's (1978) description of the role that equality and equity may play in negotiations between interdependent actors is quite similar to that proposed by Komorita and Chertkoff (1973) in their theoretical paper on bargaining. In fact, one of their 10 major theoretical assumptions states: "A person strong in resources is more likely to expect and advocate the parity norm as a basis for reward division, while a person weak in resources is more likely to expect and advocate the equality norm" (p. 151).

Cook and Emerson (1978) also examine the case of fairness rules within relationships of direct exchange. They observe first, and we concur, that the proportional formulations of equity set forth by such theorists as Homans (1961, 1974), Adams (1965), and Walster *et al.* (1973) are more applicable to settings in which some "central allocator or third party" distributes rewards between contributors than to settings in which there is a direct two-party exchange of resources. Thus, these researchers view the preceding equity statements as more applicable to instances of allocation than to those in which there is reciprocity and outcome interdependence.

Cook and Emerson (1978) go on to use the economic paradigm of bilateral monopoly to formulate one of the few formal definitions of equity that applies to direct two-party exchange relationships. Within the bilateral monopoly paradigm, it is assumed that two persons (A and B) each have a monopoly position on a single resource (x and y respectively). In such a situation, the input of one person to an exchange becomes the other person's outcome. The equity of the exchange is assumed to be determined by comparing the relative values of the resources given and received by each party using what Cook and Emerson term the *rule of equitable exchange*. This rule according to Cook and Emerson can be specified in terms of the following equation:

$$ayY - axX = bxX - byY \tag{1}$$

where ax and ay are the unit values of the resources x and y to Person A, and bx and by are the unit values of the resources x and y to Person B. X and Y refer to the number of units *exchanged* between the two actors, and the equality expression defines an equilibrium state of equal psychic profits.

Cook and Emerson (1978), following earlier work by Emerson (1976), further postulate that equity as a solution rule will be obtained in a situation of bilateral monopoly when two conditions are met: (1) Both participants know how much each profits from the transaction relative to the other, which is likely to occur if both share a common culture and a history of prior interaction; and (2) the rule of equitable exchange is activated and honored. This becomes more likely if future interaction is anticipated and if the utilities of x and y are high. Gamson (1961) proposed a somewhat similar process in his early formulation regarding coalition formation: "Our general hypothesis stated that participants will expect others to demand from a coalition a share of the payoffs which is proportional to the amount of the resources which they are contributing to it.

Each participant will estimate the value of any coalition strategy as the total payoff to a coalition multiplied by his share'' (p. 382).

Hollander (1980), although not specifying the particular rules of equity that are applied in exchange relationships, does observe that two factors define the relationship between leaders and followers in exchange relationships, namely, *system progress* and *equity*. System progress refers to movement in the direction of group goals. Equity implies that followers perceive that they are being treated fairly through time: "Simply put, where they have a choice, followers require a sufficient feeling of being fairly rewarded to remain inside the group and participate. This sense of equity often depends upon a comparison with what others, of comparable characteristics and responsibility, are receiving relative to their inputs'' (p. 118).

There have been several, very tentative attempts to look at how exchange relationships develop through time, and in a few instances the relation between fairness and reciprocity is also considered. Such analyses have been made primarily for male–female interactions of progressive intimacy and interdependence. For example, Huesmann and Levinger (1976) have recently developed a computer simulation model of incremental exchange through time. Its assumptions are based upon both expected value theory and some of the previously described assertions in Thibaut and Kelley's (1959) interdependence formulation. The model provides a more systematic way to describe the development of varying patterns of male–female exchange and mutual involvement through time than does Blau's (1964a) earlier described effort in the section "Blau's Exchange Theory''. It does not address, however, the issue of how perceptions of fairness emerge and influence exchange process.

IV. Exchange, Interdependence, and Fairness

In this and the subsequent section, we propose a continuum of interdependence between two or more actors and provide examples of empirical research that illustrate how the structure of exchange influences fairness behavior. In the present section, we consider the first five points of the continuum, beginning with relationships in which one actor has unilateral control over immediate outcomes for the self and others and ending with an exchange relationship in which there exists strong, mutual control of outcomes and in which interdependence is restricted to an immediate setting. In the subsequent section, we consider the strongest form of interdependence, namely, exchange as it occurs in intimate relationships.

At the *first* point on the continuum, in which interdependence is weakest, one actor unilaterally and anonymously controls the distribution of available resources to the self and others. Interdependence is here generally operationalized as the actors having prevously contributed to a common task. The unilateral control of resources by the allocator represents a form of fate control that serves to minimize both the normative demands and the strategic considerations of interpersonal influence. Another contributing factor to the minimization of these factors is that the allocation occurs at only one time point. Van Avermaet (1975) has observed that adults having such outcome control are likely to select fairness rules isomorphic with self-interest. At a judgmental level, Severts (1976) found that in a private condition, children favorably evaluated unjust favorable allocations made to them by a third party, but expressed disfavor of such allocations when they were made public. In a behavioral study Reis and Gruzen (1976,) found that allocators increased their own rewards beyond normative values only when their choices were completely private. Lane and Messé (1971) obtained similar results. These research examples suggest that anonymity and unilateral control enhance self-interested behaviors.

The *second* point on the continuum is represented by research settings in which an allocator unilaterally controls the outcome distribution on a one-time basis, but knows that the experimenter and/or the other task contributor will be aware of both the task input and the distribution of outcomes. Such a situation adds normative demands to the minimal setting described previously. Most prior behavioral research on fairness falls on this point at the allocation end of the continuum. It attempts to answer questions regarding what allocations actors make when charged with the responsibility of distributing a fixed set of resources between the self and another under varying conditions of relative task input. Attention is focused on the normative demands of the situation, and the fact of interdependence is generally neglected. For example, the question of future interaction between participants is generally left ambiguous. Hence, the contribution of the subject's concern about another's possible future response to his or her allocation is not known. Theoretically, however, if such interpersonal considerations are controlled by removing strategic considerations, findings at this second continuum point should be useful in providing a description of distribution behavior that includes normative demands.

The *third* point on the continuum involves instances in which an actor has fate control at a given point in time over the outcome distribution but expects to interact with another in the future. Von Grumbkow, *et al.* (1976) have found that possible future interactions between the allocator and the other affect the former's allocation behavior. Advantaged actors, who expected future interaction, distributed outcomes in a manner approximating equality; those expecting no future interaction approximated an equity rule. Future interaction is also implied in the manipulation and measurement of the effects of friendship (Benton, 1971; Morgan & Sawyer, 1967; Wright, 1942). Under conditions of friendship, one might expect that the anticipation of a continuing interaction would affect allocation behavior. Benton, for example, has found a sex by friendship interaction: Boys made equity choices both with friends and nonfriends; whereas girls made equality choices with friends but equity choices with nonfriends.

At this third point on the proposed continuum, perceived reciprocity or exchange begins to become a factor insofar as actors anticipate that others will react to their resource distribution in some way. Conceptually, the situation is even more complex because the actor is not only likely to perceive that the other will react, but also that the other may affect his or her own future outcomes. Thus, the setting for the actor becomes one of perceived interdependence, and his or her behavior toward another is likely to be defined both by considerations of interpersonal strategy and by normative demands.

The *fourth* point on the continuum is reached when an allocator actually expects to exchange roles or to take turns with the recipient in the future in the same or a similar task. At this point, the time frame is expanded, and the eventual control of resources is seen as bilateral rather than unilateral. Thus, we might expect to observe on the part of the subjects task-specific strategies that are designed to influence the other to make more favorable future allocations to the subjects. Greenberg (1978) recently examined the effects of anticipated reciprocity upon the distributional behaviors of adults and reports that justice standards were adhered to by allocators expecting exchanges with equally powerful co-workers. Self-interested responses were made when recipients had no retalitative power, particularly when the reward was lucrative.

Shapiro (1975) used the presence or absence of expectations of future interaction to explain differences between the findings reported by Leventhal and his coworkers (Leventhal & Anderson, 1970; Leventhal & Lane, 1970; Leventhal & Michaels, 1969) that indicated that equity is the principal distributional response to unequal inputs and those reported by others (Gamson, 1961; Morgan & Sawyer, 1967; Wiggins, 1966) that implied that equality was the principal rule. In his own research, Shapiro found that allocators with higher inputs, when future interaction was expected, divided the reward equally; when future interaction was not expected, rewards were divided according to equity. At this fourth continuum point, the exchange characteristics of the setting are still implicit, although the expanded time frame and the shift to bilateral control of resources adds a complexity that more closely approximates full exchange relationships.

The *fifth* point on the continuum is one in which the exchange relationship is explicit; and there is a strong form of outcome interdependence that is restricted to the immediate setting. Thus, although a reciprocal relationship exists within the time period of the exchange, there is little concern with future interaction, and hence with long-term considerations of interpersonal strategy. Laboratory studies of bargaining and negotiation as well as of coalition formation are the best examples of research at this continuum point. In a broader context, Homans (1961, 1974) defines this form of relationship as an impersonal one that is characterized by a single exchange of a single reward that is readily available elsewhere. It is the nature of the reward and not the identity of the particular other person that is important to this form of exchange. Homans defines a relationship as personal when it involves multiple exchanges of reward that are specific to the particular actors involved. Similar distinctions have been made by Boulding (1978) and by Kelley and Thibaut (1978).

Most of the theoretical and empirical work concerned with a decision theoretical and empirical understanding of bargaining and coalition formation that fall at this point on the continuum have assumed that actors are fundamentally self-interested in orientation and have attempted to define what strategies they employ to optimize their own outcomes. Pruitt (1977) in discussing various intergrative approaches to conflict resolution has observed that bargaining, whereby parties attempt to coerce or persuade their adversaries into making great concessions while conceding as little as possible, is but one of several general approaches to conflict resolution. Another involves the application of rules or norms, including those that define various kinds of fairness. However, as Kelley and Thibaut (1978) have observed and previous research has demonstrated, the availability of multiple rules of fairness enables actors to select those most consistent with self-interest. For example, a bargainer with less inputs and/or power may recommend equality as a fair distribution rule; whereas one with greater inputs or power will recommend equity as a fair distribution rule.

Komorita and Kravitz (1979) have also looked at the role various fairness rules may play in the distribution of outcomes, given various alternative outcomes that each actor will realize if a bargain is not reached. For example, they consider an instance where Person A would receive 40 points and Person B would receive 20 if an agreement were not reached; and both could split 100 points if a bargain were reached. They suggest that three fairness rules might provide a bargained outcome: the rule of equality, in which each party takes 50 units; the rule of equity, in which Person A would take two-thirds, Person B one-third; and finally the rule of equal excess, in which each player takes points directly comparable to the points he or she would receive without an agreement, and the remainder is then equally split between actors. The latter, given that the outcomes for nonagreement are specified, is comparable to the well-known bargaining solutions of Nash (1950, 1953) and Shapeley (1953). Komorita and Kravitz found empirically that on differing occasions all three of these rules are used. Although we do not yet know under what conditions one or the other will dominate, this research provides an example of how various fairness rules may affect the exchange of outcomes in a bargaining task.

As regards research in coalition formation, Komorita and Brinberg (1977) on the basis of a review of the literature and their own findings, conclude that the motives associated with self-interest and with fairness are present in most coalition tasks:

> Equal strategic power (players can form an equal number of alternative winning coalitions) but unequal outcomes (players with larger resources received a larger share)—suggests that there are two opposing motivational forces operating in a coalition situation: the motive to maximize one's own share of the prize, based upon strategic bargaining power, and a norm of equity (distributive justice) which prescribes that an individual with larger resources should receive larger outcomes. (p. 359)

In general, self-interest has been found to be a stronger determinant of outcomes in coalition studies than fairness. This probably is obtained because, as Stryker (1972) has noted, the differential allocation of resources to subjects is accomplished in a nonmeaningful way, that is, randomly or without reason. Furthermore, to the extent that the relations in coalition studies are impersonal in Homans's (1961) sense, then fairness should be weaker than when they are personal in nature. We will examine, in somewhat more detail, the *sixth* point on the continuum, exchange and fairness in close personal relationships.

V. Exchange and Fairness in Close Personal Relationships

Social exchange theory, as described here, in many respects provides an excellent foundation for a general theory of human social interaction. Its emphasis on the importance of considering the individual's perception of the hedonic value or utility of resources is consistent with most contemporary scientific and philosophical conceptions of human motivation and decision making. In addition, the analysis of interdependence and social interaction in terms of the exchange of material, social, and psychological resources is obviously applicable to a very broad spectrum of social relationships. The relationship between broker and investor, physician and patient, professor and graduate student, and prostitute and client all entail the explicit or tacit exchange of goods, services, and benefits. Thus, intuitively, social exchange theory satisfies at least one requirement of a good theory, namely, that it be sufficiently broad.

Another aspect of a good theory, however, is the extent to which it provides compelling interpretations or clarifications of very specific domains. In this section, therefore, we review research applying social exchange theory to what might be called *intimate* or *close personal relationships* (cf. Kelley, 1979). The study of fairness and exchange in such relationships is important for a number of reasons. First, it provides for a particularly stringent test of the explanatory power of exchange theory. In the absence of a close personal relationship or the existence of strong affiliative bonds, it is not surprising that individuals rely heavily upon simple distribution rules and procedures. In most laboratory studies of exchange, for example, the interpersonal knowledge of the coactors is extremely limited and their interdependence quite temporary and task dependent. In such contexts, one would expect that normative, socially endorsed rules and procedures (e.g., use of an equality rule for allocating some rewards) would be salient to and utilized by subjects. Even in the natural world, we often conduct our exchanges by executing role-appropriate procedures, for example, exchanging a 15% tip for decent service in a restaurant.

As interpersonal knowledge and the depth and duration of interdependence increase, however, reliance upon such role- and rule-mediated standards and procedures might be expected to produce less satisfactory or less desirable results. One test of the breadth or power of a social exchange theory is its ability to explain and predict interpersonal interactions when coactors have extensive knowledge about each other, can anticipate future interactions or ongoing exchange, and are interdependent along dimensions that each party perceives as being of significant value to them.

We will maintain here that it is under such conditions that the deficiencies of the economic and anthropological models of exchange, with their respective emphases on rational decision-making processes and supraindividualistic factors, are most apparent. More specifically, economic and decision-theory models of exchange do not generally make sufficient allowance for the role of emergent properties like trust, feelings of mutuality, and long-term expectations of reciprocity in exchange in such relationships. The anthropological conception of exchange, although clearly relevant to the analysis of exchange in institutional settings or between groups, adopts a *level* of analysis that is not particularly suitable for describing intimate or close dyadic relationships. Social psychological analyses of social exchange, in contrast, are very useful in such cases.

Before proceeding, it might be helpful to address a common critical reaction to attempts to explain close personal relationships in terms of social exchange theory. Huston and Burgess (1979) have succinctly described this reaction in a recent and thoughtful review of research on social exchange in developing relationships:

> The recent application by social scientists of exchange principles to intimate relationships is interesting in part because the basic tenets of exchange theory seem contrary to Western views about the nature of love and intimacy. Love is supposed to involve caring, altruism, communion, and selflessness. . . . The view that love is tied to the exchange of rewards seems crass. (p. 10)

Although Rubin (1973) made the same point a number of years earlier, the resistance is still apparent.

The reluctance to apply exchange theory to close personal relationships suggest two unfortunate but recurrent misunderstandings—one regarding the assumptions about human nature that are often associated with exchange theories and the other about the nature of close personal relationships. First, many of the assumptions of exchange theories, particularly those of the economic models, appear to imply an extreme, unflattering, and ultimately unsatisfying reductionism. The conceptualization of individuals as rational, decision-oriented, information-processing organisms has seemingly little relevance to our attempts to understand close interpersonal relationships, unless they are modified to take into account social values and psychological interdependence. Certainly, use of concepts such as cost–reward ratios, own–gain maximization, and indifference curves seems to account only imperfectly for the rich behavioral and phenomenological data of the intimate relationship. With regard to the second misunderstanding, there is an enduring prejudice against the application of scientific constructs and laws to intimate relationships. It is as if any suggestion that the spontaneous giving of affection or the exchange of intimacies are determined implies that such acts are mechanical, and thereby depersonalized.

Fortunately, recent theoretical and empirical work in exchange theory has done much to overcome both of these limitations. It is now clear that with suitable enrichment of their assumptions, exchange theories can be meaningfully applied even to close personal relationships. In fact, considerable progress has already been made towards understanding altruistic and collective acts from an exchange perspective.

A. INTIMACY AND THE HETEROSEXUAL DYAD

Not surprisingly, much of the research on exchange in close personal relationships has focused on the heterosexual dyad. As Kelley (1979) has cogently observed, "In its various manifestations in dating, marriage, cohabition, and romantic liasons, the heterosexual dyad is probably the single most important type of relationship in the life of the individual and in the history of society" (p. 2). Despite our focus on such relationships, however, we will assume here that this research is suggestive of processes that may be common to other kinds of dyadic exchange in which comparable affiliative bonds, interpersonal knowledge, and ongoing interdependence exist.

There are two broad questions that divide research on exchange in heterosexual dyads. First, how does the use of various fairness rules and exchange processes change over time? In other words, we may approach interpersonal exchange from a developmental perspective. Presumably, it is reasoned, in the evolution of a relationship there is some kind of orderly progression from the use of simple normative rules and procedures to more complex and specialized ones. This movement may broadly be conceived of as a change from relatively depersonalized to more personalized forms of exchange, as suggested by the con-tinuum mentioned earlier. The second question which might be asked is how the use of fairness rules and exchange processes differ in close personal relationships as compared to other kinds of relationships?

A number of general and important theoretical issues are raised by these questions. First, are the rules and processes that govern exchange relationships the same, irrespective of the kind of relationship? In other words, is there a set of primitive rules and fundamental processes that are useful in describing the sim-plist to the most complex exchange relations? The general equity model proposed by Walster *et al.* (1978) is representative of this orientation. Or, on the other hand, are there emergent properties that are essential to understanding the condi-tions of exchange in the later stages of a close personal relationship? Scanzoni's (1979) developmental conception of exchange in intimate relationships may be taken as an example of this point of view. Our position here will be that both perspectives are somewhat accurate insofar as general exchange principles are useful in understanding exchange in intimate relations, provided that allowances are made for emergent properties. A parsimonious assumption is that a relatively small set of principles (e.g., proportional equity and equality) are widely used by individuals in a given society across a broad range of settings and are applicable to diverse relationships. At the same time, we try to show how exchange in heterosexual relationships can be better analyzed if we include the influence of emergent properties that are not reducible to general or more fundamental processes.

Emerson (1981) has been particularly articulate about this latter perspective. He notes that, "the temporal aspects of exchange relations allow the develop-ment of 'emergent' aspects of the relation, such as trust, commitment, solidarity, 'investments,' concerns about 'justice' and equity, and contractual agreement" (p. 43). One reason that many laboratory investigations of allocation and re-source distribution may be limited in their representations of real-world ex-changes (especially those characteristic of close relationships) is that these emergent properties are seldom if ever given an opportunity to come into play. By their very nature, laboratory experiments tend to highlight factors evident in cross-sectional analysis and to minimize factors that a more longitudinal ap-proach might disclose. We conclude our analysis by briefly examining two issues: the development of exchange in heterosexual relationships, and the nature of fairness in intimate relationships.

B. EXCHANGE IN THE DEVELOPMENT
    OF THE HETEROSEXUAL RELATIONSHIP

Several researchers have preferred to characterize the development of ex-change in personal relationships in terms of a sequence of stages. Scanzoni

(1979), for example, has proposed three stages: an *exploration* stage characterized by tentative and relatively low-risk initial investments or exchanges, an *expansion* stage characterized by deepening and broadening interdependence and collective goals, and finally a *commitment* stage in which the individuals perceive the relationship as fairly stable, long term, and invested in heavily. The dynamic underlying this progression is the coactors' mutual expectations of reciprocity. "Relationships are maintained," Scanzoni asserts, "when actors perform valued services for other and vice versa; and also when these performances continue to generate ongoing feelings of moral obligation to reciprocate benefits received" (p. 64). Scanzoni's model nicely illustrates how emergent properties may operate to maintain or sustain relationships, eliminating the need for each partner in the dyad to evaluate the costs and benefits of the relationship frequently. This approach, incidentally, seems quite compatible with Altman and Taylor's (1973) conception of relationship development in terms of social penetration and privacy regulation.

Along similar lines, Huesmann and Levinger (1976) have proposed an "incremental exchange theory" based upon the assumption that the expected value of the coactors' rewards increases as the depth of the relationship increases (p. 196). Using Foa and Foa's paradigm (1974), we might expect that over time there would be an increase in *particularistic* rewards (those only available from the personal other) as well as those that are more symbolic on the concreteness dimension (e.g., self-esteem). Huesmann and Levinger's theory is important because it suggests how relationships progress from one interpersonal state to another. They suggest that dyadic partners are concerned with maximizing both their own and other's gains (expressed as a weighted sum that varies with the duration and intensity of the relationship) and that the weight accorded to the other's outcome increases with the depth of the relationship. This model includes the costs of terminating the relationship and assessing the other's probable behavior. This is comparable to Thibaut and Kelley's notion of comparison level for alternatives.

Levinger (1979) presents a model based upon the coactors' perceptions of the exchange balance or the credit balance in the relationship and traces the maintenance, formation, and dissolution of a relationship. As does Scanzoni (1979), he proposes three distinct stages. In the formative stage interactions are relatively superficial and tentative. In the plateau stage there is an "economy of surplus" whereby each partner invests in the relationship; this eliminates the need to attend closely to net costs and benefits because both actors perceive the relationship as productive, worthwhile, and rewarding. So long as reciprocity continues, the relationship is relatively stable. Finally, he describes a declining stage characterized by increasing attendance to current rewards and costs, and especially to concern with "benefits forgone by not attending to alternatives" (p. 178).

Lee (1984) outlined a similar although more detailed model of the terminal or end-stages of a romantic dyad. He proposed a five-stage linear progression of events from (1) the intial *discovery* of the problem or dissatisfaction, to (2) *exposure* or communication of the discovery to one's partner, then (3) a phase of *negotiation* characterized by attempts at solving the problem, leading to (4) reaching some kind of *resolution,* and finally, (5) the resulting *transformation* or change made in the relationship. This model describes the events that presumably unfold during separation in romantic dyads. It is worthwhile to note that one might expect that the final three stages would be characterized by changes in the structure of the dyad's exchange relationships with respect to negotiated bilateral exchanges, spontaneous unilateral exchanges by one or both partners, or even the cessation of specific positive and negative exchanges. Although their preliminary data was based entirely on retrospective survey interviews and included only the perspective of one member of a dyad, the model is very promising and highly relevant to exchange theory.

C.   FAIRNESS AND EXCHANGE IN INTIMATE RELATIONSHIPS

As noted earlier, there are two broad theoretical orientations one might take toward the question of fairness in intimate relationships. The first is that the rules and processes that are held to govern exchange relationships in general provide both necessary and sufficient accounts of exchange in close relationships as well. Walster, Traupmann, and Walster (1978), for example, have declared, "Equity is a *general theory* (and) equity principles steer *all human interactions*" (p. 82, italics ours). According to this perspective the exchange of a husband's wealth and power for his spouse's physical attractiveness could be described using a simple proportional formula, in much the same way as workers in a factory presumably weigh the relative inputs (costs) and outputs (rewards) they receive relative to their coworkers. The second orientation holds that obvious emergent properties and dynamic features of developing relationships require the addition of special rules and processes (cf. Emerson, 1981). For example, one might argue that individuals may be more trustful towards those to whom they feel close or that they are inclined to be more self-sacrificing in their personal relationships. The application of normative fairness rules or general exchange principles that do not take into consideration these special features of the close personal relationship may consequently prove unsatisfactory.

With respect to the first perspective, there has been some success in applying general conceptions of equity and exchange to intimate relationships. Walster *et al.* (1978), for example, have reviewed empirical evidence showing how equity concepts can be applied to romantic and marital relationships. In summarizing the results of a number of studies, they conclude that, "Romantic choices appear to be a delicate compromise between one's desire to capture an ideal partner and one's realization that he must settle for what he deserves'' (p. 176). In other words, consistent with the kind of proportional formula described by Adams (1965, pp. 267–299), an individual weighs his wealth and prestige, which are tangible ''inputs'' he can offer a prospective relationship against what his partner can provide in turn.

This kind of analysis has led Walster *et al.* to propose that partners who are well matched along salient dimensions will feel happier and more content with their relationships. Those who are in unbalanced or inequitable relationships, on the other hand, will feel distress and perceive the relationship as less satisfactory. Walster *et al.* (1978) empirically tested this hypothesis using students who were either casually or steadily dating. Using their Global Measure of Participants' Inputs, Outcomes, and Equity/Inequity, they could classify individuals as either underbenefited, overbenefited, or equitably treated. They argued that those who were underbenefited should generally feel more resentment and anger because their rewards were less than their contributions to the relationship, whereas those who were overbenefited would feel guilt and fear because they were not entitled to the rewards or benefits they were receiving. On the other hand, those who are equitably treated should perceive themselves as getting pretty much what they deserve. They obtained strong support for their hypotheses: Individuals in equitable relationships were happier than those who were underbenefited or overbenefited. Furthermore, those who were the most underbenefited felt more anger, whereas those who were overbenefited seemed to experience more guilt about the relationship.

These findings suggest that equitable relationships are more likely to be stable because both partners are content with their current ''balance of trade.'' Inequitable relationships, on the other hand, are less stable and susceptible to more extreme attempts to restore psychological equity. Because the partners must continually renegotiate the terms of their relationship (e.g., demand more, or give less) or make more extreme or severe cognitive distortions (e.g., deny or suppress unsatisfied sexual feelings), they will inevitably experience more distress within the relationship, coupled with increased surveillance of their social environment for more profitable alternatives.

Additional support for this analysis has been provided by Schafer and Keith (1980) who studied the relationship between perceived equity and depression among married couples. They found that marriage partners who perceived themselves to be either overbenefited or underbenefited in the performance of their marital roles experienced higher psychological distress and depression than did partners who perceived the relationship as equitable. Their results suggest that one of the psychological costs of inequitable relationships may be affective disorders and cognitive distortions of one's self-concept and esteem.

A number of investigators have tried to develop models to describe the "cost–benefit analysis" of relationships implied by these results. Caldwell (1979), for example, in a study of negotiation in sexual encounters, proposed that partners in an intimate relationship "keep books on one another in order to regulate transactions on the basis of justice" (p. 124). In order to assess dyadic exchange we should, therefore, examine the perceived debits and balances of the partners' "books." Both persons, in a sense, perceive the relationship in terms of their own capital investments (i.e., how much they put into the relationship) and in terms of the assets and liabilities (costs and rewards) they accrue. Although this metaphor is creative (she goes on to talk about "book-juggling" and "black markets") and allows us to make some predictions about partners' relative satisfactions with their current relationships and the likelihood that they might seek out others, it is not clear that this theory extends our understanding of the actual processes that underly exchange in personal relationships.

A more sophisticated analysis of social exchange in couple relationships has been put forth by Willis and Frieze (1980). Their approach also has a distinctively economic flavor to it. Willis and Frieze assume that couples form as a result of a kind of matching of the relative "social desirability value" of the partners. Individuals exist, they assert, in a "partner marketplace" that is divided into two fields, one containing the "field of availables" and the other a "field of eligibles." Partners ultimately select their mates on the basis of both their eligibility as a partner and the availability of other suitable perspective mates. The matching that underlies partner selection in this model is very similar to the kind of proportional balance that Walster et al. (1978) talk about and, of course, similar to Kelley's (1979) notion of "comparison level" and the "comparison level for alternatives."

As noted earlier, the majority of studies on social exchange in personal relationships have taken one of two directions. First, there have been attempts to describe the rules and processes underlying, and perhaps unique to, exchange in such relationships. These conceptions usually emphasize the role of emergent processes and properties in dyadic interaction. The other approach has been to study exchange from a developmental perspective. These conceptions have viewed exchange relations in terms of sequential, stage-like, and somewhat segmented units. Unfortunately, these two lines of research have remained somewhat independent. For example, the exciting developmental models put forth by Huesmann and Levinger (1976) and more recently by Lee (1984) provide a useful mapping of the exchange relationship along a longitudinal dimension. Yet, they do not clearly specify possible *intrastage* and *interstage* differences in general rule use. A logical next step would seem to be, therefore, to attempt some integration of both perspectives. We might suggest, for example, that social exchange relationships can be mapped along a horizontal continuum that differentiates between various levels or kinds of interdependence (e.g., as described previously) and then *add* a vertical dimension that maps longitudinal or developmental changes. Such an organizational scheme would be a first step in integrating contemporary research and at clarifying the complex between-category and within-category relationships evident in social exchange.

VI. Conclusion

It is fair to say that as yet there exist neither sophisticated nor powerful theories of social interaction and exchange that are capable of being tested empirically. In part, this is a function of the complexity of human interaction. Similarly, theories of fairness apply only to the simplest form of human interdependence—the unilateral allocation of outcome. We have made some progress from the early theoretical speculations of Mauss (1925/1954) and others on reciprocity in gift giving and other human activities. The major theoretical advances in exchange theory that have occurred can be traced primarily to the field of economics and its concern with understanding the exchange of economic commodities. But even here the assumptions concerning the motives of human actors as well as the structure of their interdependence have been very narrow, if not naive. Similarly, the range of exchange situations, as well as resources, to which economic theories are applicable are limited. Still the economists can hardly be faulted for making greater advances in modeling human exchange and interdependence than have other social scientists. An exception to the foregoing is to be found in the very strong conceptualization of social interdependence stated by the social psychologists Kelley and Thibaut (1978) and Kelley (1979) which represent an attempt to formulate structural properties of the exchange of social as well as economic resources.

Given the limitations in current theorizing on interdependence and exchange, as well as the current fixation of the energies of social psychologists upon processes of social cognition, it is perhaps not surprising that most social psychological theories of equity are not primarily concerned with how fairness regulates interpersonal relations, but with how perceived inequities are defined and rationalized by the favored, the disfavored, or some external observer. Such an emphasis is consistent with those individualistic models of human behavior that have dominated the social sciences and social psychology in particular over the past several decades. Descriptions of the processes which give rise to perceptions of injustice, as well as various attempts to determine what extrinsic or intrinsic factors may predispose individuals towards such judgments, are undoubtedly essential to understanding the role that fairness plays in human behavior. But the greatest advances in understanding how the rules of fairness influence human behavior will occur when we begin to understand how they help both to define and to determine the overall structure and the ongoing processes that characterize human interdependence and exchange. Such an understanding can have profound implications for both theoretical and empirical advances in all of the social sciences. To date the uneven progress towards this kind of understanding has been facilitated by efforts within a number of disciplines. One would hope that more rapid progress will occur in the future with social psychology playing a more central role than it has thus far.

REFERENCES

Adams, J. S. Inequity in social exchange. In L. Berkowitz (Ed.), *Advances in Experimental Social Psychology* (Vol. 2). NY: Academic Press, 1965.

Altman, I., & Taylor, D. A. *Social penetration: The development of interpersonal relationships.* New York: Holt, Rinehart, & Winston, 1973.

Benton, A. Productivity, distributive justice, and bargaining among children. *Journal of Personality and Social Psychology*, 1971, *18*, 68–78.

Blau, P. *Exchange and power in social life.* NY: Wiley, 1964a.

Blau, P. Justice in social exchange. *Sociological Inquiry*, 1964b, *34*, 193–206.

Boulding, K. *Ecodynamics*, Beverly Hills, CA: Sage, 1978.

Brickman, P., & Bryan, J. Equity vs. equality in children's moral judgment of thefts, charity, and third party transfers. *Journal of Personality and Social Psychology*, 1976, *34*, 757–761.

Caldwell, M. *Negotiation in social encounters.* Unpublished doctoral dissertation, University of California, Santa Barbara, 1979.

Cook, K., & Emerson, R. Power, equity and commitment in exchange networks. *American Sociological Review*, 1978, *43*, 721–739.

Eckhoff, T. *Justice: Its determinants in social interaction.* Rotterdam: Rotterdam University Press, 1974.

Emerson, R. Social exchange. In M. Rosenberg & R. Turner (Eds.), *Social psychology: Sociological perspectives.* NY: Basic Books, 1981.

Engels, F. Socialism: Utopian and scientific. In L. S. Fever (Ed.), *Marx and Engels: Basic writings on politics and philosophy.* NY: Doubleday, 1880/1959.

Festinger, L. *A theory of cognitive dissonance.* Evanston, IL: Row Peterson, 1957.

Foa, E. B., & Foa, U. G. Resource theory: Interpersonal behavior as exchange. In K. J. Gergen, M. S. Greenberg, & R. H. Willis (Eds.), *Social exchange: Advances in theory and research.* NY: Plenum, 77–97, 1980.

Foa, U. G. Interpersonal and economic resources. *Science*, 1971, *171*, 345–351.

Folger, R. Distributive and procedural justice: Combined impact of "voice" and improvement on experienced inequity. *Journal of Personality and Social Psychology*, 1977, *35*, 108–119.

Folger, R., Rosenfield, D., Grove, J. & Corkran, L. Effects of "voice" and peer opinions on responses to inequity. *Journal of Personality and Social Psychology*, 1979, *37*, 2253–2261.

Gamson, W. A theory of coalition formation. *American Sociological Review*, 1961, *26*, 372–382.

Gouldner, A. The norm of reciprocity: A preliminary statement. *American Sociological Review*, 1960, *25*, 161–179.

Greenberg, J. Effects of reward value and retaliative power on allocation decisions: Justice, generosity vs. greed? *Journal of Personality and Social Psychology*, 1978, *36*, 367–379.

Griesinger, D., & Livingston, J., Jr. Toward a model of interpersonal motivation in experimental games. *Behavioral Science*, 1973, *18*, 173–188.

Gulliver, P. H. Dispute settlements without courts: The Ndendevil of Southern Tanzania. In L. Nader (Ed.), *Law in culture and society.* Chicago: Aldine, 1969.

Heath, A. *Rational choice and social exchange: A critique of exchange theory.* Cambridge: Cambridge University Press, 1976.

Hollander, E. Leadership and social exchange process. In K. Gergen, M. S. Greenberg, & R. Willis (Eds.), *Social exchange: Advances in theory and research.* New York: Plenum Press, 1980.

Homans, G. The cash posters. *American Sociological Review,* 1954, *19,* 724–733.

Homans, G. *Social behavior: Its elementary forms.* NY: Harcourt, Brace & World, 1961.

Homans, G. *Social behavior: Its elementary forms* (Rev. ed.). NY: Harcourt, Brace, & World, 1974.

Homans, G. Commentary. In L. Berkowitz & E. Walster (Eds.), *Equity theory: Toward a general theory of social interaction. Advances in experimental social psychology* (Vol. 9). NY: Academic Press, 1976.

Huesmann, L. P., & Levinger, G. Incremental exchange theory: A formal model for progression in dyadic social interaction. In L. Berkowitz & E. Walster (Eds.), *Equity theory: Toward a general theory of social interaction. Advances in experimental social psychology* (Vol. 9). NY: Academic Press, 1976.

Huston, T. L., & Burgess, R. L. Social exchange in developing relationships: An overview. In R. L. Burgess & T. L. Huston (Eds.), *Social exchange in developing relationships.* NY: Academic Press, 1979.

Kames, Lord. *The principles of equity.* Edinburg, 1760.

Katz, D., & Kahn, R. *The social psychology of organizations* (2nd Ed.). NY: Wiley, 1978.

Kelley, H. *Personal relationships: Their structures and processes.* Hillsdale, NJ: Erlbaum, 1979.

Kelley, H., & Thibaut, J. *Interpersonal relations: A theory of interdependence.* NY: Wiley, 1978.

Komorita, S. S., & Brinberg, D. The effects of equity norms in coalition formation. *Sociometry,* 1977, *40,* 351–361.

Komorita, S., & Chertkoff, J. A bargaining theory of coalition. *Psychological Review,* 1973, *80,* 149–162.

Komorita, S., & Kravitz, D. The effects of alternatives in bargaining. *Journal of Experimental Social Psychology,* 1979, *15,* 147–157.

Lane, I. M., & Messé, L. A. Equity and the distribution of rewards. *Journal of Personality and Social Psychology,* 1971, *20,* 1–17.

Lee, L. Sequences in separation: A framework for investigating endings of the personal (romantic) relationship. *Journal of Social and Personal Relationships,* 1984, *1,* 49–73.

Leventhal, G., & Anderson, D. Self-interest and the maintenance of equity. *Journal of Personality and Social Psychology,* 1970, *15,* 57–62.

Leventhal, G. S., & Lane, D. W. Sex, age, and equity behavior. *Journal of Personality and Social Psychology,* 1970, *15,* 312–316.

Leventhal, G. S., & Michaels, J. W. Extending the equity model: Perception of inputs and allocations of reward as a function of duration and quantity of performance. *Journal of Personality and Social Psychology,* 1969, *12,* 303–309.

Lévi-Strauss, C. *The elementary structures of kinship.* Boston: Beacon Press, 1969.

Levinger, G. A social exchange view on the dissolution of pair relationships. In R. Burgess, & T. Huston (Eds.), *Social exchange in developing relationships.* NY: Academic Press, 1979.

Luce, D., & Raiffa, H. *Games and decisions: Introduction and critical survey.* NY: Wiley, 1957.

McClintock, C. G. Social motivation: A set of propositions. *Behavioral Science,* 1972, *17,* 438–454.

McClintock, C. G. Social motivations in settings of outcome interdependence. In D. Druckman (Ed.), *Negotiation behavior.* Beverly Hills, CA: Sage, 1977.

McClintock, C. G. Value orientation, interdependence, and the encoding and decoding of affect. Unpublished National Science Foundation Proposal, Grant BNS 82-14500, 1982.

McClintock, C. G., & Keil, L. Equity and social exchange. In G. Greenberg and L. Cohen (Eds.), *Equity and justice in social behavior*. NY: Academic Press, 1982.

MacCrimmon, K., & Toda, M. The experimental determination of indifference curves. *Review of Economic Studies*, 1969, *XXXVI*, 433–452.

Malinowski, B. *Argonauts of the Western Pacific*. London: Routledge & Kegan Paul, 1922.

Mauss, M. *The gift*. London: Cohen & West, 1954. (Original work published 1925)

Milgram, S. *Obedience to authority*. NY: Harper & Row, 1974.

Morgan, W., & Swayer, J. Bargaining, expectations, and the preference for equality over equity. *Journal of Personality and Social Psychology*, 1967, *6*, 139–149.

Nash, J. F. The bargaining problem. *Econometrica*, 1950, *18*, 155–162.

Nash, J. F. Two-person cooperative games. *Econometrica*, 1953, *21*, 128–140.

Olson, M. *The logic of collective action*. Cambridge, MA: Harvard University Press, 1965.

Presthus, R. Authority in organizations. *Public Administration Review*, 1960, *20*, 88–91.

Pruitt, D. Twenty years of experimental gaming. Critique, synthesis and suggestions for the future. *Annual Review of Psychology*, 1977, *28*, 363–392.

Rawls, J. *A theory of justice*. Cambridge, MA: Harvard University Press, 1972.

Reis, H. The multidimensionality of justice. In R. Folger (Ed.), *The sense of injustice: Social psychological perspectives*. NY: Plenum, 1984.

Reis, H. T., & Gruzen, J. On mediating equity, equality, and self-interest: The role of self-presentation in social exchange. *Journal of Experimental Social Psychology*, 1976, *12*, 487–503.

Rescher, N. *Distributive justice*. NY: Bobbs-Merrill, 1966.

Robbins, L. *An essay on the nature and significance of economic science*. London: MacMillan, 1932.

Roethlisberger, F., & Dickson, W. *Management and the worker*. Cambridge, MA: Harvard University Press, 1939.

Roloff, M. *Interpersonal communication: The social exchange approach*. Beverly Hills, CA: Sage, 1981.

Rubin, Z. *Liking and loving*. NY: Holt, 1973.

Scanzoni, J. Social exchange and behavioral interdependence. In R. L. Burgess & T. Huston (Eds.), *Social exchange in developing relationships*. NY: Academic Press, 1979.

Schafer, R. B., & Keith, P. M. Equity and depression among married couples. *Social Psychology Quarterly*, 1980, *43*, 430–435.

Severts, A. Billykheid en gelijkheid en het verdeelgedrag van 6-jarige kinderen. Unpublished manuscript, K. U. Lueven, 1976.

Shapeley, L. S. A value for n-person games. In H. W. Kuhn & A. W. Tucker (Eds.), *Contributions to the theory of games* (Vol. II). Princeton, NJ: Princeton University Press, 1953.

Shapiro, E. G. Effect of expectations of future interaction on reward allocations in dyads: Equity or equality. *Journal of Personality and Social Psychology*, 1975, *31*(5), 873–880.

Simon, H. Authority. In C. M. Arensberg *et al.* (Eds.), *Research in industrial human relations*. NY: Harper, 1957.

Skinner, B. F. *Science and human behavior*. NY: MacMillan, 1973.

Stryker, S. Coalition behavior. In C. G. McClintock (Ed.), *Experimental social psychology*. NY: Holt, Rinehart & Winston, 1972.

Thibaut, J., & Kelley, H. *The social psychology of groups*. NY: Wiley, 1959.

Thibaut, J., & Walker, L. *Procedural justice: A psychological analysis*. Hillsdale, NJ: Erlbaum, 1975.

Van Avermaet, E. *Equity: A theoretical and experimental analysis*. Unpublished doctoral dissertation, University of California, Santa Barbara, 1975.

Van Avermaet, E., & McClintock, C., & Moskowitz, J. Alternative approaches to equity: Dissonance reduction, pro-social motivation and strategic accommodation. *European Journal of Social Psychology,* 1978, *8,* 419–437.

Von Grumbkow, J., Deen, E., Steensma, H., & Wilke, H. The effect of future interaction on the distribution of rewards. *European Journal of Social Psychology,* 1976, *6*(1), 119–123.

Walster, E., Berscheid, E., & Walster, G. New directions in equity research. *Journal of Personality and Social Psychology,* 1973, *25,* 151–176.

Walster, E., Traupmann, J., & Walster, G. W. Equity and extramarital sex. *Archives of Sexual Behavior,* 1978, 121–141.

Walster, E., Walster, G. W., & Berscheid, E. Equity: Theory and Research. Boston: Allyn and Bacon, 1978.

Walster, E., Walster, G. W., & Traupmann, J. Equity and premarital sex. *Journal of Personality and Social Psychology,* 1978, *36,* 82–92.

Weber, M. In T. Parsons (Ed.), *The theory of social and economic organization* (A. M. Henverson & T. Parsons, trans.). NY: Oxford University Press, 1947.

Whyte, W. *Street corner society.* Chicago: Chicago University Press, 1943.

Wiggins, J. Status differentiation, external consequences and alternative reward distributions. *Sociometry,* 1966, *29,* 89–103.

Willis, R. H., & Frieze, I. Sex roles, social exchange, and couples. In K. C. Gergen & M. Greenberg (Eds.), *Social exchange: Advances in theory and research.* NY: Plenum, 1980.

Wright, B. The development of the ideology of altruism and fairness in children. *Psychological Bulletin,* 1942, *39,* 485–486.

Wyer, R. Prediction of behavior in two-person games. *Journal of Personality and Social Psychology,* 1969, *13,* 222–228.

Wyer, R. The effects of outcome matrix and partner's behavior in two-person games. *Journal of Experimental Social Psychology,* 1971, *1,* 190–210.

A NEW LOOK AT DISSONANCE THEORY

Joel Cooper

DEPARTMENT OF PSYCHOLOGY
PRINCETON UNIVERSITY
PRINCETON, NEW JERSEY

Russell H. Fazio

DEPARTMENT OF PSYCHOLOGY
INDIANA UNIVERSITY
BLOOMINGTON, INDIANA

I. Introduction

Cognitive dissonance theory is now more than a quarter of a century old.
The theory has generated more than 1000 published research entries and a con-

siderable amount of controversy. Starting with an elegantly simple proposition, the theory has provided rich insights into the way in which people deal with the consequences of cognitive inconsistency. In addition, the theory has had no lack of critics, who have questioned some or all of the proposed theoretical relationship.

From the myriad of supporting and critical discoveries, one conclusion is clear: The definition of dissonance as originally proposed by Festinger (1957) is no longer adequate to account for the data that have accumulated. As Jones (in press) concluded in his analysis of the history of modern social psychology, "From Festinger's extremely simple, rather vague theoretical statement, the theory evolved with the aid of experimental feedback to include a set of well articulated systematic relationships." In the present paper, we examine those relationships and propose a new definition of cognitive dissonance that is, we believe, more in tune with the current state of empirical findings.

Festinger (1957) proposed that cognitive dissonance occurs when one cognition that a person holds follows from the obverse of another. Moreover, dissonance was described as a state of psychological discomfort akin to the drive states of hunger or thirst. In this paper, we examine the state of the empirical findings in order to move toward a more comprehensive view of dissonance. Moreover, we will argue that once we understand what produces dissonance, we still need further elaboration of the process in order to understand adequately the cognitive changes that ensue. We propose that the concept of dissonance must, in turn, be differentiated into the concepts of dissonance arousal and dissonance motivation. It is the latter that leads to the cognitive changes that are generally associated with cognitive dissonance.

When Festinger and Carlsmith (1959) conducted the first experiment in induced compliance, they set off a flurry of theoretical and empirical controversy. College students were asked to tell a supposedly unsuspecting fellow student that an experimental task which they knew to be dull and boring was in fact interesting and exciting. The investigators argued that the cognition, "I thought the task was dull" and the cognition, "I said to this student that the task was interesting" would produce the kind of inconsistency that would lead to the arousal of dissonance. The arousal of dissonance, an uncomfortable tension state, was predicted to lead to a change of one of the cognitions to restore harmony. Because the behavioral cognition (i.e., what the subject said) could be expected to be more resistant to change, Festinger and Carlsmith predicted that attitudes toward the task would change. This is what they found—and more.

Festinger and Carlsmith (1959) also offered an incentive for subjects to make their counterattitudinal statement. Some subjects were offered the sum of one dollar. Other subjects had been offered $20 for participating (and also for being on call for the rest of the semester). It was argued that the more incentive a participant was given, the more justification there was for the counterattitudinal behavior. This, in turn, should lead to less dissonance. A paltry sum of money, on the other hand, would not provide much of a supporting cognition and therefore would arouse dissonance. The results showed significantly more positive attitudes toward the task in the low incentive condition than in the high incentive condition or in a control condition. This three-condition experiment marked the birth of the induced compliance paradigm.

In Jones's (in press) view, one of the reasons that dissonance theory and the induced compliance paradigm engendered much critical debate in the 1960s was its willingness to take on the conventional wisdom of the role played by secondary reinforcement notions. The idea of predicting great degrees of attitude change in the face of a small magnitude of incentive and a small degree of change in the presence of a large incentive seemed at variance with secondary reinforcement principles. Research critics found several reasons to be skeptical of the induced compliance work. Chapanis and Chapanis (1964) published a review that pointed out methodological ambiguities with a number of the early studies in dissonance theory, including Festinger and Carlsmith's (1959). They pointed out, for example, that the role played by a $20 inducement may have seemed like a bribe rather than an incentive. Rosenberg (1965) speculated that such a bribe might have evoked participants' "evaluation apprehension"—the concern that they would be evaluated by the psychologist and look particularly unworthy if they changed their attitudes after having received a bribe. Although some of the alternative explanations raised by critics of particular studies may have been justified, the volume of replications in a variety of situations has left the basic finding intact.

Nevertheless, Festinger and Carlsmith's (1959) interpretation of the induced compliance finding has not gone unchallenged. Aronson and his colleagues (e.g., Aronson, 1968; Nel, Helmreich, & Aronson, 1969) suggested that it was not inconsistency per se that caused counterattitudinal statements to lead to cognitive dissonance and to eventual changes in attitudes, but rather behavior that threatened one's self-esteem. Convincing a student to believe that a boring task was exciting and interesting might lead a person of high self-regard to believe that he or she has just committed an act not in keeping with what a truly worthy person should have done.

Similarly, Steele and Liu (1981, 1983) have argued that self-justificatory attitude change following counterattitudinal advocacy may be based upon an ego-based need to reaffirm that one has behaved in accord with positive values. Individuals who write an essay or make a speech that is contrary to a valued position may feel that their self-image has been lowered. What these people need, then, is a way to reaffirm their values. Steele and Liu propose that attitude change is one way for individuals to view their behavior as an affirmation of their values.

The idea of threats to self-esteem, although provocative, probably has not addressed sufficient data to be a complete theory of the causes of cognitive dissonance. Direct tests that have attempted to vary self-esteem have been equivocal (e.g., Cooper & Duncan, 1971). Nonetheless, research in the tradition of self-esteem variance did arrive at some very provocative findings (Deutsch, Krauss, & Rosenau, 1962; Gerard, Blevans & Malcolm, 1964; Worchel & McCormick, 1963).

II. The First Step Toward Dissonance Arousal: Aversive Consequences

Nel, Helmreich, and Aronson (1969) conducted a study based on the view that dissonance is created by threats to self-esteem. What they succeeded in showing was that inconsistency per se is not sufficient to produce dissonance-related attitude change. In their empirical study, Nel *et al.* had all subjects deliver an address that was counterattitudinal under conditions that have typically been associated with the arousal of dissonance. With choice and commitment set high and incentive magnitude set low, Nel *et al.* had subjects volunteer to give speeches in which they advocated legalization of marijuana. Nel *et al.* manipulated the characteristics of the audience. Subjects were informed that the audience to whom the speech was to be given was firmly committed against the position they were to advocate, was firmly committed in favor of it, or was noncommittal (a group of school children). Nel *et al.* found that the making of a counterattitudinal statement to a noncommittal group was the only treatment that produced attitude change. They reasoned that agreeing to make a speech to a group that is genuinely persuasible is an act not worthy of a self-respecting person.

This study begins to shed light on the question of what is needed to arouse cognitive dissonance. For example, if individuals were to speak quietly in the confines of their bedroom, would making a counterattitudinal speech arouse dissonance and result in cognitive changes? There is ample evidence to suggest that such logical inconsistency would not produce cognitive dissonance; in order for cognitive dissonance to occur, a product must result from the counterattitudinal behavior. And that product is the bringing about of—or the possibility of the occurrence of—an aversive event. If there is no aversive event that might be expected to occur following an action, then that action will not lead to the arousal of cognitive dissonance.

By an aversive event, we mean an event that blocks one's self-interest or an event that one would rather not have occur. Thus, making a statement contrary to one's attitude while in solitude does not have the potential for bringing about an aversive event. Similarly, the chance that Nel, Helmreich, and Aronson's (1969) subjects would bring about an aversive event when the audience was committed to a position opposed to the speech was very small. And when the audience was committed to the counterattitudinal position, the chances of bringing about an aversive event were nonexistent, because the unwanted event already existed. Only in the condition in which the audience was uncommitted did the counterattitudinal speech of the subject have the clear chance of bringing about a shift in the children's opinions in the unwanted direction.

How, then, did the Festinger and Carlsmith (1959) subjects come to experience dissonance if inconsistency is not sufficient to produce that arousal state? A re-examination of Festinger and Carlsmith's study reveals that, in addition to creating conditions of psychological inconsistency, the subjects in that experiment were also induced to bring about an aversive event. Not only did the participants have to say something that was at variance with their private beliefs, but they also convinced an unsuspecting fellow student to expect great things from a task which the participant knew was, in fact, dull and boring. Duping and deceiving a fellow student may well have been perceived as an aversive event, just as deceiving school children to accept marijuana may have been aversive in the Nel et al. study.

This reasoning was tested by Cooper and Worchel (1970), who repeated the Festinger and Carlsmith (1959) study while varying the consequences of the counterattitudinal behavior as an independent variable. Participants performed the dull, boring task created by Festinger and Carlsmith and, for varying degrees of incentive, agreed to tell a fellow student that the task was really exciting. For half of the subjects, the "fellow student" appeared convinced by the subject's statements. For these subjects, the unwanted event of deceiving a fellow student was made to occur. However, this unwanted event was specifically eliminated for the other half of the subjects. Although they made their counterattitudinal statements, these subjects learned that the "waiting subject" remained unconvinced and still expected the tasks to be uninteresting. The results of the study showed that only those subjects who believed that they had successfully deceived the waiting subject showed dissonance-produced attitude change. Subjects for whom the aversive consequence had been eliminated did not come to believe that the task was interesting.

Note, too, that it is difficult to interpret studies such as Cooper and Worchel's (1970) as consistent with self-esteem versions of dissonance. If it is contrary to one's self-esteem to volunteer to tell someone that a dull task is interesting, it should make little difference if one's colleague does or does not fall for the untruth. Agreeing to convince the unsuspecting student constitutes a dastardly act—one that a worthy person would not commit. It is just as dastardly an act regardless of whether or not the other student successfully resists the persuasion.

A study by Cooper, Zanna, and Goethals (1974) carried this reasoning regarding the necessity of aversive consequences one step further. They argued that if producing an aversive consequence is the key to understanding the effects of induced compliance, then merely convincing a waiting student should not always lead to dissonance in the experimental paradigm under discussion. Duping a fellow student may be counterattitudinal and may lead one to feel that he or she has done a very good job of persuasion, but it is an aversive event only to the extent that one has positive feelings toward the one who has been duped. Deceiving a disliked other to anticipate that a dull task might be exciting is hardly aversive. But convincing a liked person to look forward to something when it is known that he or she will soon be disappointed is, indeed, aversive. So Cooper, Zanna, and Goethals set out to ascertain the precise conditions that lead to dissonance-produced attitude change. In their experiment, subjects were led either to like or to dislike a fellow student. They then attempted to convince the fellow student that a dull task was actually exciting and something to look forward to. Half of the liked and half of the disliked confederates were convinced by the subject's remarks; the other half indicated that they were unconvinced. Cooper et al. (1974) found that the only subjects who changed their attitudes about the task were those who successfully convinced a student that they liked. Convincing a disliked student or failing to convince a liked student did not lead to attitude change, despite the fact that the subjects' remarks were inconsistent with their private attitudes.

The implication of this line of reasoning is that dissonance has precious little to do with the inconsistency among cognitions per se, but rather with the production of a consequence that is unwanted. Behaving in ways that are counterattitudinal often facilitates the arousal of dissonance because it is related to the bringing about of an unwanted event. In the dull task paradigm, the fact that the behavioral statement is counterattitudinal sets the stage for the possibility of making the situation aversive. But the counterattitudinal nature of the behavior is not a sufficient condition to lead to cognitive dissonance.

This implication is equally apparent in the research involving the making of political statements that are at variance with private attitudes. Advocating a disliked position often runs the risk of having that position brought about. Persons who are actually in a position to effect policy changes might become convinced by the argument and institute a disliked policy. In early research by Cohen (1962), for example, it was implied that counterattitudinal essays written by university students might be used by a university institute to adopt an antistudent position. Linder, Cooper, and Jones (1967) had students write essays favoring a ban against inflammatory speakers on college campuses. Students disagreed with this position but knew that their essays were to be shown to a panel who had the power to effect such a policy.

Goethals and Cooper (1972) manipulated the degree to which another person was convinced to believe in a subject's counterattitudinal statement. In one study, subjects made attitude-discrepant speeches in which they advocated the position that people should not be allowed to vote until the age of 21. Another person (actually a confederate) overheard the subject's advocacy and reported that he either was or was not convinced by what the subject said. Dissonance was apparently aroused only in the condition in which the listener was convinced. In similar research, Goethals and Cooper (1975) found that students showed changes of attitudes when they made counterattitudinal statements to a campus group that might effect a disliked policy at the university, but showed no attitude change when the same counterattitudinal statement was made but was not to be shown to the campus agency.

Of course, aversive consequences need not actually occur for dissonance to be aroused. It is the subjects' *perceptions* that the consequences will result from their actions that are important. In fact, there is abundant research indicating that even the counterattitudinal behavior itself can be anticipated rather than experienced. *Agreeing* to perform attitude-discrepant behavior produces the same dissonance effects that actually performing the behavior produces (Linder, Cooper, & Wicklund, 1968; Waterman, 1969; Wicklund, Cooper, & Linder, 1967).

An important corollary to the notion that the expectation of an aversive consequence is necessary for the arousal of dissonance is that the consequence must be irrevocable. A person making a political statement or a person convincing a colleague of something that is not true must not feel that he or she can "take it back." If a political leftist makes a conservative statement to a group of politically naive students, he will probably not experience dissonance if he knew that in a moment or two he could rescind his remarks, tell them he was only cooperating with an experimenter, and then tell them of his true beliefs. Similarly, a student in the dull task research might not experience dissonance if she knew she would be able to catch her colleague and set the record straight before the colleague participated in the task.

This assumption was tested experimentally by Davis and Jones (1960). Male participants were induced to deliver rather negative personal characterizations of a fellow student. It was known that these characterizations were counterattitudinal for the subjects. Half of the subjects believed that they would meet their fellow student and therefore have the chance to tell him that the assessment were merely part of the experimenter's research. The other half expected no such opportunity. The results showed that dissonance-produced attitude change occurred only when the consequence was irrevocable and not at all when the subject believed he could rescind the consequence of the statement.

All the research just discussed shares a common element. Successful attempts to change attitudes through the arousal of dissonance all contain an element of bringing about—or potentially bringing about—an irrevocable aversive event. The recognition that an aversive event has resulted or might result from one's behavior is the first essential ingredient in the arousal of cognitive dissonance. But it is only the first step.

III.   Personal Responsibility: A Necessary Link

Aversive consequences lead to the tension state that we call cognitive dissonance only under a special combination of circumstances. This occurs when a person is led to make a personal or internal attribution for having brought about an unwanted event. We call such an attribution the assumption of *personal responsibility* and define it as the *attribution that the locus of causation for an event is internal* (see Cooper, 1971; Wicklund & Brehm, 1976).

Because dissonance is generally associated with an unpleasant hedonic state, it follows that people are motivated to avoid it. This can be accomplished by denying personal responsibility for the unwanted event. The two most commonly used vehicles for denying responsibility are the attribution that an action has been coerced by environmental pressures and the attribution that the unwanted event is an unforeseeable consequence of the individual's behavior. If either coercion or unforeseeability can be claimed, then the individual need not experience dissonance arousal. We consider each of these concepts in turn.

A.   PERCEIVED FREEDOM

The first essential ingredient of personal responsibility is the perception that an action was undertaken freely without having been constrained by the environment. Environmental constraints can be of various forms and strengths. Deciding not to cross the street while the "wait" light is on may not be perceived as a free decision, but rather as an action forced by the environment. A policeman standing conspicuously at the street corner may aid this attribution. Similarly, deciding to hand over money to an armed robber will, in all probability, also be attributed to environmental pressures. In a laboratory study in which an investigator orders a participant to write an attitude-discrepant statement, the participant need not attribute personal responsibility to her- or himself for the action. The locus of causation for that behavior properly belongs to the high-status experimenter, and thus responsibility can be denied. "Why did I behave in this way?" the subject may query. "Because the investigator told me to," would be the logical reply. Without having to take responsibility, dissonance can be avoided.

The notion that freedom is necessary for dissonance arousal has been known for some time. Indeed, Davis and Jones (1960) showed that a subject who is induced to make derogatory statements about a person whom the subject actually liked changed his attitudes toward the subject only if the statements were made under conditions of perceived high choice. Linder *et al.* (1967) conducted two studies to test the importance of choice in arousing cognitive dissonance. In the more straightforward of their studies, the subjects' task was to write an essay favoring a disliked policy that might have been invoked on their college campus. Some of the subjects were asked if they would like to write the essays and were told that the decision was completely their own and that they could leave the laboratory if they so desired. The other half were merely told to write the essay.

The investigators also varied the magnitude of the incentive that was offered for writing the essay. Half of the subjects were offered a small financial induce-ment whereas the other half were offered a larger sum. The dissonance theory prediction regarding the role of incentive magnitude is that small inducements are effective in having attitude-discrepant behavior lead to attitude change whereas large inducements are not. The results of Linder *et al.*'s (1967) study showed that the inverse relationship between incentive magnitude and attitude change did not occur when the participants were told, rather than asked, to write their essay. The dissonance-predicted relationship occurred only under the high-choice instructions. As dissonance theory would predict, attitudes changed as an inverse function of incentive magnitude.

Subsequent studies continued to demonstrate that counterattitudinal behav-ior committed under conditions of low-perceived freedom does not produce attitude change (e.g., Cooper & Brehm, 1971; Collins & Hoyt, 1972; Goethals & Cooper, 1972; Sherman, 1970a). However, perceiving one's own behavior as having brought about an aversive event still does not ensure that responsibility will be attributed internally. We have stressed that responsibility is a joint func-tion of perceived freedom and perceived foreseeability of the consequences of the behavior. Foreseeability is a subtle but crucial determinant of whether an individual will accept responsibility and consequently will experience dissonance arousal.

B.   FORESEEABILITY: THE LINK TO RESPONSIBILITY

Imagine a man driving down a dark country road. He decides to travel at 55 miles per hour (mph). Imagine, too, that the driver notices a warning signal indicating that the road is slippery ahead. He continues to drive at 55 mph, slides around the curve, and causes the unwanted event of driving off the road. Will he feel responsible for bringing about the aversive event? We can compare his probable attribution to a similar scene of a driver who decides to travel at 55 mph on the same road, but has no idea of danger ahead. He sees no road sign warning of the imminent danger. Would he feel as responsible for having caused the event? Most likely the first driver would attribute more responsibility to himself than would the second driver. The difference in the two scenarios is only that the first driver should have been able to foresee the consequence of his continuing to drive at the speed limit, whereas the second driver could not.

Responsibility attribution in the induced-compliance research paradigm possesses similar properties. An aversive consequence that is foreseeable should lead to the attribution of responsibility and hence lead to the arousal of dissonance. When an event's occurrence is unforeseeable, then engaging in behavior that brings about that event will not lead to dissonance, regardless of the level of perceived choice and the degree of aversiveness of the event.

Cooper and Brehm (1971) had subjects agree to perform a boring and noxious task. Some subjects knew that they would be suffering the consequence of not receiving any payment for their participation and that most other subjects were being paid. Other subjects did not know of their relative deprivation until after their agreement had been obtained. The prediction derived from dissonance theory was that the greater the degree of aversiveness (i.e., the higher the relative deprivation or the more the remuneration that subjects were *not* getting), then the greater the dissonance and ultimately the more the subjects would think that the task they performed was satisfying. The results showed this to be true—but only if the aversive event (the relative deprivation) was foreseeable prior to agreeing to participate.

Cooper (1971) tested the importance of the combined effect of decision freedom and foreseeability. Female subjects either made a choice or were coerced to play a game with a partner that could result in winning a financial prize. However, the partner was described as having a specific personality trait that might make her a poor choice as a partner because both players had to be successful in order for either to win the desired money. As the subject and her partner began to play, it became obvious that the partner was not being successful, thus causing the subject to lose the prize. In this experiment all subjects behaved in a way that caused an aversive event. All lost money because they played the game with a partner whose personality trait made her an unsuccessful player. But subjects who had no choice but to work with the partner could absolve themselves of responsibility by viewing the environment (i.e., the experimenter) as the locus of causation for playing with the unsuccessful partner.

Some subjects were also given the chance to view their partner's unfortunate personality trait as being unforeseeable. As the game began, it became apparent for half of the subjects that the trait that was causing the partner to be unsuccessful was the opposite trait to the one they had been led to expect. The other half of the subjects found the trait to be precisely the one they had been led to expect. It was possible for the former half to deny responsibility for working with a partner who had a game-losing personality trait by believing that they had no way of anticipating their partner's actual trait. The data from the experiment showed that only subjects who chose to work with their partner *and* who accurately knew which personality trait their partner actually had changed their attitudes about their partner as a function of the arousal of dissonance. If subjects could claim that the event was unforeseeable or that they were not given the freedom to choose their partner, then responsibility was avoided and dissonance was not aroused.

1.   On the Meaning of Foreseeability

Several studies have employed the concept of foreseeability and concluded that subjects deny responsibility if the unwanted consequences of their behavior are unforeseen. There are some contrary examples, however, in which a consequence that was seemingly introduced after the fact did lead to attitude change (Aronson, Chase, Helmreich, & Ruhnke, 1974; Sherman, 1970b; Sogin & Pallak, 1976). Taken together, these studies call for a sharper focus on the meaning of foreseeability. Just when does an individual conclude that a consequence was foreseeable? Is it the same as a consequence that is foreseen? If not, what are the differences?

Goethals, Cooper, and Naficy (1979) attempted to clarify the concept of foreseeability. They differentiated between the concepts of foreseeable and foreseen. They argued that consequences that are not foreseen at the time that a behavior is undertaken may still be foreseeable. That is, there are some consequences that are not explicitly expected or foreseen but which, retrospectively, might reasonably have been anticipated. These consequences are regarded as foreseeable and lead to cognitive dissonance arousal. If an unwanted consequence follows a behavior, people ask themselves not only whether the consequence was known but also whether the consequence should or could reasonably have been known at the time of the decision to act. If the answer to that question is affirmative, then the consequence was foreseeable. Foreseeable consequences, as well as those that were clearly foreseen, have the potential to arouse dissonance.

In an empirical demonstration of this distinction, Goethals *et al.* (1979) had subjects write counterattitudinal essays. Some subjects believed that the essays were only for the eyes of the experimenter. A second group of subjects believed that the essays would be sent to a committee that could create unwanted consequences for the essay writers. A third group knew that some other people might be interested in the essays, but they were not told who they were. For all groups, it turned out that the essays were to be sent to the committee that could bring about the unwanted consequence. For the first group of subjects, such a consequence was not knowable at the time of the decision to write the essay. It did not lead to attitude change. For the second group, the consequence was foreseen, and it did lead to attitude change. The crucial group was the third. The consequence was not explicitly foreseen but, in retrospect, it could have been known. Indeed, this group of subjects did change their attitude to bring them in line with the counterattitudinal behavior.

2. Implications of Foreseeability: Eliminating Cognitive Dissonance

The notion that cognitive dissonance is aroused by freely bringing about aversive consequences that are foreseeable has some interesting implications on the other side of the ledger. To what extent can dissonance be eliminated if an aversive consequence is removed? The answer may depend again on the concept of foreseeability. Imagine a situation in which we induce an advocate of expanding nuclear energy systems to make a statement urging an end to nuclear expansion. In this situation, our subject agrees to make his antinuclear speech as a tape recording, which he fully expects will be played on the local radio station. Thus far, all of the ingredients for the arousal of dissonance are present. An aversive event (i.e., the probability of convincing at least some of the listeners to oppose nuclear expansion) will be brought about through the personal responsibility of the speaker. Now suppose that, after making the speech, the speaker learns that the tape recorder malfunctioned. The speech cannot be played on the radio; the aversive consequence will not arise. Has dissonance arousal been eliminated?

Cooper and Goethals (1974) conducted such a study at Williams College. Students were induced to make speeches in favor of a college parietal system that the students actually opposed. They were led to believe that the speeches were intended to be played at the meeting of a college council that had the authority to make policy with regard to this issue. Some of the subjects were led to believe that their speech would definitely be played to the council. Others believed that the tape might or might not be played. Thus, all subjects agreed to the possibility of bringing about an aversive event. However, for some of the subjects, that event was an assured outcome of agreeing to make the tape, whereas for other subjects the event's occurrence was only a possible outcome of making the counterattitudinal tape.

As it turned out, half of the subjects in each condition learned that their tape would indeed be played to the college council. The aversive consequence then was clearly in prospect. On the other hand, the remaining subjects learned that their tape would not be used. For these subjects, no aversive event would occur. The aversive consequence not occurring was a foreseeable event for those subjects who initially knew their tape might not be used. But the elimination of the aversive event was completely unforeseeable for subjects who were led to believe that the tape assuredly would be used.

All subjects had their attitudes toward the parietal system assessed at the end of the study. As expected, dissonance was apparently aroused and reduced via attitude change for all subjects who learned that their tape would be used. After all, they had brought about a potentially aversive event, freely and foreseeably. Subjects in these conditions came to believe in the validity and value of parietals more than did a group of control subjects. For subjects whose tape recordings were not to be used, those for whom the tape's not being used was an unforeseeable event continued to show evidence of dissonance arousal. They changed their attitudes toward parietals just as much as subjects who learned that the aversive event would occur. The only subjects whose dissonance arousal was eliminated were those for whom the tape's not being used was a foreseeable event at the time they decided to make the tape recording. It would appear then that the elimination of dissonance also relies upon foreseeability—the foreseeability that an event is going to occur.

Other evidence supporting the crucial role played by the foreseeability of an event was contributed by Brehm and Jones (1970). They demonstrated that the introduction of *positive* consequences were ineffective in eliminating dissonance if those consequences were unforeseeable. Brehm and Jones had participants make a choice between two attractive consumer items. The dissonance created by rejecting one of the attractive items was made more bearable by the surprise introduction of a bonus gift. The gift was expected to be a cognition consonant with the choice and therefore would reduce dissonance. The subjects' eventual ratings of the consumer items showed that the gift was not effective in reducing dissonance if its occurrence was not foreseeable at the time the subjects made their decision between the two items.

IV.   Summary of the Conditions Necessary
for Dissonance Arousal

Figure 1 summarizes the discussion thus far. Cognitive dissonance is not simply brought about by the perception of inconsistency among cognitions but rather by the perception of having brought about an aversive and irrevocable event. The dissonance process begins with the performance of a behavior whose consequences are judged to be aversive in nature. That is, the behavior produces, or has the possibility of producing, an event that one would rather not have occur.

One way to conceptualize this is to view the consequence as aversive if it is sufficiently discrepant from the individual's desires that it falls within a latitude of rejection. Indeed, it has been demonstrated that the endorsement of a political position within one's latitude of rejection and the consequent possibility of convincing others to adopt such a political stance does produce dissonance

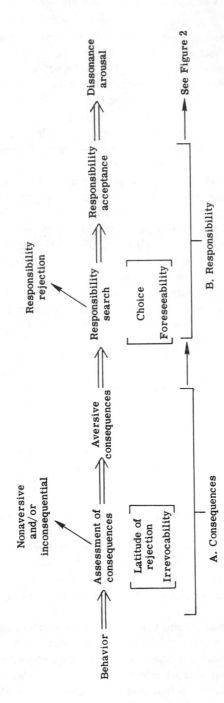

Fig. 1. The sequence of events leading to dissonance arousal. The symbols are ⇒ dissonance path, → alternative possibilities, and [] factors considered.

(Fazio, Zanna, & Cooper, 1977). The same potential consequence does not produce dissonance when the position endorsed falls within the latitude of acceptance.

Notice, too, that person's behavioral commitment takes on added emphasis in the present view. For Festinger (1957), the perception of behavior is one of the many cognitions that a person holds. It is an important cognition because, compared to attitudes, it is highly resistant to change. The present view accepts the importance of behavior, but not just because of its resistance to change. It is the behavioral commitment that produces consequences and the perception of the foreseeability and aversiveness of those consequences that determine the arousal of dissonance.

The occurrence or the forecast of an objectionable event is not sufficient to produce the state of dissonance, however. What such an event does, we argue, is to prompt an attempt to identify the agent responsible for the aversive consequences. There is nothing novel about such an assertion. Indeed, it has long been argued that attribution processes are instigated by the occurrence of novel, unexpected, or extreme events (Berlyne, 1960; Pyszczynski & Greenberg, 1981; Swann, Stephenson, & Pittman, 1981; Wong & Weiner, 1981). Likewise, the aversive event prompts an attempt to identify the locus of causality. If this event occurs because of something for which the actor is responsible, then and only then will it lead to the state of dissonance. If responsibility can be avoided by the actor by perceiving him- or herself to have been coerced or by perceiving the aversive event to have been an unforeseeable consequence of his or her decision, then that event—no matter how aversive—will not lead to the state of dissonance.

What properties does this state of dissonance possess? Our analysis thus far has accepted Festinger's (1957) assumption that dissonance is akin to a drivelike arousal state that is psychologically uncomfortable and that necessarily produces pressure to undergo cognitive changes. Research on the properties of dissonance arousal has advanced to the point in which we are now able to examine these assumptions. In the following sections we look at the evidence supporting the notion that dissonance is a state of arousal. However, the arousal state by itself may not be sufficient to lead to the pressure for cognitive changes that are typically associated with dissonance.

V. Dissonance Arousal: Does It Occur?

Beginning with Festinger's (1957) original statements in which he drew an analogy between dissonance and drive states such as hunger, it has been presumed that dissonance involves an arousal state. Fazio and Cooper (1983) have proposed that dissonance arousal be viewed as a conditioned emotional response. Originally neutral stimuli (e.g., a light or a tone) can take on negative qualities following repeated pairings with noxious events (e.g., electric shock). When only the previously neutral stimulus is presented later, the organism displays evidence of emotional arousal, presumably in anticipation of the expected noxious event (Kamin, 1969; cf. Mowrer, 1947, 1960). Likewise, a child may learn on the basis of early experiences that being responsible for some negative consequence leaves him or her open to some form of negative sanctions from parents and/or peers. In anticipation of such retribution, the individual may become aroused. Given a sufficient number of such experiences, an association is apt to develop between personally producing negative effects and arousal.

A considerable body of research now allows us to infer the existence of such an arousal state as a consequence of dissonance manipulations. (See Fazio and Cooper, 1983, for a detailed review of this body of literature.) The evidence stems from three very different lines of research: (1) Dissonance manipulations tend to energize dominant responses, just as arousal states are known to do. (2) Dissonance manipulations produce measurable physiological arousal. (3) Like the arousal involved in emotions, the state of dissonance requires appropriate interpretation and labeling for attitude change to occur.

A. ENERGIZING PROPERTIES OF DISSONANCE AROUSAL

Early research attempts focused on the notion that if dissonance manipulations produce arousal, that arousal state should operate as do other known arousal states in energizing dominant responses (Spence, Farber, & McFann, 1956). Arousal typically facilitates performance on simple tasks but interferes with performance on more complex tasks.

In the first use of this principle in order to examine dissonance arousal, Waterman and Katkin (1967) found that, in comparison to writing a consonant essay, writing a dissonant essay facilitated performance on both a simple and a complex task. They suggested that the latter task may not have been complex enough to produce the interference effect. Cottrell and Wack (1967) and Waterman (1969) were able to demonstrate the predicted interaction between levels of dissonance and dominance of response. However, as Pallak and Pittman (1972) have pointed out, these studies failed to provide any direct evidence of dissonance reduction (i.e., attitude change). Thus, it is unclear as to whether dissonance was properly manipulated, and it is conceivable that the manipulations produced some other form of emotional arousal.

Pallak and Pittman (1972) did, however, succeed in demonstrating in a series of studies both the energizing effects and the attitude-change effects of dissonance. In a first study, the experimenters found that a dissonance manipulation both facilitated performance on a simple task and interfered with performance on a complex task. A second study demonstrated that the dissonance manipulation employed was effective in producing attitude change and also provided a partial replication of the first experiment. Although the conditions necessary to establish the facilitation of simple learning were not included in the design, decrements in performance on a complex task as a consequence of the dissonance manipulation were demonstrated. In conclusion, the data from these various studies suggest that dissonance arousal is characterized by drivelike energizing properties.

B. PHYSIOLOGICAL MEASUREMENT OF DISSONANCE AROUSAL

Very few reports of attempts to measure dissonance arousal directly exist in the literature. Fazio and Cooper (1983) provide a detailed review of these few experiments. All reports provide some evidence suggesting the existence of physiological arousal. Yet, in each case, the results are rather inconclusive because of the failure to employ standard dissonance paradigms and/or to find independent evidence of dissonance reduction with attitudinal measurements.

Croyle and Cooper (1983) provide strong evidence that dissonance involves an arousal state. These investigators employed a standard induced-compliance procedure that they demonstrated to be effective at producing the typical attitude-change effect in an initial experiment. In a second experiment, subjects drawn from the same population were assigned to the identical conditions for physiological recording. Physiological arousal was measured by the frequency of spontaneous electrodermal activity. Subjects in each of the three conditions—high-choice, counterattitudinal essay; low-choice, counterattitudinal essay; and high-choice, proattitudinal essay—manifested arousal during the actual essay writing. However, only subjects in the high-dissonance condition (i.e., high-choice, counterattitudinal) maintained this elevated arousal level during a rest period immediately following the essay writing. Subjects in the other two conditions rapidly habituated to their base rates during the rest period. In sum, freely choosing to write a counterattitudinal essay that might potentially influence an important policy decision, and thus might produce an aversive consequence, resulted in measurable physiological arousal.

C. INTERPRETATION OF DISSONANCE AROUSAL

The third line of research concerning the issue of dissonance arousal has been particularly informative because it has provided not only evidence regarding dissonance as a state of arousal but also evidence regarding the processes by which individuals who are experiencing dissonance interpret the arousal state (see Fig. 2). If dissonance manipulations produce arousal, then that arousal state should be amenable, as other known arousal states are, to cognitive labeling. That is, dissonance arousal should operate in the same manner as other emotional states. According to Schachter and Singer's (1962) theory, emotional states result from arousal that is cognitively labeled in accordance with cues provided by the situation. Thus, the same state of autonomic arousal can be labeled as euphoria due to the playful antics of a confederate or in a different situational context as a very different emotion (Schachter & Singer, 1962).

1. Misattribution of Dissonance Arousal to an External Source

Utilizing the attributional approach of Schachter and Singer, Zanna and Cooper (1974) suggested that dissonance arousal could also be mistakenly attributed to some external source, i.e., to some source other than being responsible for an aversive consequence. Given a situational cue that the emotion they are experiencing is not tension due to their counterattitudinal behavior, subjects in a dissonance situation, Zanna and Cooper argued, should experience no need to modify their attitude. The findings supported this prediction. When subjects ingested a placebo that ostensibly produced, as a side effect, feelings of tension, attitude change was attenuated. That is, the classic induced-compliance effect did not occur; subjects in the high-choice condition displayed no more attitude change than did those in a low-choice condition. This attenuation occurred despite the fact that the dissonance manipulation was clearly effective. Subjects who ingested a pill that was said to produce no side effects displayed the typical induced-compliance effect.

The attenuation of attitude change that Zanna and Cooper (1974) found to occur as a consequence of the misattribution of arousal to an external source has been conceptually replicated in other experimental investigations. Pittman (1975) found that the threat of shock in an upcoming experiment served as a cue that reduced the dissonance effect. Fazio et al. (1977) found misattribution to an aversive booth in which the subject was seated, and Gonzalez and Cooper (1976) found misattribution to new fluorescent lighting, to accomplish the same effect. In each of these experiments, the presence of the external source served to attenuate attitude change. The findings suggest that an arousal state follows the acceptance of responsibility for having produced an aversive event and that the arousal plays a mediating role in the attitude-change process.

More direct evidence that dissonance arousal is produced by induced compliance is provided by a study conducted by Cooper, Zanna, and Taves (1978). In the conditions that concern us at the moment, subjects advocated a counterat-

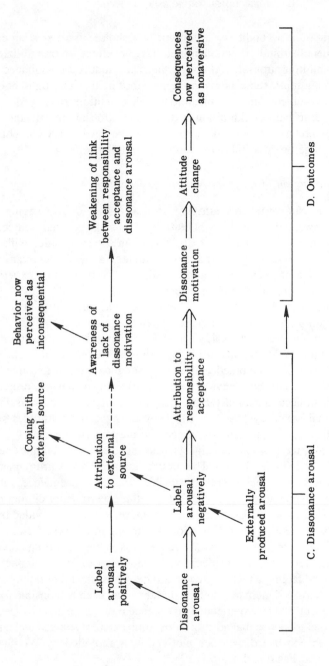

Fig. 2. The sequence of events leading from dissonance arousal to attitude change. The symbols are ⟹ dissonance path, → alternative possibilities, and – –→ tentative link.

titudinal position under conditions of high or low choice after ingesting either a placebo or phenolbarbital. (Phenolbarbital has the effect of tranquilizing the subject and inhibiting arousal.) Although the usual induced-compliance effect was found among those subjects given the placebo, neither the high-choice nor the low-choice subjects in the phenolbarbital condition displayed attitude change. Thus, drug-induced inhibition of dissonance arousal prevents the typical attitude-change process. Arousal, then, appears to be a necessary component of the attitude-change process following induced compliance.

2. Misattribution of External Arousal to Dissonance

Just as one can mistakenly attribute arousal that is due to having freely produced an unwanted event to a potentially arousing external source, it is possible to confuse arousal that is actually due to an external source with dissonance. Attributing externally caused arousal to one's own counterattitudinal behavior is likely to increase the amount of dissonance motivation experienced and thus the amount of attitude change displayed.

In the study described earlier by Cooper, Zanna, and Taves (1978), two additional conditions were included in the design that bear on the additive nature of arousal. Some of the subjects advocated a counterattitudinal position under conditions of high or low choice after ingesting an amphetamine. Therefore, amphetamine arousal is combined with any dissonance arousal that may occur for the high-choice subjects. Having been led to believe that the drug was a placebo, these subjects apparently attributed their amphetamine arousal to the counterattitudinal advocacy (see Fig. 2). They changed their attitudes significantly more than any other group of subjects in the experiment.

Interestingly, the low-choice subjects who ingested amphetamines also exhibited significant attitude change. The arousal created by the drug apparently convinced subjects that they were responsible for the consequences of their counterattitudinal behavior, despite the fact that the experimenter did not permit them any decision freedom. Evidence for this interpretation is provided by data on the subjects' perception of their freedom to decline to perform the counterattitudinal behavior. Although the low-choice subjects in the other drug conditions accurately perceived their lack of decision freedom, those in the amphetamine condition reported feeling a high degree of choice. Thus, the arousal they experienced seems to have led them to conclude that they had been responsible for their action. Consequently, they experienced dissonance motivation and changed their attitudes. (Further evidence that arousal from some external source can be misattributed and can enhance dissonance motivation is provided by Worchel and Arnold, 1974, and Fazio and Martin, 1983).

To summarize, our answer to the question of whether responsibility for an aversive consequence produces a state of dissonance arousal must be a resounding yes. We have reviewed evidence suggesting that dissonance arousal has general drivelike energizing properties and that it is physiologically measurable. We have seen that attitude change can be attenuated by providing subjects with an opportunity to misattribute dissonance arousal to some external source. And we have seen that attitude change can be accentuated by the misattribution of externally produced arousal to one's own aversive consequence-producing behavior. Furthermore, when dissonance arousal is inhibited by a tranquilizing drug, the usual induced-compliance effects fail to occur.

VI. Arousal and Alternate Theoretical Approaches

The evolution of any theory can, and often does, profit from the challenge of alternative approaches. Weaving alternative interpretations, finding proper domains and limits for each theory, and testing alternative predictions help a theory mature. By these criteria, dissonance is a mature theory indeed, for it has not been wanting for competing points of view. Fortunately, the identification of arousal properties following induced compliance has helped to distinguish dissonance from several alternative conceptual approaches. We single out two of the major alternatives to dissonance theory as explanations for attitude change in the induced-compliance situation.

A. SELF-PERCEPTION

As we have seen earlier, induced-compliance research set off a flurry of criticism that focused on possible methodological artifacts in producing attitude change. The first major competitor to accept the basic data of induced compliance research but to offer a plausible alternative causal mechanism was Bem's (1965) model of self-perception. Utilizing concepts borrowed from behavior analysis, Bem distinguished between those behaviors that are under the control of environmental stimuli and those that are not. The former are called mands and the latter are tacts. Only tacted behaviors are considered descriptive of an individual's true state.

Suppose we were observing a participant in Festinger and Carlsmith's (1959) induced-compliance experiment. A $20 inducement for telling a waiting subject that a task was interesting should render the behavior a mand. What conclusion would we draw about the actor's real attitude toward the task? We would assume that the behavior was forced by the environment and therefore tells us very little about the actor's true belief. On the other hand, the same behavior that was induced for a trivial sum ($1) would render the actor's behavior more of a tact. That behavior, then, would be useful in deducing that the actor's real attitude was consistent with the actor's behavior.

The novelty of Bem's (1965) approach is his assertion that both the observer and the participant would use the degree to which a behavior is under the control of the environment as a way of deducing the participant's attitude. Bem challenged dissonance theorists to demonstrate that involved participants are functioning as more than observers of their own behavior in deducing their attitudes. Bem (1965) conducted a series of demonstrations to show that the results of induced-compliance experiments could be replicated quite well by observers— people who are not actually in the experiment, who only read descriptions of the procedures, and who presumably do not experience any relevant internal state. A flurry of research (e.g., Jones, Linder, Kiesler, Zanna, & Brehm, 1968) and rejoinders (e.g., Bem, 1968) failed to find a convincing distinction between the two approaches. A series of supposedly critical tests between dissonance theory and self-perception theory on the role of the salience of participants' initial attitudes prior to the attitude-discrepant behavior yielded conflicting predictions, not to mention conflicting data (Ross & Schulman, 1973; Snyder & Ebbesen, 1972). Greenwald (1975) reviewed this literature and concluded that a critical test was not possible on this particular dimension (if on any).

The question of whether arousal exists following induced compliance is a crucial issue in the argument between the dissonance and the self-perception analyses. Finding that arousal accompanies counterattitudinal advocacy provides the evidence that attitude change can not be interpreted exclusively as a matter of self-perception (cf. Zanna & Cooper, 1976). Using the concept of arousal as an indicator of the presence of dissonance, Fazio et al. (1977) proposed that dissonance might account for attitude change when behavior is truly counterattitudinal, but that self-perception might play a role when behavior is only slightly discrepant from one's attitudes. The former is considered to occur when a behavior falls within a person's latitude of rejection, whereas the latter occurs when the behavior is within the latitude of acceptance. In a study designed to test this hypothesis, Fazio et al. (1977) found arousal to be present when behaviors are within the latitude of rejection but found no arousal when the behaviors are within the acceptable range. Abelson (1983) has referred to this finding as a "truce" between the dissonance and the self-perception points of view because the range of applicability of the two approaches has been more firmly established.

B. IMPRESSION MANAGEMENT

Tedeschi, Schlenker, and Bonoma (1971) proposed the notion of impression management to account for the data of induced compliance. They reasoned that participants in any research want to appear to be worthy persons to others of high status. Any attitude change that might exist in an induced-compliance experiment is said to be at the service of interpersonal appearances. It is not that people are trying to resolve unpleasant tension states. Rather, they try at all costs not to appear unworthy in the eyes of the experimenter. In induced-compliance experiments, for example, people do not want to look as though they would sell their souls for a paltry sum of money. So, they lie to the experimenter to convince him that they said what they did because it was consistent with their true beliefs.

The essence of Tedeschi *et al.*'s (1971) original impression-management approach is that a subject's mark on an attitude scale does not represent genuine attitude change. It is feigned purely for managing the impression that one is giving to the high-status experimenter. There is no dilemma of internal consistency, no state of arousal, and no resolution of an uncomfortable tension state. Unlike the self-perception theory, there is no effort to deduce one's genuine attitude from a consideration of the behavior. This analysis is an intriguing one and leads to some potentially testable propositions. Interpretation of the data from that research has been less than clear.

One of the propositions that Tedeschi *et al.* (1971) put forth is that attitude change would follow from induced compliance if and only if the experimenter who collects the attitudinal data also knows about the behavior (i.e., the essay writing or speech making) of the subject. Research designs in which the behavior of the subject is anonymous or in which there are two experimenters who are perceived to have no connection with each other should provide a test of the impression-management point of view. Such tests have been undertaken. In fact, Festinger and Carlsmith's (1959) original experiment utilized two separate experimenters. One requested and obtained the subject's aggreement to engage in the counterattitudinal advocacy. A departmental secretary, supposedly asking questions after the conclusion of the experiment, assessed the subjects' attitudes toward the spool-turning task. Tedeschi and Rosenfeld (1981) explain such attitude change by contending that the "attitude scales could have served as cues to associate the measurement with the previous experimenter" (p. 167). Similarly, Hoyt, Henley, and Collins (1972) ran a study in which subjects' counterattitudinal essays were anonymous—that is, unsigned and supposedly untraceable. Attitude change consistent with dissonance predictions was obtained. In responding to these data, Gaes, Kalle, and Tedeschi (1978) suggested that subjects may have believed that the seats were coded with some form of identifier that would enable the investigator to decode the essays and find out who wrote what. With such tortuous logic, it is very difficult indeed to find a reasonable test that would support the notion that only feigned attitudes are involved in the induced-compliance paradigm.

An alternative approach to examining the process of attitude change in the induced-compliance paradigm is the use of the "bogus pipeline" as a dependent measure (Jones & Sigall, 1971). With a bogus pipeline, the participants are convinced that the experimenter can accurately read their true, internal feelings with the use of an electronic device. In the impression management view, this should eliminate attitude change. With no possibility of fooling the experimenter, there is no utility in attitude change. Studies in this area in the past few years have provided mixed support (Reiss, Kalle, & Tedeschi, 1981; Gaes et al. 1978; Paulhus, 1982).

The first study that applied the bogus-pipeline procedure as a measure of dissonance-produced attitude change was conducted by Cooper (1971). In that study, which was described in detail earlier, the bogus-pipeline measure showed stronger support for the dissonance predictions than did the traditional paper-and-pencil measures. Gaes et al. (1978), on the other hand, did find that attitude change was eliminated using the bogus pipeline. Scheier and Carver (1980) suggested that Gaes et al. (1978) may have inadvertently focused subjects' attention on their initial attitudes, making them more resistant to change.

An experiment by Stults, Messe, and Kerr (1984) suggests yet another explanation for the Gaes et al. (1978) finding of no attitude change given the use of a bogus-pipeline procedure. These experimenters replicated the finding of less attitude change in a bogus-pipeline condition than in a condition involving a traditional attitude scale. However, in a second bogus-pipeline condition that provided for habituation to the apparatus, attitude change was obtained. Stults et al. (1984) suggest that, without the opportunity to get accustomed to the supposed physiological apparatus, subjects may interpret dissonance arousal as nervousness due to the novel hardware and hence not change their attitudes.

Like self-perception theory, impression management as originally proposed (Tedeschi et al., 1971) requires no assumption of internal states, discomfort, or arousal. Consequently, the discovery of arousal might be construed as evidence inconsistent with the impression-management approach. However, there has appeared a "revisionist impression management theory" (Tedeschi & Rosenfeld, 1981). An essential difference between the old and new versions is the central role now played by a concept called social anxiety. The experience of the state of social anxiety is what occurs when a high-status experimenter may hold the participant blameworthy for an action that has produced an embarrassing or unwanted consequence. Tedeschi and Rosenfeld assert that the degree of attitude change following induced compliance is "directly related to the degree of embarrassment or social anxiety experienced by subjects" (p. 156). The assertion that an individual is aroused as a consequence of having freely brought about an aversive event makes it very difficult to find many lingering points of contrast between impression management and dissonance.

Nonetheless, it is important to note that some research on dissonance has revealed attitude change that is difficult to interpret as feigned in any manner. Some research has found evidence not only of attitude change but also of behavioral change weeks after the dissonance manipulation. For example, Staw (1974) investigated the attitudes and behavior of students who had committed themselves to Reserve Officer Training Corps just prior to the institution of the draft lottery system. Those who subsequently received high lottery numbers (naturally-occurring random assignment to a high-dissonance condition) found themselves committed to ROTC with little external justification. They subsequently indicated more satisfaction with ROTC than did those students who received low lottery numbers. Furthermore, those with high lottery numbers actually performed better and received higher grades in their military science courses the next semester than did those with low numbers. It is difficult to understand how such behavioral change could have occurred except through actual internalized, rather than feigned, attitude change.

A modified view of impression management that does not rely upon the notion of feigned attitude has been proposed by Schlenker (1982). The basis of this approach is that people's major concern is to protect a positive view of their identity. When faced with the possibility of being responsible for reprehensible events, they undertake a variety of accounts and explanations to excuse their behavior. Attitude change is one such excuse and is at the service of identity protection. The concern of subjects in Schlenker's view is not all that dissimilar from the subjects' dilemma according to our dissonance analysis. In both instances, people are concerned with being responsible for behavior that has produced aversive consequences. From the dissonance perspective, the motivation to change attitudes as a result of accepting responsibility emanates from the arousal of a tension state. From Schlenker's version of impression management, the motivation arises from wanting to protect one's positively valued identity to others and to oneself.

Schlenker's (1982) version of impression management places the participant in a different perspective from the original impression-management view. It does not see the participant as necessarily feigning attitude change in order to impress an experimenter. There is no assumption that attitude change is merely a Machiavellian public demonstration of an attitude that bears little relationship to one's private belief. On the contrary, Schlenker's identity approach acknowledges that attitude change following counterattitudinal advocacy may indeed be genuine. As such, Schlenker's view bears a close resemblance to the earlier self-esteem versions of dissonance theory.

We do not doubt at all that subjects are concerned with the impression that they are having on other subjects, the experimenter, and any other participant in the interpersonal sphere. What has been at issue in the controversy between the two approaches is whether the management of impressions is the *only* phenomenon that transpires in induced-compliance studies or whether the bringing about of aversive consequences creates an unpleasant tension that, in turn, motivates attitude change (cf. Paulhus, 1982). In their review of the attitude-change literature, Cialdini, Petty, and Cacioppo (1981) conclude, "We cannot agree with the claim that self-presentational influences are the sole mediators of the compliance effects" (p. 382).

VII. Dissonance Arousal:
A General or an Aversive State?

Given that dissonance arousal occurs following the acceptance of responsibility for an unwanted event, what sort of arousal state is it? Is the dissonance arousal specifically aversive or is it a general and undifferentiated state? The research described to this point does not address this issue. That dissonance arousal can be misattributed or that it has energizing properties is consistent with either viewpoint.

A set of studies have attempted to answer this question, however. The issue was first addressed by Zanna, Higgins, and Taves (1976), who employed the misattribution paradigm to explore whether dissonance arousal is capable of misattribution only to negative labels. The design of the study is largely a replication of the original Zanna and Cooper (1974) study with the addition of a condition in which subjects were led to believe that a pill they were taking produces side-effect feelings of "pleasant excitement". The interesting comparison concerns the degree of attitude change in the pleasant excitement relative to change among the group of subjects who were told that the pill would make them feel "tense". Both the "tense" and "pleasant excitement" labels imply arousal, but the two labels differ in their aversiveness. Zanna et al. (1976) reasoned that the tense label, and not the pleasant excitement one, should mitigate attitude change if dissonance arousal is uniquely aversive. If the arousal is a more general state, then both labels should mitigate attitude change. The findings are consistent with the view that dissonance arousal is aversive. Subjects in the tense condition did not change their attitudes, whereas those in the pleasant excitement condition did.

Although the Zanna et al. (1976) data are consistent with the view that dissonance is specifically aversive, the data do not exclude, as Cooper, Fazio, and Rhodewalt (1978) have pointed out, an interpretation that is consistent with the notion that dissonance involves a more malleable and general heightened state of arousal. Could not the subjects in the Zanna et al. study have experienced a heightened state of arousal that they subsequently labeled as negative? Recall that subjects believed that they were taking an experimental pill, one which was still being tested and which potentially produced side effects. Thus, there exists a strong situational cue for the subject to label any general arousal experienced as a negative emotion. Only in the pleasant excitement condition, does the subject have any indication that the pill may not be responsible for the negative feelings experienced. Having labeled the arousal as negative, subjects may be searching specifically for a source of negative arousal. Thus, only the tense pill could serve as a misattribution stimulus.

This explanation can also account for the findings in a study by Higgins,

Rhodewalt, and Zanna (1979). Using the now familiar "pill paradigm," the investigators examined four different side-effect labels arranged in a 2 (arousal–nonarousal) by 2 (pleasant–unpleasant) factorial design. The labels employed were "pleasantly excited", "tense", "relaxed", and "unpleasantly sedated." From the results, which indicated an attenuation of attitude change in the two unpleasant conditions, the authors inferred that discomfort, and not arousal per se, is the critical component of the dissonant state. Although we say more about this conclusion at a later point, it should be clear that subjects may have experienced a general state of arousal, interpreted that arousal as discomfort, and then misattributed their unpleasantness only in those conditions in which the pill was said to produce feelings of discomfort.

The extent to which arousal states are malleable in terms of the labeling they permit has been questioned (e.g., Berkowitz, 1978; Cotton, 1981; Marshall & Zimbardo, 1979; Maslach, 1979). However, it appears that the "pill paradigm" may not be a feasible approach to the investigation of the issue of whether dissonance arousal is a general or an aversive state. Cooper, Fazio, and Rhodewalt (1978) employed a different procedure to investigate whether dissonance arousal is a sufficiently labile state that it can be interpreted as a positive emotion (see also Drachman & Worchel, 1976). Subjects were committed to counterattitudinal advocacy under conditions of high or low choice. All subjects then observed a humorous cartoon. Schachter and Wheeler (1962) have demonstrated that increasing a subject's arousal level by an injection of epinephrine increases the degree to which the subject is amused by a humorous film. Cooper, Fazio, and Rhodewalt (1978) reasoned that the same outcome should occur if one is aroused by having freely chosen to behave counterattitudinally—provided that dissonance arousal is sufficiently general that it can be interpreted positively. The investigators manipulated the timing of the cartoon presentation. For half the subjects the cartoon was presented immediately following the counterattitudinal commitment; and hence, the cartoon could serve as a misattribution stimulus. For the other subjects, the cartoon was not presented until the subjects had completed a postcommitment attitude measure and, hence, was not available as a cue for interpreting the arousal state. This order manipulation was found to affect greatly the attitude and humor ratings of the high-choice subjects (those subjects who theoretically experience arousal). Those who were presented with the cartoon prior to the attitude measure tended to find the film relatively funnier and to change their attitudes less. Those who were presented with the attitude measure first tended to change their attitudes relatively more and to find the cartoon less funny. As expected, however, the order manipulation had no significant effect upon the low-choice subjects.

The suggestion that dissonance arousal is a highly malleable state is also supported by a study by Rhodewalt and Comer (1979). Subjects performed an induced-compliance task under conditions of high choice. Prior to the actual counterattitudinal commitment, electrodes were attached to the subject's face ostensibly in order to record various physiological data. Allegedly so as to improve the quality of the recordings, the subject's face was positioned so as to form a smile or a frown or was not positioned at all. This latter group of subjects displayed the typical induced-compliance effect of attitude change. In the other conditions, however, the smile or frown apparently served as a cue to the subject that aided him in labeling his dissonance arousal. The subjects who were frowning displayed significantly more attitude change than any other group in the experiment. The frowning facial expression apparently provided a cue, stronger than any cue in the control condition, that the arousal was unpleasant. Smiling subjects, on the other hand, did not change their attitudes at all. Their facial expression apparently led them to interpret their arousal positively (and in fact, they reported feeling happier than did other subjects on a mood measure) and, consequently, they experienced no aversive pressure to alter their attitudes.

From the data from the just described two studies, it appears that dissonance arousal is sufficiently general and malleable that it can be interpreted as a positive emotion. There appears to be no need to postulate that it is intrinsically aversive, although it typically may lead to negative affect.

VIII. Dissonance Arousal versus Dissonance Motivation

Figure 2 presents a flow diagram of the steps leading from dissonance arousal to final attitude change. Dissonance arousal, we would suggest, is a general and undifferentiated state of arousal. If it is labeled positively and attributed to an external source of positive arousal, then dissonance motivation, that is, aversive pressure to change one's attitude, does not occur. Nor does dissonance motivation occur if the arousal is interpreted negatively and attributed to some external source. In these two cases, the individual has succeeded in transforming that arousal into one typically produced by that external agent, for example, a humorous reaction to a cartoon or anger toward an insulting party. If the emotional experience is unpleasant, the individual may attempt to cope with the emotion in a manner appropriate to that external agent. He might allow sufficient time to elapse for the effects of a pill to dissipate, he might decide to leave an aversive environment, or in the case of misattribution to another person who has insulted him, he might engage in some aggressive behavior.

Dissonance motivation only occurs when the individual labels his state of arousal negatively and attributes that arousal to his having freely produced an aversive consequence. It is in this case that dissonance motivation, as Festinger (1957) described it, occurs. The individual experiences an aversive state which he should desire to reduce.

The reader should have noted by now that we draw a distinction between what we term dissonance arousal and dissonance motivation. To review this distinction, *dissonance arousal* refers to the general heightened arousal that is presumed to follow the acceptance of responsibility for an unwanted event. This arousal is open to varied interpretations. The individual searches the environment to determine the nature of the emotion and its cause. Given that the arousal is interpreted to be discomfort due to the acceptance of responsibility for an aversive consequence, *dissonance motivation,* that is, aversive pressure to change one's attitude, occurs.

The Higgins *et al.* (1979) study described earlier in the section "Dissonance Arousal: General or Aversive State?" is relevant to this distinction. Recall that the experimental results displayed an attenuation of attitude change when a pill that the subjects ingested was described as producing feelings of tension or of unpleasant sedation, but not when it was described as producing pleasant excitement or relaxation. On the basis of these findings the authors suggest that "attitude change following counterattitudinal behavior is motivated by the unpleasantness of the dissonant state, and that arousal per se is irrelevant. Thus it would appear that arousal is not even a necessary component of the *motivation* to reduce dissonance; the unpleasantness of the dissonance state is sufficient" (p. 28, italics ours). In light of the data, we can concur with the statement that attitude change is motivated not so much by arousal as by the feeling of discomfort. That is, subjects may experience and consider what we call dissonance motivation primarily as a state of unpleasantness. However, it is important to note that this state of discomfort is preceded by a state of undifferentiated arousal and that this dissonance arousal is a necessary component of dissonance motivation. Some arousal must occur to provoke any labeling of the state as unpleasant. Evidence for the occurrence of dissonance arousal is provided by the research on the energizing properties of dissonance and by the research on direct physiological assessment. Once dissonance arousal is present and is interpreted in the manner we have suggested, dissonance motivation can occur. Subjects experiencing dissonance motivation may, as Higgins *et al.* suggest, change their attitudes largely because of the unpleasantness of the state, but the arousal and a particular interpretation of that arousal are necessary to create dissonance motivation.

1. Alternatives to Attitude Change

It has been our intent to specify the course of events that lead to attitude change via a dissonance process. In fact, Fig. 1 and Fig. 2 together summarize our characterization of the sequence. The main or "dissonance path" displays the steps that are necessary for attitude change to occur. Once dissonance motivation is experienced, attitude change constitutes a means of handling the discomfort one is experiencing over having been personally responsible for the production of an aversive consequence. In effect, attitude change serves to modify one's perception of the consequences in the direction of viewing them as not that aversive after all.

What if such attitude change were essentially not available as a means of dealing with the dissonance motivation? It is quite easy to imagine attitudes that are so central to one's system of beliefs and values and to one's self-identity that attitude change is not a viable option. One possibility is that the individual will review the course of events that led up to the experience of dissonance motivation and conceivably "discover" that an "error" had been made at some previous step. For example, one might review one's assessment of the arousal state that is being experienced and come to the conclusion that it is some emotional reaction other than dissonance motivation. Such appears to have been the case in an experiment conducted by Cooper and Mackie (1983). Student members of a campus group supporting the 1980 presidential election of Ronald Reagan freely complied with a request to write pro-Carter arguments. Yet, given that their attitudes so clearly defined their group membership, these subjects could not very well change their attitudes toward the candidates. Instead, these subjects seem to have misattributed their arousal to the existence of rival outgroups supporting Carter, as evidenced by their enhanced derogation of such outgroup members.

Gonzalez and Cooper (1976) observed a similar phenomenon among members of Princeton eating clubs who had freely agreed to write an essay supporting the abolition of such clubs. Although nonmembers displayed the typical induced-compliance effect after performing the behavior under conditions of high versus low choice, the eating club members did not. Clearly, a change in attitude toward the clubs was very difficult for these latter individuals. After they completed the attitude scale and just before they left the experimental room, the experimenter provided the subjects with a possible alternative explanation for their discomfort. He implied that the new fluorescent lighting in the room had been making some people feel uneasy and asked subjects to indicate whether they had found the lights bothersome. Sure enough, the eating club members seized upon this opportunity to make an external attribution for their discomfort. High-choice subjects who were eating club members rated the lights as more aversive than did any other group of subjects.

Alternatively, individuals for whom attitude change is not a viable option might review their assessment of the consequences that were presumably made possible by the behavior. Such reassessment might lead to the distorted conclusion that the consequences can be viewed as trivial or nonexistent. The essay, speech, or whatever might be perceived as very weak and unconvincing and, hence, unlikely to produce or to have produced any aversive consequence. A recent series of experiments by Scheier and Carver (1980) found evidence for this possibility among subjects for whom initial attitudes were very salient either because of their status with respect to an individual difference measure (high private self-consciousness) or because of a manipulation that presumably increased attention to the self (the presence of a mirror). Rather than change their attitudes, these subjects came to perceive the counterattitudinal essays that they had written as relatively weak, when in actuality the essays were objectively no different in quality from essays written by control subjects.

In each of the cases just discussed, there exists the suggestion that individuals may reassess their behavior, its consequences, their personal responsibility, or their feeling state when they find attitude change to be an unproductive manner with which to cope with dissonance motivation. Yet another possibility exists. It is conceivable that there can be no denying that one did produce an aversive consequence and that one is upset over having done so. In such a situation, individuals may attempt to make amends for their transgression. Either behaviorally or cognitively, they may try to reaffirm or bolster their initial attitude. The results of a study by Sherman and Gorkin (1980) provide evidence of such attitude bolstering. In the critical condition, profeminist subjects failed to solve a difficult logic problem concerning sex roles and, in so doing, displayed stereotypic sexist behavior. Because the sexist behavior was clearly self-generated, a high degree of personal responsibility was involved. Furthermore, such sexist action implied the potential for future aversive consequences by suggesting that sexism is so pervasive and subtle that even the confirmed feminist can fall prone to its influence. Finally, there was no way that the subject could deny the evidence of having exhibited sexist thought. How then did the subjects deal with this situation? When given the opportunity to reaffirm their feminist attitudes, they did so. In an ostensibly separate experiment, the subjects considered a simulated sex discrimination court case and expressed decisions about the appropriate verdict. Subjects who failed the sex-role problem were more favorable toward the female plaintiff than control subjects. Furthermore, this enhanced vigilance with regard to sex discrimination was particularly evident on the part of those subjects who were initially extremely supportive of feminism as opposed those who were only midly feminist. Because their stance with regard to feminism was so extreme and the issue so important to them, the former subjects especially could not very well modify their opinions of sexism. Instead, they sought to make amends for their sexist behavior and to reaffirm their original attitudes.

What we seem to see evidence of in all the described research is what may be characterized as some form of a "gate-keeping" function. If the critical attitude is so highly central or salient that changing the attitude would be problematic, individuals appear to arrive at other ways of coping with the dissonance motivation. They may reassess the events that led them to experience dissonance motivation in a distorted fashion, or they may acknowledge their transgression and strive to make amends. Attitude change following dissonance motivation is not a sure thing. Nevertheless, dissonance motivation and the various intervening steps are necessary if the occurrence of an aversive consequence is to have any possibility of affecting the attitude in question.

IX.   Some Concluding Thoughts

We have seen that dissonance motivation and, hence, attitude change are apt to follow an attribution of dissonance arousal to one's own behavior. We have also suggested that if dissonance arousal is misattributed to some external source, a person may attempt to cope with that external agent in some appropriate manner. But, given the misattribution of dissonance arousal, does the person attend at all to the cognitions that prompted the arousal process? No data relevant to this question have yet been collected. The issue appears important enough, however (see Ronis & Greenwald, 1979; Fazio, Zanna, & Cooper, 1979), to warrant a few speculative thoughts.

An individual who has misattributed his dissonance arousal does not experience the state that usually follows from having freely produced an aversive event. Although dissonance motivation usually follows from such behavior, it did not occur in this case. Whether the individual attends to his earlier acceptance of responsibility would appear to depend upon the extent to which that person is aware of this lack of dissonance motivation. (We have indicated the tentative nature of this notion by a dotted line in our flow chart of the dissonance process in Fig. 2.) If the individual realizes that what he usually experiences after behavior of the sort he performed (a feeling of discomfort) did not occur in this particular instance, then he may modify his perception of the consequences of his counterattitudinal action. If he does not feel uncomfortable about having produced this consequence, then it is likely that the consequence was not very severe.

For example, in the typical induced-compliance study, a subject writes a counterattitudinal essay that is to be employed in a future attitude change study or is to be shown to some officials or organization. Consequently, the subject's essay may convince some people or an organization to adopt a position that the individual him- or herself opposes. If dissonance motivation occurs, the individual may consider his or her lack of dissonance motivation as a signal, say, that the probability of the essay actually convincing someone and producing that unwanted state of affairs is very minimal. In other words, the perception of the consequences of the subject's action might be altered by the awareness that he or she does not feel upset about the behavior.

Misattribution may bring about yet another effect. We have argued that an individual learns early in life an association between personally producing negative effects and dissonance arousal. This learned arousal state eventually develops to the point that it occurs whenever the individual feels responsible for a negative consequence. Furthermore, interpretation of that arousal state usually leads the subject to feel discomfort over his behavior. Because the discomfort does not occur in an instance of misattribution, the association between responsibility acceptance and dissonance arousal may be weakened. If misattribution were to occur frequently enough, the association may decay to the point that the individual may not experience dissonance arousal following freely performed counterattitudinal behavior. One wonders whether a subject who is led to misattribute dissonance arousal in each of a succeeding number of induced-compliance situations would exhibit any attitude change in a later situation in which no misattribution opportunity is provided.

Unfortunately, there are no data to ascertain the adequacy of these speculations. Nevertheless, it is encouraging to note that our view of the dissonance process suggests some new directions for future research. We find our theoretical proposal (and our speculations) provocative and hope that this review will prompt additional research on dissonance processes.

1. Summary: A Look at the Past and the Future

Dissonance theory has come a long way since 1957. The view that people are driven by logical inconsistency has changed. The changes in emphasis stand as a case study in the evolution of a theory (Greenwald & Ronis, 1978). An original theory sets the directions and foci for inquiry. Some of what Festinger wrote in 1957 remains; some has been modified. New postulates have replaced or altered older ones. But in the accumulation of data, the theory has evolved.

In the present chapter, we speculate that attitude change is a consequence of a multifaceted process that includes both the concept of dissonance arousal and of dissonance motivation. Both processes require a complex set of attributions. Dissonance arousal is facilitated by attributions about consequences and responsibility. Attributions about the valence and the causes of the arousal may lead to dissonance motivation. Such mediating steps were not envisioned in 1957. Yet, they represent theoretical postulates necessitated by the accumulation of data. At the same time, the central concepts of motivation and arousal still lie at the heart of the dissonance process. The original theory pointed to general directions— directions that are still bearing fruit in terms of our understanding of attitude-change phenomena and our understanding of basic motivational processes. Whether one views the present formulation as such a profound shift from the original theory as to necessitate considering the original disproved (and, in turn, the present in need of a new name) appears inconsequential.

It would have been naive to believe that Festinger's original statement of dissonance would capture all of the nuances of what more than a quarter century of empirical data has shown us is a complex process. Likewise, it would be naive of us to believe that our modified formulation of dissonance motivation will account for all of the data to come. Yet as we have seen, it does point to some new directions for research.

ACKNOWLEDGMENTS

The authors thank George R. Goethals for his assistance with an early draft of the manuscript and Edward E. Jones, Charles Lord, Steven J. Sherman, and Yaacov Trope for their helpful comments on an earlier draft. Preparation of this chapter was assisted by National Science Foundation Grant BNS 76-19384 to the first author and National Institute of Mental Health Grant MH 38832 to the second author.

REFERENCES

Abelson, R. P. Whatever became of consistency theory? *Personality and Social Psychology Bulletin,* 1983, *9,* 37–54.

Aronson, E. Dissonance theory: Progress and problems. In R. Abelson, E. Aronson, W. McGuire, T. Newcomb, M. Rosenberg, & P. Tannebaum (Eds.), *The cognitive consistency theories: A source book.* Chicago: McNally, 1968.

Aronson, E., Chase, T., Helmreich, R., & Ruhnke, R. A two-factor theory of dissonance reduction: The effect of feeling stupid or feeling "awful" on opinion change. *International Journal of Communication Research,* 1974, *3,* 59–74.

Bem, D. J. An experimental analysis of self-persuasion. *Journal of Experimental Social Psychology,* 1965, *1,* 199–218.

Bem, D. J. The epistemological status of interpersonal simulations: A reply to Jones, Linder, Kiesler, Zanna, and Brehm. *Journal of Experimental Social Psychology,* 1968, *4,* 270–274.

Berkowitz, L. Do we have to believe we are angry with someone in order to display "angry" aggression toward the person? In L. Berkowitz (Ed.), *Cognitive theories in social psychology,* NY: Academic Press, 1978.

Berlyne, D. E. *Conflict, arousal, and curiosity.* NY: McGraw-Hill, 1960.

Brehm, J. W., & Jones, R. A. The effect on dissonance of surprise consequences. *Journal of Experimental Social Psychology,* 1970, *6,* 420–431.

Chapanis, N. P., & Chapanis, A. Cognitive dissonance: Five years later. *Psychological Bulletin,* 1964, *61,* 1–22.

Cialdini, R. B., Petty, R. E., & Cacioppo, J. T. Attitude and attitude change. In M. R. Rosenzweig & L. W. Porter (Eds.), *Annual Review of Psychology* (Vol. 32). Palo Alto, CA: Annual Reviews, 1981.

Cohen, A. R. An experiment on small rewards for discrepant compliance and attitude change. In J. W. Brehm & A. R. Cohen (Eds.), *Explorations in cognitive dissonance.* NY: Wiley, 1962.

Collins, B. E., & Hoyt, M. G. Personal responsibility for consequences: An integration and extension of the "forced compliance" literature. *Journal of Experimental Social Psychology,* 1972, *8,* 558–593.

Cooper, J. Personal responsibility and dissonance: The role of foreseen consequences. *Journal of Personality and Social Psychology,* 1971, *18,* 354–363.

Cooper, J., & Brehm, J. W. Prechoice awareness of relative deprivation as a determinant of cognitive dissonance. *Journal of Experimental Social Psychology,* 1971, *7,* 571–581.

Cooper, J., & Duncan, B. L. Cognitive dissonance as a function of self-esteem and logical inconsistency. *Journal of Personality,* 1971, *39,* 289–302.

Cooper, J., Fazio, R. H., & Rhodewalt, F. Dissonance and humor: Evidence for the undifferentiated nature of dissonance arousal. *Journal of Personality and Social Psychology,* 1978, *36,* 280–285.

Cooper, J., & Goethals, G. R. Unforeseen events and the elimination of cognitive dissonance. *Journal of Personality and Social Psychology,* 1974, *29,* 441–445.

Cooper, J., & Mackie, D. Cognitive dissonance in an intergroup context. *Journal of Personality and Social Psychology,* 1983, *44,* 536–544.

Cooper, J., & Worchel, S. Role of undesired consequences in arousing cognitive dissonance. *Journal of Personality and Social Psychology,* 1970, *16,* 199–206.

Cooper, J., Zanna, M. P., & Goethals, G. R. Mistreatment of an esteemed other as a consequence affecting dissonance reduction. *Journal of Experimental Social Psychology,* 1974, *10,* 224–233.

Cooper, J., Zanna, M. P., & Taves, P. A. Arousal as a necessary condition for attitude change following induced compliance. *Journal of Personality and Social Psychology,* 1978, *36,* 1101–1106.

Cotton, J. L. A review of research on Schachter's theory of emotion and the misattribution of arousal. *European Journal of Social Psychology,* 1981, *11,* 365–397.

Cottrell, N. B., & Wack, D. L. The energizing effect of cognitive dissonance on dominant and subordinate responses. *Journal of Personality and Social Psychology,* 1967, *16,* 132–138.

Croyle, R., & Cooper, J. Dissonance arousal: Physiological evidence. *Journal of Personality and Social Psychology,* 1983, *45,* 782–791.

Davis, K. E., & Jones, E. E. Changes in interpersonal perception as a means of reducing cognitive dissonance. *Journal of Abnormal and Social Psychology,* 1960, *61,* 402–410.

Deutsch, M., Krauss, R. M., & Rosenau, N. Dissonance or defensiveness? *Journal of Personality,* 1962, *30,* 16–28.

Drachman, D. & Worchel, S. Misattribution of dissonance arousal as a means of dissonance reduction. *Sociometry,* 1976, *39,* 53–59.

Fazio, R. H., & Cooper, J. Arousal in the dissonance process. In J. T. Cacioppo & R. E. Petty (Eds.), *Social Psychophysiology.* NY: Guilford, 1983.

Fazio, R. H., & Martin, F. *Dissonance arousal and the transfer of residual excitation.* (Data reported in Fazio & Cooper, 1983).

Fazio, R. H., Zanna, M. P., & Cooper, J. Dissonance and self-perception: An integrative view of each theory's proper domain of application. *Journal of Experimental Social Psychology,* 1977, *13,* 464–479.

Fazio, R. H., Zanna, M. P., & Cooper, J. On the relationship of data to theory: A reply to Ronis and Greenwald. *Journal of Experimental Social Psychology,* 1979, *15,* 70–76.

Festinger, L. *A theory of cognitive dissonance.* Stanford, CA: Stanford University Press, 1957.

Festinger, L., & Carlsmith, J. M. Cognitive consequences of forced compliance. *Journal of Abnormal and Social Psychology,* 1959, *58,* 203–211.

Gaes, G. G., Kalle, R. J., & Tedeschi, J. T. Impression management in the forced compliance situation: Two studies using the bogus pipeline. *Journal of Experimental Social Psychology,* 1978, *14,* 493–510.

Gerard, H. B., Blevans, S. A., & Malcolm, T. Self-evaluation and the evaluation of choice alternatives. *Journal of Personality,* 1964, *32,* 395–410.

Goethals, G. R., & Cooper, J. The role of intention and postbehavioral consequences in the arousal of cognitive dissonance. *Journal of Personality and Social Psychology,* 1972, *3,* 293–301.

Goethals, G. R., & Cooper, J. When dissonance is reduced: The timing of self-justificatory attitude change. *Journal of Personality and Social Psychology,* 1975, *32,* 361–367.

Goethals, G. R., Cooper, J., & Naficy, A. Role of foreseen, foreseeable, and unforeseeable behavioral consequences in the arousal of cognitive dissonance. *Journal of Personality and Social Psychology*, 1979, *37*, 1179–1185.

Gonzalez, A. E. J., & Cooper, J. *What to do with leftover dissonance: Blame it on the lights.* (Data reported in Zanna & Cooper, 1976).

Greenwald, A. G. On the inconclusiveness of "crucial" cognitive tests of dissonance vs. self-perception theories. *Journal of Experimental Social Psychology*, 1975, *11*, 490–499.

Greenwald, A. G., & Ronis, D. L. Twenty years of cognitive dissonance: Case study of the evolution of a theory. *Psychological Review*, 1978, *85*, 53–57.

Higgins, E. T., Rhodewalt, F., & Zanna, M. P. Dissonance motivation: Its nature, persistence, and reinstatement. *Journal of Experimental Social Psychology*, 1979, *15*, 16–34.

Hoyt, M. F., Henley, M. D., & Collins, B. E. Studies in forced compliance: The confluence of choice and consequences on attitude change. *Journal of Personality and Social Psychology*, 1972, *23*, 205–210.

Jones, E. E. Major developments in social psychology since 1930. In G. Lindzey & E. Aronson (Eds.), *Handbook of Social Psychology* (3rd Ed.). Reading, MA: Addison-Wesley, in press.

Jones, E. E., & Sigall, H. The bogus pipeline: A new paradigm for measuring affect and attitude. *Psychological Bulletin*, 1971, *76*, 349–364.

Jones, R. A., Linder, D. E., Kiesler, C., Zanna, M., & Brehm, J. W. Internal states or external stimuli: Observers' attitude judgments and the dissonance theory—self-persuasion controversy. *Journal of Experimental Social Psychology*, 1968, *4*, 247–269.

Kamin, L. J. Predictability, surprise, attention, and conditioning. In B. A. Campbell & R. M. Church (Eds.), *Punishment and Aversive Behavior*. NY: Appleton-Century-Crofts, 1969.

Linder, D. E., Cooper, J., & Jones, E. E. Decision freedom as a determinant of the role of incentive magnitude in attitude change. *Journal of Personality and Social Psychology*, 1967, *6*, 245–254.

Linder, D. E., Cooper, J., & Wicklund, R. A. Pre-exposure persuasion as a result of commitment to pre-exposure effort. *Journal of Experimental Social Psychology*, 1968, *4*, 470–482.

Marshall, G. D., & Zimbardo, P. G. Affective consequences of inadequately explained physiological arousal. *Journal of Personality and Social Psychology*, 1979, *37*, 970–988.

Maslach, C. Negative emotional biasing of unexplained arousal. *Journal of Personality and Social Psychology*, 1979, *37*, 953–969.

Mowrer, O. H. On the dual nature of learning: A reinterpretation of "conditioning" and "problem-solving." *Harvard Educational Review*, 1947, *17*, 102–148.

Mowrer, O. H. *Learning Theory and Behavior*. NY: Wiley, 1960.

Nel, E., Helmreich, R., & Aronson, E. Opinion change in the advocate as a function of the persuasibility of his audience: A clarification of the meaning of dissonance. *Journal of Personality and Social Psychology*, 1969, *12*, 117–124.

Pallak, M. S., & Pittman, T. S. General motivation effects of dissonance arousal. *Journal of Personality and Social Psychology*, 1972, *21*, 349–358.

Paulhus, D. Individual differences, self-presentation, and cognitive dissonance: Their concurrent operation in forced compliance. *Journal of Personality and Social Psychology*, 1982, *43*, 838–852.

Pittman, T. S. Attribution of arousal as a mediator in dissonance reduction. *Journal of Experimental Social Psychology*, 1975, *11*, 53–63.

Pyszczynski, T. A., & Greenberg, J. Role of disconfirmed expectancies in the instigation of attributional processing. *Journal of Personality and Social Psychology*, 1981, *40*, 31–38.

Reiss, M., Kalle, R. J., & Tedeschi, J. T. Bogus pipeline attitude assessment, impression management and misattribution in induced compliance settings. *Journal of Social Psychology*, 1981, *115*, 247–258.

Rhodewalt, F., & Comer, R. Induced-compliance attitude change: Once more with feeling. *Journal of Experimental Social Psychology*, 1979, *15*, 35–47.

Ronis, D. L., & Greenwald, A. G. Dissonance theory revised again: Comment on the paper by Fazio, Zanna, and Cooper. *Journal of Experimental Social Psychology*, 1979, *15*, 62–69.

Rosenberg, M. J. When dissonance fails: On eliminating evaluation apprehension from attitude measurement. *Journal of Personality and Social Psychology*, 1965, *1*, 28–42.

Ross, M., & Shulman, R. F. Increasing the salience of initial attitudes: Dissonance versus self-perception theory. *Journal of Personality and Social Psychology*, 1973, *28*, 138–144.

Schachter, S., & Singer, J. E. Cognitive, social and physiological determinants of emotional state. *Psychological Review*, 1962, *69*, 379–399.

Schachter, S., & Wheeler, L. Epinephrine, chlorpromazine, and amusement. *Journal of Abnormal and Social Psychology*, 1962, *65*, 121–128.

Scheier, M. F., & Carver, C. S. Private and public self-attention, resistance to change, and dissonance reduction. *Journal of Personality and Social Psychology*, 1980, *39*, 390–405.

Schlenker, B. R. Translating actions into attitudes: An identity-analytic approach to the explanation of social conduct. In L. Berkowitz (Ed.), *Advances in Experimental Social Psychology* (Vol. 15). NY: Academic Press, 1982.

Sherman, S. J. Effects of choice and incentive on attitude change in a discrepant behavior situation. *Journal of Personality and Social Psychology*, 1970, *15*, 245–252. (a)

Sherman, S. J. Attitudinal effects of unforeseen consequences. *Journal of Personality and Social Psychology*, 1970, *16*, 510–520. (b)

Sherman, S. J., & Gorkin, L. Attitude bolstering when behavior is inconsistent with central attitudes. *Journal of Experimental Social Psychology*, 1980, *16*, 388–403.

Snyder, M., & Ebbesen, E. Dissonance awareness: A test of dissonance theory versus self-perception theory. *Journal of Experimental Social Psychology*, 1972, *8*, 502–517.

Sogin, S. R., & Pallak, M. S. Bad decisions, responsibility, and attitude change: Effects of volition, foreseeability, and locus of causality of negative consequences. *Journal of Personality and Social Psychology*, 1976, *33*, 300–306.

Spence, K. W., Farber, I. E., & McFann, H. H. The relation of anxiety (drive) level to performance in competitive paired-associates learning. *Journal of Experimental Psychology*, 1956, *52*, 296–305.

Staw, B. M. Attitudinal and behavioral consequences of changing a major organizational reward: A natural field experiment. *Journal of Personality and Social Psychology*, 1974, *29*, 742–751.

Steele, C. M., & Liu, T. J. Making the dissonance act unreflective of self: Dissonance avoidance and the expectancy of a value-affirming response. *Personality and Social Psychology Bulletin*, 1981, *7*, 393–397.

Steele, C. M., & Liu, T. J. Dissonance processes as self-affirmation. *Journal of Personality and Social Psychology*, 1983, *45*, 5–19.

Stults, D. M., Messe, L. A., & Kerr, N. L. Belief discrepant behavior and the bogus pipeline: Impression management or arousal attribution? *Journal of Experimental Social Psychology*, 1984, *20*, 47–54.

Swann, W. B., Stephenson, B., & Pittman, T. S. Curiosity and control: On the determinants of the search for social knowledge. *Journal of Personality and Social Psychology*, 1981, *40*, 635–642.

Tedeschi, J. T., & Rosenfeld, P. Impression management theory and the forced compliance situation. In J. T. Tedeschi (Ed.), *Impression management theory and social psychological research*. NY: Academic Press, 1981.

Tedeschi, J. T., Schlenker, B. R., & Bonoma, T. V. Cognitive dissonance: Private ratiocination or public spectacle? *American Psychologist*, 1971, *26*, 685–695.

Waterman, C. K. The facilitating and interfering effects of cognitive dissonance on simple and complex paired associates learning tasks. *Journal of Experimental Social Psychology*, 1969, *5*, 31–42.

Waterman, C. K., & Katkin, E. S. The energizing (dynamogenic) effect of cognitive dissonance on task performance. *Journal of Personality and Social Psychology*, 1967, *6*, 126–131.

Wicklund, R. A., & Brehm, J. W. *Perspectives on cognitive dissonance*. Hillsdale, NJ: Erlbaum, 1976.

Wicklund, R. A., Cooper, J., & Linder, D. E. Effects of expected effort on attitude change prior to exposure. *Journal of Experimental Social Psychology*, 1967, *3*, 416–428.

Wong, P. T. P., & Weiner, B. When people ask "why" questions, and the heuristics of attributional search. *Journal of Personality and Social Psychology*, 1981, *40*, 650–663.

Worchel, P., & McCormick, B. L. Self-concept and dissonance reduction. *Journal of Personality*, 1963, *31*, 588–599.

Worchel, S., & Arnold, S. E. The effect of combined arousal states on attitude change. *Journal of Experimental Social Psychology*, 1974, *10*, 549–560.

Zanna, M. P., & Cooper, J. Dissonance and the pill: An attribution approach to studying the arousal properties of dissonance. *Journal of Personality and Social Psychology*, 1974, *29*, 703–709.

Zanna, M. P., & Cooper, J. Dissonance and the attribution process. In J. H. Harvey, W. J. Ickes, & R. F. Kidd (Eds.), *New directions in attribution research*. Hillsdale, NJ: Erlbaum, 1976.

Zanna, M. P., Higgins, E. T., & Taves, P. A. Is dissonance phenomenologically aversive? *Journal of Experimental Social Psychology*, 1976, *12*, 530–538.

COGNITIVE THEORIES OF PERSUASION

Alice H. Eagly

DEPARTMENT OF PSYCHOLOGICAL SCIENCES
PURDUE UNIVERSITY
WEST LAFAYETTE, INDIANA

Shelly Chaiken

DEPARTMENT OF PSYCHOLOGY
VANDERBILT UNIVERSITY
NASHVILLE, TENNESSEE

ADVANCES IN EXPERIMENTAL
SOCIAL PSYCHOLOGY, VOL. 17

I. Introduction

A. SCOPE OF THE CHAPTER

Theories of persuasion are designed to account for the attitude and belief change that occurs in people who are exposed to relatively complex messages that consist of a position advocated by a communicator and (usually) one or more arguments designed to support that position. Traditionally, psychologists have accounted for such changes in attitudes and beliefs by presuming that communications affect one or more psychological processes that are causally prior to the changes. During the past 15 years, theorizing about these mediating psychological processes has increasingly focused on some aspect of information processing, although the particular aspect of information processing considered important varies widely among theories.

The dominance of cognitive theories in the persuasion area mirrors the increased emphasis on cognition that has characterized American psychology in general during this period. Although attitude researchers have no doubt followed this intellectual trend in their enthusiastic acceptance of cognitive frameworks, the extent of the turn toward cognition may be surprising because several other perspectives (e.g., learning theory) were once moderately popular in this area. Indeed, it is doubtful that there is any other area of social psychology, aside from person perception (see Schneider, Hastorf, & Ellsworth, 1979) and social cognition (see Fiske & Taylor, 1984), in which cognitive theories have become as dominant. Because of this focus on information processing, this chapter scrutinizes in detail those theories that have elaborated the cognitive mediation of persuasion.

In considering cognitive theories of persuasion, it is important to keep in mind that their emphasis on cognitive mediation reflects a relatively long-standing tradition in this area (e.g., Hovland & Rosenberg, 1960; Osgood & Tannenbaum, 1955). Having developed over a long period of time, many cognitive theories of persuasion have been tested in numerous empirical studies and refined in various ways. Although new variants of information-processing theories continue to appear (and we give such approaches some consideration), the general worth and limitations of the cognitive perspective should be apparent by now. Such an evaluative stance would probably be premature in relation to cognitive theorizing in other areas of social psychology that have only more recently been approached systematically from a cognitive perspective. For example, cognitive theories are a more recent innovation in areas such as interpersonal attraction and close relationships (e.g., Orvis, Kelley, & Butler, 1976) and small-group processes (e.g., Brändstatter, Davis, & Stocker-Kreichgauer, 1980).

In order to reveal some of the limitations of the almost exclusively cognitive emphasis of most contemporary theories of persuasion, we also consider several viewpoints that emphasize motivation at least as much as cognition. For example, some discussion is devoted to reactance theory (Brehm, 1966), which assumes that recipients of persuasive messages attempt to maintain and restore threatened freedoms, as well as to public and private self-identity formulations (e.g., Carver & Scheier, 1981) that assume that people tend to express attitudes and beliefs that are consistent with their public and private self-identities. Such approaches, with their clear-cut motivational assumptions, were once very popular in the attitudes area and may again regain popularity if, as we suspect, a nearly exclusive emphasis on cognition prevents consideration of a full range of persuasion phenomena.

The fact that a relatively large number of theories are discussed in this chapter should not surprise readers familiar with the attitude-change literature.[1] The tradition in this area has long been one of many theories, no one of which has gained dominance. This multiplicity of viewpoints is not an embarrassment; rather, it is a sign of vigorous intellectual health. We agree wholeheartedly with McGuire's (1969) recommendation, "Let a hundred flowers blossom together, let a hundred schools of thought contend" (p. 265). Moreover, we believe that multiple theoretical perspectives are needed to reflect adequately the complexity of the processes that attitude-change investigators seek to understand.

Lasswell's (1948, p. 37) frequently cited question, "Who says what in which channel to whom with what effect?" nicely captures the intricacies of the persuasion process. The categories of persuasion variables (e.g., who, what, in which channel) highlighted by Lasswell have served a heuristic function for persuasion researchers, and research on these variables has cumulated at a moderately steady pace. The first four of these categories—source, message, channel, and recipient—identify the primary types of independent variables that have been empirically investigated. As already noted, psychologists have proposed that the persuasive effects of such distal independent variables are mediated by underlying psychological processes proximal to the persuasion dependent variable. Because numerous psychological processes may be affected by these distal variables, it is advantageous that the study of persuasion has been approached

---

[1]The theories discussed in this chapter are selected from a much wider set of models of social inference (see Hastie, 1983) because the implications of these theories have been developed in a persuasion context. Other social inference formulations such as Bayesian models (e.g., Edwards, Lindman, & Savage, 1963) may hold some promise for persuasion, yet their potential applications have not been pursued in detail. For general reviews of the classic theories of attitude change that precede the cognitive theories that are emphasized in this chapter, see Himmelfarb and Eagly (1974), Insko (1967), Kiesler, Collins, and Miller (1969), and McGuire (1969). It should also be noted that the goal of understanding persuasion is shared by social psychologists with other social scientists, especially those in the fields of communication (e.g., Reardon, 1981; Roloff & Miller, 1980) and sociology (e.g., Holz & Wright, 1979). Although their work is important to achieving a complete understanding of persuasion, it is given scant attention in this chapter.

from several directions. Differing theories have illuminated differing distal variables as well as differing intervening processes.

As a consequence of their varied foci, the theoretical perspectives considered in this chapter are rarely in strict contention with one another. In fact, two or more persuasion theories have only infrequently been brought to bear on exactly the same empirical problem, in the manner that dissonance theory (Festinger, 1957) and self-perception theory (Bem, 1972) have provided competing explanations for the attitudinal effects of counterattitudinal behavior. Of course, persuasion theories can occasionally be made to generate conflicting predictions for the effects of particular variables. However, these theories are more frequently complementary because they often pertain to different variables, and when relevant to the same variables, they make similar predictions. Despite this relative lack of conflict between theories, it has proven difficult to integrate them within a single overarching framework. Although we do not propose such a framework in this chapter, we hope that by sharply delineating the role of each theory and explicating its relation to others, we can contribute to a more generalized understanding of a wide range of persuasion phenomena.

Our presentations of persuasion theories give primary emphasis to their strengths. Those theories that have survived long enough to inspire empirical tests have at least heuristic value in relation to certain persuasion variables. It is this core of explanatory power within each theory that deservedly merits attention. Although proponents of certain theories have often taxed the resources of their frameworks to show that various empirical phenomena can be reinterpreted in their terms, such exercises in breadth often result in retrospective accounts that are not particularly compelling. Necessarily, then, we also draw attention to the areas in which theories lack predictive power or have only the weak powers that derive from post hoc accounts of known phenomena. Another standard imposed in our evaluation of cognitive theories is their ability to account for the effects of distal persuasion variables (source, message, etc.) that are potentially controllable by practitioners of persuasion. Agreeing with those who have seconded Lewin's (1951, p. 169) statement that "there is nothing so practical as a good theory," we believe that persuasion theories should possess obvious applied value for persons who design information campaigns.

Our review of cognitive theories of persuasion considers the effects of persuasive communications on attitude change but does not evaluate the many other ways in which attitudes and beliefs may be changed. Most notably we will not discuss the large body of theory and research on how one's own behavior changes one's attitudes and beliefs (e.g., Schlenker, 1982; Wicklund & Brehm, 1976). Also absent is any explicit discussion of conformity—the change of attitudes and beliefs through exposure to unelaborated statements of other persons' positions, usually in a group setting (e.g., Allen, 1965; Asch, 1956). Although some of the theories that we discuss have explanatory power in relation to such phenomena, in order to limit the scope of this chapter, we have chosen to forego exploration of the implications that persuasion theories have for other kinds of social influence.

In this chapter we first review the information-processing paradigm proposed by McGuire (e.g., 1968a). This approach, which is very closely linked to the seminal work of Hovland, Janis, and Kelley (1953), provides a very broad framework for thinking about cognitive processes that may be relevant to persuasion. There follows a consideration of three contemporary persuasion theories, each of which treats persuasion as a product of a distinctive cognitive process: (1) cognitive responding or thinking about message- or issue-relevant information, (2) causal reasoning, and (3) heuristic processing. Next, three quantitatively formulated combinatorial models are considered: (1) probabilogical model, (2) expectancy–value models, and (3) information-integration theory. These approaches predict the attitudes or beliefs that result from message recipients combining items of information with one another and with their prior cognitions. Finally, we contrast these two sets of cognitive theories with several viewpoints that take into account message recipients' motives in persuasion settings.

B. MCGUIRE'S INFORMATION-PROCESSING PARADIGM

The first explicit information-processing interpretation of persuasion was proposed by McGuire (1968a, 1968b, 1969, 1972). McGuire's analysis followed directly from Hovland, Janis, and Kelley's (1953) suggestion that the impact of persuasive communications could be understood in terms of three phases: (1) attention to the message, (2) comprehension of its content, and (3) acceptance of its conclusions. According to this approach, independent variables that influence attitude change (e.g., communicator credibility or the order of presentation of messages) act not only directly on recipients' tendencies to accept the position recommended in the message but also indirectly through their impact on processes such as attention and comprehension that are causally prior to attitude change. To examine these prior processes empirically, Hovland and his colleagues often assessed recipients' memory for the content of the message as well as their acceptance of its conclusions (e.g., Hovland & Weiss, 1951; Janis & Feshbach, 1953).

The role that these prior processes play in persuasion was developed more systematically in the late 1960s by McGuire (1968a), who proposed that the persuasive impact of messages is a product of their initial presentation by communicators and of five subsequent information-processing steps: (1) attention, (2) comprehension, (3) yielding, (4) retention, and (5) action.[2] According to this

---

[2]In McGuire's numerous discussions of the information-processing paradigm, varying numbers of steps have been explored, with his latest presentation (McGuire, in press) suggesting 12 processing steps: (1) tuning in that produces exposure to the communication, (2) attending to it, (3) liking and taking an interest in it, (4) comprehending its content, (5) generating related cognitions, (6) acquiring

approach, once a message is presented, the recipient must pay attention to it in order for it to produce attitude change. Provided that the message attracts the recipient's attention, the position recommended by the communicator must be comprehended (and often the arguments supporting the position must be understood to some extent as well). It is also necessary that the recipient yield to the message content that he or she comprehends if any attitude change is to be detectable. If this change is to persist over a period of time, the message recipient must retain this changed attitude. Furthermore, in order for the attitude-relevant behaviors to be changed by the message, the recipient must behave on the basis of the changed attitude.

McGuire argued that the failure of any of the steps to occur causes the sequence of processes to be broken, with the consequence that subsequent steps do not occur. McGuire (1972) further elaborated these ideas by formulating this causal chain as a stochastic model—a chain of responses with uncertainty at every link. These uncertain steps are then related according to the mathematics of probability. Because of the assumption that subsequent steps depend on current ones, the probability of any step is proportional to the joint probability that all previous steps occur. Given that the probability of each step is unlikely to approach unity, the model suggests that it often may be difficult to induce attitude change or behavior change through information campaigns. For example, even if attention, comprehension, yielding, and retention all had probabilities of .8, the upper limit of the probability that a relevant behavior would be changed is $.8^4$ or .41 (provided that the probabilities of the separate steps are independent).

Although all of the information-processing stages are important in effecting persisting attitude change that influences behavior, only three steps—attention, comprehension, and yielding—are relevant to the typical persuasion experiment, which assesses attitudes and beliefs immediately after presentation of the message. Further, in experiments designed to test this paradigm, the first two steps—attention and comprehension—have been combined into a single step of *reception* of message content because of the difficulty of obtaining separate measures of attention and comprehension in a persuasion experiment. This focus on reception constitutes the distinctive contribution of the McGuire (1972) paradigm as a theory of persuasion. The key assumption of this model is that distal independent variables can influence attitude change through their effect on the reception of message content as well as on yielding or message acceptance.

The importance of the proposition that message reception can play a mediating role in persuasion can be appreciated in view of the neglect of reception by

---

relevant skills, (7) agreeing with the communication position, (8) storing the change in memory, (9) retrieving the relevant material from memory, (10) decision making on basis of the retrieved material, (11) acting in accord with the decision that is made, and (12) postaction consolidating of the new pattern.

· other investigators. Aside from the research of Hovland and his associates (Hovland et al., 1953), most persuasion researchers both prior and subsequent to McGuire's work on the information-processing paradigm have not given serious consideration to reception as a possible mediator of persuasion. Most investigators either have not included measures of message reception (e.g., Brock & Becker, 1965; Petty, Cacioppo, & Goldman, 1981) or have assessed reception in order to insure that they held it constant when manipulating independent variables (e.g., Norman, 1976; Osterhouse & Brock, 1970).

1. Empirical Evidence that Reception Mediates Persuasion

When the proposition that reception mediates persuasion is examined empirically, investigators typically have proceeded by manipulating independent variables that might influence persuasion through their impact on reception (see reviews by McGuire, 1966, 1969) and have included recognition or recall measures of retention of message content to assess reception. In such studies, researchers have then examined whether independent variables exerted parallel effects on attitude change and retention (e.g., whether high credibility increased retention as well as persuasion). Investigators have also determined whether measures of attitude change and retention were positively correlated. In general, the majority of the studies that have employed one or both of these methods of examining reception have not produced statistically significant evidence for a positive relation between retention of message content and attitude change (e.g., Cacioppo & Petty, 1979b; Harkins & Petty, 1981; Hovland & Weiss, 1951; Millman, 1968; Osterhouse & Brock, 1970; Petty & Cacioppo, 1979b; Petty, Cacioppo, & Heesacker, 1981; Thistlethwaite, deHaan, & Kamenetzky, 1955; Zimbardo & Ebbesen, 1970). Nevertheless, numerous findings that are favorable to the reception-as-mediator hypothesis have been obtained (e.g., Chaiken & Eagly, 1976; Eagly, 1974; Eagly & Warren, 1976; Haaland & Venkatesan, 1968; Janis & Rife, 1959; McGuire, 1957; Miller & Campbell, 1959; Romer, 1979a).

The absence of consistent covariation between retention of message content and persuasion has been interpreted by many investigators as proving that reception is unimportant in accounting for attitude change (e.g., Fishbein & Ajzen, 1972; Greenwald, 1968). Yet there are several reasons why this conclusion is probably wrong. Most importantly, reception was never believed to be a general, all-purpose mediator of persuasion. McGuire (e.g., 1972) argued that reception plays a mediating role under some circumstances (e.g., for messages that are difficult to understand) but not other circumstances (e.g., for messages that are easily understood).[3]

[3]Further complexities arise when the effects of an independent variable on persuasion are mediated by both reception and yielding. If an independent variable (e.g., self-esteem) has opposite

The interpretation of empirical tests of the relation between reception and persuasion is also clouded by the use of recognition and recall of message content as measures of reception. Such measures are inherently poor indexes of reception, which refers to the encoding of the message content *prior* to its integration with the message recipient's initial opinion. In addition to encoding, measures of retention encompass the storage of message content in memory and its subsequent retrieval. Because the details of message content may be forgotten after they are encoded and perhaps stored in a verbal memory system different from the system in which attitudes and overall impressions are stored (e.g., Anderson & Hubert, 1963; Watts & McGuire, 1964), the contribution of verbal memory to variability in retention severely contaminates retention as a measure of reception. Unfortunately, most investigators have obscured the important distinction between the reception of message content and its retention in memory by treating the relation between message *learning* and attitude change as the critical issue (e.g., Fishbein & Ajzen, 1972, 1975, 1981; Greenwald, 1968; Petty & Cacioppo, 1981). Learning of content generally refers to the encoding of message content, the storage of this content in memory, and its retrieval. Within the information-processing paradigm, it is the reception or encoding of content, not its storage and retrieval, that is at issue.

In addition to these validity limitations, retention measures may lack adequate reliability. Typical measures consist of a small number of multiple-choice questions (e.g., Hendrick & Shaffer, 1970). Such measures are likely to have low reliability and sometimes may even be misinterpreted by subjects as measures of their own beliefs, as Fishbein and Ajzen (1972) claimed. As an alternative to recognition measures, subjects are often asked to list the arguments given in the message (e.g., Petty, Cacioppo, & Heesacker, 1981). However, given the relatively few arguments in most messages used in persuasion research, such recall measures would also tend to lack adequate reliability.

It should also be noted that in most experiments the effect of message reception on persuasion may have been severely attenuated (compared to its usual impact in natural settings) because of typical aspects of laboratory research methodology that tend to insure a high and relatively invariant level of reception: (1) Persuasive messages are usually too simple to be easily misunderstood, (2) Subjects are usually college students and therefore are relatively verbally skilled, (3) Laboratory settings and instructions constrain subjects to pay close attention to messages. Therefore, the within-cell correlations that are often used to examine the reception–persuasion relation may often be attenuated by the restricted range of the recall variable (see Insko, Lind, & LaTour, 1976). In contrast,

---

impact on the two processes (e.g., increases reception and decreases yielding), persuasion would not be expected to correlate positively with reception because it is presumed to be predicted by the product of the probability of reception and the probability of yielding.

comprehension of information presented in nonlaboratory settings appears to be quite variable and generally not very accurate. For example, on the basis of the responses of a large sample of adult respondents who viewed 30-second television segments in a shopping mall testing situation and answered simple questions about them, it was found that 30 to 40% of the information (Jacoby & Hoyer, 1982; Jacoby, Hoyer, & Sheluga, 1980) or even more (Schmittlein & Morrison, 1983) was miscomprehended and there was considerable variability in comprehension across subjects. Similar rates of miscomprehension were reported by Lipstein (1980) for the CBS show "Sixty Minutes," viewed in a home situation.

Because of the ambiguity of most tests of the reception–persuasion relationship, Eagly (1974) manipulated message comprehensibility in order to influence reception directly. In three experiments, lowering comprehensibility lessened acceptance of the position recommended by the communicator. This effect of comprehensibility appeared robust because it was obtained for two different comprehensibility manipulations and did not interact with the extremity of the message, the expertise of the communicator, or instructions to counterargue the message. Because lowering comprehensibility decreases persuasion by lessening the amount of information received, it is also relevant to note research that has varied the number of persuasive arguments presented in messages (Calder, Insko, & Yandell, 1974; Insko, Lind, & LaTour, 1976). This research has documented a reliable tendency for persuasion to decrease when fewer arguments are presented, although the slope for the regression of argument recall on persuasion was relatively flat. This research, along with Eagly's (1974) comprehensibility studies, suggests that substantial differences in the amount of argumentation received by subjects do have detectable effects on persuasion.[4]

Although Eagly's (1974) research established that impaired reception of argumentation *can* lessen persuasion, it did not answer the question of whether naturally occurring variations of distal persuasion factors interfere with reception sufficiently that the persuasiveness of communications is lessened. The comprehensibility manipulations used by Eagly (1974) had a very strong impact on subjects' understanding of the messages, and these effects were no doubt stronger than those that might commonly occur due to the influence of source, message, channel, and recipient variables. Nevertheless, there are certain classes of such distal persuasion variables that may often exert a sufficiently strong impact on reception to have a significant effect on attitude change. For example, there is good evidence that strong distractions interfere with message reception (e.g., Haaland & Venkatesan, 1968; Romer, 1979a; Zimbardo, Snyder, Thomas,

[4]Although lowered reception of message content in the McGuire paradigm was assumed to decrease persuasion by lessening the number of message-supportive cognitions held by message recipients, the Eagly (1974) studies suggested that the mechanism by which reception affected persuasion is not exclusively informational: Recipients' negative affective reaction to attempting to comprehend information that was difficult to understand appeared to be important as well.

Gold, & Gurwitz, 1970), and this lessened reception appears to be one of the processes by which distraction affects persuasion. Also, Chaiken and Eagly (1976) found that communication modality had a sufficiently strong impact on the reception of messages that were inherently difficult to comprehend. In this experiment, subjects were exposed to either an easy- or difficult-to-understand message presented via the written, audiotaped, or videotaped modality. With difficult messages, both persuasion and comprehension of persuasive material were greater when the message was written as compared to when it was videotaped or audiotaped. Moreover, regression analyses suggested that the lesser amount of information received by the subjects (and their negative affective reaction) contributed to the lowered persuasion obtained with difficult-to-understand videotaped and audiotaped messages. With easily comprehended messages, persuasion was greatest when the message was videotaped, moderate when audiotaped, and least when written; but comprehension was equivalent regardless of modality. Thus, with less demanding messages, differences in reception did not account for message persuasiveness.

When searching for independent variables whose persuasive impact may be mediated by message reception, it is especially important to examine the message recipients' attributes because McGuire (1968a, 1968b) spelled out the implications of his information-processing model most completely in relation to the personality–persuasibility problem. McGuire argued that individual-difference variables, such as self-esteem or intelligence, usually relate positively to reception (i.e., persons higher in self-esteem or intelligence are better able to receive information) and negatively to yielding (i.e., persons lower in self-esteem or intelligence are more likely to yield to the communicator's view). According to McGuire's theory, these opposing effects of personality variables on reception and yielding often result in an overall nonmonotonic relationship between such variables and attitude change; thus, individuals with midscale positions on personality dimensions are more easily influenced than those positioned higher or lower. The information-processing model gained additional power to account for persuasion by including a postulate that the relative importance of reception and yielding changes with the nature of the situation. For example, reception is assumed to be more important than yielding for complex, well-argued messages, whereas yielding is assumed to be more important than reception for simple, poorly argued messages. Hence, the shape of the relation between an independent variable (such as a personality trait) and persuasion depends on whether reception or yielding (or both processes) function as mediators.

McGuire's predictions regarding the persuasive effects of personality variables have fared only moderately well in empirical tests (Eagly & Warren, 1976; Johnson & Izzett, 1969; Johnson & Stanicek, 1969; Johnson, Torcivia, & Poprick, 1968; Lehmann, 1970; Millman, 1968; Nisbett & Gordon, 1967; Zellner, 1970). These studies concerned anxiety, authoritarianism, intelligence, and self-esteem, and although positive findings were obtained for some predictions, most of these were relatively weak in magnitude. Also, the experiments obtained little direct evidence regarding the mediational role of reception. Of the four studies that assessed comprehension (Eagly & Warren, 1976; Johnson et al., 1968; Millman, 1968; Zellner, 1970), only the Johnson et al. and the Eagly and Warren studies found a significant positive relation between respondents' measured level on a personality trait and retention of message content. Further, only the Eagly and Warren study is free from the criticism that this relation may have been an artifact of premessage knowledge differences among people at different levels of a personality trait. It is noteworthy that only the Eagly and Warren (1976) experiment concerned the effects of verbal intelligence, the dimension of individual differences that should have the most dramatic effect on comprehension of verbal materials. Because other personality traits should have a weaker impact on comprehension, it is perhaps not surprising that most of this literature has failed to generate definitive evidence that individual differences in message reception can account for personality–persuasibility relationships.

In summary, in terms of its ability to account for the effects of distal variables on persuasion, the reception-as-mediator model has proven to be predictive within the laboratory context (where it has been tested) only with respect to certain independent variables. These variables all have a notably strong impact on message reception: for example, very strong distractions, recipients' verbal intelligence, and communication modality when a very difficult message is presented. Although there is little evidence that reception functions as a mediator of persuasion for a broad range of the independent variables that have been manipulated in laboratory experiments, reception may be a considerably more important mediator in many natural settings.

2. New Directions in Investigating Reception

Another important limitation of existing research on reception is that researchers have not seriously examined the mediational role of attention. Although lumping attention with comprehension and labeling the composite reception may have been a reasonable first step in examining the mediational role of these processes, numerous issues concerning the role of attention have been ignored (see McGuire, 1976). Because attention is the assignment of processing capacity to stimuli (Kahneman, 1973) and comprehension is the encoding or interpretation of stimuli to which processing capacity has been assigned, these two processes are likely to have somewhat different effects in relation to persuasion.

A testimony to the importance of attention is the fact that advertisers and media workers devote considerable time and effort to designing attention-getting appeals. Psychologists investigating consumer behavior from an information-processing standpoint (e.g., Bettman, 1979) claim that the attentional step in message processing controls a substantial portion of the variability in consumer decisions. It is unlikely that this emphasis is misplaced. Attention has been explored extensively by cognitive psychologists (see Eysenck, 1982; Kahneman, 1973) and merits careful consideration in relation to persuasion. The laboratory persuasion experiment, with its implicit and explicit pressures on subjects to be extremely attentive to communications, is a limited setting for examining attention. Nevertheless, it is possible that greater variability in attention could be obtained in laboratory contexts by presenting messages as incidental stimuli— for example, in a "waiting room" situation such as Ickes used in his studies of social interaction (e.g., Ickes & Barnes, 1978). In addition, there is an obvious need for creative use of field settings, in which there is very often considerable variability in attention to messages. Some of the methods that consumer psychologists have developed to measure recall and persuasion in natural settings (e.g., Ross, 1982) may be useful.

Theorizing and research on the "vividness" of information signals increased interest in how attentional processes affect persuasion. Vivid information is information that presumably attracts and holds people's attention because it is, for example, concrete, imagery-provoking, or proximal in a sensory, temporal, or spatial way (Nisbett & Ross, 1980). Although vividly presented information has been hypothesized to exert a greater impact on judgments than nonvividly presented information (Nisbett & Ross, 1980), in a recent review paper Taylor and Thompson (1982) concluded that, despite the intuitive appeal of this hypothesis, empirical evidence is equivocal. Yet, any conclusions about the effect of vividly presented information on persuasion should be viewed with skepticism until experimental vividness manipulations are carefully examined to determine *what information* they make vivid. It is not necessarily persuasive message content that is made more vivid by typical vividness manipulations (e.g., videotaped versus audiotaped versus written communications; pictorially versus not pictorially illustrated information; concrete versus abstract information; case history versus base rate or other statistical information). Certain manipulations (e.g., concrete versus abstract information) may make message content vivid, whereas other manipulations (e.g., videotaped versus audiotaped versus written information) may, for example, make communicator-related information vivid. As Chaiken and Eagly (1983) showed, increasing the vividness of communicator-related information increases the impact of communicator variables on persuasion and, as a consequence, increases message persuasiveness if the communicator has positive characteristics and decreases persuasiveness if the communicator has negative characteristics. Further work on vividness and salience effects, including research bearing on their cognitive mediation (e.g., Fiske & Taylor, 1984; McArthur, 1980; Taylor & Thompson, 1982), may help specify the conditions under which vivid information is especially persuasive.

To profit from the increased understanding of attentional processes being gained by social psychologists, a more refined theory is needed concerning how aspects of attention and comprehension may relate to persuasion. In developing such a theory, invesitgators would be well advised to consider more carefully how the reception of various components of the message might affect persuasion. For example, as noted in relation to vividness effects, reception of communicator-related information may have different effects than reception of message content. Further, reception of the details of argumentation might relate differently to persuasion than does reception of the message topic or of the communicator's position on this topic (Watts & McGuire, 1964).[5]

The hypothesis that good reception of argumentation enhances persuasion (e.g., Eagly, 1974) rests not only on the obvious assumption that the message contains high-quality argumentation but also on the assumption that recipients base their decision to accept the advocated position on their understanding of persuasive argumentation rather than on other cues. According to the heuristic model of persuasion (Chaiken, 1980, 1982), which we will discuss later in this chapter, there are many conditions under which recipients rely, not on the semantic meaning of arguments, but on cues such as the source's identity, the number of arguments, or other superficial cues in deciding whether to accept a message's conclusions. Under such conditions, reception of argumentation may be unrelated to persuasion, whereas under conditions in which recipients do rely on arguments, good reception should relate to persuasion (Chaiken, 1980).

3. Persuasion Theories as Theories of Yielding

Most theories of persuasion specify various mechanisms involved in accepting or yielding to the communicator's position. Although McGuire (e.g., 1969, 1972) defined yielding as the extent to which recipients accept *what they comprehend of the message,* most researchers have not adopted this definition because, as noted earlier, they have assumed that reception was constant across

---

[5]Concerning reception of the communicator's position, it should be noted that the relation between perception of this position and persuasion was an issue of some importance in the Sherifs' social judgment theory (Sherif, Sherif, & Nebergall, 1965; Sherif & Hovland, 1961). According to this theory, messages that are relatively consistent with one's own attitude are assimilated or seen as closer to one's own position than others would see them, and messages that are relatively inconsistent with one's own position are contrasted or seen as farther from one's own position than others would see them. Although these subjective displacements of message content are likely to lessen pressure to change one's attitude toward the message, a detailed understanding of the relation between the encoding of the position advocated in a message and attitude change was not developed in social judgment theory. Further, although this issue has received some attention from researchers (e.g., Atkins, Deaux, & Bieri, 1967; Eagly & Telaak, 1972; Kelman & Eagly, 1965; Sherif & Hovland, 1961), the theoretical principles underlying existing empirical findings have yet to be satisfactorily resolved (see Keisler, Collins, & Miller, 1969; Ostrom & Upshaw, 1968).

experimental conditions. Instead, they have treated agreement with the communicator's advocated position (compared to a premessage or control-group baseline) as the major dependent variable and labeled it persuasion, opinion change, or attitude change. Theories of yielding (or agreement with the communication) describe how individuals discern the importance of incoming information for their attitudes and beliefs.

Although most contemporary theories of yielding treat persuasion as a constructive process that involves both the information stored in memory and the stimulus input itself, they differ considerably in their descriptions of the processes that account for yielding. A major difference between the various information-processing theories of yielding is that some provide verbal descriptions of particular mechanisms or processes involved in accepting the communicator's position, whereas others provide a mathematical description of how recipients combine or integrate the various cues that are available to them. For convenience, theories that primarily provide verbal descriptions of particular mechanisms involved in yielding will be referred to as *process theories*, whereas those that primarily provide quantitative descriptions of the integration or combination problem will be referred to as *combinatorial theories*. These process and combinatorial theories are illustrated and their merits explored in subsequent sections of the chapter.

II. Process Theories of Persuasion

A. COGNITIVE RESPONSE APPROACH

The cognitive response approach to understanding attitude change shares with the earlier information-processing models of Hovland, Janis, and Kelley (1953) and McGuire (e.g., 1972) the assumption that some kind of learning or concept formation plays a major role in determining opinion change and the temporal persistence of this change. Hovland *et al.* (1953) emphasized the mediational role of recipients' learning of the specific content of a communication, and McGuire (1972) emphasized the role of reception of message content. In contrast, the cognitive response approach asserts that the persuasive impact of a communication is primarily determined by the nature of the idiosyncratic thoughts or "cognitive responses" that recipients presumably *generate* (and, thus, rehearse and learn) as they anticipate, receive, or, subsequently, reflect upon a persuasive communication (Greenwald, 1968; Petty & Cacioppo, 1981; Petty, Ostrom, & Brock, 1981). Indeed, the impetus for Greenwald's (1968) general hypothesis that recipients' cognitive responses to persuasion, rather than their learning of persuasive communication content, are a fundamental determinant of opinion change, stemmed from his desire to "salvage an associative learning interpretation of persuasion" (Greenwald, 1981, p. 127) in light of previous findings (reviewed earlier in the section "Empirical Evidence that Reception Mediates Persuasion") suggesting little relation between persuasion and the retention of communication content.

The idea that a message recipient's associations or stream of thought plays at least some role in determining persuasion had some precedent in prior persuasion research. For example, findings obtained in the Yale research program regarding active versus passive participation in persuasion (e.g., Janis & King, 1954; Kelman, 1953; King & Janis, 1956) as well as data pertaining to the relative effectiveness of one- versus two-sided persuasive messages (e.g., Hovland, Lumsdaine, & Sheffield, 1949; Lumsdaine & Janis, 1953) were interpreted, at least in part, in terms of recipient-generated cognitions. The superiority of active improvisation (versus passive exposure) in influencing persuasion was explained in terms of the active participant's greater tendency to add to and to cognitively elaborate on communication content (see Hovland *et al.*, 1953, Ch. 7). In contrast to this focus on the enhancement of persuasion by recipient-generated supportive cognitions, results showing that two-sided messages (those in which opposing arguments are mentioned and refuted) induced greater persuasion than one-sided messages (those mentioning only supportive argumentation) were viewed as compatible with the notion that two-sided communications reduced recipients' motivations to counterargue (see Hovland *et al.*, 1953, Ch. 4). Subsequent work by McGuire (1964) on inoculating people against persuasion (stimulated by findings indicating that two-sided communications conferred resistance to subsequent counterpropaganda) also implicated covert counterarguing. In this research, McGuire argued that exposing subjects to weak arguments countering their opinions along with refutations of these arguments facilitated resistance to subsequent stronger counterattitudinal messages because such an inoculation procedure stimulated subjects to generate supporting cognitions and practice refuting opposing arguments.

Although the ideas that recipients of messages are active information processors and that their own cognitive reactions play a mediational role in persuasion were not new to researchers, Greenwald (1968) was the first to offer an explicit cognitive response account of persuasion. Moreover, although some previous attempts had been made to tap the thoughts of recipients as they listened to persuasive communications (e.g., Hovland, Lumsdaine, & Sheffield, 1949; Janis & Terwilliger, 1962), Greenwald (1968) and Brock (1967) introduced the "thought-listing" task as a means of monitoring and categorizing subjects' cognitive responses to a persuasive message. In this task, subjects (typically under some time constraint) are asked to list their thoughts or ideas relevant to the message topic. Subsequently, subjects' thoughts are coded by judges into various theoretically relevant categories. Cognitive response researchers typically classify subjects' thoughts into two major categories: those favorable (i.e., supportive thoughts) and those unfavorable (i.e., counterarguments) to the overall position advocated in the persuasive message.

According to the cognitive response approach (Greenwald, 1968; Petty, Ostrom, & Brock, 1981), recipients actively relate information in a persuasive message (or anticipated message, e.g., Petty & Cacioppo, 1977) to their existing feelings and beliefs regarding the message topic. Cognitive responses represent the content of this *internal* communication on the part of message recipients and reflect recipient-generated thoughts that are not merely repetitions of message content. The crux of the cognitive response approach is that these recipient-generated thoughts *mediate* the effect of the persuasive message on opinion change. To the extent that a communication elicits predominantly favorable thoughts, persuasion is enhanced. To the extent that the message evokes predominantly unfavorable thoughts, persuasion is inhibited. Moreover, because recipients process the information in the message more or less extensively, persuasion should be a function of the amount of message-relevant thinking that occurs as well as its favorability. For a message that elicits favorable thinking, increased message-relevant thinking increases persuasion. For a message that elicits unfavorable thinking, increased processing decreases persuasion. In essence, then, the cognitive response approach asserts that the cognitions generated in response to a persuasive message determine both the direction and magnitude of opinion change.

1. Empirical Evidence Supporting Cognitive Response Approach

The strategy underlying most research guided by the cognitive response approach has been (1) to identify persuasion variables that influence the favorability of subjects' cognitive responses and those that influence the amount of message-relevant thinking and (2) to explore the simultaneous effects of such variables on cognitive responding and persuasion. Petty, Cacioppo, and their colleagues (see Petty & Cacioppo, 1981) have conducted a series of experiments using this strategy and have mustered an impressive amount of support for the cognitive response framework.

Distraction was the first major persuasion variable to be systematically investigated from the cognitive response perspective. Earlier, Festinger and Maccoby (1964) found that distracting (versus not distracting) recipients from attending carefully to message content enhanced persuasion and, further, suggested that this effect occurred because distraction inhibited recipients' abilities to effectively counterargue message content. Subsequent research by Osterhouse and Brock (1970) replicated these persuasion findings and also provided more direct evidence (via inclusion of a thought-listing task) that the increased persuasive impact of distraction was due to its negative impact on counterargument production. Petty, Wells, and Brock (1976) addressed the issue more generally by arguing that increased distraction inhibits recipients' *dominant* cognitive responses to message content. Consequently, distraction would tend to enhance persuasion for messages that elicit primarily unfavorable thoughts from recipients but inhibit persuasion for messages that elicit primarily favorable thoughts. In support of this reasoning, Petty *et al.* (1976) found that for subjects receiving a message containing weak, specious arguments (i.e., a message that elicited predominantly unfavorable thoughts), increased distraction decreased production of unfavorable thoughts and increased agreement with the persuasive message. In contrast to this finding, for subjects receiving a message containing strong, compelling arguments (i.e., a message that elicited predominantly favorable thoughts), increased distraction decreased production of favorable thoughts and decreased persuasion.

Petty and Cacioppo (1979a, 1979b) have successfully applied this same cognitive response logic to the variable of personal involvement (defined in terms of the importance or personal relevance of the message topic). In contrast to the research stimulated by social judgment theory (Sherif & Hovland, 1961) that had suggested that heightened involvement typically increases resistance to persuasion (e.g., Miller, 1965), other research had shown that involvement sometimes facilitates persuasion, especially for proattitudinal (versus counterattitudinal) messages (e.g., Apsler & Sears, 1968; Eagly, 1967; Pallak, Mueller, Dollar, & Pallak, 1972). Petty and Cacioppo (1979a, 1979b) reasoned that heightened involvement increases a recipient's motivation to engage in message-relevant thinking (see Chaiken, 1978, 1980, for a similar argument) and, consequently, hypothesized that increased involvement should decrease persuasion for messages that elicit predominantly unfavorable thoughts from recipients but should increase persuasion for messages that elicit predominantly favorable thoughts. Consistent with this hypothesis, Petty and Cacioppo (1979b) found that increased involvement enhanced the production of unfavorable thoughts and inhibited persuasion when a message consisted of weak, specious arguments, but enhanced the production of favorable thoughts and thus facilitated persuasion when a message consisted of strong, compelling arguments.

Similar studies by Petty, Cacioppo, and their colleagues (see Petty & Cacioppo, 1981) have examined the interactive effects on cognitive responses and on persuasion of (1) argument strength, which controls the favorability of recipients' cognitive responses, and (2) other persuasion variables that were selected because they presumably affect motivation and/or ability to engage in message-relevant thinking. These studies have yielded findings similar to those described earlier with respect to distraction and involvement. For example, Harkins and Petty (1981) assumed that multiple sources presenting multiple arguments (versus one communicator who presents the same arguments) enhance recipients' motivation to scrutinize a message. Consistent with this assumption, when multiple sources presented multiple arguments, these authors found that subjects receiving a strong message generated more favorable thoughts and were more persuaded by the message and that subjects receiving a weak message generated more unfavorable thoughts and were less persuaded. Also, Petty, Harkins, and Williams (1980) assumed that the presence (versus absence) of other recipients who share the task of evaluating a message decreases any one recipient's motivation to evaluate a messsage. Consistent with this assumption, when other subjects did not share responsibility for message evaluation, these authors found that subjects receiving a strong message generated more favorable thoughts and were more persuaded by the message and that subjects receiving a weak message generated more unfavorable thoughts and were less persuaded by the message. Furthermore, Petty and Cacioppo (1979b) assumed that repeating a message several times (versus presenting it once) enhances recipients' abilities to think about a message's implications. Thus, consistent with this assumption, when a message was presented three times, rather than only once, these authors found that subjects receiving a message consisting of strong arguments produced more favorable thoughts and manifested greater persuasion, whereas subjects receiving a message containing weak arguments apparently generated more unfavorable thoughts and manifested less persuasion (Cacioppo & Petty, unpublished manuscript cited in Petty & Cacioppo, 1981).

2. Evaluation of Cognitive Response Approach

For persuasion variables that seem intuitively to be clearly related to recipients' abilities or motivation to engage in message-relevant thinking (e.g., distraction, involvement, message repetition), the cognitive response framework has provided some important insights concerning the cognitive mediation of the effect of these variables on persuasion. Indeed, the predicted interaction effects that have been observed when such variables are crossed with a variable (argument quality) that affects the valence of recipients' thoughts have a subtle and often nonobvious quality. For example, Petty, Cacioppo, and Heesacker (1981) analyzed the persuasive impact of arguments posed in *statement* form (e.g., Thus, instituting a comprehensive exam would be an aid to those who seek admission to graduate and professional schools) versus *rhetorical* form (e.g., Wouldn't instituting a comprehensive exam be an aid to those who seek admission to graduate and professional schools?). They assumed that with relatively uninvolving issues, the use of rhetoricals (versus statements) would enhance recipients' motivation to engage in message-relevant thinking, whereas with highly involving issues (which already motivate recipients to process and elaborate on message content), the use of rhetoricals (versus statements) would disrupt recipients' "natural" train of thought and therefore tend to reduce their ability to elaborate effectively on message content. On the basis of these assumptions, these researchers predicted and found that under conditions of low involvement with the message topic, the use of arguments in rhetorical (versus statement) form increased persuasion for messages consisting of strong arguments but decreased persuasion for messages consisting of weak arguments. Conversely, under conditions of high involvement, the use of rhetoricals decreased persuasion for strong messages but increased persuasion for weak messages.

Research that has tested the above class of interaction predictions has yielded findings congenial to the role of recipient-generated cognitive responses in persuasion and important information regarding the mechanisms responsible for the persuasive impact of a number of distal persuasion variables. However, the generality of these research findings has not been fully demonstrated. To date, research exploring the persuasive impact of variables postulated to influence *amount* of message-relevant thinking (e.g., distraction or message repetition) has typically crossed these factors with one variable that is assumed to control the favorability of the subjects' cognitive responses—argument strength. In general, this research has yielded the predicted Extent of Processing × Valence of Thought interactions. However, message discrepancy, which should also influence the valence of thoughts, has generally not produced reversed effects of the extent-of-processing variables when discrepancy has been manipulated by presenting proattitudinal versus counterattitudinal versions of messages (Cacioppo & Petty, 1979b; Petty *et al.*, 1976). Other variables that should influence the valence of the dominant thoughts (e.g., mood inductions or pleasant or unpleasant message context) have not been researched in conjunction with factors that influence extent of processing. Therefore, confidence in the generality of claims that distraction (or other variables affecting extent of processing) can increase or decrease persuasion (depending upon the valence of dominant cognitive responses elicited by a message) awaits research that employs a broader range of favorability-of-thought manipulations. It might also be noted that cognitive response research has relied heavily on just a few student-oriented persuasion topics (e.g., comprehensive exams or tuition). Whether strong versus weak renditions of messages on broader social issues (about which people may be more knowledgeable and thus less reliant on the implications they draw from experimenter-provided information) would interact in the same way with variables such as distraction and involvement remains to be seen.

Beyond the class of variables for which interaction predictions such as the above can be generated, the utility of the cognitive response framework is limited. The approach lacks clear implications regarding the persuasive impact of variables that are less obviously related to recipients' abilities or motivations to engage in message-relevant thinking. For example, source variables such as credibility might *increase* the extensiveness of message-relevant thinking (e.g., Hass, 1981)[6] or might *decrease* recipients' tendencies to process message content (e.g., Cook, 1969; Petty & Cacioppo, 1981; Sternthal, Dholakia, & Leavitt, 1978). Alternatively, a variable such as source credibility may not have its major impact on the extent of message-relevant thinking, but rather (like argument strength) on the *favorability* of recipients' cognitive responses (e.g., Cook, 1969; Gillig & Greenwald, 1974). Most existing research demonstrating that credibility manipulations affect both cognitive responding and persuasion cannot differentiate clearly among these possible effects on the extent and valence of message-relevant thinking. For example, studies showing that heightened credibility is associated with fewer unfavorable thoughts (e.g., Baron & Miller, 1969; Cook, 1969; Gillig & Greenwald, 1974; Sternthal, Dholakia & Leavitt, 1978) suggest that credibility decreases message-relevant thinking or increases favorability of thinking or both. Similarly, demonstrations that heightened credibility increases unfavorable thoughts (e.g., Hass, unpublished manuscript cited in Hass, 1981) indicate that credibility increases thinking or decreases favorability of thinking or both.

Because a variable such as credibility might have a range of possible effects on cognitive responding, the most reasonable strategy is to search for conditions under which the variable is most likely to enhance or inhibit message-relevant thinking. Then under these conditions, one could test for the interaction effects on opinion change and cognitive responses of the sort predicted for variables, such as distraction, that are more directly related to extent of processing. For example, variables that might affect whether high (versus low) credibility communicators increase or decrease recipients' tendencies to scrutinize message content include involvement (Heesacker, Petty, & Cacioppo, 1983; Petty & Cacioppo, 1981), commitment to one's own attitudinal position (Hass, 1981), and message discrepancy (Sternthal, Dholakia, & Leavitt, 1978). Yet the rationale for why such variables should control the impact of credibility on the extensiveness of information processing is not inherent in the cognitive response framework. Nor, for that matter, do cognitive response researchers' assumptions regarding *why* variables such as involvement, multiple sources and recipients, message repetition, and rhetorical questions influence the extent of processing

---

[6]Heesacker, Petty, and Cacioppo (1983) have argued that with highly involving issues, credibility increases message-relevant thinking. In partial support of this hypothesis, these researchers found (for field-dependent subjects only) that heightened credibility decreased the persuasiveness of messages containing weak arguments (which presumably elicited primarily unfavorable thoughts) but negligibly increased the persuasiveness of messages containing strong arguments (which presumably elicited primarily favorable thoughts). However, because this interaction between credibility and argument strength was *not* obtained on measures of subjects' favorable and unfavorable thoughts, this study does not provide unambiguous evidence regarding whether credibility (even with highly involving issues) affects extensiveness of message-relevant thinking.

stem directly from the cognitive response approach. Rather, such assumptions require the importation of extratheoretical postulates and concepts. For example, Hass's (1981) hypothesis that under high commitment, high (versus low) credibility sources stimulate greater counterarguing is based on the assumption (derived from Jones and Gerard's [1967] concept of "basic antinomy," but which could also be derived from Brehm's [1966] reactance theory) that in such situations, recipients are primarily motivated to defend their own attitudinal positions. Similarly, the hypothesis that distraction inhibits message-relevant thinking presumably rests on the implicit assumption that manipulations making a task more difficult disrupt information processing (see Shiffrin & Schneider, 1977; Schneider & Shiffrin, 1977).

In summary, although research guided by the cognitive response framework has contributed and should continue to contribute to our knowledge of the cognitive mediation of opinion change, the framework itself lacks predictive power with respect to most distal persuasion variables and, thus, does not constitute a general theory of persuasion. Although the framework may yet be enlarged to encompass other variables, clear-cut predictions are limited to a relatively narrow class of persuasion variables that affect extent of processing when these variables are crossed with argument strength or perhaps with other variables affecting the valence of message recipients' thoughts. As cognitive response researchers have themselves noted (e.g., Greenwald, 1981; Ostrom, 1981; Petty & Cacioppo, 1981), the approach is best viewed as a "conceptual orientation" (Ostrom, 1981, p. 287) that emphasizes the role that recipient-generated thought plays in persuasion. Its demonstrated and ultimate success in explaining persuasion, however, is dependent on the bridges that can be built between this approach and insights provided by other theoretical perspectives.

Assessing Cognitive Responses. Because of the crucial mediational role ascribed to recipient-generated thoughts by the cognitive response framework, it is important to assess the adequacy of the "thought-listing" task (Brock, 1967; Greenwald, 1968), which is so heavily relied upon in cognitive response research. The traditional criticism of the technique has been to question whether the thoughts listed by subjects (usually after they have received a communication) validly reflect the content and amount of covert cognitive responses they theoretically generate *during* exposure to the persuasive message (or when anticipating the message). Miller and Baron (1973) have pointed out that if subjects view the thought-listing procedure (which is typically temporally contiguous with the assessment of the subjects' post-message opinions) as an opportunity to justify their post-message opinions, then their responses to the thought-listing task could be the result, rather than the cause, of opinion change. More generally, demonstrations that cognitive responses covary with opinion change or that a given independent variable exerts parallel effects on cognitive responses and opinion change are vulnerable to the criticism that cognitive responses represent an alternative dependent measure of persuasion rather than an intervening variable that is antecedent to opinion change. Unfortunately, unequivocal evidence regarding the mediational role of cognitive responses would necessitate the development of nonreactive direct assessments of ongoing cognitive responding (see Greenwald, 1981; Miller & Colman, 1981). Nevertheless, studies that have employed analyses of covariance or regression techniques to test the causal direction of the relation between cognitive responses and persuasion have generally supported the mediational role of cognitive responses (e.g., Heesacker, Petty, & Cacioppo, 1983; Insko, Turnbull, & Yandell, 1974; Osterhouse & Brock, 1970). Yet, as Greenwald (1981) has noted, such analyses do not provide definitive evidence of causation.

Cacioppo's recent research on potential physiological correlates of cognitive responding also suggests optimism with respect to the mediational role of cognitive responding in persuasion (Cacioppo, 1979; Cacioppo & Petty, 1979a; Cacioppo, Sandman, & Walker, 1978). Cacioppo and his colleagues have shown that physiological responses such as accelerated heart rate and oral-electromyographic (EMG) activity, although they are not diagnostic of the favorability of cognitive responses, are, nevertheless, associated with more extensive cognitive processing (as indexed by thought protocols) in persuasion settings. There is preliminary evidence suggesting that the valence of individuals' thoughts can be detected through the patterning of facial-EMG activity (Cacioppo & Petty, 1981). Further, this research indicates that subtle manipulations of physiological responses exert predictable effects on cognitive responses. For example, Cacioppo (1979) found that increasing subjects' heart rate without their awareness (through adjusting their cardiac pacemakers) was associated with increased counterargument production for messages that elicited predominantly unfavorable thoughts.

Finally, it should be noted that a variety of categories could be employed in content analyses of experimental subjects' thought protocols (e.g., counterarguments, supportive arguments, source derogations, recipient-originated thoughts, message-originated thoughts, message-modified thoughts; see Cacioppo, Harkins, & Petty, 1981 for a review). Yet researchers have typically classified thoughts into two main categories: favorable and unfavorable message-relevant cognitions. In order to capture more of the richness and subtlety of people's reactions to persuasive messages and persuasion settings, researchers who utilize thought-listing techniques might undertake more sophisticated content analyses of subjects' thought protocols guided by categories pertinent to the specific persuasion hypotheses under investigation. Chaiken and Eagly (1983), for example, coded subjects' listed thoughts into two major categories—communicator-oriented thoughts and message-oriented thoughts—in exploring the hypothesis that communicator characteristics exert a greater persuasive impact when recipients receive video- or audio-taped (versus written) communications. By virtue of this coding scheme, these researchers were able to demonstrate not only that a manipulation of communicator likability exerted a stronger impact on the post-message opinions of subjects receiving video- or audio-taped (versus written) messages but also that subjects receiving broadcast (versus written) messages engaged in more thinking about the communicator.

B. ATTRIBUTION APPROACHES

Drawing on Heider's (1958) seminal analysis of causal attributions, Kelley (1967, 1972a) provided a provocative analysis of the attributional inferences that underlie persuasion. The theoretical principles suggested by Kelley and others who have subsequently analyzed persuasion within an attribution framework explain how message recipients utilize principles of causation to evaluate the validity of persuasive messages. According to Kelley, the message recipient faces the problem of attributing or explaining the communicator's message. In more exact terms, the recipient observes that the communicator takes a particular stand in the message. Then the recipient decides why this stand has been taken. This stand may be attributed to that part of the environment that is under discussion in the message, to characteristics of the communicator (e.g., preferences, ideology, traits), or to pressures in the communicator's situation. Attribution of the message to the environment (or "external reality") under discussion is termed an *entity* or *stimulus attribution* within Kelley's framework. Such an attribution increases message persuasiveness because it implies that the recipient believes that the message provides a veridical description of the environment it purports to describe.

Kelley suggested that perceivers may decide whether to attribute the communicator's stand to the environment under discussion by carrying out a subjective analysis of variance (ANOVA) on information arranged in a Persons × Occasions × Entities matrix. Within such a matrix, the probability of an entity attribution was assumed to be increased by a data pattern of *consensus* across persons, *consistency* across occasions (and modalities), and *distinctiveness* to the entity described. Although numerous questions have been raised concerning aspects of this ANOVA model (see Kelley & Michela, 1980), this assumption about consensus, consistency, and distinctiveness has proven to be generally valid. With respect to persuasive communications, then, an entity attribution would be favored (and therefore the message would be considered valid) if a communicator took a position that (1) was in agreement with that of other relevant information sources (consensus), (2) was stated on various occasions to various audiences (consistency), and (3) was tailored to the particular issue under consideration (distinctiveness).

1. Fulfillment of Consensus, Consistency, and Distinctiveness Criteria from Multiple Observations

The relevance of Kelley's (1967) ANOVA analysis to understanding persuasion is clearest when message recipients have multiple observations of communicators and messages that would enable them to fulfill consensus, consistency, and distinctiveness criteria with respect to communicators' positions on issues. Although most persuasion experiments have not provided subjects with such multiple observations, there are some studies that have involved multiple sources and repeated presentations of messages. Multiple sources, which have been shown to be more persuasive than single sources (e.g., Harkins & Petty, 1981; Himmelfarb, 1972), may enhance persuasion by increasing the consensus associated with the communicator's stand. Also, repeated messages or multiple messages advocating a similar viewpoint, which within limits are more persuasive than messages delivered once (e.g., Cacioppo & Petty, 1979b; Himmelfarb, 1972; Sawyer, 1981), may enhance persuasion by increasing the consistency of the communicator's stand. In further support of the consistency principle, Moscovici (e.g., Moscovici, 1976; Moscovici & Nemeth, 1974) has argued that persistent repetition of the same position by group members holding a minority opinion enhances their influence on other group members. Moscovici termed this aspect of communicators' behavioral style *behavioral consistency* and proposed that its effects on group members' opinions are mediated by their causal inferences.

The potential of the ANOVA analysis of attribution to account for perceivers' evaluations of persuasive messages in natural settings is enormous because very often people have extensive experience with various communicators who state their positions on related issues on multiple occasions. Examples include observations of politicians' stands on social and legislative issues as well as observations of friends' and family members' views on a host of everyday issues. In such realms, the ANOVA model is highly relevant to predicting message persuasiveness.

2. Fulfillment of Consensus, Consistency, and Distinctiveness Criteria from Single Observations

Because laboratory persuasion experiments typically present subjects with a single message in which a communicator takes a position on a single issue, it may seem that Kelley's (1967) ANOVA analysis has limited usefulness. Available information in such settings is usually not adequate to allow recipients to build a Persons × Occasions × Entities matrix based on multiple observations of communicators' positions on issues. Nevertheless, various cues in such persuasion situations may allow perceivers to make reasonable assumptions about how such a data matrix would be completed if more detailed information were available. Some relevant cues may be placed into the message itself by communicators' claims that their positions are consensual with those of other persons, consistent across occasions, and distinctive to the issue discussed. Communicator cues can provide other information relevant to the ANOVA data matrix. For example, inexpert communicators, who are generally less persuasive than experts (e.g., Bochner & Insko, 1966), may be regarded as lacking sufficient knowledge to make statements distinctive to the entities under discussion.

Although it is plausible to assume that recipients' use of consensus, consistency, and distinctiveness rules may mediate the persuasive effects of a number of persuasion cues, few independent variables have been systematically studied from this perspective. An exception is the work of Goethals and his associates (Goethals, 1976; Goethals & Nelson, 1973) on communicator similarity. Although subjects' judgmental confidence (rather than persuasion) was the dependent variable in these studies, documentation was obtained for the attributional mediation of the impact of communicator–recipient similarity on judgmental confidence. This research showed that, on matters of fact, agreement from a dissimilar other increased judgmental confidence more than agreement from a similar other. This finding is consistent with the attribution principle that consensus information increases perceivers' confidence that their judgment accurately reflects the true nature of the entity. If the agreeing others are similar, they might have the same biasing characteristics as message recipients and therefore generate inaccurate judgments on the same basis as the recipients. If the agreeing others are dissimilar, they are unlikely to share the same error-producing characteristics. Their agreement is especially likely to reduce the plausibility of person-based explanations of the advocated position and to increase the likelihood that the position accurately reflects the true nature of the world. In a similar vein, Himmelfarb (1972) has shown that consistency in other persons' descriptions of an actor is more effective in enhancing the persuasiveness of the descriptions if this consistency is based on observations in dissimilar rather than in similar situations. Consistency across dissimilar situations is especially likely to reduce the plausibility of situation-based explanations of messages and to increase the likelihood of entity attributions. Perhaps other cues whose effects on persuasion have been given a variety of other interpretations may prove to be mediated, at least partially, by their relevance to the consensus, consistency, and distinctiveness criteria that attribution theory postulates that message recipients use to judge message validity.

3. Multiple Plausible Causes and Message Persuasiveness

Kelley (1972a) also suggested that recipients of persuasive messages may engage in a simpler analysis of causation based not on the ANOVA cube, but on the plausibility of possible causes of the communicator's position. According to this analysis, perceivers scan available information for possible causes of the communicator's stand, and take into account whether there are one or more causes that seem plausible and whether these causes would be facilitative or inhibitory in relation to the position that the communicator states in the message.

The implications of Kelley's analysis of multiple plausible causes for persuasion were developed by Eagly and her colleagues (see Eagly, Chaiken, & Wood, 1981) who studied recipients' causal explanations that were based on single observations of a communicator's message. According to their analysis, cues leading recipients to infer possible causes of the communicator's position include information about the communicator's personal attributes (e.g., attitudes or personality traits) and the pressures in his or her situation. Recipients search for causes and often initiate their causal analysis on the basis of causally relevant information that they have available prior to receiving the message. Of course, such information is also frequently embedded in the message itself (e.g., information about the communicator's personality) or presented simultaneously with the message (e.g., audience reactions to the communicator).

Using causally relevant cues, recipients construct a minitheory of the communicator's behavior. That is, the recipient reasons, "A communicator with these attributes (or under these pressures) would probably take this type of position on the issue." This causal analysis, then, creates an expectancy about the position the communicator should take on the issue, and this expectancy is either confirmed or disconfirmed by the position the communicator actually takes in the message.

When recipients' expectancies are confirmed, they tend to attribute the communicator's view to the personal characteristic or situational pressure that generated their expectancy. Such a causal inference accounts for the message in terms of a personal or situational factor instead of the external reality the message purports to describe. This weakening of the entity or stimulus attribution is consistent with Kelley's (1972a) discounting principle, which predicts that a viable person- or situation-based cause lessens the plausibility of external reality as the cause. As a consequence of this attribution of the message to a person- or situation-based cause, message recipients believe that the communicator is biased. This inference about bias compromises the validity of the message as an accurate representation of the environment it describes. Thus, recipients are persuaded relatively little by such a message.

When a communicator disconfirms an expectancy by not taking the predicted position, recipients must generate a new theory of why the communicator took the position he or she did. Usually the most likely alternative theory is that especially compelling evidence made the communicator overcome the bias that was expected to affect his or her behavior. This strengthening of the entity attribution is consistent with Kelley's (1972a) augmentation principle. According to this principle, when an expectation based on a personal or situational cause is disconfirmed, this cause is assumed to have functioned in an inhibitory sense, with the consequence that the strength of the facilitating external reality cause is enhanced. Under such circumstances, a communicator is regarded as especially unbiased, and the message is relatively persuasive. In summary, because of the impact of the discounting principle when messages confirm expectancies and of the augmentation principle when messages disconfirm expectancies, messages that are unexpected in view of the communicator's attributes and situation are more persuasive than messages that are expected.

In developing the implications of this analysis for recipients' perceptions of communicators, Eagly, Wood, and Chaiken (1978) distinguished between two types of communicator bias that characterize recipients' expectancies about the communicator's position and that can underlie their causal explanations for this position. *Knowledge bias* refers to the recipient's belief that a communicator's knowledge of message-relevant information is nonveridical. A knowledge-biased communicator has a distorted view of the evidence but does not willfully mislead the audience. In contrast, *reporting bias* refers to the belief that a communicator's willingness to convey an accurate version of message-relevant information is compromised. A reporting-biased communicator willfully misleads the audience.

In one experiment testing this framework, Eagly, Wood, and Chaiken (1978) established knowledge-bias or reporting-bias expectancies, which were either confirmed or disconfirmed. When explaining the communicator's position, subjects took into account whether the message confirmed or disconfirmed their expectancies. They attributed the communicator's view more strongly to the relevant cue (the communicator's background in the knowledge-bias conditions and the audience's opinions in the reporting-bias conditions) when their expectancy was confirmed rather than disconfirmed. When the communicator confirmed the subjects' expectancies, he was judged more biased than when he disconfirmed them. Yet confirmation of expectancies based on reporting bias, but not knowledge bias, was associated with inferences of communicator insincerity and manipulativeness. However, regardless of the type of bias that subjects expected, they were more persuaded when their expectancies were disconfirmed. This tendency for unexpected stands to be more persuasive than expected stands was also obtained in several other experiments in this research program (Eagly & Chaiken, 1975; Eagly & Chaiken, 1976; Wood & Eagly, 1981).

The attribution framework has proven useful for interpreting the findings of a number of earlier persuasion experiments that had been formulated in terms of various aspects of communicator trustworthiness. For example, Walster, Aronson, and Abrahams (1966) demonstrated that, regardless of overall prestige, a communicator was more persuasive when arguing against rather than in accord with his or her own self-interest. In these and other experiments (e.g., Birnbaum

& Stegner, 1979; Koeske & Crano, 1968; Mills & Jellison, 1967), communicators were more persuasive advocating positions that were unexpected (versus expected) in terms of their personal attributes and situational pressures. Although it is useful to understand such effects in terms of recipients' causal inferences, there is a need for direct assessments of recipients' causal explanations (as carried out by Eagly, Wood, and Chaiken [1978]) to determine whether subjects actually used a trustworthiness cue in a causal theory of the communicator's behavior.

4.   The Theory of Correspondent Inferences

Jones and Davis (1965) proposed a version of attribution theory that concerns perceivers' inferences that others' behaviors are manifestations of their underlying dispositions, such as their attitudes and personality traits. This analysis has some relevance to persuasion because message recipients often must infer communicators' personal attributes. Inferences about communicators' message-relevant attitudes are of special interest. Following a distinction introduced by Jones and McGillis (1976), inferences concerning the communicator's attitudes may be category based (derived from recipients' knowledge that the communicator is a member of a particular class, category, or reference group) or target based (derived from prior information about the specific communicator).

Jones and Davis suggested, and others have demonstrated (Ajzen, 1971; Lay, Burron, & Jackson, 1973), that the less a behavior is expected, given the actor's situation, the stronger is the perceiver's inference that the actor's dispositions correspond to the actor's behavior. When applied to persuasion, this principle suggests that the less a communicator's position is expected, given the pressures in his or her situation, the stronger is the recipient's inference that the communicator's attitudes correspond to the position taken in the message. Eagly, Wood, and Chaiken (1978) found support for this proposition when the situational pressure on the communicator stemmed from the opinions of the members of the audience. Numerous studies (e.g., Himmelfarb & Anderson, 1975; Jones & Harris, 1967; Jones, Worchel, Goethals, & Grumet, 1971; Miller, 1976) on the attribution of attitudes have also supported this principle, in relation to a variety of situational pressures.

Despite the relevance of the Jones and Davis (1965) analysis to understanding recipients' inferences about communicators' attitudes, for predicting persuasion we find it less useful than Kelley's (1967, 1972a) analyses, which concern causal attributions about the message itself. When recipients are deciding whether to adopt the communicator's advocated position, causal explanation of this position is the central problem. Recipients may also use a causal analysis to infer the communicator's dispositions. Yet, to decide whether to accept the communicator's position, they must determine whether these dispositions, along with situational pressures, can or cannot be ruled out as causes of the position taken in the message.

Although it may seem that inferences about the communicator's attitudes may have direct implications for message persuasiveness, it is doubtful that this is so. It is true that an inference that the communicator's attitude does not correspond to the position taken in the message covaries with perceived lack of communicator trustworthiness and with lowered message persuasiveness (Eagly et al., 1978). Yet these inferences of attitude-message noncorrespondence and communicator untrustworthiness stem from the congruence of the communicator's position with external pressures acting on him or her. And it is the causal prominence of these pressures, and the consequent discounting of external reality as a cause of the message, that are critical to lowering the persuasiveness of the message. Thus, the impact of attributions about the communicator's attitudes is, at best, indirect in relation to persuasion.

5. Evaluation of Attribution Framework

As we have shown, a number of researchers have utilized some aspect of attribution theory to make predictions about persuasion. Further, other writers have recognized the general importance of attribution principles as explanations of persuasion (e.g., Sternthal, Phillips, & Dholakia, 1978) and other forms of social influence (Gottlieb & Ickes, 1978). Yet attribution theory has not been developed to the fullest possible extent as a theory of persuasion, and attributional principles have recieved only limited testing in persuasion studies. Although Kelley's (1972a) analysis of multiple plausible causes has been developed as a persuasion model by Eagly and her colleagues (Eagly, Chaiken, & Wood, 1981) and tested in a number of attitude change experiments, his ANOVA analysis in terms of consensus, consistency, and distinctiveness has received less attention, despite its obvious relevance to popular persuasion variables such as message repetition and multiple sources. Still other aspects of attribution theory (e.g., Kelley's, 1972b, analysis of causal schemata) have not been explored at all in relation to persuasion.

Sufficient persuasion research has been conducted in an attribution framework to demonstrate that message recipients' causal attributions concerning the communicator's stand are an important determinant of message persuasiveness. Messages are persuasive if they are believed to reflect the facts—that is, the qualities of the environment described by the message. Messages are relatively unpersuasive if they are attributed to biasing personal characteristics of the communicator or to pressures in his or her situation. Perceivers of messages search for causes and assess the believability of messages according to the outcome of this search. Existing research suggests that message recipients make causal inferences on the basis of (1) consensus, consistency, and distinctiveness of multiple observations of communicators and messages, (2) cues in single messages or their context allowing reasonable guesses about consensus, consistency, and distinctiveness, and (3) causally relevant communicator attributes or situational pressures observed in the persuasion situation. Causal reasoning stemming from these informational bases has been shown to be important to understanding how contextual features of social influence situations, such as communicator characteristics and audience reactions, affect message persuasiveness.

Despite the considerable potential of attributional principles for understanding persuasion, such principles provide only a partial theory of the conditions under which attitudes and beliefs are changed by persuasive communications. These limitations arise because only some cues in persuasion settings have causal relevance. Although this set of cues may be larger than most investigators have suspected, there are many kinds of information whose effects on persuasion are no doubt mediated by inferences of other types.

C. HEURISTIC MODEL

Implicit in the more traditional information-processing models of persuasion such as McGuire's (1972) reception–yielding framework and the cognitive response approach is the view that message recipients engage in a considerable amount of message- and/or issue-relevant information processing in deciding whether to accept a message's overall position. In contrast to this *systematic* conceptualization of persuasion, Chaiken (1978, 1980, 1982, 1983; Chaiken & Eagly, 1983) has recently proposed a *heuristic* processing model of persuasion. According to the heuristic conceptualization, people sometimes exert little cognitive effort in judging message validity. Instead, recipients may base their agreement with a message on a rather superficial assessment of a variety of persuasion cues, such as surface or structural characteristics of persuasive messages (e.g., their length or number of arguments), communicator characteristics (e.g., likability or expertise), and audience characteristics (e.g., positive or negative audience reactions to the message).

The heuristic model asserts that many persuasion cues are processed by means of simple schemas or decision rules (or cognitive heuristics) that people have presumably learned on the basis of past experiences and observations (Abelson, 1976; Nisbett & Ross, 1980; Stotland & Canon, 1972). For example, with respect to communicator expertise, people may have learned that statements by experts are more veridical than statements by persons who lack expertise and may then apply the expert credo, "Statements by experts can be trusted," in response to a cue conveying high expertise. Given a cue conveying that a communicator is likable, people may call on a liking–agreement heuristic such as "people agree with people they like" or "people I like usually have correct opinions on issues." With respect to message cues, people's past experiences may have taught them that strong, compelling persuasive messages typically contain more arguments, longer and more detailed arguments, arguments supported by statistics, or arguments derived from highly credible sources. If so, it is likely that people will have abstracted rules such as "length implies strength," "more arguments are better arguments," "statistics don't lie," and "arguments based on expert opinions are valid." According to the heuristic model, people may apply such rules in judging the probable validity of communications. Thus, without fully absorbing the semantic content of persuasive argumentation, people may agree more with meassages containing many (versus few) arguments, with messages that are longer (versus shorter), or with messages containing arguments that are embellished with statistics or ascribed to credible sources.

In essence, whereas the more systematic information-processing approaches emphasize relatively detailed processing of message content and the role of message- and topic-relevant cognitions in determining opinion change, the heuristic model de-emphasizes detailed processing and asserts that simple decision rules often mediate the persuasive impact of a variety of distal persuasion variables. Consistent with Shiffrin and Schneider's (1977; Schneider & Shiffrin, 1977) ideas about automatic processing, heuristic processing of persuasion cues may occur without much active control or attention by message recipients. Thus, people may typically be unaware of the extent to which they apply simple rules in processing persuasion cues. Nevertheless, there no doubt are circumstances in which such decision rules are applied quite self-consciously (Chaiken, 1982). For example, an investor may self-consciously decide to accept a stockbroker's recommendations about stock purchases because the broker is an expert on such matters and the investor feels unable to evaluate the evidential base underlying the broker's recommendations.

Although other theoretical perspectives in persuasion such as Kelman's (1961) identification model and the attributional approaches we have already discussed share with the heuristic processing model the view that persuasion is not invariably the outcome of recipients' reception and/or acceptance of persuasive argumentation, the heuristic perspective is novel in its explicit cognitive focus on the mediational role of simple schemas or cognitive heuristics. Yet the heuristic model is in accord with the implicit motivational assumption of most information-processing models that a recipient's primary motivation in a persuasion setting is to assess the validity of a message's overall conclusion.

It is also important to note that the heuristic model is not synonymous with what Petty and Cacioppo (1981) refer to as the "peripheral route to persuasion." As most clearly articulated in their 1981 text (pp. 255–256), the "central versus peripheral'' framework represents a *typological* distinction between various attitude-change processes. Under the central route (which does correspond closely to what Chaiken [1978, 1980] calls the "systematic" perspective), Petty and Cacioppo classify persuasion models that emphasize detailed processing of argumentation and the importance of issue-relevant thinking. In contrast, approaches that specify factors or *motives* in persuasion settings that produce attitude change without any active message- or issue-relevant thinking are classified under the peripheral route. The heuristic model would, in the Petty and Cacioppo framework, be classified as a peripheral approach. However, the two formulations are not identical because Petty and Cacioppo (1981) also use the peripheral label to refer to theoretical approaches that feature assumptions about the psychological mediation of persuasion and motivational goals of message recipients that are not shared by the heuristic model. For example, the peripheral label is used to refer to classical and to operant conditioning models of attitude change as well as approaches such as Kelman's (1961) identification model, Schlenker's (1980) impression-management theory, and Brehm's (1966) reactance theory that feature motivational orientations other than assessing the validity of persuasive messages (see the section ''Other Motivational Bases of Persuasion'').

1. Empirical Evidence Supporting the Heuristic Model

Consistent with the heuristic conceptualization, there are numerous studies suggesting that communicator attributes may exert a relatively direct impact on persuasion (see Chaiken, 1978, for a more detailed review). For example, Norman (1976) found that argumentative support provided for a communicator's position failed to increase the persuasiveness of an attractive source (although it did increase an expert source's persuasiveness). If the attractiveness cue were mediated by recipients' processing of message content, the attractive communicator should have been more persuasive with the message that included (versus excluded) argumentation. Similar findings were reported by Mills and Harvey (1972). Further, Miller, Maruyama, Beaber, and Valone (1976) found that fast-talking (versus slow-talking) communicators were perceived as more credible and were more persuasive. Yet there was no evidence that this greater persuasiveness was mediated either by the recipients' comprehension of message content or by their message- and issue-relevant thinking. Apparently, the Miller *et al.* (1976) subjects based their opinion judgments directly on their perceptions of the communicator's credibility.

More evidence that persuasion cues may often be heuristically processed stems from experiments that have examined subjects' motivation or ability to engage in effortful cognitive processing. Because heuristic processing is relatively effortless and may be activated without much active control or attention by message recipients, whereas systematic processing is effortful and may generally be avoided, heuristic processing of persuasion cues may predominate in many persuasion settings. However, when motivation to engage in message- and issue-relevant thinking is high, and at least a modicum of ability to do so exists, people may be more likely to engage in systematic processing of messages. These considerations suggest that persuasion cues that may typically be processed heuristically should exert a greater persuasive impact when recipients are un-motivated or unable to systematically process message content. Conversely, such cues should exert a lesser impact under conditions of high motivation or high ability. Although in such situations heuristic processing may proceed in parallel with systematic processing or at least be initiated, systematic processing may reduce the impact of persuasion cues that are typically processed heuristically (Chaiken, 1982, 1983). For example, although long messages may often lead to greater persuasion than short messages because recipients apply the "length implies strength" heuristic, careful scrutiny of the semantic content of argumentation may provide information contradicting this simple heuristic. Thus, in such situations, a variable like message length may not exert a detectable impact on persuasion.

Consistent with the above reasoning, in experiments that have presumably varied recipients' motivation to process systematically by manipulating issue involvement (personal importance of a topic) or response involvement (consequentiality of recipients' opinion judgments), manipulations of source credibility have significantly affected persuasion under conditions of low, but not high, involvement (Johnson & Scileppi, 1969; Rhine & Severance, 1970). In a more definitive pair of experiments, Chaiken (1980) found that the persuasive impact of communicator likability was greater under low (versus high) involvement; and, further, was able to document that under high-involvement conditions, recipients based their opinion judgments primarily on their responses to persuasive argumentation, whereas under low involvement, opinion judgments were primarily determined by recipients' perceptions of the communicator. In a conceptually similar study, Petty, Cacioppo, and Goldman (1981) replicated these persuasion findings using a manipulation of communicator expertise.

Compatible findings have been obtained in studies that have examined the persuasive impact of surface or structural characteristics of persuasive messages. Langer, Blank, and Chanowitz (1978) found that compliance with a small, inconsequential request was equally high regardless of whether the request (to make 5 Xerox copies) was supported by a vacuous reason ("May I use the Xerox machine because I have to make copies") or a more valid reason ("May I use the Xerox machine because I'm in a rush"); however, given a larger, more consequential request (to make 20 Xerox copies), compliance was substantially lower when the request was justified with a vacuous (versus valid) reason. This suggests that the mere inclusion of arguments in a message, regardless of their quality, can enhance persuasion under uninvolving conditions. In a more definitive test of this hypothesis, Petty and Cacioppo (1983) found that, under low issue involvement, recipients were more persuaded by messages containing nine rather than three arguments, regardless of the quality of these arguments. Under high involvement, however, recipients agreed more with messages containing nine (versus three) strong arguments but less with messages containing nine (versus three) weak arguments. Moreover, recipients' opinion judgments were more highly related to message-relevant thinking under high (versus low) involvement. Finally, in a study that examined ability to engage in systematic processing of persuasive argumentation, Wood, Kallgren, and Priesler (1983) obtained evidence consistent with the idea that persuasion cues that are typically processed heuristically will exert a greater impact on the opinion judgments of recipients who have less ability to evaluate argumentation. In one experiment, subjects with little prior knowledge about the message topic, as compared to highly knowledgeable subjects, showed greater agreement with long, rather than short, messages, even though these messages contained an equivalent number of arguments. In a second experiment, low- but not high-knowledge subjects showed greater agreement with a likable (versus unlikable) communicator. And in both experiments, low-knowledge subjects evidenced less extensive processing of persuasive argumentation. Presumably, people lacking in ability to carefully scrutinize message content are more likely to apply simple decision rules such as "length implies strength" or "people generally agree with people they like." Alternatively, as noted earlier, although such rules may also be activated when highly knowledgeable recipients receive a persuasive communication, their greater ability to carefully analyze message content and engage in issue-relevant thinking may provide them with information that tends to override the impact of these simple decision rules on their opinion judgments.

    The research just reviewed suggests that when recipient involvement is low or when, regardless of involvement, people have little ability to engage in issue-relevant thinking, persuasion is more likely to reflect recipients' use of simple decision rules. In addition, Chaiken and Eagly (1983) have obtained findings suggesting that increasing the salience (and/or vividness) of persuasion cues that are typically processed in heuristic fashion may increase the likelihood that recipients will apply simple decision rules in judging message validity. In two experiments, subjects were presented with either a video-taped, audio-taped, or written persuasive message that was attributed to either a likable or unlikable communicator. Based on the assumption that nonverbal communicator-related cues in the two broadcast modalities would draw recipients' attention to the communicator, Chaiken and Eagly reasoned that the liking–agreement rule ("people generally agree with people they like") would be more likely to be activated when recipients were exposed to video-taped or audio-taped, rather than written, messages. Consistent with this reasoning, the communicator likability manipulation exerted a significantly greater impact on the postmessage opinions expressed by recipients of video-taped or audio-taped (versus written) messages. Moreover, additional findings indicated that subjects thought more about the communicator in the two broadcast modalities and, to a greater extent than recipients of written messages, based their opinion judgments on their perceptions of the communicator. The findings of this experiment, which are consistent with prior research on salience effects (e.g., McArthur, 1981; Taylor & Fiske, 1978) as well as the hypothesis that vivid (versus nonvivid) information is more impactful (Nisbett & Ross, 1980; Taylor & Thompson, 1982), suggest that manipulations that make other types of persuasion cues salient (relative to other cues) or inherently more vivid should also increase their persuasive impact. Of course, manipulations that make message content more salient (e.g., instructional sets that lead recipients to focus attention on persuasive argumentation) should enhance the likelihood that recipients engage in systematic processing and reduce the persuasive impact of cues that are typically processed heuristically. Also, increasing the salience or vividness of cues such as communicator likability, communicator expertise, or message length should increase their persuasive impact. Moreover, according to the heuristic model, the enhanced persuasive impact of such cues would be ascribed to the effect of their increased salience or vividness on recipients' tendencies to utilize the simple decision rules that are associated with these cues.

Consistent with this reasoning about the effects of increasing attention to cues that are typically processed heuristically, Pallak (1983) obtained findings suggesting that increasing the vividness of a communicator's physical attractiveness (by presenting subjects with a color photograph versus a degraded Xerox copy of the photo) enhances the likelihood that recipients retrieve and make use of the liking–agreement rule in making their opinion judgments. When the communicator's physical appearance was not vivid, subjects apparently processed the persuasive message systematically: They agreed more with high- (versus low-) quality messages, and their post-message opinions were highly correlated with their message-oriented cognitions. In contrast, when the communicator's appearance was vivid, subjects evidenced less systematic processing and greater heuristic processing: In this condition, post-message opinions were unaffected by the argument-strength manipulation and were more highly correlated with the subjects' perceptions of the communicator than with their own message-oriented thoughts.

2. Evaluation of the Heuristic Model

Because the heuristic-processing model is relatively new, its worth as a theory of persuasion has not yet been fully developed. Although a growing body of literature supports its potential utility, direct evidence regarding the cognitive mediation specified by the heuristic model is, at present, lacking. Existing empirical evidence has been indirect: Under conditions of low motivation and/or low ability to process message content, and perhaps under conditions of high cue salience, persuasion cues such as number of arguments, message length, and communicator likability, expertise, or physical attractiveness appear to have an enhanced impact on opinion change (relative to conditions of high motivation and/or ability and low cue salience). Moreover, those studies that have included measures designed to index more effortful, systematic processing of message content (e.g., measures of argument recall and of message- and issue-relevant thinking) have indicated that the observed persuasive impact of these communicator and superficial message cues has *not* been mediated by recipients' attention to, comprehension of, or elaboration of persuasive argumentation (Chaiken, 1980; Chaiken & Eagly, 1983; Pallak, 1983; Pallak, Murroni, & Koch, 1983; Petty & Cacioppo, 1983; Wood, Kallgren, & Priesler, 1983). At the same time, however, this research has provided little *direct* evidence that subjects in these studies have actually employed the kinds of simple decision rules specified by the heuristic model (e.g., the liking–agreement rule, the expertise credo, the "length implies strength" rule). For example, in the only study that included a measure designed to assess subjects' possible use of a simple decision rule, Chaiken (1980, Exp. 2) found only a partial correspondence between the subjects' self-reported use of the liking–agreement rule and the extent to which they agreed more with a likable (versus unlikable) communicator's message. (Of course, self-report measures may not prove very helpful in documenting the role that cognitive heuristics play in persuasion because recipients may often be unaware that such processing has occurred.) Clearly, more direct evidence for the cognitive mediation of opinion change specified by the heuristic model necessitates research that utilizes experimental manipulations of the strength, reliability, or salience of decision rules. For example, tasks designed to prime a decision rule such as "length implies strength" could be examined for their impact on recipients' tendencies to agree with long (versus short) messages in a subsequent persuasion setting (see Chaiken, 1983).

Among the implications that the heuristic model has for understanding persuasion phenomena is the idea that opinion change in response to persuasive communications is often the outcome of only minimal information processing on the part of recipients and, further, that recipients may often not even be aware of the extent to which they employ simple decision rules or heuristics in forming their opinion judgments. The idea that people often perform tasks and make decisions and other judgments after only minimal information processing has gained increasing attention in both cognitive psychology (e.g., Craik & Lockhart, 1972; Schneider & Shiffrin, 1977; Shiffrin & Schneider, 1977) and social psychology (e.g., Abelson, 1976; Bargh, 1982; Bargh & Pietromonaco, 1982; Langer, 1978). Yet, aside from the heuristic model and a few past informal observations (e.g., McGuire's [1969] discussion of the "lazy organism" message recipient), this idea is largely absent in contemporary cognitive accounts of persuasion. Research stimulated by the heuristic model should, therefore, help redress other theoretical perspectives' possible overestimation of the extent to which people carefully scrutinize argumentation and engage in issue-relevant thinking when exposed to persuasive messages.

In terms of specific implications for persuasion phenomena, the heuristic model suggests an alternative mediational explanation for the impact of a number of distal variables that have traditionally been thought to influence persuasion via other psychological mechanisms. For example, Kelman (1961) distinguished between internalization-based and identification-based attitude change and postulated that source credibility and source attractiveness, respectively, may be antecedent conditions for these two qualitatively different modes of social influence. Following this distinction, researchers have traditionally assumed that the persuasive impact of credibility can be attributed to the impact of this variable on recipients' processing of argumentation, whereas the heightened persuasive impact of attractive communicators is independent of recipients' processing of message content and instead reflects their desires to establish a self-defining relationship with the communicator. Although existing empirical evidence (e.g., Kelman, 1961; Mills & Harvey, 1972; Norman, 1976) suggests that there are some circumstances under which these two source variables *do* influence opinion change via these qualitatively different mechanisms, the heuristic model suggests that very often the persuasive impact of *both* source variables can be attributed to recipients' use of simple decision rules and that (1) credibility effects, like attractiveness effects, may often be independent of recipients' processing of persuasive argumentation, and (2) heightened agreement with liked communicators, like heightened agreement with credible communicators, may often be motivated by recipients' desires to hold correct opinions. Moreover, research stimulated by the heuristic model has provided some insights regarding the *conditions* (e.g., low involvement, low ability to engage in issue-relevant thinking, high cue salience) under which source variables (as well as other cues that may often be processed heuristically) are most likely to be important determinants of persuasion. Research has also explored the consequences of heuristic processing of persuasion cues for opinion persistence (Chaiken, 1980; Chaiken & Eagly, 1983) and attitude-behavior relations (Pallak *et al.,* 1983), as well as the conditions under which the elusive sleeper-effect phenomenon (cf. Cook, Gruder, Hennigan, & Flay, 1979) is most likely to be observed (Chaiken, 1980).

Other research that has been guided by the heuristic conceptualization of persuasion has shown that message variables such as message length (Wood, Kallgren, & Priesler, 1983) and number of distinct persuasive arguments (Petty & Cacioppo, 1983) can, under some circumstances (e.g., low involvement or low ability), also influence persuasion without engendering any message- or issue-relevant thinking on the part of message recipients. Speculative hypotheses that other message, contextual, and recipient variables (Chaiken, 1980) may also be processed heuristically in some settings await empirical verification. Nevertheless, such speculations do suggest that the heuristic model may have some general applicability with respect to a variety of distal persuasion cues.

Despite the potential of the heuristic model for increasing our understanding of certain persuasion phenomena, it, like the other processing theories considered in this chapter, does not constitute a general theory of persuasion. First, although the range of cues whose persuasive impact may sometimes be mediated by simple decision rules may prove broader than those that have been identified by existing research, this set will obviously not exhaust the variety of distal variables that have long interested attitude-change researchers. In addition, although some of these other distal variables (e.g., involvement) have been shown to influence the likelihood that heuristic (versus systematic) processing of persuasion cues will predominate in a given persuasion setting, assumptions about why such variables influence processing mode are not inherent in the heuristic model. Rather, like many of the assumptions made by cognitive response researchers, such assumptions require the importation of concepts from other theoretical perspectives.

D. EVALUATION OF PROCESS THEORIES

The process theories (the cognitive response approach, attribution theory, and the heuristic model) that we have reviewed all describe particular mechanisms or cognitive processes that are postulated to underlie message-recipients' tendencies to agree with persuasive messages they receive from outside sources. The major distinction among these theories is that they specify differing *modes* of information processing. Both the heuristic model and the attributional perspective provide molecular descriptions of yielding to a persuasive message's overall position. The heuristic model specifies simple decision rules that message recipients apply on the basis of cues available in the message or the context in which it is received, whereas the attribution model specifies particular causal inferences that recipients make on the basis of such cues. Such simple rules or causal inferences are postulated to underlie recipients' tendencies to accept or reject a message's overall position. In contrast, the cognitive response approach provides a more molar description of yielding that does not focus on particular causal inferences or decision rules, but instead focuses on general characteristics of the cognitive processing or thinking that is elicited by exposure to persuasive communications. Thus, recipients' agreement with a communication is typically predicted from the extent to which their issue-relevant thinking is favorable or unfavorable to the message's recommendation.

Assuming the validity of each of these differing modes of information processing, it is important to develop an understanding of the conditions under which recipients process persuasion cues by means of one or another of the intervening processes that theorists have described and, further, to consider the extent to which these processing modes represent parallel or mutually exclusive processes. Although we do not undertake an exhaustive analysis of these issues, we offer some observations and preliminary speculations regarding factors that affect recipients' tendencies to utilize these differing processing modes.

Prior learning is clearly one determinant of whether message recipients utilize the causal reasoning processes specified by attribution theory as well as the simple rules and schemas specified by the heuristic model. To employ such inferences and decision rules in evaluating message validity, people must have learned and stored in memory the particular knowledge structures that are relevant to available persuasion cues. Further, these knowledge structures must be activated upon the presentation of the persuasion cues that are associated with them. For example, in order for a cue such as communicator expertise to be processed heuristically, recipients via their past experiences with experts must have learned and stored in memory the expert credo. Moreover, the persuasive impact of such cues should be a function of the *strength* of the decision rule or schema: Recipients whose past experiences with likable persons, for example, have yielded few exceptions to the liking–agreement rule (i.e., the schema has "low" probabilism, Stotland & Canon, 1972) should perceive a relatively strong associative connection between the concepts of liking and interpersonal agreement and should thus be more likely to agree with likable communicators than will recipients whose past experiences have yielded many exceptions to the liking–agreement rule (i.e., the liking–agreement schema has "high" probabilism). Similarly, message recipients can perform the kind of causal reasoning specified by the attributional perspective only to the extent that they possess relevant knowledge structures. For example, to attribute a senator's statement on social security reform to his political attitudes or general ideology, recipients must have observed (or abstracted from other observations) a general relation between political attitudes and stands on the social security issue (or on related issues) and recognize the relevance of this general relation to interpreting the senator's behavior. Also, as noted earlier in relation to heuristic processing, recipients' confidence in such an attributional judgment should be a function of the *strength* of the general relation or schema that forms the basis for their causal inference.

Prior learning also plays a role in determining whether recipients engage in the sort of cognitive processing described by the cognitive response model. Thus, in order to engage in the message- and issue-relevant thinking highlighted in this approach, recipients must have at least some prior knowledge related to the topic discussed in the persuasive message. As Wood *et al.* (1983) have shown, subjects who possess little issue-relevant knowledge tend to manifest little message- and issue-relevant thinking in response to a persuasive communication.

The extent to which recipients engage in attributional reasoning or heuristic processing also depends on whether relevant knowledge structures are *activated* upon presentation of the persuasion cues that are associated with them. Although little research exists on this issue, the Chaiken and Eagly (1983) experiments suggest that increasing attention to persuasion cues (e.g., communicator likability) may enhance the likelihood that recipients retrieve from memory and utilize relevant knowledge structures (e.g., the liking–agreement rule) in forming their opinion judgments. Another factor that may influence whether relevant knowledge structures are activated in a particular setting is the recipient's motivational goals in that setting. Clearly, if a recipient is relatively uninterested in assessing the validity of a communicator's statements (and, instead, has other goals that are unrelated to such an assessment), it is less likely that knowledge structures of potential relevance for judging message validity would be activated. Finally, an obvious factor that affects whether recipients utilize the causal reasoning specified by attribution theory as well as the simple rules specified by the heuristic model is whether the persuasion setting contains cues that have causal implications for the validity of the message (attribution model) or cues that can be processed heuristically.

The extent to which differing modes of information processing require *effortful thinking* on the part of message recipients is also an important consideration in predicting which processing mode may predominate in a particular persuasion setting. It seems reasonable to assert that the three modes of processing that have been described—the issue-relevant thinking specified in the cognitive response model, the induction of causal reasoning specified by attribution theory, and the elicitation of simple decision rules postulated by the heuristic model—can be ordered along a continuum with issue-relevant thinking as the most demanding processing mode and simple schemas and decision rules the least effortful mode. Indeed, to the extent that heuristic processing of persuasion cues sometimes occurs outside of recipients' conscious awareness, this mode would require virtually no active thinking on the part of recipients. As Chaiken (1980, 1982) and Petty and Cacioppo (1981) have suggested, people may prefer less effortful modes of processing messages unless they are especially motivated to engage in a more effortful process. Research on the role of involvement in persuasion (see the section ''Heuristic Model'') suggests that involvement is a critical motivational variable that affects processing. Moderate to high levels of involvement may be necessary to motivate recipients to engage in the kind of message- and issue-relevant thinking implied by the cognitive response model. Because causal reasoning is presumably less effortful than such thinking, it may be a preferred mode at lower levels of involvement. Because of its least effortful nature, heuristic processing of persuasion cues may represent the predominant mode of information processing in persuasion settings characterized by extremely low levels of involvement. It is important to point out that this analysis of the influence of involvement on mode of processing does not assert that at particular levels of involvement *only one* mode of processing occurs. Rather, the analysis suggests that whereas heuristic processing may predominate in low involvement situations, as involvement increases to some moderate level, both heuristic processing and causal reasoning may occur and predominate over issue-relevant thinking; and as involvement increases beyond this point, recipients may be likely to engage in all three of these differing modes of processing information.

Finally, the extent to which recipients utilize one mode of processing information rather than another may depend in part on the *sufficiency* of a particular processing mode for determining the validity of a persuasive message's overall recommendation. An implicit (and often explicit) assumption underlying research guided by all three of the processing theories we have considered is that recipients are primarily motivated to maximize the validity of their own opinions (see discussion in the section ''Other Motivational Bases of Persuasion''). Thus, if a particular mode of processing does not provide a relatively clear-cut assessment of message validity, another processing mode may be invoked. Wood and Eagly (1981) explored this general hypothesis in a study that examined the persuasive impact of subjects' causal attributions regarding the position advocated by a communicator in a persuasive message. In this study, when message recipients could not unambiguously determine message validity on the basis of their causal reasoning, they scrutinized message content more carefully, presumably in order to clarify whether the message was indeed a valid description of external reality. Thus, the Wood and Eagly findings suggest that when a relatively less effortful processing mode (e.g., causal reasoning) does not yield a confident judgment regarding the probable validity of a persuasive message, recipients may be more likely to turn to a more effortful mode of processing (e.g., message- and issue-relevant thinking) in order to assess message validity more confidently.

It may also be true that engaging in the message- and issue-relevant thinking highlighted in the cognitive response approach is a more *reliable* method of judging message validity than the causal reasoning specified by the attribution perspective, which in turn is a more reliable processing stragegy than the simple rules postulated by the heuristic model. Nevertheless, the sufficiency principle does not necessarily imply that in attempting to confidently assess message validity, recipients *always* move from less effortful to more effortful processing modes. Indeed, as Chaiken (1980, 1982) has suggested, even when recipients are highly motivated and quite able to engage in message- and issue-relevant thinking, they may sometimes fall back on and employ simple decision rules in evaluating message validity because their processing of message content has provided them with an insufficient informational base on which to predicate an opinion judgment.

These ideas regarding the conditions that may influence modes of processing information in persuasion settings are quite speculative, and the principles we discuss (prior learning, least effort, and sufficiency) are, no doubt, neither completely independent nor exhaustive of factors that potentially influence processing mode. Nevertheless, these principles may prove useful to researchers interested in exploring the interrelations among the differing modes of processing that are highlighted in current verbally formulated process theories of persuasion. Before concluding this section, it is wise to underscore our assumption that these differing modes of processing persuasion information should be viewed as parallel rather than mutually exclusive processes. Thus, we would not want to argue that recipients either do or do not engage in heuristic processing (or causal reasoning or issue-relevant thinking) and, if not, that they do or do not engage in causal reasoning and so on. Rather, we assume that these modes of processing may occur simultaneously, albeit to a greater or lesser extent depending upon other factors (e.g., involvement, preference for less effortful thinking, sufficiency of processing mode). Future research should not only address the extent to which the principles we have discussed influence the modes of information processing that predominate in particular persuasion settings, but also the extent to which message recipients do or do not self-consciously select or switch between processing modes.

III.   Combinatorial Theories of Persuasion

A.   PROBABILOGICAL MODEL

Probabilogical approaches to understanding the processes underlying the acquisition and change of beliefs define beliefs as subjective probability judgments (e.g., the perceived likelihood that a nuclear war will occur within the next 10 years). Because these models examine the general proposition that the relations among beliefs obey the laws of mathematical probability theory, they are normative models in the sense that they specify how beliefs *ought* to be related to one another within the individual's cognitive system and how beliefs *should* change when other probabilistically-related beliefs are formed, modified, or made salient to the individual.

Working within a cognitive consistency framework, McGuire (1960a, 1960b, 1960c) developed a probabilogical model of cognitive structure and belief change that provided a quantitative definition and assessment of consistency among beliefs. Formulated in the context of logical syllogisms, the McGuire model pertains to sets of syllogistically-related belief propositions such as the following:

A (Minor premise): A major nuclear war will occur within the next 10 years.
B (Major premise): A major nuclear war would result in violent death to at least half the earth's population.
C (Conclusion): At least half the earth's population will meet violent death within the next 10 years.

If a person's beliefs in the above three propositions are assessed in terms of subjective probabilities (e.g., the person's judgment of the probability that the minor premise is true) and if the person's beliefs manifest complete logical consistency, then according to the laws of formal logic and probability theory, the relations among these beliefs should conform to the equation,

$$p(C) = p(A)p(B) + p(K) \qquad (1)$$

where $p(A)$, $p(B)$, and $p(C)$ are the person's beliefs in the minor premise, major premise, and conclusion, respectively. The final term in the equation, $p(K)$, represents the person's belief in the conclusion "on bases other than the conjunction of A and B" (McGuire, 1960c, p. 346); for example, that "factors other than nuclear war are going to result in violent death to at least half the earth's population within the next ten years" (McGuire, 1960a, p. 68).

More recently, Wyer (Wyer, 1970, 1974; Wyer & Goldberg, 1970; Wyer & Hartwick, 1980) has proposed a conditional inference model of cognitive organization and change. Although neither developed within the general framework of cognitive consistency theory nor applied exclusively to syllogistically related belief propositions, Wyer's model is virtually identical to the McGuire (1960a, 1960b, 1960c) model of cognitive structure. Conditional inferences refer to judgments concerning the validity of one proposition, given the validity of others. To the extent that conditional inference processes play a role in belief formation and change, we might expect, for example, that people's belief in the proposition, "marijuana should be legalized," might be dependent on their beliefs associated with a second proposition such as "marijuana is harmless."

According to Wyer's (1970) conditional inference model, a person's belief (assessed in probabilistic terms) in a target proposition C should be related to his or her beliefs associated with a second proposition A in the following manner:

$$p(C) = p(A)p(C/A) + p(A')p(C/A') \qquad (2)$$

In this equation $p(C)$ is a person's belief in C, $p(A)$ and $p(A')$ [where $p(A') = 1 - p(A)$] are beliefs that A is and is not true, respectively, and $p(C/A)$ and $p(C/A')$ are conditional beliefs that the target proposition C is true if A is and is not true, respectively. For the marijuana example, Equation 2 states that a person's belief that marijuana should be legalized [$p(C)$] should be equivalent in strength to his or her belief that marijuana is harmless [$p(A)$], weighted by the conditional belief that marijuana should be legalized if it is harmless [$p(C/A)$], plus his or her belief that marijuana is not harmless [$p(A')$], weighted by the conditional belief that marijuana should be legalized even if it is not harmless [$p(C/A')$].

Reexamining the nuclear war example introduced earlier, the similarity between the Wyer (1970) and McGuire (1960a) models becomes evident. According to Wyer, a person's belief in the conclusion "At least half the earth's population will meet violent death within the next 10 years" (C) should be a function of his or her beliefs and conditional beliefs associated with the *minor premise,* "A major nuclear war will occur within the next 10 years" (A). In the McGuire model (Equation 1), belief in the *major premise,* "A major nuclear war would result in violent death to at least half the earth's population," is denoted $p(B)$. Because belief in this major premise is essentially the person's conditional belief that the conclusion C is true *if* the minor premise A is true, the $p(B)$ term in Equation 1 (McGuire model) is equivalent to the $p(C/A)$ term in Equation 2 (Wyer model). Finally, Wyer (Wyer, 1970; Wyer & Goldberg, 1970) has pointed out that the $p(K)$ term in the McGuire model—the belief that the conclusion is true on the basis of factors *other* than the conjunction of the two premises—can be denoted more precisely by the person's belief that the minor premise is *false* [i.e., $p(A')$], weighted by his or her conditional belief that the conclusion C is true *if* the minor premise A is not true [i.e., $p(C/A')$]. In summary, as both Wyer (Wyer, 1970; Wyer & Goldberg, 1970) and McGuire (1981) have agreed, Equation 1 (the McGuire formulation) is identical to Equation 2 (the Wyer formulation) when the Equation 1 terms $p(B)$ and $p(K)$ are assumed to be equivalent to $p(C/A)$ and $p(A')p(C/A')$, respectively.

1.   Empirical Evidence Supporting Probabilogical Model

When applied to interrelations among beliefs, considerable support for the McGuire–Wyer probabilogical model has been obtained. In relevant studies, subjects were presented with sets of belief propositions like the previous examples and then provided probability estimates for each term in Equation 2 [i.e., $p(C)$, $p(A)$, $p(A')$, $p(C/A)$, $p(C/A')$]. In such studies, predicted and observed values of $p(C)$ have generally shown a high degree of correspondence, although errors in predicting individual subjects' beliefs have typically been greater than errors based on grouped data (e.g., Wyer, 1970; Wyer & Goldberg, 1970). Analysis of variance tests have provided additional evidence that subjects' beliefs associated with the premises of a syllogism [i.e., $p(A)$, $p(A')$, $p(C/A)$, $p(C/A')$] combine functionally to affect their belief in its conclusion [$p(C)$] in the

manner prescribed by Equation 2. For example, Wyer (1975) presented information to subjects that manipulated their estimates of $p(A)$ and $p(C/A)$ (e.g.,
Persons usually versus sometimes versus rarely have gene x; Persons who have
gene x usually versus sometimes versus rarely have attribute X). The interaction
produced by these manipulations took the following form: subjects' judgments of
$p(C)$ (i.e., the probability that a particular person has attribute X) increased as
$p(C/A)$ increased but, in accord with the model, this increase was greater when
$p(A)$ was high, rather than low.

In addition to specifying how beliefs ought to be interrelated within the
individual's cognitive system, the probabilogical model also predicts how a
person's belief in some target proposition should change when beliefs associated
with a probabilistically related proposition undergo revision. According to
Wyer's (Wyer, 1970; Wyer & Goldberg, 1970; Wyer & Hartwick, 1980) formulation, changes in a person's belief in a conclusion C should be related to
changes in his or her beliefs associated with a related premise A in the following
manner:

$$\Delta p(C) = \Delta[p(A)p(C/A) + p(A')p(C/A')] \tag{3}$$

Research that has examined the effect of changing subjects' beliefs in the minor
premise of a syllogism [i.e., $p(A)$] on changes in their beliefs in its conclusion
[i.e., $p(C)$] has generally supported the utility of the probabilogical model for
understanding belief change. McGuire (1960a), Wyer (1970), and others (e.g.,
Dillehay, Insko, & Smith, 1966; Holt, 1970; Holt & Watts, 1969) have shown
that persuasive messages that successfully change subjects' beliefs in minor
premises do result in significant changes in their beliefs in logically related
conclusions, even though these conclusions are not, themselves, mentioned in
the persuasive messages that subjects receive. Moreover, as both the model and
popular wisdom would suggest, the *extent* to which subjects' beliefs in a conclusion change as a function of changes in their beliefs in a minor premise should
depend on the *relation* between the two propositions [i.e., $p(C/A)$ and $p(C/A')$,
the strength of the conditional beliefs that C is true if A is and is not true,
respectively]. In line with this expectation, Wyer (1970) found that a persuasive
communication that induced a change in subjects' beliefs in a minor premise A
(e.g., Governor Smith will be reelected) resulted in a large change in their belief
in an unmentioned conclusion C (e.g., state aid to education will be increased)
when a strong relation existed between the two propositions [e.g., $p(C/A)$ was
high and $p(C/A')$ was low], but resulted in little change in their beliefs in the
conclusion when only a weak relation existed between the conclusion and minor
premise [e.g., $p(C/A)$ and $p(C/A')$ were equivalent].

In addition to demonstrating that messages that change people's beliefs in
one proposition can lead to changes in related but unmentioned beliefs, research
stimulated by the probabilogical model also indicates that belief change can be

produced simply by asking people to express their beliefs in related issues (e.g., McGuire, 1960c; Henninger & Wyer, 1976; Watts & Holt, 1970; Wyer, 1974). McGuire (1960c) dubbed this phenomenon the "Socratic effect." For example, investigators have documented increased logical consistency among conditionally related beliefs from the first to a second administration of a questionnaire that solicits these beliefs (e.g., McGuire, 1960c; Henninger & Wyer, 1976). In these studies, logical consistency was defined in terms of the discrepancy between observed and predicted (on the basis of Equation 2) beliefs in some conclusion. McGuire (1960a, 1960c) originally postulated that the Socratic effect was due to a process of cognitive restructuring motivated by the desire to reduce logical inconsistencies among beliefs made salient as a result of reporting them on an initial belief questionnaire. Wyer and his colleagues (Henninger & Wyer, 1976; Wyer & Hartwick, 1980), however, have suggested that the reduction of inconsistency over repeated questionnaire administrations may be due to a relatively passive inference process in which a person's beliefs in a syllogism's premises are made salient during the first administration of a questionnaire and, consequently, are more likely to be used in evaluating one's belief in the conclusion during the second administration of the questionnaire. In support of this reasoning, Henninger and Wyer (1976) found a greater reduction in logical inconsistency over time when, during the first questionnaire administration, subjects' beliefs in the premises of syllogisms were assessed *after* (versus *before*) their beliefs in these syllogisms' conclusions. Moreover, when subjects indicated their beliefs in premises *before* (versus *after*) indicating their beliefs in conclusions, the level of logical inconsistency manifested during the first questionnaire administration was quite small, as predicted by the passive inference explanation.

2. Evaluation of the Probabilogical Model

The main contribution of the probabilogical model is the molecular analysis it provides of recipients' conditional inferences about premises and (mentioned or unmentioned) conclusions of messages and of the process by which these inferences combine to affect belief change. Its usefulness is limited to exploring the role that conditional inferences play in persuasion, and such inferences represent only one of a variety of inference processes (e.g., algebraic, Anderson, 1974; pseudological, Abelson & Rosenberg, 1958; configural, Abelson, 1976; attributional, Kelley, 1967) that have been postulated to underlie belief change and other social judgments. Another possible limitation is that research that has explored the utility of the model has focused heavily on subjects' inferences about *nonevaluative* propositions (e.g., whether marijuana *will* be legalized); and as Wyer and Hartwick (1980) have argued, when people are asked to make judgments about *evaluative* propositions (e.g., whether marijuana *should* be legalized), conditional inference processes (versus other combinatorial processes) may be less likely to occur. Thus, the probabilogical model may be more applicable to understanding the persuasive impact of messages designed to change particular beliefs than messages designed to influence more molar attitudes. Finally, in terms of its utility as a theory of persuasion, the most severe limitation of the probabilogical model is that it lacks an explicit account of how most distal persuasion variables (i.e., source, message, contextual variables) influence the subjective probabilities of the model. Thus, although the model helps explicate some of the psychological processes that may underlie persuasion, its lack of predictive power with respect to distal persuasion variables renders it inadequate as a general theory of persuasion.

Despite these limitations, the probabilogical model possesses a number of unique and important implications for persuasion. Among these is the consistently replicated finding that a persuasive message that induces a change in one belief can have a remote impact on other logically related beliefs, even though these latter beliefs are neither directly attacked nor mentioned in the persuasive message. Although there is evidence that messages are more persuasive if the communicator explicitly draws the conclusions for the audience rather than allows the audience to infer these (same) conclusions on the basis of their understanding of the messages' premises (e.g., Hovland *et al.*, 1949; Hovland & Mandell, 1952; McKeachie, 1954; Thistlethwaite, de Haan, & Kamenetzky, 1955), research stemming from the probabilogical model has demonstrated that messages that do not explicitly draw conclusions for recipients can, in fact, induce significant opinion changes.

Perhaps the most provocative implication of the model stems from research on the Socratic effect. This research shows that belief change in a target proposition can be induced merely by making salient logically related beliefs that have positive implications for the target belief. For example, in a study by Wyer and Henninger (Wyer & Henninger, 1978, reported in Wyer & Hartwick, 1980), subjects were asked to report their beliefs in premises that were constructed to have positive implications for logically related conclusions (i.e., the conclusion C was believed more likely to be true if the premise A was true rather than false). This study predicted and found that by making these premises salient to subjects in a first experimental session (by having them indicate their beliefs in these premises), subjects' beliefs in the conclusions associated with these premises became significantly more positive in the second session of the experiment. This research suggests that persuasive messages could bring about a desired change in some (mentioned or unmentioned) conclusion either by presenting individuals with *new* information with positive implications for the conclusion or by simply presenting assertions (again with positive implications for the conclusion) with which the individual already agrees. The latter technique is reminiscent of Rokeach's (1968) work showing that beliefs in target propositions (e.g., civil rights) can be changed simply by making salient for individuals their existing values (e.g., equality) that have positive implications for the target proposition.

The idea that persuasion may, in part, be a function of the information most salient to respondents at the time they indicate their opinion judgments suggests that any factor that enhances the salience of information may, consequently, affect persuasion. For example, Wyer and Hartwick (1980) have argued that persuasive argumentation that is processed more extensively should, subsequently, be easily retrieved and thus exert a greater impact on future opinion judgments than argumentation that is initially processed less extensively. Wyer and Henninger (Wyer & Henninger, 1978, cited in Wyer & Hartwick, 1980) obtained some counterintuitive findings consistent with this general argument. These researchers hypothesized that messages containing relatively implausible premises (e.g., Edward Kennedy is a good friend of Richard Nixon) with relatively weak or unclear implications for a target proposition (e.g., Edward Kennedy made illegal contributions to Nixon's campaign fund) would be more thought provoking and thus engender more cognitive activity on the part of the subjects than messages containing relatively plausible premises (e.g., vast oil resources lie under the frozen earth of Antarctica) with fairly strong implications for a target proposition (e.g., the settlement of Antarctica will be vastly accelerated in the next few years). Consistent with this hypothesis, subjects showed superior recall for premises and conclusions when the premises were implausible (versus plausible); moreover, this tendency was particularly evident when the implications of the premises for the conclusions were weak (versus strong). Most intriguing, this research found suggestive evidence that subjects increased their beliefs in conclusions to the extent that they had more extensively processed the premises and the premises' implications for conclusions; that is, more belief change occurred when subjects had initially been exposed to messages containing relatively implausible premises with weak implications for the conclusion rather than messages containing fairly plausible premises with strong implications for the conclusion. Although this somewhat surprising finding requires more extensive examination, the Wyer and Henninger (1978) study (cited in Wyer & Hartwick, 1980) does illustrate the kinds of hypotheses that could be tested, given the assumption that factors that influence the salience of persuasive information exert corresponding effects on opinion change (also see previous discussion on vividness and persuasion in the section "New Directions in Investigating Reception").

3. Probabilogical Model of Reception and Yielding

Before concluding this section, it is worth noting that Wyer (1974) has attempted a more molar application of his conditional inference model to persuasion. According to this version of the model, the probability that a recipient is influenced by a given persuasive message, $p(\mathrm{I})$, is given by the equation,

$$p(\mathrm{I}) = p(\mathrm{R})p(\mathrm{I/R}) + p(\mathrm{R'})p(\mathrm{I/R'}) \tag{4}$$

where $p(\mathrm{R})$ and $p(\mathrm{R'})$ [where $p(\mathrm{R'}) = 1 - p(\mathrm{R})$] are the probabilities of receiving and comprehending and not receiving and comprehending a message's arguments, and $p(\mathrm{I/R})$ and $p(\mathrm{I/R'})$ are the probabilities of being influenced, given that the individual does and does not receive a message's arguments, respectively. Wyer further assumes that $p(\mathrm{I/R}) = p(\mathrm{Y})$ where $p(\mathrm{Y})$ is the probability of yielding to the message given that it is received and that this probability can be estimated by the equation,

$$p(\mathrm{Y}) = p(\mathrm{CA})p(\mathrm{Y/CA}) + p(\mathrm{CA'})p(\mathrm{Y/CA'}) \tag{5}$$

where $p(\mathrm{CA})$ and $p(\mathrm{CA'})$ are the probabilities that persuasive argumentation is and is not refuted through counterarguing, and $p(\mathrm{Y/CA})$ and $p(\mathrm{Y/CA'})$ are the probabilities of yielding, given that the arguments are and are not refuted, respectively. Thus, Equation 4 becomes:

$$p(\mathrm{I}) = p(\mathrm{R}) \, (p(\mathrm{CA})p(\mathrm{Y/CA}) + p(\mathrm{CA'})p(\mathrm{Y/CA'})) + p(\mathrm{R'})p(\mathrm{I/R'}) \tag{6}$$

Equation 6 asserts that the probability that a persuasive message will change a recipient's opinion [i.e., $p(\mathrm{I})$] is a multiplicative function of (1) the probability that its arguments are comprehended [i.e., $p(\mathrm{R})$], (2) the probability that its arguments are counterargued [i.e., $p(\mathrm{CA})$], and (3) the degree to which yielding is contingent upon counterarguing message content [i.e., $p(\mathrm{Y/CA})$].

The astute reader will note that Equation 6 represents an extension of the McGuire (e.g., 1972) reception–yielding framework discussed earlier (see section "McGuire's Information-Processing Paradigm"). As in the McGuire model, Wyer's (1974) formulation suggests that situational and individual difference variables influence the impact of a persuasive message via their influence on one or more of the components of Equation 6. The primary differences between the two models are that (1) Wyer (1974) explicitly defines "reception" as the understanding of a message's persuasive arguments, (2) yielding in the Wyer formulation is explicitly tied to the degree to which recipients engage in effective counterarguing of message content and to the extent to which yielding is contingent upon the counterargumentation, and (3) the additional term in the Wyer formulation [$p(\mathrm{R'})p(\mathrm{I/R'})$], unlike the original McGuire model, explicitly recognizes the possibility that recipients' acceptance of a persuasive communication's conclusion may not be dependent upon their reception of message content. Although identical in most respects to the earlier McGuire model, the Wyer (1974) formulation does incorporate the possibility that recipients may often accept a message even though they have not attempted to assess the validity of its arguments [i.e., $p(Y/CA')$]. Thus Wyer's (1974) revised formulation of McGuire's information-processing framework is more amenable to theories of persuasion such as Chaiken's (1980, 1982) heuristic framework and Kelman's (1961) identification model, which assume that persuasion is not invariably the product of recipients' processing of persuasive argumentation.

B. EXPECTANCY–VALUE MODELS

Expectancy–value models provide a popular framework for describing how beliefs are combined to form attitudes. The central idea of these models is that an attitude (interpreted as the evaluation of an attitude object) is a function of the sum of the expected values of the attributes of the attitude object. The expectancy associated with an attribute is the subjective probability that the attitude object has the attribute, and the value of an attribute is the evaluation of it. For example, if a person believes that a new play is witty yet lacks character development, these attributes would be represented by the subjective probability that the play has each attribute (i.e., the high probability of wittiness and the low probability of character development), as well as by the evaluation of each attribute (i.e., the positive evaluations of wittiness and character development). To predict an attitude, the expectancy and value terms associated with each attribute are multiplied together, and these products are summed. Thus, expectancy–value models of attitudes are represented as follows:

$$\text{Attitude} = \Sigma \ (\text{Expectancy} \times \text{Value}) \tag{7}$$

In utilizing the expectancy–value principle, attitude theorists have built on a well-established tradition in psychology (see Feather, 1982). The principle has been central in several influential theories of motivation (e.g., Atkinson, 1958; Lewin, 1938; Tolman, 1958). Other well known applications include subjective expected utility models of decision making (e.g., Edwards, 1954) and Rotter's (1954) social learning theory. In the first published presentation of an expectancy–value theory of attitudes, Peak (1955) analyzed attitudes in terms very close to those of the expectancy–value theories of motivation that were influential in the 1950s. She defined *attitude* as the evaluation or affect associated with an attitude object and proposed that an attitude is determined by the individual's "attitude structure." Structure was formulated as the *instrumentality* of the attitude object for aiding or interfering with goal attainment and the *satisfaction* derived from attaining goals. Thus, attitude was assumed to be a function of the subjective probability that the attitude object leads to good or bad consequences and the intensity of the affect anticipated from these consequences.

This framework was explored empirically in experiments carried out by two of Peak's doctoral students, Rosenberg and Carlson. Rosenberg (1953, 1956) assessed the instrumentality of an attitude object (e.g., free speech for Communists) by having subjects judge the extent to which it would lead to or block the attainment of each of 35 goals (e.g., all human beings having equal rights, or people being well educated). Subjects also indicated the amount of satisfaction or dissatisfaction they would gain from reaching each goal. The subjective probability and satisfaction scores were then multiplied for each goal, and these products were summed according to the Expectancy × Value equation. These summed products were found to relate positively to a self-report evaluative measure of attitude. In Carlson's (1953, 1956) research, subjects listed their own reasons and listened to a communicator's reasons why an attitude object (abolishing housing segregation) would lead to the attainment of four relevant goals (e.g., maintaining property values). Among subjects not already extremely prejudiced or extremely unprejudiced, attitudes changed toward greater approval of desegregation, and attitude change related positively to change in the subjective probability that desegregation would lead to the four goals.

Following the cognitive consistency theme that dominated the study of attitudes in the late 1950s and the 1960s, Rosenberg (1960, 1968) then explored the implications of consistency between affect (directly measured attitudes) and beliefs defined in expectancy–value terms. The task of developing the expectancy–value approach as a more general framework for understanding attitudes was undertaken by Fishbein (1961, 1963, 1967), who proposed that attitudes are a function of beliefs about the attitude object (the subjective probability that the attitude object has each attribute) and the evaluative aspect of these beliefs (the evaluation of each attribute). This expectancy–value formulation is expressed algebraically as follows:

$$A_o = \sum_{i=1}^{n} b_i e_i \tag{8}$$

where A_o is the attitude toward the object, action, or event o; b_i is the belief i about o (expressed as the subjective probability that o has attribute i); e_i is the evaluation of attribute i; and n is the number of salient attributes. In his early work on this expectancy–value model, Fishbein (1961, 1963) showed that attitudes, as directly measured by evaluative semantic differential items, were highly correlated with their summed expectancy–value products, presumably because attitudes derive from beliefs about attitude objects.

Fishbein (1967) also proposed an expectancy–value equation for predicting behavior that is under volitional control. Building on a theory that Dulany (1961, 1968) proposed to explain the role of awareness in verbal conditioning, Fishbein suggested that behavior is a function of one's intention to engage in the behavior, which is, in turn, a function of the expected consequences of the behavior. In this particular version of the Expectancy × Value equation, consequences are divided into two classes—personal consequences and social consequences in terms of approval or disapproval from significant others (called "referents"). This expectancy–value equation can be expressed algebraically as follows:

$$B \sim BI = \left[\sum_{i=1}^{n} b_i e_i \right] w_1 + \left[\sum_{i=1}^{r} b_j m_j \right] w_2 \qquad (9)$$

where b_i is the "behavioral belief" that performing behavior leads to some consequence i (subjective probability that behavior has the consequence i); e_i is the evaluation of consequence i; n is the number of salient consequences; b_j is the "normative belief" that performing behavior leads to approval or disapproval from some referent j (subjective probability that behavior leads to approval or disapproval from j); m_j is the motivation to comply with referent j; r is the number of relevant referents; and w_1 and w_2 are the empirical weights indicating relative importance of first and second terms. Fishbein defined the first term on the right-hand side of the equation as forming an attitude toward the behavioral act (A_B) and the second term as forming a subjective norm (SN).

It should be recognized that Equation 9 is a variant of the familiar expectancy–value formulation. The first term on the right (A_B) matches Equation 8 if it is assumed that consequences are the salient attributes of an attitude object that is a behavior. As Fishbein and Ajzen (1975) have acknowledged, the second term in the equation (SN) can be considered as one particular instance of the first term A_B because (1) consequences of approval and disapproval are but one class of consequences that individuals may believe are contingent on performing behaviors and (2) motivation to comply specifies the affective value of a referent's approval or disapproval. From this perspective, the second term SN can be considered as an additional determinant of attitude toward the behavior, which in a situation free of anticipated external barriers would be synonymous with intention to perform a behavior. With these assumptions, Equation 9 reduces to Equation 8, the simple Expectancy × Value formulation. Substantiating this interpretation are findings that measures of behavioral intentions are very highly correlated with direct measures of attitudes toward behaviors (e.g., Davidson & Jaccard, 1975; Loken & Fishbein, 1980). Nevertheless, Fishbein has preferred to maintain separate "attitudinal" and "normative" terms for predicting behavioral intentions, and this equation has provided a framework for considerable empirical work on the relation between attitudes and behavior. In general, intentions to engage in volitional acts are highly correlated with the expectancy–value products calculated from the equation, and behavioral intentions are moderately correlated with overt behaviors (Ajzen & Fishbein, 1973, 1977, 1980).

1. The Expectancy-Value Principle as a Theory of Persuasion

Fishbein and Ajzen have developed a number of the implications that the Expectancy × Value framework has for persuasion (Ajzen & Fishbein, 1980; Fishbein & Ajzen, 1975, 1981). According to the model, in order to change an attitude or an intention in a favorable direction, the summed expectancy–value products must become more positive than the summed products prior to the influence attempt (and similarly, change in an unfavorable direction is produced by negative change in these summed products). In other words, to change an attitude or intention, the beliefs underlying the attitude or intention (the so-called *primary beliefs*) must be changed correspondingly. According to the model, these changes in beliefs occur in either the subjective probabilities of the attributes or consequences (b_i) or the evaluations of these attributes or consequences (e_i). In research by Carlson (1953, 1956) and McArdle (1972; Fishbein, Ajzen, & McArdle, 1980), communications relevant to attitude objects have been shown to change message-recipients' beliefs about the attitude objects and to have corresponding effects on their overall attitudes. Further investigations have demonstrated that exposure to advertisements brings about changes in beliefs about products and product use and corresponding changes in attitudes toward using or purchasing products (Lutz, 1975, 1977; Mitchell & Olson, 1981; Pomazal, 1983). Less research has addressed changing attitudes through changing evaluations of attributes or consequences. Further, those few messages that have been designed explicitly to change attribute evaluations have had relatively little effect on these evaluations and little corresponding effect on overall attitudes toward the attitude object (Lutz, 1975), perhaps because evaluations of attributes are often well anchored in extensive prior learning.

Fishbein and Ajzen (1975) have emphasized that an individual's attitude or intention is a function of the beliefs that are salient at the point in time when the attitude or the intention is assessed. Therefore, a change in an attitude or an intention could occur through changing the beliefs that were already salient for message recipients prior to receiving the message or by making beliefs salient that were not previously salient. Although Ajzen and Fishbein (1980) have recommended that persuasion researchers use detailed pretesting to determine the salient beliefs that message recipients hold concerning the target attitude object, such pretesting does not solve the problem of whether communicators should attempt to change already salient beliefs or to introduce new beliefs in hope that these will become salient. Yet such pretesting would help persuaders to avoid including arguments that merely reiterate recipients' preexisting beliefs. With argumentation tailored to the underlying beliefs of the members of the target audience, communications designed to change target attitudes or intentions could probably be written more efficiently. Nevertheless, if a communication designed with or without the benefits of such pretesting is effective in changing attitudes or intentions, change in underlying beliefs has taken place, according to the assumptions of the expectancy–value model.

Ajzen and Fishbein (Ajzen & Fishbein, 1980; Fishbein & Ajzen, 1981) have also pointed out that the arguments contained in a message are more likely to be persuasive if they are carefully tailored to whether the persuader's goal is changing an attitude, a belief, or a behavior. For example, if the goal is changing an attitude, the expectancy–value principle implies that the communication should address the salient attributes of the attitude object. If, however, the goal is changing a behavior, the communication should address the consequences of the behavior, in an effort to change the behavioral intention that presumably controls the behavior. Of course, consistent with the process theories already reviewed, messages containing appropriately tailored arguments may nevertheless be ineffective in producing desired changes because other persuasion cues (e.g., low communicator credibility or negative audience reactions) induce resistance to persuasion.

2. Evaluation of Expectancy–Value Models

Although the Expectancy × Value approach has important implications for choosing arguments to include in messages, the framework has a narrow scope as a theory of persuasion. One limitation of the approach is that it pertains only to the change of attitudes (evaluations of attitude objects) and behavioral intentions. The model has no implications for change of specific beliefs. Fishbein and Ajzen (Fishbein & Ajzen, 1981; Ajzen & Fishbein, 1980) have recommended that the McGuire–Wyer probabilogical approach and other formal probability models be applied to the problem of predicting change of beliefs, yet they have also agreed with our position that such models describe only one of the possible types of inferences that may account for belief change.

The other principal limitation of the model is that it provides no mechanism for predicting the effects of persuasion variables other than those message–content variables that can be directly coordinated to the terms of the expectancy–value equation (i.e., subjective probabilities of attributes or consequences, and the evaluations of these attributes or consequences). Not only does the model have no explicit way to predict the effects of source, recipient, and contextual variables, but also it has few implications for predicting the effects of molar message–content variables such as order of presentation. Fishbein and Ajzen (1981) have suggested that such variables be treated as variables "external" to the terms of the Expectancy × Value equation and have argued that these variables have impact on the target attitude or intention only to the extent that they change the expectancies or values associated with the primary beliefs underlying the attitude or intention. Although this proposition has yet to be tested extensively by structural equation and other regression procedures (Kenny, 1979) that allow an examination of the causal ordering of variables, there is some evidence that effects of messages on attitudes are not always mediated by changes in beliefs as defined by summed expectancy–value products (e.g., Mitchell & Olson, 1981). Further, it is consistent with the heuristic model and the attribution approaches (reviewed earlier) to expect that some persuasion cues have direct impact on target attitudes or intentions without mediation by the processing of argumentation or the retrieval of the attributes of the attitude object. Even in the case of variables whose impact is mediated by their effects on underlying beliefs, Fishbein and Ajzen's "external variable" perspective merely allows investigators to *track* the effects of such cues but does not suggest novel predictions about them. Linkages to other theories or to known persuasion findings are required to predict the effects of persuasion cues that affect attitudes and intentions through impact on the beliefs that are the terms of the expectancy–value equation.

Finally, another application of the expectancy–value principle to persuasion should be noted—Rogers's (1975) "protection motivation" theory of fear appeals. Rogers proposed that the important aspects of a fear appeal are the evaluation of the danger portrayed in the message (the perceived noxiousness of the danger) as well as two variables that determine whether the recommended behavior lessens the probability of the danger: (1) the subjective probability that the dangerous event will occur if no adaptive behavior is performed, and (2) the perceived efficacy of the recommended coping responses in averting the danger. Relevant research (e.g., Hass, Bagley, & Rogers, 1975; Rogers & Mewborn, 1976) has failed to support the detailed predictions of the expectancy–value equation but has shown that the variables proposed by Rogers are important determinants of the acceptance of fear appeals. As in the case of other applications of expectancy–value theory to persuasion, the Rogers work contributes to our understanding of persuasion by providing useful guidance concerning the types of arguments that should be included in persuasive appeals designed to change attitudes or behavioral intentions.

C. INFORMATION-INTEGRATION THEORY

The most general theory for describing the process by which stimuli are combined to form an attitude or a belief is Anderson's information-integration theory (e.g., 1971, 1981a, 1981b). According to this theory, attitudes or beliefs are formed and modified as people receive and interpret information and then integrate it with their prior attitudes or beliefs.

The two basic operations of information integration are the *valuation* of the incoming information and its *integration* into the current attitude or belief. Valuation is the determination of the meaning of the information and its relevance for the judgment-at-hand. This valuation operation is represented in information-integration theory in terms of the determination of two components—the *scale value* and the *weight* of information. The scale value of information is its location on the relevant dimension of judgment, and its weight is its importance or psychological impact in relation to the individual's judgment. For example, the scale value of a persuasive message on the topic of the nuclear test ban is its location on a pro versus con scale of favorability toward the ban. The weight of the message is its importance as a determinant of the individual's opinion on the issue.

Integration refers to the process of combining items of information. The central assumption of the theory is that integration can be described in terms of simple algebraic models. For example, if a person receives n items of information, and the scale value of stimulus i is represented by s_i and its weight by w_i, the response to the total set could be described by the following model:

$$R = w_0 s_0 + w_1 s_1 + w_2 s_2 + \ldots + w_n s_n \tag{10}$$

In this equation w_0 and s_0 are the weight and the scale value of the person's initial attitude. This equation specifies an adding model. To transform this model to an averaging model, the additional requirement is made that the weights sum to one. The averaging model is also frequently written in the following form:

$$R = (w_0 s_0 + \sum_{i=1}^{n} w_i s_i)/(w_0 + \sum_{i=1}^{n} w_i) \tag{11}$$

The breadth of the information-integration approach stems from its inclusion of a variety of specific integration rules as plausible combinatorial models. Yet the integration rule that has proven to have the widest applicability is averaging, and most critical tests of averaging versus adding rules have favored averaging (e.g., Anderson, 1965; Anderson, 1968; Gollob & Lugg, 1973; Hamilton & Huffman, 1971; Hendrick, 1968; Himmelfarb, 1973). Subtracting models appear to be appropriate for some judgmental problems, such as determining the degree of preference for one object over another (Shanteau & Anderson, 1969). A multiplying rule is appropriate for still other judgmental problems, such as the determination of subjective-expected value (i.e., evaluation) from subjective probability and subjective value (e.g., Anderson & Shanteau, 1970), which we have discussed in relation to expectancy–value models. Of course, a multiplying rule (Weight × Scale Value) is a component of the averaging rule itself.

The flexibility of information-integration theory with respect to the specific integration rule that is posited sets it apart from most competing theories that have been applied to attitude change. For example, as noted earlier, Fishbein and Ajzen (e.g., 1975) proposed a single rule—an Expectancy × Value adding equation; and earlier Osgood and Tannenbaum (1955) proposed a quantitative cognitive-consistency model of persuasion, which consisted of a weighted-averaging equation in which the weight of each item of information increases as its scale value becomes more polarized. Numerous other rules have been suggested by investigators for specific problems of stimulus combination (see Anderson, 1981a).

In empirical applications of information-integration theory, weights and scale values are coordinated with various aspects of the stimulus information and the judgment task. As already noted, the scale value of a persuasive message is the position the communicator advocates on the issue, and the weight or the importance of the message would be identified with other parameters of the persuasion situation, such as the credibility of the communicator. The recipient's initial opinion can be represented in terms of its scale value and its weight. The scale value of the initial opinion is its location on the scale of favorability toward the attitude object, and the weight of the initial opinion would typically be identified with recipient factors such as degree of involvement with the issue.

With an appropriate experimental design varying the position advocated in messages and/or other persuasion parameters, it is possible simultaneously to test the adequacy of one or more stimulus combination models as descriptions of persuasion, test various hypotheses about weights and/or scale values, and also obtain an interval scaling of weights and/or scale values. Neither the scale values nor the weights of the information that is integrated need be known a priori because measurement is an integral part and by-product of the subject's responses. Anderson (e.g., 1970, 1976, 1981a) has termed these scaling procedures *functional measurement*.

A simple application of the theory to persuasion is illustrated by an experiment on attitudes toward United States' presidents (Anderson, 1973). In this experiment, subjects read biographical paragraphs about the lives and deeds of various presidents and judged the presidents on their statesmanship. The sets of paragraphs presented to subjects on each president varied according to the 2 × 3 design represented in Fig. 1. The two rows of the design represent positive or negative paragraphs, and the three columns represent positive, neutral, or negative paragraphs. As shown by the data points plotted in the figure, subjects judged statesmanship by averaging the information in the paragraphs that were presented. The adequacy of the averaging model to account for the data is documented by the parallelism of the two curves. In general, if data exhibit parallelism, an averaging or adding model is adequate to describe the findings.[7]

The very general terms in which integration theory is formulated allow it to

---

[7]However, nonparallelism does not necessarily invalidate such models (see Anderson, 1981a, p. 112; Himmelfarb & Anderson, 1975). It should also be noted that, although parallelism has been taken to support an adding or averaging model, Birnbaum (1982) has pointed out that parallelism is consistent with other, more complex models as well.

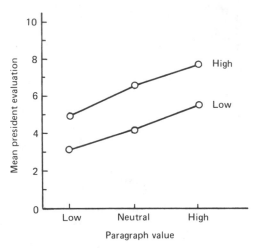

Fig. 1.   Mean judgment of general statesmanship for presidents. (From Anderson, 1973, p. 5). Copyright 1973 by the American Psychological Association. Reprinted/Adapted by permission of the author.

be applied very flexibly in areas of psychology, ranging from psychophysics to clinical judgment, impression formation, group dynamics, and persuasion (Anderson, 1981a, 1982). This flexibility stems in part from the freedom that investigators have to apply the model at differing levels of analysis. Thus, the units of information that are integrated may be relatively molar (e.g., entire communications) or relatively molecular (e.g., single words). In a persuasion paradigm, there are several possibilities for defining the units that are integrated in forming a new opinion. The relevant units may be entire communications, arguments within communications, or even sentences or words. Although the theory provides no explicit guidance concerning the most appropriate level of analysis for persuasion (or other) settings, the units that are integrated are assumed to be defined at a level that is meaningful in relation to the judgment being made (e.g., statesmanship) and the type of stimuli that are presented (e.g., descriptive paragraphs).

1.   Predictions from the Averaging Model

There are numerous specific attitude-change predictions inherent in the averaging model, which is the stimulus combination rule most commonly applied to persuasion. Most obviously, the model predicts that the attitude of an individual who is exposed to messages advocating divergent viewpoints is a composite or average of the various messages. This prediction seems to be generally accurate (e.g., Anderson, 1973). Further, when messages advocating differing positions are arranged in a factorial design, the parallelism prediction is made (provided that the messages in a row or column of the design are weighted equally). Although parallelism has been obtained in experiments on impression formation (e.g., Anderson, 1962) and persuasion (e.g., Anderson, 1973), many investigators have obtained findings that deviate from parallelism (e.g., Birnbaum, 1979).

The model also makes an exact prediction concerning the consequences of exposure to multiple messages that advocate the same position. This prediction is based on the inclusion of the individual's prior attitude position in the averaging equation. The equation then makes the prediction, known as the "set-size effect," that adding information of equal value creates a more extreme attitude, although at a decreasing rate as more items of information are added. Following Anderson (1981b), a demonstration of the ability of the averaging model to predict a set-size effect is readily accomplished if we assume that the initial attitude has a scale value of 50 (the neutral point) on a 0 to 100 scale and a weight of 1. If every piece of information has a scale value of 100 and a weight of 1, the response to a set of k pieces of information is the following, according to the averaging equation given earlier:

$$R = (50 + 100 \ k)/(1 + k) \tag{12}$$

It can easily be calculated that R takes on the values 50, 75, 83.3, 87.5, . . . , for 0, 1, 2, 3, . . . items of information and approaches 100 as an asymptote. This weighted-averaging explanation for the set-size effect is in accord with empirical tests (e.g., Anderson, 1965, 1967; Sloan & Ostrom, 1974). Although the original impetus for adding the initial attitude (or impression) term to the averaging model may have been that it would enable the model to account for the set-size effect (Anderson, 1965), subsequent research by Kaplan (e.g., 1971a, 1973) has systematically explored the concept of initial attitude and documented several of its implications for information integration. For example, Kaplan (1971a, 1971b, 1972) demonstrated that, consistent with the averaging model, initial attitudes have less impact on final attitudes as the amount of information from external sources increases.

Other interesting predictions are inherent in the averaging property by which the weights in the equation sum to one. One simple illustration of the implications of this property can be given for a situation in which the communication and the recipient's prior attitude are integrated, and the weight of the message is coordinated to source credibility, and the weight of the initial opinion to the recipient's involvement in the topic of the communication. Because of the averaging property in which the weights must sum to one, the lower weight for the initial opinion under low involvement implies a higher weight for the message and hence a more pronounced source-credibility effect. The predicted finding that source credibility has more impact under low than high involvement is common in the persuasion literature (e.g., Chaiken, 1980; Johnson & Scileppi, 1969; Petty, Cacioppo, & Goldman, 1981). Numerous other predictions of interactions between variables that are coordinated to weights on differing items of information would also follow from the weighted-averaging model. In particular, the model predicts interactions between recipient variables and communicator or message variables because the recipient's prior attitude and the message are represented as two items of information that are integrated.

One of the additional advantages of the information-integration approach is that it provides rigorous methods of distinguishing between various combinatorial models. In other tests of such models (e.g., Jaccard & Fishbein, 1975), investigators have relied on correlations between observed attitudes and those predicted by various equations, or they have merely examined scatterplots of predicted versus obtained values. As numerous investigators have shown (e.g., Anderson, 1971, 1982; Birnbaum, 1973; Slovic & Lichtenstein, 1971), models seriously in error can yield very high correlations between predicted and obtained values as well as scatterplots in which the points fall close to the diagonal line of perfect fit. Anderson (e.g., 1962, 1965) pioneered the use of more exact analysis-of-variance tests of models. The parallelism prediction, for example, is tested by analysis of variance: The absence of a statistically significant interaction in an appropriate design indicates parallelism.

2.   Relation of Information-Integration Theory to Process Theories of Persuasion

Process theories of persuasion can be related to information-integration theory in terms of Anderson's (1981a) valuation process—the determination of the weight and the scale value of information. That is, the processes postulated by other theories could be seen to affect attitude change through their impact on the weight or the scale value of the information. Although shifts in scale value may occur under some circumstances, Anderson has assumed that the scale value of information is ordinarily constant. Therefore, if the impact of an item of information varies from one situation to another, it is usually assumed to occur through changes in the weight of the information (see Himmelfarb, 1975).

Although information-integration theory does not include a formal theory of weighting, Anderson (1981a) suggested that there are four main determinants of the weight parameter: (a) relevance, defined as the implicational relation between the stimulus information and the dimension of judgment, (b) salience, defined in terms of attentional factors, (c) reliability, defined as the subjective probability that the information is valid, and (d) quantity, defined as amount of information. Empirical work by Anderson and his colleagues, most notably research on order effects on persuasion (Anderson & Farkas, 1973) and impression formation (e.g., Anderson, 1968; Hendrick & Costantini, 1970), lends credibility to some of these proposed determinants of weights. For example, primacy effects may reflect attentional decrements over a series of stimuli, which cause later items in a series of stimuli to be weighted less heavily (see Anderson, 1981a).

Process theories of persuasion can provide additional insights into the determinants of weighting. For example, the reception processes emphasized by McGuire (1968a) are included in the salience determinant of weighting. The attribution and the heuristic analyses of persuasion provide a theory of the inferences underlying the reliability aspect of weights. The cognitive elaboration emphasized in the cognitive response framework could be interpreted as one process underlying the quantity aspect of weights. There are, then, numerous possibillties for joining information-integration theory to process theories of persuasion. The advantages of such linkages are twofold: (1) From the perspective of information-integration theory, additional ability is gained to identify the determinants of weights. (2) From the perspective of the process theories, a mathematical description is gained of the impact of process-relevant cues, including the simultaneous impact of several such cues.

The use of information-integration techniques to test the predictions of process models and to provide a systematic description of the effects of processes is illustrated by Himmelfarb's attributional research (1972; Himmelfarb & Anderson, 1975). Himmelfarb (1972) examined the persuasiveness of trait descriptions made by single or multiple sources, who had observed a person behave in one situation, in several similar situations, or in several dissimilar situations. As noted earlier, attribution predictions for this experiment were based on the consensus principle (greater persuasiveness for multiple versus single sources) and the consistency principle (greater persuasiveness for information gathered in multiple versus single situations, especially if these situations are dissimilar). These predictions were upheld, and the data proved to be consistent with the information-integration assumption that multiple sources and multiple situations both produced increased weighting of the target trait descriptions.

In Himmelfarb and Anderson's (1975) research, subjects inferred the true opinions of writers who had made statements under varying degrees of constraint. Although attribution researchers have established that statements made under constraint are less informative about a person's true opinion than statements made under no constraint (e.g., Jones & Harris, 1967; Jones et al., 1971), they had not dealt with the more complex issue of opinion inferences based on observations of multiple statements that were made on multiple occasions under varying constraints. To deal with this complex type of multiple-cue prediction, the methods of information-integration theory are a decided asset. In the Himmelfarb and Anderson (1975) experiments, several predictions of the averaging model were confirmed, including the attribution predictions that (1) perceived freedom of choice affects the weights that were attached to statements used to infer a writer's opinion and (2) such weights reflect both the discounting and augmentation principles.

The effects of communicator characteristics on the persuasiveness of messages have also been of interest within the information-integration framework. At one level, the predictions of information-integration theory for source effects are quite simple. Communicators with evaluatively positive attributes are assumed to be more persuasive than communicators with less positive attributes, and communicator variables are usually assumed to affect persuasion through their effect on the weight parameter. Consequently, source variables (e.g., communicator credibility), interpreted as weights, would multiply the scale value of the message. This assumption that source variables typically influence the weight parameter has specific quantitative implications within designs in which communicators of differing credibility advocate differing positions.

To illustrate the implications of these assumptions for source credibility effects, it is helpful to examine research by Birnbaum, Wong, and Wong (1976). In one of their studies, hypothetical persons were described by two acquaintances, each of whom contributed one trait description conveying high, medium, or low likableness. Communicator credibility was manipulated by specifying how long the acquaintance had known the person: one meeting, 3 months, or 3 years. The information-integration assumption that source credibility affects the weight of the message implies that factorial combinations of the position advocated and of source credibility plot as a linear fan—that is, more extreme judgments will be obtained for information provided by more credible sources. As shown in Fig. 2, this linear fan prediction was substantiated by Birnbaum, Wong, and Wong (1976). This outcome supports the multiplying rule derived from the averaging model.

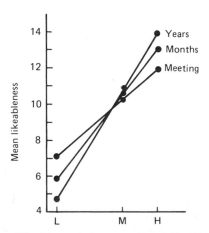

Fig. 2.   Mean rating of likeableness for source–adjective combinations, plotted as a function of adjective value (L = low, M = medium, H = high value) with a separate curve for each source (the source has known the target person for either one meeting, 3 months, or 3 years). (From Birnbaum, Wong, & Wong, 1976.)

Birnbaum and Stegner (1979) provided a more complex application of information-integration principles to the prediction of source effects. In this research, the simultaneous effects of three variables were studied: communicator expertise, communicator bias, and the respondent's point of view (i.e., as a buyer or seller). Respondents estimated the monetary value of used cars, given their "blue book" value and the value estimated by a communicator. The communicator's expertise was manipulated by ascribing either a low, medium, or high level of automotive expertise to him, and his bias was manipulated by describing him as either a friend of the buyer, a friend of the seller, or an independent individual with no relationship to the buyer or seller. In addition, subjects were instructed to adopt the point of view of either the buyer, the seller, or an independent person.

Although the individual effects of these variables are understandable in terms of prior research and other theories, evaluation of the simultaneous effects of such variables is extremely difficult. Thus, classic persuasion research (e.g., Hovland *et al.*, 1953) established that persuasiveness generally increases with communicator expertise, yet it is not clear how expertise might interact with the other two independent variables. Similarly, the communicator's bias has been examined within an attribution framework (e.g., Eagly, Chaiken, & Wood, 1981), but it is not clear how this variable would interact with the other two variables. Although information-intergration theory does not provide a priori predictions of the effects of combining such cues, it does provide a technology suitable for evaluating various models that describe how such cues simultaneously affect respondents' judgments (see Anderson, 1982).

Birnbaum and Stegner (1979) examined the fit of several models to their data. In general, the averaging model was adequate, and the effects of bias, expertise, and the respondent's point of view were accounted for by effects on both weight and scale value. Expertise affected weighting, whereas the communicator-bias manipulation had its primary effect on the scale value of messages: Scale values were adjusted up or down by roughly $30 according to whether the source was a buyer's friend or a seller's friend. The respondent's point of view also affected the scale value, together with a complex configural-weighting effect (by which the relative weight of the estimates of the car's value changed across points of view).

3. *Evaluation of Information-Integration Theory*

In general, the potential of information-integration techniques within persuasion research is considerable. Certain predictions are inherent in particular combinatorial models—for example, the parallelism prediction, the set-size effect, and Credibility × Involvement and other interactions follow from the averaging model. More importantly, the approach provides a means of assessing the relative contribution or influence of various parameters of the persuasion situation. The limitations of the theory for predicting persuasion stem from the absence of a general theory of weighting as well as the absence of a theory of the conditions under which one rather than another stimulus combination rule is utilized. Yet, with links to frameworks such as attribution theory that do deal systematically with the determinants of weights, predictions can be made with respect to the effects of various persuasion variables. The technology associated with information-integration theory provides powerful methods of testing these predictions and of determining the integration model underlying the effects that are obtained.

D. EVALUATION OF COMBINATORIAL THEORIES

Although the three combinatorial models we have discussed are considerably broader than their applications to persuasion, explaining how the change of attitudes and beliefs is accomplished by persuasive communications is a central problem to which all of these approaches have been applied. Despite this common focus on persuasion, the scope of the three models varies considerably. The probabilogical model has been directed to the problem of predicting change in target beliefs that are induced by changing or by making salient other probabilistically related beliefs. As we have noted, this model may be less appropriate for predicting change in molar attitudes. In contrast, the expectancy–value model is directed specifically to predicting change in molar attitudes, as well as change in behavioral intentions.

In contrast to the more limited emphases of the probabilogical and expectancy–value models, information-integration theory claims as its domain all classes of judgments or inferences. The generality of the approach is both a strength and a weakness. One strength (and the primary reason for the breadth of the approach) is that it encompasses a wide range of algebraic integration rules. Further, the weights and the scale values utilized in these equations can be coordinated to various aspects of incoming stimuli and preexisting cognitions of perceivers. Given that each of the integration rules can be applied at both molar or molecular levels to aspects of persuasion settings, it seems that most persuasion phenomena could potentially be described by some form of "cognitive algebra." Yet this extreme generality is also a weakness in the absence of explicit theory concerning which stimulus-combination rule is appropriate under what conditions or which aspects of the persuasion situation should be coordinated to weights and scale values. As illustrated by Birnbaum and Stegner's (1979) research on source characteristics, investigators studying persuasion within the information-integration framework must select, from among numerous possibilities, an appropriate combinatorial rule to accommodate the effects of variables such as communicator credibility.

It is possible to consider the expectancy–value model as one member of the family of stimulus-combination rules inherent in information-integration theory. In information-integration terms, the weights of the expectancy–value equation are the expectancies or subjective probabilities attached to attributes (or consequences) of the attitude object, and the scale values are simply the values or affect attached to the attributes (or consequences). It is less clear that the probabilogical model can be encompassed within the information-integration framework. Probabilistic models provide a fundamentally different account of combinatorial processes than do algebraic models because the content of beliefs is not represented by a scale value. Rather, beliefs are represented only in terms of their subjective probabilities and not in terms of their scale values on other dimensions of meaning (e.g., evaluation). Beliefs influence judgments, not through an aggregation of their semantic content (i.e., weighted scale-values), but through the aggregation of probabilistically related beliefs, as specified by the mathematical laws of probability (e.g., Equation 2).

The combinatorial models share the problem of providing no explicit account of the effects of distal persuasion variables (e.g., source, context, recipient) on belief and attitude change. Such variables would presumably have their impact on attitudes and beliefs through effects on the terms of each model: (1) in the probabilogical model, through the subjective probabilities that determine belief change, (2) in the expectancy–value model, through the expectancies and perceived values associated with attributes or consequences, and (3) in information-integration theory, through the weights (and occasionally the scale values) of the terms of the particular combinatorial rule utilized. Yet, as we have explained in relation to each theory, this assumption of mediation via the terms of each model yields relatively few a priori predictions about the effects of most persuasion variables. Nevertheless, the models can be used descriptively to track the effects of many persuasion variables. Along these lines, Fishbein and Ajzen (Ajzen & Fishbein, 1980; Fishbein & Ajzen, 1981), as we have noted, claimed that variables that are external to the terms of the expectancy–value equation affect persuasion *only* through their impact on these terms (i.e., through effects on primary beliefs). Yet for the purpose of providing post hoc descriptions of the impact of persuasion variables, information-integration theory, with its variety of specific models and its methodology based on functional measurement and analysis-of-variance tests of these models, probably provides a more powerful technology for generating a mathematical description of the effects of persuasion variables.

IV. Other Motivational Bases of Persuasion

The cognitive theories of persuasion reviewed in this chapter do not provide a detailed account of the motivations of people who are exposed to persuasive communications. Message recipients are assumed to engage in one or another kind of information processing, yet the motivations underlying this processing for the most part remain unelaborated in the theories. To the extent that there is an assumption about motivation in these theories, this assumption might be broadly characterized by the statement that message recipients process information in a relatively unbiased manner in order to attain valid opinions that are in line with the relevant facts. This assumption is most explicit in applications of attribution theory to persuasion (e.g., Eagly, Chaiken, & Wood, 1981), in which message recipients are assumed to screen available information to determine whether an entity (or stimulus) attribution is plausible for the message, as opposed to a person or situation attribution. Because an entity attribution accounts for message content in terms of "external reality," the assumption that recipients desire to hold accurate opinions is inherent in the theory. This assumption is also explicit in the heuristic model, which asserts that people often judge message validity on the basis of simple decision rules. In the cognitive response framework (e.g., Cacioppo, Harkins, & Petty, 1981), motivational assumptions are more difficult to discern, except perhaps for a motive to actively process and elaborate the information given in messages rather than passively receive it. In McGuire's (e.g., 1972) information-processing framework, any motivational assumptions are also left unstated, yet a concern with achieving valid opinions seems implicit in the theory's emphasis on the reception of and yielding to message content.

The combinatorial theories we have reviewed share the assumption that message recipients are motivated to follow rational or systematic rules in combining information. This rule-following quality of information processing is implied by the assumption that people take the available items of information into account in forming an overall evaluation or impression. The rationality of stimulus-combination processes is relatively explicit in Fishbein and Ajzen's approach, which they recently have labeled a theory of *reasoned* action (Ajzen & Fishbein, 1980; Fishbein, 1980). In the McGuire–Wyer probabilogical model (e.g., Wyer, 1974), a type of rationality would seem inherent in the assumption that people follow mathematical laws of probability in combining information.[8] Finally, in at least most of its applications, Anderson's (e.g., 1981a) cognitive algebra formulation seems to imply the rationality of stimulus-combination processes, although Anderson (1978, 1981a, 1982) has acknowledged that various motivational orientations could impact on the valuation aspect of the model as determinants of weights and/or scale values.

---

[8]It should be noted, however, that McGuire's (1960a, 1981) research, but not Wyer's, incorporated the extralogical postulate of "hedonic consistency," in addition to the logical consistency postulate emphasized in the probabilogical model. This postulate recognizes that wishful thinking, in addition to more rational thinking, may often affect belief formation and change.

This contemporary focus on information processing and on maximizing the validity of one's opinions implies an openness to information that contrasts sharply with views once popular in the attitude change area. For example, in earlier accounts of attitude change, stemming from theories such as cognitive dissonance (e.g., Festinger, 1957), reactance (e.g., Brehm, 1966), and social judgment (e.g., Sherif & Hovland, 1961), people were thought to be motivated to defend their attitudes and beliefs from the implications of information that might disturb existing cognitions to which they were importantly committed. In addition, some earlier attitude theories featured explicit attempts to delineate the range of motivations that may guide people's reactions to persuasive messages. The most general of these functional approaches was proposed by Katz (Katz, 1960; Katz & Stotland, 1959), who defined four motivational bases of attitudes. Message recipients were assumed to be motivated to (1) gain reward and minimize punishment (instrumental or utilitarian function), (2) maintain a stable, organized, and valid representation of the world (knowledge function), (3) protect themselves from facing threats from the external world or their own unacceptable impulses (ego-defensive function), or (4) express their values or enhance their self-identity (value-expressive function). In terms of Katz's typology of motives, contemporary information-processing theories of persuasion might be thought to elaborate only the knowledge function of attitudes and beliefs.

Because of the relative neglect of motivational issues in contemporary cognitive theories of persuasion, this section briefly reviews aspects of some theoretical perspectives that provide important insights into motivational issues—insights that are generally absent from the information-processing theories emphasized in this chapter. We suspect that the motivational concerns highlighted in these other viewpoints will be increasingly recognized as important issues for persuasion research and theory, as investigators begin to realize that an overemphasis on cognition limits the range of persuasion phenomena that can be explained.

A. RESTORATION OF THREATENED FREEDOMS

Brehm's theory of psychological reactance (Brehm, 1966, 1968, 1972; Brehm & Brehm, 1981) asserts that when individuals perceive their freedom to engage (or not engage) in some behavior as threatened or eliminated, they experience "reactance," a state of motivational arousal that leads them to attempt to restore their lost or threatened freedoms. With respect to persuasion, the theory assumes that people want to feel free to adopt particular positions on issues (e.g., pro or con) or to not adopt any position at all (e.g., to remain neutral) and that persuasive messages that attempt to influence recipients to adopt particular positions may sometimes threaten this attitudinal freedom. Moreover, the more important the attitudinal freedom that is threatened and the greater the coercive pressure exerted on the individual to adopt a particular position, the greater will be the magnitude of reactance experienced (Brehm, 1968). Thus, the theory predicts that when people receive persuasive messages that they construe to be threats to their attitudinal freedom, they may attempt to reassert their freedom by maintaining their initial opinions or, more provocatively, by changing their opinions in a direction *opposite* to the position advocated in the message (''boomerang effect'').

Research exploring the persuasive impact of *overt* attempts to force recipients to take certain attitudinal positions on issues (e.g., Brehm & Krasin, reported in Brehm, 1966; Heller, Pallak, & Picek, 1973; Sensenig & Brehm, 1968; Snyder & Wicklund, 1976; Wicklund & Brehm, 1968; Worchel & Brehm, 1970) has generally supported reactance theory predictions. Yet the original hypothesis that due to their greater discrepancy, counterattitudinal (versus proattitudinal) messages would cause greater reactance and thus greater negative attitude change has not been supported (e.g., Snyder & Wicklund, 1976; Worchel & Brehm, 1970). For example, Worchel and Brehm (1970) presented subjects with a message advocating that the Communist party should be treated like any other political party in the United States. For half the subjects (high-threat condition) the message contained extra statements of the sort ''you cannot believe otherwise'' or ''you have no choice but to believe this'' (Worchel & Brehm, 1970, p. 19), whereas for the remaining subjects (low-threat condition), these statements were omitted. Worchel and Brehm found that the predicted lesser positive and greater negative persuasive impact of the high- (versus low-) threat message was significant only for subjects who were in initial agreement with the position advocated in the message.

The fact that reactance theory's predictions regarding boomerang attitude change have been substantiated primarily for proattitudinal messages, rather than for counterattitudinal messages, has been interpreted in terms of ''prior exercise of freedom'' (Snyder & Wicklund, 1976; Wicklund, 1974). According to this interpretation, recipients of counterattitudinal messages have already asserted their freedom by expressing initial attitudes that oppose those advocated by the message and thus can maintain their initial opinions. In contrast, in order to restore their attitudinal freedom, recipients of proattitudinal messages must change their opinions away from the position advocated in the message (see Brehm & Brehm, 1981).

Brehm (1968) has also suggested that more *subtle* pressures to adopt an attitudinal position, such as the communicator's stated intention or desire to influence recipients, can also arouse reactance (albeit to a lesser extent than more overt pressures) and thus inhibit persuasion or even produce negative attitude change. In support of this reasoning, Heller, Pallak, and Picek (1973) found that subjects who (without coercion) wrote proattitudinal essays changed their attitudes *away* from their initial positions and in their essays generated more arguments *against* their initial positions after an experimental accomplice expressed a desire to persuade people on the topic (versus expressed little interest in the topic). In addition, a number of studies have shown that, at least under some conditions, forewarning recipients of a communicator's intent to influence them tends to inhibit persuasion (e.g., Freedman & Sears, 1965; Hass & Grady, 1975; Kiesler & Kiesler, 1964; Petty & Cacioppo, 1979a). Nevertheless, other research indicates that recipients' perceptions of a communicator's persuasive intent may often have no impact on opinion change (e.g., Allyn & Festinger, 1961; McGuire & Millman, 1965; McGuire & Papageorgis, 1962) and under some conditions may even enhance persuasion (e.g., Mills, 1966; Mills & Aronson, 1965). Thus, if even relatively subtle pressures, such as the communicator's intent to persuade, can lead recipients to resist influence in the interest of maintaining or restoring freedom, the conditions under which such pressures are likely to instill reactance have yet to be delineated.

Because reactance is presumably aroused in only a subset of persuasion settings in which communications from outside sources threaten recipients' attitudinal freedom, Brehm's (1968) theory is unlikely to prove useful as a general theory of resistance to persuasive communications. Nevertheless, it has proven useful in relation to some variables, most notably in explicating why forewarning manipulations sometimes inhibit persuasion (e.g., Hass & Grady, 1975; Petty & Cacioppo, 1979a) and why highly credible or attractive sources could sometimes engender greater counterargumentation and less persuasion (Brehm & Brehm, 1981). In a more applied vein, the theory has generated predictions regarding the possible impact of censorship on people's attitudes and responses to "censored" materials (Worchel & Arnold, 1973; Worchel, Arnold, & Baker, 1975).

For more cognitively oriented persuasion researchers, an interesting and largely unexplored issue is the extent to which a motivational orientation, such as the desire to maintain or restore attitudinal freedom, influences how recipients process information in persuasion settings. In this regard, it should be noted that researchers should also pay greater attention to assessing the extent to which subjects in persuasion experiments, who are hypothesized to experience reactance, actually experience this motivational state and, if so, the extent to which obtained persuasion findings can be ascribed to the subjects' attempts to restore attitudinal freedom. Unfortunately, researchers who have used reactance theory to generate predictions or to explain obtained persuasion findings have rarely attempted to assess subjects' motivations. Thus, many persuasion findings that have been interpreted in terms of reactance theory can also be interpreted within other theoretical frameworks. For example, an alternative to Brehm's (1968) reactance interpretation of the lesser persuasive impact of direct (versus overheard) communications (e.g., Brock & Becker, 1965; Walster & Festinger,

1962) is provided by attribution theory (see Eagly, Chaiken, & Wood, 1981). Finally, an extremely important question to address in settings in which reactance is postulated to influence persuasion (especially settings in which a boomerang effect is predicted) is the extent to which the attitudes that subjects express in these settings represent genuine changes in belief or affect versus more strategic, and therefore temporary, shifts designed to manage an impression of being free or independent (see Baer, Hinkle, Smith, & Fenton, 1980; Brehm & Brehm, 1981, Chapter 10; Heilman & Toffler, 1976).

B.   MAINTENANCE OF SELF-DEFINING ROLE RELATIONSHIPS

In a functional theory of social influence, Kelman (1958, 1961) distinguished between three influence processes (internalization, identification, and compliance) that differ in terms of the motivational significance of the message-recipient's relationship to the communicator. Kelman defined *internalization* as opinion change that occurs because the communicator's recommended opinion is congruent with one's value system. Kelman's assumption that message recipients scrutinize information to determine its consistency with their existing knowledges structures (i.e., values) places the motivational base of this process in the same category with those of most information-processing theories of persuasion.

In contrast, Kelman's *identification* process provides a distinctive account of the motivations that affect the extent to which message recipients are persuaded by communications. According to Kelman, identification occurs when a recipient changes his or her opinion because the adoption of the new position helps establish or maintain a positive self-defining relationship with the communicator. This changed opinion is accepted privately as well as publicly, although it is thought to be maintained only in the context of the role relationship on which the identification was based. The changed opinion is integrated with the individual's other cognitions only by becoming a part of a self-defining role relationship.

The place of interpersonal goals such as maintaining role relationships is a neglected concern in cognitive persuasion theories, even though in natural settings, such goals are often paramount. It is likely, as Kelman (1958, 1961) has implied, that when self-definition in relation to a communicator is a major goal, recipients may process persuasion information differently than they do when their major goal is maximizing the validity of their opinions. Along these lines, Kelman (1961, 1974) has suggested that for identification and internalization (1) different aspects of the communicator's image are salient (attractiveness or likability for identification, and credibility for internalization), (2) different situational constraints control acceptance of the advocated opinion (role requirements for identification, and the relevance of the issue to one's values for internalization), and (3) different knowledge structures are integrated with the advocated opinion when opinion change occurs (role expectations for identification, and one's value system for internalization).

Predictions derived from Kelman's distinction between identification and internalization are supported by a few empirical tests (e.g., Kelman, 1958; Kelman & Eagly, 1965; Romer, 1979b). Especially interesting from an information-processing standpoint are several findings consistent with the interpretation that a communicator's credibility or expertise affects persuasion through its impact on issue-relevant thinking whereas a communicator's attractiveness affects persuasion without issue-related mediation and presumably through the mediation of beliefs about one's relation to the communicator (Mills & Harvey, 1972; Norman, 1976; but see Maddux & Rogers, 1980). Although Kelman's analysis of internalization and identification has been influential at a theoretical level, it has spawned relatively few thorough attempts to evaluate the model empirically, perhaps because of the general difficulty of testing such typological theories (see Eagly & Himmelfarb, 1974). Kelman's ideas about the importance of self-defining relationships with communicators deserve more detailed elaboration at a theoretical level, as well as more experimentation directed to testing them.

Finally, Kelman's third process, *compliance,* should also be mentioned because its motivational base, the desire to gain a favorable effect from the communicator, was assumed to bring about influence at a superficial overt response level of verbal agreement or behavioral compliance with the communicator. Although in the research literature, persuasion is generally assumed to occur at the level of recipients' private opinions, persuasion studies that have been formulated in impression-management terms (see the following section) have demonstrated the utility of sometimes regarding apparent changes of opinion as more strategic responses to immediate situational pressures.

C. MAINTENANCE OF PUBLIC AND PRIVATE SELF-IDENTITY

In a recent analysis of the ego-involvement construct, Greenwald (1982) abstracted three major meanings that theorists and researchers have traditionally attributed to this term. In one usage, ego-involvement refers to a concern about evaluation by others and portrays the ego-involved person as engaged in the task of seeking satisfactory evaluations from other persons. Greenwald labeled this first kind of ego-task *impression management* and noted its compatibility with psychological constructs such as evaluation apprehension (e.g., Rosenberg, 1969), need for approval (Crowne & Marlowe, 1964), impression management (e.g., Goffman, 1959; Schlenker, 1980; Tedeschi, Schlenker, & Bonoma,

1971), public self-consciousness (Fenigstein, Scheier, & Buss, 1975; Scheier & Carver, 1980), and high self-monitoring (Snyder, 1974). A second meaning of ego-involvement refers to a concern with self-evaluation and portrays the ego-involved person as engaged in the task of seeking a satisfactory self-evaluation. Greenwald (1982) labeled this second ego-task *self-image management* and noted its similarity to constructs such as private self-consciousness (Fenigstein, Scheier, & Buss, 1975; Scheier & Carver, 1980), subjective self-awareness (Duval & Wicklund, 1972), and low self-monitoring (Snyder, 1974). Finally, a third usage of the term ego-involvement connotes personal importance and portrays the ego-involved person as engaged in the task of evaluating or reevaluating important social objects (e.g., attitudes or beliefs). Noting that this sense of ego-involvement primarily emerged from the attitude change literature (e.g., Sherif & Cantril, 1947; Sherif, Sherif, & Nebergall, 1965) and has often been used to designate important or central beliefs that implicate personal values (Ostrom & Brock, 1968), Greenwald labeled this third ego-task *value management*.[9]

As explained earlier, contemporary cognitive theories of persuasion tend to share the assumption that recipients process information in order to attain valid opinions. This assumption corresponds closely to the ego-task of value management (i.e., evaluating or reevaluating important social objects). Moreover, ego-involvement defined in terms of personal importance, which was first investigated in relation to persuasion from the perspective of social judgment theory (Sherif & Hovland, 1961; Sherif, Sherif, & Nebergall, 1965), continues to be systematically investigated by contemporary cognitively oriented persuasion researchers (see earlier sections on processing theories).

The conceptions of ego-involvement as concern about others' evaluation (i.e., impression management) and as concern about self-evaluation (i.e., self-image management) are reflected in earlier functional approaches to persuasion. The ego-task of impression management is reminiscent of Kelman's (1961) compliance mode of social influence and Katz's (1960) instrumental or utilitarian function, and the ego-task of self-image management is reminiscent of Katz's idea that attitudes often function to express people's values or enhance their self-identities (value-expressive function). These two additional senses of ego-involvement have also occasionally been brought to bear on various empirical findings in the attitude-change literature. For example, the finding in the dissonance-inspired counterattitudinal advocacy literature that people change their attitudes to be more consistent with the attitudes implied by their overt behaviors has been interpreted by some theorists as reflecting their desire to maintain a favorable self-evaluation (e.g., Aronson, 1969; Greenwald & Ronis, 1978) and

---

[9]Still other ego-tasks may be relevant to persuasion. See, for example, Greenwald's (1982) discussion of the "communal" orientation and Eagly's (1978) discussion of how this orientation might give rise to sex differences in influenceability.

by others, as reflecting their desire to *appear* consistent to others (Tedeschi, Schlenker, & Bonoma, 1971). Another finding that has been interpreted in impression-management terms is the tendency for people who expect to discuss their opinions with others to moderate their opinion expressions by moving toward a more neutral position prior to the discussion and then to shift back to their original opinions when the anticipated discussion is cancelled (Cialdini, Levy, Herman, & Evenbeck, 1973; Cialdini, Levy, Herman, Kozlowski, & Petty, 1976; Cialdini & Petty, 1981). Consistent with the impression-management interpretation of this finding, Scheier (1980) found that subjects who were high in public self-consciousness and therefore were especially attuned to the publicly displayed aspects of themselves (Fenigstein *et al.*, 1975) showed this type of moderation effect more strongly than subjects who were low in public self-consciousness.

Unfortunately, the motivational orientations of impression management and self-image management are not elaborated in contemporary cognitive theories of persuasion and, aside from occasional post hoc theorizing, are rarely brought to bear on empirical findings in the persuasion literature. Clearly, the implicit (and typically unexamined) assumption underlying most cognitively oriented persuasion research that message recipients are engaged in the ego-task of value management is too narrow. As in other life situations, persuasion settings may vary widely in the extent to which they evoke differing motivational orientations. Further, as illustrated by research on the individual difference constructs of public and private self-consciousness (Fenigstein *et al.*, 1975) and self-monitoring (Snyder, 1974), recipients, themselves, may be differentially predisposed to engage in the ego-tasks of impression management, self-image management, and value management.

One exception to the general neglect of these motivational issues is, as already noted, Kelman's (1961) analysis of opinion change, which included a relatively careful analysis of features of persuasion settings that evoke the differing motivational orientations he discussed. Along with Kelman's analysis of identification (discussed earlier), his analysis of compliance is of interest in relation to ego-relevant motives. In particular, Kelman argued that surveillance by the influencing agent—a variable of considerable importance in contemporary impression-management analyses of social behavior—and the influencing agent's reward or coercive power are associated with opinion change that takes the form of compliance and is therefore not internalized by the message recipient. Another exception to the neglect of ego-relevant motivational issues is found in the literature on warning recipients of impending persuasive messages: Cialdini, Levy, Herman, Kozlowski, and Petty (1976) provided an instructive analysis of how the importance of issues and the expectation of discussing one's opinions might interact to influence subjects' predominant motives in social influence settings. In contrast to these efforts, current persuasion researchers ordinarily pay little attention to analyzing their research settings in terms of the kinds of motives they are most likely to evoke in recipients.

Persuasion researchers have also paid little attention' to individual differences in recipients' motivational orientations despite their long-term interest in exploring how recipient characteristics influence persuasion (see Eagly, 1981). Greenwald's (1982) ego-task analysis and, perhaps, Bem and Funder's (1978) template-matching technique provide models for persuasion researchers interested in developing a common language to describe both recipients of communications and persuasion situations in terms of ego-involved tasks. Once a more formal method is developed to identify what factors in persuasion settings tend to evoke differing motives in message recipients and what kinds of persons are most likely to be predisposed to engage in behavior in the service of these motives, researchers could begin to examine more systematically how differing recipient motivations influence the processing of information in persuasion settings. Such research could shed much needed light on the ability of contemporary cognitive theories to account for persuasion effects across a wide range of settings. Further, this kind of research might indicate how information-processing models could be expanded to take account of the multiplicity of motives that no doubt underlie persuasion effects in everyday settings.[10]

V. Summary and Conclusions

There has been substantial progress in understanding persuasion in the last 30 years. Building on the base provided by the pioneering work of Hovland, Janis, and Kelley (1953), social psychologists have continued to be concerned

---

[10]There are several reasons why we have omitted reduction of cognitive inconsistency as a motivational base of persuasion. A derivation from cognitive dissonance theory in its early form (e.g., Aronson, Turner, & Carlsmith, 1963; Festinger, 1957; Festinger & Aronson, 1960) was that exposure to counterattitudinal messages from outside sources would induce dissonance. Thus, persuasion could be viewed as a product of dissonance reduction. In subsequent refinements of dissonance theory (e.g., Brehm & Cohen, 1962), however, dissonance was thought to occur only in situations in which subjects committed themselves to a counterattitudinal position. This more limited definition of the situations in which dissonance is likely to be aroused led to an increasing empirical emphasis on exploring the effects of counterattitudinal behavior on attitude change (an area not reviewed in this chapter). Because of the rarity of commitment to counterattitudinal positions in persuasion settings, dissonance ceased to be a viable theory of persuasion.

Balance theory is a very general model for representing perceivers' cognitions and thus has potential relevance to understanding persuasion. Most obviously, a recipient's evaluation of a communicator and agreement with that communicator on some issue can be represented by a p-o-x triad (see Insko, 1981). Yet in its original form (Heider, 1958), balance theory seems to have limited utility as a persuasion theory because of its inability to account for the persuasive impact of distal

with explaining the psychological mediation of the effects of persuasive communications. The work accomplished has grown in sophistication as theories have been formulated and brought to bear on persuasion in an increasingly rigorous and systematic manner. The high quality of much of this theory-oriented research can be contrasted with the somewhat disparaging opinions that some commentators expressed concerning persuasion research after the first wave of research following in the Hovland, Janis, and Kelley tradition. Brown's (1965) characterization of this work expressed a common view: "The work has been well done . . . but it lacks something of intellectual interest because the results do not fall into any general compelling pattern. They summarize as a set of elaborately contingent, and not very general, generalizations" (p. 549). During a period when many researchers studied variables such as level of fear, communicator credibility, and order of presentation in a way that sometimes seemed somewhat less than thoughtful, new theoretical perspectives were born, inspired in part by the work of McGuire (e.g., 1960a, 1969, 1972) on conditional inferences and on reception and yielding as mediators of persuasion. Not surprisingly, these contemporary persuasion theories have focused on the cognitive issues that have dominated most of social psychology during the 1960s and 1970s. The worth of these newer cognitive theories has become very apparent (see also Eagly & Himmelfarb, 1974, 1978). Persons having more than a superficial knowledge of persuasion research do not view the field now as a haphazard collection of unintegrated findings, but as sets of studies organized in terms of coherent theoretical perspectives with substantial predictive power and at least moderate scope and generality.

The dismay sometimes expressed over the inconsistency supposedly characterizing the persuasion literature (e.g., Fishbein & Ajzen, 1972, 1975; Jaccard, 1981) may reflect a bias toward defining consistency in terms of the persuasive impact of particular independent variables (e.g., with respect to distraction, whether distraction manipulations uniformly facilitate or uniformly inhibit persuasion) rather than defining consistency in terms of the persuasive impact of the cognitive processes that are often influenced by such independent variables (e.g., the impact on persuasion of distraction-induced decrements of message reception and issue-relevant thinking). The literature indicates that particular distal variables such as distraction are often mediated by different cognitive processes (e.g., reception versus issue-relevant thinking), depending on other factors in persuasion situations (e.g., strength of distraction manipulation or difficulty of message content; see Baron, Baron, & Miller, 1973; Regan & Cheng, 1973).

---

variables other than some communicator characteristics and message discrepancy. Although there have been some attempts to apply more sophisticated versions of balance theory to aspects of persuasion (Feather, 1967; Insko, in press), explicit balance analyses have, in general, not been developed in relation to persuasion.

Thus, although the persuasive impact of variables such as distraction may often be heterogeneous across studies, their effects on persuasion are nevertheless predictable to the extent that the cognitive processes underlying them are understood.[11]

If there is disappointment to be expressed at the conclusion of a review of contemporary theories of persuasion, it concerns the absence of a general theory. With the possible exception of Anderson's (e.g., 1981a) information-integration theory, each member of the current generation of theories has a limited scope. The three verbally formulated process theories we have reviewed each provides important insights into particular sets of distal persuasion variables. The cognitive response framework predicts the effects of those independent variables that are assumed to affect the extent of message- and issue-relevant thinking (e.g., distraction or involvement), when these variables are crossed with a variable known to affect the valence of such thinking (e.g., the strength of the message's arguments). Attribution theory predicts the effects of those persuasion cues that elicit causal explanations of the communicator's viewpoint by means of either (1) the consensus, consistency, and distinctiveness criteria of the ANOVA model or (2) the discounting and augmentation principles. The heuristic model predicts the effects of a set of persuasion cues that are linked to agreement with persuasive messages by means of simple decision rules. Because all of these approaches are still under development, it is not yet known how large a set of persuasion variables will potentially be illuminated by each theory. Nevertheless, it is clear that none of these theories functions as a general theory of persuasion or is likely ever to achieve such status.

The mathematically formulated combinatorial models reviewed in this chapter have explanatory value primarily in relation to the effects of the content of the persuasive message itself rather than in relation to distal source, context, and recipient variables. The McGuire-Wyer probabilogical model specifies a conditional inference process by which arguments in persuasive messages affect belief in the conclusions advocated in such messages. The expectancy–value model focuses on the argumentation in messages as well, but provides a model of how arguments, when interpreted as beliefs about attributes (or consequences) of attitude objects, are combined by message recipients to form global attitudes or intentions. The information-integration model, as noted earlier, is more difficult to characterize because of its flexibility about specific integration rules and the

---

[11]It might also be noted that some of the pessimism with respect to the consistency of persuasion findings may reflect reviewers' traditional adherence to statistical significance as a criterion for evaluating the consistency of research findings. A more sophisticated approach to synthesizing findings utilizes quantitative methods that assess the magnitude of effects, regardless of their statistical significance (e.g., Glass, McGaw, & Smith, 1981), and in addition, evaluate the homogeneity of effects across studies (e.g., Hedges, 1982, Rosenthal & Rubin, 1982). Such techniques offer promise for future reviewers of the persuasion literature.

level of analysis at which it is applied. Although it has been applied, like the probabilogical and expectancy–value models, at a level that illuminates issues of message content, it is relevant to other issues as well. Information-integration theory does achieve greater generality than other theories because of this flexibility, yet it achieves this generality at a considerable loss of descriptive content in relation to psychological processes. Information-integration theory provides little information about the types of inferences that underlie information integration, whereas each of the other theories we have considered does provide a description of a particular class of inferences.

At the present stage of theory development in the persuasion area, some increase in generality of theoretical frameworks may be achieved by building bridges between theoretical perspectives. Indeed, we have noted instances in which such bridges have been or could be built—for example, between information-integration theory and attribution theory. Multiple opportunities exist for linking the theories we have labeled process theories to those we have labeled combinatorial theories. In particular, because expectancy–value and information-integration theories weight the information that is combined to form or change an opinion, verbally formulated process theories could be invoked to provide hypotheses about the determinants of these weights.

Growth of knowledge may also be facilitated by research that contrasts the predictions of various theories for given sets of variables. For example, the three process theories we have reviewed all have implications for the effects of communicator variables (see Eagly, 1983). According to the cognitive response framework, a variable such as communicator credibility affects persuasion through its effects on the favorability of cognitive responses and/or the extent of issue-relevant thinking. According to attribution theory, credibility affects persuasion through its impact on perceivers' explanations of the communicator's viewpoint. And according to the heuristic model, cues such as credibility are linked to simple schemas such as the expert credo. Although all three theories usually make similar predictions about the effects of a variable such as communicator credibility, in some circumstances differing predictions are generated as well. For example, mediation by the effortful cognitive processing that is postulated by the cognitive response framework suggests enduring effects of credibility cues, whereas mediation by the less effortful heuristic processes suggests ephemeral effects that would not endure over an extended period of time. Thus, opinion persistence (Cook & Flay, 1978) is one area in which these theories may make contrasting predictions.

As we have indicated, the relative neglect of motivational issues in the contemporary literature on persuasion is striking. The renewed interest that social psychologists have shown in motivation (e.g., Carver & Scheier, 1981; Greenwald, 1982) suggests that motivational issues are beginning to be reintegrated into the study of attitudes. Researchers might consider adopting a perspective that can be termed *functional,* following from the use of this term by an earlier generation of attitude theorists (Katz, 1960; Kelman, 1961). Functional perspectives take into account the message recipients' motivational goals in persuasion settings, and assume that these goals are influenced by features of the persuasion setting itself as well as ingrained dispositions of the recipients. From a functional perspective, research could examine whether the information processing carried out by message recipients is altered or biased by differing motivational orientations. A few issues of this sort have already been studied extensively in the social cognition literature—for example, research has addressed the question of whether there is a self-serving bias in causal attributions (e.g., Miller & Ross, 1975; Zuckerman, 1979).

This chapter pays little attention to the applications of persuasion theory to more practical concerns. In a world in which changing attitudes is a primary goal of health professionals, advertisers, and politicians, persuasion theory has potentially important applied value. A primary question in considering applications is whether the social psychological perspectives we review have been developed fully enough to be useful to practitioners. There is sufficient information about the role of some distal variables in persuasion that could prove to be of substantial value to practitioners, when coupled with knowledge of the underlying cognitive processes operative in a given situation. Yet, if called upon to consult with practitioners about persuasion strategies, investigators should proceed with caution because these practitioners may possess naive theories of persuasion that, when combined with their intuitive knowledge of the many variables operative in their unique persuasion settings, may in fact have substantial predictive power. Nevertheless, as more psychologists knowledgeable about attitude theory become employed in nonacademic settings and in applied academic programs in specialties such as marketing and medical sciences, there will inevitably be more extensive efforts to apply systematic theories of persuasion in natural settings. If theory and research continue to grow at the rapid pace of the past decades, a certain optimism about applications is warranted.

ACKNOWLEDGMENTS

The authors thank Norman Anderson, Susan Fiske, Samuel Himmelfarb, Chester Insko, Judson Mills, Eliot Smith, Valerie Steffen, Donald Thistlethwaite, Sharon Wolf, and Wendy Wood for their helpful comments on a draft of this chapter.

REFERENCES

Abelson, R. P. Script processing in attitude formation and decision making. In J. S. Carroll & J. W. Payne (Eds.), *Cognition and social behavior.* Hillsdale, NJ: Erlbaum, 1976.

Abelson, R. P., & Rosenberg, M. J. Symbolic psycho-logic: A model of attitudinal cognition. *Behavioral Science*, 1958, *3*, 1–13.

Ajzen, I. Attribution of dispositions to an actor: Effects of perceived decision freedom and behavioral utilities. *Journal of Personality and Social Psychology*, 1971, *18*, 144–156.

Ajzen, I., & Fishbein, M. Attitudinal and normative variables as predictors of specific behaviors. *Journal of Personality and Social Psychology*, 1973, *27*, 41–57.

Ajzen, I., & Fishbein, M. Attitude-behavior relations: A theoretical analysis and review of empirical research. *Psychological Bulletin*, 1977, *84*, 888–918.

Ajzen, I., & Fishbein, M. *Understanding attitudes and predicting social behavior*. Englewood Cliffs, NJ: Prentice-Hall, 1980.

Allen, V. L. Situational factors in conformity. In L. Berkowitz (Ed.), *Advances in experimental social psychology* (Vol. 2). NY: Academic Press, 1965.

Allyn, J., & Festinger, L. The effectiveness of unanticipated persuasive communications. *Journal of Abnormal and Social Psychology*, 1961, *62*, 35–40.

Anderson, N. H. Application of an additive model to impression formation. *Science*, 1962, *138*, 817–818.

Anderson, N. H. Averaging versus adding as a stimulus-combination rule in impression formation. *Journal of Experimental Psychology*, 1965, *70*, 394–400.

Anderson, N. H. Averaging model analysis of set-size effect in impression formation. *Journal of Experimental Psychology*, 1967, *75*, 158–165.

Anderson, N. H. Application of a linear-serial model to a personality-impression task using serial presentation. *Journal of Personality and Social Psychology*, 1968, *10*, 354–362.

Anderson, N. H. Functional measurement and psychophysical judgment. *Psychological Review*, 1970, *77*, 153–170.

Anderson, N. H. Integration theory and attitude change. *Psychological Review*, 1971, *78*, 171–206.

Anderson, N. H. Information integration theory applied to attitudes about U.S. Presidents. *Journal of Educational Psychology*, 1973, *64*, 1–8.

Anderson, N. H. Cognitive algebra: Integration theory applied to social attribution. In L. Berkowitz (Ed.), *Advances in experimental social psychology* (Vol. 7). NY: Academic Press, 1974.

Anderson, N. H. How functional measurement can yield validated interval scales of mental quantities. *Journal of Applied Psychology*, 1976, *61*, 677–692.

Anderson, N. H. Methods & designs: Measurement of motivation and incentive. *Behavior Research Methods & Instrumentation*, 1978, *10*, 360–375.

Anderson, N. H. *Foundations of information integration theory*. NY: Academic Press, 1981. (a)

Anderson, N. H. Integration theory applied to cognitive responses and attitudes. In R. E. Petty, T. M. Ostrom, & T. C. Brock (Eds.), *Cognitive responses in persuasion*. Hillsdale, NJ: Erlbaum, 1981. (b)

Anderson, N. H. *Methods of information integration theory*. NY: Academic Press, 1982.

Anderson, N. H., & Farkas, A. J. New light on order effects in attitude change. *Journal of Personality and Social Psychology*, 1973, *28*, 88–93.

Anderson, N. H., & Hubert, S. Effects of concomitant verbal recall on order effects in personality impression formation. *Journal of Verbal Learning and Verbal Behavior*, 1963, *2*, 379–391.

Anderson, N. H., & Shanteau, J. C. Information integration in risky decision making. *Journal of Experimental Psychology*, 1970, *84*, 441–451.

Apsler, R., & Sears, D. O. Warning, personal involvement, and attitude change. *Journal of Personality and Social Psychology*, 1968, *9*, 162–166.

Aronson, E. The theory of cognitive dissonance: A current perspective. In L. Berkowitz (Ed.), *Advances in experimental social psychology* (Vol. 4). NY: Academic Press, 1969.

Aronson, E., Turner, J. A., & Carlsmith, J. M. Communicator credibility and communication discrepancy as determinants of opinion change. *Journal of Abnormal and Social Psychology,* 1963, *67,* 31–36.

Asch, S. E. Studies of independence and conformity: I. A minority of one against a unanimous majority. *Psychological Monographs,* 1956, *70* (9, Whole No. 416), 1–70.

Atkins, A. L., Deaux, K. K., & Bieri, J. Latitude of acceptance and attitude change: Empirical evidence for a reformulation. *Journal of Personality and Social Psychology,* 1967, *6,* 47–54.

Atkinson, J. W. (Ed.). *Motives in fantasy, action, and society: A method of assessment and study.* Princeton, NJ: Van Nostrand, 1958.

Baer, R., Hinkle, S., Smith, K., & Fenton, M. Reactance as a function of actual versus projected autonomy. *Journal of Personality and Social Psychology,* 1980, *38,* 416–422.

Bargh, J. A. Attention and automaticity in the processing of self-relevant information. *Journal of Personality and Social Psychology,* 1982, *43,* 425–436.

Bargh, J. A., & Pietromonaco, P. Automatic information processing and social perception: The influence of trait information presented outside of conscious awareness on impression formation. *Journal of Personality and Social Psychology,* 1982, *43,* 437–449.

Baron, R. S., Baron, P. H., & Miller, N. The relation between distraction and persuasion. *Psychological Bulletin,* 1973, *80,* 310–323.

Baron, R. S., & Miller, N. Credibility, distraction, and counterargument in a forewarning situation. *Proceedings of the 77th Annual Convention of the American Psychological Association,* 1969, *4,* 411–412.

Bem, D. J. Self-perception theory. In L. Berkowitz (Ed.), *Advances in experimental social psychology* (Vol. 6). NY: Academic Press, 1972.

Bem, D. J. & Funder, D. C. Predicting more of the people more of the time: Assessing the personality of situations. *Psychological Review,* 1978, *85,* 485–501.

Bettman, J. R. *An information processing theory of consumer choice.* Reading, MA: Addison-Wesley, 1979.

Birnbaum, M. H. Morality judgment: Test of an averaging model with differential weights. *Journal of Experimental Psychology,* 1973, *99,* 395–399.

Birnbaum, M. H. The nonadditivity of personality impressions. *Journal of Experimental Psychology,* 1974, *3,* 543–561.

Birnbaum, M. H. Controversies in psychological measurement. In B. Wegener (Ed.), *Social attitudes and psychophysical measurement.* Hillsdale, NJ: Erlbaum, 1982.

Birnbaum, M. H., & Stegner, S. E. Source credibility in social judgment: Bias, expertise, and the judge's point of view. *Journal of Personality and Social Psychology,* 1979, *37,* 48–74.

Birnbaum, M. H., Wong, R., & Wong, L. K. Combining information from sources that vary in credibility. *Memory & Cognition,* 1976, *4,* 330–336.

Bochner, S., & Insko, C. A. Communicator discrepancy, source credibility, and opinion change. *Journal of Personality and Social Psychology,* 1966, *4,* 614–621.

Brändstatter, H., Davis, J. H., & Stocker-Kreichgauer, G. (Eds.). *Contemporary problems in group decision-making.* NY: Academic Press, 1980.

Brehm, J. W. *A theory of psychological reactance.* NY: Academic Press, 1966.

Brehm, J. W. Attitude change from threat to attitudinal freedom. In A. G. Greenwald, T. C. Brock, & T. M. Ostrom (Eds.), *Psychological foundations of attitudes.* NY: Academic Press, 1968.

Brehm, J. W. *Responses to loss of freedom: A theory of psychological reactance.* Morristown, NJ: General Learning Press, 1972.

Brehm, J. W., & Cohen, A. R. *Explorations in cognitive dissonance.* NY: Wiley, 1962.

Brehm, S. S., & Brehm, J. W. *Psychological reactance: A theory of freedom and control.* NY: Academic Press, 1981.

Brock, T. C. Communication discrepancy and intent to persuade as determinants of counterargument production. *Journal of Experimental Social Psychology,* 1967, *3,* 296–309.

Brock, T. C., & Becker, L. A. Ineffectiveness of "overheard" counterpropaganda. *Journal of Personality and Social Psychology*, 1965, *2*, 654–660.

Brown, R. *Social psychology*. NY: Free Press, 1965.

Cacioppo, J. T. The effects of exogenous changes in heart rate on the facilitation of thought and resistance to persuasion. *Journal of Personality and Social Psychology*, 1979, *37*, 489–498.

Cacioppo, J. T., Harkins, S. G., & Petty, R. E. The nature of attitudes and cognitive responses and their relationships to behavior. In R. E. Petty, T. M. Ostrom, & T. C. Brock (Eds.), *Cognitive responses in persuasion*. Hillsdale, NJ: Erlbaum, 1981.

Cacioppo, J. T. & Petty, R. E. Attitudes and cognitive response: An electrophysiological approach. *Journal of Personality and Social Psychology*, 1979, *37*, 2181–2199. (a)

Cacioppo, J. T., & Petty, R. E. Effects of message repetition and position on cognitive response, recall, and persuasion. *Journal of Personality and Social Psychology*, 1979, *37*, 97–109. (b)

Cacioppo, J. T. & Petty, R. E. Electromyograms as measures of extent and affectivity of information processing. *American Psychologist*, 1981, *36*, 441–456.

Cacioppo, J. T., Sandman, C., & Walker, B. The effects of operant heart rate conditioning on cognitive elaboration and attitude change. *Psychophysiology*, 1978, *15*, 330–338.

Calder, B. J., Insko, C. A., & Yandell, B. The relation of cognitive and memorial processes to persuasion in a simulated jury trial. *Journal of Applied Social Psychology*, 1974, *4*, 62–93.

Carlson, E. R. *Attitude change through modification of attitude structure*. Unpublished doctoral dissertation, University of Michigan, 1953.

Carlson, E. R. Attitude change through modification of attitude structure. *Journal of Abnormal and Social Psychology*, 1956, *52*, 256–261.

Carver, C. S., & Scheier, M. F. *Attention and self-regulation: A control-theory approach to human behavior*. NY: Springer-Verlag, 1981.

Chaiken, S. *The use of source versus message cues in persuasion: An information processing analysis*. Unpublished doctoral dissertation, University of Massachusetts-Amherst, 1978.

Chaiken, S. Heuristic versus systematic information processing and the use of source versus message cues in persuasion. *Journal of Personality and Social Psychology*, 1980, *39*, 752–766.

Chaiken, S. *The heuristic/systematic processing distinction in persuasion*. Paper presented at the Symposium on Automatic Processing, Society for Experimental Social Psychology, Nashville, IN, October 1982.

Chaiken, S. *Heuristic processing of persuasion cues*. Invited paper presented at Midwestern Psychological Association Mettings, Chicago, IL, May 1983.

Chaiken, S., & Eagly, A. H. Communication modality as a determinant of message persuasiveness and message comprehensibility. *Journal of Personality and Social Psychology*, 1976, *34*, 605–614.

Chaiken, S., & Eagly, A. H. Communication modality as a determinant of persuasion: The role of communicator salience. *Journal of Personality and Social Psychology*, 1983, *45*, 241–256.

Cialdini, R. B., Levy, A., Herman, C. P., & Evenbeck, S. Attitudinal politics: The strategy of moderation. *Journal of Personality and Social Psychology*, 1973, *25*, 100–108.

Cialdini, R. B., Levy, A., Herman, C. P., Kozlowski, L. T., & Petty, R. E. Elastic shifts of opinion: Determinants of direction and durability. *Journal of Personality and Social Psychology*, 1976, *34*, 663–672.

Cialdini, R. B., & Petty, R. E. Anticipatory opinion effects. In R. E. Petty, T. M. Ostrom, & T. C. Brock (Eds.), *Cognitive responses in persuasion*. Hillsdale, NJ: Erlbaum, 1981.

Cook, T. D. Competence, counterarguing, and attitude change. *Journal of Personality*, 1969, *37*, 342–358.

Cook, T. D., & Flay, B. R. The persistence of experimentally induced attitude change. In L. Berkowitz (Ed.), *Advances in experimental social psychology* (Vol. 11). NY: Academic Press, 1978.

Cook, T. D., Gruder, C. L., Hennigan, K. M., & Flay, B. R. History of the sleeper effect: Some logical pitfalls in accepting the null hypothesis. *Psychological Bulletin*, 1979, *86*, 662–679.

Craik, F. I. M., & Lockhart, R. S. Levels of processing: A framework for memory research. *Journal of Verbal Learning and Verbal Behavior*, 1972, *11*, 671–684.

Crowne, D. P., & Marlowe, D. *The approval motive: Studies in evaluative dependence.* NY: Wiley, 1964.

Davidson, A. R., & Jaccard, J. J. Population psychology: A new look at an old problem. *Journal of Personality and Social Psychology*, 1975, *31*, 1073–1082.

Dillehay, R. C., Insko, C. A., & Smith, M. B. Logical consistency and attitude change. *Journal of Personality and Social Psychology*, 1966, *3*, 646–654.

Dulany, D. E. Hypotheses and habits in verbal "operant conditioning." *Journal of Abnormal and Social Psychology*, 1961, *63*, 251–263.

Dulany, D. E. Awareness, rules, and propositional control: A confrontation with S-R behavior theory. In D. Horton & T. Dixon (Eds.), *Verbal behavior and general behavior theory.* Englewood Cliffs, NJ: Prentice-Hall, 1968.

Duval, S., & Wicklund, R. A. *A theory of objective self-awareness.* NY: Academic Press, 1972.

Eagly, A. H. Involvement as a determinant of response to favorable and unfavorable information. *Journal of Personality and Social Psychology*, 1967, *7*,(3, Pt. 2), 1–15.

Eagly, A. H. Comprehensibility of persuasive arguments as a determinant of opinion change. *Journal of Personality and Social Psychology*, 1974, *29*, 758–773.

Eagly, A. H. Sex differences in influenceability. *Psychological Bulletin*, 1978, *85*, 86–116.

Eagly, A. H. Recipient characteristics as determinants of responses to persuasion. In R. E. Petty, T. M. Ostrom, & T. C. Brock (Eds.), *Cognitive responses in persuasion.* Hillsdale, NJ: Erlbaum, 1981.

Eagly, A. H. *Who says so? The processing of communicator cues in persuasion.* Invited address presented at the Eastern Psychological Association, Philadelphia, April 1983.

Eagly, A. H., & Chaiken, S. An attribution analysis of the effect of communicator characteristics on opinion change: The case of communicator attractiveness. *Journal of Personality and Social Psychology*, 1975, *32*, 136–144.

Eagly, A. H., & Chaiken, S. Why would anyone say that? Causal attribution of statements about the Watergate scandal. *Sociometry*, 1976, *39*, 236–243.

Eagly, A. H., Chaiken, S., & Wood, W. An attribution analysis of persuasion. In J. H. Harvey, W. J. Ickes, & R. F. Kidd (Eds.) *New directions in attribution research* (Vol. 3). Hillsdale, NJ: Erlbaum, 1981.

Eagly, A. H., & Himmelfarb, S. Current trends in attitude theory and research. In S. Himmelfarb & A. H. Eagly (Eds.), *Readings in attitude change.* NY: Wiley, 1974.

Eagly, A. H., & Himmelfarb, S. Attitudes and opinions. *Annual Review of Psychology*, 1978, *29*, 517–554.

Eagly, A. H., & Telaak, K. Width of the latitude of acceptance as a determinant of attitude change. *Journal of Personality and Social Psychology*, 1972, *23*, 388–397.

Eagly, A. H., & Warren, R. Intelligence, comprehension, and opinion change. *Journal of Personality*, 1976, *44*, 226–242.

Eagly, A. H., Wood, W., & Chaiken, S. Causal inferences about communicators and their effect on opinion change. *Journal of Personality and Social Psychology*, 1978, *36*, 424–435.

Edwards, W. The theory of decision making. *Psychological Bulletin*, 1954, *51*, 380–417.

Edwards, W., Lindman, H., & Savage, L. J. Bayesian statistical inference for psychological research. *Psychological Review*, 1963, *70*, 193–242.

Eysenck, M. W. *Attention and arousal, cognition and performance.* NY: Springer-Verlag, 1982.

Feather, N. T. A structural balance approach to the analysis of communication effects. In L.

Berkowitz (Ed.), *Advances in experimental social psychology* (Vol. 3). NY: Academic Press, 1967.

Feather, N. T. (Ed.). *Expectations and actions: Expectancy-value models in psychology.* Hillsdale, NJ: Erlbaum, 1982.

Fenigstein, A., Scheier, M. F., & Buss, A. H. Public and private self-consciousness: Assessment and theory. *Journal of Consulting and Clinical Psychology,* 1975, *43,* 522–527.

Festinger, L. *A theory of cognitive dissonance.* Stanford, CA: Stanford University Press, 1957.

Festinger, L., & Aronson, E. Arousal and reduction of dissonance in social contexts. In D. Cartwright & A. Zander (Eds.), *Group dynamics: Research and theory* (2nd ed.). Evanston, IL: Row, Peterson, 1960.

Festinger, L., & Maccoby, N. On resistance to persuasive communications. *Journal of Abnormal and Social Psychology,* 1964, *68,* 359–366.

Fishbein, M. *A theoretical and empirical investigation of the interrelation between beliefs about an object and the attitude toward the object.* Unpublished doctoral dissertation, University of California at Los Angeles, 1961.

Fishbein, M. An investigation of the relationships between beliefs about an object and the attitude toward that object. *Human Relations,* 1963, *16,* 233–240.

Fishbein, M. A behavior theory approach to the relations between beliefs about an object and the attitude toward the object. In M. Fishbein (Ed.), *Readings in attitude theory and measurement.* NY: Wiley, 1967.

Fishbein, M. A theory of reasoned action: Some applications and implications. In H. E. Howe & M. M. Page (Eds.), *Nebraska Symposium on Motivation, 1979.* Lincoln, NE: University of Nebraska Press, 1980.

Fishbein, M., & Ajzen, I. Attitudes and opinions. *Annual Review of Psychology,* 1972, *23,* 487–544.

Fishbein, M., & Ajzen, I. *Belief, attitude, intention, and behavior: An introduction to theory and research.* Reading, MA: Addison-Wesley, 1975.

Fishbein, M., & Ajzen, I. Acceptance, yielding, and impact: Cognitive processes in persuasion. In R. E. Petty, T. M. Ostrom, & T. C. Brock (Eds.), *Cognitive responses in persuasion.* Hillsdale, NJ: Erlbaum, 1981.

Fishbein, M., Ajzen, I., & McArdle, J. Changing the behavior of alcoholics: Effects of persuasive communication. In I. Ajzen & M. Fishbein, *Understanding attitudes and predicting social behavior.* Englewood Cliffs, NJ: Prentice-Hall, 1980.

Fiske, S. T., & Taylor, S. E. *Social cognition.* Reading, MA: Addison-Wesley, 1984.

Freedman, J. L., & Sears, D. Warning, distraction and resistance to influence. *Journal of Personality and Social Psychology,* 1965, *1,* 262–266.

Gillig, P. M., & Greenwald, A. G. Is it time to lay the sleeper effect to rest? *Journal of Personality and Social Psychology,* 1974, *29,* 132–139.

Glass, G. V., McGaw, B., & Smith, M. L. *Meta-analysis in social research.* Beverly Hills, CA: Sage Publications, 1981.

Goethals, G. R. An attributional analysis of some social influence phenomena. In J. H. Harvey, W. J. Ickes, & R. F. Kidd (Eds.), *New directions in attribution research* (Vol. 1). Hillsdale, NJ: Erlbaum, 1976.

Goethals, G. R., & Nelson, R. E. Similarity in the influence process: The belief-value distinction. *Journal of Personality and Social Psychology,* 1973, *25,* 117–122.

Goffman, E. *The presentation of self in everyday life.* NY: Doubleday, 1959.

Gollob, H. F., & Lugg, A. M. Effects of instruction and stimulus presentation on the occurrence of averaging responses in impression formation. *Journal of Experimental Psychology,* 1973, *98,* 217–219.

Gottlieb, A., & Ickes, W. J. Attributional strategies of social influence. In J. H. Harvey, W. J. Ickes, & R. F. Kidd (Eds.), *New directions in attribution research* (Vol. 2). Hillsdale, NJ: Erlbaum, 1978.

Greenwald, A. G. Cognitive learning, cognitive response to persuasion, and attitude change. In A. G. Greenwald, T. C. Brock, & T. M. Ostrom (Eds.), *Psychological foundations of attitudes.* NY: Academic Press, 1968.

Greenwald, A. G. Cognitive response analysis: An appraisal. In R. E. Petty, T. M. Ostrom, & T. C. Brock (Eds.), *Cognitive responses in persuasion.* Hillsdale, NJ: Erlbaum, 1981.

Greenwald, A. G. Ego task analysis: An integration of research on ego-involvement and self-awareness. In A. H. Hastorf & A. M. Isen (Eds.), *Cognitive social psychology.* NY: Elsevier/North-Holland, 1982.

Greenwald, A. G., & Ronis, D. L. Twenty years of cognitive dissonance: Case study of the evolution of a theory. *Psychological Review,* 1978, *85,* 53–57.

Haaland, G. A., & Venkatesan, M. Resistance to persuasive communications: An examination of the distraction hypothesis. *Journal of Personality and Social Psychology,* 1968, *9,* 167–170.

Hamilton, D. L., & Huffman, L. J. Generality of impression-formation processes for evaluative and nonevaluative judgments. *Journal of Personality and Social Psychology,* 1971, *20,* 200–207.

Harkins, S. G., & Petty, R. E. Effects of source magnification of cognitive effort on attitudes: An information-processing view. *Journal of Personality and Social Psychology,* 1981, *40,* 401–413.

Hass, J. W., Bagley, G. S., & Rogers, R. W. Coping with the energy crisis: Effects of fear appeals upon attitudes toward energy consumption. *Journal of Applied Psychology,* 1975, *60,* 754–756.

Hass, R. G. Effects of source characteristics on cognitive responses and persuasion. In R. E. Petty, T. M. Ostrom, & T. C. Brock (Eds.), *Cognitive responses in persuasion.* Hillsdale, NJ: Erlbaum, 1981.

Hass, R. G., & Grady, K. Temporal delay, type of forewarning, and resistance to influence. *Journal of Experimental Social Psychology,* 1975, *11,* 459–469.

Hastie, R. Social inference. *Annual Review of Psychology,* 1983, *34,* 511–542.

Hedges, L. V. Estimation of effect size from a series of independent experiments. *Psychological Bulletin,* 1982, *92,* 490–499.

Heesacker, M., Petty, R. E., & Cacioppo, J. T. Field dependence and attitude change: Source credibility can alter persuasion by affecting message-relevant thinking. *Journal of Personality,* 1983, *51,* 653–666.

Heider, F. *The psychology of interpersonal relations.* NY: Wiley, 1958.

Heilman, M. D., & Toffler, B. L. Reacting to reactance: An interpersonal interpretation of the need for freedom. *Journal of Experimental Social Psychology,* 1976, *12,* 519–529.

Heller, J. F., Pallak, M. S., & Picek, J. M. The interactive effects of intent and threat on boomerang attitude change. *Journal of Personality and Social Psychology,* 1973, *26,* 273–279.

Hendrick, C. Averaging vs. summation in impression formation. *Perceptual and Motor Skills,* 1968, *27,* 1295–1302.

Hendrick, C., & Costantini, A. F. Effects of varying trait inconsistency and response requirements on the primacy effect in impression formation. *Journal of Personality and Social Psychology,* 1970, *15,* 158–164.

Hendrick, C., & Shaffer, D. R. Effects of arousal and credibility on learning and persuasion. *Psychonomic Science,* 1970, *20,* 241–243.

Henninger, M., & Wyer, R. S. The recognition and elimination of inconsistencies among syllogistically related beliefs: Some new light on the "Socratic effect." *Journal of Personality and Social Psychology,* 1976, *34,* 680–693.

Himmelfarb, S. Integration and attribution theories in personality impression formation. *Journal of Personality and Social Psychology,* 1972, *23,* 309–313.

Himmelfarb, S. General test of a differential weighted averaging model of impression formation. *Journal of Experimental Social Psychology*, 1973, *9*, 379–390.

Himmelfarb, S. On scale value and weight in the weighted averaging model of integration theory. *Personality and Social Psychology Bulletin*, 1975, *1*, 580–583.

Himmelfarb, S., & Anderson, N. H. Integration theory applied to opinion attribution. *Journal of Personality and Social Psychology*, 1975, *31*, 1064–1072.

Himmelfarb, S., & Eagly, A. H. Orientations to the study of attitudes and their change. In S. Himmelfarb & A. Eagly (Eds.), *Readings in attitude change*. NY: Wiley, 1974.

Holt, L. E. Resistance to persuasion on explicit beliefs as a function of commitment to and desirability of logically related beliefs. *Journal of Personality and Social Psychology*, 1970, *16*, 583–591.

Holt, L. E., & Watts, W. A. Salience of logical relationships among beliefs as a factor in persuasion. *Journal of Personality and Social Psychology*, 1969, *11*, 193–203.

Holz, J. R., & Wright, C. R. Sociology of mass communications. *Annual Review of Sociology*, 1979, *5*, 193–217.

Hovland, C. I., Janis, I. L., & Kelley, H. H. *Communication and persuasion: Psychological studies of opinion change*. New Haven, CT: Yale University Press, 1953.

Hovland, C. I., Lumsdaine, A. A., & Sheffield, F. D. *Experiments on mass communication*. Princeton, NJ: Princeton University Press, 1949.

Hovland, C. I., & Mandell, W. An experimental comparison of conclusion-drawing by the communicator and by the audience. *Journal of Abnormal and Social Psychology*, 1952, *47*, 581–588.

Hovland, C. I., & Rosenberg, M. J. (Eds.). *Attitude organization and change*. New Haven, CT: Yale University Press, 1960.

Hovland, C. I., & Weiss, W. The influence of source credibility on communication effectiveness. *Public Opinion Quarterly*, 1951, *15*, 635–650.

Ickes, W. J., & Barnes, R. D. Boys and girls together—and alienated: On enacting stereotyped sex roles in mixed-sex dyads. *Journal of Personality and Social Psychology*, 1978, *36*, 669–683.

Insko, C. A. *Theories of attitude change*. NY: Appleton-Century-Crofts, 1967.

Insko, C. A. Balance theory and phenomenology. In R. E. Petty, T. M. Ostrom, & T. C. Brock (Eds.), *Cognitive responses in persuasion*. Hillsdale, NJ: Erlbaum, 1981.

Insko, C. A. Balance theory, the Jordan paradigm, and the Weist tetrahedron. In L. Berkowitz (Ed.), *Advances in Experimental Social Psychology*, in press.

Insko, C. A., Lind, E. A., & LaTour, S. Persuasion, recall, and thoughts. *Representative Research in Social Psychology*, 1976, *7*, 66–78.

Insko, C. A., Turnbull, W., & Yandell, B. Facilitative and inhibiting effects of distraction on attitude change. *Sociometry*, 1974, *37*, 508–528.

Jaccard, J. J. Toward theories of persuasion and belief change. *Journal of Personality and Social Psychology*, 1981, *40*, 260–269.

Jaccard, J. J., & Fishbein, M. Inferential beliefs and order effects in personality impression formation. *Journal of Personality and Social Psychology*, 1975, *31*, 1031–1040.

Jacoby, J., & Hoyer, W. D. Viewer miscomprehension of televised communication: Selected findings. *Journal of Marketing*, 1982, *46*, 12–26.

Jacoby, J., Hoyer, W. D., & Sheluga, D. A. *Miscomprehension of televised communications*. NY: American Association of Advertising Agencies, 1980.

Janis, I. L., & Feshbach, S. Effects of fear-arousing communications. *Journal of Abnormal and Social Psychology*, 1953, *48*, 78–92.

Janis, I. L., & King, B. The influence of role playing on opinion change. *Journal of Abnormal and Social Psychology*, 1954, *49*, 211–218.

Janis, I. L., & Rife, D. Persuasibility and emotional disorder. In I. L. Janis & C. I. Hovland (Eds.), *Personality and persuasibility*. New Haven, CT: Yale University Press, 1959.

Janis, I. L., & Terwilliger, R. An experimental study of psychological resistances to fear arousing communications. *Journal of Abnormal and Social Psychology*, 1962, *65*, 403–410.

Johnson, H. H., & Izzett, R. R. Relationship between authoritarianism and attitude change as a function of source credibility and type of communication. *Journal of Personality and Social Psychology*, 1969, *13*, 317–321.

Johnson, H. H., & Scileppi, J. A. Effects of ego-involvement conditions on attitude change to high and low credibility communicators. *Journal of Personality and Social Psychology*, 1969, *13*, 31–36.

Johnson, H. H., & Stanicek, F. F. Relationship between authoritarianism and attitude change as a function of implicit and explicit communications. *Proceedings of the 77th Annual Convention of the American Psychological Association*, 1969, *4*, 415–416.

Johnson, H. H., Torcivia, J. M., & Poprick, M. A. Effects of source credibility on the relationship between authoritarianism and attitude change. *Journal of Personality and Social Psychology*, 1968, *9*, 179–183.

Jones, E. E., & Davis, K. E. From acts to dispositions: The attribution process in person perception. In L. Berkowitz (Ed.), *Advances in experimental social psychology* (Vol. 2). NY: Academic Press, 1965.

Jones, E. E., & Gerard, H. B. *Foundations of social psychology*. NY: Wiley, 1967.

Jones, E. E., & Harris, V. A. The attribution of attitudes. *Journal of Experimental Social Psychology*, 1967, *3*, 1–24.

Jones, E. E., & McGillis, D. Correspondent inferences and the attribution cube: A comparative reappraisal. In J. H. Harvey, W. J. Ickes, & R. F. Kidd (Eds.), *New directions in attribution research* (Vol. 1). Hillsdale, NJ: Erlbaum, 1976.

Jones, E. E., Worchel, S., Goethals, G. R., & Grumet, J. F. Prior expectancy and behavioral extremity as determinants of attitude attribution. *Journal of Experimental Social Psychology*, 1971, *7*, 59–80.

Kahneman, D. *Attention and effort*. Englewood Cliffs, NJ: Prentice-Hall, 1973.

Kaplan, M. F. Dispositional effects and weight of information in impression formation. *Journal of Personality and Social Psychology*, 1971, *18*, 279–284. (a)

Kaplan, M. F. The effect of judgmental dispositions on forming impressions of personality. *Canadian Journal of Behavioural Science*, 1971, *3*, 259–267. (b)

Kaplan, M. F. The modifying effect of stimulus information on the consistency of individual differences in impression formation. *Journal of Experimental Research in Personality*, 1972, *6*, 213–219.

Kaplan, M. F. Stimulus inconsistency and response dispositions in forming judgments of other persons. *Journal of Personality and Social Psychology*, 1973, *25*, 58–64.

Katz, D. The functional approach to the study of attitudes. *Public Opinion Quarterly*, 1960, *24*, 163–204.

Katz, D., & Scotland, E. A preliminary statement to a theory of attitude structure and change. In S. Koch (Ed.), *Psychology: A study of a science* (Vol. 3). NY: McGraw-Hill, 1959.

Kelley, H. H. Attribution theory in social psychology. In D. Levine (Ed.), *Nebraska Symposium on Motivation* (Vol. 15). Lincoln, NE: University of Nebraska Press, 1967.

Kelley, H. H. Attribution in social interaction. In E. E. Jones, D. E. Kanouse, H. H. Kelley, R. E. Nisbett, S. Valins, & B. Weiner (Eds.), *Attribution: Perceiving the causes of behavior*. Morristown, NJ: General Learning Press, 1972. (a)

Kelley, H. H. Causal schemata and the attribution process. In E. E. Jones, D. E. Kanouse, H. H. Kelley, R. E. Nisbett, S. Valins, & B. Weiner (Eds.), *Attribution: Perceiving the causes of behavior*. Morristown, NJ: General Learning Press, 1972. (b)

Kelley, H. H., & Michela, J. L. Attribution theory and research. *Annual Review of Psychology*, 1980, *31*, 457–501.

Kelman, H. C. Attitude change as a function of response restriction. *Human Relations*, 1953, *6*, 185–214.

Kelman, H. C. Compliance, identification, and internalization: Three processes of attitude change. *Journal of Conflict Resolution*, 1958, *2*, 51–60.

Kelman, H. C. Processes of opinion change. *Public Opinion Quarterly*, 1961, *25*, 57–78.

Kelman, H. C. Social influence and linkage between the individual and the social system: Further thoughts on the processes of compliance, identification, and internalization. In J. Tedeschi (Ed.), *Perspectives on social power*. Chicago: Aldine, 1974.

Kelman, H. C., & Eagly, A. H. Attitude toward the communicator, perception of communication content, and attitude change. *Journal of Personality and Social Psychology*, 1965, *1*, 63–78.

Kenny, D. A. *Correlation and causality*. NY: Wiley, 1979.

Kiesler, C. A., Collins, B. E., & Miller, N. *Attitude change: A critical analysis of theoretical approaches*. NY: Wiley, 1969.

Kiesler, C. A., & Kiesler, S. B. Role of forewarning in persuasive communications. *Journal of Abnormal and Social Psychology*, 1964, *68*, 547–549.

King, B. T., & Janis, I. L. Comparison of the effectiveness of improvised versus non-improvised role-playing in producing opinion changes. *Human Relations*, 1956, *9*, 177–186.

Koeske, G. F., & Crano, W. D. The effect of congruous and incongruous source-statement combinations upon the judged credibility of a communication. *Journal of Experimental Social Psychology*, 1968, *4*, 384–399.

Langer, E. J. Rethinking the role of thought in social interaction. In J. H. Harvey, W. J. Ickes, & R. F. Kidd (Eds.), *New directions in attribution research* (Vol. 2). Hillsdale, NJ: Erlbaum, 1978.

Langer, E. J., Blank, A., & Chanowitz, B. The mindlessness of ostensibly thoughtful action: The role of "placebic" information in interpersonal interaction. *Journal of Personality and Social Psychology*, 1978, *36*, 635–642.

Lasswell, H. D. The structure and function of communication in society. In L. Bryson (Ed.), *The communication of ideas*. NY: Harper, 1948.

Lay, C. H., Burron, B. F., & Jackson, D. N. Base rates and informational value in impression formation. *Journal of Personality and Social Psychology*, 1973, *28*, 390–395.

Lehmann, S. Personality and compliance: A study of anxiety and self-esteem in opinion and behavior change. *Journal of Personality and Social Psychology*, 1970, *15*, 76–86.

Lewin, K. *The conceptual representation and the measurement of psychological forces*. Durham, NC: Duke University Press, 1938.

Lewin, K. *Field theory in social science: Selected theoretical papers*. New York: Harper, 1951.

Lipstein, B. Theories of advertising and measurement systems. In R. W. Olshavsky (Ed.), *Attitude research enters the '80s*. Chicago: American Marketing Association, 1980.

Loken, B., & Fishbein, M. An analysis of the effects of occupational variables on childbearing intention. *Journal of Applied Social Psychology*, 1980, *10*, 202–223.

Lumsdaine, A. A., & Janis, I. L. Resistance to "counterpropaganda" produced by one-sided and two-sided "propaganda" presentations. *Public Opinion Quarterly*, 1953, *17*, 311–318.

Lutz, R. J. Changing brand attitudes through modification of cognitive structure. *Journal of Consumer Research*, 1975, *1*(4), 49–59.

Lutz, R. J. An experimental investigation of causal relations among cognitions, affect, and behavioral intention. *Journal of Consumer Research*, 1977, *3*, 197–208.

Maddux, J. E., & Rogers, R. W. Effects of source expertness, physical attractiveness, and supporting arguments on persuasion: A case of brains over beauty. *Journal of Personality and Social Psychology*, 1980, *39*, 235–244.

McArdle, J. B. *Positive and negative communications and subsequent attitude and behavior change in alcoholics*. Unpublished doctoral dissertation, University of Illinois, Urbana-Champaign, 1972.

McArthur, L. Z. Illusory causation and illusory correlation: Two epistemological accounts. *Personality and Social Psychology Bulletin*, 1980, *6*, 507–519.

McArthur, L. Z. What grabs you? The role of attention in impression formation and causal attribution. In E. T. Higgins, C. P. Herman, & M. P. Zanna (Eds.), *Social cognition: The Ontario Symposium* (Vol. 1). Hillsdale, NJ: Erlbaum, 1981.

McGuire, W. J. Order of presentation as a factor in "conditioning" persuasiveness. In C. I. Hovland (Ed.), *The order of presentation in persuasion*. New Haven, CT: Yale University Press, 1957.

McGuire, W. J. A syllogistic analysis of cognitive relationships. In C. I. Hovland & M. J. Rosenberg (Eds.), *Attitude organization and change*. New Haven, CT: Yale University Press, 1960. (a)

McGuire, W. J. Cognitive consistency and attitude change. *Journal of Abnormal and Social Psychology*, 1960, *60*, 345–353. (b)

McGuire, W. J. Direct and indirect persuasive effects of dissonance producing messages. *Journal of Abnormal and Social Psychology*, 1960, *60*, 354–358. (c)

McGuire, W. J. Inducing resistance to persuasion: Some contemporary approaches. In L. Berkowitz (Ed.), *Advances in experimental social psychology* (Vol. 1). NY: Academic Press, 1964.

McGuire, W. J. Attitudes and opinions. *Annual Review of Psychology*, 1966, *17*, 475–514.

McGuire, W. J. Personality and attitude change: An information-processing theory. In A. G. Greenwald, T. C. Brock, & T. M. Ostrom (Eds.), *Psychological foundations of attitudes*. NY: Academic Press, 1968. (a)

McGuire, W. J. Personality and susceptibility to social influence. In E. F. Borgatta & W. W. Lambert (Eds.), *Handbook of personality theory and research*. Chicago: McNally, 1968. (b)

McGuire, W. J. The nature of attitudes and attitude change. In G. Lindzey & E. Aronson (Eds.), *The handbook of social psychology* (Vol. 3, 2nd ed.). Reading, MA: Addison-Wesley, 1969.

McGuire, W. J. Attitude change: The information-processing paradigm. In C. G. McClintock (Ed.), *Experimental social psychology*. NY: Holt, Rinehart, & Winston, 1972.

McGuire, W. J. Some internal psychological factors influencing consumer choice. *Journal of Consumer Research*, 1976, *2*, 302–319.

McGuire, W. J. The probabilogical model of cognitive structure and attitude change. In R. E. Petty, T. M. Ostrom, & T. C. Brock (Eds.), *Cognitive responses in persuasion*. Hillsdale, NJ: Erlbaum, 1981.

McGuire, W. J. Attitudes and attitude change. In G. Lindzey & E. Aronson (Eds.), *Handbook of social psychology* (3rd ed.). Reading, MA: Addison-Wesley, in press.

McGuire, W. J., & Millman, S. Anticipatory belief lowering following forewarning of a persuasive attack. *Journal of Personality and Social Psychology*, 1965, *2*, 471–479.

McGuire, W. J., & Papageorgis, D. Effectiveness of forewarning in developing resistance to persuasion. *Public Opinion Quarterly*, 1962, *26*, 24–34.

McKeachie, W. J. Individual conformity to attitudes of classroom groups. *Journal of Abnormal and Social Psychology*, 1954, *49*, 282–289.

Miller, A. G. Constraint and target effects in the attribution of attitudes. *Journal of Experimental Social Psychology*, 1976, *12*, 325–339.

Miller, D. T., & Ross, M. Self-serving biases in the attribution of causality: Fact or fiction? *Psychological Bulletin*, 1975, *82*, 213–255.

Miller, N. Involvement and dogmatism as inhibitors of attitude change. *Journal of Experimental Social Psychology*, 1965, *1*, 121–132.

Miller, N., & Baron, R. S. On measuring counterarguing. *Journal for the Theory of Social Behaviour*, 1973, *1*, 101–118.

Miller, N., & Campbell, D. T. Recency and primacy in persuasion as a function of the timing of speeches and measurements. *Journal of Abnormal and Social Psychology*, 1959, *59*, 1–9.

Miller, N., & Colman, D. E. Methodological issues in analyzing the cognitive mediation of persuasion. In R. E. Petty, T. M. Ostrom, & T. C. Brock (Eds.), *Cognitive responses in persuasion.* Hillsdale, NJ: Erlbaum, 1981.

Miller, N., Maruyama, G., Beaber, R. J., & Valone, K. Speed of speech and persuasion. *Journal of Personality and Social Psychology,* 1976, *34,* 615–624.

Millman, S. Anxiety, comprehension, and susceptibility to social influence. *Journal of Personality and Social Psychology,* 1968, *9,* 251–256.

Mills, J. Opinion change as a function of the communicator's desire to influence and liking for the audience. *Journal of Experimental Social Psychology,* 1966, *2,* 152–159.

Mills, J., & Aronson, E. Opinion change as a function of the communicator's attractiveness and desire to influence. *Journal of Personality and Social Psychology,* 1965, *1,* 173–177.

Mills, J., & Harvey, J. Opinion change as a function of when information about the communicator is received and whether he is attractive or expert. *Journal of Personality and Social Psychology,* 1972, *21,* 52–55.

Mills, J., & Jellison, J. M. Effect on opinion change of how desirable the communication is to the audience the communicator addressed. *Journal of Personality and Social Psychology,* 1967, *6,* 98–101.

Mitchell, A., & Olson, J. Are product attribute beliefs the only mediator of advertising effects on brand attitude? *Journal of Marketing Research,* 1981, *18,* 318–332.

Moscovici, S. *Social influence and social change.* London: Academic Press, 1976.

Moscovici, S., & Nemeth, C. Social influence II: Minority influence. In C. Nemeth (Ed.), *Social psychology: Classic and contemporary integrations.* Chicago: McNally, 1974.

Nisbett, R. E., & Gordon, A. Self-esteem and susceptibility to social influence. *Journal of Personality and Social Psychology,* 1967, *5,* 268–276.

Nisbett, R., & Ross, L. *Human inference: Strategies and shortcomings of social judgment.* Englewood Cliffs, NJ: Prentice-Hall, 1980.

Norman, R. When what is said is important: A comparison of expert and attractive sources. *Journal of Experimental Social Psychology,* 1976, *12,* 294–300.

Orvis, B. R., Kelley, H. H., & Butler, D. Attributional conflict in young couples. In J. H. Harvey, W. J. Ickes, & R. F. Kidd (Eds.), *New directions in attribution research* (Vol. 1). NY: Wiley, 1976.

Osgood, C. E., & Tannenbaum, P. H. The principle of congruity in the prediction of attitude change. *Psychological Review,* 1955, *62,* 42–55.

Osterhouse, R. A., & Brock, T. C. Distraction increases yielding to propaganda by inhibiting counterarguing. *Journal of Personality and Social Psychology,* 1970, *15,* 344–358.

Ostrom, T. M. Theoretical perspectives in the analysis of cognitive responses. In R. E. Petty, T. M. Ostrom, & T. C. Brock (Eds.), *Cognitive responses in persuasion.* Hillsdale, NJ: Erlbaum, 1981.

Ostrom, T. M., & Brock, T. C. A cognitive model of attitudinal involvement. In R. P. Abelson, E. Aronson, W. J. McGuire, T. M. Newcomb, M. J. Rosenberg, & P. H. Tannenbaum (Eds.), *Theories of cognitive consistency: A sourcebook.* Chicago: McNally, 1968.

Ostrom, T. M., & Upshaw, H. S. Psychological perspective and attitude change. In A. G. Greenwald, T. C. Brock, & T. M. Ostrom (Eds.), *Psychological foundations of attitudes.* NY: Academic Press, 1968.

Pallak, M. S., Mueller, M., Dollar, K., & Pallak, J. Effect of commitment on responsiveness to an extreme consonant communication. *Journal of Personality and Social Psychology,* 1972, *23,* 429–436.

Pallak, S. R. Salience of a communicator's physical attractiveness and persuasion: A heuristic versus systematic processing interpretation. *Social Cognition,* 1983, *2,* 156–168.

Pallak, S. R., Murroni, E., & Koch, J. Communicator attractiveness and expertise, emotional vs.

rational appeals, and persuasion: A heuristic versus systematic processing interpretation. *Social Cognition*, 1983, *2*, 120–139.

Peak, H. Attitude and motivation. In M. R. Jones (Ed.), *Nebraska Symposium on Motivation* (Vol. 3). Lincoln, NE: University of Nebraska Press, 1955.

Petty, R. E., & Cacioppo, J. T. Forewarning, cognitive responding, and resistance to persuasion. *Journal of Personality and Social Psychology*, 1977, *35*, 645–655.

Petty, R. E., & Cacioppo, J. T. Effects of forewarning of persuasive intent and involvement on cognitive responses and persuasion. *Personality and Social Psychology Bulletin*, 1979, *5*, 173–176. (a)

Petty, R. E., & Cacioppo, J. T. Issue involvement can increase or decrease persuasion by enhancing message-relevant cognitive responses. *Journal of Personality and Social Psychology*, 1979, *37*, 1915–1926. (b)

Petty, R. E., & Cacioppo, J. T. *Attitudes and persuasion: Classic and contemporary approaches.* Dubuque, IA: Wm. C. Brown, 1981.

Petty, R. E., & Cacioppo, J. T. The effects of involvement on responses to argument quantity and quality: Central and peripheral routes to persuasion. *Journal of Personality and Social Psychology*, 1983, *46*, 69–81.

Petty, R. E., Cacioppo, J. T., & Goldman, R. Personal involvement as a determinant of argument-based persuasion. *Journal of Personality and Social Psychology*, 1981, *41*, 847–855.

Petty, R. E., Cacioppo, J. T., & Heesacker, M. Effects of rhetorical questions on persuasion: A cognitive response analysis. *Journal of Personality and Social Psychology*, 1981, *40*, 432–440.

Petty, R. E., Harkins, S. G., & Williams, K. D. The effects of group diffusion of cognitive effort on attitudes: An information processing view. *Journal of Personality and Social Psychology*, 1980, *38*, 81–92.

Petty, R. E., Ostrom, T. M., & Brock, T. C. Historical foundations of the cognitive response approach to attitudes and persuasion. In R. E. Petty, T. M. Ostrom, & T. C. Brock (Eds.), *Cognitive responses in persuasion.* Hillsdale, NJ: Erlbaum, 1981.

Petty, R. E., Wells, G. L., & Brock, T. C. Distraction can enhance or reduce yielding to propaganda: Thought disruption versus effort justification. *Journal of Personality and Social Psychology*, 1976, *34*, 874–884.

Pomazal, R. J. Salient beliefs and attitude change over time: An experimental approach. *Representative Research in Social Psychology*, 1983, *13*, 11–22.

Reardon, K. K. *Persuasion: Theory and context.* Beverly Hills, CA: Sage Publications, 1981.

Regan, D. T., & Cheng, J. B. Distraction and attitude change: A resolution. *Journal of Experimental Social Psychology*, 1973, *9*, 138–147.

Rhine, R. J., & Severance, L. J. Ego-involvement, discrepancy, source credibility, and attitude change. *Journal of Personality and Social Psychology*, 1970, *16*, 175–190.

Rogers, R. W. A protection motivation theory of fear appeals and attitude change. *Journal of Psychology*, 1975, *91*, 93–114.

Rogers, R. W., & Mewborn, C. R. Fear appeals and attitude change: Effects of a threat's noxiousness, probability of occurrence, and the efficacy of coping responses. *Journal of Personality and Social Psychology*, 1976, *34*, 54–61.

Rokeach, M. *Beliefs, attitudes, and values: A theory of organization and change.* San Francisco: Jossey-Bass, 1968.

Roloff, M. E., & Miller, G. R. (Eds.) *Persuasion: New directions in theory and research.* Beverly Hills, CA: Sage Publications, 1980.

Romer, D. Distraction, counterarguing and the internalization of attitude change. *European Journal of Social Psychology*, 1979, *9*, 1–17. (a)

Romer, D. Internalization versus identification in the laboratory: A causal analysis of attitude change. *Journal of Personality and Social Psychology*, 1979, *37*, 2171–2180. (b)

Rosenberg, M. J. *A value theory of attitude*. Unpublished doctoral dissertation, University of Michigan, 1953.

Rosenberg, M. J. Cognitive structure and attitudinal affect. *Journal of Abnormal and Social Psychology*, 1956, *53*, 367–372.

Rosenberg, M. J. An analysis of affective-cognitive consistency. In C. I. Hovland & M. J. Rosenberg (Eds.), *Attitude organization and change*. New Haven, CT: Yale University Press, 1960.

Rosenberg, M. J. Hedonism, inauthenticity, and other goads toward expansion of a consistency theory. In R. P. Abelson, E. Aronson, W. J. McGuire, T. M. Newcomb, M. J. Rosenberg, & P. H. Tannenbaum (Eds.), *Theories of cognitive consistency: A sourcebook*. Chicago: McNally, 1968.

Rosenberg, M. J. The conditions and consequences of evaluation apprehension. In R. Rosenthal & R. L. Rosnow (Eds.), *Artifact in behavioral research*. NY: Academic Press, 1969.

Rosenthal, R., & Rubin, D. B. Comparing effect sizes of independent studies. *Psychological Bulletin*, 1982, *92*, 500–504.

Ross, H. L., Jr. Recall versus persuasion: An answer. *Journal of Advertising Research*, 1982, *22*, 13–16.

Rotter, J. B. *Social learning and clinical psychology*. NY: Prentice-Hall, 1954.

Sawyer, A. Repetition, cognitive responses, and persuasion. In R. E. Petty, T. M. Ostrom, & T. C. Brock (Eds.), *Cognitive responses in persuasion*. Hillsdale, NJ: Erlbaum, 1981.

Scheier, M. F. Effects of public and private self-consciousness on the public expression of personal beliefs. *Journal of Personality and Social Psychology*, 1980, *39*, 514–521.

Scheier, M. F., & Carver, C. S. Private and public self-attention, resistance to change, and dissonance reduction. *Journal of Personality and Social Psychology*, 1980, *39*, 390–405.

Schlenker, B. R. *Impression management: The self-concept, social identity, and interpersonal relations*. Monterey, CA: Brooks/Cole, 1980.

Schlenker, B. R. Translating actions into attitudes: An identity-analytic approach to the explanation of social conduct. In L. Berkowitz (Ed.), *Advances in experimental social psychology* (Vol. 15). NY: Academic Press, 1982.

Schmittlein, D. C., & Morrison, D. G. Measuring miscomprehension in televised communications using true–false questions. *Journal of Consumer Research*, 1983, *10*, 147–156.

Schneider, D. J., Hastorf, A. H., & Ellsworth, P. C. *Person perception* (2nd ed.). Reading, MA: Addison-Wesley, 1979.

Schneider, W., & Shiffrin, R. M. Controlled and automatic human information processing: I. Detection, search, and attention. *Psychological Review*, 1977, *84*, 1–66.

Sensenig, J., & Brehm, J. W. Attitude change from an implied threat to attitudinal freedom. *Journal of Personality and Social Psychology*, 1968, *8*, 324–330.

Shanteau, J. C., & Anderson, N. H. Test of a conflict model for preference judgment. *Journal of Mathematical Psychology*, 1969, *6*, 312–325.

Sherif, C. W., Sherif, M., & Nebergall, R. E. *Attitude and attitude change: The social judgment-involvement approach*. Philadelphia: Saunders, 1965.

Sherif, M., & Cantril, H. *The psychology of ego-involvements: Social attitudes and identifications*. NY: Wiley, 1947.

Sherif, M., & Hovland, C. I. *Social judgment: Assimilation and contrast effects in communication and attitude change*. New Haven, CT: Yale University Press, 1961.

Shiffrin, R. M., & Schneider, W. Controlled and automatic human information processing: II. Perceptual learning, automatic attending, and a general theory. *Psychological Review*, 1977, *84*, 127–190.

Sloan, L. R., & Ostrom, T. M. Amount of information and interpersonal judgment. *Journal of Personality and Social Psychology*, 1974, *29*, 23–29.

Slovic, P., & Lichtenstein, S. Comparison of Bayesian and regression approaches to the study of information processing in judgment. *Organizational Behavior and Human Performance*, 1971, *6*, 649–744.

Snyder, M. L. Self-monitoring of expressive behavior. *Journal of Personality and Social Psychology*, 1974, *30*, 526–537.

Snyder, M. L., & Wicklund, R. A. Prior exercise of freedom and reactance. *Journal of Experimental Social Psychology*, 1976, *12*, 120–130.

Sternthal, B., Dholakia, R., & Leavitt, C. The persuasive effect of source credibility: Tests of cognitive response. *Journal of Consumer Research*, 1978, *4*, 252–260.

Sternthal, B., Phillips, L. W., & Dholakia, R. The persuasive effect of source credibility: A situational analysis. *Public Opinion Quarterly*, 1978, *42*, 285–314.

Stotland, E., & Canon, L. K. *Social psychology: A cognitive approach*. Philadelphia: Saunders, 1972.

Taylor, S. E., & Fiske, S. T. Salience, attention, and attribution: Top of the head phenomena. In L. Berkowitz (Ed.), *Advances in experimental social psychology* (Vol. 11). NY: Academic Press, 1978.

Taylor, S. E., & Thompson, S. C. Stalking the elusive "vividness" effect. *Psychological Review*, 1982, *89*, 155–181.

Tedeschi, J. T., Schlenker, B. R., & Bonoma, T. V. Cognitive dissonance: Private ratiocination or public spectacle? *American Psychologist*, 1971, *26*, 685–695.

Thistlethwaite, D. L., de Haan, H., & Kamenetzky, J. The effects of "directive" and "nondirective" communication procedures on attitudes. *Journal of Abnormal and Social Psychology*, 1955, *51*, 107–113.

Tolman, E. C. *Behavior and psychological man: Essays in motivation and learning*. Berkeley: University of California Press, 1958.

Walster, E., Aronson, E., & Abrahams, D. On increasing the persuasiveness of a low prestige communicator. *Journal of Experimental Social Psychology*, 1966, *2*, 325–342.

Walster, E., & Festinger, L. The effectiveness of "overheard" persuasive communications. *Journal of Abnormal and Social Psychology*, 1962, *65*, 395–402.

Watts, W. A., & Holt, L. E. Logical relationships among beliefs and timing as factors in persuasion. *Journal of Personality and Social Psychology*, 1970, *16*, 571–582.

Watts, W. A., & McGuire, W. J. Persistence of induced opinion change and retention of the inducing message contents. *Journal of Abnormal and Social Psychology*, 1964, *68*, 233–241.

Wicklund, R. A. *Freedom and reactance*. Potomac, MD: Erlbaum, 1974.

Wicklund, R. A., & Brehm, J. W. Attitude change as a function of felt competence and threat to attitudinal freedom. *Journal of Experimental Social Psychology*, 1968, *4*, 64–75.

Wicklund, R. A., & Brehm, J. W. *Perspectives on cognitive dissonance*. Hillsdale, NJ: Erlbaum, 1976.

Wood, W., & Eagly, A. H. Stages in the analysis of persuasive messages: The role of causal attributions and message comprehension. *Journal of Personality and Social Psychology*, 1981, *40*, 246–259.

Wood, W., Kallgren, C. A., & Priesler, R. M. *Access to attitude-relevant information in memory as a determinant of persuasion: The role of message and communicator attributes*. Unpublished manuscript, Texas A & M University, 1983.

Worchel, S., & Arnold, S. E. The effects of censorship and attractiveness of the censor on attitude change. *Journal of Experimental Social Psychology*, 1973, *9*, 365–377.

Worchel, S., Arnold, S. E., & Baker, M. The effects of censorship on attitude change: The influence of censor and communication characteristics. *Journal of Applied Social Psychology*, 1975, *5*, 227–239.

Worchel, S., & Brehm, J. W. Effect of threats to attitudinal freedom as a function of agreement with the communicator. *Journal of Personality and Social Psychology*, 1970, *14*, 18–22.

Wyer, R. S. Quantitative prediction of belief and opinion change: A further test of a subjective probability model. *Journal of Personality and Social Psychology,* 1970, *16,* 559–570.

Wyer, R. S. *Cognitive organization and change: An information-processing approach.* Potomac, MD: Erlbaum, 1974.

Wyer, R. S. Functional measurement methodology applied to a subjective probability model of cognitive functioning. *Journal of Personality and Social Psychology,* 1975, *31,* 94–100.

Wyer, R. S., & Goldberg, L. A probabilistic analysis of the relationships among beliefs and attitudes. *Psychological Review,* 1970, *77,* 100–120.

Wyer, R. S., & Hartwick, J. The role of information retrieval and conditional inference processes in belief formation and change. In L. Berkowitz (Ed.), *Advances in experimental social psychology* (Vol. 13). NY: Academic Press, 1980.

Zellner, M. Self-esteem, reception, and influenceability. *Journal of Personality and Social Psychology,* 1970, *15,* 87–93.

Zimbardo, P. G., & Ebbesen, E. B. Experimental modification of the relationship between effort, attitude, and behavior. *Journal of Personality and Social Psychology,* 1970, *16,* 207–213.

Zimbardo, P., Snyder, M., Thomas, J., Gold, A., & Gurwitz, S. Modifying the impact of persuasive communications with external distraction. *Journal of Personality and Social Psychology,* 1970, *16,* 669–680.

Zuckerman, M. Attribution of success and failure revisited, or: The motivational bias is alive and well in attribution theory. *Journal of Personality,* 1979, *47,* 245–287.

HELPING BEHAVIOR AND ALTRUISM: AN EMPIRICAL AND CONCEPTUAL OVERVIEW

John F. Dovidio

DEPARTMENT OF PSYCHOLOGY
COLGATE UNIVERSITY
HAMILTON, NEW YORK

ADVANCES IN EXPERIMENTAL
SOCIAL PSYCHOLOGY, VOL. 17

I. Introduction

A. HISTORICAL AND CONCEPTUAL OVERVIEW

Although helping behavior and altruism have only recently been examined in depth by experimental psychologists, these topics have a long and rich philosophical and theoretical history. Questions over whether humans are by nature good or bad, selfless or selfish, altruistic or egoistic have been the subject of debate for centuries (e.g., by Aristotle, Socrates). Scientific interest in altruism was initially stimulated in the late 1800s by the work of Charles Darwin. In addition, social psychologists seem to have been interested in altruistic motivation for as long as social psychology has been recognized as a distinct field. In the discipline's first text, *An Introduction to Social Psychology,* McDougall (1908) hypothesized that instincts formed the basis for human altruistic activity and that these ''sympathetic instincts'' were stronger in women than in men.

The 20-year period from 1962 to 1982 clearly represents the ''golden age'' of research on helping behavior and altruism. These two decades are characterized by unprecedented empirical activity. When the total number of articles and chapters in psychology-related journals and books is examined, the amount of research is impressive. There have been over 1050 scholarly papers published on human altruism and helping behavior (Dovidio, 1982). As Fig. 1 illustrates, over 98% of this research has been published since 1962! In 1975 alone, the year of peak activity, there were more than 100 articles and chapters published on these topics.

The research of the early and the mid-1960s typically focused on norms, such as social responsibility and reciprocity, that seemed to govern help giving. In the later 1960s, the influence of social learning theory was evident. Experiments examined the effects of models on both children and adults. By the end of the decade and into the early 1970s, investigators, stimulated by public outrage at bystander apathy and guided by the pioneering research of Latané and Darley (1970), explored factors that reduced the likelihood of intervening in crisis and emergency situations. The research of the mid-1970s appeared dedicated to detailing the factors that inhibit and promote helping. This period is also characterized by considerable interest in the development of altruism and helping behavior. During the late 1970s and the early 1980s, there has been increasing concern with developing theories that not only describe *when* people will or will not intervene but also explain *why*. Current theorists in this area are attempting to understand some of the more basic and more general motivational issues, often in terms of the initial philosophical debates (e.g., egoism versus altruism).

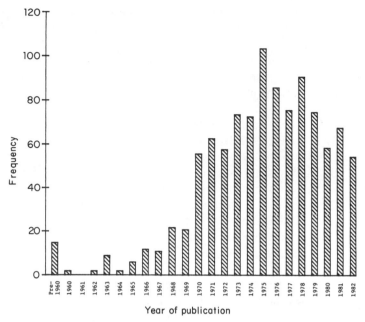

Fig. 1.   Frequency of studies published each year on helping behavior and altruism.

Despite (or perhaps because of) the impressive amount of research that has focused on prosocial, helping, and altruistic behaviors, there is little consensus concerning how these terms should be defined or distinguished from one another. Comte (1851–1875) introduced the term altruism in reference to sympathetic instincts (which he believed were anatomically localized) and sympathetic motivations for social behavior. Current definitions of *altruism* vary quite widely, and many bear little resemblance to Comte's original concept. The four dimensions that researchers have most frequently used to identify altruistic behavior are (1) the consequence of the act for the recipient, (2) the locus of reinforcement (i.e., internal or external), (3) the intent of the benefactor, and (4) the motivation underlying helping.

Definitions of altruism become more restrictive as they move from consideration of consequence to intention then to motivation. Dawkins (1976), like many sociobiologists, defines altruistic behavior broadly—based only on the consequences of the action: "An entity . . . is said to be altruistic if it behaves in such a way as to increase another such entity's welfare at the expense of its own" (p. 4). Psychologists, in contrast, generally emphasize the importance of intention as well as outcome. Underwood and Moore (1982a) define altruism as "behaviors done with the apparent intent of benefiting another more than oneself" (p. 7); Krebs (1982) describes altruism as a "willingness to sacrifice one's own welfare for the sake of another" (p. 55). Macaulay and Berkowitz's (1970) definition of altruism, one that is widely recognized in the field, refers to the consequences, the intention, and the potential source of rewards. Specifically, they define altruism as "behavior carried out to benefit another without anticipation of rewards from external sources" (p. 3). Still other investigators (e.g., Bar-Tal & Raviv, 1982; Batson & Coke, 1981) have argued that a conceptual distinction between altruism and other types of helping behavior can be made only if motivational bases are considered. Bar-Tal and Raviv's (1982) conceptualization represents the restrictive end of a broad-to-narrow continuum of definitions. It includes all four critical dimensions: outcome, intent, locus of reinforcement, and motivation. They propose: "Altruism, as one type of helping act that is at the highest level of quality, is defined as voluntary and intentional behavior carried out for its own end to benefit a person, as a result of moral conviction in justice and without expectations for external rewards" (p. 199).

In the present chapter, prosocial, helping, and altruistic behavior are distinguished from one another. The first terminological distinction is between the broad category of prosocial behavior and other types of behaviors (i.e., antisocial and nonsocial acts). As Piliavin, Dovidio, Gaertner, and Clark (1981) suggest, *prosocial behavior* means no more, and no less, than behavior that is valued by the individual's society. Assisting others, donating to charity, cooperating with others, and intervening to save another person's life are all acts that societies generally value. In some instances, however, there may be inconsistencies in the standards that different societies apply to evaluate behavior. "Good Samaritan" laws that required citizens to come to the aid of others were legislated in Nazi Germany; one purpose was to enlist the assistance of citizens in the government's campaign against Jews.

Helping behavior can be considered to be a subcategory of prosocial behavior. Helping behaviors are defined as voluntary acts performed with the intent to provide some benefit to another person. These behaviors may or may not require personal contact with the recipient, and they may or may not involve anticipation of external rewards. It is important to note that this definition is based on the perspective of the benefactor. It is possible that the recipient does not share the benefactor's perception of benefit or that the action does not actually improve the welfare of the recipient. Actually, few studies attempt to assess the intentions of a bystander. Thus, in practice, helping behavior generally refers to apparently intentional acts that either seem to or actually do benefit the recipient. The term altruism is reserved for a special type of helping that involves favorable consequences for the recipient, an intent to help by the benefactor, no obvious external reinforcement, and a motivation "directed toward the end-state goal of increasing the other's welfare" (Batson & Coke, 1981, p. 173). Unless researchers make a strong empirical or theoretical case that each of these criteria is satisfied, the act is considered to be helping or prosocial behavior.

B. CHAPTER OVERVIEW

The major purpose of the present chapter is to review the determinants of intervention in response to problems, crises, and emergencies and to provide an integrative overview of current theoretical perspectives on helping behavior and altruism. The chapter is generally structured around the arousal: cost–reward model that was introduced by Piliavin, Rodin, and Piliavin (1969) and revised by Piliavin, Dovidio, Gaertner, and Clark (1981, 1982). This model attempts to integrate a wide variety of factors involved in helping behavior (see Fig. 2). The model identifies two conceptually separate but functionally interdependent factors that influence helping behavior. The first factor, arousal in response to the need or distress of others, is basically an emotional response and can be considered the fundamental motivational construct of the model. Arousal is the process through which bystanders are mobilized for action that could lead to intervention and helping. The second factor is a cost–reward component. This involves the cognitive processes through which bystanders weigh various anticipated costs and rewards associated with action and inaction. Although these two components are conceptually distinct, often times they are functionally related (see Fig. 2). Many of the situational, social, and personality variables that increase arousal also affect perceived costs. Variations in arousal can also produce changes in the perceptions or assessment of costs; the recognition of potential costs can, in turn, influence arousal.

Although it is beyond the scope of the chapter to develop the arousal: cost–

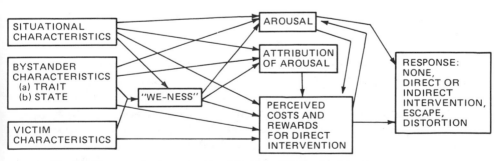

Fig. 2.   The arousal: cost–reward model. (From Piliavin, Dovidio, Gaertner, & Clark III, 1981.)

reward model fully and to discuss its implications completely, it can be summarized briefly. (See Piliavin *et al.*, 1981, for a thorough description.) A fundamental proposition of the model is that the observation of an emergency arouses a bystander. The degree of arousal is directly related to the severity and clarity of the emergency and to the proximity and emotional involvement with the victim. The model also proposes that the arousal occasioned by observation of an emergency becomes more unpleasant as it increases, and the bystander is therefore motivated to reduce it. It is further hypothesized that the bystander will choose to respond in a way that will most rapidly and completely reduce arousal, incurring in the process as few net costs (costs minus rewards) as possible. There are, however, certain specifiable circumstances that give rise to rapid, impulsive, noncalculative, "irrational" emergency-helping behavior.

In the present review of the determinants of prosocial, helping, and altruistic behavior, the propositions of the arousal: cost–reward model are discussed in order. At each step, the arousal: cost–reward model is used as a basis for comparing and contrasting different conceptual and empirical approaches. The data related to the model are first considered. Then, where additional theory and empirical evidence exist, these approaches and findings are reviewed. The section "Motivational Constructs" begins with a discussion of internal mediators and reviews the data on arousal and helping behavior. Empathy and feelings of moral obligation, as well as related motivational constructs, are also considered. The section "Cost and Reward Considerations" reviews the effects of costs and rewards on helping. Next, in the section "Moods and Helping" research on moods is summarized. The presence of other bystanders, situational factors related to impulsive intervention, and the relationship between the victim and the bystander are examined in the section "The Social Context of Helping." In the last section of the chapter, the arousal: cost–reward model is evaluated, and implications for future research are discussed.

Because it is not possible to review all of the altruism and helping behavior literature in one chapter, it is also important to indicate what is not covered. The extensive literature on helping in nonhuman species and on sociobiological approaches is not discussed in detail. Also, there is no separate section devoted to personality factors. This is not to suggest (as some writers believe) that personality does not relate to helping. Rather, the decision was based on *how* personality seems to relate to helping. Empirically and theoretically, researchers have made a strong case for a person × situation approach (see Staub, 1978). Thus, studies of personality factors are discussed within the topic sections that take a situational approach. For more extended reviews of how personality relates to helping, the reader is directed to Piliavin *et al.* (1981), Staub (1980), and Rushton (1980, 1981). For reasons similar to those for personality, no separate section on the development of altruism appears. Reviews of the developmental literature can be found in Rushton (1980), Rushton and Sorrentino (1981), and Eisenberg

(1982). In addition, only help giving is discussed. For reviews of help seeking and recipient reactions to aid, consult Fisher, DePaulo, and Nadler (1981) and Fisher, Nadler, and Witcher-Alagna (1982).

II. Motivational Constructs

According to the arousal: cost–reward model, there are both emotional and cognitive determinants of intervention. In particular, it is hypothesized that bystanders are motivated to help because intervention is perceived as being an effective way to reduce unpleasant arousal generated by witnessing another person's distress. In less severe situations, psychological tensions associated with anticipated costs and rewards can also motivate helping. This section, therefore, examines both affective and cognitive mediators of prosocial, helping, and altruistic behavior.

A. AFFECTIVE MEDIATORS OF HELPING BEHAVIOR AND ALTRUISM

Several models of helping behavior rely on arousal or empathy as primary motivational constructs underlying helping and altruism. Arousal is a central motivational concept in the Piliavin *et al.* (1981, 1982) model. Specifically, the arousal: cost–reward model proposes that arousal is generated by witnessing the distress of another person. This arousal is related to a "defense reaction" (Lynn, 1966), a physiological response characterized by strong sympathetic nervous system activation. When the arousal is attributed to the emergency, it is emotionally experienced as unpleasant; and the bystander is therefore motivated to reduce it. Other researchers (e.g., Aronfreed, 1968; Batson & Coke, 1981; Hoffman, 1981a, b) use empathic arousal or empathy as their primary motivational constructs. Hoffman (1981a), for example, defines *empathy* as "an affective response appropriate to someone else's situation rather than to one's own" (p. 128). Batson and Coke (1981) supply an even more restrictive definition of empathy. According to these authors, empathy is "an emotional response elicited by and congruent with the perceived welfare of someone else" (p. 169).

1. Arousal

There is considerable empirical support for the hypothesis, which the Piliavin *et al.* (1981, 1982) model shares with several other models of helping, that people are aroused by the distress of others. In fact, the evidence is sufficiently persuasive that Hoffman (1981a) proposes that empathic arousal "appears to be

a universal human response for which there is a constitutional basis'' (p. 128).
Studies using indirect measures of arousal such as reaction time (e.g., Weiss,
Buchanan, Altstatt, & Lombardo, 1971) and direct physiological measures of
arousal (e.g., Gaertner & Dovidio, 1977; Krebs, 1975) consistently demonstrate
that individuals are aroused by the distress and suffering of another. This
vicarious arousal is generally similar to but less intense than the arousal caused
by a more direct threat to the self. There is also evidence showing similar
affective reactions in the response of the bystander and of the victim. In an
experiment by Vaughn and Lanzetta (1980), subjects witnessed a person showing strong facial distress in response to repeated, apparently painful, electric
shocks. The subjects reacted not only with physiological arousal but also with
affective facial expressions that resembled those of the person who was being
shocked. Moreover, there is evidence that even 1- and 2-day old infants respond
to the distress of another infant (Martin & Clark, 1982; Sagi & Hoffman, 1976;
Simner, 1971).

Supportive of the arousal: cost–reward model, contextual factors, such as
the severity of the situation and the relationship with the victim, systematically
influence arousal. For both indirect and direct measures of arousal, emergencies
of greater clarity and severity generate higher levels of bystander arousal (e.g.,
Byeff, 1970; Sterling, 1977). In addition, there is evidence indicating that
arousal increases as the length of the observer's exposure to the emergency
increases if no intervention occurs (Gaertner & Dovidio, 1977; Gaertner,
Dovidio, & Johnson, 1982). Although research directly examining the effects of
the bystander's relationship with a victim on arousal is surprisingly infrequent,
the evidence that does exist (Krebs, 1975; Stotland, 1969) supports the hypothesis that closer relationships with a victim increase a bystander's level of arousal.

The arousal: cost–reward model further proposes that the arousal generated
by the observation of another's distress is unpleasant and, consequently, the
bystander is motivated to reduce it. Piliavin et al. (1981, 1982) find substantial
evidence that supports this hypothesis. Studies that have measured both arousal
and helping behavior consistently demonstrate a positive relationship. Greater
levels of arousal, measured by self-report (e.g., Clark & Word, 1974; Gaertner
& Dovidio, 1977), galvanic skin response (GSR) (e.g., Byeff, 1970), or by heart
rate (e.g., Gaertner & Dovidio, 1977; Gaertner et al., 1982) are associated with
faster rates of intervention. When a bystander is the only witness to an emergency in which are are low costs for intervention, the correlations between the
physiological arousal and the speed of helping range from .45 to .77.

Additional empirical evidence demonstrates that arousal is not merely associated with helping but that it can, in fact, motivate helping behavior. Weiss and
his colleagues (Weiss et al., 1971; Weiss, Boyer, Lombardo, & Stich, 1973)
showed that vicarious arousal can activate instrumental responses that relieve the

suffering of victims. These researchers concluded that an aversive state is aroused by the suffering of another and that this state behaves like other drive states in motivating a person to alleviate another's distress. In a series of experiments based on excitation-transfer theory, Mueller and Donnerstein demonstrated that arousal generated by media violence (Mueller, Nelson, & Donnerstein, 1977), aggressive films (Mueller, Donnerstein & Hallam, 1983), and erotic films (Mueller & Donnerstein, 1981) facilitated later helping behavior, particularly when subjects had an emotional bond with the person in need. In addition, attribution of one's arousal to the other's distress is an important factor affecting a bystander's motivation to intervene in an emergency. Gaertner and Dovidio (1977) demonstrated that subjects who misattributed arousal that was generated by an ambiguous emergency to a placebo showed significant decreases in helpfulness. Furthermore, Sterling and Gaertner (in press) report that arousal from physical exercise that could be attributed to an unambiguous emergency increased the speed of bystander intervention. In an ambiguous emergency situation in which emergency-generated arousal could be attributed to previous physical activity, however, higher levels of exercise were associated with slower helping. Attribution-related effects have also been observed in less emergencylike situations (e.g., Coke, Batson, & McDavis, 1978; Harris & Huang, 1973). Coke et al. (1978) found that subjects who were administered a placebo described as having side effects of autonomic arousal volunteered less time for baby-sitting to a student who lost her parents in an accident than did subjects who attributed their arousal to the student's need.

Although many researchers agree that general arousal and empathic arousal seem to motivate intervention, there is much less consensus about the affective nature of this arousal. Depending upon the situation, arousal may sometimes be interpreted as one emotion, sometimes as a quite different emotion. In severe emergency situations subjects respond with upset and distress (Gaertner & Dovidio, 1977); in less critical, less intense problem situations, arousal may be conceptualized as promotive tension (Hornstein, 1982) or may be interpreted as empathic concern and compassion (Batson & Coke, 1981). Weiner (1980) proposes a general attributional framework that emphasizes a three-step cognition-affect-helping process. Specifically, he suggests that another's need for help, especially when it occurs unexpectedly, stimulates a search for causes. The perceived causes are then examined and analyzed (with locus and controllability being particularly important dimensions). These attributions, in turn, create an affective experience that motivates helping. The nature of the affective experience (e.g., sympathy or disgust) is determined by the attributions that the bystander makes. Thus, Weiner (1980) suggests that "attributions guide our feelings, but emotional reactions provide the motor and the direction for behavior" (p. 186).

2. Promotive Tension

Hornstein and his colleagues (see Hornstein, 1976, 1982) have applied the concept of promotive tension, which is based on the Lewinian (see Lewin, 1951) tension system construct that relates tension to psychological needs and intentions in an attempt to understand the motivation underlying helping behavior. Promotive tension is defined as "tension coordinated with *another's* need or goals" (Hornstein, 1982, p. 230). That is, one's own need state can become coordinated to that of another, which then motivates behavior to reduce this tension. A feeling of "we-ness," however, must characterize the relationship with the other person before promotive tension can be aroused (Hornstein, Marton, Rupp, Sole, & Tartell, 1980). We-ness can be based on similarity, group identification, or interdependence.

Hornstein and his colleagues propose that, because people often require assistance to achieve their goals, promotive tension often mediates helping behavior. In support of this reasoning, Hornstein, Masor, Sole, and Heilman (1971) arranged for pedestrians in a Jewish section of New York City to find two envelopes clipped together, apparently dropped by accident. Similarity was manipulated by whether the person's attitudes (which were expressed on a questionnaire in one of the envelopes) were pro-Israeli or pro-Arab. The contents of the second envelope, a check and a contribution card indicating whether the enclosed contribution to the "Institute for Research in Medicine" was the second or ninth in a series of 10 planned contributions, set the stage for the test of Lewinian assumptions about psychological tension. As Hornstein *et al.* (1971) hypothesized, the interrupted goal-related activity of liked others was completed (i.e., the lost envelope was mailed) more often when the people were close to completing their goal of 10 contributions. For dissimilar strangers, closeness to the goal had no effect. These findings, plus the results of several other experiments, provide strong evidence for the hypothesized influence of "socially mediated Zeigarnik effects" in which promotive tension, an unpleasant arousal state, mediates helping behavior (see Hornstein, 1982).

3. Empathic Concern

Batson and his colleagues (e.g., Batson & Coke, 1981; Coke *et al.*, 1978) present a theoretical model of altruistic behavior in which arousal is a central construct. These authors have attempted to demonstrate that empathic concern, which is created by the distress of another and is characterized by feelings of compassion and softheartedness, motivates altruism. Batson and Coke (1981) propose that this model is fundamentally different from other arousal models in that (1) empathic concern is conceptually distinct from unpleasant feelings that bystanders might experience but which are not feelings *for* the victim, and (2) empathic concern evokes an *altruistic* motivation that has the goal of increasing the other person's welfare (rather than by the bystander's own welfare). Batson and Coke (1981) do not refute the possibility that helping can be motivated by the desire to alleviate one's own distress that is associated with observing the plight of a victim. Rather, they suggest that under certain specifiable conditions empathic concern will be aroused and will motivate *altruistic* action.

There appears to be consistent empirical support for the basic assumptions of Batson's model. Five studies (Batson & Coke, 1981; Batson, O'Quin, Fultz, Vanderplas, & Isen, 1983) demonstrate that feelings of personal distress (i.e., upset, troubled, alarmed, disturbed, and distressed) are qualitatively distinct from feelings of empathic concern (i.e., empathic, concerned, warm, soft-hearted, and compassionate). In further support of Batson's distinction, Davis (1980) developed a multidimensional empathy inventory, the Interpersonal Reactivity Index, in which two of the subscales measure separate emotional reactions. One of the subscales, the empathic concern scale, measures other-oriented feelings such as sympathy and concern; the other emotional subscale, the personal distress scale, assesses self-oriented emotions such as anxiety and unease. Additional research (Davis, 1983a) demonstrates that scores on the empathic concern and personal distress subscales display different patterns of relationship with other measures (e.g., egotism or self-esteem). Thus, although feelings of empathic concern and personal distress in response to a victim's plight (e.g., the need for assistance on a research project or the experience of pain from repeated electric shocks) are typically highly associated (Davis, 1983b, reports an average correlation of .52 across five experiments conducted by Batson and his colleagues, see Batson & Coke, 1981), there is evidence that these emotions are empirically as well as conceptually distinct.

A second fundamental assumption of Batson's (see Batson & Coke, 1981) model is that empathy motivates altruistic behavior. Several experiments (e.g., Archer, Diaz-Loving, Gollwitzer, Davis, & Foushee, 1981; Batson et al., 1983; Coke et al., 1978) have demonstrated a positive relationship between feelings of empathic concern and helping behavior. Empathic concern was simply measured or was manipulated indirectly by varying bystander similarity with the victim (e.g., Batson, Duncan, Ackerman, Buckley, & Birch, 1981) or by giving the instructional set to imagine the feelings of the victim (Toi & Batson, 1982). More direct evidence that empathic concern has motivational properties distinct from personal distress comes from a series of experiments that manipulated factors designed to elicit greater empathic concern or greater personal distress and manipulated factors related to the ease of escaping from the situation without helping. Specifically, Batson and his colleagues (see Batson & Coke, 1981) reasoned that if bystanders are egoistically motivated, then ease of escape would affect intervention. Subjects would be expected to be less helpful when the costs for escaping are low than when they are high. If, however, helping is altruistically motivated by empathic concern, then Batson and his colleagues suggest that ease of escape would be unrelated because escaping would not reduce the other person's distress. There is consistent empirical support for these hypotheses (e.g., Batson *et al.,* 1981, Experiment 2; Batson *et al.,* 1983; Toi & Batson, 1982). Therefore, research has indicated that arousal in the form of empathic concern, as well as in the form of distress, is capable of motivating prosocial behavior.

In the experiments by Batson and his colleagues that manipulated similarity to the victim or instructional set (Batson *et al.,* 1981; Toi & Batson, 1982), it is possible to explain the different patterns of helping associated with the ease of escape within the arousal: cost–reward framework. The costs (e.g., guilt or blame) for not helping a similar victim or a victim with whom one identifies are likely to be higher than the costs for not helping a dissimilar victim or one with whom one does not identify. Thus, even when situational factors make escape easy, social factors differentially influence the costs for not helping and hence the rates of helping. The experiment in which the preponderance of empathic concern or personal distress was influenced by leading subjects to misattribute specific emotions to a placebo (Batson *et al.,* 1981, Experiment 2), however, poses a more direct challenge to the arousal: cost–reward model. This experiment indicates that there are two dynamically distinct emotional responses to the need of another person: personal distress and empathic concern. Consistent with the arousal: cost–reward framework, bystanders were motivated to reduce their personal distress generated by the plight of the victim. However, inconsistent with the assumption that bystanders are motivated to reduce their *own* arousal, empathic concern appears to motivate a bystander to reduce *another's* distress. Thus, there seem to be special costs for not helping that are inherent in empathic concern that are not involved in personal distress.

4. Developmental Trends Involving Arousal, Empathy, and Helping

Underwood and Moore (1982b) provide a comprehensive review of the literature on developmental trends in the relationship between individual differences in empathy and in helping behavior. Individual differences in empathy are most frequently assessed in children by the Feshbach and Roe (1968) scale in which responses associated with fear, anger, sadness, and happiness are summed into a single empathy score. (Feshbach, 1982 has introduced a new empathy test that assesses emotional responses to videotapes involving children experiencing strong emotion in common childhood situations.) The Mehrabian and Epstein (1972) scale, which measures emotional response to others' needs, and the Davis (1980) Interpersonal Reactivity Index, which is a multidimensional measure of empathy with empathic concern, personal distress, perspective taking, and fantasy subscales, are most commonly used with adolescents and adults.

After combining the results of 10 studies of trait empathy (and empathic arousal) and helping behavior, Underwood and Moore (1982b) concluded, as did Kurdek (1978) and Krebs and Russell (1981) in previous literature reviews, that there is no systematic relationship between trait measures of empathy and helping behavior among children. Two studies conducted with adolescents also yielded inconsistent results. Why are trait measures of empathy unrelated to helping behavior in children? One explanation proposed by Krebs and Russell (1981) is based on the observation that there is little consistent relationship among measures of prosocial behavior. Rushton (1976) reviewed various measures and concluded that the typical intercorrelation was around .30. If there is little consistency among measures of helping, then it should not be surprising that there is little consistency in the relationship between empathy and helping. Yet, the relationship between measured empathy and helping is consistent among adults. A second explanation of the lack of relationship focuses on the measures of empathy. Hoffman (1977, 1981b) questioned the psychometric properties of scales that were used to assess empathy in children. Indeed, a relatively consistent pattern emerges when studies are organized by empathy measures. There appears to be little systematic relationship between empathy, as measured by the Feshbach and Roe (1968) scale, and helping; the correlations are more consistent when the Mehrabian and Epstein (1972) and the Davis (1980) scales are used.

Because age of the subject and measure of empathy are generally confounded across studies, it is also possible that developmental trends may account for the different patterns of results across experiments. Hoffman (1975, 1977, 1981b), for example, presents a developmental model of empathy. According to Hoffman, children in the first year of life are capable of experiencing empathic distress in response to the distress of another person. Infants, however, are unable to distinguish between their own experience and the experience of the other person. By the age of one, the child can recognize the physical distinction between the self and another person, and by the age of two or three the child can sense that others have inner states. The child at this stage, though, is not able to clearly identify what these inner states are. By late childhood and early adolescence, greater cognitive complexity and greater role-taking ability develop, and empathically aroused affect combines with an image of the other person's plight. At this stage, people's empathic distress may be transformed in part into a feeling of concern for the victim, and this concern motivates helping. Thus according to Hoffman's model, the affective component of empathy is experienced differently as the child matures socially and cognitively. It is often not until early adolescence that this affect leads to a motivation to reduce another's distress. It is also around this age that the relatively consistent relationship between measured empathy and helping begins to emerge. In further support of the hypothesized developmental changes in the relation between empathy and helping, Zahn-Waxler, Friedman, and Cummings (1983) showed that although children from preschool age to preadolescence reported empathy (in response to infants' cries) to about the same degree, there were significant increases with age in prosocial intentions. Also consistent with the finding that the link between empathy and helping becomes stronger with age, research by Eisenberg, Lennon, and Roth (1983) demonstrates that the importance of empathic reasoning for prosocial moral judgments becomes greater with age throughout the elementary school years. Thus, the finding of no systematic relationship between empathy and helping among younger chuldren may reflect their empathic immaturity.

The work of Cialdini and his colleagues (*e.g.,* Cialdini & Kenrick, 1976; Cialdini, Baumann, & Kenrick, 1981) also suggests that developmental and socialization factors may mediate the relationship between arousal and helping. In particular, if, as the arousal: cost–reward model proposes, helping behavior is motivated by a desire to reduce unpleasant arousal associated with the distress of another, then empathic arousal and intervention will be related only if the bystander perceives that helping will be instrumental in relieving his or her unpleasant state. Because children learn through the socialization process that helping has rewarding properties, Cialdini and Kenrick (1976) predicted age-related differences in the extent that children would engage in helping as a way of alleviating an unpleasant affective state. Consistent with this hypothesis, there were no significant differences between the helping actions of younger children (6- to 8-year olds and 10- to 12-year olds) who experienced a negative mood state and of control subjects who did not experience a negative affect. Among older children (15- to 18-year olds) who had presumably internalized the reward properties of prosocial behavior, there was an effect for mood. Subjects who experienced negative affect helped more than did control subjects. Thus, although the model proposed by Cialdini and his colleagues does not directly address the effects of empathy, it does suggest that an understanding of the rewarding properties of helping must develop before a consistent arousal-helping link can occur. Younger children may recognize the distress of others and may even experience negative arousal themselves, but they might not intervene because they do not understand that helping will reduce their unpleasant arousal state. Consistent with the developmental trends revealed in Underwood and Moore's (1982b) review of the empathy literature, Cialdini's work indicated that this understanding is not fully developed until early adolscence.

B.   LEARNED HELPFULNESS

A considerable amount of social psychological research has investigated the acquisition and maintenance of helping behavior from a learning theory perspective. Three basic processes have been implicated: classical conditioning, operant conditioning, and social learning. With respect to the arousal: cost–reward model, learning affects the arousal in response to another's crisis, the understanding that helping can reduce unpleasant arousal, and the anticipation of costs and rewards. The fundamental assumption of learning-oriented approaches is that helping develops rewarding properties in the same manner as do other types of behavior. This research can be summarized on the basis of the types of experimental paradigms that are commonly used: direct reinforcement, persuasion, role playing, and modeling.

1. Direct Reinforcement

The work of Aronfreed and Paskal (1966) first demonstrated the importance of classical conditioning in the acquisition of helping behavior. In one phase of their experiment involving 7- and 8-year-old girls, an adult's expression of distress (the conditioned stimulus) was paired with a loud, unpleasant noise (the unconditioned stimulus) played through the children's earphones. In the second phase of the experiment, children who had previous conditioning experience with the distress of another were more helpful to another child who displayed distress cues than were children in a control group who had no previous conditioning experience. Aronfreed and Paskal proposed that the conditioned negative response to another person's distress increased the subject's motivation to help.

From an operant perspective, people learn to help others because they have made helping responses that have been positively reinforced in the past. Moss and Page (1972), for example, demonstrated the effects of reinforcement associated with helping on subsequent help giving by adults. A confederate asked a subject for directions, and then in some conditions reacted pleasantly and politely and in other conditions responded unpleasantly and impolitely. Compared to a control group, subjects who had the positive experience were more likely to help, and subjects who had the unpleasant experience were less likely to help. Behavior modification techniques (e.g., Barton & Ascione, 1979) are also very effective at teaching children how to act prosocially and at increasing the probability that they will perform helping behaviors. In general, researchers (e.g., Gelfand & Hartmann, 1982; Grusec, 1981, 1982; Rushton, 1976; 1980, 1982; Staub, 1979, 1981) who have reviewed the development and socialization of prosocial behavior have concluded that previous learning is an important determinant of helping behavior.

2. Persuasion and Role Playing

Although helping is a very common activity, even during the first 2 years of life (Rheingold, 1982), it is sometimes necessary or desirable to use verbal persuasion or role playing to increase helping among children. Several experiments (e.g., Eisenberg-Berg & Geisheker, 1979; Midlarsky & Bryan, 1972; Rushton, 1975) demonstrate that persuasion (e.g., telling children that it is good to give to others) can generally be an effective way to facilitate helping. Several important factors, however, must be considered: the nature of the message (e.g., Grusec, Saas-Kortsaak, & Simutis, 1978; Zahn-Waxler, Radke-Yarrow, & King, 1979), the consistency between the message and observed behavior (e.g., Rushton, 1975), and the degree of reactance generated by the message (e.g., Rice & Grusec, 1975). Staub (1979, 1981) suggests that persuasion is most effective when it is used in conjunction with prosocial behavior that the child is already exhibiting. In this way, the verbal communication provides reasons why they are engaging in prosocial behavior, and the children's behavior increases the salience of the prosocial inductions. Staub (1979, 1981) also proposes that children can learn through participation in helping activities. Allowing children to play the role of helpers, of people being helped, or both increases their subsequent prosocial activity.

3. Modeling

The effects of models on the helping behavior of both adults and children have been extensively researched (see Rushton [1976, 1982] for reviews). Much of this research has been conducted in the laboratory, but studies in naturalistic settings generally show similar results. Krebs (1970) proposed that models can affect helping by providing an example of how to perform a prosocial act, by reminding observers of norms and appropriate behaviors, or by increasing observers' confidence in being able to help. More typically, researchers have emphasized the role of modeling in the socialization and development of prosocial behavior. With respect to the arousal: cost–reward model, the consequences of a model's behavior primarily influences an observer's perceptions of costs and rewards.

Consistent with predictions based on social learning theory, both the consequences to the model and the characteristics of the model can mediate the influence of prosocial models. As with direct learning experience, vicarious positive outcomes increase the model's effectiveness at promoting helping, whereas vicarious negative outcomes decrease the likelihood that the observer will subsequently help (Hornstein, Fisch, & Holmes, 1968). Midlarsky and Bryan (1972) demonstrate that vicarious reinforcement can either increase selfishness or selflessness. The observation of a generous model who showed a positive emotional reaction increased helping; the observation of a selfish model who displayed pleasant feelings reduced helping.

The influences of a model's power and nurturance on the effectiveness of modeling have also been investigated. In particular, people who are perceived to have direct control over reinforcements for the observer are more effective prosocial models than are people who do not possess the power to control the observer's outcomes (Grusec, 1971; Rushton, 1975). With respect to nurturance,

Grusec (1981) concludes (as did Rushton [1976] in an earlier review) that the findings are more equivocal. Laboratory manipulations of nurturance, which typically involve brief interactions in which an adult model behaves either pleasantly and warmly or unpleasantly and coldly toward the subject, do not seem generally to increase children's imitation of prosocial acts (e.g , Staub, 1971a; Weissbrod, 1976). These null results, however, may reflect weaknesses in the manipulations. Studies that have examined longer term relationships (Rosenhan, 1969; Rutherford & Mussen, 1968; Yarrow, Scott, & Waxler, 1973) suggest that nurturance can enhance the effectiveness of prosocial models.

Krebs (1970) argues that if modeling truly contributes to the internalization of prosocial behavior, then the effects should be durable across time and generalizable across situations. Both Rushton (1976) and Grusec (1981) conclude that the effects of modeling are lasting in that exposure to a model can affect the behavior of 7- to 11-year-old children over 4 months later. The effects of modeling also appear to be generalizable to some extent across situations (e.g., Elliot & Vasta, 1970; Grusec, Kuczynski, Rushton, & Simutis, 1978). Thus, the overall pattern of results for modeling experiments seem to satisfy Krebs' (1970) criteria for genuine learning and internalization.

In summary, then, the direct reinforcement, behavior modification, verbal persuasion, role playing, and modeling techniques all rely explicitly or implicitly on learning-based theories of behavior. The activity of the individual is directly or indirectly shaped into a prosocial response and then reinforcements are provided. Reinforcers may be direct or vicarious, primary or secondary, immediate or delayed, continuous or partial, and social or nonsocial. Nevertheless, the principles and assumptions are fundamentally the same. People learn to be helpful. Of course, these forces similarly influence selfish and aggressive behaviors. In the context of the arousal: cost–reward model, learning provides the mechanism through which children come to understand the relationship between helping and the reduction of their distress associated with another's needs. Learning also influences children's appreciation of potential cost and reward consequences associated with their action or inaction.

C. SOCIAL NORMS AND INTERNAL STANDARDS

Several researchers have referred to social norms to explain the motivation underlying helping behaviors. These normative theories emphasize that people help others because they have expectations based on previous social learning or the current behavior of others that it is the socially appropriate response. Thus, helping is viewed as "a function of pressure to comply with shared group expectations about appropriate behavior that are backed by social sanctions and rewards" (Schwartz & Howard, 1982, p. 346). In terms of the arousal: cost–

reward model, norms can operate in two ways to influence helping. First, social norms can have an arousal component. According to Schwartz and Howard (1982), social norms can elicit affective feelings such as shame, fear, or pride in anticipation of how other people will react. Second, norms can directly influence perceived costs (e.g., social sanctions as well as personal guilt if norms are internalized) and rewards (e.g., social reinforcement).

Two types of norms related to helping have generally been proposed. The first type, which Karylowski (1982) terms "norms of aiding," refers to a widespread norm that people are supposed to help a person who is dependent upon them. Berkowitz (1972) calls this the norm of social responsibility and Leeds (1963) refers to it as the norm of giving. The second type of norm that has received considerable empirical attention in the helping behavior literature is related to feelings of fairness. Gouldner (1960) proposed a norm of reciprocity. According to this norm, people are supposed to help someone who has previously helped them. Norms of equity (Walster, Walster, & Berscheid, 1978) and norms of justice (Lerner, 1970, 1980) may also be classified in this category of norms.

1. Norms of Aiding

The research conducted by Berkowitz and his colleagues during the early 1960s focused on a generalized social responsibility norm that prescribed that individuals should help those who are dependent upon them. Using a supervisor–worker paradigm, Berkowitz and his associates (e.g., Berkowitz & Connor, 1966; Berkowitz & Daniels, 1963) found, consistent with the hypothesized social responsibility norm, that the more dependent a supervisor was for assistance, the more people helped. This finding occurred even when people believed that the supervisor would not learn of the help for several weeks and that they would have no future interaction with their supervisor. Thus, it is unlikely that subjects' helping was motivated primarily by a desire to gain approval from their supervisor.

Although there is considerable evidence supporting the norm of social responsibility and a direct dependency–helping relationship, research also demonstrates some limitations. First, people are more likely to help a person whose dependency is seen as caused by forces beyond the individual's control than to assist people whose dependency is seen as reflecting personal weakness (e.g., Piliavin et al., 1969; Weiner, 1980). Second, when the situation threatens a person's freedom of action and arouses reactance, there is an inverse relationship between dependency and helping (see Berkowitz, 1973). Third, males and females often respond in quite different ways to dependency manipulations. Males often respond to high dependency by providing less rather than more help (e.g., Enzle & Harvey, 1979; Schopler & Matthews, 1965). Fourth, in any given situation a variety of norms may exist, but the action taken often can only be consistent with one of them (Latané & Darley, 1970). People are frequently confronted with a dilemma in which they feel socially responsible to two people simultaneously, but can only help one (e.g., Batson, Cochran, Biederman, Blosser, Ryan, & Vogt, 1978). Unfortunately, there is no clearcut guideline for telling which norm of social responsibility will have the greater impact. Thus, the generalizability of the social responsibility norm was called into question.

Whereas general norms of social responsibility may provide only a vague guide for behavior in concrete situations, the use of *personal* norms may be valuable in accounting for how a *particular* person will behave in a specific situation. Schwartz's (Schwartz, 1977; Schwartz & Howard, 1981, 1982) normative model of helping behavior describes a five stage decision-making process through which personal and social norms mediate helping behavior. The five stages are (1) attention, (2) motivation, (3) evaluation, (4) defense, and (5) behavior. In the first stage, the bystander's degree and direction of attention mediate readiness for action. The bystander must become aware of the other person's need, identify actions that might relieve the needs of the other person, and recognize that he or she can engage in these actions. The decision made at this step is related to the person's perceptions of costs and rewards for helping and for not helping. Schwartz (1974) has found that scores on an Awareness of Consequences scale (Schwartz, 1968a), which measures the tendency to be aware of the consequences of others' needs, relates to helping behavior, particularly when situational salience is relatively low. The second stage of Schwartz's model involves feelings of obligation that are based on internalized moral values and personal norms. Personal norms are an individual's expressions of feelings of obligation to behave in a particular manner in a particular type of situation. Feelings of moral obligation represent the central motivational construct in this model. They have both cognitive and affective properties. The cognitive property involves expectations of behavior that are associated with self-based standards; the affective component concerns the emotional arousal (e.g., anticipating guilt, pride, fear) related to these expectations. Within Schwartz's framework, empathic arousal as an emotional response is elicited only when reactions to another's need have implications for the bystander's internalized values (Schwartz & Howard, 1981; 1982). Consistent with Schwartz's model, Underwood and Moore's (1982b) review of 19 different experiments revealed a strong relationship between moral reasoning and helping behavior. The relationship appears to be quite generalizable; it is obtained across several different age groups and across diverse measures of prosocial behavior. Schwartz's research on personal norms also provides strong support for his model. Schwartz and other researchers have found that individuals' statements of feelings of moral responsibility toward specific issues predict whether or not they will help (Pomazal & Jaccard, 1976; Schwartz, 1968a, 1970, 1974; Zuckerman & Reis, 1978).

In the evaluation stage of Schwartz's normative model, anticipated costs and rewards associated with various actions are considered. If feelings of moral obligation and cost–reward considerations favor the same response, the defense stage becomes unnecessary, and the person directly enters the behavior stage. If, however, there are conflicting feelings based on feelings of obligation and anticipation of costs and benefits, then a decision about what action to take is delayed as the person enters the defense stage. In the defense stage, conflict is most commonly alleviated by weakening the feelings of moral obligation through redefining aspects of the situation. For example, individual differences in tendencies to accept or deny responsibility mediate the relationship between personal norms and helping. Several experiments (Schwartz, 1968b; 1973; Schwartz & BenDavid, 1976; Schwartz & Fleischman, 1978, 1982) have demonstrated a relatively strong relationship between personal norms and helping among people who are likely to accept responsibility, but they found little correlation among people who are likely to deny responsibility. Once a decision is reached after considering or reconsidering moral obligation and costs and rewards, the person enters the behavior stage of the model. The person helps or does not help. Schwartz and Howard (1981, 1982), though, do not consider this to be a terminal point in the model. Feedback and consequences of each action taken at the behavior stage can alter the structure of internalized values and perceptions of costs, rewards, and social norms. Thus, a future response to a similar situation may differ considerably from past behavior.

2. Norms of Fairness

It has been proposed that another expectation that people learn through the socialization process is that they should help those who have helped them; they should not harm those who have not harmed them; and they should not help those who have denied them help for no apparent legitimate reason (Gouldner, 1960). This norm of reciprocity implies that people attempt to maintain stable reciprocal relationships with others. An imbalance in which one person invests more in the relationship than the other is experienced as uncomfortable and motivates a person to respond. Although there is considerable evidence of reciprocal helping (e.g., Berkowitz & Daniels, 1964), including cross-cultural (e.g., Gergen, Ellsworth, Maslach, & Seipel, 1975) and cross-species data (e.g., Trivers, 1971), the generality of the reciprocity norm is influenced by several aspects of the situation. Reciprocity is less likely when the initial recipient of aid perceives the motive for helping as selfish rather than as unselfish (e.g., Worchel, Andreoli, & Archer, 1976), or when a favor appears to be accidental or required rather than intentional (e.g., Greenberg & Frisch, 1972). Reciprocity is also less likely to occur when people feel pressured to reciprocate or feel resentful for receiving the favor (Fraser & Fujitomi, 1972). In fact, if receiving an unwanted favor makes a person feel that his or her personal freedom is threatened by the obligation to return a favor, individuals may experience psychological reactance and respond with less help in order to reassert their independence (e.g. Brehm & Cole, 1966). Thus, the perception of the benefactor's intentions critically influences whether or not reciprocity motives will be aroused.

Another popular theory used to explain helping behavior involves distributive justice or equity (Adams, 1963; Walster *et al.*, 1978). Equity theory suggests that people try to maintain a proper balance between their inputs and outcomes in a relationship. Fairness, or equity, will be seen to exist when the contributions and outcomes for individuals who are engaged in social exchange appear to balance out. When inequity is perceived, people are motivated to seek an equitable solution. Thus, as Hatfield, Walster, and Piliavin (1978) propose, distress as a function of inequity, like other types of unpleasant arousal, can motivate helping behavior. People who have been inequitably advantaged, who receive too much based on their inputs, often spontaneously choose to redistribute some of their rewards (e.g., Leventhal, Weiss, & Long, 1969). When equity cannot be readily restored by a redistribution of resources, people typically feel guilty or distressed (Lerner & Matthews, 1967). Hence, people who receive help in a manner that does not allow them to restore equity may very likely find it to be an unpleasant experience (e.g., Gross & Latané, 1974).

Equity theory suggests that helping is not the only way that people can respond to the injury or need of another person. There are several responses that a person can make to restore equity: compensating the victim, punishing the perpetrator, or distorting perceptions of the situation (for example, rationalizing that the victim got what he or she deserved). In fact, Lerner and his colleagues (see Lerner, 1970, 1980, 1982) have demonstrated that because people are motivated to see the world as a fair and just place, they often derogate and devalue a victim in need. According to Lerner's original just-world hypothesis, people have a need to believe that the world is fair so that they can maintain feelings of control over their own eventual fate. The observation of an innocent person suffering disconfirms this view of a just-world and threatens one's own fate because good behavior and innocence do not guarantee positive outcomes. Thus, to protect feelings of security and sanity people become motivated to respond in ways that will make things seem fair again. If helping is a possibility, most people will choose to intervene. However, if the person cannot be helped, the just-world hypothesis suggests that bystanders will disparage the victim, thus making the world right again—a world in which people get what they deserve (e.g., Miller, 1977). Lerner and Meindl (1981), however, argue that belief in a just world represents more than self-interest. They present evidence (e.g., Comer

& Laird, 1975; Rubin & Peplau, 1975) that the "threat to a victim's sense of self-worth is of less consequence than the importance of finding justice in their fate" (Lerner and Meindl, p. 221). Consequently, they propose that in adults, the justice motive is "functionally autonomous." Thus, in contrast to most of the traditional normative theories of helping behavior, Lerner and Meindl (1981) believe that self-interest is a "trivial motive" compared with the justice motive.

D. SELF-CONCEPT AND HELPING

Karylowski (1982) proposes that, in general, there are two types of motivations that mediate helping behavior: exocentric and endocentric motivations. In *exocentric motivation,* attention is focused on the need of another person. Improvement in the other's condition, regardless of the cause, is inherently rewarding. Batson's (see Batson and Coke, 1981) conceptualization of empathic concern fits nicely into the exocentric motivation category. In *endocentric motivation,* attention is focused on the self and the self's moral standards, and therefore, improvement in another person's condition is reinforcing only if the individual has an instrumental role in alleviating the other's distress. Karylowski (1982) suggests that Berkowitz's (1972) social norm approach and Schwartz's (1977) personal norm framework represent endocentric approaches to helping behavior. An implication of Karylowski's conceptualization of endocentric motivation is that a person may sometimes offer assistance primarily to reaffirm a self-image as a caring, helpful individual. Thus, general self-image, as well as social expectations and personal moral standards, may mediate helping behavior.

A variety of studies do, in fact, indicate that people who are led to make dispositional self-attributions about their helpfulness subsequently show relatively high levels of helping behavior (e.g., Batson, Harris, McCaul, Davis, & Schmidt, 1979, Strenta & DeJong, 1981). For example, Swinyard and Ray (1979) had door-to-door interviewers tell some of their respondents that they were "interested in their fellow man." This labeling produced an increase in expressing the intention to volunteer for Red Cross activities in response to later mailings. Grusec and her colleagues have also investigated the effects of attributions of helpfulness in children. The results are generally consistent with those for adults. In one experiment (Grusec, Kuczynski, Rushton & Simutis, 1978) 7- to 10-year old children were induced by observing a model to share some of their winnings from a game with poor children. They were given an internal attribution (they were the kind of people who liked to help others), an external attribution (they donated because the experimenter wanted them to give), or no attribution for behavior. As the researchers predicted, children who were given the internal attribution were most likely to help again during the same experimental session. The effect of attribution seemed to endure; 2 weeks later in a separate test, children who had previously been given the internal attribution donated more privately than did children who had been given the external explanation. The fact that this effect occurred for subsequent private generosity in a different situation suggests that the greater helping was a function of self-definition. Additional research (Grusec & Redler, 1980) demonstrated that prosocial attribution and social reinforcement for donating were equally effective in facilitating later donating behavior. The effects of prosocial attribution appeared to be more generalizable, although there appear to be developmental limits to the effectiveness of prosocial attribution. Internal prosocial attributions facilitated generalized prosocial behavior among 8-year-old children but not among 4- and 5-year-olds (Grusec & Redler, 1980).

In summary, internalized standards related to one's self-concept, as well as personal norms and feelings of moral obligation, appear to mediate helping behavior. The consequences of action and inaction on one's self-concept and moral standards are straightforwardly related to cost–reward considerations. Furthermore, it is possible that this influence has an arousal as well as a cognitive component. Perry, Perry, Bussey, English, and Arnold (1980) have suggested that prosocial attribution is effective because failure to live up to these standards can lead to self-criticism. Clearly, negative affective reactions are likely to be aroused by self-criticism. In addition, to the extent that cognitive dissonance is created by behavior that is inconsistent with one's self-image, then helping behavior by people who view themselves as helpful persons may be motivated, in part, by a desire to reduce or to avoid unpleasant arousal.

III. Cost and Reward Considerations

Another proposition of the arousal: cost–reward model asserts that the bystander will choose a response that will most rapidly and completely reduce his or her arousal and that incurs the fewest net costs (i.e., costs minus rewards) as possible. This analysis is based on costs as perceived by the bystander who is involved in the situation and not on costs as assessed by detached observers. Several other researchers have used a cost–benefit analysis to understand helping behavior (Epstein & Hornstein, 1969; Latané & Darley, 1970; Piliavin et al., 1969; Wagner & Wheeler, 1969). These researchers have also generally assumed an economic view of human behavior—individuals are motivated to minimize costs and to maximize rewards.

In the arousal: cost–reward model, there are two basic categories of potential costs and rewards for a bystander. One category is personal costs for helping. These costs involve negative outcomes directly imposed on the benefactor for making a direct helping response. Injury, effort, and embarrassment are examples of potential costs for helping. The other category is costs for the victim not receiving help. It contains two conceptually different subcategories. First, there are personal costs for not helping, which are direct negative outcomes for the bystander for failing to aid a victim. These include guilt and public censure. Second, there are empathic costs for the victim receiving no help, which are based primarily on the bystander's awareness of the victim's continued distress. In particular, these empathic costs involve internalizing the victim's need and distress as well as more sympathetic and concerned feelings for the victim (see Batson & Coke, 1981).

Within the context of the arousal: cost–reward framework, predictions about a bystander's response are a function of both costs for helping and costs for the victim not receiving help. As can be seen in Table 1, when the costs for the victim not receiving help are relatively low, direct helping is predicted to decrease as the costs for helping increase. When the costs for helping are low, helping is predicted to increase as the costs, both personal and empathic, for the victim not receiving help increase. When both types of costs are high, however, victims are predicted to receive either indirect assistance (e.g., calling others to aid the victim) or no help. In the latter case, the bystander is expected to derogate the victim, deny personal responsibility for intervention, or redefine the situation as one not requiring assistance. These responses will serve to reduce perceived personal costs for not helping and/or reduce empathic costs (e.g., unpleasant arousal) associated with the belief that the victim is still needy.

TABLE I

PREDICTED MODAL RESPONSES OF MODERATELY AROUSED OBSERVER AS A JOINT FUNCTION OF COSTS FOR DIRECT HELP AND COSTS FOR NO HELP TO VICTIM

		Costs for direct help		
		Low		High
	High	Direct intervention	Indirect intervention or $\rightarrow$	Redefinition of the situation, disparagement of victim, etc., which lowers costs for no help, allowing $\downarrow$
Costs for no help to victim				
	Low	Variable: will be largely a function of perceived norms in situation		Leaving the scene, ignoring, denial

Note: From Piliavin & Piliavin, 1972. Copyright 1972 by the American Psychological Association. Reprinted by permission.

A. COSTS FOR HELPING

In a review of the literature by Piliavin *et al.* (1981, 1982) of the effects of personal costs for helping on bystander intervention, a consistent pattern emerges. As costs increase, helping decreases. This relationship is obtained even though costs are operationalized in a very wide variety of ways: psychological aversion based on the victim's drunkeness or physical stigma (e.g., Piliavin *et al.*, 1969; Piliavin, Piliavin, & Rodin, 1975), possible physical harm (e.g., Shotland & Straw, 1976); effort and time (e.g., Darley & Batson, 1973), money expended or foregone (e.g., Bleda, Bleda, Byrne, & White, 1976), threat to personal freedom (Berkowitz, 1973), and potential social sanction for violating rules or for giving assistance incorrectly (e.g., Staub, 1971b, 1974). Individual differences in the degree to which subjects feel able to deal effectively with the costs generally reduce the effect (e.g., Ashton & Severy, 1976; Midlarsky & Midlarsky, 1973, 1976; Schwartz & BenDavid, 1976).

Although few experiments have directly examined the effects of rewards (Bickman, 1976; Katz, Farber, Glass, Lucido & Emswiller, 1978; McGovern, Ditizian, & Taylor, 1975; Paulhus, Shaffer, & Downing, 1977; Wilson & Kahn, 1975), the overall pattern of results indicates that rewards (e.g., a "thank you" or monetary compensation) tend to facilitate intervention. Research on similarity and attraction, although very indirect indicators of anticipated rewards, also suggests that anticipated positive outcomes promote helping. In addition, person variables that seem to relate to anticipated rewards have sometimes been shown to influence helping. Wilson (1976) demonstrated that "esteem-oriented" subjects were more likely to help in an emergency than were "safety-oriented" subjects and subjects with a mixed orientation. The effects of rewards, however, appear to be much weaker than those of costs, and there are some inconsistencies in the literature. This may reflect the fact that experimenters ordinarily use less potent manipulations of positive outcomes than of negative outcomes, or it may indicate a theoretical weakness in the cost–reward models. It is also likely, though, that the weaker effect of rewards relative to costs may reflect an important aspect of human decision-making processes: People weigh negative consequences more heavily than positive consequences when they make social decisions (Lynch, 1979).

B. COSTS FOR THE VICTIM RECEIVING NO HELP AND COSTS
   FOR HELPING COMBINED

According to the arousal: cost–reward model, helping should increase as the costs associated with the victim receiving no help increase, except when the costs for helping are high. The results are relatively consistent despite the fact that very different manipulations of costs (e.g., focused responsibility, need and dependency of the victim, anticipated future interaction with the victim) and diverse measures of helping (e.g., emergency and nonemergency intervention) have been used (see Piliavin *et al.*, 1981, 1982). Higher costs for no help typically relate to higher rates of helping (e.g., Berkowitz, 1978; Gottlieb & Carver, 1980; Moriarty, 1975; Schwartz & BenDavid, 1976).

The arousal: cost–reward model suggests, however, that the impact of costs for not helping depends upon the level of costs for helping. Several experiments have simultaneously manipulated costs for helping and costs for the victim receiving no help. The overall pattern of results for eight emergency and non-emergency experiments reviewed by Piliavin *et al.* (1981) plus four other studies (Shotland & Stebbins, 1983, Experiments 1 and 2; Wagner & Wheeler, 1969; Weyant, 1978) suggests that costs for helping have greater impact than do costs for the victim not receiving help. Across all of these studies, helping decreased as costs for helping increased. The effects of costs for the victim receiving no help were weaker, more inconsistent, and often appeared only in interactions with other variables. In general, consistent with the arousal: cost–reward model, costs for *not* helping affect prosocial behavior primarily when the costs *for* helping are low.

Because many real-life emergencies involve both high costs for helping and high costs for not helping, the upper right-hand cell of the cost–reward matrix presented in Table 1 is of particular interest. Piliavin *et al.* (1981) reviewed 14 experiments (see Table 2) that examined amounts of both direct and indirect helping (e.g., phoning for assistance). The findings indicate that although indirect helping does occur more frequently when costs for helping are high, indirect intervention is relatively infrequent. It primarily occurs when an indirect response is made clearly available, is salient during the emergency, and does not require complex activity. Otherwise, inaction is the likely response. Because relatively severe emergencies are arousing and can capture the attention of a bystander, even apparently obvious instruments for indirect helping may be forgotten or too complicated to use.

Cognitive reinterpretation seems to be a common way that bystanders resolve the high costs for helping–high costs for not helping dilemma. In particular, Piliavin *et al.* (1981) propose that the bystander, whose attention is focused primarily on the plight of the victim, first attempts to reduce the perceived costs for not helping. Reinterpreting the costs for not helping by defining the situation as less serious, by diffusing responsibility, or by denigrating the victim can reduce a bystander's unpleasant state of arousal or anticipated guilt and blame for not intervening. With high costs for helping and relatively low costs for not helping, bystanders become less likely to intervene. This process, which also seems related to the defense stage in Schwartz's (Schwartz, 1977; Schwartz &

TABLE II

STUDIES EXAMINING DETERMINANTS OF DIRECT AND INDIRECT HELP

Study	Situation	Subject sex	Percentage helping overall	Percentage helping indirectly	Comments
Schwartz & Gottlieb (1980, Expt. II)	Audio–visually presented seizure	F	92	82	Phone available (done at night)
Schwartz & Gottlieb (1976)	Audio only: theft, physical attack	M	65	67	Bell to summon experimenter (done at night)
Ashton & Severy (1976)	Audio only: falling bookshelves	F	91	55	E^a location explicitly stated
Clark & Word (1974, Expt. I)	Electrical emergency	M	70	37	E location vague
Schwartz & Gottlieb (1980, Expt. I)	Audio–visually presented theft, physical attack	M & F	89	35	Phone available (done at night) anonymous Ss^b help less and help indirectly more (52% versus 79%)
Clark & Word (1974, Expt. II)	Electrical emergency	M	65	29	E location vague

(continued)

TABLE II (*Continued*)

Study	Situation	Subject sex	Percentage helping overall	Percentage helping indirectly	Comments
Shotland & Straw (1976)	Male attacks female	M & F	44	24	Phone available
Schwartz & Clausen (1970)	Audio only seizure	M & F	68	18	E location known both sex (F more) and information (none more) affect level of indirect help
Byeff (1970, unpub.)	Audio or audio—visual fall	M	45	16	Alone Ss more likely to help indirectly than Ss in separated pairs (36% versus 0%)
Piliavin & Piliavin (1972)	Collapse in subway	M & F	85	9	Indirect help all in blood condition
Clark and Word (1972, Expt. I)	Audio:falling workman	M	100	0	In pairs, one would help directly, the other indirectly; E location vague
Clark & Word (1972, Expt. II)	Audio:falling workman	M	100% high ambiguous: 30% low ambiguous	0	Same as Expt. I

Note. From Piliavin, Dovidio, Gaertner, & Clark III, 1981.

[a]E = Experimenter

[b]Ss = Subjects

Howard, 1981, 1982) normative model of helping, underscores the iterative, cyclical processes hypothesized in the arousal: cost–reward and other recent models of helping behavior.

In summary, conceptualizing decision making as a process in which various costs and rewards are weighed is a useful approach to understanding helping behavior. It allows diverse manipulations to be summarized along a limited number of theoretical dimensions and the similarities and differences in the effects of clusters of variables to be analyzed systematically. A weakness of this approach is the tendency to use post hoc cost explanations in ways that imply causality when such inferences are not warranted. For example, because a variable reduces helping it does not necessarily mean that is does so because costs are reduced. Cost explanations too often become circular arguments. In addition, because costs are presumably based on the individual's perceptions, it is often difficult to generate unequivocal predictions. Although many researchers rely on manipulations for which most people's perceptions will be similar, it is also important that an independent assessment of the bystander's perceptions of costs be included in these experimental designs. Heuristically, however, cost–reward analyses seem to add rather than to detract from our understanding of the processes involved in decisions about whether or not to intervene in the crises and problems of others.

IV. Moods and Helping

A considerable amount of study has been devoted to the effects of mood on helping behavior. Nevertheless, the processes by which positive and negative moods influence helping are not clearly understood. Many of the theories that researchers have proposed are related to arousal and cost–reward considerations and bear some resemblance to the affective and cognitive models that have been proposed as general explanations about why people help others. For example, it has been proposed that good moods promote attention to the needs of others and increase the sense of we-ness. Thus, good moods could mediate helping by influencing the bystander's experience of empathic arousal and by affecting the costs for not helping. Other researchers have suggested that people who experience negative states help because it is perceived as a way of reducing unpleasant arousal. Unfortunately, in many of the experiments in this area the arousal, attention, costs, and even the subjective mood state are not independently assessed. Thus the results often appear complex and contradictory, and no comprehensive theory of moods and helping has yet emerged.

A. THE EFFECTS OF GOOD MOODS
    AND POSITIVE FEELINGS

    Although moods are complex experiences (see Polivy, 1981) and obviously
there are many types of "good moods," the effect of feeling good on helping is
remarkably consistent. The results of many experiments involving a variety of
subject populations, research settings, ways of inducing feelings, and types of
helping situations have found that people who feel good, successful, happy, and
fortunate are more likely to help someone else than are people who are not in a
positive state or who feel bad, unsuccessful, sad, or depressed (see Rosenhan,
Salovey, Karylowski, & Hargis, 1981). Several explanations concerning why
good moods facilitate helping have been proposed. One suggests that manipulations of success and failure create differences both in affect and in feelings of
competence. Feelings of competence, in turn, may reduce the impact of costs for
helping, or they may motivate people to reaffirm this self-image, thereby increasing the costs for not helping. Experiments (e.g., Midlarsky & Midlarsky,
1976; Schwartz & BenDavid, 1976) have consistently demonstrated that individuals who feel competent to deal with costs for helping are more likely to
intervene than are people who feel unable to cope with the situation. In fact,
Kazdin and Bryan (1971) found that generalized feelings of competence, even if
unrelated to the potential helping situation, can promote helping behavior.
    The competency explanation, although quite plausible for the studies that
manipulated success and failure, does not address why moods that are induced in
ways unrelated to competence also systematically affect helping. For example,
people who found a dime in a phonebooth, an event that presumably produces
good feelings, were much more likely to help a person pick up papers that she
had dropped, to mail a stamped envelope that was lost, and to mail an unstamped
envelope than were individuals who did not have the good fortune of finding
money (Isen & Levin, 1972; Levin & Isen, 1975). Also, people are in better
moods and are more helpful on sunny, temperate days than on overcast, cold
days (Cunningham, 1979). Thus, good moods can influence helping in ways that
are unrelated to feelings of competence.
    Isen and her colleagues have presented an information processing model of
how moods affect helping. This model, which is dynamically different from
most of the general motivational models of helping, suggests that mood states
influence how individuals process and recall information. A positive mood increases the accessibility of cognitions that are consistent with that affect. People
who are in a good mood are more likely to think positive thoughts, to retrieve
positive thoughts from memory, and to have a more positive outlook on life than
are people who have not recently had a mood-enhancing experience (Isen, Clark,
& Schwartz, 1976; Isen, Shalker, Clark, & Karp, 1978). These people might
also be more likely to consider prosocial activity and perhaps to think more about
the rewards than the cost for helping. Engaging in prosocial behavior, then,

would be consistent with these cognitions associated with positive mood states. In support of this hypothesis, Isen and Levin (1972) found that good moods facilitated subjects' willingness to volunteer to help another person but did not increase their willingness to volunteer to harass another. Also, Isen and Simonds (1978) demonstrated that people who had recently found a dime were willing to read more positive-mood statements but fewer negative mood statements, in response to a request, than did controls. Thus, consistent with Isen's affect–cognition model, positive moods seem to lead to positive thoughts; positive thoughts, in turn, relate to prosocial action.

Hornstein (1982) relates the effects of positive events on helping behavior to his general theory of promotive tension. In particular, he proposes that exposure to positive events, like radio newscasts conveying positive social information, can increase prosocial behavior by fostering a "sense of community" that allows promotive tension to develop. Hornstein (1982) presents empirical evidence that social outlook, which is a cognitive variable, rather than affect, is the mechanism through which positive social information mediates helping behavior. It should be noted, however, that Hornstein's work in this area has been limited to the effects of information provided by newscasts and does not consider the effects of good moods in the ways that other researchers have manipulated them. It is also possible that these other mood-enhancing events (e.g., finding a dime or succeeding on a task) could have an effect through the social outlook on helping behavior and altruism. Indeed, good moods have been shown to increase social interest (Crandall, 1978). Thus one hypothesis might be that good moods generally promote a more positive social outlook, a greater sense of community, and a more embracing definition of we-ness, which then affect responsiveness to another's distress and facilitate prosocial response.

B. THE EFFECTS OF BAD MOODS AND NEGATIVE FEELINGS

Although good moods consistently promote helping behavior, it does not necessarily follow that bad moods inhibit helping. The data for bad moods, in fact, are mixed. Bad moods sometimes increase helpfulness, sometimes decrease helpfulness, and sometimes do not affect helping behavior. Consequently, unlike the case with good moods, it is necessary to distinguish among different types of bad moods to begin to understand how negative states can influence help giving.

Substantial empirical attention has been directed at investigating the effects of an individual's transgression on his or her subsequent willingness to engage in helping behavior. Researchers have frequently used guilt (e.g., Hoffman, 1982) to describe the negative feelings that the person experiences as a result of transgressing, but few studies directly assess the nature of the subjects' affective states. Nevertheless, the results of numerous experiments (see Table 3) consistently demonstrate that people who have accidentally injured somebody or

TABLE III

TRANSGRESSION AND HELPING BEHAVIOR[a]

Study	Transgression	Dependent measure	Subject:	Help directed toward:	Result (trans. vs. control)
Brock & Becker (1966)	Damaged equipment	Sign petition	Participant	Victim	49% vs. 0%*
Darlington & Macker (1966)	Failure caused harm	Donate blood	Participant	Other	100% vs. 57%*
Wallace & Sadalla (1966)	Damaged equipment	Volunteer for experiment	Participant	Other	69% vs. 15%*[a]
Berscheid & Walster (1967)	Deprived partner	Give away green stamps	Participant	Victim	59% vs. 13%*
Freedman, Wallington, & Bless (1967)	Told a lie	Volunteer for experiment	Participant	Other	61% vs. 33%*
	Knocked over cards	Volunteer for experiment	Participant	Other	75% vs. 39%*
	Knocked over cards	Work on research	Participant	Victim	55% vs. 28%*
Silverman (1967)	Cheated on task	Volunteer for experiment	Participant	Victim	85% vs. 92%
Rawlings (1968)	Gave shocks	Distribution of shock to self or other	Participant Witness	Victim Victim	T > C* T > C*
Carlsmith & Gross (1969)	Gave shocks	Make phone calls	Participant	Other	75% vs. 25%*
	Gave shocks	Make phone calls	Participant	Victim	T > C*
			Participant Witness	Other Victim	T > C* T = C
McMillen (1970)	Cheated on task	Circulate petition	Participant	Victim	50% vs. 31%
McMillen (1971)	Cheated on task	Score tests	Participant	Victim	64% vs. 41%
McMillen & Austin (1971)	Cheated on task	Score questionnaire	Participant	Victim	T > C*[b]
J. Regan (1971)	Allowed rat to be shocked	Donate money	Participant Witness	Other Other	56% vs. 43% 73% vs. 43%*
Heilman, Hodgson, & Hornstein	Knocked over slides	Report accident	Participant	Victim	57% vs. 17%*

(continued)

TABLE III (*Continued*)

Study	Transgression	Dependent measure	Subject:	Help directed toward:	Result (trans. vs. control)
(1972)		Volunteer to proofread	Participant	Victim	T = C
Konecni (1972)	Knocked over cards or books	Pick up cards	Participant	Victim	39% vs. 16%*
			Participant	Other	42% vs. 16%*
			Witness	Victim	64% vs. 16%*
Regan, Williams, & Sparling (1972)	Broke camera	Inform person about broken bag	Participant	Other	55% vs. 15%*
Cialdini, Darby, & Vincent (1973)	Knocked over cards	Make phone calls	Participant	Other	60% vs. 50%[b]
			Witness	Other	86% vs. 50%
Noel (1973)	Read bad evaluation	Make phone calls	Participant	Victim	T = C
Wallington (1973)	Cheated on task	Willingness to be shocked	Participant	Other	T > C*
DePalma (1974)	Played roughly	Donate candy	Participant	Other	T > C*
McMillen, Jackson, & Austin (1974)	Cheated on task	Circulate petition	Participant	Victim	T > C*
Donnerstein, Donnerstein, & Munger (1975)	Viewed negative affect slides	Volunteer for experiment	Witness	Other	T > C*
Stewart & Rosen (1975)	Knocked over cards	Address envelopes	Participant	Victim	70% vs. 45%
Harris, & Samorette (1976)	Allowed radio to be stolen	Comply with request for 50 cents	Participant	Other	53% vs. 18%*
Keating & Brock (1976)	Shocked partner	Reward partner with money	Participant	Victim	T > C*
Katsev, Edelsack, Steinmentz, Walker, & Wright (1978)	Touched museum objects	Pick up pencils	Participant	Other	52% vs. 35%[a]
	Fed zoo animals	Pick up fallen articles	Participant	Other	46% vs. 25%

(*continued*)

TABLE III (*Continued*)

Study	Transgression	Dependent measure	Subject:	Help directed toward:	Result (trans. vs. control)
Katz, Glass, Lucido, & Farber (1979)	Read negative evaluation	Work on tedious task	Participant	Victim	T = C
	Controlled noise	Work on tedious task	Participant	Victim	T = C
	Told data not usable	Recruit subjects	Participant	Victim	T > C*
Silverman, Rivera, & Tedeschi (1979)	Cheated on task	Volunteer for experiment	Participant	Victim	T = C
	Lied to the experimenter	Complete questionnaires	Participant	Victim	T = C
Konoske, Staple, & Graf (1979)	Knocked over cards	Make phone calls	Participant	Other	T > C*
Cunningham, Steinberg, & Grev (1980)	Broke camera	Pick up papers	Participant	Other	80% vs. 44%*[b]
	Broke camera	Donate to charity (appeal emphasizes positive outcome)	Participant	Other	10% vs. 15%
		Donate to charity (appeal emphasizes obligation)	Participant	Other	50% vs. 15%*[b]

[a] When positive outcome follows transgression, subjects in control group tend to help more than subjects in transgression condition.

[b] Publicly recognized transgression facilitates helping more than private transgression.

*Indicates statistically significant test.

caused some damage show an increase in helpfulness. The generality of the transgression-induced helping effect is quite impressive. A wide variety of experimental manipulations and measures of helping have been employed with consistent results.

One explanation for the relationship between transgression and helping is the image-reparation hypothesis. This approach focuses on the cognitive impact of transgression on self-image and is related to perceived costs and rewards for helping or for not helping. It shares with some of the more general models of helping the assumption that people are motivated to reaffirm or restore positive self-images. When people unintentionally transgress, their self-concept suffers, and they become motivated to make some positive response that will restore their self-esteem. Helping is one such response. This explanation is consistent not only for the research that shows that people who unintentionally transgress show an increased likelihood of helping the victim, but also with the studies that show that they are more willing to help anyone else who needs assistance (e.g., Regan, Williams & Sparling, 1972). The image-reparation hypothesis also explains why failure can sometimes promote helpfulness. The experience of failure leads to helping primarily when a person has a public opportunity to repair his or her reputation (e.g., Isen, Horn, & Rosenhan, 1973).

Although the notion that people are motivated to repair or reaffirm their self-images seems to account for why individuals who feel responsible for their transgression help more than do nontransgressors, it does not explain other findings in this area. For instance, people who simply witness transgression against someone else also become more helpful (see Table 3). Consequently, Cialdini and his colleagues (see Cialdini, Kenrick, & Baumann, 1982) have proposed a negative-state relief model as an alternative to the image-reparation hypothesis. According to this model, unintentionally harming another person or observing another person being harmed produces a negative emotional state that motivates a response to relieve this negative feeling. Helping others can be instrumental in alleviating this negative state (Harris, 1977). Helping, though, is only one of the many possible mood-enhancing events that can serve to relieve negative affect—other pleasant events like receiving money or praise can also make people feel better. Thus, the negative-state relief model predicts that transgressors and witnesses of transgression are only more likely to help others if no pleasant experiences occur between the transgression and the helping opportunity. If pleasant experiences follow soon after the transgression, transgressors and witnesses should be no more likely to help than nontransgressors.

The negative-state relief model as an explanation for transgression-related helping has received consistent empirical support. People do seem to experience unpleasant emotions after they unintentionally transgress against another person (Cunninghan, Steinberg, & Grev, 1980; Wallington, 1973). In addition, experiments (e.g., Cialdini, Darby, & Vincent, 1973) have demonstrated that causing or witnessing harm to another person promotes helping behavior, except among people who experience a mood-enhancing event (such as receiving money or praise) between the occurrence of the transgression and the opportunity to help. Furthermore, consistent with the hypothesized instrumental link between helping and relief from a negative state, negative moods facilitate helping only if people believe that their moods are alterable (Manucia, Baumann, & Cialdini, 1984). Individual differences in emotional responsiveness (McPeek & Cialdini, 1977) and the degree to which people see helping as a positive activity (Cialdini & Kenrick, 1976) are also important mediators of this relationship.

Although the arousal processes hypothesized in the negative-state relief model appear quite similar to the processes involved in the arousal: cost–reward model, Piliavin *et al.* (1981) identify two important differences. First, the arousal: cost–reward model suggests that transgression will facilitate helping behavior primarily when the residual arousal from the transgression can be attributed to the need of the person requiring aid; Cialdini and his associates imply that misattribution is not necessary. Second, Piliavin *et al.* (1981) emphasize the importance of cost considerations, whereas Cialdini and his colleagues have generally postulated a direct relationship between arousal and helping. Kenrick, Baumann, and Cialdini (1979), however, have recently qualified their model by suggesting that costs and rewards must also be considered in making predictions concerning transgression-induced moods and helping.

C. MOOD, ATTENTION, AND HELPING

Although the negative-state relief model seems to provide a good integrative framework for understanding how some bad moods, particularly transgression-induced states, can influence helping, there are a number of experiments with adults that have not found that bad moods increase helping (e.g., Isen, 1970; Moore, Underwood, & Rosenhan, 1973; Thompson, Cowan, & Rosenhan, 1980). Thus additional factors must be operating. One factor that has sometimes been implicated in the research on both the effects of bad and good moods is attention. In particular, it has been hypothesized that good moods direct one's attention toward others and the environment, whereas certain bad moods like sadness and depression turn one's attention inward. Attention directed toward others is presumed to facilitate helping; a preoccupation with oneself inhibits helping (Aderman & Berkowitz, 1983). An experiment reported by McMillen, Sanders, & Solomon (1977) investigated the three-step process linking mood to attention, then attention to helping, by varying the mood of the subject (through self-esteem feedback) and the salience of the other person's need. As McMillen *et al.* (1977) predicted, when the salience of the need was low, subjects who were in bad moods (and who were less attentive to their environment) helped less frequently than did subjects who were in good moods. When the person in need attracted the attention of the subject, however, subjects in bad moods helped as often as subjects in good moods.

Important questions about how attention combines with emotions and cognitions remain to be answered. Increased attention toward others could intensify a bystander's affective response to another person's need and could simultaneously influence the perceptions or the impact of costs and rewards (e.g., Weyant, 1978). Self-awareness theory (Duval & Wicklund, 1972), which concerns the interrelationships among attention, affect, values and behavior, may provide a valuable framework for understanding how temporary states can influence helping. Research indicates that self-awareness can either inhibit or facilitate helping. Gibbons and Wicklund (1982) propose that self-focus can interfere with the helping process by reducing attentiveness to others and by inhibiting empathy; self-focus can also increase the likelihood of helping when the salience of situational helping norms (e.g., social norms of responsibility) or internal prosocial standards (e.g., personal norms) is high (Hoover, Wood, & Knowles, 1983). This suggests that future research on mood, attention, and helping should consider not only whether attention is directed toward others or toward the self, but also on the aspects of the self on which attention is focused.

Rosenhan and his colleagues (Rosenhan, Salovey, & Hargis, 1981; Rosenhan, Salovey, Karylowski, & Hargis, 1981) have proposed a comparative efficacy model, which is similar in some ways to the "fairness" models of helping that have previously been discussed, in which affect and direction of attention are critical factors. These authors state that when people have an opportunity to help another person a social comparison process is initiated. When an imbalance of resources is perceived, people will respond in ways to restore balance. Affect and attention play important roles in one's perceptions of relative wealth or efficacy. Specifically, according to the comparative efficacy model, people examine their own emotional state to see if it is more or less positive than that of the person who needs assistance. If one perceives that the other person is experiencing more sadness, then helping will occur. Consistent with this prediction, attention to the negative feelings of another person facilitates helping (Thompson et al., 1980). If, however, one perceives that the other person is experiencing more happiness or joy than oneself, helping will be unlikely to occur. Supportive of this hypothesis, Rosenhan, Salovey, and Hargis (1981) found that subjects who attended to their *own* joy were more helpful than control subjects, whereas subjects who attended to *another person's* joy were less helpful than controls.

In summary, moods can affect helping and altruistic behavior through a variety of arousal and cost–reward mechanisms. Good moods can influence attentiveness toward others, perception of the relative need of others, a sense of we-ness with others, feelings of competence, and the salience of rewards for helping. These factors, in turn, can increase arousal, empathic concern, and promotive tension associated with witnessing a victim's distress, can increase the costs for not helping, and can increase the perceived rewards and decrease the perceived costs for helping. In contrast, some bad moods (like depression) may decrease a bystander's attentiveness toward others, may reduce the likelihood that a bystander feels that the victim is relatively needy (compared to himself or herself), may inhibit the formation of we-ness bonds between the bystander and the victim, and may relate to feelings of helplessness that increase the perceived costs and decrease the perceived rewards for helping. Helping that is associated with a previous transgression can be motivated by a desire to reduce an unpleasant arousal state or by a concern to reaffirm a positive self-image. Thus, transgression affects arousal, the rewards for helping, and the costs for not helping. Again, it is important to emphasize that there are many different types of good and bad moods. It is therefore unlikely that any single factor can generally explain the influence of moods on helping behavior.

V.   The Social Context of Helping

This section examines the influences of the presence of other bystanders and the relationship between a bystander and a victim. It begins with a discussion of how the presence of other bystanders can influence the decision of whether or not to intervene, and it concludes with a review of how interpersonal similarity, and the attractiveness and race of a victim determine helping behavior.

A.   THE PRESENCE OF OTHER BYSTANDERS

Probably the most widely known research on helping behavior concerns the effects of the presence of other witnesses on a bystander's response to an emergency. This work was stimulated by Latané and Darley's (1970, 1976) classic decision model of intervention that provided a social psychological explanation concerning why citizens sometimes do not respond to another person's crisis. Their model describes a series of decisions that must be made if an individual is to intervene in another's crisis, problem, or emergency. There are five steps that a bystander must take: (1) Notice the event, (2) Decide whether or not the event is an emergency, (3) Decide on the degree of one's personal responsibility, (4) Decide on a manner of intervention, (5) Implement the decision to intervene. Latané and Darley propose that the presence of others can affect a bystander's response in three ways. First, the presence of others or the belief that others can intervene may allow a person to diffuse not only feelings of responsibility for helping but also guilt and blame for not helping. Second, the reactions of other witnesses to an emergency can provide social information concerning the seriousness of the situation. Third, the behavior of others can affect a bystander's perceptions about what actions are normatively appropriate.

The effects of perceived group size on helping are well documented. Latané and Nida (1981) and Latané, Nida, and Wilson (1981) provide comprehensive reviews of the literature. Latané et al. (1981) report:

> We are aware of some 4 dozen published or unpublished studies from nearly 3 dozen different laboratories reporting data from over 5000 persons faced with the opportunity to help either alone or in the presence of others. With very few exceptions, individuals faced with a sudden need for action exhibit a markedly reduced likelihood of response if other people actually are, or are believed to be available. (p. 290)

Latané and his associates (Latané, Nida, & Wilson, 1981) report that in 48 out of 56 comparisons, people who were in the presence of confederates or who merely believed that other people were present helped less frequently than did people who were alone. Of the people who were alone, 75% intervened; of the people who were actually with confederates or who simply believed that other bystanders were aware of the emergency, 53% helped. Another set of 37 comparisons involved differences in helping between bystanders who were alone and those who were in actual groups of naive subjects. In 31 of these cases the "effective individual probability" of helping for people in groups was lower than the rate for persons who were alone. Of the people who were alone, 50% intervened, but the effective individual response rate for people in groups was only 22%. The inhibiting effect of the presence of others on intervention consistently occurs across a variety of field and laboratory situations (for example, in situations involving staged injuries and accidents, "accidentally" dropped objects, and criminal acts). Clearly, this is a very robust phenomenon.

1. Diffusion of Responsibility

Diffusion of responsibility refers to a bystander's willingness, either consciously or unconsciously, to accept or deny personal responsibility for intervening. When bystanders believe that someone else can help, the pressure that any given bystander must intervene if the victim is to be rescued is reduced. In the classic Darley and Latané (1968) experiment, subjects overheard a victim suffer an apparently severe epileptic seizure. Before the end of the seizure, 85% of the subjects who believed that they were alone intervened, but only 62% of those who believed that one other witness was present and 31% of those who thought that there were four other bystanders helped the victim. A review by Piliavin et al. (1981) of 10 experiments that manipulated the conditions for diffusion to occur reveals additional supporting evidence. Awareness of the presence of other capable bystanders generally inhibits or delays intervention. In addition, Berkowitz (1978) demonstrates that diffusion of responsibility operates in non-emergency situations by minimizing feelings of *personal responsibility* for helping.

Schwartz and Gottlieb (1976) argue that "pure diffusion" effects can only be isolated when the bystander believes that "others are present and that neither he/she nor they are aware of each other's responses" (p. 119). That is, when a subject is aware of how others are responding, informational social influence is involved. When a subject believes that others can monitor his or her behavior, normative processes may operate. Therefore, in studies that have manipulated conditions for diffusion to occur but have also allowed people to monitor each other's responses, diffusion effects are confounded with other types of social influence. Schwartz and Gottlieb (1976), however, were able to demonstrate a pure diffusion effect. Thus, the belief that others are available to help, independent of other types of social influence, can strongly affect helping behavior.

2. Informational Social Influence

Information provided by the reactions of other witnesses is another way that the presence of other bystanders can influence intervention. Whether a confederate acts in a passive or alarmed manner strongly affects a person's response to an emergency. For example, Latané and Darley (1970) found that, compared to being alone, the presence of two confederates who acted calmly as a steady stream of smoke filled the room dramatically reduced the likelihood that subjects would seek assistance. Furthermore, subjects who did not respond to the incident generally concluded that the situation was not dangerous. Other experiments, in which subjects overheard or witnessed an accident involving another person, replicated this finding (e.g., Latané & Rodin, 1969). When other bystanders react with alarm, however, intervention is facilitated (e.g., Staub, 1974; Wilson, 1976).

The effect of informational social influence is most pronounced in ambiguous emergency conditions. Clark and Word (1972) found that under unambiguously critical emergency situations victims were no less likely to be helped by groups of naive subjects than by bystanders who witnessed the emergency alone. The victim received 100% help in both cases. When the emergency was ambiguous, thereby increasing the relative importance of social information provided by others, the victim received help relatively less frequently from bystanders in groups than from bystanders who were alone. Similarly, Solomon, Solomon, and Stone (1978) showed that the inhibiting effect of other bystanders was more pronounced when subjects only heard the sounds of an emergency than when they could both see and hear the incident. Furthermore, social comparison theory suggests that individuals would be more influenced by the reactions of people who are similar to them than of people who are dissimilar to them. Consistent with this hypothesis, Smith, Smythe, and Lien (1972) found that although subjects with a passive confederate helped less often when an emergency occurred than did subjects who were alone, the inhibiting effect of the confederate was much greater when the passive confederate was described as similar to the subject rather than as dissimilar.

3. Normative Social Influence

Normative social influence, which is based on a concern for the evaluation of others, can either inhibit or facilitate intervention. The critical factor is what the bystander believes that others feel is appropriate. If a person believes that it is normatively appropriate to help, then others' awareness of the bystander's behavior should facilitate helping. For example, two experiments by Schwartz and Gottlieb (1976, 1980) were designed to isolate normative social influence effects from diffusion and informational social influence effects. In both studies, bystanders who believed that others were aware of their behavior were more likely to help than were bystanders who believed that their behavior was not being monitored by others. Subjects reported that the awareness that they were being monitored by others increased their feelings of obligation to intervene. If, however, people witness a unanimously nonresponsive reaction by a group, they may come to believe that helping is not appropriate in that situation (e.g., Gaertner, 1975) and, consequently, helping should be inhibited.

Rutkowski, Gruder, and Romer (1983) hypothesize that group cohesiveness mediates how groups norms influence intervention. These investigators reasoned that greater group cohesiveness should make bystanders more responsive to social responsibility norms, thereby increasing their likelihood of helping in an emergency. In one experiment, increased group size (i.e., from two to four) inhibited intervention only in low cohesive groups; in high cohesive groups there was a tendency for a higher proportion of subjects in the larger groups to help. In a second experiment, cohesiveness facilited intervention primarily in the conditions in which the need of the victim was high and the norm of social responsibility was salient. An experiment by Firestone, Lichtman, and Colamosca (1975) also demonstrates the importance of group charasteristics. Groups with a legitimate leadership structure helped more often than groups in which the leader was appointed or in which the election for the leader was rigged. The designs of the Rutkowski et al. (1983) and the Firestone et al. (1975) experiments, however, do not allow comparisons between the responses of group members and the reactions of people who believe that they are the only witness to the emergency. It is possible that groups with a structure and a degree of cohesiveness may behave as a unit and respond in ways more like alone bystanders than like the collection of individuals that form the groups in most of the bystander intervention studies.

4. Processes Mediating the Effects of the Presence of Others

Several investigators have developed models of helping behavior specifically to explain the effects of the presence of others on bystander intervention (e.g., Morgan, 1978). Other researchers have attempted to apply more general models such as the social impact theory (Latané, 1981), objective self-awareness theory (Wegner & Schaefer, 1978), and normative theory (Schwartz & Howard, 1981, 1982). (See Latané, Nida, and Wilson [1981] for a review of these approaches.) The arousal: cost–reward model, one of these general models, suggests that the inhibition of helping due to diffusion of responsibility may be mediated by both cost and arousal factors. If a bystander comes to believe that someone else has intervened or will intervene, then costs for not helping are reduced because the victim will not be left to suffer. In addition, because arousal is hypothesized to be associated with the victim's distress, the belief that the victim could be or is being aided should also lower the bystander's arousal. Gaertner and Dovidio (1977) found that bystanders who overheard an emergency alone showed more arousal in response to the accident than did bystanders who believed that other bystanders were present. Furthermore, much of the inhibiting effect of the presumed presence of others on helping was mediated by this decreased arousal. Thus, both cognitive and arousal factors seem to contribute to bystander inhibition that is based on diffusion of responsibility.

If the social information provided by the face-to-face presence of others inhibits helping by influencing bystanders' perceptions of the seriousness of the situation, then within the arousal: cost–reward framework both personal costs for not helping and empathic costs for the victim receiving no help may be affected. To the extent that the behavior of others leads a person to believe that help is not needed, personal costs for not helping should be reduced because the bystander should feel less social pressure to intervene and should anticipate less blame for not helping. Because a decrease in arousal accompanies the no-help-needed conclusion frequently reached in these situations (Byeff, 1970), empathic costs for not helping are also reduced. Changes in arousal and cost factors are also implicated in the way normative social influence affects helping, but in a way different than that related to informational social influence effects. Because normative influence involves group pressure, personal costs for helping and for not helping are directly affected. In addition, level and attribution of arousal are influenced. Gaertner et al. (1982) found the expected decrease in subjects' speed of intervention as a function of the presence of face-to-face passive confederate bystanders. There was also an increase in heart rate among subjects with non-responsive others, which is perhaps a manifestation of group pressure. Most importantly, however, there was a direct correlation between arousal and speed of intervention for subjects who were alone, but there was an inverse correlation for subjects placed in a unanimously nonresponsive group. Thus, increased arousal due only to the emergency led to faster intervention; arousal beyond that level, which was attributable to normative pressures, produced a hesitancy to intervene.

The arousal: cost–reward model also suggests that under special circumstances impulsive (i.e., rapid, noncalculative) helping may occur and the presence and the behavior of other bystanders will have little effect on intervention. What are the variables that promote impulsive helping? Piliavin et al. (1981) conclude that they are the factors that elicit high levels of arousal: the clarity of the situation (operationally defined as the victim either being visible or calling for help), the reality of the situation (based on whether it was a field or laboratory experiment), and the relationship with the victim (defined as whether or not the bystander and the victim have prior personal contact). Severity was not included in this list because of difficulties in operationalizing this concept across diverse studies. Specifically, it is hypothesized that under highly arousing conditions the bystander's attention becomes focused primarily on the plight of the victim and, consequently, on the costs for the victim receiving no help. Personal costs for helping, including those related to the presence of others, become peripheral and are not attended to. Consistent with this reasoning, a review by Piliavin et al. (1981) of 39 experiments involving 78 separate comparisons indicates that group inhibition effects are less likely to occur under conditions that promote relatively high levels of arousal. In particular, among the studies that had none of the three factors (i.e., clarity and reality of the situation and a prior relationship between the bystander and the victim) that have been shown to relate to high levels of arousal, 59% of the comparisons showed effects associated with the presence of others. Among the studies containing one of the three elements, 64% revealed group-size effects. However, 40% of the comparisons for studies with two of the three factors and only 18% of the comparisons for experiments in which all three factors were involved demonstrated an effect related to the presence of other bystanders. Thus, this review of the literature provides some support, although clearly not conclusive evidence, that certain, specifiable situational factors can elicit rapid intervention that is generally unaffected by cost factors, including those related to the presence of other bystanders.

Morgan (1978) and Lynch and Cohen (1978) present cognitive models of intervention that emphasize cost and benefit factors. In the Morgan model, response latency is hypothesized to be a function of the net expected group benefits (which is related to the degree that the person who needs help will benefit and to the costs to the bystander for not helping) and of the net expected individual benefit (which is a function of personal costs and rewards for helping). Morgan (1978) concludes, with some empirical support, that the inhibiting effect of diffusion of responsibility becomes greater as the costs for helping increase relative to the net individual benefits. Lynch and Cohen (1978) use a subjective utility model to understand group effects on intervention. According to this approach, situational factors affect helping through their influence on the subjective probabilities of consequences that are associated with helping or not helping, the perceived utility of those consequences, and the salience of the consequences. Their model assumes that people will try to choose behaviors with consequences that maximize personal benefits. Thus, this approach is also conceptually similar to the cost–reward formulation of the Piliavin *et al.* (1981, 1982) model. Lynch and Cohen (1978) successfully applied the subjective expected utility model to explain the results of the Darley and Latané (1968) diffusion of responsibility study. They also used it to predict intentions to help, in one experiment, and how badly people would feel for not helping, in a second study. Lynch and Cohen's results did not fit a simple additive subjective expected utility model; certain features apparently received more attention in the decision process than did others. Specifically, Lynch and Cohen suggest that their results demonstrate that bystanders give greatest weight to consequences with extreme implications.

Latané *et al.* (1981) note in their review of cognitive approaches that the situations used to test these cognitive models (e.g., Fishbein, 1967; Lynch & Cohen, 1978; Pomazal & Jaccard, 1976; Zuckerman & Reis, 1978) do not involve significant time pressure, which could significantly influence the decision process. Latané *et al.* (1981) conclude that in nonemergency, as compared to emergency, situations "there is ordinarily more opportunity for a coherent cognitive structure (i.e., intention and its determinants) to emerge as a clearly identifiable and accurate predictor of helping behavior. Whether such cognitive processes operate in the same fashion (if at all) under the stressful circumstances of a real emergency remains, however, an open question" (p. 302).

B. THE NATURE OF THE BYSTANDER–VICTIM RELATIONSHIP

The arousal: cost–reward model predicts that relationships with a victim that are closer and more involving will faciliate helping. Similarity and attention to the victim are proposed to increase the bystander's arousal response as well as to affect cost–reward considerations. Guilt and blame for not helping, for example, would likely be relatively high when feelings of closeness, attraction, intimacy, or we-ness characterize the bystander–victim relationship. Supportive of the model, research consistently demonstrates that people exhibit greater physiological arousal and empathy in response to the distress of similar others than to the distress of dissimilar others (Krebs, 1975; Shotland, 1969). Furthermore, Krebs (1975) reports data consistent with the hypothesis that similarity induces a higher level of arousal, which then promotes helping. Other experiments that have used self-report measures demonstrate the role of arousal and empathic concern induced by feelings of similarity in mediating helping (e.g., Batson *et al.*, 1981).

A review of the effects of similarity on helping reveal a consistent pattern of results. Table 4 presents a summary of experiments that have examined similarity of attitudes and personality, political and national identification, and even dress. Supportive of the predictions of the arousal: cost–reward framework, feelings of similarity systematically promote helping. It is important to note, however, that a similarity-helping prediction can also be derived from a number of other models (e.g., Hornstein's (1982) promotive tension model). The effects of similarity are quite robust; they appear relatively consistent across a variety of manipulations and a variety of dependent measures. The relationship occurs in situations in which help is directly requested and in situations when it is not. Also, it is found in both face-to-face and remote helping situations, and it appears even in circumstances in which it is highly unlikely the benefactor will ever meet the recipient.

Feelings of closeness with a victim that are based on interpersonal attraction are also hypothesized to increase helping behavior. Because similarity typically leads to attraction (e.g., Byrne, 1971), research on similarity can be interpreted as support for the prediction that attraction promotes helping. More direct evidence comes from studies that have varied the physical attractiveness (e.g., Harrell, 1978), the dress and appearance (e.g., Kleinke, 1977), the interpersonal behavior (e.g., Kelley & Byrne, 1976), and the intellectual qualities (Dovidio & Gaertner, 1981) of the person in need. The influence of attraction is quite powerful. Despite diverse operationalizations of attraction, conditions that are assumed to increase attraction systematically facilitate helping. Unfortunately, researchers have not directly examined the intervening mechanisms, although cost–reward explanations have been frequently proposed. One explanation for why physical attractiveness promotes helping, particularly from members of the other sex, is because it increases potential rewards (related, for example, to the opportunity to initiate a relationship). This explanation is plausible but can not explain all of the results. For example, Benson, Karabenick, and Lerner (1976) manipulated attractiveness by varying the picture on a lost application. The dependent measure was the subject's willingness to mail the packet. People more often mailed the application containing a physically attractive applicant's photograph than a physically unattractive one, even though helping was anonymous and it was highly improbable that the subject would ever meet the confederate. Thus, the specific processes by which attraction increases helping have yet to be clearly identified.

Because racial dissimilarity often leads to assumptions of belief dissimilarity (e.g., Stein, Hardyck, & Smith, 1965) and because emotional involvement, similarity, and perceptions of we-ness systematically promote prosocial behaviors, the predictions concerning the effects of racial similarity–dis-

TABLE IV

SIMILARITY AND HELPING

Study	Manipulation	Dependent measure	Result: similarity vs. dissimilarity	Significance
Daniels & Berkowitz (1963)	Personality similarity	Task performance	S > D	*
Feldman (1968)	Compatriot vs. foreigner (American sample)	Give directions	79% vs. 80%	
		Mail stamped letter	85% vs. 75%	*
		Mail unstamped letter	56% vs. 40%	*
Baron (1971)	Attitude similarity	Return books	97% vs. 57%	*
Emswiller, Deaux, & Willits (1971)	Similarity of dress	Comply with request for dime	68% vs. 46%	*
Hornstein, Masor, Sole, & Heilman (1971)	Attitude similarity	Mail lost check	70% vs. 50%	*
		Mail lost questionnaire	69% vs. 30%	*
Suedfeld, Bochner, & Matas (1971)	Similarity of dress	Sign petition	80% vs. 65%	*
Darley & Cooper (1972)	Similarity of dress	Accept leaflets	86% vs. 80%	*
Graf & Riddell (1972)	Similarity of dress	Stop for disabled car	S > D	*
Hodgson, Hornstein, & LaKind (1972)	Attitude similarity	Mail lost check	52% vs. 42%	
		Mail lost questionnaire	46% vs. 27%	*
Raymond & Ungar (1972)	Similarity of dress	Comply with request for change	83% vs. 68%	*
Samuel (1972)	Similarity of dress	Sign petition	57% vs. 44%	*
Suedfeld, Bochner, & Wnek (1972)	Similarity of dress	Help injured person	S = D	

(continued)

TABLE IV (*Continued*)

Study	Manipulation	Dependent measure	Result: similarity vs. dissimilarity	Significance
	Similarity of political orientation	Help injured person	S > D	*
Ehlert, Ehlert, & Merrens (1973)	Similarity of political orientation	Turn off car headlights	23% vs. 8%	*
Karabenick, Lerner, & Beecher (1973)	Similarity of political orientation	Pick up dropped materials	71% vs. 46%	*
Stapleton, Nacci, & Tedeschi (1973)	Attitude similarity	Give away points	S = D	
Chaikin, Derlega, Yoder, & Phillips (1974)	Similarity of dress	Sign petition	41% vs. 20%	*
Pandey & Griffitt (1974)	Attitude similarity	Task assistance	S > D	*
Schiavo, Sherlock, & Wicklund (1974)	Similarity of dress	Give directions	52% vs. 38%	*
Dovidio & Morris (1975)	Similarity of fate	Pick up pencils	73% vs. 43%	*
Karylowski (1975)	Personality similarity	Task performance	S > D	*
Krebs (1975)	Personality similarity	Money-shock trade-off	S > D	*
Sole, Marton, & Hornstein (1975)	Attitude similarity (100% vs. 75% vs. 50% vs. 25% vs. 0%)	Mail lost check	51% vs. 38% vs. 36% vs. 30% vs. 19%	*
Karylowski (1976)	Personality similarity	Task performance	S > D	*
McGovern & Holmes (1976)	Similarity of dress	Sign petition	S = D	
Hansson & Slade (1977)	Similarity of political orientation	Mail lost letter	49% vs. 14%	*
Batson et al. (1979)	Attitude similarity	Donate tokens	S = D	

(*continued*)

TABLE IV (*Continued*)

Study	Manipulation	Dependent measure	Result: similarity vs. dissimilarity	Significance
Batson *et al.* (1981)	Personality similarity	Take shock for partner	86% vs. 41%	*
Hensley (1981)	Similarity of dress	Give dime for phone call	S > D	*
Wagner, Hornstein, & Holloway (1982)	Attitude similarity (100% vs. 67% vs. 33% vs. 0%)	Mail lost packet	58% vs. 41% vs. 39% vs. 33%	*

*Indicates a statistically significant difference.

similarity seem to be straightforward. Racially similar victims would be expected to be helped more frequently than racially dissimilar victims. However, the results are not so simple to interpret. For example, Piliavin *et al.* (1981) found that seven experiments report that whites are less likely to help black victims than white victims, and four studies show no effect for the victim's race. In addition, five studies indicate that depending upon the experimental treatment black victims are helped either less frequently or as frequently as white victims, and six experiments demonstrated that under some experimental conditions black victims are helped more often than white victims. Three recent helping-behavior experiments with white subjects also show mixed results (Brigham & Richardson, 1979; Dovidio & Gaertner, 1981; Rosenfield, Greenberg, Folger, & Borys, 1982). Also, the effect of racial similarity–dissimilarity sometimes appears to be mediated by the bystander's race. Several experiments show that the effect of the victim's race has a stronger effect among white than among black subjects (e.g., Gaertner & Bickman, 1971; Graf & Riddell, 1972). Other experiments demonstrate equally strong biases among blacks and whites in favor of racially similar victims (Wegner & Crano, 1975; West, Whitney, & Schnedler, 1975).

Crosby, Bromley, and Saxe (1980) and Piliavin *et al.* (1981) propose ways of integrating the apparently contradictory results that frequently appear for white subjects. Crosby *et al.* concluded that in the remote helping situations white subjects help black victims less frequently than they help white victims, whereas in the face-to-face situations discrimination against blacks does not occur. Piliavin *et al.* (1981), building on the work of Gaertner and Dovidio (1977, 1981), present a theoretical orientation concerning contemporary racial attitudes that integrates with the arousal: cost–reward model. Briefly, Gaertner and Dovidio (1977, 1981) suggest that the racial attitudes of many people who claim to be low in prejudice may be characterized as a special type of ambivalence—aversiveness (Kovel, 1970). The aversive type is characterized by a conflict between negative feelings toward blacks, which are not always conscious, and a conscience that seeks to dissociate these feelings from a nonprejudiced self-image. Because of this conflict and their concern with reaffirming their egalitarian self-image, aversive racists are especially motivated to avoid acting in negative socially inappropriate ways toward blacks. Thus, just as a desire to reaffirm a helpful self-image can motivate helping behavior, concern with maintaining an egalitarian image can promote prosocial behavior toward blacks.

The importance of maintaining a fair and egalitarian self-image represents the key link to the arousal: cost–reward model. Specifically, Gaertner and Dovidio (1977, 1981) propose that in addition to the personal costs associated with not helping a white victim, there is a special cost, the threat to self-esteem incurred with not helping a black victim. Most whites, therefore, will not withhold assistance solely on the basis of the victim's race. That is, when no non-race-related justification to avoid intervention is readily available, white bystanders are expected to help black victims at least as often as white victims. According to this framework, however, whites may discriminate against blacks when a failure to help can be attributable to factors other than the victim's race. Because of latent negative feelings toward blacks, variables that ordinarily increase costs for helping or decrease personal costs for not helping are hypothesized to have an exaggerated effect for black victims. The review of the literature on this topic presented by Piliavin *et al.* (1981, see pp. 150–159) is generally consistent with this framework.

In summary, closer relationships with victims can increase a bystander's level of arousal and the costs for not helping (e.g., guilt). In addition, the presence of other bystanders can affect both cost and arousal factors. For example, arousal, costs for helping, rewards for helping, and costs for not helping can be influenced by the information that other bystanders provide about the seriousness of the situation or about relevant norms. The opportunity to diffuse responsibility also affects both arousal and cognitive factors related to intervention. Thus, social factors seem to affect helping behavior by influencing both the degree of arousal and the perception of costs and rewards.

VI. Summary and Implications

The preceding sections have presented an overview of motivational, cognitive, and situational factors that influence helping behavior and altruism. In general, the data are supportive of the arousal: cost–reward model. People experience arousal as a result of another person's distress. Furthermore, situations of greater severity and clarity consistently generate higher levels of arousal (e.g.,

Byeff, 1970). Similarity and feelings of involvement with a victim also increase bystander arousal (e.g., Krebs, 1975). Consistent with another major proposition of the arousal: cost–reward model, unpleasant arousal occasioned by the observation of another's distress motivates a person to respond.

The emotional experience of arousal as well as the overall level of arousal appears to be a critical determinant of prosocial behavior. In particular, there are several different types of emotion that can mediate intervention. Strong feelings of upset associated with high levels of psychophysiological activity (i.e., a defense reaction) motivates helping in emergency situations (e.g., Gaertner & Dovidio, 1977). In nonemergency situations, empathic concern (e.g., Batson & Coke, 1981), promotive tension (e.g., Hornstein, 1982), feelings of inequity (e.g., Walster et al., 1978), or feelings of moral obligation (e.g., Schwartz & Howard, 1981, 1982) influence whether or not a person intervenes with assistance. Piliavin et al. (1981) concluded that "despite apparent variations in emotional content, the process by which another's need promotes helping seems dynamically similar across situations" (p.236). The work of Batson and his colleagues (e.g., Batson et al., 1981), though, suggests that different emotional experiences of arousal influence intervention in different ways. In particular, within the arousal: cost–reward framework, the costs for not helping the victim may be perceived as higher when arousal is labeled as warmth and compassion than as upset and alarm. Therefore, even when situational factors make it easy to leave the scene, bystanders who interpret their arousal as empathic concern may show relatively high levels of helping behavior compared to bystanders who label their arousal as personal distress. However, when the costs for helping are high and outweigh the costs for not helping, people who experience mainly empathic concern are as unlikely to help as are people who feel a preponderance of personal distress (Batson et al., 1983).

Another basic assumption of the arousal: cost–reward model is that a bystander will consider potential costs and rewards in choosing a response to relieve his or her arousal. Overall, the literature supports the "economic man" approach; people tend to behave as if to minimize costs and maximize rewards. All costs and rewards, though, are not weighed equally in the decision. In nonemergency situations, the impact of costs for helping is greater than the influence of either costs for not helping or rewards for helping. In highly arousing emergency situations, costs for not helping have the greatest impact. Because of the arousal, the bystander's attention can become focused almost exclusively of the costs for the victim receiving no help, and consequently the bystander may respond impulsively with little apparent concern for the costs for helping or the response of other bystanders. Under conditions in which the costs for helping and the costs for the victim receiving no help are both high and salient, either indirect intervention or cognitive reinterpretation tends to occur. For example, to resolve this dilemma people often reinterpret the severity of the situation or the need for personal involvement. Thus, the arousal: cost–reward model considers iterative, cyclical processing effects and emphasizes the notion that cost–reward considerations and arousal are not independent. In general, the arousal: cost–reward model provides a useful framework for organizing previous research. By focusing on the *processes* involved in intervention, the model can be used to explain the effects of diverse manipulations concerning characteristics of the victim's need, temporary states of the bystander, the presence of other bystanders, and the relationship between the bystander and the victim.

The model may also be valuable for encouraging the orderly theoretical development of this area of inquiry and for suggesting new research, new ideas, and new regions for study. There are two general directions that future research can take—inward, toward greater empirical and theoretical refinement, and outward, toward regions largely unexplored in the current literature. Focusing inward, there is continued need for work in theoretical synthesis and integration. In each section of this chapter several empirical contradictions were identified, and related questions were raised. What are the precise interrelationships in the cognition-affect-helping sequence? Are there fundamental differences in the ways costs for helping and not helping, and rewards are processed by bystanders? Do moods primarily affect helping through affective, cognitive, or attentional mechanisms? Does altruism exist or can all helping be explained by egoistic motivations? An unequivocal demonstration that altruistic motivations exist would suggest limitations to the economic man models of human behavior, illustrate inadequacies of the drive-reduction models of human motivation, and challenge the traditional individualistic bias of empirical social psychology in the United States.

The finding that various conditions produce different emotions and levels of arousal and differentially influence the relative impact of costs and rewards suggests that there may be different *types* of helping situations and different *types* of motivations. Thus, it is unlikely that prosocial behavior can be understood by referring to a single factor. Analogous to the person × situation approach, a motivation × situation approach may contribute to a better understanding of when and why people help. What *types* of situations are there? Two different approaches, theoretical and empirical, seem to be converging on an answer. In 1970, Latané and Darley theorized that there were two kinds of helping situations, nonemergency and emergency. They characterized emergencies as being threatening, unusual, different from one another, unforeseen, and requiring immediate action. Using an empirical procedure, in which subjects made judgments about 96 problem situations, Shotland and Huston (1979) concluded that the most important defining characteristic of an emergency is that "harm increases with time." Other researchers have proposed more elaborate classification schemes. Wispé (1972) distinguished six categories of prosocial behavior: altruism, sympathy, cooperation, helping, aiding, and donating. The genotype similarities and differences among these categories, however, have yet to be empirically examined. After reviewing the literature, Lau and Blake (1976) suggested that there seemed to be four major types of helping: donating resources to individuals or organizations, sharing of one's own resources with others, offering help to the needy, and crisis intervention.

In contrast to the approaches used by Wispé (1972) and Lau and Blake (1976), Pearce and Amato (1980) have attempted to develop a taxonomy of helping behaviors by using multidimensional scaling procedures. Pearce and Amato found three fundamental dimensions. The first dimension involves the characteristics of planned versus spontaneous help, formal versus informal help, and other-initiated versus self-initiated help. The second dimension is related to nonserious versus serious (i.e., emergency) situations. The third dimension of helping concerns "giving what I have" versus "doing what I can," and indirect versus direct helping. Behaviors like sharing or giving money represent one end of this dimension, whereas breaking up a fight and picking up computer cards characterize the other end. Smithson and Amato (1982) found an additional dimension. Characteristics of this dimension are help that is personal and is given to a friend versus help that is anonymous and is given to a stranger. Pearce and Amato propose that an understanding of different types of helping will assist researchers in organizing and interpreting past research and in suggesting new manupulations for future research, and it will advance psychological theory on helping behavior and altruism.

What *types* of motivations are there for helping behavior and altruism? Karylowski (1982) in his distinction between endocentric and exocentric motivations suggests two. Alternatively, Batson and Coke (1981) distinguish between altruistic and egoistic motivations. The arousal: cost–reward framework suggests a different scheme: affective and cognitive motivational categories. The affective category includes unpleasant arousal generated by witnessing an emergency (Piliavin et al., 1981, 1982) or by transgression (Cialdini et al., 1982), promotive tension (Hornstein, 1982), empathic arousal (Hoffman, 1981), empathic concern (Batson & Coke, 1981), or guilt (Hoffman, 1982). The cognitive category includes helping based on anticipation or rewards and avoidance of potential costs, compliance with norms (i.e., external standards), and a desire to reaffirm one's self-concept (i.e., internal standards). This category also includes manipulative helping. Although this type of motivation has only infrequently been discussed in the literature, it is quite possible that helping is sometimes used as an impression management, ingratiation, or appeasement strategy (e.g., Dovidio & Gaertner, 1981; Dutton & Lennox, 1974). There are, of course, many other possible categories of motivations that have not been considered. For example, helping may be based on aesthetic motivations similar to those that move people to paint. Or, helping can be related to motivations that underlie children's play. Rheingold (1982) observed that even children as young as 18 months spontaneously participated in housekeeping tasks performed by adults. Of course, one danger of a motivation × situation approach is a proliferation of proposed motivations, such that the number of motivational categories soon approaches the number of possible individual helping situations.

Looking outward, several aspects of helping behavior and altruism remain largely unexplored. It is important to recognize that much of what is known about helping behavior and altruism is based on information gathered in social psychological laboratories. Researchers can feel somewhat reassured, however, by the support that field experiments frequently provide. In general, many of the phenomena observed in the laboratory (e.g., bystander inhibition effects) seem to occur in similar ways outside of the laboratory, for example on the streets of New York. Thus, the laboratory conclusions generally seem to possess external validity. This, though, only partially addresses the questions of ecological validity. Typically, field research on helping behavior is modeled after laboratory work: They make similar assumptions and employ analogous methods. Consequently, the scope of the field work is limited by the types of questions that are asked in the laboratory. Ironically, although this approach increases our confidence along certain dimensions, it may reduce the likelihood that questions that can uniquely be addressed in the field will be asked.

There are, for example, a number of areas that are largely overlooked in the current literature. Shotland and Heinold (1982) point out that although bystander *intervention* in emergencies is well researched, *helping* behavior in emergencies is not commonly studied. Most of the emergency studies measure only whether or not a person makes a behavioral response (e.g., leaving the room) in reaction to another's apparent injury. Studies rarely investigate how a subject actually tries to give assistance. Intervention in emergency situations typically presents a bystander with unexpected circumstances, produces high levels of stress, and requires relatively complex and precise activities to aid the victim. Thus, it is quite possible that one set of variables may relate to whether or not a bystander intervenes, whereas another set of factors may determine whether or not a bystander can help effectively. This is, in fact, what Shotland and Heinold found. Ambiguity and bystander sex were related to intervention; previous first-aid training influenced the type of help that was given to a victim of serious arterial bleeding.

In addition, common experience indicates that much, if not most, of the daily helping that occurs is between friends or between family members. Yet, Smithson and Amato (1982), in their attempt to develop a cognitively based typology of helping, conclude that the area of helping characterized by intimacy and prior personal relationship between the benefactor and the recipient has been largely neglected by empirical study. A review of the over 1000 studies conducted on helping behavior indicates that only a dozen refer to "friend" in the title. Nevertheless, observational research by Strayer (1981) demonstrates the

importance of conceptualizing helping as an aspect of ongoing social relationships. Among young children, there were consistently high correlations (.79
to .88) between how much help children initiated with their peers and how much
assistance they received from others. In addition, the experiments that have
examined help giving (e.g., Tesser & Smith, 1980) and help seeking (e.g.,
Shapiro, 1978) among friends often demonstrate different patterns of results than
those obtained among strangers. Some fundamental differences would also be
expected as a function of familial relationship. Specifically, kin selection theory
(Hamilton, 1964), a sociobiological approach, hypothesizes that the evolutionary
basis for helping is genetic relatedness.

Furthermore, the traditional experimental approach, although it seems to
provide valuable information about the processes that mediate intervention, gives
us little information about how often people typically engage in prosocial, helping, and altruistic behavior. The nature of contemporary experimental methods,
statistical procedures, and publishing policies leads researchers to construct situations that maximize differences between experimental conditions, avoiding
both ceiling and basement effects. The overall amounts of helping in these
contrived situations therefore probably do not accurately reflect naturally occurring rates of helpfulness. Thus, although much of our research has refuted the
assumption that people are apathetic, it it quite likely that the nature of our
laboratory situations lead even active researchers in this area to underestimate the
amount of helping that occupies people's daily lives. Rushton (1978) and Latané
and Darley (1970) show that between 85% to 97% of people in small towns and
large cities will readily comply with requests for the time of day or for directions.
Based on an observational study of 3- to 5-year-old children in free play sessions,
Strayer, Wareing, and Rushton (1979) estimated that each child engaged, on the
average, in over 15 prosocial acts per hour. Helping also seems to be a dominant
form of activity throughout the human life span. Rheingold Hay, and West
(1976) found that giving and sharing are a very common activity of children 18-
months-old and younger; Midlarsky and Kahana (1981) also find that helping is a
characteristic activity of the elderly. These arguments do not necessarily imply
that the laboratory and the experimental approaches should be abandoned. What
is suggested, though, is that alternative approaches may generate new hypotheses
and new insights, many of which can then be further examined under the more
controlled conditions of the laboratory.

ACKNOWLEDGMENTS

Work on this chapter was supported by the Colegate University Research Council. The author
wishes to acknowledge the contributions of Jane Piliavin, Sam Gaertner, and Russ Clark, whose
ideas are represented in this chapter, and the intellectual support provided by Bibb Latané and

colleagues at the 1982 and 1983 Nags Head Conferences on Altruism. The author also wishes to express his appreciation to Sam Gaertner, Carrie Keating, and Russ Clark, who made very thoughtful and helpful comments on an earlier version of the manuscript.

REFERENCES

Adams, J. S. Toward an understanding of inequity. *Journal of Abnormal and Social Psychology,* 1963, *67,* 422–436.

Aderman, D., & Berkowitz, L. Self-concern and the unwillingness to be helpful. *Social Psychology Quarterly,* 1983, *46,* 293–301.

Archer, R. L., Diaz-Loving, R., Gollwitzer, P. M., Davis, M. H., & Foushee, H. C. The role of dispositional empathy and social evaluation in the empathic mediation of helping. *Journal of Personality and Social Psychology,* 1981, *40,* 786–796.

Aronfreed, J. *Conduct and conscience: The socialization of internalized control over behavior.* NY: Academic Press, 1968.

Aronfreed, J., & Paskal, V. *The development of sympathetic behavior in children: An experimental test of a two-phase hypothesis.* Unpublished manuscript, University of Pennsylvania, 1966.

Ashton, N. L., & Severy, L. J. Arousal and costs in bystander intervention. *Personality and Social Psychology Bulletin,* 1976, *2,* 268–272.

Baron, R. A. Behavioral effects of interpersonal attraction: Compliance with requests from liked and disliked others. *Psychonomic Science,* 1971 *25,* 325–326.

Bar-Tal, D., & Raviv, A. A cognitive-learning model of helping behavior development: Possible implications and applications. In N. Eisenberg (Ed.), *The development of prosocial behavior.* NY: Academic Press, 1982.

Barton, E. J., & Ascione, F. R. Sharing in preschool children: Facilitation, stimulus generalization, response generalization, and maintenance. *Journal of Applied Behavior Analysis,* 1979, *12,* 417–430.

Batson, C. D., Cochran, P. J., Biederman, M. F., Blosser, J. L., Ryan, M. J., & Vogt, B. Failure to help when in a hurry: Callousness or conflict? *Personality and Social Psychology Bulletin,* 1978, *4,* 97–101.

Batson, C. D., & Coke, J. S. Empathy: A source of altruistic motivation for helping? In J. P. Rushton & R. M. Sorrentino (Eds.), *Altruism and helping behavior: Social, personality, and developmental perspectives.* Hillsdale, NJ: Erlbaum, 1981.

Batson, C. D., Duncan, B., Ackerman, P., Buckley, T., & Birch, K. Is empathic emotion a source of altruistic motivation? *Journal of Personality and Social Psychology,* 1981, *40,* 290–302.

Batson, C. D., Harris, A. C., McCaul, K. D., Davis, M., & Schmidt, T. Compassion or compliance: Alternative dispositional attributions for one's helping behavior. *Social Psychology Quarterly,* 1979, *42,* 405–409.

Batson, C. D., O'Quin, K., Fultz, J., Vanderplas, M., & Isen, A. M. Influence of self-reported distress and empathy on egoistic versus altruistic motivation to help. *Journal of Personality and Social Psychology,* 1983, *45,* 706–718.

Benson, P. L., Karabenick, S. A., & Lerner, R. M. Pretty pleases: The effects of physical attractiveness, race, and sex on receiving help. *Journal of Experimental Social Psychology,* 1976, *12,* 409–415.

Berkowitz, L. Social norms, feelings, and other factors affecting helping behavior and altruism. In L. Berkowitz (Ed.), *Advances in experimental social psychology* Vol. 6. NY: Academic Press, 1972.

Berkowitz, L. Reactance and the unwillingness to help others. *Psychological Bulletin,* 1973, *79,* 310–317.

Berkowitz, L. Decreased helpfulness with increased group size through lessening the effects of the needy individual's dependency. *Journal of Personality,* 1978, *46,* 299–310.

Berkowitz, L., & Connor, W. H. Success, failure, and social responsibility. *Journal of Personality and Social Psychology,* 1966, *4,* 664–669.

Berkowitz, L., & Daniels, L. R. Responsibility and dependency. *Journal of Abnormal and Social Psychology,* 1963, *66,* 429–436.

Berkowitz, L., & Daniels, L. R. Affecting the salience of the social responsibility norm: Effects of past help on the responses to dependency relationships. *Journal of Abnormal and Social Psychology,* 1964, *68,* 275–281.

Berscheid, E., & Walster, E. When does a harm-doer compensate a victim? *Journal of Personality and Social Psychology,* 1967, *6,* 435–441.

Bickman, L. Attitude toward an authority and the reporting of a crime. *Sociometry,* 1976, *39,* 76–82.

Bleda, P. R., Bleda, S. T., Byrne, D., & White, L. A. When a bystander becomes an accomplice: Situational determinants of reaction to dishonesty. *Journal of Experimental Social Psychology,* 1976, *12,* 9–25.

Brehm, J. W., & Cole, A. H. Effect of a favor which reduces freedom. *Journal of Personality and Social Psychology,* 1966, *3,* 420–426.

Brigham, J. C., & Richardson, C. B. Race, sex, and helping in the maketplace. *Journal of Applied Social Psychology,* 1979, *9,* 314–322.

Brock, T. C., & Becker, L. A. "Debriefing" and susceptibility to subsequent experimental manipulations. *Journal of Experimental Social Psychology,* 1966, *22,* 314–323.

Byeff, P. Helping behavior in audio and audio-video conditions. Senior honors thesis, University of Pennsylvania, 1970.

Byrne, D. *The attraction paradigm,* NY: Academic Press, 1971.

Carlsmith, J. M., & Gross, A. E. Some effects of guilt on compliance. *Journal of Personality and Social Psychology,* 1969, *11,* 232–239.

Chaikin, A. L., Derlega, V. J., Yoder, J., & Phillips, D. The effects of appearance on compliance. *Journal of Social Psychology,* 1974, *92,* 199–200.

Cialdini, R. B., Baumann, D. J., & Kenrick, D. T. Insights from sadness: A three-step model of the development of altruism as hedonism. *Developmental Review,* 1981, *1,* 207–223.

Cialdini, R. B., Darby, B. K., & Vincent, J. E. Transgression and altruism: A case for hedonism. *Journal of Experimental Social Psychology,* 1973, *9,* 502–516.

Cialdini, R. B., & Kenrick, D. T. Altruism as hedonism: A social Development perspective on the relationship of negative mood state and helping. *Journal of Personality and Social Psychology,* 1976, *34,* 907–914.

Cialdini, R. B., Kenrick, D. T., & Baumann, D. J. Effects of mood on prosocial behavior in children and adults. In N. Eisenberg (Ed.), *The development of prosocial behavior.* NY: Academic Press, 1982.

Clark, R. D., III, & Word, L. E. Why don't bystanders help? Because of ambiguity? *Journal of Personality and Social Psychology,* 1972, *24,* 392–400.

Clark, R. D., III, & Word, L. E. Where is the apathetic bystander? Situational characteristics of the emergency. *Journal of Personality and Social Psychology,* 1974, *29,* 279–287.

Coke, J. S., Batson, C. D., & McDavis, K. Empathic mediation of helping: A two-stage model. *Journal of Personality and Social Psychology,* 1978, *36,* 752–766.

Comer, R., & Laird, J. D. Choosing to suffer as a consequence of expecting to suffer: Why do people do it? *Journal of Personality and Social Psychology,* 1975, *32,* 92–101.

Comte, A. *System of positive polity* (4 Vols.). London: Longmans, 1875–1877. (Original work published in French 1851–1854)

Crandall, J. E. Effects of threat and failure on concern for others. *Journal of Research in Personality*, 1978, *12*, 350–360.

Crosby, F., Bromley, S., & Saxe, L. Recent unobtrusive studies of black and white discrimination and prejudice: A literature review. *Psychological Bulletin*, 1980, *87*, 546–563.

Cunningham, M. R. Weather, mood, and helping behavior: Quasi experiments with the sunshine samaritan. *Journal of Personality and Social Psychology*, 1979, *37*, 1947–1956.

Cunningham, M. R., Steinberg, J., Grev, R. Wanting to and having to help: Separate motivations for positive mood and guilt-induced helping. *Journal of Personality and Social Psychology*, 1980, *38*, 181–192.

Daniels, L. R., & Berkowitz, L. Liking and response to dependency relationships. *Human Relations*, 1963, *16*, 141–148.

Darley, J. M., & Batson, C. D. From Jerusalem to Jericho: A study of situational and dispositional variables in helping behavior. *Journal of Personality and Social Psychology*, 1973, *27*, 100–108.

Darley, J. M., & Cooper, J. The "Clean for Gene" phenomenon: The effects of student appearance on political campaigning. *Journal of Applied Social Psychology*, 1972, *2*, 24–33.

Darley, J. M., & Latané, B. Bystander intervention to emergencies: Diffusion of responsibility. *Journal of Personality and Social Psychology*, 1968, *8*, 377–383.

Darlington, R. B., & Macker, C. E. Displacement of guilt-produced altruistic behavior. *Journal of Personality and Social Psychology*, 1966, *4*, 442–443.

Davis, M. H. Measuring individual differences in empathy. *JSAS Catalog of Selected Documents in Psychology*, 1980, *10*, 85.

Davis, M. H. Measuring individual differences in empathy: Evidence for a multidimensional approach. *Journal of Personality and Social Psychology*, 1983, *44*, 113–126. (a)

Davis, M. H. The effects of dispositional empathy on emotional reactions and helping: A multidimensional approach. *Journal of Personality*, 1983, *51*, 167–184. (b)

Dawkins, R. *The selfish gene*. Oxford: Oxford University Press, 1976.

DePalma, D. J. Effects of social class, moral orientation, and severity of punishment on boys' moral responses to transgression and generosity. *Developmental Psychology*, 1974, *10*, 890–900.

Donnerstein, E., Donnerstein, M., & Munger, G. Helping behavior as a function of pictorially induced moods. *Journal of Social Psychology*, 1975, *97*, 21–25.

Dovidio, J. F. Helping behavior: A bibliography. Unpublished manuscript, Colgate University, New York, 1982.

Dovidio, J. F., & Gaertner, S. L. The effects of race, status, and ability on helping behavior. *Social Psychology Quarterly*, 1981, *44*, 192–203.

Dovidio, J. F., & Morris, W. N. Effects of stress and commonality of fate on helping behavior. *Journal of Personality and Social Psychology*, 1975, *31*, 145–149.

Dutton, D. G., & Lennox, V. L. Effect of prior "token" compliance on subsequent interracial behavior. *Journal of Personality and Social Psychology*, 1974, *29*, 65–71.

Duval, S., & Wicklund, R. A. *A theory of objective self-awareness*. NY: Academic Press, 1972.

Ehlert, J., Ehlert, N., & Merrens, M. The influence of idealogical affiliation on helping behavior. *Journal of Social Psychology*, 1973, *89*, 315–316.

Eisenberg, N. (Ed.). *The development of prosocial behavior*. NY: Academic Press, 1982.

Eisenberg, N., Lennon, R., & Roth, K. Prosocial development: A longitudinal study. *Developmental Psychology*, 1983, *19*, 846–855.

Eisenberg-Berg, N., & Geisheker, E. Content of preachings and power of the model preacher: The effect on children's generosity. *Developmental Psychology*, 1979, *15*, 168–175.

Elliot, R., & Vasta, R. The modeling of sharing: Effects associated with vicarious reinforcement, symbolization, age, and generalization. *Journal of Experimental Child Psychology*, 1970, *10*, 8–15.

Emswiller, T., Deaux, K., & Willits, J. E. Similarity, sex and requests for small favors. *Journal of Applied Social Psychology,* 1971, *1,* 284–291.

Enzle, M. E., & Harvey, M. D. Recipient mood states and helping behavior. *Journal of Experimental Social Psychology,* 1979, *15,* 170–182.

Epstein, Y. M., & Hornstein, H. A. Penalty and interpersonal attraction as factors influencing the decision to help another person. *Journal of Experimental Social Psychology,* 1969, *5,* 272–282.

Feldman, R. Response to compatriot and foreigner who seek assistance. *Journal of Personality and Social Psychology,* 1968, *10,* 202–214.

Feshbach, N. D. Sex differences in empathy and social behavior in children. In N. Eisenberg (Ed.), *The development of prosocial behavior.* NY: Academic Press, 1982.

Feshbach, N. D., & Roe, K. Empathy in six- and seven-year olds. *Child Development,* 1968, *39,* 133–145.

Firestone, I. J., Lichtman, C. M., & Colamosca, J. V. Leader effectiveness and leadership conferral as determinants of helping in a medical emergency. *Journal of Personality and Social Psychology,* 1975, *31,* 343–348.

Fishbein, M. Attitudes and the prediction of behavior. In M. Fishbein (Ed.), *Readings in attitude theory and measurement.* NY: Wiley, 1967.

Fisher, J. D., DePaulo, B. M., & Nadler, A. Extending altruism beyond the altruistic act: The mixed effects of aid on the help recipient. In J. P. Rushton & R. M. Sorrentino (Eds.), *Altruism and helping behavior: Social, personality, and developmental perspectives.* Hillsdale, NJ: Erlbaum, 1981.

Fisher, J. D., Nadler, A., & Whitcher-Alagna, S. J. Recipient reactions to aid: A conceptual review and a new theoretical framework. *Psychology Bulletin,* 1982, *91,* 27–54.

Fraser, S. C., & Fujitomi, I. Perceived prior compliance, psychological reactance and altruistic contributions. *Proceedings of the 80th Annual Convention of the American Psychological Association,* 1972, *7,* 247–248.

Freedman, J. C., Wallington, S. A., & Bless, E. Compliance without pressure: The effect of guilt. *Journal of Personality and Social Psychology,* 1967, *7,* 117–124.

Gaertner, S. L. The role of racial attitudes in helping behavior. *Journal of Social Psychology,* 1975, *97,* 95–101.

Gaertner, S. L., & Bickman, L. Effects of race on the elicitation of helping behavior: The wrong number technique. *Journal of Personality and Social Psychology,* 1971, *20,* 218–222.

Gaertner, S. L., & Dovidio, J. F. The subtlety of white racism, arousal, and helping behavior. *Journal of Personality and Social Psychology,* 1977, *35,* 691–707.

Gaertner, S. L., & Dovidio, J. F. Racism among the well-intentioned. In E. G. Clausen & J. Bermingham (Eds.), *Pluralism, racism, and public policy: The search for equality.* Boston: Hall, 1981.

Gaertner, S. L., Dovidio, J. F., & Johnson, G. Race of victim, nonresponsive bystanders, and helping behavior. *The Journal of Social Psychology,* 1982, *117,* 69–77.

Gelfand, D. M., & Hartmann, D. P. Response consequences and attributions: Two contributors to prosocial behavior. In N. Eisenberg (Ed.), *The development of prosocial behavior.* NY: Academic Press, 1982.

Gergen, K. J., Ellsworth, P., Maslach, C., & Seipel, M. Obligation, donor resources, and reactions to aid in three cultures. *Journal of Personality and Social Psychology,* 1975, *31,* 390–400.

Gibbons, F. X., & Wicklund, R. A. Self-focused attention and helping behavior. *Journal of Personality and Social Psychology,* 1982, *43,* 462–474.

Gottlieb, J., & Carver, C. S. Anticipation of future interaction and the bystander effect. *Journal of Experimental Social Psychology,* 1980, *16,* 253–260.

Gouldner, A. W. The norm of reciprocity: A preliminary statement. *American Sociological Review,* 1960, *25,* 161–178.

Graf, R. G., & Riddell, J. C. Helping behavior as a function of interpersonal perception. *Journal of Social Psychology*, 1972, *86*, 227–231.

Greenberg, M. S., & Frisch, D. M. Effect of intentionality on willingness to reciprocate a favor. *Journal of Experimental Social Psychology*, 1972, *8*, 99–111.

Gross, A. E., & Latané, J. G. Receiving help, reciprocation, and interpersonal attraction. *Journal of Applied Social Psychology*, 1974, *4*, 210–223.

Grusec, J. E. Power and the internalization of aversive behaviors. *Child Development*, 1971, *42*, 93–105.

Grusec, J. E. Socialization processes and the development of altruism. In J. P. Rushton & R. M. Sorrentino (Eds.), *Altruism and helping behavior: Social, personality, and developmental perspectives*. Hillsdale, NJ: Erlbaum, 1981.

Grusec, J. The socialization of altruism. In N. Eisenberg (Ed.), *The development of prosocial behavior*. NY: Academic Press, 1982.

Grusec, J. E., Kuczynski, L. Rushton, J. P., & Simutis, Z. Modeling, direct instruction, and attributions: Effects on altruism. *Developmental Pychology*, 1978, *14*, 51–57.

Grusec, J. E., & Redler, E. Attribution, reinforcement, and altruism. *Developmental Psychology*, 1980, *16*, 525–534.

Grusec, J. E., Saas-Kortsaak, P., & Simutis, Z. M. The role of example and moral exhortation in the training of altruism. *Child Development*, 1978, *49*, 920–923.

Hamilton, W. D. The genetic evolution of social behavior. *Journal of Theoretical Biology*, 1964, *7*, 1–52.

Hansson, R., & Slade, K. Altruism toward a deviant in city and small town. *Journal of Applied Social Psychology*, 1977, *7*, 272–279.

Harrell, W. A. Physical attractiveness, self-disclosure, and helping behavior. *Journal of Social Psychology*, 1978, *104*, 15–17.

Harris, M. B. Effects of altruism on mood. *Journal of Social Psychology*, 1977, *102*, 197–208.

Harris, M. B., & Huang, L. C. Helping and the attribution process. *Journal of Social Psychology*, 1973, *90*, 291–297.

Harris, M. B. & Samerotte, G. C. The effects of actual and attempted theft, need, and a previous favor on altruism. *Journal of Social Psychology*, 1976, *99*, 193–202.

Hatfield, E., Walster, G. W. & Piliavin, J. A. Equity theory and helping relationship. In L. Wispé (Ed.), *Altruism, sympathy, and helping: Psychological and sociological principles*. NY: Academic Press, 1978.

Heilman, M. E., Hodgson, S. A., & Hornstein, H. A. Effects of magnitude and rectifiability of harm and information value on the reporting of accidental harm-doing. *Journal of Personality and Social Psychology*, 1972, *23*, 211–218.

Hensley, W. E. The effects of attire, location, and sex on aiding behavior: A similarity explanation. *Journal of Nonverbal Behavior*, 1981, *6*, 3–11.

Hodgson, S. A., Hornstein, H. A., & LaKind, E. Socially mediated Ziegarnik effects as a function of sentiment, valence, and desire for goal attainment. *Journal of Experimental Social Psychology*, 1972, *8*, 446–456.

Hoffman, M. L. Developmental synthesis of affect and cognition and its implications for altruistic motivation. *Developmental Psychology*, 1975, *11*, 607–622.

Hoffman, M. L. Empathy, its development and prosocial implications. In C. B. Keasey (Ed.), *Nebraska Symposium on Motivation* (Vol. 25), Lincoln, NE: University of Nebraska Press, 1977.

Hoffman, M. L. Is altruism part of human nature? *Journal of Personality and Social Psychology*, 1981, *40*, 121–137.(a)

Hoffman, M. L. The development of empathy. In J. P. Rushton & R, M. Sorrentino (Eds.), *Altruism and helping behavior: Social, personality, and developmental perspectives*. Hillsdale, NJ: Erlbaum, 1981. (b)

Hoffman, M. L. Development of prosocial motivation: Empathy and guilt. In N. Eisenberg (Ed.), *The development of prosocial behavior*. NY: Academic Press, 1982.

Hoover, C. W., Wood, E. E., & Knowles, E. S. Forms of social awareness and helping. *Journal of Experimental Social Psychology*, 1983, *18*, 577–590.

Hornstein, H. A. *Cruelty and kindness: A new look at aggression and altruism*. Englewood Cliffs, NJ: Prentice-Hall, 1976.

Hornstein, H. A. Promotive tension: Theory and research. In V. J. Derlega & J. Grzelak (Eds.), *Cooperation and helping behavior: Theories and research*. NY: Academic Press, 1982.

Hornstein, H. A., Fisch, E., & Holmes, L. Influence of a model's feelings about his behavior and his relevance as a comparison on other observers' helping behavior. *Journal of Personality and Social Psychology*, 1968, *10*, 222–226.

Hornstein, H. A., Marton, J., Rupp, A., Sole, K., & Tartell, R. The propensity to recall another's completed and uncompleted tasks as a consequence of varying social relationships. *Journal of Experimental Social Psychology*, 1980, *16*, 362–375.

Hornstein, H. A., Masor, H. N., Sole, K., & Heilman, M. Effects of sentiment and completion of a helping act on observer helping: A case for socially mediated Ziegarnik effects. *Journal of Personality and Social Psychology*, 1971, *17*, 107–112.

Isen, A. M. Success, failure, attention, and reaction to others: The warm glow of success. *Journal of Personality and Social Psychology*, 1970, *15*, 294–301.

Isen, A. M., Clark, M., & Schwartz, M. Duration of the effect of good mood on helping: "Footprints on the sands of time." *Journal of Personality and Social Psychology*, 1976, *34*, 385–393.

Isen, A. M., Horn. N., & Rosenhan, D. C. Effects of success and failure on children's generosity. *Journal of Personality and Social Psychology*, 1973, *27*, 239–247.

Isen, A. M., & Levin, P. F. Effect of feeling good on Helping: Cookies and kindness. *Journal of Personality and Social Psychology*, 1972, *21*, 384–388.

Isen, A. M., Shalker, T. E., Clark, M., & Karp, L. Affect, accessibility of material in memory, and behavior: A cognitive loop? *Journal of Personality and Social Psychology*, 1978, *36*, 1–12.

Isen, A. M., & Simonds, S. F. The effect of feeling good on a helping task that is incompatible with good mood. *Social Psychology*, 1978, *41*, 346–349.

Karabenick, S. A., Lerner, R. M., & Beecher, M. D. Relation of political affiliation to helping behavior on election day, November 7, 1972. *Journal of Social Psychology*, 1973, *91*, 223–227.

Karylowski, J. Altruism and interpersonal attraction as a function of perceived self-partner similarity and self-esteem. *Polish Psychology Bulletin*, 1975, *6*, 63–71.

Karylowski, J. Self-esteem, similarity, liking, and helping. *Personality and Social Psychology Bulletin*, 1976, *2*, 71–74.

Karylowski, J. Two types of altruistic behavior: Doing good to feel good or to make the other feel good. In V. J. Derlega & J. Grzelak (Eds.), *Cooperation and helping behavior: Theories and research*. NY: Academic Press, 1982.

Katsev, R., Edelsack, L., Steinmetz, G., Walker, T., & Wright, R. The effect of reprimanding transgressions on subsequent helping behavior: Two field experiments. *Personality and Social Psychology Bulletin*, 1978, *4*, 326–329.

Katz, I., Farber, J., Glass, D. C., Lucido, D., & Emswiller, T. When courtesy offends: Effects of positive and negative behavior by the physically disabled on altruism and anger in normals. *Journal of Personality*, 1978, *46*, 506–518.

Katz, I., Glass, D. C., Lucido, D., & Farber, J. Harm-doing and victim's racial or orthopedic stigma as determinants of helping behavior. *Journal of Personality*, 1979, *47*, 340–364.

Kazdin, A. E., & Bryan, J. H. Competence and volunteering. *Journal of Experimental Social Psychology*, 1971, *7*, 87–97.

Keating, J. P., & Brock, T. C. The effects of prior reward and punishment on subsequent reward and punishment: Guilt versus consistency. *Journal of Personality and Social Psychology*, 1976, *34*, 327–333.

Kelley, K., & Byrne, D. Attraction and altruism: With a little help from my friends. *Journal of Research in Personality*, 1976, *10*, 59–68.

Kenrick, D. T., Baumann, D. J., & Cialdini, R. B. A step in the socialization of altruism as hedonism: Effects of negative mood on children's generosity under public and private conditions. *Journal of Personality and Social Psychology*, 1979, *37*, 756–768.

Kleinke, C. L. Effects of dress on compliance to requests in a field setting. *Journal of Social Psychology*, 1977, *101*, 223–224.

Konecni, V. J. Some effects of guilt on compliance: A field replication. *Journal of Personality and Social Psychology*, 1972, *23*, 30–32.

Konoske, P., Staple, S., & Graf, R. G. Complaint reactions to guilt: Self-esteem or self-punishment. *Journal of Social Psychology*, 1979, *108*, 207–211.

Kovel, J. *White racism: A psychohistory*. NY: 1970.

Krebs, D. L. Altruism—An examination of the concept and a review of the literature. *Psychological Bulletin*, 1970, *73*, 258–302.

Krebs, D. Empathy and altruism. *Journal of Personality and Social Psychology*, 1975, *32*, 1134–1146.

Krebs, D. Altruism—A rational approach. In N. Eisenberg (Ed.), *The development of prosocial behavior*. NY: Academic Press, 1982.

Krebs, D., & Russell, C. Role-taking and altruism: When you put yourself in the shoes of another, will they take you to to their owner's aid? In J. P. Rushton & R. M. Sorrentino (Eds.), *Altruism and helping behavior: Social, personality, and developmental perspectives*. Hillsdale, NJ: Erlbaum, 1981.

Kurdek, L. A. Perspective-taking as the cognitive basis of children's moral development: A review of the literature. *Merrill-Palmer Quarterly*, 1978, *24*, 3–28.

Latané, B. Psychology of social impact. *American Psychologist*, 1981, *36*, 343–356.

Latané, B., & Darley, J. M. *The unresponsive bystander: Why doesn't he help?* NY: Appleton-Centruy-Crofts, 1970.

Latané, B., & Darley, J. M. *Help in a crisis: Bystander response to an emergency*. Morristown, NJ: General Learning Press, 1976.

Latané, B., & Nida, S. Ten years of research on group size and helping. *Psychological Bulletin*, 1981, *89*, 308–324.

Latané, L., Nida, S. A., & Wilson, D. W. The effects of group size on helping behavior. In J. P. Rushton & R. M. Sorrentino (Eds.), *Altruism and helping behavior: Social, personality, and developmental perspectives*. Hillsdale, NJ: Erlbaum, 1981.

Latané, B., & Rodin, J. A lady in distress: Inhibiting effects of friends and strangers on bystander intervention. *Journal of Experimental Social Psychology*, 1969, *5*, 189–202.

Lau, S., & Blake, B. F. Recent research on helping behavior: An overview and bibliography. American Psychological Association, Wasnington, D. C. *Journal Supplement Abstract Service*, 1976, p. 42.

Leeds, R. Altruism and the norm of giving. *Merrill-Palmer Quarterly*, 1963, *9*, 229–240.

Lerner, M. J. Desire for justice and reactions to victims. In J. Macaulay & L. Berkowitz (Eds.), *Altruism and helping behavior*. NY: Academic Press, 1970.

Lerner, M. J. *The belief in a just world: The fundamental delusion*. NY: Plenum, 1980.

Lerner, M. J. The justice motive in human relations and the economic model of man: A radical analysis of facts and fictions. In V. J. Derlega & J. Grzelak (Eds.), *Cooperation and helping behavior: Theories and research*. NY: Academic Press, 1982.

Lerner, M. J., & Matthews, G. Reactions to suffering of others under conditions of indirect responsibility. *Journal of Personality and Social Psychology*, 1967, *5*, 319–325.

Lerner, M. J., & Meindl, J. R. Justice and altruism. In J. P. Rushton & R. M. Sorrentino (eds.),

Altruism and helping behavior: Social, personality, and developmental perspectives. Hillsdale, NJ: Erlbaum, 1981.

Leventhal, G. S., Weiss, T., & Long, G. Equity, reciprocity, and reallocating the rewards in the dyad. *Journal of Personality and Social Psychology,* 1969, *13,* 300–305.

Levin, P. F., & Isen, A. M. Further studies on the effect of feeling good on helping. *Sociometry,* 1975, *38,* 141–147.

Lewin, K. *Field theory in social science.* New York: Harper, 1951.

Lynch, J. G., Jr. Why additive utility models fail as descriptors of choice behavior. *Journal of Experimental Social Psychology,* 1979, *15,* 397–417.

Lynch, J. G., Jr., & Cohen, J. L. The use of subjective expected utility theory as an aid to understanding variables that influence helping behavior. *Journal of Personality and Social Psychology,* 1978, *36,* 1138–1151.

Lynn, R. *Attention, arousal, and the orientation reaction.* Oxford: Pergamon Press, 1966.

Macaulay, J. R., & Berkowitz, L. *Altruism and helping behavior.* NY: Academic Press, 1970.

Manucia, G. K., Baumann, D. J., & Cialdini, R. B. Mood influences in helping: Direct effects or side effects? *Journal of Personality and Social Psychology,* 1984, *46,* 357–364.

Martin, G. B., & Clark, R. D., III Distress crying in neonates: Species and peer specificity. *Developmental Psychology,* 1982, *18,* 3–9.

McDougall, W. *An introduction to social psychology* (5th ed.). Boston: Luce, 1913. (Original work published 1908)

McGovern, L. P., Ditzian, J. L., & Taylor, S. P. The effect of one positive reinforcement on helping with cost. *Bulletin of Psychonomic Society,* 1975, *5,* 421–423.

McMillen, D. L. Transgression, fate control, and compliant behavior. *Psychonomic Science,* 1970, *21,* 103–104.

McMillen, D. L. Transgression, self-image, and compliant behavior. *Journal of Personality and Social Psychology,* 1971, *20,* 176–179.

McMillen, D. L., & Austin, J. B. Effect of positive feedback on compliance following transgression. *Psychonomic Science,* 1971, *20,* 179–179.

McMillen, D. L., Jackson, J. A., & Austin, J. B. Effects of positive and negative effects on compliance following transgression. *Bulletin of the Psychonomic Society,* 1974, *3,* 80–82.

McMillen, D. L., Sanders, D. Y., & Solomon, G. S. Self-esteem, attentiveness, and helping behavior. *Personality and Social Psychology Bulletin,* 1977, *3,* 257–261.

McPeek, R., & Cialdini, R. Social anxiety, emotion and helping. *Motivation and Emotion,* 1977, *1,* 225–233.

Mehrabian, A., & Epstein, N. A measure of emotional empathy. *Journal of Personality,* 1972, *40,* 525–543.

Midlarsky, E., & Bryan, J. H. Affect expressions and children's imitative altruism. *Journal of Experimental Research in Personality,* 1972, *6,* 195–203.

Midlarsky, E., & Kahana, E. Altruism in the aged: An alternative to helplessness. *Gerontologist,* 1981, *21,* 218–219.

Midlarsky, E., & Midlarsky, M. Some determinants of aiding under experimentally induced stress. *Journal of Personality,* 1973, *41,* 305–327.

Midlarsky, M., & Midlarsky, E. Status inconsistency, aggressive attitude, and helping behavior. *Journal of Personality,* 1976, *44,* 371–391.

Miller, D. T. Personal deservingness versus justice for others: An exploration of the justice motive. *Journal of Experimental Social Psychology,* 1977, *13,* 1–13.

Moore, B. S., Underwood, B., & Rosenhan, D. L. Affect and altruism. *Developmental Psychology,* 1973, *8,* 99–104.

Morgan, C. J. Bystander intervention: Experimental test of a formal model. *Journal of Personality and Social Psychology,* 1978, *36,* 43–55.

Moriarty, T. Crime, commitment, and the responsive bystander: Two field experiments. *Journal of Personality and Social Psychology,* 1975, *31,* 370–376.

Moss, M. K., & Page, R. A. Reinforcement and helping behavior. *Journal of Applied Social Psychology,* 1972, *2,* 360–371.

Mueller, C., Nelson, R., & Donnerstein, E. Facilitative effects of media violence on helping. *Psychological Reports,* 1977, *40,* 775–778.

Mueller, C. W., & Donnerstein, E. Film-facilitated arousal and prosocial behavior. *Journal of Experimental Social Psychology,* 1981, *17,* 31–41.

Mueller, C. W., Donnerstein, E., & Hallam, J. Violent films and prosocial behavior. *Personality and Social Psychology Bulletin,* 1983, *9,* 83–89.

Noel, R. C. Transgression—compliance: A failure to confirm. *Journal of Personality and Social Psychology.* 1973, *27,* 151–153.

Pandey, J., & Griffitt, W. Attraction and helping. *Bulletin of the Psychonomic Society,* 1974, *3,* 123–124.

Paulhus, D. L., Shaffer, D. R., & Downing, L. L. Effects of making blood donor motives salient upon donor retention: A field experiment. *Personality and Social Psychology Bulletin,* 1977, *3,* 99–102.

Pearce, P. L., & Amato, P. R. A taxonomy of helping: A multidimensional scaling analysis. *Social Psychology Quarterly,* 1980, *43,* 363–371.

Perry, D. G., Perry, L. C., Bussey, K., English, D., & Arnold, G. Processes of attribution and children's self-punishment following misbehavior. *Child Development,* 1980, *51,* 545–552.

Piliavin, I. M., Piliavin, J. A., & Rodin, S. Costs, diffusion, and the stigmatized victim. *Journal of Personality and Social Psychology,* 1975, *32,* 429–438.

Piliavin, I. M., Rodin, J., & Piliavin, J. Good samaritanism: An underground phenomenon? *Journal of Personality and Social Psychology,* 1969, *13,* 289–299.

Piliavin, J. A., Dovidio, J. F., Gaertner, S. L., & Clark, R. D., III. *Emergency intervention.* NY: Academic Press, 1981.

Piliavin, J. A., Dovidio, J. F., Gaertner, S. L., & Clark, R. D. III. Responsive bystanders: The process of intervention. In V. J. Derlega and J. Grzelak (Eds.), *Cooperation and helping behavior: Theories and research.* NY: Academic Press, 1982.

Piliavin, J. A., & Piliavin, I. M. The effect of blood on reactions to a victim. *Journal of Personality and Social Psychology,* 1972, *23,* 253–261.

Polivy, J. On the induction of emotion in the laboratory: Discrete moods or multiple affective states? *Journal of Personality and Social Psychology,* 1981, *41,* 803–817.

Pomazal, R. S., & Jaccard, J. J. An informational approach to altruistic behavior. *Journal of Personality and Social Psychology,* 1976, *33,* 317–327.

Rawlings, E. I. Witnessing harm to another: A reassessment of the role of guilt in altruistic behavior: *Journal of Personality and Social Psychology,* 1968, *10,* 377–380.

Raymond, B. J., & Unger, R. K. "The apparel oft proclaims the man": Cooperation with deviant and conventional youths. *Journal of Social Psychology,* 1972, *87,* 75–82.

Reagan, D. T., Williams, M., & Sparling, S. Voluntary expiation of guilt: A field experiment. *Journal of Personality and Social Psychology,* 1972, *24,* 42–45.

Regan, J. Guilt, perceived injustice, and altruistic behavior. *Journal of Personality and Social Psychology,* 1971, *18,* 124–132.

Rheingold, H. Little children's participation in the work of adults, a nascent prosocial behavior. *Child Development,* 1982, *53,* 114–125.

Rheingold, H. L., Hay, D. F., & West, M. J. Sharing in the second year of life. *Child Development,* 1976, *47,* 1148–1158.

Rice, M. E., & Grusec, J. E. Saying and doing: Effects on observer performance. *Journal of Personality and Social Psychology,* 1975, *32,* 584–593.

Rosenfield, D., Greenberg, J., Folger, R., & Borys, R. Effect of an encounter with a black panhandler on subsequent helping for blacks: Tokenism or confirming a negative stereotype? *Personality and Social Psychology Bulletin*, 1982, 8, 664–671.

Rosenhan, D. Some origins of concern for others. In P. H. Mussen, J. Langer, & M. Covington (Eds.), *Trends and issues in developmental psychology*. NY: Holt, Rinehart, & Winston, 1969.

Rosenhan, D. L., Salovey, P., Karylowski, J., & Hargis, K. Emotion and altruism. In J. P. Rushton and R. M. Sorrentino (Eds.), *Altruism and helping behavior: Social, personality, and developmental perspectives*. Hillsdale, NJ: Erlbaum, 1981.

Rosenhan, D. L., Salovey, P., & Hargis, K. The joys of helping: Focus of attention mediates the impact of positive affect on altruism. *Journal of Personality and Social Psychology*, 1981, 40, 899–905.

Rubin, Z., & Peplau, A. Who believes in a just world? *Journal of Social Issues*, 1975, 31, 65–89.

Rushton, J. P. Generosity in children: Immediate and long-term effects of modeling, preaching, and moral judgment. *Journal of Personality and Social Psychology*, 1975, 31, 459–466.

Rushton, J. P. Socializations and the altruistic behavior of children. *Psychological Bulletin*, 1976, 83, 898–913.

Rushton, J. P. Urban density and altruism: Helping strangers in a Canadian city, suburb, and small town. *Psychological Reports*, 1978, 43, 887–900.

Rushton, J. P. *Altruism, socialization, and society*. Englewood Cliffs, NJ: Prentice-Hall, 1980.

Rushton, J. P. The altruistic personality. In J. P. Rushton & R. M. Sorrentino (Eds.), *Altruism and helping behavior: Social, personality, and developmental perspectives*. Hillsdale, NJ: Erlbaum, 1981.

Rushton, J. P. Social learning theory and the development of prosocial behavior. In N. Eisenberg (Ed.), *The development of prosocial behavior*. NY: Academic Press, 1982.

Rushton, J. P., & Sorrentino, R. M. (Eds.), *Altruism and helping behavior: Social, personality, and developmental perspectives*. Hillsdale, NJ: Erlbaum, 1981.

Rutherford, E., & Mussen, P. Generosity in nursery school boys. *Child Development*, 1968, 39, 755–765.

Rutkowski, G. K., Gruder, C. L., & Romer, D. Group cohesiveness, social norms, and bystander intervention. *Journal of Personality and Social Psychology*, 1983, 44, 545–552.

Sagi, A., & Hoffman, M. Empathic distress in the newborn. *Developmental Psychology*, 1976, 12, 175–176.

Samuel, W. Response to bill of rights paraphrases as influenced by the hip or straight attire of the opinion solicitor. *Journal of Applied Social Psychology*, 1972, 2, 47–62.

Schiavo, R. S., Sherlock, B., & Wicklund, G. Effect of attire on obtaining directions. *Psychological Reports*, 1974, 34, 245–246.

Schopler, J., & Matthews, M. The influence of perceived causal locus of partner's dependence on the use of interpersonal power. *Journal of Personality and Social Psychology*, 1965, 2, 609–612.

Schwartz, S. H. Awareness of consequences and the influence of moral norms on interpersonal behavior. *Sociometry*, 1968, 31, 355–368. (a)

Schwartz, S. H. Words, deeds, and the perception of consequences and responsibility in action situations. *Journal of Personality and Social Psychology*, 1968, 10, 243–250. (b)

Schwartz, S. H. Elicitation of moral obligation and self-sacrificing behavior: An experimental study of volunteering to be a bone marrow donor. *Journal of Personality and Social Psychology*, 1970, 15, 283–293.

Schwartz, S. H. Normative explanation of helping behavior: A critique, proposal and empirical test. *Journal of Experimental Social Psychology*, 1973, 9, 349–364.

Schwartz, S. H. Awareness of interpersonal consequences, responsibility denial, and volunteering. *Journal of Personality and Social Psychology*, 1974, 30, 57–63.

Schwartz, S. H. Normative influences on altruism. In L. Berkowitz (Ed.), *Advances in experimental social psychology* (Vol. 10). NY: Academic Press, 1977.

Schwartz, S. H., & BenDavid, T. Responsibility and helping in an emergency: Effects of blame, ability, and denial of responsibility. *Sociometry*, 1976, *39*, 406–415.

Schwartz, S. H., & Clausen, G. T. Responsibility, norms, and helping in an emergency. *Journal of Personality and Social Psychology*, 1970, *16*, 229–310.

Schwartz, S. H., & Fleischman, J. Personal norms, legitimacy, and helping. *Social Psychology Quarterly*, 1978, *41*, 306–315.

Schwartz, S. H., & Fleischman, J. A. Effects of negative personal norms on helping behavior. *Personality and Social Psychology Bulletin*, 1982, *8*, 81–86.

Schwartz, S. H., & Gottlieb, A. Bystander reactions to a violent theft: Crime in Jerusalem. *Journal of Personality and Social Psychology*. 1976, *34*, 1188–1199.

Schwartz, S. H., & Gottlieb, A. Bystander anonymity and reactions to emergencies. *Journal of Personality and Social Psychology*, 1980, *39*, 418–430.

Schwartz, S. H., & Howard, J. A. A normative decision-making model of altruism. In J. P. Rushton & R. M. Sorrentino (Eds.), *Altruism and helping behavior: Social, personality, and developmental perspective*. Hillsdale, NJ: Erlbaum, 1981.

Schwartz, S. H., & Howard, J. Helping and cooperation: A self-based motivational model. In V. J. Derlega & J. Grzelak (Eds.), *Cooperation and helping behavior: Theories and research*. NY: Academic Press, 1982.

Shapiro, E. G. Help-seeking: Effects of visibility of task performance and seeking help. *Journal of Applied Social Psychology*, 1978, *8*, 163–173.

Shotland, R. L., & Heinold, W. D. Bystander responses to arterial bleeding: Differentiating the helping response and the impact of training. Unpublished manuscript, Pennsylvania State University, 1982.

Shotland, R. L., & Hutson, T. L. Emergencies: What are they and do they influence bystanders to intervene? *Journal of Personality and Social Psychology*, 1979, *37*, 1822–1834.

Shotland, R. L., & Stebbins, C. A. Emergency and cost as determinants of helping behavior and the slow accumulation of psychological knowledge. *Social Psychology Quarterly*, 1983, *46*, 36–46.

Shotland, R. L., & Straw, M. K. Bystander response to an assault: When a man attacks a woman. *Journal of Personality and Social Psychology*, 1976, *34*, 990–999.

Silverman, L. J., Rivera, A. N., & Tedeschi, J. T. Transgression-compliance: Guilt, negative affect, or impression management? *Journal of Social Psychology*, 1979, *108*, 57–62.

Silverman, L. W. Incidence of guilt reactions in children. *Journal of Personality and Social Psychology*, 1967, *7*, 338–340.

Simner, M. Newborn's repsonse to the cry of another infant. *Developmental Psychology*, 1971, *5*, 136–150.

Smith, R. E., Smythe, L., & Lien, D. Inhibition of helping behavior by a similar or dissimilar nonreactive fellow bystander, *Journal of Personality and Social Psychology*, 1972, *23*, 414–419.

Smithson, M., & Amato, P. An unstudied region of helping: An extension of the Pearce-Amato cognitive taxonomy. *Social Psychology Quarterly*, 1982, *45*, 67–76.

Sole, K., Marton, J., & Hornstein, H. A. Opinion similarity and helping: Three field experiments investigating the bases of promotive tension. *Journal of Experimental Social Psychology*, 1975, *11*, 1–13.

Solomon, L. Z., Solomon, H., & Stone, R. Helping as a function of number of bystanders and ambiguity of emergency, *Personality and Social Psychology Bulletin*, 1978, *4*, 318–321.

Stapleton, R. E., Nacci, P., & Tedeschi, J. T. Interpersonal attraction and the reciprocation of benefits. *Journal of Personality and Social Psychology*, 1973, *28*, 199–205.

Staub, E. A child in distress: The influence of nurturance and modeling on children's attempts to help. *Developmental Psychology*, 1971, *5*, 124–132. (a)

Staub, E. Helping a person in distress: The influence of implicit and explicit "rules" of conduct on children and adults. *Journal of Personality and Social Psychology*, 1971, *17*, 137–144. (b)

Staub, E. Helping a distressed person: Social, personality, and stimulus determinants. In L. Berkowitz (ed.), *Advances in experimental social psychology* (Vol. 7). NY: Academic Press, 1974.

Staub, E. *Positive social behavior and morality. Vol. 1: Social and personal influences.* NY: Academic Press, 1978.

Staub, E. *Positive social behavior and morality. Vol. 2: Socialization and development.* NY: Academic Press, 1979.

Staub, E. Social and prosocial behavior: Personal and situational influences and their interactions. In E. Staub (Ed.), *Personality: Basic aspects and current research.* Englewood Cliffs, NJ: Prentice-Hall, 1980.

Staub, E. Promoting positive behavior in schools, in other educational settings, and in the home. In J. P. Rushton & R. M. Sorrentino (Eds), *Altruism and helping behavior: Social, personality, and developmental perspectives.* Hillsdale, NJ: Erlbaum, 1981.

Stein, D. D., Hardyck, J. A., & Smith, M. B. Race and belief: An open and shut case. *Journal of Personality and Social Psychology*, 1965, *1*, 281–289.

Sterling, B. The effects of anger, ambiguity, and arousal on helping behavior (Doctoral dissertation, University of Delaware, 1977). *Dissertation Abstracts International*, 1977, *38*(4), 1962.

Sterling, B., & Gaertner, S. L. The attribution of arousal and emergency helping: A bi-directional process. *Journal of Experimental Social Psychology*, in press.

Stewart, J. E., II, & Rosen, S. Adequacy of compensation, worthiness of recipient, and their effects on transgressor compliance to render aid. *Journal of Social Psychology*, 1975, *97*, 77–82.

Stotland, E. Exploratory investigations of empathy. In L. Berkowitz (Ed.), *Advances in experimental social psychology* (Vol. 4). NY: Academic Press, 1969.

Strayer, F. F. The nature and organization of altruistic behavior among preschool children. In J. P. Rushton & R. M. Sorrentino (Eds.), *Altruism and helping behavior: Social, personality, and developmental perspectives.* Hillsdale, NJ: Erlbaum, 1981.

Strayer, F. F., Wareing, S., & Rushton, J. P. Social constraints on naturally occurring preschool altruism. *Ethology and Sociobiology*, 1979, *1*, 3–11.

Strenta, A., & DeJong, W. The effect of prosocial labeling on helping behavior. *Social Psychology Quarterly*, 1981, *44*, 142–147.

Suedfield, P., Bochner, S., & Matas, C. Petitioner's attire and petition signing by peace demonstrators: A field experiment. *Journal of Applied Social Psychology*, 1971, *1*, 278–283.

Suedfeld, P., Bochner, S., & Wnek, D. Helper-sufferer similarity and specific request for help: Bystander intervention during a peace demonstration. *Journal of Applied Social Psychology*, 1972, *2*, 17–23.

Swinyard, W. R., & Ray, M. L. Effects of praise and small requests on receptivity to direct-mail appeals. *Journal of Social Psychology*, 1979, *108*, 177–184.

Tesser, A., & Smith, J. Some effects of task relevance and friendship on helping: You don't always help the one you like. *Journal of Experimental Social Psychology*, 1980, *16*, 582–590.

Thompson, W. C., Cowan, C. L., & Rosenhan, D. L. Focus of attention mediates the impact of negative affect on altruism. *Journal of Personality and Social Psychology*, 1980, *38*, 291–300.

Toi, M., & Batson, C. D. More evidence that empathy is a source of altruistic motivation. *Journal of Personality and Social Psychology*, 1982, *43*, 281–292.

Trivers, R. L. The evolution of reciprocal altruism. *Quarterly Review of Biology*, 1971, *46*, 35–37.

Underwood, B., & Moore, B. S. The generality of altruism in children. In N. Eisenberg (Ed.), *The development of prosocial behavior.* NY: Academic Press, 1982. (a)

Underwood, B., & Moore, B. S. Perspective-taking and altruism. *Psychological Bulletin, 1982, 91,* 143–173. (b)

Vaughn, K. B. & Lanzetta, J. T. Vicarious instigation and conditioning of facial expressive and autonomic responses to a model's expressive display of pain. *Journal of Personality and Social Psychology, 1980, 38,* 909–923.

Wagner, C., & Wheeler, L. Model, need, and cost effects in helping behavior. *Journal of Personality and Social Psychology, 1969, 12,* 111–116.

Wagner, S., Hornstein, H. A., & Holloway, S. Willingness to help a stranger: The effects of social context and opinion similarity. *Journal of Applied Social Psychology, 1982, 12,* 429–443.

Wallace, J., & Sadalla, E. Behavioral consequences of transgressions: I. The effects of social recognition. *Journal of Experimental Research in Personality, 1966, 1,* 187–194.

Wallington, S. A. Consequences of transgression: Self-punishment and depression. *Journal of Personality and Social Psychology, 1973, 28,* 1–7.

Walster, E., Walster, G. W., & Berscheid, E. *Equity: Theory and research.* Boston: Allyn & Bacon, 1978.

Wegner, D. M., & Crano, W. D. Racial factors in helping behavior: An unobtrusive field experiment. *Journal of Personality and Social Psychology, 1975, 32,* 901–905.

Wegner, D. M., & Schaefer, D. The concentration of responsibility: An objective self-awareness analysis of group size effects in helping situations. *Journal of Personality and Social Psychology, 1980, 36,* 147–155.

Weiner, B. A cognitive (attribution)-emotion-action model of motivated behavior: An analysis of judgments of help-giving. *Journal of Personality and Social Psychology, 1980, 39,* 186–200.

Weiss, R. F., Boyer, J. L., Lombardo, J. P., & Stich, M. H. Altruistic drive and altruistic reinforcement, *Journal of Personality and Social Psychology, 1973, 25,* 390–400.

Weiss, R. F., Buchanan, W., Altstatt, L., & Lombardo, J. P. Altruism is rewarding. *Science, 1971, 171,* 1262–1263.

Weissbrod, C. S. Noncontingent warmth induction, cognitive style, and children's imitative donation and rescue effort behaviors. *Journal of Personality and Social Psychology, 1976, 34,* 274–281.

West, S. G., Whitney, G., & Schnedler, R. Helping a motorist in distress: The effects of sex, race, and neighborhood. *Journal of Personality and Social Psychology, 1975, 31,* 691–698.

Weyant, J. M. Effects of mood states, costs, and benefits on helping. *Journal of Personality and Social Psychology, 1978, 36,* 1169–1176.

Wilson, D. W., & Kahn, A. Rewards, costs, and sex differences in helping behavior. *Psychological Reports, 1975, 36,* 31–34.

Wilson, J. P. Motivation, modeling and altruism: A person × situation analysis. *Journal of Personality and Social Psychology, 1976, 34,* 1078–1986.

Wispé, L. G. Positive forms of social behavior: An overview. *Journal of Social Issues, 1972, 28,* 1–20.

Worchel, S., Andreoli, V. A., & Archer, R. When is a favor a threat to freedom: The effects of attribution and importance of freedom on reciprocity. *Journal of Personality, 1976, 44,* 294–310.

Yarrow, M. R., Scott, P. M., & Waxler, C. Z. Learning concern for others. *Developmental Psychology, 1973, 8,* 240–260.

Zahn-Waxler, C., Friedman, S. L. & Cummings, E. M. Children's emotions and behaviors in response to infant's cries. *Child Development, 1983, 54,* 1522–1528.

Zahn-Waxler, C., Radke-Yarrow, M., & King, R. A. Child rearing and children's prosocial initiations toward victims of distress. *Child Development, 1979, 50,* 319–330.

Zuckerman, M., & Reis, H. T. Comparison of three models for predicting altruistic behavior. *Journal of Personality and Social Psychology, 1978, 36,* 498–510.

INDEX

CONTENTS OF OTHER VOLUMES